Frommer's

New York City
from $90 a Day

7th edition

by Brian Silverman

Here's what the critics say about Frommer's:

"Amazingly easy to use. Very portable, very complete."
—*Booklist*

"Detailed, accurate, and easy-to-read information for all price ranges."
—*Glamour Magazine*

"Hotel information is close to encyclopedic."
—*Des Moines Sunday Register*

"Frommer's Guides have a way of giving you a real feel for a place."
—*Knight Ridder Newspapers*

WILEY
Wiley Publishing, Inc.

About the Author

Brian Silverman has written about travel, food, sports, and music for publications such as *Saveur, Caribbean Travel & Life, Islands, American Way, The New Yorker,* and the *New York Times.* He is the author of several books, including *Going, Going, Gone: The History, Lore and Mystique of the Home Run* and co-editor of *The Twentieth Century Treasury of Sports.* Brian lives in New York City with his wife and children.

Published by:

Wiley Publishing, Inc.

111 River St.
Hoboken, NJ 07030-5774

ISBN 0-7645-7648-8

Editor: Kathleen Warnock
Production Editor: Suzanna R. Thompson
Cartographer: Elizabeth Puhl
Photo Editor: Richard Fox
Production by Wiley Indianapolis Composition Services

Front cover photo: New Yorkers enjoying Central Park
Back cover photo: A room at the Gershwin Hotel

For information on our other products and services or to obtain technical support, please contact our Customer Care Department within the U.S. at 800/762-2974, outside the U.S. at 317/572-3993 or fax 317/572-4002.

Wiley also publishes its books in a variety of electronic formats. Some content that appears in print may not be available in electronic formats.

Manufactured in the United States of America

5 4 3 2 1

Contents

iv CONTENTS

8   Shopping for Big Apple Bargains   258

9   New York City After Dark   288

List of Maps

An Invitation to the Reader

In researching this book, we discovered many wonderful places—hotels, restaurants, shops, and more. We're sure you'll find others. Please tell us about them, so we can share the information with your fellow travelers in upcoming editions. If you were disappointed with a recommendation, we'd love to know that, too. Please write to:

Frommer's New York City from $90 a Day, 7th Edition
Wiley Publishing, Inc. • 111 River St. • Hoboken, NJ 07030-5774

An Additional Note

Please be advised that travel information is subject to change at any time—and this is especially true of prices. We therefore suggest that you write or call ahead for confirmation when making your travel plans. The authors, editors, and publisher cannot be held responsible for the experiences of readers while traveling. Your safety is important to us, however, so we encourage you to stay alert and be aware of your surroundings. Keep a close eye on cameras, purses, and wallets, all favorite targets of thieves and pickpockets.

Other Great Guides for Your Trip:

Frommer's NYC for Free & Dirt Cheap
Frommer's New York City
Frommer's New York City with Kids
Frommer's Memorable Walks in New York
Frommer's Irreverent Guide to Manhattan
The Unofficial Guide to New York City
New York City For Dummies
Frommer's New York State

Frommer's Star Ratings, Icons & Abbreviations

Every hotel, restaurant, and attraction listing in this guide has been ranked for quality, value, service, amenities, and special features using a **star-rating system.** In country, state, and regional guides, we also rate towns and regions to help you narrow down your choices and budget your time accordingly. Hotels and restaurants are rated on a scale of zero (recommended) to three stars (exceptional). Attractions, shopping, nightlife, towns, and regions are rated according to the following scale: zero stars (recommended), one star (highly recommended), two stars (very highly recommended), and three stars (must-see).

In addition to the star-rating system, we also use **seven feature icons** that point you to the great deals, in-the-know advice, and unique experiences that separate travelers from tourists. Throughout the book, look for:

Finds	Special finds—those places only insiders know about
Fun Fact	Fun facts—details that make travelers more informed and their trips more fun
Kids	Best bets for kids and advice for the whole family
Moments	Special moments—those experiences that memories are made of
Overrated	Places or experiences not worth your time or money
Tips	Insider tips—great ways to save time and money
Value	Great values—where to get the best deals

The following **abbreviations** are used for credit cards:

AE	American Express	DISC	Discover	V	Visa
DC	Diners Club	MC	MasterCard		

Frommers.com

Now that you have the guidebook to a great trip, visit our website at **www.frommers.com** for travel information on more than 3,000 destinations. With features updated regularly, we give you instant access to the most current trip-planning information available. At Frommers.com, you'll also find the best prices on airfares, accommodations, and car rentals—and you can even book travel online through our travel booking partners. At Frommers.com, you'll also find the following:

- Online updates to our most popular guidebooks
- Vacation sweepstakes and contest giveaways
- Newsletter highlighting the hottest travel trends
- Online travel message boards with featured travel discussions

What's New in New York City

GETTING AROUND After much anticipation and millions of dollars, the **JFK AirTrain** opened in late 2003. Though taking the AirTrain to JFK airport will save you money, it may not save you time. If you aren't lugging a family or bags around, then it might work for you. It's far cheaper than a cab to or from Manhattan, and during rush hours can be faster than the various buses and shuttles.

Good news on the subway lines in 2004: After a 2-year construction project on the Manhattan Bridge disrupted service on the **B** and **D** lines, construction has been completed and those two lines have resumed their routes from Manhattan to Brooklyn.

Almost 2 years since being destroyed in the September 11, 2001, terrorist attacks, a new **PATH Station** at the World Trade Center opened in 2004.

Taxi fares increased in 2004 from a base fare of $2 to $2.50. Also increasing is the rate for every ⅕ block from 30¢ to 40¢. Also, the flat rate from JFK Airport has gone up to $45 from $35 and a surcharge of $1 has been added on all rides from 4 to 8pm, Monday through Friday.

More potential bad news, as we go to press, the **MTA** (**www.mta.nyc.ny. us/metrocard**) claiming a deficit, has floated the idea of an increase in the 30-day MetroCard from $70 to $76 and the 7-day card from $21 to $26.

ACCOMMODATIONS We've added a couple of hotels outside Manhattan (but not by much) in nearby Long Island City. The **Comfort Inn Long Island City** (*C* **718/303-3700**) and **Best Western City View** (*C* **718/ 392-8400**) are minutes from Midtown on the 7 train, and if you're in town for the U.S. Open, are also convenient to the same 7 train that takes you out to Flushing.

DINING In 2003 and 2004, a number of restaurant institutions closed including the venerable **Lutece,** four-star **Lespinasse,** 45-year-old **La Cote Basque, La Caravelle,** and the Brooklyn landmark, **Gage & Tollner.** But not to worry, there's never a lull in restaurant opening in New York and many of the 2003 and 2004 additions might be institutions in the making.

The larger spinoff of SoHo's Bread, **Bread Tribeca** (*C* **212/334-8282**) features those amazing sandwiches along with some interesting pastas at reasonable prices in a comfortable, communal atmosphere.

Bubby's, a TriBeCa institution, branched out with another location in

---

⌐ *Tips* **Times Square Relief**

When ya gotta go, ya gotta go and if you're in Times Square, you are in luck. In the busy Times Square subway station (btwn Broadway and 7th Ave. at 42nd St.), new, very clean restrooms have been constructed. The restrooms are open almost all day (7am–1am) and there is a 5-minute time limit for use. So make the most of your time there.

Mmmmmm . . . Toys & Chocolate!

As we went to press, an old favorite returned and a trendy newcomer opened its doors. The 142-year-old toy store **F.A.O. Schwarz** (✆ **212/644-9400;** www.faoschwarz.com), which closed its doors in January 2004 after declaring bankruptcy, reopened under new management at its old location, 757 Fifth Ave. (at 58th St.), with a redesigned interior just in time for Thanksgiving 2004. And Berkeley-based **Scharffen Berger** (✆ **212/362-9734;** www.scharffenberger.com) joined the chocolate revolution in New York City (chocolate is the new coffee!), opening a store at 473 Amsterdam Ave. (at 83rd St.) and providing chocoholics with another source of fine small-batch gourmet chocolate.

---

the fashionable DUMBO section of Brooklyn (✆ **212/222-0666**).

The lines at the **Clinton St. Baking Company** are long for breakfast on weekends, as people wait patiently for their incredible pancakes in the ultra-trendy Lower East Side (✆ **646/602-6263**).

The East Village continues to attract interesting new restaurants and one of the best of those is **Mojo** (✆ **212/539-1515**).

Serving arguably the best hamburger in New York, **Prime Burger** (✆ **212/759-4729**) in Midtown was named an "American Classic" by the James Beard Foundation.

For ice cream lovers, the Arizona-based **Cold Stone Creamery** and its incredible creations entered the New York market with two stores, one on 42nd Street the other on the Upper East Side.

Also new is the seasonal (late spring to Nov) **Shake Shack,** created by restaurateur Danny Meyer in Madison Square Park. Featuring hot dogs, hamburgers, and fries, best of all are the Shake Shack's milkshakes and frozen custard.

EXPLORING NEW YORK CITY

After being denied access to the interior of the **Statue of Liberty** since the September 11 attacks, visitors were once more able to explore the Statue of Liberty museum, peer into the

intricate inner structure through a glass ceiling near the base of the statue, and enjoy the 360-degree views from the observation deck on top of the 16-story pedestal.

A concept was chosen after an open competition where over 5,000 entries of a design for a **memorial** to be built on the **World Trade Center site** (✆ **212/484-1222;** www.downtown ny.com) commemorating the tragic events of 9/11. The winning entry was titled "Reflecting Absence" and will consist of two large voids, cascading pools 30 feet into the footprints of the Twin Towers with the names of the victims of the attacks listed around the pool. Groundbreaking for the Freedom Tower was in summer 2004.

The Manhattan location for the **Museum of Modern Art,** 11 W. 53rd St. (✆ **212/708-9400**), closed since 2002, reopened in November 2004. The good news is that after a $650-million renovation, there's more than double the previous exhibit space. The bad news is that the admission charge has gone up to a whopping $20!

Opening too late for us to review this edition is the **Rubin Museum of Art,** 150 W. 17th St. (✆ **212/620-5000;** www.rmanyc.org), which aims to "present, preserve and document a permanent collection that reflects the vitality, complexity and historical significance of Himalayan art."

And since our last edition, the **Louis Armstrong House Museum,** 34–56 107th St., Corona, Queens (© **718/478-8274;** www.satchmo. net), has opened to glowing reviews.

AFTER DARK   The Time Warner Center is the new home of **Jazz at Lincoln Center** (© **212/258-9800;** www.jazzatlincolncenter.org).   The $115-million, 100,000-square-foot facility is the first performing arts center designed specifically for jazz.

SHOPPING   Perhaps the most ambitious project in New York the past several years has been the construction and opening of the **Time Warner Center** at Columbus Circle. *The Shops at Columbus Circle,* a collection of some of the most upscale retailers in the world including **Sephora, A/X Armani Exchange, Williams-Sonoma, Eileen Fisher, Hugo Boss,** and a huge **Whole Foods Supermarket** opened in early 2004.

1

The Best of the Big Apple

New York is the concentrate of art and commerce and sport and religion and entertainment and finance, bringing to a single compact arena the gladiator, the evangelist, the promoter, the actor, the trader and the merchant. It carries on its lapel the unexpungeable odor of the long past, so that no matter where you sit in New York you feel the vibrations of great times and tall deeds, of queer people and events and undertakings.

New York is nothing like Paris; it is nothing like London; and it is not Spokane multiplied by sixty, or Detroit multiplied by four. It is by all odds the loftiest of cities.

Novelist and essayist E. B. White wrote these words in 1948; and in the more than half-century since, his description of New York remains accurate. And though the grandeur and importance of New York has not changed, New York is constantly changing. Restaurants and nightclubs become trendy overnight, and then die under the weight of their own popularity. (As the philosopher Yogi Berra said: "Nobody goes there anymore; it's too crowded.") Broadway shows, exercise fads, city politics, even neighborhoods are all subject to the same Big Apple fickleness.

But within this ebb and flow lies the answer to why we New Yorkers persist in loving our city so, despite the high rents, the noise, the crowds, the cab drivers who don't know Lincoln Center from the Lower East Side, and the more stark realities of high-security-alert days and living in the shadow of great tragedy. Nowhere else is the challenge so tough, the pace so relentless, the stimuli so ever changing and insistent—and the payoff so rewarding. It is why we go on; it is why we proudly persist in living our vibrant lives here.

Come witness New York's resilience for yourself—it's reason enough to visit.

1 How This Guide Can Save You Money

New York City is perpetually short on space and overflowing with people. It's a situation that turns the economy of supply and demand in the seller's favor, with vendors charging what the market will bear. The result has been stratospheric prices, some of the highest in the country. If you're used to getting a simple, comfortable motel room for $60 or so, get set for a shock.

That's the bad news—but there's plenty of good news, too. You *can* stay in New York City comfortably, eat well, and see and do everything you want without blowing your budget. There are plenty of great deals for the traveler who knows where to look for value.

You've already taken the first step: buying this book. I've done the initial legwork, scouring the city and loading the pages that follow with money-saving advice, the top values and bargains, and the kind of New York travel know-how that comes only with years of research and experience.

On New York

The only credential the city asked was the boldness to dream. For those who did, it unlocked its gates and its treasures, not caring who they were and where they came from.

—Moss Hart

Accommodations will be your biggest hurdle, although visitors have regained their bargaining power in the post-9/11 world. Every other aspect of New York is manageable if you look before you leap, which is how regular New Yorkers manage. The city tends to snag people who, exhausted, sit down at the first restaurant they see and end up with a huge bill—or those who stumble into a chic boutique to buy a souvenir that can be had for a fraction of the price with a little effort. Keep an eye on the goal, and you'll see New York has more affordable culinary and bargain hunters' delights than you'll have time to enjoy.

With average museum admissions hovering around 10 bucks a pop and guided bus tours starting at $30 for the basic look-see, you could spend a fortune on sightseeing and activities—but you don't have to. Start perusing these pages, and you'll find more to see and do for free and on the cheap than you could squeeze into one vacation (or two or three or four). I'm not suggesting that you skip everything that has a price tag; certain New York experiences shouldn't be missed. But read the pages that follow and you should glean enough insight to know what's worth your hard-earned dough—and what's not.

THE NEW-YORK-FROM-$90-A-DAY PREMISE

The idea is this: With good planning and a watchful eye, you can keep your basic daily costs—accommodations and three meals—down to as little as $90. This budget model works best for two adults traveling together who have at least $180 a day to work with

and can share a double room. (Single rooms are less cost-efficient.) This way, if you aim for accommodations that cost around $120 for a double—a reasonable budget—you'll be left with about $30 per person per day for food (less drinks and tips). Snare a room for less—doable in this economic climate, especially in a less-busy season or if you're willing to share a bathroom—and you'll have more left over from your $180-per-day budget for dining.

In defining this premise, we assume you want to travel comfortably, with your own room rather than a hostel bunk (even if it does mean a shared bathroom), and dining on good food. This book will serve you well even if you don't need to keep your two-person budget to a strict $180 a day, but you want to get the most for your money. It will, on the other side of the coin, also meet your needs if you want to travel on the ultracheap—for less than $90 a day—by staying in hostels and eating super-inexpensively.

Sightseeing, transportation, and entertainment are all extra. But I've got plenty of suggestions on how to keep those costs down, too. What you choose for entertainment will have a huge effect on your overall budget. If you go to nightclubs every night, you'll come home with a lighter wallet than if you spend time taking in free concerts or browsing galleries. If you seek top-name entertainment on Broadway or the cabaret circuit, you'll pay more than if you take a risk on tomorrow's stars at an Off-Broadway show or a no-cover bar. Only you know how much money you have to spend—but if you follow my advice, you'll be able to make informed decisions so that it's money well spent.

Even if you stick with freebies, the Big Apple guarantees a memorable time. After all, to the late, great Quentin Crisp, every flat surface in New York was a stage—and you're guaranteed a nonstop show.

2 Cheap Thrills: Frommer's Favorite Free & Affordable Experiences

- **Best Attraction:** If you have time to do only one thing on your visit to New York, sail to the **Statue of Liberty.** No other monument embodies the nation's, and the world's, notion of political freedom and economic potential more than Lady Liberty. It is also the ultimate symbol of New York, the personification of the city's vast diversity and tolerance. See p. 202.

- **Best Building:** The **Empire State Building,** once again the tallest building in New York, is one of the city's definitive icons.

  Runners-up include the Art Deco masterpiece, the **Chrysler Building,** and the triangular **Flatiron Building.** See chapter 7.

- **Best Street:** This is a tough choice. Fifth Avenue has the reputation, but has lost some luster the past few years with the proliferation of chain and theme stores, so my pick is **Broadway.** Beginning at the southern tip of the island downtown, Broadway runs from Wall Street, up through Chinatown, SoHo, and Greenwich Village, past the Flatiron building at 23rd Street, into the heart of Times Square, and then up to Columbus Circle, past Lincoln Center and the Upper West Side, all the way to the northern tip of the island. No street better captures the diversity of Manhattan than Broadway.

- **Best Bridge:** Manhattan has five major bridges connecting the island to other shores, and the most historic and fascinating is the **Brooklyn Bridge.** For a close-up look at what was a marvel of civic engineering when it was built in 1883, and a real New York experience, walk across the bridge from Manhattan to Brooklyn. See p. 196.

- **Best Historic Building:** Despite all the modern steel and glass skyscrapers in New York, there are still many historic marvels standing, and the best of those is the Beaux Arts gem, **Grand Central Terminal.** This railroad station, built in 1913, was restored in the 1990s to recapture its initial brilliance. Even if you don't have to catch a train, make sure you visit. See p. 198.

- **Best Museum:** You could spend your entire visit to New York at **American Museum of Natural History** and not run out of things to see. From the famed dinosaur halls to the wondrous *Hall of Ocean Life,* the 4-square-block Museum of Natural History houses the world's greatest natural science collection. See p. 195.

- **Best Art Museum:** The **Metropolitan Museum of Art** is not only the best art museum in New York, but also the best in North America. The number of masterworks here is mind-boggling. See p. 199.

- **Best Park:** Though New York has many very wonderful parks, there is no real competition here. **Central Park** is one of the world's greatest urban refuges, a center of calm and tranquillity amongst the noise and bustle that is Manhattan. See p. 227.

- **Best location in Central Park for a picnic: The Pool,** at 100th Street, is like being in another world. It's relatively quiet and undiscovered, and with weeping willows, ducks, geese, egrets, and a hawk or two, an oasis of tranquility. See p. 231.
- **Best Park excluding Central Park: Riverside Park,** a 4-mile-long park along the picturesque Hudson River, is a welcome alternative to the sometimes overcrowded Central Park. See p. 234.
- **Best Place to Take the Kids:** With a carousel, a zoo, two ice-skating rinks, and numerous playgrounds and ball fields, **Central Park** is a children's wonderland.
- **Best Neighborhood to Stroll:** Though I'm partial to the Upper West Side, I have to give the nod to **Greenwich Village.** With its historic streets, hidden cafes, cozy restaurants, and eccentric characters, Greenwich Village is a constant but pleasant barrage on the senses. See chapter 4.
- **Best Mode of Transportation:** There's no better way to see New York than **on foot.** It is certainly the cheapest way to get around, and at times, it's also the fastest.

    Runner-Up: Fast and still economical and despite the constant upheavals in schedules and routes, the **subway** is the fastest way to get from point A to point B in New York.
- **Best Jogging Path:** The 1.5-mile **Reservoir in Central Park** (also known as Jacqueline Kennedy Onassis Reservoir) is the preferred path of most New Yorkers, this one included. See chapter 7.
- **Best Parade:** New York is famous for its parades, notably the Macy's Thanksgiving Day Parade and the St. Patrick's Day Parade, but the best parade in New York is the lesser-known **West Indian-American Day Parade.** Held on Eastern Parkway in Brooklyn, this is the biggest parade in the city. The music—calypso, soca, reggae, and Latin—the carnival costumes, and incredible Caribbean food make this an unforgettable experience. If you are lucky enough to be here on Labor Day, don't miss it. See chapter 2.
- **Best Street Festival:** For one weekend in the middle of May, the **Ninth Avenue International Food Festival** is the perfect illustration of ethnic diversity in the city. You'll be able to taste foods from restaurants and cuisines from Afghani to Peruvian. See chapter 2.
- **Best New Year's Eve Celebration:** Avoid the madness of Times Square and head to **Central Park** where, at midnight, fireworks are set off and a midnight running race commences. See chapter 2.
- **Best Free Event:** Perennial favorites **SummerStage** in Central Park, which is now drowning in corporate sponsorship and slowly becoming a "paid" event; and **Shakespeare in the Park,** which is becoming more of a showcase for the celebrity of the moment; are losing their luster, leaving **Lincoln Center Out-of-Doors** as the winner. I've seen many great performances at the 4-week festival each August, on the plaza of Lincoln Center, including jazz great Sonny Rollins, the traditional Spanish dance troupe Danzas Espanolas, and a children's singalong my son still talks fondly about. There is something for everyone at this wonderful free event. See chapter 9.
- **Best Performance Space:** There are few greater spaces in the world than **Carnegie Hall.** Visually and

acoustically brilliant, Carnegie Hall attracts an amazing array of talent. But remember: Never ask a New Yorker how you get there. (Practice, practice, practice!) See p. 302.

- **Best Jazz Club:** The acoustics and sight lines aren't great, but you can't do better than **The Village Vanguard** for finding consistently good-quality jazz. The Vanguard is a New York institution. See p. 314.
- **Best Budget Jazz Club: Smoke,** a cozy Upper West Side jazz club, is emerging as one of the best in the city. There's no cover Sunday through Thursday, with Tuesday, for the tremendous "Hammond Organ" night and Wednesday, for the "Hot Pants Funk Sextet," not to be missed. See p. 314.
- **Best Harlem Jazz Club:** I like my jazz without hassle. At **St. Nick's Pub** I can come in just about anytime, not worry about reservations, sit at the bar, and hear great music. And you never know who, from the neighborhood, might join in and jam. See p. 314.
- **Best New Club: Satalla** is an intimate club that features music from around the world. In a cozy, comfortable setting, you'll hear music from everywhere from Finland to Cameroon. See p. 314.
- **Best Dive Bar:** Sure, we know you came to New York to go to a dive bar. Enter the **Subway Inn** and it's as if you stepped into a 1940s moody film noir—minus the cigarette smoke. See p. 321.
- **Best Crime Bookstore:** New York is fodder for crime writers and as result, the city has many crime bookstores. With its spiral staircase and musty rows of manuscripts, **The Mysterious Bookshop** is not only a fun place to browse, but also the perfect setting for a crime novel. See p. 268.
- **Best Way to Spend a Day in the Boroughs:**

    The Bronx: Spend the morning at the **Bronx Zoo** or the **Bronx Botanical Gardens** and then head to Arthur Avenue, the Little Italy of the Bronx, for an authentic Italian feast.

    Brooklyn: First take a look at what's on exhibit at always exciting **Brooklyn Museum,** and then get some fresh air with a stroll in nearby, lovely **Prospect Park** capped off by a sandwich and a slice of cheesecake at **Junior's** on Flatbush Avenue.

    Queens: Take the **7 train,** the International Express, out to the **Queens Museum of Art,** on the grounds of the 1964 World's Fair, or the new **Louis Armstrong House Museum.** On your way back, stop for a meal at any number of ethnic restaurants you will find within close proximity of the 7 train. See p. 247.
- **Best Day to Come to New York:** You've skipped the insanity of New Year's Eve and arisen fresh and sober. On **New Year's Day** get out on the town early; you'll have the city practically to yourself.

    Runner-Up: The city clears out during the dog days of August and on the weekends in particular. On **Sunday mornings in August** the city is as close to deserted as it ever is.

    And: Start **any Sunday morning** early and experience a calm, quiet, almost serene feel to the city that can be positively invigorating.
- **Best Photo Op:** On the **Brooklyn Heights Promenade,** with the New York skyline behind you, your friends won't have any difficulty knowing where you are.

3 Best Low-Cost Hotel Bets

You'll likely spend more than you like on a hotel room; it's a fact of life in the big city. But New York has a wealth of wallet-friendly choices for bargain hunters who know where to look. For the details on these and other afford-able hotels, see chapter 5.

- **Best Overall Value—Down-town:** It's hard to beat the **Cos-mopolitan Hotel–TriBeCa,** 95 W. Broadway (© **888/895-9400;** www.cosmohotel.com), for value. Each of the small, comfy, modern rooms comes with its own petite but immaculate private bathroom for as little as $119 a night. The high-rent neighborhood is hip as can be and subway-convenient to the rest of the city. See p. 98.

- **Best Overall Value—Midtown:** The excellent Apple Core Hotels group's premier property, the **Red Roof Inn,** 6 W. 32nd St. (© **800/ 567-7720;** www.applecorehotels. com) is a combination of location, quality, comforts, and space at rates that are a bargain in any town, much less New York—as low as $89 double, with breakfast, this one is hard to beat. See p. 118.

- **Best Overall Value—Uptown:** The **Hotel Newton,** 2528 Broad-way (© **888/HOTEL-58;** www. newyorkhotel.com), doesn't expect you to put up with a tiny room or myriad inconveniences because you aren't spending a fortune. With rates starting at $85 double, you'll get more than your money's worth here—and you'll save an additional 10% if you're a AAA member. See p. 124.

- **Best Value for Bargain Hunters Who Don't Mind Sharing:** If you're willing to share a bathroom, you'll be pleased with the **Larch-mont Hotel,** in the loveliest part of Greenwich Village at 27 W. 11th St. (© **212/989-9333;** www. larchmonthotel.com). See p. 103.

- **Best Value for Bargain Hunters Who Do Mind Sharing:** Kudos to **SoHotel,** 341 Broome St. (© **212/226-1482;** www.pioneer hotel.com), which has done some-thing no one else has managed: offer clean, friendly accommoda-tions with private bathrooms for just $77 double year-round. The staff is professional, the decor is more attractive than most hotels in the shoestring category, and the edge-of-Chinatown location is safe and convenient. See p. 99.

- **Best for Bargain Hunters Will-ing to Compromise:** Chelsea Lodge, 318 W. 20th St. (© **800 /373-1116;** www.chelsealodge. com), offers the perfect compro-mise: You'll have an in-room sink and shower, so all you have to share is a toilet in the hall. If you're willing to do that, you'll find yourself in one of the cutest, cleanest, most comfortable hotels in New York—and at one of the cheapest rates (from $105 for a double) in town. One of my all-time budget favorites! See p. 103.

- **Best Service for the Budget-Minded:** The staff at the **Broad-way Inn,** 264 W. 46th St. (© **800/826-6300;** www.broad wayinn.com), might be the most helpful in the city. They're so com-mitted to making their guests feel welcome that they give you a hot line number to call when you're out and about if you need direc-tions, advice on where to eat, or any other assistance. And you thought New Yorkers weren't friendly! See p. 112.

- **Best for Creative Spirits:** Remi-niscent of Warhol's Factory at the height of its creativity and style, the supercool **Gershwin Hotel,** 7 E. 27th St. (① 212/545-8000; www.gershwinhotel.com), after a recent renovation and the addition of a hip bar, is the winner in this category. See p. 109.

- **Best for Families:** On the Upper West Side, one of the city's most kid-friendly residential neighborhoods, is **The Milburn,** 242 W. 76th St. (① 800/833-9622; www.milburnhotel.com), which offers the best value-for-dollar ratio on suites in town. A queen-size sleeper sofa in the living room makes the junior and one-bedroom suites large enough for four, and a kitchenette with microwave, minifridge, and coffeemaker means you can save on breakfast. Kids under 13 stay free in parent's room. See p. 124.

- **Best for Gay & Lesbian Travelers:** New York is such a hub of gay life and culture that virtually all of the city's hotels welcome gay and lesbian visitors. But if you're looking for like-minded folks, try the fabulous Hollywood-themed **Chelsea Pines Inn,** 317 W. 14th St. (① 888/546-2700; www. chelseapinesinn.com; see p. 104), or the more low-key but equally welcoming **Colonial House Inn,** 318 W. 22nd St. (① 800/

689-3779; www.colonialhouse inn.com; see p. 105).

- **Best Freebies:** The **Travel Inn,** 515 W. 42nd St. (① 800/869-4630; www.newyorkhotel.com), wins on *two* counts. First is the free garage parking—a $25-a-day value at minimum for visitors driving to the city—and free in-and-out privileges. Summer visitors can take advantage of the rooftop swimming pool and sun deck.

- **Best for Travelers with Disabilities:** The comfortable, budget-minded **Skyline Hotel,** 725 10th Ave. (① 800/433-1982; www.sky linehotelny.com), has seven generously sized wheelchair-accessible rooms, ramps, and fire-safety alarms for deaf and blind visitors, plus free parking. See p. 119.

- **Best Splurge:** The Art Deco–style **Hotel Metro,** 45 W. 35th St. (① 800/356-3870; www.hotel metronyc.com), is a midpriced Midtown gem that feels much more expensive than it is, with stylish furnishings, marble bathrooms, an attentive staff, and a rooftop terrace with the best view of the Empire State Building in town. You'll get a surprisingly good value for your dollar here, and free continental breakfast softens the blow. See p. 116.

4 Best Low-Cost Dining Bets

- **Best Newcomer: Bread Tribeca,** 301 Church St. (① 212/334-8282). This bigger version of SoHo's delicious Bread features great sandwiches, but also a wood-burning oven that spins out specialties from the Ligurian region of Italy.

- **Best Chinese Cuisine:** With all the culinary wonders that Chinatown has to offer, this is a tough choice. **New York Noodletown,**

28½ Bowery (① 212/349-0923), where the soups are always fresh and comforting and anything that's salt-baked is guaranteed to be sublime, is my favorite of the moment. See p. 139.

- **Best Diner:** The eclectic **Big Nick's Burger and Pizza Joint,** 2175 Broadway (① 212/362-9232), has offered culinary comfort any time of day or night for over 40 years. The variety of burgers is as mind-boggling as the collection of unidentifiable celebrity photos on the walls.

- **Best Burger: Burger Joint,** at Le Parker Meridien hotel, 118 W. 57th St. (℃ **212/708-7460**), serves great burgers at great prices. Who woulda thunk a fancy hotel like Le Parker Meridien would be the home to a place like that?
- **Best Pizza: Patsy's Pizzeria,** 2287 1st Ave. (℃ **212/534-9783**), has been cranking out coal-oven pies since 1932. It was a favorite of Frank Sinatra, who used to have Patsy's pizzas shipped to him from East Harlem. You can also order by the slice, but do it only if the pie is fresh out of the oven.
- **Best Breakfast:** Uptown, head to **Good Enough To Eat,** 483 Amsterdam Ave. (℃ **212 496-0163**), but try to avoid weekends when the wait sometimes can last until lunch. See p. 174.

   Downtown, head to the trendy Lower East Side and the **Clinton St. Baking Company,** 4 Clinton St. (℃ **646/602-6263**), where the pancakes are worth tasting any time of day. See p. 142.
- **Best Late-Night Hangout:** Half authentic French bistro, half all-American diner, **Florent,** 69 Gansevoort St. (℃ **212/989-5779**), is the hipster crowd's favorite after-hours hangout. Thanks to its good food, great people-watching, and sense of humor, it's mine, too. See p. 150.
- **Best Times Square Restaurant: Virgil's Real BBQ,** 152 W. 44th St. (℃ **212/921-9494;** www. virgilsbbq.com). Times Square is a restaurant wasteland with bad theme restaurants or overpriced national chains. Virgil's, in a sense, is a theme restaurant; the theme being barbecue, but they do an excellent job smoking their

meats. The barbecued lamb is not to be missed. See p. 167.
- **Best Old New York Experience: Eisenberg's Coffee Shop,** 174 5th Ave. (℃ **212/675-5096**), has served the same retro fare since 1929—and prices are retro, too. New Yorkers consider this the best tuna salad in town, but the Reuben is my ticket to culinary happiness. See p. 157.
- **Best Deli: Katz's Delicatessen,** 205 E. Houston St. (℃ **212/254-2246**), is the choice among those who know their kreplach, knishes, and pastrami. No cutesy sandwiches named for celebrities here—just top-notch Jewish classics. See p. 142.
- **Best for Families:** Kids of all ages love **Serendipity 3,** 225 E. 60th St. (℃ **212/838-3531**), a classic ice-cream parlor like your childhood memories, but *better*. See p. 177. For more kid-friendly choices, see "Family-Friendly Restaurants," in chapter 6.
- **Best Hot Chocolate:** The lines begin forming as soon as the doors open on weekends in the winter at **Jacques Torres Chocolate,** 60 Water St., Brooklyn (℃ **718/875-9772;** www.mrchocolate.com). And for good reason: rich, creamy, satiny smooth; really indescribable. Also at 350 Hudson St. in TriBeCa. See p. 276.
- **Best Post-Museum Treat:** After visiting the very interesting **Lower East Side Tenement Museum,** 90 Orchard St. (℃ **212/431-0233;** www.tenement.org), and seeing how some of New York's early-20th-century immigrants struggled to make ends meet, reward yourself by going next door to sample New York's best gelato at **Il Laboratorio del Gelato,** 95 Orchard St. (℃ **212/343-9922;** www.laboratoriodelgelato.com).

- **Best Bagels: Absolute Bagels,** 2788 Broadway (© **212/932-2105**). They're not huge like some bagels these days, but they are always hot and cooked to perfection.
- **Best Baked Goods & Sweets:** There's a lot of competition in this category, but the ultimate kudos go to Franco-Brussels import **Le Pain Quotidien,** 100 Grand St. (© **212/625-9009**), for its fresh-baked breads (baked in small batches five times daily) and scrumptious pastries and sweets, served in a SoHo-loft-goes-farmhouse setting. (You'll find locations in the Flatiron District and on the Upper West and Upper East Sides, too.) See p. 144.
- **Best Cheap Meal:** Though the $2.45 "recession special"—two hot dogs and a fruit drink—at **Gray's Papaya,** 2090 Broadway (© **212/799-0243**), is almost a $1 increase from the previous recession, it's still a bargain. But is it any good? Witness the lines out the door every day for lunch.
- **Best Ice Cream:** A stop at **Brooklyn Ice Cream Factory,** Fulton Ferry Landing Pier, Brooklyn (© **718/246-3963**), is the perfect reward for a brisk walk across the Brooklyn Bridge. A rich, homemade ice cream with a view of the Manhattan skyline is a hard combination to beat.

- **Best 24-Hour Restaurant:** Ukrainian diner **Veselka,** 144 2nd Ave. (© **212/228-9682**), will meet almost all your food needs any time of day or night. If you want borscht at midnight, you can get it. If you want French toast at 4am, you can have it. It's a comfort to know they will make pretty much whatever you want when you want it. See p. 148.
- **Best Soul Food:** Not only is **Charles' Southern Style Kitchen,** 2841 8th Ave. (© **877/813-2920**), the best soul food in the city, it's also the best buffet. For $9.95 on weekdays and $12 on weekends, the down-home offerings at this tiny Harlem restaurant will tempt you to make an obscene number of visits to the buffet line. See p. 178.
- **Best Taqueria:** With the influx of Mexican immigrants to El Barrio (East Harlem) a number of very good Mexican restaurants and groceries have opened. **El Paso Taqueria,** 1642 Lexington Ave. (© **212/831-9831**), is the best of the bunch.
- **Best Neighborhood for Food:** **Hell's Kitchen,** the area comprising 9th Avenue from the 30s through the 50s, features so many inexpensive and exciting ethnic choices (so devilishly good!), you'd need at least a month's visit here to sample them all.

Planning an Affordable Trip to New York City

In the pages that follow, you'll find everything you need to know to handle the practical details of planning your trip in advance—airlines and area airports, a calendar of events, resources for those with special needs, and much more—plus time-tested advice on how to save money at every turn.

1 Visitor Information

For information before you leave home, your best source (besides this book, of course) is **NYC & Company,** the organization that fronts the New York Convention & Visitors Bureau (NYCVB), 810 7th Ave., New York, NY 10019. You can call ✆ **800/NYC-VISIT** to order the **Official NYC Visitor Kit,** which contains the *Official NYC Guide* detailing hotels, restaurants, theaters, attractions, events, and more; a foldout map; a decent newsletter on the latest goings-on in the city; and brochures on attractions and services. It costs $5.95 to receive the packet (payable by credit card) in 7 to 10 days, $9.95 for rush delivery (3–4 business days) to U.S. addresses and international orders. (*Note:* I have received complaints that packages don't always strictly adhere to these time frames.)

You can also find a wealth of free information on the bureau's website, **www.nycvisit.com**. To speak with a travel counselor who can answer specific questions, call ✆ **212/484-1222,** which is staffed weekdays from 8:30am to 6pm Eastern Standard Time, weekends from 9am to 5pm Eastern Standard Time.

FOR U.K. VISITORS The **NYCVB Visitor Information Center** is at 36 Southwark Bridge Rd., London, SE1 9EU (✆ **020/7202 6368**). You can order the Official NYC Visitor Kit by sending an A5-size self-addressed envelope and 72p postage to the above address. For New York–bound travelers in the London area, the center also offers free one-on-one travel-planning assistance.

2 Money

You never have to carry too much cash in New York (although always make sure you have at least $20 in taxi fare on hand).

In most Manhattan neighborhoods, you can find a bank with **ATMs** every couple of blocks. The only places you may have some difficulty are in more far-flung neighborhoods like the far East Village or uptown in Harlem (though it seems like every deli or bodega has an ATM these days).

The easiest and best way to get cash away from home is from an ATM (automated teller machine). The **Cirrus** (℃ 800/424-7787; www.master card.com) and **PLUS** (℃ 800/843-7587; www.visa.com) networks span the globe; look at the back of your bank card to see which network you're on, then call or check online for ATM locations at your destination. Be sure you know your personal identification number (PIN) before you leave home and be sure to find out your daily withdrawal limit before you depart. Also keep in mind that many banks impose a fee every time a card is used at a different bank's ATM, averaging from $1 to $3. On top of this, the bank from which you withdraw cash may charge its own fee. To compare banks' ATM fees within the U.S., use www.bankrate.com.

You can also get cash advances on your credit card at an ATM. Keep in mind that credit card companies try to protect themselves from theft by limiting the funds someone can withdraw outside their home country, so call your credit card company before you leave home.

TRAVELER'S CHECKS

Traveler's checks are something of an anachronism from the days before the ATM made cash accessible at any time. Traveler's checks used to be the only alternative to traveling with dangerously large amounts of cash. They are as reliable as currency, and can be replaced if lost or stolen.

These days, traveler's checks are less necessary because most cities have 24-hour ATMs that allow you to withdraw small amounts of cash as needed. However, keep in mind that you will likely be charged an ATM withdrawal fee if the bank is not your own, so if you're withdrawing money every day, you might be better off with traveler's checks—provided that you don't mind showing identification every time you want to cash one.

You can get traveler's checks at almost any bank. **American Express** offers denominations of $20, $50, $100, $500, and (for cardholders only) $1,000. You'll pay a service charge ranging from 1% to 4%. You can also get American Express traveler's checks over the phone by calling ℃ 800/221-7282; Amex gold and platinum cardholders who use this number are exempt from the 1% fee.

Visa offers traveler's checks at Citibank locations nationwide, as well as at several other banks. The service charge ranges between 1.5% and 2%; checks come in denominations of $20, $50, $100, $500, and $1,000. Call ℃ 800/732-1322 for information. AAA members can obtain Visa checks without a fee at most AAA offices or by calling ℃ 866/339-3378. **MasterCard** also offers traveler's checks. Call ℃ 800/223-9920 for a location near you.

If you choose to carry traveler's checks, be sure to keep a record of their serial numbers separate from your checks in the event that they are stolen or lost. You'll get a refund faster if you know the numbers.

CREDIT CARDS

Credit cards are a safe way to carry money, they provide a convenient record of all your expenses, and they generally offer good exchange rates. You can also withdraw cash advances from your credit cards at banks or ATMs, provided you know your PIN. If you've forgotten yours, or didn't even know you had one, call the number on the back of your credit card and ask the bank to send it to you. It usually takes 5 to 7 business days, though some banks will provide the number over the phone if you tell them your mother's maiden name or some other personal information.

New York Metro Area

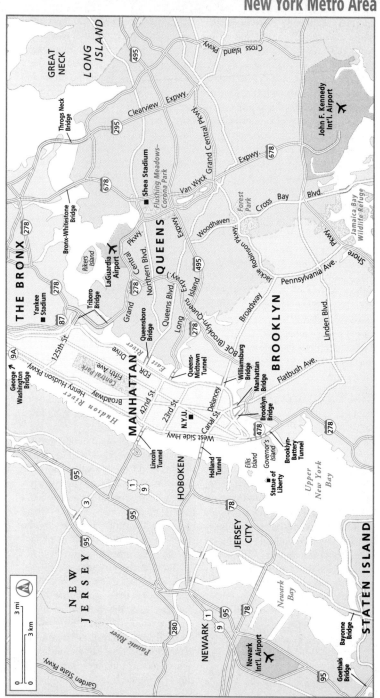

3 When to Go

Summer or winter, rain or shine, there's always great stuff going on in New York City, so there's no real "best" time to go.

Culture hounds might come in fall, winter, and early spring, when the theater and performing arts seasons reach their heights (though summer performance festivals have been springing up over the last few years). During summer, many top cultural institutions, especially Lincoln Center, offer free, alfresco entertainment. Those who want to see the biggest hits on Broadway usually have the best luck getting tickets in the slower months of January and February.

Gourmands might find it easiest to land the best tables during July and August, when New Yorkers escape the city on weekends. If you prefer to walk every city block to take in the sights, spring and fall usually offer the mildest and most pleasant weather.

New York is a nonstop holiday party from early December through the start of the New Year. Celebrations of the season abound in festive holiday windows and events like the lighting of the Rockefeller Center tree and the Radio City Christmas Spectacular—not to mention those seasonal sales that make New York a holiday shopping bonanza. However, keep in mind that hotel prices go sky high (more on that below), and the crowds are almost intolerable. If you'd rather have more of the city to yourself—a better chance at restaurant reservations and show tickets, easier access to museums and other attractions—choose another time of year to visit.

MONEY MATTERS Hotel prices are more flexible than they've been in years, but New York hotels are by no means throwing a fire sale. Therefore, if money is a big concern, you might want to follow these rough seasonal guidelines.

The least expensive time to visit is in winter, between the first of the year and early April. Sure, you might have to bear some cold weather, but that's when hotels are suffering from the post-holiday blues, and rooms often go for a relative song—a song in this case meaning a room with a private bathroom for as little as $125, or even lower. AAA cardholders could even do better in many cases (generally a 5%–10% savings, if the hotel offers a AAA discount). However, be aware that the occasional convention or event, such as February's annual Fashion Week, can sometimes throw a wrench in your winter savings plans.

Spring and fall are traditionally the busiest, and most expensive, seasons after holiday time. Don't expect hotels to be handing you deals, but you may be able to negotiate a decent rate.

The city is drawing more families these days, and they usually visit in the summer. Still, the prospect of heat and humidity keeps some people away, making July and the first half of August a significantly cheaper time to visit than later in the year; good hotel deals are often available.

Christmas is *not* a good time for budget-minded travelers. The first 2 weeks of December—the shopping weeks—are the absolute worst when it comes to scoring an affordable hotel room; that's when shoppers from around the world converge on the town to catch the holiday spirit and spend, spend, spend.

But Thanksgiving can be a great time to come, believe it or not: Business travelers have gone home for the holiday, and the holiday shoppers haven't yet arrived. It's a little-known secret that most hotels away from the Thanksgiving Day Parade route have empty rooms, and they're usually willing to make deals to fill them.

WEATHER The worst weather in New York is during that long week or 10 days that usually arrive each summer between mid-July and mid-August, when temperatures go up to around 100°F (38°C) with 90% humidity. You feel sticky all day, the streets smell horrible, everyone's cranky, and the concrete canyons become furnaces. It can be no fun walking around in this weather. Don't get put off by this—summer has its compensations, such as wonderful free open-air concerts and other events, as I've already mentioned—but bear it in mind. But if you are at all temperature sensitive, your odds of getting comfortable weather are better in June or September.

Another period when you might not like to stroll around the city is during January or February, when temperatures are commonly in the 20s (–7° to –2° Celsius) and those concrete canyons turn into wind tunnels. The city looks gorgeous for about a day after a snowfall, but the streets soon become an ugly, slushy mess. Again, you never know—temperatures have regularly been in the 30s (–1° to 4° Celsius) and mid-40s (about 7° Celsius) during the past few winters. If you hit the weather jackpot, you could have a bargain bonanza (see "Money Matters," above).

Fall and spring are the best times in New York. From April to June and September to November, temperatures are mild and pleasant, and the light is beautiful. With the leaves changing in Central Park and just the hint of crispness in the air, October is a fabulous time to be here—but expect to pay for the privilege.

If you want to know how to pack just before you go, check the Weather Channel's online 10-day forecast at **www.weather.com**; I like to balance it against CNN's online 5-day forecast at **www.cnn.com/weather**. You can also look up the local weather anywhere in the country online at any of many sites, including Yahoo.com.

New York's Average Temperature & Rainfall

	Jan	Feb	Mar	Apr	May	June	July	Aug	Sept	Oct	Nov	Dec
Daily Temp. (°F)	38	40	48	61	71	80	85	84	77	67	54	42
Daily Temp. (°C)	3	4	9	16	22	27	29	29	25	19	12	6
Days of Precipitation	11	10	11	11	11	10	11	10	8	8	9	10

NEW YORK CITY CALENDAR OF EVENTS

The following information is always subject to change. Always confirm information before you make plans around a specific event. Call the venue or the NYCVB at © 212/484-1222, go to **www.nycvisit. com**, or pick up a copy of *Time Out New York* once you arrive in the city for the latest details.

January

Chinese New Year. Every year, Chinatown rings in its own New Year (based on a lunar calendar) with 2 weeks of celebrations, including parades with dragon and lion dancers, plus vivid costumes of all kinds. The parade usually winds throughout Chinatown along Mott, Canal, and Bayard streets, and along East Broadway. Chinese New Year falls on February 9 in 2005 and it's the Year of the Rooster. Call the NYCVB hot line at © **212/484-1222** or the Asian American Business Development Center at © **212/966-0100.**

Restaurant Week. Twice a year some of the best restaurants in New

York offer three-course prix-fixe meals at almost affordable prices. At lunch, the deal is $20, while dinner is $30. Reserve immediately. Call ℂ 212/484-1222 for info, or visit www.nycvisit.com. Late January.

February

Westminster Kennel Club Dog Show. The ultimate purebred pooch fest. Some 30,000 dog fanciers from the world over congregate at **Madison Square Garden** for the 129th "World Series of Dogdom." All 2,500 dogs are American Kennel Club Champions of Record, competing for the best-in-show trophy. Check the website www.westminsterkennelclub.org for further information. Tickets become available after January 1 through **Ticketmaster** (ℂ 212/307-7171; www.ticketmaster.com). Mid-February.

March

St. Patrick's Day Parade. More than 150,000 marchers join in the world's largest civilian parade, as 5th Avenue from 44th to 86th streets rings with the sounds of bands and bagpipes. The parade usually starts at 11am, but go extra early if you want a good spot. Call ℂ 212/484-1222. March 17.

Easter Parade. This isn't a traditional parade, per se: There are no marching bands, no baton twirlers. Once upon a time, New York's gentry came out to show off their tasteful but discreet toppings. Today, if you were planning to slip on a tasteful little number—say something delicately woven in straw with a simple flower or two that matches your gloves—you will *not* be the grandest lady in this springtime hike along 5th Avenue from 48th to 57th streets. It's more about flamboyant exhibitionism, with hats and costumes that get more outrageous every year—and anybody can join in for free. The parade generally runs Easter Sunday from about 10am to 3 or 4pm. Call ℂ 212/484-1222. March 27.

April

New York International Auto Show. Here's the irony: You don't need a car in New York, yet this is the largest car show in the United States. Held at the **Jacob K. Javits Convention Center,** many concept cars show up that will never roll off the assembly line but are fun to dream about. Call ℂ 718/746-5300, or point your browser to www.autoshowny.com or www.javitscenter.com. Early April.

May

Bike New York: The Great Five Boro Bike Tour. The largest mass-participation cycling event in the United States attracts about 30,000 cyclists from all over the world. After a 42-mile ride through the five boroughs, finalists are greeted with a traditional New York–style celebration of food and music. Call ℂ 212/932-BIKE (2453) or visit www.bikenewyork.org to register. First or second Sunday in May.

Ninth Avenue International Food Festival. Street fairs are part of the New York landscape each spring and summer, but this is one of the best. Here you can spend the day sampling sizzling Italian sausages, homemade pierogies, spicy curries, and an assortment of other ethnic dishes. Street musicians, bands, and vendors add to the festive atmosphere at the city's best street fair, stretching along 9th Avenue from 37th to 57th streets. Call ℂ 212/484-1222. One weekend in mid-May.

Fleet Week. About 10,000 navy and Coast Guard personnel are "at liberty" in New York for the annual Fleet Week at the end of May. Usually from 1 to 4pm daily, you can watch the ships and aircraft carriers as they dock at the piers on the west side of Manhattan, tour them with on-duty personnel, and watch some dramatic exhibitions by the U.S. Marines. Even if you don't take in any of the events, you'll know it's Fleet Week, because those 10,000 sailors invade Midtown in their starched white uniforms. It's wonderful—just like *On the Town* come to life. Call ✆ **212/245-0072,** or visit www.fleetweek.com (your best source for a full list of events) or www.intrepidmuseum. org. Late May.

June

Museum Mile Festival. Fifth Avenue from 82nd to 104th streets is closed to cars from 6 to 9pm as 20,000-plus strollers enjoy live music, from Broadway tunes to string quartets; street entertainers, from juggling to giant puppets; and free admission to nine Museum Mile institutions, including the Metropolitan Museum of Art and the Guggenheim. Call ✆ **212/606-2296** or any of the participating institutions for details. Usually the second Tuesday in June.

Summer Parades. During the summer there is a parade for almost every nationality or ethnicity. June is the month for (among others) the very colorful **Puerto Rican Day Parade** and the **Lesbian and Gay Pride March,** where 5th Avenue goes wild as the GLBT community celebrates with bands, marching groups, floats, and plenty of panache. The parade starts on upper 5th Avenue around 52nd Street and continues into the Village, where a street festival and a waterfront dance party with fireworks cap the day. Call ✆ **212/807-7433** or check www.hopinc. org. Mid- to late June.

SummerStage. A summer-long festival of outdoor performances in **Central Park,** featuring world music, pop, folk, and jazz artists ranging from Steve Earle to Craig David to Basement Jaxx to the New York Grand Opera (always performing Verdi) to the Chinese Golden Dragon Acrobats. Performances are often free, but certain events require purchased tickets (usually less than $30). Call ✆ **212/360-2756** or visit www.summer stage.org. June through August.

Shakespeare in the Park. The Delacorte Theater in **Central Park** is the setting for first-rate free performances under the stars—often with TV and film stars on the stage. For details, see "Park It! Shakespeare, Music & Other Free Fun," in chapter 9. Call ✆ **212/539-8750,** or go to www.publictheater. org. Late June through August.

Restaurant Week. For information, see "January," above. Late June.

July

Independence Day Harbor Festival and Fourth of July Fireworks Spectacular. Start the day amid the crowds at the Great July Fourth Festival in Lower Manhattan, and then catch Macy's fireworks extravaganza (one of the country's most fantastic) over the East River (the best vantage point is from FDR Dr., which closes to vehicle traffic several hours before sunset). Call ✆ **212/484-1222,** or Macy's Visitor Center at 212/494-2922. July 4.

Lincoln Center Festival. This festival celebrates the best of the performing arts from all over the world—theater, ballet, contemporary dance, opera, nouveau circus performances, even puppet and media-based art. Recent editions have featured performances by

Ornette Coleman, the Royal Opera, the Royal Ballet, and the New York Philharmonic. Schedules are usually available in mid-March, and tickets go on sale in late May or early June. Call ⓒ **212/546-2656,** or visit www.lincolncenter.org. Throughout July.

Midsummer Night's Swing. Dancing duos head to the **Lincoln Center Fountain Plaza** for romantic evenings of Big Band swing, salsa, and tango under the stars to the sounds of top-flight bands. Dance lessons are offered with the purchase of a ticket. Call ⓒ **212/875-5766,** or visit www.lincolncenter.org. July and August.

Mostly Mozart. World-renowned ensembles and soloists (Alicia de Larrocha and André Watts have performed in the past) are featured at this month-long series at **Avery Fisher Hall.** Schedules are usually available in mid-April, and tickets in early May. Call ⓒ **212/875-5030** or 212/546-2656 for information, 212/721-6500 to order tickets, or visit www.lincolncenter.org. Late July through August.

Siren Festival. The *Village Voice* sponsors this annual free outdoor music festival at Coney Island. The bands are generally a mix of beloved cult acts and up-and-coming cult acts (Mission of Burma, Death Cab for Cutie). The crowd often exceeds 100,000, driving the hipster quotient to stratospheric levels. Call ⓒ **212/475-3333** for info, or visit www.villagevoice.com. Late July.

August

Lincoln Center Out-of-Doors. This series of free music and dance performances is held outdoors on the plazas of **Lincoln Center.** Call ⓒ **212/875-5108** or 212/546-2656, or visit www.lincolncenter.org for this year's schedule (usually available in mid-July). Throughout August.

Harlem Week. The world's largest black and Hispanic cultural festival actually spans almost the whole month to include the Black Film Festival, the Harlem Jazz and Music Festival, and the Taste of Harlem Food Festival. Expect a full slate of music, from gospel to hip-hop, and lots of other festivities. Call ⓒ **212/484-1222.** Throughout August.

New York International Fringe Festival. Held in a variety of downtown venues and park spaces for a mainly hipster crowd, this arts festival presents alternative as well as traditional theater, musicals, dance, comedy, and all manner of performance art, including new media. Literally hundreds of events are held at all hours over about 10 days in late August. The quality can vary wildly (lots of performers use Fringe as a workshop to develop their acts and shows), and some performances really push the envelope. Nonetheless, you'd be surprised at how many shows are actually *good.* (The Tony-award-winning Broadway musical *Urinetown* started out at the Fringe). Call ⓒ **888/FRINGE-NYC** or 212/279-4488, or visit www.fringenyc.org. Late August.

HOWL Festival. In addition to the Fringe, other theater/performance festivals have started to fill the traditional August vacuum. The HOWL Festival (named for the Allan Ginsberg poem) became an instant classic when it debuted in 2003. HOWL celebrates the Bohemian history and flash and trash of the East Village with events ranging from marathon poetry readings to the revived drag festival Wigstock. Call ⓒ **212/505-2225** or visit www.howlfestival.com. Late August.

U.S. Open Tennis Championships. The final Grand Slam event of the tennis season is held at the Arthur Ashe Stadium at the USTA National Tennis Center, the largest public tennis center in the world, at **Flushing Meadows Park** in Queens. Tickets go on sale in May or early June. The event sells out immediately because many of the tickets are held by corporate sponsors who hand them out to customers. (It's worth it to check the list of sponsors to determine if anyone you know has a connection for getting tickets.) You can usually buy scalped tickets outside the complex (an illegal practice, of course), which is right next to Shea Stadium. The last few matches of the tournament are the most expensive, but you'll see a lot more tennis early on, when your ticket allows you to wander the outside courts and view several different matches. Call ✆ **888/OPEN-TIX** or 718/760-6200 well in advance; visit www.usopen.org or www.usta.com for additional information. Two weeks around Labor Day.

September

West Indian–American Day Parade. This annual Brooklyn event is New York's largest and best street celebration. Come for the extravagant costumes, pulsating rhythms (soca, calypso, reggae), bright colors, folklore, food (jerk chicken, oxtail soup, Caribbean soul food), and two million hip-shaking revelers. The route can change from year to year, but it usually runs along Eastern Parkway from Utica Avenue to Grand Army Plaza (at the gateway to Prospect Park). Call ✆ **212/484-1222** or 718/625-1515. Labor Day.

Broadway on Broadway. This free alfresco afternoon show features the songs and casts from virtually every Broadway production, performing on a stage erected in the middle of Times Square. Call ✆ **212/768-1560,** or visit www.timessquare bid.org and click on "Events." Sunday in early September.

New York Film Festival. Legendary hits *Pulp Fiction* and *Mean Streets* both had their U.S. premieres at the Film Society of Lincoln Center's 2-week festival, a major stop on the film fest circuit. Screenings are held in various Lincoln Center venues; advance tickets are a good bet always, and a necessity for certain events (especially evening and weekend screenings). Call ✆ **212/875-5600** for information, 212/875-5050 for tickets, or check out www.filmlinc.com. Two weeks from late September to early October.

BAM Next Wave Festival. One of the city's most important cultural events takes place at the **Brooklyn Academy of Music.** The months-long festival showcases experimental new dance, theater, and music works by both renowned and lesser-known international artists. Recent celebrated performances have included Astor Piazzolla's *Maria de Buenos Aires* (featuring Piazzolla disciple Gidon Kremer), the 25th anniversary of the Kronos Quartet, and choreographer Bill T. Jones's *We Set Out Early . . . Visibility Was Poor* (set to the music of Igor Stravinsky, John Cage, and Peteris Vask). Call ✆ **718/636-4100** or visit www.bam.org. September through December.

October

New York is Book Country. One of our favorite street fairs is this celebration of the written word, which relocated to Washington Square Park in 2004. Hundreds of exhibitors, from huge publishers to small presses, and other literary-minded organizations present their wares, along with author readings and book signings. It's a book-lover's paradise. Visit www.nyis bookcountry.com for schedule. First weekend in October.

Feast of St. Francis. Animals from goldfish to elephants are blessed as thousands of Homo sapiens look on at the **Cathedral of St. John the Divine.** A magical experience—pets, of course, are welcome. A festive fair follows the blessing and music events. Buy tickets in advance because they can be hard to come by. Call © **212/316-7540** or 212/662-7133 for tickets, or visit www.stjohndivine.org. First Sunday in October.

Outdoor Ice-Skating. Show off your skating style in the limelight at the diminutive **Rockefeller Center** rink (© **212/332-7654;** www. rockefellercenter.com), open from mid-October to mid-March or early April (you'll skate under the magnificent Christmas tree for the month of Dec). In Central Park, try **Wollman Rink** on the east side of the park between 62nd and 63rd streets (© **212/439-6900;** www.wollmanskatingrink.com), and **Lasker Rink,** midpark between 106th and 108th streets (© **917/492-3850**). Both Central Park rinks usually close in early April.

Greenwich Village Halloween Parade. This is Halloween at its most outrageous. You may have heard Lou Reed singing about it on his classic album *New York*—he wasn't exaggerating. Drag queens and assorted other flamboyant types parade through the Village in wildly creative costumes. The parade route has changed over the years, but most recently it has started after sunset at Spring Street and marched up 6th Avenue to 23rd Street or Union Square. Call

the *Village Voice* Parade hot line at © **212/475-3333,** ext. 14044; go to www.halloween-nyc.com; or check the papers for the exact route so you can watch—or participate, if you have the threads and the imagination. October 31.

November

The Chocolate Show. You know about New York's car, boat, and antiques shows, but they have nothing on this burgeoning 4-day event. My perennial favorite, this show is devoted solely to chocolate; it takes place each year 2 weeks before Thanksgiving and is open to the public. The event is held at the Metropolitan Pavilion in Chelsea and features booths representing over 50 of the world's best chocolate makers, chocolate tastings, demonstrations by top pastry chefs, and activities for children. For more information call **866/CHOC-NYC** or 212/889-5112, or visit the show's website, www.chocolateshow.com. Second week of November.

New York City Marathon. Some 30,000 hopefuls from around the world participate in the largest U.S. marathon, and more than a million fans cheer them on as they follow a route that visits all five New York boroughs and finishes at Central Park. Call © **212/423-2249** or 212/860-4455, or point your Web browser to www.nyrrc.org, where you can find applications to run. November 6 in 2005.

Radio City Music Hall Christmas Spectacular. A rather gaudy extravaganza, but lots of fun nonetheless. Starring the Radio City Rockettes and a cast that includes live animals (just try to picture the camels sauntering in the 6th Ave. entrance!). For information, call © **212/247-4777** or visit www.radiocity.com; buy tickets at the box office or via Ticketmaster's **Radio City Hot**

Line (℅ 212/307-1000), or visit www.ticketmaster.com. Throughout November and December.

Macy's Thanksgiving Day Parade. The procession from Central Park West and 77th Street and down Broadway to Herald Square at 34th Street continues to be a national tradition. Huge hot-air balloons in the forms of Rocky and Bullwinkle, Snoopy, Underdog, the Pink Panther, Bart Simpson, and other cartoon favorites are the best part of the fun. The night before, you can usually see the big blow-up on Central Park West at 79th Street; call in advance to see if it will be open to the public. Call ℅ **212/484-1222,** or Macy's Visitor Center at 212/494-2922. November 24 in 2005.

Big Apple Circus. New York City's homegrown performing-arts circus is a favorite with children and everyone who's young at heart. Big Apple is committed to maintaining the classical circus tradition with sensitivity, and only features animals that have a traditional working relationship with humans. A tent is pitched in **Damrosch Park** at **Lincoln Center.** Call ℅ **212/268-2500,** or visit www.bigapplecircus. org. November through January.

The Nutcracker. Tchaikovsky's holiday favorite is performed by the New York City Ballet at **Lincoln Center.** The annual schedule is available from mid-July, and tickets usually go on sale in early October. Call ℅ **212/870-5570,** or go online to www.nycballet.com. Late November through early January.

Lighting of the Rockefeller Center Christmas Tree. The annual lighting ceremony is accompanied by an ice-skating show, singing, entertainment, and a huge crowd. The tree stays lit around the clock until after the new year. Call ℅ 212/332-6868 or visit www.

rockefellercenter.com for this year's date. Late November or early December.

December

Holiday Trimmings. Stroll down festive 5th Avenue and you'll see a 27-foot sparkling snowflake floating over the intersection outside **Tiffany's,** the **Cartier** building ribboned and bowed in red, wreaths warming the necks of the **New York Public Library**'s lions, and fanciful figurines in the windows of **Saks Fifth Avenue** and **Lord & Taylor.** Madison Avenue between 55th and 60th streets is also a good bet; **Sony Plaza** usually displays something fabulous, as does **Barneys New York.** Throughout December.

Christmas Traditions. In addition to the **Radio City Music Hall Christmas Spectacular** and the New York City Ballet's staging of *The Nutcracker* (see "November," above), traditional holiday events include *A Christmas Carol* at **The Theater at Madison Square Garden** (℅ 212/465-6741; www.thegarden.com; for tickets, call ℅ 212/307-7171 or go to www.ticketmaster.com), usually featuring a big name playing Scrooge to draw in the crowds (Roger Daltrey, Ben Vereen). At **Avery Fisher Hall** is the National Chorale's singalong performances of Handel's *Messiah* (℅ 212/875-5030; www.lincoln center.org) for a week before Christmas. Don't worry if the only words you know are "Alleluia, Alleluia!"—a lyrics sheet is given to ticket holders. Throughout December.

Lighting of the Hanukkah Menorah. Everything is done on a grand scale in New York, so it's no surprise that the world's largest menorah (32 ft. high) is at Manhattan's **Grand Army Plaza,** 5th Avenue and 59th Street. Hanukkah celebrations begin at sunset, with the lighting of the first of the giant electric candles. December 26, 2005.

New Year's Eve. The biggest party of them all happens in **Times Square,** where hundreds of thousands of raucous revelers count down in unison the year's final seconds until the new lighted ball drops at midnight at 1 Times Square. This one, in the cold surrounded by thousands of very drunk revelers, almost all from out of town, is definitely a masochist's delight. Call ✆ **212/768-1560,** 212/484-1222, or visit www.times squarebid.org. December 31.

Runner's World **Midnight Run.** Enjoy **fireworks** followed by the New York Road Runners Club's annual run in **Central Park,** which is fun for runners and spectators alike; call ✆ **212/860-4455** or visit www.nyrrc.org. December 31.

Brooklyn's fireworks celebration. Head to Brooklyn for the city's largest New Year's Eve **fireworks** celebration at Prospect Park; call ✆ **718/965-8999** or visit www. prospectpark.org. December 31.

New Year's Eve Concert for Peace. The Cathedral of St. John the Divine is known for its annual concert, whose performers have included the Manhattan School of Music Chamber Sinfonia, Tony award–winning composer Jason Robert Brown *(Parade),* American soprano Lauren Flanigan, and the Forces of Nature Dance Company. Call ✆ **212/316-7540** for info, 212/662-2133 for tickets, or visit www.stjohndivine. org. December 31.

4 Travel Insurance

Check your existing insurance policies and credit card coverage before you buy travel insurance. You may already be covered for lost luggage, canceled tickets, or medical expenses. The cost of travel insurance varies widely, depending on the cost and length of your trip, your age, your health, and the type of trip you're taking.

TRIP-CANCELLATION INSURANCE Trip-cancellation insurance helps you get your money back if you have to back out of a trip, if you have to go home early, or if your travel supplier goes bankrupt. Allowed reasons for cancellation can range from sickness to natural disasters to the State Department declaring your destination unsafe for travel. (Insurers usually won't cover vague fears, though, as many travelers discovered who tried to cancel their trips in Oct 2001 because they were wary of flying.) In this unstable world, trip-cancellation insurance is a good buy if you're getting tickets well in advance—who

knows what the state of the world, or of your airline, will be in 9 months? Insurance policy details vary, so read the fine print—and especially make sure that your airline or cruise line is on the list of carriers covered in case of bankruptcy. For information, contact one of the following insurers: **Access America** (✆ 866/807-3982; www. accessamerica.com), **Travel Guard International** (✆ 800/826-4919; www.travelguard.com), **Travel Insured International** (✆ 800/243-3174; www.travelinsured.com), and **Travelex Insurance Services** (✆ 888/457-4602; www.travelex-insurance.com).

MEDICAL INSURANCE Most health insurance policies cover you if you get sick away from home—but check, particularly if you're insured by an HMO.

LOST-LUGGAGE INSURANCE On domestic flights, checked baggage is covered up to $2,500 per ticketed passenger. If you plan to check items more valuable than the standard liability, see if your valuables are covered by your homeowner's policy, get baggage insurance as part of your comprehensive travel-insurance package, or buy Travel Guard's "BagTrak" product. Don't buy insurance at the airport, as it's usually overpriced. Be sure to take any valuables or irreplaceable items with you in your carry-on luggage, as many valuables (including books,

money, and electronics) aren't covered by airline policies.

If your luggage is lost, immediately file a lost-luggage claim at the airport, detailing the luggage contents. For most airlines, you must report delayed, damaged, or lost baggage within 4 hours of arrival. The airlines are required to deliver luggage, once found, directly to your house or destination free of charge.

5 Health & Safety

WHAT TO DO IF YOU GET SICK AWAY FROM HOME

If you suffer from a chronic illness, consult your doctor before your departure. For conditions like epilepsy, diabetes, or heart problems, wear a **Medic Alert Identification Tag** (© 888/633-4298; www.medicalert. org), which will immediately alert doctors to your condition and give them access to your records through Medic Alert's 24-hour hot line.

If you do get sick, ask the concierge at your hotel to recommend a local doctor, even his or her own. This will probably yield a better recommendation than any 800 number would. There are several walk-in medical centers, like **DOCS at New York Healthcare,** 55 E. 34th St. (btwn Park and Madison aves.; © 800/673-3627), for non-emergency illnesses. The clinic, affiliated with Beth Israel Medical Center, is open Monday through Thursday from 8am to 8pm, Friday from 8am to 7pm, Saturday from 9am to 3pm, and Sunday from 9am to 2pm. The **NYU Downtown Hospital** offers physician referrals at © 888/698-3362.

If you have dental problems, a nationwide referral service known as **1-800-DENTIST** (© 800/336-8478) will provide the name of a nearby dentist or clinic.

If you can't find a doctor who can help you right away, try the emergency

room at the local hospital. For a list of local hospitals, see "Fast Facts: New York City," in chapter 4.

Most health insurance policies cover you if you get sick away from home—but check, particularly if you're insured by an HMO.

In most cases, your existing health plan will provide the coverage you need. But double-check; you may want to buy **travel medical insurance** instead. (See the section on insurance, above.) Bring your insurance ID card with you when you travel.

Pack **prescription medications** in your carry-on luggage, and carry prescription medications in their original containers, with pharmacy labels—otherwise they won't make it through airport security. Also bring along copies of your prescriptions in case you lose your pills or run out. Don't forget an extra pair of contact lenses or prescription glasses.

STAYING SAFE

In 2004, the FBI rated New York City as the safest large city in the United States and it remains one of the safest, but it is still a large city and crime most definitely exists. Here are a few tips for staying safe. For more, see "Playing it Safe" in chapter 4.

Trust your instincts, because they're usually right.

You'll rarely be hassled, but it's always best to walk with a sense of purpose and self-confidence. Don't stop in the middle of the sidewalk to pull out and peruse your map.

Anywhere in the city, if you find yourself on a deserted street that feels unsafe, it probably is; leave as quickly as possible.

If you do find yourself accosted by someone with or without a weapon, remember to keep your anger in check and that the most reasonable response (maddening though it may be) is not to resist.

6 Specialized Travel Resources

TRAVELERS WITH DISABILITIES

Most disabilities shouldn't stop anyone from traveling. There are new options and resources out there all the time, and New York is more accessible to travelers with disabilities than ever before. The city's bus system is wheelchair friendly, and most of the major sightseeing attractions are easily accessible. Even so, **always call first** to be sure that the places you want to go to are fully accessible.

Most hotels are ADA-compliant, with suitable rooms for wheelchair-bound travelers as well as those with other disabilities. But before you book, **ask lots of questions based on your needs.** Many city hotels are housed in older buildings that have had to be modified to meet requirements; still, both elevators and bathrooms can be on the small side, and other impediments may exist. If you have mobility issues, you'll probably do best to book one of the city's newer hotels, which tend to be more spacious and accommodating. At **www.access-able.com** (see below), you'll find links to New York's best accessible accommodations (click on "World Cities"). Some Broadway theaters and other performance venues provide total wheelchair accessibility; others provide partial accessibility. Many also offer lower-priced tickets for theatergoers with disabilities and their companions, though you'll need to check individual policies and reserve in advance.

GENERAL TRAVEL INFORMATION Organizations that offer assistance to travelers with disabilities include the **Moss Rehab Hospital** (www.mossresourcenet.org), which provides a library of accessible-travel resources online; the **Society for Accessible Travel and Hospitality** (© 212/447-7284; www.sath.org; annual membership fees: $45 adults, $30 seniors and students), which offers a wealth of travel resources for all types of disabilities and informed recommendations on destinations, access guides, travel agents, tour operators, vehicle rentals, and companion services; and the **American Foundation for the Blind** (© 800/232-5463; www.afb.org), which provides information on traveling with Seeing Eye dogs.

Access-Able Travel Source (© 303/232-2979; www.access-able.com) is another excellent online source. You'll also find relay and voice numbers for airlines and car-rental companies on Access-Able's user-friendly site, as well as links to New York's best accessible accommodations, attractions, transportation, tours, local medical resources and equipment repair, and much more.

In New York, **Hospital Audiences, Inc.** (© 212/575-7676; www.hospitalaudiences.org), arranges attendance and provides details about accessibility at cultural institutions as well as cultural events adapted for people with disabilities. Services include "Describe!," which allows visually impaired theatergoers to enjoy theater events; and the invaluable **HAI Hot Line** (© 212/575-7676), which offers accessibility information for hotels, restaurants, attractions, cultural venues, and much more. This nonprofit organization also publishes *Access for All,* a guidebook on accessibility, available by calling © **212/575-7663** or by sending a $5 check to 548 Broadway, third floor, New York, NY 10012-3950.

Another terrific source for travelers with disabilities in New York City is **Big Apple Greeter** (© **212/669-8159;** www.bigapplegreeter.org). All of its employees are well versed in accessibility issues. They can provide a resource list of agencies that serve the city's community with disabilities, and sometimes have discounts available to theater and music performances. Big Apple Greeter even offers one-to-one tours that pair volunteers with visitors with disabilities; they can even introduce you to the public transportation system. Reserve at least 1 week ahead.

For more information specifically targeted to travelers with disabilities, the community website **iCan** (www.icanonline.net) has destination guides and several regular columns on accessible travel. Also check out the quarterly magazine **Emerging Horizons** ($14.95 per year, $19.95 outside the U.S.; www.emerginghorizons.com); **Twin Peaks Press** (© **360/694-2462;** http://home.pacifier.com/~twinpeak), offering travel-related books for travelers with special needs; and *Open World Magazine,* published by the Society for Accessible Travel and Hospitality (see above; subscription $18 per year, $35 outside the U.S.).

GETTING AROUND Express **Shuttle USA** (© **800/451-0455** or 212/315-3006; www.graylinenewyork.com) operates minibuses with lifts from Newark airports to Midtown hotels by reservation; arrange pickup 3 or 4 days in advance. **Olympia Trails** (© **877/894-9155** or 212/964-6233; www.olympiabus.com) provides service from Newark Airport, with half-price fares for travelers with disabilities

(be sure to prepurchase your tickets to guarantee the discount fare, as drivers can't sell discounted tickets). Not all buses are appropriately equipped, so call ahead for the daily schedule of accessible buses (press "0" to reach a real person).

Taxis are required to carry people who have folding wheelchairs and guide or therapy dogs. However, don't be surprised if they don't run each other down trying to get to you; even though you shouldn't have to, you may have to wait a bit for a friendly (or fare-desperate) driver to come along.

Public buses are an inexpensive and easy way to get around New York. All buses' back doors are supposed to be equipped with wheelchair lifts (though the city has had complaints that not all are in working order). Buses also "kneel," lowering their front steps for people who have difficulty boarding. Passengers with disabilities pay half-price fares ($1). The **subway** isn't yet fully wheelchair accessible, but a list of about 30 accessible subway stations and a guide to wheelchair-accessible subway itineraries is on the MTA website. Call © **718/596-8585** for bus and subway transit info, or go to www.mta.nyc.ny.us/nyct and click on the wheelchair symbol.

You're better off not trying to rent your own car to get around the city. But if you consider it the best mode of transportation for you, **Wheelchair Getaways** (© **800/642-2042** or 800/344-5005; www.wheelchair-getaways.com) rents specialized vans with wheelchair lifts and other features for travelers with disabilities throughout the New York metropolitan area.

Many travel agencies offer customized tours and itineraries for travelers with disabilities. **Flying Wheels Travel** (© **507/451-5005;** www.flyingwheelstravel.com) offers escorted tours and cruises that emphasize sports and private tours in minivans with lifts. **Accessible Journeys** (© **800/846-4537** or 610/521-0339; www.disabilitytravel.com) caters specifically to slow walkers and wheelchair travelers and their families and friends.

GAY & LESBIAN TRAVELERS

Gay and lesbian culture is as much a part of New York's basic identity as yellow cabs, high-rises, and Broadway theater. Indeed, in a city with one of the world's largest, loudest, and most powerful gay and lesbian populations, homosexuality is squarely in the urban mainstream. So city hotels tend to be neutral on the issue, and gay couples shouldn't have a problem; for particularly gay-friendly accommodations, see "Best for Gay & Lesbian Travelers" under "Best Low-Cost Hotel Bets," in chapter 1. For nightlife suggestions, see "The Gay & Lesbian Scene" in chapter 9.

The **International Gay & Lesbian Travel Association** (IGLTA; © **800/ 448-8550** or 954/776-2626; www. iglta.org) is the trade association for the gay and lesbian travel industry, and offers an online directory of gay- and lesbian-friendly travel businesses; go to their website and click on "Members."

Many agencies offer tours and travel itineraries specifically for gay and lesbian travelers. **Above and Beyond Tours** (© **800/397-2681;** www.abovebeyondtours.com) is the exclusive gay and lesbian tour operator for United Airlines. **Now, Voyager** (© **800/255-6951;** www.nowvoyager. com) is a well-known San Francisco–based gay-owned and -operated travel service.

All over Manhattan, but especially in neighborhoods like the **West Village** (particularly Christopher St., famous the world over as the main drag of New York gay male life) and **Chelsea** (especially 8th Ave., from 16th to 23rd sts., and W. 17th to 19th sts., from 5th to 8th aves.), shops, services, and restaurants have a lesbian and gay flavor. The **Oscar Wilde Bookshop,** 15 Christopher St. (© **212/255-8097;** www.oscarwilde books.com), is the city's best gay and lesbian bookstore, and a good source for information on the city's gay community.

The **Lesbian and Gay Community Services Center** is at 208 W. 13th St. (btwn 7th and 8th aves.; © **212/620-7310;** www.gaycenter. org). The center is the meeting place for more than 400 lesbian, gay, and bisexual organizations. You can check the online events calendar, which lists hundreds of happenings—lectures, dances, concerts, readings, films—or call for the latest. Their site offers links to additional gay-friendly hotels and guesthouses in and around New York, plus tons of other information; the staff is also exceedingly friendly and helpful in person or over the phone.

Other good sources for lesbian and gay events are glossy listings magazines *HX* (www.hx.com), and lesbian-oriented *GONYC Magazine* (www.go nycmagazine.com), and *Next* magazine (www.nextnyc.com), as well as the weekly LGBT newspapers *Gay City News* (www.gaycitynews.com) the *New York Blade* (www.nyblade. com), that you can pick up in appropriate bars, clubs, stores, and sidewalk boxes throughout town.

The free weekly *Village Voice* (www.villagevoice.com)—has excellent listings, including LGBT events/ venues. The glossy weekly *Time Out New York* (www.timeoutny.com) boasts a terrific gay and lesbian section. The Lesbian and Gay Community Services Center (see above) publishes a monthly guide listing dozens of events (also listed on its website).

In addition, there are lesbian and gay musical events, such as performances by the **New York City Gay Men's Chorus** (✆ 212/242-1777; www.nycgmc.org); health programs sponsored by the **Gay Men's Health Crisis** (**GMHC;** ✆ 800/AIDS-NYC or 212/807-6655; www.gmhc.org); the **Gay & Lesbian National Hot Line** (✆ **212/989-0999;** www.glnh. org), offering peer counseling and information on upcoming events; and many other organizations.

You can find GLBT travel-related publications before you go, including *Out and About* (✆ **800/929-2268** or 415/644-8044; www.outandabout. com), which offers guidebooks and a newsletter 10 times a year packed with solid information on the global gay and lesbian scene; *Spartacus International Gay Guide* (Bruno Gmunder Verlag) and *Odysseus: The International Gay Travel Planner* (Odysseus Enterprises Ltd.), both good, annual English-language guidebooks focused on gay men; the *Damron* guides (Damron Company), with separate, annual books for gay men and lesbians; and *Gay Travel A to Z: The World of Gay & Lesbian Travel Options at Your Fingertips* by Marianne Ferrari (Ferrari Publications; Box 35575, Phoenix, AZ 85069), a very good gay and lesbian guidebook series.

SENIOR TRAVEL

Mention the fact that you're a senior when you make your travel reservations. Although all of the major U.S. airlines except America West have canceled their senior discount and coupon book programs, many hotels still offer discounts for seniors. In most cities, people over the age of 60 qualify for reduced admission to theaters, museums, and other attractions, as well as discounted fares on public transportation.

New York subway and bus fares are half price ($1) for people 65 and older.

Many museums and sights (and some theaters and performance halls) offer discounted admittance and tickets to seniors, so don't be shy about asking. Always bring an ID card, especially if you've kept your youthful glow.

Many hotels offer senior discounts; **Choice Hotels** (which include Comfort Inns, some of my favorite affordable Midtown hotels; see chapter 5), for example, gives 30% off their published rates to anyone over 50, provided you book your room through their nationwide toll-free reservations number (that is, not directly with the hotels or through a travel agent). For a complete list of Choice Hotels, visit **www.hotelchoice.com**.

Members of **AARP** (formerly known as the American Association of Retired Persons), 601 E St. NW, Washington, DC 20049 (✆ **888/ 687-2277** or 202/434-2277; www. aarp.org), get discounts on hotels, airfares, and car rentals. AARP offers members a wide range of benefits, including *AARP: The Magazine* and a monthly newsletter. Anyone over 50 can join.

Many reliable agencies and organizations target the 50-plus market. **Elderhostel** (✆ **877/426-8056;** www.elderhostel.org) arranges study programs for adults 55 and over (and a spouse or companion of any age) in the U.S. and in more than 80 countries around the world. Most courses last 5 to 7 days in the U.S. and many include airfare, accommodations in university dormitories or modest inns, meals, and tuition. New York City is a popular destination for Elderhostel courses.

Recommended publications offering travel resources and discounts for seniors include the quarterly magazine *Travel 50 & Beyond* (www.travel50 andbeyond.com); *Travel Unlimited: Uncommon Adventures for the Mature Traveler* (Avalon); *101 Tips for Mature Travelers,* available from

Grand Circle Travel (☏ **800/221-2610** or 617/350-7500; www.gct.com); *The 50+ Traveler's Guidebook* (St. Martin's Press); and *Unbelievably Good Deals and Great Adventures That You Absolutely Can't Get Unless You're Over 50* (McGraw-Hill).

FAMILY TRAVEL

If you have enough trouble getting your kids out of the house in the morning, dragging them thousands of miles away may seem like an insurmountable challenge. But family travel can be immensely rewarding, giving you new ways of seeing the world through smaller pairs of eyes.

For more extensive recommendations, check out a copy of *Frommer's New York City with Kids,* an entire guidebook dedicated to family visits to the Big Apple.

Good bets for the most timely information include the "Weekend" section of Friday's *New York Times,* which has a whole section dedicated to the week's best kid-friendly activities; the weekly *New York* magazine, which has a full calendar of children's events in its "Cue" section; and *Time Out New York,* which also has a great weekly kids section with a bit of an alternative bent. The *Big Apple Parents' Paper* is usually available, for free, at children's stores and other locations in Manhattan; you can also find good information from the folks behind the paper at **www.parentsknow.com**.

The first place to look for **babysitting** is in your hotel (better yet, ask about babysitting when you reserve). Many hotels have babysitting services or will provide you with lists of reliable sitters. If this doesn't pan out, call the **Baby Sitters' Guild** (☏ **212/682 0227**; www.babysittersguild.com). The sitters are licensed, insured, and bonded, and can even take your child on outings.

Familyhostel (☏ **800/733-9753**; www.learn.unh.edu/familyhostel) takes the whole family, including kids ages 8 to 15, on moderately priced domestic and international learning vacations. Lectures, field trips, and sightseeing are guided by a team of academics.

You can find good family-oriented vacation advice on the Internet from sites like the **Family Travel Network** (www.familytravelnetwork.com); **Traveling Internationally with Your Kids** (www.travelwithyourkids.com), a comprehensive site offering sound advice for long-distance and international travel with children; and **Family Travel Files** (www.thefamilytravel files.com), which offers an online magazine and a directory of off-the-beaten-path tours and tour operators for families.

How to Take Great Trips with Your Kids (The Harvard Common Press) is full of good general advice that can apply to travel anywhere.

FOR STUDENTS

Many museums, sights, and theaters offer reduced admission to students, so don't forget to bring your student ID and valid proof of age.

Your best resource is the **Council on International Educational Exchange** (**CIEE**; www.ciee.org). They can set you up with an International Student ID card, and their travel branch, **Council Travel Service** (☏ **800/226-8624**; www.counciltravel.com), the world's biggest student-travel agency, has joined with STA Travel (☏ **800/781-4040**; www.statravel.com) to get you discounts on plane tickets and the like. STA has offices at 254 Greene St., 10 Downing St. (6th Ave. at Bleecker St.; ☏ **212/627-3111**); 30 3rd Ave. (☏ **212/473-6100**); in Greenwich Village (☏ **212/254-2525**); in Midtown at 205 E. 42nd St. (btwn 2nd and 3rd aves.; ☏ **212/822-2700**); and locations at Columbia University, in Alfred Learner Hall, 2871 Broadway (© **212/854-0150**), and 2871 Broadway (© **212/865-2700**).

In Canada, **Travel CUTS** (© **866/ 246-9762** or 416/614-2887; www. travelcuts.com) offers similar services. In London, **USIT World** (© **0171/ 730-3402;** www.usitworld.com/index. html), opposite Victoria Station, is a specialist in student and youth travel.

Hostelling International–American Youth Hostels (© **202/783-6161;** www.hiayh.org) has its largest hostel in New York City at 891 Amsterdam Ave., at 103rd Street (© **212/**

932-2300;** www.hinewyork.org); see chapter 5 for a review. Reserve well ahead. You'll also find other, privately run hostels with cheap dorm beds in chapter 5. For additional hostelling choices in the city (and North America), order *The Hostel Handbook* by sending a check or money order for $5 (payable to Jim Williams) to The Hostel Handbook, Dept: HHB, 722 St. Nicholas Ave., New York, NY 10031. You can also find ordering information and a selection of listings at **www.hostelhandbook.com**. More info and recommendations can also be found online at **Hostels.com**.

7 Planning Your Trip Online

SURFING FOR AIRFARES

The "big three" online travel agencies, **Expedia.com, Travelocity.com,** and **Orbitz.com** sell most of the air tickets bought on the Internet. (Canadian travelers should try expedia.ca and Travelocity.ca; U.K. residents can go to expedia.co.uk and opodo.co.uk.) Each has different business deals with the airlines and may offer different fares on the same flights, so it's wise to shop around. Expedia and Travelocity will also send you **e-mail notification** when a cheap fare becomes available to your favorite destination. Of the smaller travel agency websites, **Side-Step** (www.sidestep.com) has gotten the best reviews from Frommer's authors. It's a browser add-on that purports to "search 140 sites at once," but in reality only beats competitors' fares as often as other sites do.

Also remember to check **airline websites**, especially those for low-fare carriers such as Southwest, JetBlue, AirTran, WestJet, or Ryanair, whose fares are often misreported or simply missing from travel agency websites. Even with major airlines, you can often shave a few bucks from a fare by booking directly through the airline

and avoiding a travel agency's transaction fee. But you'll get these discounts only by **booking online:** Most airlines now offer online-only fares that even their phone agents know nothing about. For the websites of airlines that fly to and from your destination, go to "Getting There," later in this chapter.

Great **last-minute deals** are available through free weekly e-mail services provided directly by the airlines. Most of these are announced on Tuesday or Wednesday and must be purchased online. Most are only valid for travel that weekend, but some (such as Southwest's) can be booked weeks or months in advance. Sign up for weekly e-mail alerts at airline websites or check megasites that compile comprehensive lists of last-minute specials, such as **Smarter Living** (smarterliving.com). For last-minute trips, **site59.com** often offers better deals than the major-label sites.

If you're willing to give up some control over your flight details, use an **opaque fare service** like **Priceline** (www.priceline.com; www.priceline. co.uk for Europeans) or **Hotwire** (www.hotwire.com). Both offer rock-bottom prices in exchange for travel

Frommers.com: The Complete Travel Resource

For an excellent travel-planning resource, we highly recommend **Frommers.com** (www.frommers.com). We're a little biased, of course, but we guarantee you'll find the travel tips, reviews, monthly vacation giveaways, and online-booking capabilities thoroughly indispensable. Among the special features are our **Message Boards,** where Frommer's readers post queries and share advice (sometimes our authors even show up to answer questions); the **Frommers.com Newsletter,** for the latest travel bargains and insider travel secrets; and **Frommer's Destinations Section,** where you'll get travel tips, hotel and dining recommendations, and advice on the sights to see for more than 3,000 destinations around the globe. When your research is done, the **Online Reservations System** (www.frommers.com/book_a_trip) takes you to Frommer's preferred online partners for booking your vacation at affordable prices.

on a "mystery airline" at a mysterious time of day, often with a mysterious change of planes en route. The mystery airlines are all major, well-known carriers—and the possibility of being sent from Philadelphia to Chicago via Tampa is remote; the airlines' routing computers have gotten a lot better than they used to be. But your chances of getting a 6am or 11pm flight are pretty high. Hotwire tells you flight prices before you buy; Priceline usually has better deals than Hotwire, but you have to play their "name your price" game. If you're new at this, the helpful folks at **BiddingForTravel** (www.biddingfortravel.com) do a good job of demystifying Priceline's prices.

Note: In 2004 Priceline added non-opaque service to its roster. You now have the option to pick exact flights, times, and airlines from a list of offers—or opt to bid on opaque fares as before.

For much more about airfares and savvy air-travel tips and advice, pick up a copy of *Frommer's Fly Safe, Fly Smart* (Wiley Publishing, Inc.).

SURFING FOR HOTELS

Shopping online for hotels is much easier in the U.S., Canada, and certain parts of Europe than it is in the rest of the world. Also, many smaller hotels and B&Bs—especially outside the U.S.—don't show up on websites at all. Of the "big three" sites, **Expedia** may be the best choice, thanks to its long list of deals. **Travelocity** runs a close second. Hotel specialist sites **hotels.com** and **hoteldiscounts.com** are also reliable. An excellent free program, **TravelAxe** (www.travelaxe.net), can help you search multiple hotel sites at once.

Priceline and Hotwire are even better for hotels than for airfares; with both, you're allowed to pick the neighborhood and quality level of your hotel before offering up your money. *Note:* Hotwire overrates its hotels by one star—what Hotwire calls a four-star is a three-star anywhere else.

The vast number of hotels in New York means that there's plenty of competition for your business, so sometimes the best place to find a deal is to go directly to the hotel's website.

8 The 21st-Century Traveler

INTERNET ACCESS AWAY FROM HOME

Travelers have any number of ways to check their e-mail and access the Internet on the road. Of course, using your own laptop—or even a PDA (personal digital assistant) or electronic organizer with a modem—gives you the most flexibility. But even if you don't have a computer, you can still access your e-mail and even your office computer from cybercafes.

WITHOUT YOUR OWN COMPUTER

It's hard nowadays to find a city that *doesn't* have a few cybercafes. Although there's no definitive directory for cybercafes—these are independent businesses, after all—two places to start looking are at **www.cyber captive.com** and **www.cybercafe. com**.

Aside from formal cybercafes, most **youth hostels** nowadays have at least one computer you can get to the Internet on. And most **public libraries** across the world offer Internet access free or for a small charge. Avoid **hotel business centers,** which often charge exorbitant rates.

Most major airports now have **Internet kiosks** scattered throughout their gates. These kiosks, which you'll also see in shopping malls, hotel lobbies, and tourist information offices around the world, give you basic Web access for a per-minute fee that's usually higher than cybercafe prices. The kiosks' clunkiness and high price means they should be avoided whenever possible.

To retrieve your e-mail, ask your **Internet service provider (ISP)** if it has a Web-based interface tied to your existing e-mail account. If your ISP doesn't have such an interface, you can use the free **mail2web** service (www.mail2web.com) to view and reply to your home e-mail. For more flexibility, you may want to open a free, Web-based e-mail account with **Yahoo! Mail** (http://mail.yahoo.com). (Microsoft's Hotmail is another popular option, but Hotmail has severe spam problems.) Your home ISP may be able to forward your e-mail to the Web-based account automatically.

If you need to access files on your office computer, look into a service called **GoToMyPC** (www.gotomypc. com). The service provides a Web-based interface for you to access and manipulate a distant PC from anywhere—even a cybercafe—provided your "target" PC is on and has an always-on connection to the Internet (such as with Road Runner cable). The service offers top-quality security, but if you're worried about hackers, use your own laptop rather than a cybercafe to access the GoToMyPC system.

WITH YOUR OWN COMPUTER

Major ISPs have **local access numbers** around the world, allowing you to go online by simply placing a local call. Check your ISP's website or call its toll-free number and ask how you can use your current account away from home, and how much it will cost.

If you're traveling outside the reach of your ISP, the **iPass** network has dial-up numbers in most of the world's countries. You'll have to sign up with an iPass provider, who will then tell you how to set up your computer for your destination(s). For a list of iPass providers, go to www.ipass. com and click on "Reseller Locator." Under "Select a Country," pick the country that you're coming from, and under "Who is this service for?", pick "Individual." One solid provider is **i2roam** (℡ **866/811-6209** or 920/235-0475; www.i2roam.com).

Where to Check Your E-mail in the City That Never Sleeps

The **Times Square Visitors Center**, 1560 Broadway (btwn 46th and 47th sts.; ✆ **212/768-1560**; daily 8am–8pm), has computer terminals that you can use to send e-mails courtesy of Yahoo!; you can even send an electronic postcard with a photo of yourself home to Mom.

Open 24/7 in the heart of Times Square, **easyInternetCafé** ★, 235 W. 42nd St. (btwn 7th and 8th aves.; ✆ **212/398-0775**; www.easyevery thing.com), is the first stateside branch of a worldwide web of Internet cafes. Boasting 15-inch flat-screen monitors and a superfast T-3 connection, this mammoth place makes accessing the Internet cheap through the economy of scale: Access is available for $1, and the length of access time that buck buys you fluctuates depending on the occupancy at the time you log on. This will generally work out to the cheapest Web time you can buy in the city.

CyberCafe (www.cyber-cafe.com)—in Times Square at 250 W. 49th St. (btwn Broadway and 8th Ave.; ✆ **212/333-4109**), and in SoHo at 273 Lafayette St. (at Prince St.; (✆ **212/334-5140**)—is more expensive at $6.40 per half-hour, with a half-hour minimum (you're billed $3.20 for every subsequent 15 min.). But their T1 connectivity gives you superfast access, and they offer a full range of other cyber, copy, fax, and printing services.

FedEx Kinko's (www.fedex.com) charges 30¢ per minute ($15 per hour) and is open at 100 Wall St. (at Water St.; ✆ 212/269-0024); near City Hall at 105 Duane St. (btwn Broadway and Church St.; ✆ 212/406-1220); 250 E. Houston St. (btwn aves. A and B; ✆ 212/253-9020); 21 Astor Place (btwn Broadway and Lafayette St. in the Village; ✆ 212/228-9511); 245 7th Ave. (at 24th St.; ✆ 212/929-2679); 60 W. 40th St. (btwn 5th and 6th aves.; ✆ 212/921-1060); 221 W. 72nd St. (at Broadway; ✆ 212/362-5288); and about a billion other locations around town. If you want to do some advance planning, check the website for the location nearest your hotel before you leave home.

Wherever you go, bring a **connection kit** of the right power, phone adapters, a spare phone cord, and a spare Ethernet network cable.

Most business-class hotels throughout the world offer dataports for laptop modems, and a few thousand hotels in the U.S. now offer high-speed Internet access using an Ethernet network cable. You'll have to bring your own cables either way, so **call your hotel in advance** to find out what the options are.

Many business-class hotels in the U.S. also offer a form of computer-free Web browsing through the room TV set for an extra charge.

If you have an 802.11b/**Wi-Fi** card for your computer, several commercial companies have made wireless service available in airports, hotel lobbies, and coffee shops, primarily in the U.S. **T-Mobile Hotspot** (www.t-mobile.com/hotspot) serves up wireless connections at more than 1,000 Starbucks coffee shops nationwide. **Boingo** (www.boingo.com) and **Wayport** (www.wayport.com) have set up networks in airports and high-class hotel lobbies. iPass providers (see above) also give you access to a few hundred wireless hotel lobby setups. Best of all, you don't need to be staying at the Four Seasons to use the hotel's network; just set yourself up on a couch in the lobby. Unfortunately, the companies' pricing policies are Byzantine, with a variety of monthly, per-connection, and per-minute plans.

Community-minded individuals have also set up **free wireless networks** in major cities around the world. These networks are spotty, but you get what you (don't) pay for. Each network has a home page explaining how to set up your computer for their particular system; start your explorations at www.personaltelco.net/index.cgi/wirelesscommunities.

USING A CELLPHONE ACROSS THE U.S.

Just because your cellphone works at home doesn't mean it'll work elsewhere in the country (thanks to our nation's fragmented cellphone system). It's a good bet that your phone will work in major cities. But take a look at your wireless company's coverage map on its website before heading out—T-Mobile, Sprint, and Nextel are particularly weak in rural areas. If you need to stay in touch at a destination where you know your phone won't work, **rent** a phone that does from **InTouch USA** (© **800/872-7626;** www.intouchglobal.com) or a

---

Online Traveler's Toolbox

Veteran travelers usually carry some essential items to make their trips easier. Following is a selection of online tools to bookmark and use.

- **Visa ATM Locator** (www.visa.com), for locations of PLUS ATMs worldwide, or **MasterCard ATM Locator** (www.mastercard.com), for locations of Cirrus ATMs worldwide.
- **Foreign Languages for Travelers** (www.travlang.com). Learn basic terms in more than 70 languages and click on any underlined phrase to hear what it sounds like.
- **Intellicast** (www.intellicast.com) and **Weather.com** (www.weather.com). Gives weather forecasts for all 50 states and for cities around the world.
- **Mapquest** (www.mapquest.com). This best of the mapping sites lets you choose a specific address or destination, and in seconds, it will return a map and detailed directions.
- **Universal Currency Converter** (www.xe.com/ucc). See what your dollar or pound is worth in more than 100 other countries.
- **Travel Warnings** (http://travel.state.gov/travel_warnings.html, www.fco.gov.uk/travel, www.voyage.gc.ca, www.dfat.gov.au/consular/advice). These sites report on places where health concerns or unrest might threaten American, British, Canadian, and Australian travelers. Generally, U.S. warnings are the most paranoid; Australian warnings are the most relaxed.
- **Entertainment** *New York Magazine*'s website (www.nymetro.com) and the free weekly newspaper's website (www.villagevoice.com) have good coverage or arts and events.

rental-car location, but be aware that you'll pay $1 a minute or more for airtime.

If you're not from the U.S., you'll be appalled at the poor reach of our **GSM (Global System for Mobiles) wireless network,** which is used by much of the rest of the world. Your phone will probably work in most major U.S. cities. (To see where GSM phones work in the U.S., check out www.t-mobile.com/coverage/national _popup.asp.) And you may or may not be able to send SMS (text messaging) home—something Americans tend not to do anyway, for various cultural and technological reasons. (International budget travelers like to send text messages home because it's much cheaper than making international calls.) Assume nothing—call your wireless provider and get the full scoop. In a worst-case scenario, you can always rent a phone; InTouch USA delivers to hotels.

9 Getting There

BY PLANE

Three major airports serve New York City: **John F. Kennedy International Airport** (✆ 718/244-4444) in Queens, about 15 miles (1 hr. driving time) from Midtown Manhattan; **LaGuardia Airport** (✆ 718/533-3400), also in Queens, about 8 miles (30 min.) from Midtown; and **Newark International Airport** (✆ 973/961-6000) in nearby New Jersey, about 16 miles (45 min.) from Midtown. Information about all three is available online at **www.panynj. gov**; click on the "All Airports" tab on the left.

Even though LaGuardia is the closest airport to Manhattan, it has a hideous reputation for delays and terminal chaos, in both ticket-desk lines and baggage claim. You may prefer to use JFK or Newark instead. (JFK has the best reputation for timeliness among New York–area airports.)

Almost every major domestic carrier serves at least one of the New York–area airports; most serve two or all three. Among them are **America West** (✆ 800/327-7810; www.america west.com), **American** (✆ 817/967-2000; www.aa.com), **Continental** (✆ 800/525-3273; www.continental. com), **Delta** (✆ 800/221-1212; www. delta.com), **Northwest** (✆ 800/225-2525; www.nwa.com), **US Airways** (✆ 800/428-4322; www.usairways. com), and **United** (✆ 800/864-8331; www.united.com).

In recent years, there has been rapid growth in the number of start-up, no-frills airlines serving New York. You might check out Atlanta-based **AirTran** (✆ 800/AIRTRAN; www. airtran.com); Chicago-based **ATA** (✆ 800/225-2995; www.ata.com); **Independence Air** (✆ 1-800-FLY-FLYi; www.flyi.com); Denver-based **Frontier** (✆ 800/432-1359; www.

⸢Tips⸣ Choosing Your NYC-Area Airport

It's more convenient to fly into Newark than Kennedy if your destination is Manhattan, and consider that fares to Newark are often cheaper than those to the other airports. Newark is particularly convenient if your hotel is in Midtown West or downtown. Taxi fare into Manhattan from Newark is roughly equivalent to the fare from JFK—both airports now have AirTrains in place (see "Transportation to & from the New York–Area Airports," below), but the AirTrain to Newark from Manhattan is quicker.

An Airport Warning

Never accept a car ride from the hustlers who hang out in the terminal halls. They're illegal, don't have proper insurance, and aren't safe. You can tell who they are because they'll approach you with a suspicious conspiratorial air and ask if you need a ride. Not from them, you don't. Sanctioned city cabs and car services wait outside the terminals.

flyfrontier.com); Milwaukee- and Omaha-based **Midwest Airlines** (© 800/452-2022; www.midwest airlines.com); or Detroit-based **Spirit Airlines** (© 800/772-7117; www. spiritair.com).

The JFK-based cheap-chic airline **jetBlue** ✈ (© 800/JET-BLUE; www. jetblue.com) has taken New York by storm with its low fares and classy service to cities throughout the nation. The nation's leading discount airline, **Southwest** (© 800/435-9792; www. iflyswa.com), flies into MacArthur (Islip) Airport on Long Island, 50 miles east of Manhattan.

Most major international carriers also serve New York; see chapter 3 for details.

TRANSPORTATION TO & FROM THE NEW YORK–AREA AIRPORTS

Since there's no need to rent a car in New York, you're going to have to figure out how you want to get from the airport to your hotel and back.

For complete transportation information for all three airports (JFK, LaGuardia, and Newark), call **Air-Ride** (© **800/247-7433**), which offers recorded details on bus and shuttle companies and private car services registered with the New York and New Jersey Port Authority 24 hours a day. Similar information is available at **www.panynj.gov/airports**; just click on the airport at which you'll be arriving.

The Port Authority also runs staffed Ground Transportation Information counters on the baggage-claim level in each terminal at each airport, where you can get information and book on all manner of transport once you land. Most transportation companies also have courtesy phones near the baggage-claim area.

Generally, travel time between the airports and Midtown Manhattan by taxi or car is 45 to 60 minutes for JFK, 20 to 35 minutes for LaGuardia, and 35 to 50 minutes for Newark. Always allow extra time, though, especially during rush hour, peak holiday travel times, and if you're taking a bus.

SUBWAYS & PUBLIC BUSES

For the most part, your best bet is to stay away from the MTA when traveling to and from the airport. You might save a few dollars, but subways and buses that currently serve the airports involve multiple transfers, and you'll have to drag your luggage up and down staircases. Spare yourself the drama.

The only exception to this rule that I feel somewhat comfortable with is the subway service to and from JFK, which connects with the new AirTrain (see "AirTrains: Newark & JFK—The Very Good & the Not-So-Very Good," below). The subway can actually be more reliable than taking a car or taxi at the height of rush hour, but *a few words of warning:* This isn't the right option for you if you're bringing more than a single piece of luggage, since there's a good amount of walking and some stairs involved in the trip, and you'll have nowhere to put it on the subway. And *do not* use this method if you're traveling to or from

AirTrains: Newark & JFK—The Very Good & the Not-So-Very Good

First the very good: A few years back, a new rail link revolutionized the process of connecting by public transportation to New York's notoriously underserved airport: the brand-new **AirTrain Newark,** which now connects Newark Airport with Manhattan via a speedy monorail/rail link.

Even though you have to make a connection, the system is fast, pleasant, affordable, and easy to use. Each arrivals terminal at Newark Airport has a boarding station for the AirTrain, so just follow the signs once you collect your bags. All AirTrains head to **Newark International Airport Station,** where you transfer to a **NJ Transit** train. NJ Transit will deliver you directly to New York Penn Station at 33rd Street and 7th Avenue, where you can pick up a cab to your hotel.

The trip from the door of my apartment on Manhattan's Upper West Side to the Newark Alitalita terminal was under a half-hour and only cost me $13.15 ($11.15 for the AirTrain link via Penn Station plus $2 for the subway to get to Penn Station). That's a savings of at least $35 if I took a cab, not to mention the time I saved. NJ Transit trains run two to three times an hour during peak travel times (once an hour during early and late hours); you can check the schedules on monitors before you leave the airport terminal, and again at the train station. Tickets can be purchased from vending machines at both the air terminal and the train station (no ticket is required to board the AirTrain). The one-way fare is $11.15 (children under 5 ride free). (On your return trip to the airport, the AirTrain is far more predictable, time-wise, than subjecting yourself to the whims of traffic.)

Note that travelers heading to points beyond the city can also pick up Amtrak and other NJ Transit trains at Newark International Airport Station to their final destination.

the airport after dark or too early in the morning—it's just not safe. For additional subway information, see "Getting Around," in chapter 4.

TAXIS Despite significant rate hikes in 2004, taxis are still a quick and convenient way to travel to and from the airports. They're available at designated taxi stands outside the terminals, with uniformed dispatchers on hand during peak hours at JFK and LaGuardia, around the clock at Newark. Follow the GROUND TRANS-PORTATION or TAXI signs. There may be a long line, but it generally moves pretty quickly. Fares, whether fixed or metered, do not include bridge and tunnel tolls ($3.50–$4) or a tip for the cabbie (15%–20% is customary). They do include all passengers in the cab and luggage—never pay more than the metered or flat rate, except for tolls and a tip (from 8pm–6am, a $1 surcharge also applies on New York yellow cabs). Taxis have a limit of four passengers, so if there are more in your group, you'll have to take more than one cab. For more on taxis, see "Getting Around," in chapter 4.

Now the not so very good: After years of anticipation and $1.9 billion, AirTrain JFK opened late in 2003. Though you can't beat the price—$7 if you take a subway to the AirTrain, $11.75 if you take Long Island Railroad—you won't save much on time getting to the airport, except perhaps at rush hour. From Midtown Manhattan, the ride is approximately 90 minutes and the connections are confusing. Only a few lines connect with the AirTrain: the A, E, J, and Z; the E, J, and Z to Jamaica Station and Sutphin Blvd.–Archer Ave. Station, and the A to Howard Beach/JFK Airport Station. The MTA is working hard to clear up the confusion, and though they are contemplating adding connections to the AirTrain in Lower Manhattan sometime in the next decade, there's not much they can do now to speed up the trip.

A word of warning for both AirTrains: If you have mobility issues, mountains of luggage that will make connections difficult, or a bevy of small children to keep track of, skip the AirTrain. You'll find it easier to rely on a taxi, car service, or shuttle service that can offer you door-to-door transfers.

For more information on AirTrain Newark, call ✆ **888/EWR-INFO** or go online to **www.airtrainnewark.com**. For connection details, click on the links on the AirTrain website or contact **NJ Transit** (✆ **800/626-RIDE; www.njtransit.com**) or **Amtrak** (✆ **800/USA-RAIL; www.amtrak.com**).

For more information on AirTrain JFK, go online to www.airtrain jfk.com. For connection details, click on the links on the AirTrain website or the MTA site, www.mta.nyc.ny.us/mta/airtrain.htm.

- **From JFK:** A flat rate of $45 to Manhattan (plus tolls and tip) is charged. The meter will not be turned on and the surcharge will not be added. The flat rate does not apply on trips from Manhattan to the airport.
- **From LaGuardia:** Rates are $17 to $27, metered, plus tolls and tip.
- **From Newark:** The dispatcher for New Jersey taxis gives you a slip of paper with a flat rate ranging from $30 to $38 (toll and tip extra), depending on where you're going in Manhattan, so you'll have to be precise about your destination. New York yellow cabs aren't permitted to pick up passengers at Newark. The yellow-cab fare from Manhattan to Newark is the meter amount plus $15 and tolls (about $45–$55, perhaps a few dollars more with tip). New Jersey taxis aren't permitted to take passengers from Manhattan to Newark.

PRIVATE CAR & LIMOUSINE SERVICES Private car and limousine companies provide convenient

If You're Flying into Islip on Southwest

Southwest Airlines flies into the New York area via Long Island's Islip MacArthur Airport, 50 miles east of Manhattan. If you're on one of these flights, here are your options for getting into the city:

Colonial Transportation (© 631/589-3500; www.colonialtransporta tion.com), Classic Transportation (© 631/567-5100; www.classictrans. com), and Legends (© 888/LEGENDS or 888/534-3637; www.legends limousine.com) will pick you up at Islip Airport and deliver you to Manhattan via private sedan, but expect to pay about $125 plus tolls and tip for door-to-door service, which sort of erases any money you saved on a rock-bottom fare to Islip. Be sure to arrange for it at least 24 hours in advance.

For a fraction of the cost, you can catch a ride aboard a Hampton Jitney coach (© 631/283-4600; www.hamptonjitney.com) to various drop-off points on Midtown's east side. The cost is $27 per person, plus a minimal taxi fare from the terminal to the Hampton Jitney stop. Hampton Jitney can explain the details and arrange for taxi transport.

Colonial Transportation (© 631/589-3500; www.colonialtransporta tion.com) also offers regular shuttle service that traverses the 3 miles from the airport to the Ronkonkoma Long Island Rail Road Station, where you can pick up an LIRR (Long Island Rail Road) train to Manhattan. The shuttle fare is $5 per person, $1 for each additional family member accompanying a full-fare customer. From Ronkonkoma, it's about a 1½-hour train ride to Manhattan's Penn Station; the one-way fare is $12.25 at peak hours, $8.25 off-peak (half-fare for seniors 65 or older and kids 5–11). You can also catch the Suffolk County Transit bus no. S-57 between the airport and the station daily except Sundays for $1.50. Trains usually leave Ronkonkoma once or twice every hour, depending on the day and time. For more information, call © 718/ 217-LIRR or visit www.mta.nyc.ny.us/lirr.

For additional options and the latest information, call © 631/467- 3210 or visit www.macarthurairport.com.

24-hour door-to-door airport transfers for roughly the same cost of a taxi. The advantage they offer over taking a taxi is that you can arrange your pickup in advance and avoid the hassles of the taxi line. Call at least 24 hours in advance (even earlier on holidays), and a driver will meet you near baggage claim (or at your hotel for a return trip). You'll probably be asked to leave a credit card number to guarantee your ride. You'll likely be offered the choice of indoor or curbside pickup; indoor pickup is more expensive, but makes it easier to find your driver (who usually waits in baggage claim bearing a sign with your name on it). You can save a few dollars if you arrange for an outside pickup; call the dispatcher as soon as you clear baggage claim and then take your luggage out to the designated waiting area, where you'll wait for the driver to come around, which can take anywhere from 10 minutes to a half-hour. Besides the wait, the other disadvantage of this option is that curbside can be chaos during prime deplaning hours.

Vehicles range from sedans to vans to limousines and tend to be relatively clean and comfortable. Prices vary slightly by company and the size of car reserved, but expect a rate roughly equivalent to taxi fare if you request a basic sedan and have only one stop; toll and tip policies are the same. (*Note:* Car services are not subject to the flat-rate rule that taxis have for rides to and from JFK.) Ask when booking what the fare will be and if you can use your credit card to pay for the ride so there are no surprises at drop-off time. There may be waiting charges tacked on if the driver has to wait an excessive amount of time for your plane to land when picking you up, but the car companies will usually check on your flight beforehand to get an accurate landing time.

I've had the best luck with **Carmel** (℗ **800/922-7635** or 212/666-6666) and **Legends** (℗ **888/LEGENDS** or 888/534-3637; www.legends limousine.com); **Allstate** (℗ **800/ 453-4099** or 212/333-3333) and **Tel-Aviv** (℗ **800/222-9888** or 212/ 777-7777) also have reasonable reputations. (Keep in mind, though, that these services are only as good as the individual drivers—and sometimes there's a lemon in the bunch. If you have a problem, report it immediately to the main office.)

These car services are good for rush hour (no ticking meters in rush-hour traffic), but if you're arriving at a quieter time of day, taxis work fine.

PRIVATE BUSES & SHUTTLES

Buses and shuttle services provide a comfortable and less expensive (but usually more time-consuming) option for airport transfers than do taxis and car services.

SuperShuttle serves all three airports; **New York Airport Service** serves JFK and LaGuardia; **Olympia Trails and Express Shuttle USA** serves Newark. These services are my

---

Getting to the Other Boroughs & Burbs

If you're traveling to a borough other than Manhattan, call **ETS Air Service** (℗ **718/221-5341**) for shared door-to-door service. For Long Island service, call **Classic Transportation** (℗ **631/567-5100**; www. classictrans.com) for car service, or **JFK Flyer** (℗ **516/766-6722**) for bus service. For service to Westchester County or Connecticut, contact **Connecticut Limousine** (℗ **800/472-5466** or 203/878-2222; www.ct limo.com) or **Prime Time Shuttle of Connecticut** (℗ **800/377-8745**; www.primetimeshuttle.com).

If you're traveling to points in New Jersey from Newark Airport, call **Olympic Limousine** (℗ **800/822-9797** or 732/938-4300) for Ocean and Monmouth counties; the **Airporter** (℗ **800/385-4000** or 609/587-6600; www.goairporter.com) to Middlesex and Mercer counties, plus Bucks County, Pennsylvania; or **State Shuttle** (℗ **800/427-3207** or 973/729-0030; www.stateshuttle.com) for destinations throughout New Jersey.

Additionally, **New York Airport Service** express buses (℗ **718/875-8200**; www.nyairportservice.com) serve the entire New York metropolitan region from JFK and LaGuardia, offering connections to the Long Island Rail Road; the Metro North Rail Road to Westchester County, upstate New York, and Connecticut; and New York's Port Authority, where you can pick up buses to points throughout New Jersey.

Tips Don't Stow It—Ship It

If ease of travel is your main concern and money is no object, you can ship your luggage with one of the growing number of luggage-service companies that pick up, track, and deliver your luggage (often through couriers such as Federal Express) with minimum hassle for you. Traveling luggage-free may be ultra-convenient, but it's not cheap: One-way overnight shipping can cost from $100 to $200, depending on what you're sending. Still, for some people, especially the elderly or the infirm, it's a sensible solution to lugging heavy baggage. Specialists in door-to-door luggage delivery are **Virtual Bellhop** (www.virtualbellhop.com), **SkyCap International** (wwww.skycapinternational.com), and **Luggage Express** (www.usxpluggageexpress.com).

favorite option for getting to and from Newark during peak travel times because the drivers usually take lesser-known surface streets that make the ride much quicker than if you go with a taxi or car, which will virtually always stick to the traffic-clogged main route.

The familiar blue vans of **Super-Shuttle** (© **212/258-3826;** www. supershuttle.com) serve all three area airports, providing door-to-door service to Manhattan and points on Long Island every 15 to 30 minutes around the clock. As with Express Shuttle, you don't need to reserve your airport-to-Manhattan ride; just go to the ground-transportation desk or use the courtesy phone in baggage claim and ask for SuperShuttle. Hotel pickups for your return trip require 24 to 48 hours' notice; you can make your reservations online. Fares run $15 to $19 per person, depending on the airport, with discounts available for additional persons in the same party.

New York Airport Service (© **718/875-8200;** www.nyairport service.com) buses travel from JFK and LaGuardia to the Port Authority Bus Terminal (42nd St. and 8th Ave.), Grand Central Terminal (Park Ave., btwn 41st and 42nd sts.), and to select Midtown hotels between 27th and 59th streets, plus the Jamaica LIRR

Station in Queens, where you can pick up a train for Long Island. Follow the GROUND TRANSPORTATION signs to the curbside pickup or look for the uniformed agent. Buses depart the airport every 20 to 70 minutes (depending on your departure point and destination) between 6am and midnight. Buses to JFK and LaGuardia depart the Port Authority and Grand Central Terminal on the Park Avenue side every 15 to 30 minutes, depending on the time of day and the day of the week. To request direct shuttle service from your hotel, call the above number at least 24 hours in advance. One-way fare for JFK is $13, $23 round-trip; to and from LaGuardia, it's $10 one-way, $17 round-trip.

Olympia Airport Express (© **212/ 964-6233;** www.olympiabus.com) provides service every 5 to 30 minutes (depending on the time of day) from Newark Airport to Penn Station (the pickup point is the northwest corner of 34th St. and 8th Ave., and the drop-off point is the southwest corner), the Port Authority Bus Terminal (on 42nd St. btwn 8th and 9th aves.), and Grand Central Terminal (on 41st St. btwn Park and Lexington aves.). Passengers to and from the Grand Central Terminal location can connect to Olympia's Midtown shuttle vans, which service select Midtown hotels.

Call for the exact schedule for your return trip to the airport. The one-way fare runs $12, $24 round-trip; it's $5 more if you connect to the hotel shuttle. Seniors and passengers with disabilities ride for $5.

GETTING THROUGH THE AIRPORT

With the federalization of airport security, security procedures at U.S. airports are more stable and consistent than ever. Generally, you'll be fine if you arrive at the airport **1 hour** before a domestic flight; if you show up late, tell an airline employee and he or she'll probably expedite your check-in.

Bring a **current, government-issued photo ID** such as a driver's license or passport. Keep your ID at the ready to show at check-in, the security checkpoint, and sometimes even the gate. (Children under 18 do not need photo IDs for domestic flights, but the adults checking in with them should have them.)

In 2003, the TSA phased out **gate check-in** at all U.S. airports. Passengers with e-tickets can still beat the ticket-counter lines by using **electronic kiosks** or even **online check-in.** Ask your airline which alternatives are available, and if you're using a kiosk, bring the credit card you used to book the ticket or your frequent-flier card. If you're checking bags or looking to snag an exit-row seat, you will be able to do so using most airlines' kiosks; again, call your airline for up-to-date information. **Curbside check-in** is also a good way to avoid lines, although a few airlines still ban curbside check-in; call before you go.

Security checkpoint lines are getting shorter than they were during 2001 and 2002, but some doozies remain. If you have trouble standing for long periods of time, tell an airline employee; the airline will provide a wheelchair. Speed up security by **not wearing metal objects** such as big belt buckles. If you've got metallic body parts, a note from your doctor can prevent a long chat with the security screeners. Keep in mind that only **ticketed passengers** are allowed past security, except for folks escorting passengers with disabilities or children.

Federalization has stabilized **what you can carry on** and **what you can't.** The general rule is that sharp things are out, nail clippers are okay, and food and beverages must be passed through the X-ray machine—but that security screeners can't make you drink from your coffee cup. Bring food in your carry-on rather than checking it, as explosive-detection machines used on checked luggage have been known to mistake food (especially chocolate, for some reason) for bombs. Travelers in the U.S. are allowed one carry-on bag, plus a "personal item" such as a purse, briefcase,

Travel in the Age of Bankruptcy

At press time, two major U.S. airlines were struggling in bankruptcy court and most of the rest weren't doing very well either. To protect yourself, **buy your tickets with a credit card,** as the Fair Credit Billing Act guarantees that you can get your money back from the credit card company if a travel supplier goes under (and if you request the refund within 60 days of the bankruptcy). **Travel insurance** can also help, but make sure it covers against "carrier default" for your specific travel provider. And be aware that if a U.S. airline goes bust midtrip, a 2001 federal law requires other carriers to take you to your destination (albeit on a space-available basis) for a fee of no more than $25, provided you rebook within 60 days of the cancellation.

Flying with Film & Video

Never pack film—developed or undeveloped—in checked bags, as the new, more powerful scanners in U.S. airports can fog film. The film you carry with you can be damaged by scanners as well. X-ray damage is cumulative; the faster the film, and the more times you put it through a scanner, the more likely the damage. Film under 800 ASA is usually safe for up to five scans. If you're taking your film through additional scans, U.S. regulations permit you to demand hand inspections. In international airports, you're at the mercy of airport officials. Keep in mind that airports are not the only places where your camera may be scanned: Highly trafficked attractions are X-raying visitors' bags with increasing frequency.

Most photo supply stores sell protective pouches designed to block damaging X-rays. The pouches fit both film and loaded cameras. They should protect your film in checked baggage, but they also may raise alarms and result in a hand inspection.

An organization called **Film Safety for Traveling on Planes (FSTOP;** ☎ **888/301-2665;** www.f-stop.org) can provide additional tips for traveling with film and equipment.

Carry-on scanners will not damage **videotape** in video cameras, but the magnetic fields emitted by the walk-through security gateways and hand-held inspection wands will. Always place your loaded camcorder on the screening conveyor belt or have it hand-inspected. Be sure your batteries are charged, as you will probably be required to turn the device on to ensure that it's what it appears to be.

or laptop bag. Carry-on hoarders can stuff all sorts of things into a laptop bag; as long as it has a laptop in it, it's still considered a personal item. The Transportation Security Administration (TSA) has issued a list of restricted items; check its website (www.tsa.gov/public/index.jsp) for details.

Airport screeners may decide that your checked luggage needs to be searched by hand. You can now purchase luggage locks that allow screeners to open and relock a checked bag if hand-searching is necessary. Look for Travel Sentry certified locks at luggage or travel shops and Brookstone stores (you can buy them online at www.brookstone.com). These locks, approved by the TSA,

can be opened by luggage inspectors with a special code or key. For more information on the locks, visit www.travelsentry.org. If you use something other than TSA-approved locks, your lock will be cut off your suitcase if a TSA agent needs to hand-search your luggage.

FLYING FOR LESS: TIPS FOR GETTING THE BEST AIRFARE

Passengers sharing the same airplane cabin rarely pay the same fare. Travelers who need to purchase tickets at the last minute, change their itinerary at a moment's notice, or fly one-way often get stuck paying the premium rate. Here are some ways to keep your airfare costs down.

- Passengers who can book their ticket **long in advance,** who can **stay over Saturday night,** or who **fly midweek** or **at less-trafficked hours** will pay a fraction of the full fare. If your schedule is flexible, say so, and ask if you can secure a cheaper fare by changing your flight plans.

- You can also save on airfares by keeping an eye out in local newspapers for **promotional specials** or **fare wars,** when airlines lower prices on their most popular routes. You rarely see fare wars offered for peak travel times, but if you can travel in the off-months, you may snag a bargain.

- Search **the Internet** for cheap fares (see "Planning Your Trip Online," earlier in this chapter).

- **Consolidators,** also known as bucket shops, are great sources for international tickets, although they usually can't beat the Internet on fares within North America. Start by looking in Sunday newspaper travel sections; U.S. travelers should focus on the *New York Times, Los Angeles Times,* and *Miami Herald.* For less-developed destinations, small travel agents who cater to immigrant communities in large cities often have the best deals. *Beware:* Bucket shop tickets are usually nonrefundable or rigged with stiff cancellation penalties, often as high as 50% to 75% of the ticket price, and some put you on charter airlines with questionable safety records. Several reliable consolidators are worldwide and available on the Net. **STA Travel** is now the world's leader in student travel, thanks to their purchase of Council Travel. It also offers good fares for travelers of all ages. **ELT Express** (aka **Flights.com;** (℃ **800/ TRAV-800;** www.eltexpress.com) started in Europe and has excellent fares worldwide, but particularly to that continent. It also has "local" websites in 12 countries. **FlyCheap** (℃ **800/FLY-CHEAP;** www.1800flycheap.com) is owned by package-holiday megalith MyTravel and so has especially good access to fares for sunny destinations. **Air Tickets Direct** (℃ **800/778-3447;** www.air ticketsdirect.com) is based in Montreal and leverages the currently weak Canadian dollar for low fares; it'll also book trips to places that U.S. travel agents won't touch, such as Cuba.

  I've gotten great deals on many occasions from **Cheap Tickets** (℃ **888/922-8849;** www.cheap tickets.com) and **Council Travel** (℃ **800/226-8624;** www.council travel.com). **The TravelHub** (℃ **888AIR-FARE;** www.travel hub.com) represents nearly 1,000 travel agencies, many of whom offer consolidator and discount fares. Other reliable consolidators include **TFI Tours** (℃ **800/745- 8000** or 212/736-1140; www. lowestairprice.com), which serves as a clearinghouse for unused seats.

- Join **frequent-flier clubs.** Accrue enough miles, and you'll be rewarded with free flights and elite status. It's free, and you'll get the best choice of seats, faster response to phone inquiries, and prompter service if your luggage is stolen, your flight is canceled or delayed, or if you want to change your seat. You don't need to fly to build frequent-flier miles—**frequent- flier credit cards** can provide thousands of miles for doing your everyday shopping.

- For many more tips about air travel, including a rundown of the major frequent-flier credit cards, pick up a copy of *Frommer's Fly Safe, Fly Smart* (Wiley Publishing, Inc.).

Getting Your Car Out of the Pound

If you come back to the spot on the street where you left your car and it's not there, it probably hasn't been stolen, but rather towed. You can call the city general information number (☎ **311**) or call the car pound directly at ☎ **212/971-0770,** and the personnel there can help you track your car in the system. Or, just head for the Manhattan car pound at Pier 76 on the far West Side (12th Ave. and 38th St.). Take a cab; it's on the other side of the busy West Side Highway. The pound is open Monday 7am to 11pm, Tuesday until midnight, Wednesday through Saturday 24 hours, and Sunday from midnight to 6am.

If your car is towed, you should get it as quickly as possible because he pound charges you $15 a day for storage after the first day. Granted, his may be cheaper than what you're paying at a parking lot, but don't forget that big fine you already have to cover.

When you go to the car pound, bring the car's registration (if it's not in the glove box) or rental agreement and your driver's license. Pound personnel will escort you to the car, if necessary, to identify it if you don't have all the required documentation. Oh, and bring cash (or traveler's checks). It's a minimum of $185 to claim your car, and they don't take credit cards or personal checks. You don't have to pay the (additional) $55 parking ticket when you claim your car.

If you think this information sounds like a firsthand account, believe me, it is!

BY CAR

From the **New Jersey Turnpike** (I-95) and points west, there are three Hudson River crossings into the city's west side: the **Holland Tunnel** (lower Manhattan), the **Lincoln Tunnel** (Midtown), and the **George Washington Bridge** (upper Manhattan).

From **upstate New York,** take the **New York State Thruway** (I-87), which crosses the Hudson on the Tappan Zee Bridge and becomes the **Major Deegan Expressway** (I-87) through the Bronx. For the east side, continue to the Triborough Bridge and then down the FDR Drive. For the west side, take the Cross Bronx Expressway (I-95) to the Henry Hudson Parkway or the Taconic State Parkway to the Saw Mill River Parkway to the Henry Hudson Parkway south.

From **New England,** the **New England Thruway** (I-95) connects with the **Bruckner Expressway** (I-278), which leads to the Triborough Bridge and the FDR Drive on the east side. For the west side, take the Bruckner to the Cross Bronx Expressway (I-95) to the Henry Hudson Parkway south.

Note that you'll have to pay tolls along some of these roads and at most crossings.

Once you arrive in Manhattan, park your car in a garage (expect to pay $20–$45 per day) and leave it there. Don't use your car for traveling within the city. Public transportation, taxis, and walking will easily get you where you want to go without the headaches of parking, gridlock, and dodging crazy cabbies.

BY TRAIN

Amtrak (☎ **800/USA-RAIL;** www. amtrak.com) runs frequent service to

New York City's **Penn Station,** on 7th Avenue between 31st and 33rd streets, where you can easily pick up a taxi, subway, or bus to your hotel. To get the best rates, book early (as much as 6 months in advance) and travel on weekends.

If you're traveling to New York from a city along Amtrak's Northeast Corridor—such as Boston, Philadelphia, Baltimore, or Washington, D.C.—Amtrak may be your best travel bet now that they've rolled out their new high-speed Acela trains, which will have replaced all the old Metroliners by the time you read this. The Acela Express trains cut travel time from D.C. down to 2½ hours, and travel time from Boston to a lightning-quick 3 hours.

10 Packages for the Independent Traveler

Before you start your search for the lowest airfare, you may want to consider booking your flight as part of a travel package. Package tours are not the same thing as escorted tours. Package tours are simply a way to buy the airfare, accommodations, and other elements of your trip (such as car rentals, airport transfers, and sometimes even activities) at the same time and often at discounted prices—kind of like one-stop shopping. Packages are sold in bulk to tour operators—who resell them to the public at a cost that usually undercuts standard rates.

One good source of package deals is the airlines themselves. Most major airlines offer air/land packages, including **American Airlines Vacations** (© 800/321-2121; www.aavacations. com), **Delta Vacations** (© 800/221-6666; www.deltavacations.com), **Continental Airlines Vacations** (© 800/301-3800; www.coolvacations.com), and **United Vacations** (© 888/854-3899; www.unitedvacations.com). Several big **online travel agencies**—Expedia, Travelocity, Orbitz, Site59, and Lastminute.com—also do a brisk business in packages. If you're unsure about the pedigree of a smaller packager, check with the Better Business Bureau in the city where the company is based, or go online at www.bbb.org. If a packager won't tell you where it's based, don't fly with them.

Travel packages are also listed in the travel section of your local Sunday newspaper. Or check ads in the national travel magazines such as *Arthur Frommer's Budget Travel Magazine, Travel & Leisure, National Geographic Traveler,* and *Condé Nast Traveler.*

Package tours can vary by leaps and bounds. Some offer a better class of hotels than others. Some offer the same hotels for lower prices. Some offer flights on scheduled airlines, while others book charters. Some limit your choice of accommodations and travel days. You are often required to make a large payment up front. On the plus side, packages can save you money, offering group prices but allowing for independent travel. Some even let you to add on a few guided excursions or escorted day trips (also at prices lower than if you booked them yourself) without booking an entirely escorted tour.

Before you invest in a package tour, get some answers. Ask about the **accommodations choices** and prices for each. Then look up the hotels' reviews in a Frommer's guide and check their rates for your specific dates of travel online. Finally, look for **hidden expenses.** Ask whether airport departure fees and taxes, for example, are included in the total cost.

11 Escorted General-Interest Tours

Escorted tours are structured group tours, with a group leader. The price usually includes everything from airfare to hotels, meals, tours, admission costs, and local transportation.

Many people derive a certain ease and security from escorted trips. Escorted tours—whether by bus, motor coach, train, or boat—let travelers sit back and enjoy their trip without having to spend lots of time behind the wheel. All the little details are taken care of; you know your costs up front; and there are few surprises. Escorted tours can take you to the maximum number of sights in the minimum amount of time with the least amount of hassle—you don't have to sweat over the plotting and planning of a vacation schedule. Escorted tours are particularly convenient for people with limited mobility.

On the downside, an escorted tour often requires a big deposit up front, and lodging and dining choices are predetermined. As part of a cloud of tourists, you'll get little opportunity for serendipitous interactions with locals. The tours can be jam-packed with activities, leaving little room for individual sightseeing, whim, or adventure—plus they also often focus on the heavily touristed sites, so you miss out on the lesser-known gems.

Before you invest in an escorted tour, ask about the **cancellation policy:** Is a deposit required? Can they cancel the trip if they don't get enough people? Do you get a refund if they cancel? If *you* cancel? How late can you cancel if you are unable to go?

When do you pay in full? *Note:* If you choose an escorted tour, think strongly about purchasing trip-cancellation insurance, especially if the tour operator asks you to pay up front. See the section on "Travel Insurance," earlier in this chapter.

You'll also want to get a complete **schedule** of the trip to find out how much sightseeing is planned each day and whether enough time has been allotted for relaxing or wandering solo.

The **size** of the group is also important to know up front. Generally, the smaller the group, the more flexible the itinerary, and the less time you'll spend waiting for people to get on and off the bus. Find out the **demographics** of the group as well. What is the age range? What is the gender breakdown? Is this mostly a trip for couples or singles?

Discuss what is included in the **price.** You may have to pay for transportation to and from the airport. A box lunch may be included in an excursion, but drinks might cost extra. Tips may not be included. Find out if you will be charged if you decide to opt out of certain activities or meals.

Before you invest in a package tour, get some answers. Ask about the **accommodations choices** and prices for each. Then look up the hotels' reviews in a Frommer's guide and check their rates for your specific dates of travel online. Finally, if you plan to travel alone, you'll need to know if a **single supplement** will be charged and if the company can match you up with a roommate.

12 Recommended Books & Films

For the definitive history of the birth of New York City to the end of the 19th century, there is no better read than *Gotham: A History of New York*

City to 1898, by Edwin R. Burrows and Mike Wallace (Oxford University Press). Another recommended historical look at the growth of New York

City, this one told in a breezy narrative tone, is *The Epic of New York City: A Narrative History,* by Edward Robb Ellis (Kodansha).

Luc Sante's *Low Life: Lures and Snares of Old New York* (Vintage Departures) details the bad old days of brothels, drug dens, and gambling saloons in New York in the early 20th century—it's a lively, fascinating read.

One of master biographer Robert Caro's early works, *The Power Broker: Robert Moses and the Fall of New York* (Random House), focuses on how the vision of master deal maker Robert Moses transformed New York to what it became in the second half of the 20th century.

In *The Great Bridge: The Epic Story of the Building of the Brooklyn Bridge* (Simon & Schuster), author David McCullough devotes his estimable talents to the story of the building of the Brooklyn Bridge.

The companion to the PBS Series (see below) *New York,* by Ric Burns, Lisa Ades, and James Sanders (Knopf) uses lavish photographs and illustrations to show the growth of New York City.

My all-time favorite book about New York is a children's classic called *This Is New York* (Universe Publishing), written and illustrated by M. Sasek in 1960. The book was recently reissued and, with an update added, as fresh as it was 45 years ago.

There are not many places as cinematic as New York City. Filmmakers think of the city as a character unto itself. The list of movies where New York plays a crucial role are too many to mention, but here are some of the top New York City movies, worth renting before you visit.

Possibly the best New York City promotional film is the musical *On the Town,* with Gene Kelly and Frank Sinatra, about three sailors with 24 hours' leave spent exploring Gotham. Shot on location, all the landmarks, circa 1949, are captured in beautiful Technicolor.

Woody Allen is known as a New York filmmaker and proudly shoots all his films in the city. One of his best— and a good look at neurotic New York—is *Annie Hall.*

Following in Woody Allen's footsteps are director Rob Reiner and writer Nora Ephron, who made *When Harry Met Sally.* It's sort of a poorman's *Annie Hall,* but a gorgeous cinematic tribute to New York. The famous "orgasm scene" was filmed in **Katz's Delicatessen** (p. 142).

"I love this dirty town," says Burt Lancaster in the gritty, crackling *Sweet Smell of Success.* In the beautifully photographed black-and-white movie, Lancaster plays malicious gossip columnist J. J. Hunsecker, and Tony Curtis is perfectly despicable as the groveling publicist Sidney Falco.

Another filmmaker always identified with New York is Martin Scorsese. He has made many films where New York played a central role, from *Mean Streets* to *Gangs of New York* (which was actually filmed in Italy). But the one film where New York is a character, and not a very flattering one, is *Taxi Driver.* The Academy Award–nominated 1976 movie about an alienated, psychotic taxi driver is tough and bloody, but to see images of seedy Times Square as it was before its recent reincarnation, there is no better film.

The best history of New York on film is the Ric Burns documentary *New York,* which originally aired on PBS. The seven-disc, 14-hour DVD (also available on VHS) is a must-see for anyone interested in the evolution of this great city.

3

For International Visitors

New York's global media profile might make it appear familiar, but movies and TV, music videos, and news images distort as much as they reflect. The gap between image and reality can make certain situations puzzling for the foreign— or even the domestic—visitor. This chapter will help prepare you for the more common issues or problems that you may encounter.

1 Preparing for Your Trip

ENTRY REQUIREMENTS

Check at any U.S. embassy or consulate for current information and requirements. You can also obtain a visa application and other information online at the **U.S. State Department**'s website, at **www.travel.state.gov**.

VISAS The U.S. State Department has a **Visa Waiver Program** allowing citizens of certain countries to enter the United States without a visa for stays of up to 90 days. At press time these included Andorra, Australia, Austria, Belgium, Brunei, Denmark, Finland, France, Germany, Iceland, Ireland, Italy, Japan, Liechtenstein, Luxembourg, Monaco, the Netherlands, New Zealand, Norway, Portugal, San Marino, Singapore, Slovenia, Spain, Sweden, Switzerland, and the United Kingdom. Citizens of these countries need only a valid passport and a round-trip air or cruise ticket in their possession upon arrival. If they first enter the United States, they may also visit Mexico, Canada, Bermuda, and/or the Caribbean islands and return to the United States without a visa. Further information is available from any U.S. embassy or consulate. Canadian citizens may enter the United States without visas; they need only proof of residence.

Citizens of all other countries must have (1) a valid passport that expires at least 6 months later than the end of their visit to the United States, and (2) a tourist visa, available without charge from any U.S. consulate.

To obtain a visa, the traveler must submit a completed application form (either in person or by mail) with a 1½-inch-square photo, and must demonstrate binding ties to a residence abroad. Usually you can obtain a visa at once or within 24 hours, but it may take longer from June through August. If you cannot go in person, contact the nearest U.S. embassy or consulate for directions on applying by mail. Your travel agent or airline office may also be able to provide you with visa applications and instructions. The U.S. consulate or embassy that issues your visa will determine whether you will be issued a multiple- or single-entry visa and any restrictions regarding the length of your stay.

British subjects can obtain up-to-date visa information by calling the **U.S. Embassy Visa Information Line** (© 0891/200-290) or by visiting the "Consular Services" section of the American Embassy London's website at www.usembassy.org.uk.

Irish citizens can obtain up-to-date visa information through the **Embassy**

of the USA Dublin, 42 Elgin Rd., Dublin 4, Ireland (*©* **353/1-668-8777**) or by checking the "Consular Services" section of the website at www.usembassy.ie.

Australian citizens can obtain up-to-date visa information by contacting the **U.S. Embassy Canberra,** Moonah Place, Yarralumla, ACT 2600 (*©* **02/6214-5600**) or by checking the U.S. Diplomatic Mission's website at http://usembassy-australia.state.gov/consular.

Citizens of **New Zealand** can obtain up-to-date visa information by contacting the **U.S. Embassy New Zealand,** 29 Fitzherbert Terrace, Thorndon, Wellington (*©* **644/472-2068**), or get the information directly from the "Services to New Zealanders" section of the website at http://usembassy.org.nz.

MEDICAL REQUIREMENTS

Unless you're arriving from an area known to be suffering from an epidemic (particularly cholera or yellow fever), inoculations or vaccinations are not required for entry into the United States. If you have a condition that requires **syringe-administered medications,** carry a valid signed prescription from your physician—the Federal Aviation Administration (FAA) no longer allows airline passengers to pack syringes in their carry-on baggage without documented proof of medical need. If you have a disease that requires treatment with **narcotics,** you should also carry documented proof with you—smuggling narcotics aboard a plane is a serious offense that carries severe penalties in the U.S.

For **HIV-positive visitors,** requirements for entering the U.S. are somewhat vague and change frequently. According to the latest publication of *HIV and Immigrants: A Manual for AIDS Service Providers,* the Immigration and Naturalization Service (INS) doesn't require a medical exam for entry into the United States, but INS officials may stop individuals because they look sick or because they are carrying AIDS/HIV medicine.

If an HIV-positive non-citizen applies for a non-immigrant visa, the question on the application regarding communicable diseases is tricky no matter which way it's answered. If the applicant checks "no," INS may deny the visa on the grounds that the applicant committed fraud. If the applicant checks "yes" or if INS suspects the person is HIV-positive, it will deny the visa unless the applicant asks for a special waiver for visitors. This waiver is for people visiting the United States for a short time, to attend a conference, for instance, to visit close relatives, or to receive medical treatment. It can be a confusing situation. For up-to-the-minute information, contact **AIDSinfo** (*©* **800/448-0440** or 301/519-6616 outside the U.S.; www.aidsinfo.nih.gov) or the **Gay Men's Health Crisis** (*©* **212/367-1000;** www.gmhc.org).

DRIVER'S LICENSES Foreign driver's licenses are mostly recognized in the U.S., although you may want to get an international driver's license if your license is not written in English.

PASSPORT INFORMATION

Safeguard your passport in an inconspicuous, inaccessible place like a money belt. Make a copy of the critical pages, including the passport number, and store it in a safe place, separate from the passport. If you lose your passport, visit the nearest consulate of your country as soon as possible for a replacement. Passport applications are downloadable from the websites listed below.

Note: The International Civil Aviation Organization has recommended a policy requiring that *every* individual who travels by air have a passport. In response, many countries are now requiring that children must be issued their own passport to travel internationally, where before those under 16 or so may have been allowed to travel on a parent's or guardian's passport.

FOR RESIDENTS OF CANADA

You can pick up a passport application at one of 28 regional passport offices or most travel agencies. Canadian children who travel must have their own passport. However, if you hold a valid Canadian passport issued before December 11, 2001, that bears the name of your child, the passport remains valid for you and your child until it expires. Passports cost C$85 for those 16 years and older (valid 5 years), C$35 children 3 to 15 (valid 5 years), and C$20 children under 3 (valid 3 years). Applications, which must be accompanied by two identical passport-size photographs and proof of Canadian citizenship, are available at travel agencies throughout Canada or from the central **Passport Office,** Department of Foreign Affairs and International Trade, Ottawa, ON K1A 0G3 (© **800/567-6868;** www. dfait-maeci.gc.ca/passport). Processing takes 5 to 10 days if you apply in person, or about 3 weeks by mail.

FOR RESIDENTS OF THE UNITED KINGDOM

To pick up an application for a standard 10-year passport (5-year passport for children under 16), visit the nearest Passport Office, major post office, or travel agency. You can also contact the **United Kingdom Passport Service** at © **0870/571-0410** or visit its website at www.passport.gov.uk. Passports are £33 for adults and £19 for children under 16, with another £30 fee if you apply in person at a Passport Office. Processing takes about 2 weeks (1 week if you apply at the Passport Office).

FOR RESIDENTS OF IRELAND

You can apply for a 10-year passport, costing €57, at the **Passport Office,**

Setanta Centre, Molesworth Street, Dublin 2 (© **01/671-1633;** www. irlgov.ie/iveagh). Those under age 18 and over 65 must apply for a €12 3-year passport. You can also apply at 1A South Mall, Cork (© **021/272-525**) or over the counter at most main post offices.

FOR RESIDENTS OF AUSTRALIA

You can get an application from your local post office or any branch of Passports Australia, but you must schedule an interview at the passport office to present your application materials. Call the **Australian Passport Information Service** at © **131-232,** or visit the government website at www. passports.gov.au. Passports for adults are A$144 and for those under 18 are A$72.

FOR RESIDENTS OF NEW ZEALAND

You can pick up a passport application at any New Zealand Passports Office or download it from their website. Contact the **Passports Office** at © **0800/ 225-050** in New Zealand or 04/474-8100, or log on to www.passports.govt. nz. Passports for adults are NZ$80 and for children under 16 NZ$40.

CUSTOMS
WHAT YOU CAN BRING IN

Every visitor more than 21 years of age may bring in, free of duty, the following: (1) 1 liter of wine or hard liquor; (2) 200 cigarettes, 100 cigars (but not from Cuba), or 3 pounds of smoking tobacco; and (3) $100 worth of gifts. These exemptions are offered to travelers who spend at least 72 hours in the United States and who have not claimed them within the preceding 6 months. It is altogether forbidden to bring into the country foodstuffs (particularly fruit, cooked meats, and canned goods) and plants (vegetables, seeds, tropical plants, and the like). Foreign tourists may bring in or take out up to $10,000 in U.S. or foreign currency with no formalities; larger sums must be declared to U.S. Customs on entering or leaving, which includes filing form CM 4790. For more specific information regarding U.S. Customs and Border Protection, contact your nearest U.S. embassy or consulate, or the **U.S. Customs** office (℡ **202/927-1770;** www.customs. ustreas.gov).

WHAT YOU CAN TAKE HOME

U.K. citizens returning from a non-E.U. country have a customs allowance of: 200 cigarettes; 50 cigars; 250 grams of smoking tobacco; 2 liters of still table wine; 1 liter of spirits or strong liqueurs (over 22% volume); 2 liters of fortified wine, sparkling wine or other liqueurs; 60cc (ml) perfume; 250cc (ml) of toilet water; and £145 worth of all other goods, including gifts and souvenirs. People under 17 cannot have the tobacco or alcohol allowance. For more information, contact HM Customs & Excise at ℡ **0845/010-9000** (from outside the U.K., 020/8929-0152), or consult their website at www.hmce.gov.uk.

For a clear summary of **Canadian** rules, request the booklet *I Declare,* issued by the **Canada Border Services** (℡ **800/461-9999** in Canada, or 204/983-3500; www.cbsa-asfc.gc.ca). Canada allows its citizens a C$750 exemption, and you're allowed to bring back duty-free one carton of cigarettes, 1 can of tobacco, 40 imperial ounces of liquor, and 50 cigars. You're also allowed to mail gifts to Canada valued at less than C$60 a day, provided they're unsolicited and don't contain alcohol or tobacco (write on the package "Unsolicited gift, under $60 value"). All valuables should be declared on the Y-38 form before departure, including serial numbers of valuables you already own, such as foreign cameras. *Note:* The C$750 exemption can only be used once a year and only after an absence of 7 days.

The duty-free allowance in **Australia** is A$400 or, for those under 18, A$200. Citizens age 18 and over can bring in 250 cigarettes or 250 grams of loose tobacco, and 1,125 milliliters of alcohol. If you're returning with valuables you already own, such as foreign-made cameras, you should file form B263. A helpful brochure available from Australian consulates or Customs offices is *Know Before You Go.* For more information, call the **Australian Customs Service** at ℡ **1300/363-263,** or log on to www.customs.gov.au.

The duty-free allowance for **New Zealand** is NZ$700. Citizens over 17 can bring in 200 cigarettes, 50 cigars, or 250 grams of tobacco (or a mixture of all three if their combined weight doesn't exceed 250g); plus 4.5 liters of wine and beer, or 1.125 liters of liquor. New Zealand currency does not carry import or export restrictions. Fill out a certificate of export, listing the valuables you are taking out of the country; that way, you can bring them back without paying duty. Most questions are answered in a free pamphlet available at New Zealand consulates and Customs offices: *New Zealand Customs Guide for Travellers, Notice no. 4.* For more information, contact **New Zealand Customs,** The Customhouse, 17–21 Whitmore St., Box 2218, Wellington (℡ **0800/428-786** or 04/ 473-6099; www.customs.govt.nz).

HEALTH INSURANCE

Although it's not required of travelers, health insurance is highly recommended. Unlike many European countries, the United States does not usually offer free or low-cost medical care to its citizens or visitors. Doctors and hospitals are expensive, and in most cases will require advance payment or proof of coverage before they render their services. Policies can cover everything from the loss or theft of your baggage and trip cancellation to the guarantee of bail in case you're arrested. Good policies will also cover the costs of an accident, repatriation, or death. See "Travel Insurance" in chapter 2 for more information. Packages such as **Europ Assistance's "Worldwide Healthcare Plan"** are sold by European automobile clubs and travel agencies at attractive rates. **Worldwide Assistance Services, Inc.** (© **800/821-2828;** www.worldwide assistance.com) is the agent for Europ Assistance in the United States.

Though lack of health insurance may prevent you from being admitted to a hospital in non-emergencies, don't worry about being left on a street corner to die: The American way is to fix you now and bill the living daylights out of you later.

INSURANCE FOR BRITISH TRAVELERS Most big travel agents offer their own insurance and will probably try to sell you their package when you book a holiday. **Britain's Consumers' Association** recommends that you insist on seeing the policy and reading the fine print before buying travel insurance. **The Association of British Insurers** (© **020/7600-3333;** www. abi.org.uk) gives advice by phone and publishes *Holiday Insurance,* a free guide to policy provisions and prices. You might also shop around for better deals: Try **Columbus Direct** (© **020/7375-0011;** www.columbusdirect.net).

INSURANCE FOR CANADIAN TRAVELERS Canadians should check with their provincial health plan offices or call **Health Canada** (© **613/957-2991;** www.hc-sc.gc.ca) to find out the extent of their coverage and what documentation and receipts they must take home in case they are treated in the United States.

MONEY

CURRENCY The U.S. monetary system is very simple: The most common **bills** are the $1 (colloquially, a "buck"), $5, $10, and $20 denominations. There are also $2 bills (seldom encountered), $50 bills, and $100 bills (the last two are usually not welcome as payment for small purchases). All the paper money was recently redesigned, making the famous faces adorning them disproportionately large. The old-style bills are still legal tender.

There are seven denominations of coins: 1¢ (1 cent, or a penny); 5¢ (5 cents, or a nickel); 10¢ (10 cents, or a dime); 25¢ (25 cents, or a quarter); 50¢ (50 cents, or a half dollar); the new gold-colored "Sacagawea" coin worth $1; and, prized by collectors, the rare, older silver dollar.

Note: The "foreign-exchange bureaus" so common in Europe are rare even at airports in the United States, and nonexistent outside major cities. It's best not to change foreign money (or traveler's checks denominated in a currency other than U.S. dollars) at a small-town bank, or even a branch in a big city; in fact, leave any currency other than U.S. dollars at home—it may prove a greater nuisance to you than it's worth.

TRAVELER'S CHECKS Though traveler's checks are widely accepted, make sure that they're in U.S. dollars, as foreign-currency checks are often difficult to exchange. The three traveler's checks that are most widely recognized—and least likely to be denied—are **Visa, American Express,** and **Thomas Cook.** Be sure to record the numbers of the checks, and keep that information in a separate place in case they get lost or stolen. Most businesses are pretty good about taking traveler's checks, but you're better off cashing them in at a bank (in small amounts, of course) and paying in cash. Remember: You'll need identification, such as a driver's license or passport, to change a traveler's check.

CREDIT CARDS & ATMS Credit cards are the most widely used form of payment in the United States: **Visa**

(Barclaycard in Britain), **MasterCard** (EuroCard in Europe, Access in Britain, Chargex in Canada), **American Express, Diners Club, Discover,** and **Carte Blanche.** There are, however, a handful of stores and restaurants that do not take credit cards, so ask in advance. Most businesses display a sticker near their entrance to let you know which cards they accept. (***Note:*** Businesses may require a minimum purchase, usually around $10, to use a credit card.)

It is strongly recommended that you bring at least one major credit card. You must have a credit or charge card to rent a car. Hotels and airlines usually require a credit card imprint as a deposit against expenses, and in an emergency a credit card can be priceless.

You'll find **automated teller machines (ATMs)** on just about every block in Manhattan. Some ATMs will allow you to draw U.S. currency against your bank and credit cards. Check with your bank before leaving, and remember that you will need your personal identification number (PIN) to do so. Most accept Visa, MasterCard, and American Express, as well as ATM cards from other U.S. banks. Expect to be charged up to $3 per transaction, however, if you're not using your own bank's ATM.

One way around these fees is to ask for cash back at grocery stores that accept ATM cards and don't charge usage fees. Of course, you'll have to purchase something first.

ATM cards with major credit card backing, known as "debit cards," are now a commonly acceptable form of payment in most stores and restaurants. Debit cards draw money directly from your checking account. Some stores and branches of the U.S. Post Office enable you to receive "cash back" on your debit-card purchases as well.

SAFETY
GENERAL SAFETY SUGGESTIONS   Tourist areas in Manhattan are generally safe, and the city has experienced a dramatic drop in its crime rate in recent years. Still, crime is a national problem, and U.S. urban areas tend to be less safe than those in Europe or Japan. You should always stay alert, use common sense, and trust your instincts. If you're in doubt about which neighborhoods are safe, don't hesitate to make inquiries with the hotel front desk staff or the local tourist office.

Avoid deserted areas, especially at night, and don't go into parks after dark unless there's a concert or similar occasion that will attract a crowd.

Avoid carrying valuables with you on the street, and keep expensive cameras or electronic equipment bagged up or covered when not in use. If you're using a map, try to consult it inconspicuously—or better yet, study it before you leave your room. Hold onto your pocketbook, and place your billfold in an inside pocket. In theaters, restaurants, and other public places, keep your possessions in sight.

Always lock your room door—don't assume that once you're inside the hotel you are automatically safe and no longer need to be aware of your surroundings. Hotels are open to the public, and in a large hotel, security may not be able to screen everyone who enters.

For more about personal security in Manhattan, see "Playing It Safe" on p. 89.

Tips   **Travel Tip**

Be sure to keep a copy of all your travel papers separate from your wallet or purse, and leave a copy with someone at home should you need it faxed in an emergency.

Size Conversion Chart

Women's Clothing

American	4	6	8	10	12	14	16
French	34	36	38	40	42	44	46
British	6	8	10	12	14	16	18

Women's Shoes

American	5	6	7	8	9	10
French	36	37	38	39	40	41
British	4	5	6	7	8	9

Men's Suits

American	34	36	38	40	42	44	46	48
French	44	46	48	50	52	54	56	58
British	34	36	38	40	42	44	46	48

Men's Shirts

American	14½	15	15½	16	16½	17	17½
French	37	38	39	41	42	43	44
British	14½	15	15½	16	16½	17	17½

Men's Shoes

American	7	8	9	10	11	12	13
French	39½	41	42	43	44½	46	47
British	6	7	8	9	10	11	12

2 Getting to the U.S.

In addition to the domestic airlines listed in chapter 2, many international carriers serve John F. Kennedy International and Newark airports. **British Airways** (© 0845/77-333-77 or 0870/55-111-55 in the U.K., or 800/AIR-WAYS in the U.S.; www.ba.com) has daily service from London as well as direct flights from Manchester and Glasgow. **Virgin Atlantic** (© 0870/380-2007 in the U.K., or 800/862-8621 in the U.S.; www.virgin-atlantic.com) flies from Heathrow to New York.

Canadian readers might book flights on **Air Canada** (© 888/247-2262; www.aircanada.ca), which offers direct service from Toronto, Montreal, Ottawa, and other cities.

Aer Lingus flies from Ireland to New York (© 0818/365000 in Ireland, or 800/IRISH-AIR in the U.S.; www.aerlingus.ie). The following U.S. airlines fly to New York from most major European cities: **Continental** (© 0120/377-6464 in the U.K., or 800/523-3273 in the U.S.; www.continental.com), **United** (© 0845/844-4777 in the U.K., or 800/864-8331 in the U.S.; www.ual.com), **American** (© 0208/572-5555 or 0845/778-9789 in the U.K., or 800/433-7300 in the U.S.; www.aa.com), and **Delta** (© 0800/414-767 in the U.K., or 800/221-4141 in the U.S.; www.delta.com).

Qantas (© 13-13-13 in Australia, or 800/227-4500 in the U.S.; www.qantas.com.au) and **Air New Zealand** (© 0800/737-000 in New Zealand, or 800/262-1234 in the U.S.; www.airnewzealand.co.nz) fly to the West Coast and will book you through to New York City on a partner airline.

AIRLINE DISCOUNTS The smart traveler can find many ways to reduce the price of a plane ticket simply by

Tips **Prepare to Be Fingerprinted**

Starting in January 2004, many international visitors traveling on visas to the United States were being photographed and fingerprinted at Customs in a new program created by the Department of Homeland Security called **US-VISIT.** Non-U.S. citizens arriving at airports and on cruise ships must undergo an instant background check as part of the government's ongoing efforts to deter terrorism by verifying the identity of incoming and outgoing visitors. Exempt from the extra scrutiny are visitors entering by land or those from 28 countries (mostly in Europe) that don't require a visa for short-term visits. For more information, go to the Homeland Security website at **www.dhs.gov/dhspublic**.

taking time to shop around. For example, overseas visitors can take advantage of the APEX (Advance Purchase Excursion) reductions offered by all major U.S. and European carriers. For more money-saving airline advice, see "Getting There," in chapter 2. For the best rates, compare fares and be flexible with the dates and times of travel.

IMMIGRATION & CUSTOMS CLEARANCE Visitors arriving by air, no matter what the port of entry, should cultivate patience and resignation before setting foot on U.S. soil. Getting through immigration can take as long as 2 hours on some days, especially on summer weekends, so be sure to carry this guidebook or something else to read.

People traveling by air from Canada, Bermuda, and certain countries in the Caribbean can sometimes clear Customs and Immigration at the point of departure, which is much quicker.

3 Getting Around the U.S.

BY PLANE Some large airlines (for example, Northwest and Delta) offer travelers on their transatlantic or transpacific flights special discount tickets under the name **Visit USA,** allowing mostly one-way travel from one U.S. destination to another at very low prices. These discount tickets are not on sale in the United States and must be purchased abroad in conjunction with your international ticket. This system is the best, easiest, and fastest way to see the United States at low cost. You should obtain information well in advance from your travel agent or the office of the airline concerned, because the conditions attached to these discount tickets can be changed without advance notice.

BY TRAIN International visitors (excluding Canada) can also buy a **USA Rail Pass,** good for 15 or 30 days of unlimited travel on Amtrak (© **800/USA-RAIL;** www.amtrak. com). The pass is available through many foreign travel agents. Prices in 2004 for a 15-day pass were $295 off peak, $440 peak; a 30-day pass cost $385 off peak, $550 peak. With a foreign passport, you can also buy passes at some Amtrak offices in the United States, including locations in San Francisco, Los Angeles, Chicago, New York, Miami, Boston, and Washington, D.C. Reservations are generally required and should be made for each part of your trip as early as possible. Regional rail passes are also available.

BY BUS Although bus travel is often the most economical form of public transit for short hops between U.S. cities, it can also be slow and uncomfortable—certainly not an option for everyone (particularly when Amtrak, which is far more luxurious, offers similar rates). **Greyhound/Trailways** (© **800/231-2222**), the sole nationwide bus line, offers an **International Ameripass** that must be purchased before coming to the United States or by phone through the Greyhound International Office at the Port Authority Bus Terminal in New York City (© **212/971-0492**). The pass can be obtained from foreign travel agents or through Greyhound's website (order at least 21 days before your departure to the U.S.) and costs less than the domestic version. In 2004, passes cost as follows: 4 days ($160), 7 days ($219), 10 days ($269), 15 days ($329), 21 days ($379), 30 days ($439), 45 days ($489), or 60 days ($599). You can get more info on the pass at the website, or by calling © **402/330-8552.** In addition, special rates are available for seniors and students.

BY CAR   Unless you plan to spend the bulk of your vacation time in New York City, where walking is the best and easiest way to get around, the most cost-effective, convenient, and comfortable way to travel around the United States is by car. The interstate highway system connects cities and towns all over the country; in addition to these high-speed, limited-access roadways, there's an extensive network of federal, state, and local highways and roads. Some of the national car-rental companies include **Alamo** (© 800/ 327-9633; www.goalamo.com), **Avis** (© 800/331-1212; www.avis.com), **Budget** (© 800/527-0700; www. budget.com), **Dollar** (© 800/800- 4000; www.dollar.com), **Hertz** (© 800/ 654-3131; www.hertz.com), **National**

(© 800/227-7368; www.nationalcar. com), and **Thrifty** (© 800/367-2277; www.thrifty.com).

If you plan to rent a car in the United States, you probably won't need the services of an additional automobile organization. If you're planning to buy or borrow a car, automobile-association membership is recommended. The **American Automobile Association** (**AAA;** © **800/222-4357;** www. aaa.com) is the country's largest auto club and supplies its members with maps, insurance, and, most important, emergency road service. The cost of joining runs from $63 for singles to $87 for two members, but if you're a member of a foreign auto club with reciprocal arrangements, you can enjoy free AAA service in America. See below for more information.

An inviolable rule of thumb for New York: Don't even *think* of driving in the city. Like many cities, New York has its own arcane rules of the road, one-way streets, incomprehensible parking rules, and expensive parking garages. Public transit—whether buses, subways, or taxis—will get you anywhere you want quickly and easily, and that's where you'll be most comfortable.

If you do drive to New York in a rental car, return it as soon as you arrive and rent another when you're ready to leave the city. Always keep your car doors locked. Never leave any packages or valuables in sight because thieves will break car windows. If someone attempts to rob you or steal your car, don't resist. Report the incident to the police department immediately.

FAST FACTS: **For the International Traveler**

Also see "Fast Facts: New York City," in chapter 4, for more New York City–specific information.

Automobile Organizations Auto clubs will supply maps, suggested routes, guidebooks, accident and bail-bond insurance, and emergency road service. The **American Automobile Association (AAA)** is the major auto club in the United States. If you belong to an auto club in your home country, inquire about AAA reciprocity before you leave. You may be able to join AAA even if you're not a member of a reciprocal club; to inquire, call AAA (© **800/222-4357**). AAA is actually an organization of regional auto clubs; so look under "AAA Automobile Club" in the White Pages of the telephone directory. AAA has a nationwide emergency road service telephone number (© **800/AAA-HELP**).

Business Hours Offices are usually open weekdays from 9am to 5pm. Banks are open weekdays from 9am to 3pm or later and sometimes Saturday mornings. Stores typically open between 9 and 10am and close between 5 and 6pm from Monday through Saturday. Stores in shopping complexes or malls tend to stay open late: until about 9pm on weekdays and weekends, and many malls and larger department stores are open on Sunday.

Currency & Currency Exchange See "Entry Requirements" and "Money" under "Preparing for Your Trip," earlier in this chapter.

Drinking Laws The legal age for purchase and consumption of alcoholic beverages is 21; proof of age is required and often requested at bars, nightclubs, and restaurants, so it's always a good idea to bring ID when you go out. In New York State, beer may be purchased in supermarkets.

Do not carry open containers of alcohol in your car or any public area that isn't zoned for alcohol consumption. The police can fine you on the spot. And nothing will ruin your trip faster than getting a citation for DUI ("driving under the influence"), so don't even think about driving while intoxicated.

Electricity Like Canada, the United States uses 110–120 volts AC (60 cycles), compared to 220–240 volts AC (50 cycles) in most of Europe, Australia, and New Zealand. If your small appliances use 220–240 volts, you'll need a 110-volt transformer and a plug adapter with two flat parallel pins to operate them here. Downward converters that change 220–240 volts to 110–120 volts are difficult to find in the United States, so bring one with you.

Embassies & Consulates All embassies are located in the nation's capital, Washington, D.C. Some consulates are located in major U.S. cities, and most nations have a mission to the United Nations in New York City. If your country isn't listed below, call for directory information in Washington, D.C. (© **202/555-1212**), for the number of your national embassy.

The embassy of **Australia** is at 1601 Massachusetts Ave. NW, Washington, DC 20036 (© **202/797-3000**; www.austemb.org). There are consulates in New York, Honolulu, Los Angeles, and San Francisco.

The embassy of **Canada** is at 501 Pennsylvania Ave. NW, Washington, DC 20001 (© **202/682-1740**; www.canadianembassy.org). Canadian consulates are in Buffalo (N.Y.), Detroit, Los Angeles, New York, and Seattle.

The embassy of **Ireland** is at 2234 Massachusetts Ave. NW, Washington, DC 20008 (© **202/462-3939**; www.irelandemb.org). Irish consulates are in Boston, Chicago, New York, and San Francisco.

The embassy of **Japan** is at 2520 Massachusetts Ave. NW, Washington, DC 20008 (② **202/238-6700**; www.embjapan.org). Japanese consulates are located in Atlanta, Kansas City, San Francisco, and Washington, D.C.

The embassy of **New Zealand** is at 37 Observatory Circle NW, Washington, DC 20008 (② **202/328-4800**; www.nzemb.org). New Zealand consulates are in New York, Los Angeles, Salt Lake City, San Francisco, and Seattle.

The embassy of the **United Kingdom** is at 3100 Massachusetts Ave. NW, Washington, DC 20008 (② **202/588-7800**; www.britainusa.com/consular/embassy). British consulates are in Atlanta, Boston, Chicago, Houston, Los Angeles, New York, San Francisco, and Seattle.

Emergencies Call ② **911** to report a fire, call the police, or get an ambulance anywhere in the United States. This is a toll-free call (which means that no coins are required at public telephones).

If you have a medical emergency that doesn't require an ambulance, you can walk into a hospital's 24-hour emergency room (usually a separate entrance). For a list of hospitals, see "Fast Facts: New York City," in chapter 4. Because emergency rooms are often crowded and waits are long, one of the walk-in medical centers listed under "What to Do If You Get Sick Away from Home" (under "Health & Safety" in chapter 2) might be a better option.

If you encounter serious problems, contact **Traveler's Aid International** (② **202/546-1127**; www.travelersaid.org) to help direct you to a local branch. This nationwide, nonprofit, social-service organization geared to helping travelers in difficult straits offers services that might include reuniting families separated while traveling, providing food and/or shelter to people stranded without cash, or even emotional counseling. If you're in trouble, seek them out.

Gasoline (Petrol) Petrol is known as gasoline (or simply "gas") in the United States, and petrol stations are known as both gas stations and service stations. Gasoline costs about half as much here as it does in Europe (about $2 per gal. at press time), and taxes are already included in the printed price. One U.S. gallon equals 3.8 liters or .85 imperial gallons.

Holidays Banks, government offices, post offices, and many stores, restaurants, and museums are closed on the following legal national holidays: January 1 (New Year's Day), the third Monday in January (Martin Luther King Jr. Day), the third Monday in February (Presidents' Day, Washington's Birthday), the last Monday in May (Memorial Day), July 4th (Independence Day), the first Monday in September (Labor Day), the second Monday in October (Columbus Day), November 11 (Veterans' Day/Armistice Day), the fourth Thursday in November (Thanksgiving Day), and December 25 (Christmas). Also, the Tuesday following the first Monday in November is Election Day and is a federal government holiday in presidential-election years (held every 4 years).

Legal Aid If you are "pulled over" for a minor infraction (such as speeding), never attempt to pay the fine directly to a police officer; this could be construed as attempted bribery, a much more serious crime. Pay fines by mail, or directly into the hands of the clerk of the court. If accused of a more serious offense, say and do nothing before consulting a lawyer. Here the burden is on the state to prove a person's guilt beyond a reasonable doubt, and everyone has the right to remain silent, whether he or she is suspected of a crime or actually arrested. Once arrested, a person can make one telephone call to a party of his or her choice. Call your embassy or consulate.

Mail If you aren't sure what your address will be in the United States, mail can be sent to you, in your name, c/o General Delivery at the main post office of the city or region where you expect to be. (Call *©* 800/275-8777 for information on the nearest post office.) The addressee must pick up mail in person and must produce proof of identity (driver's license, passport, and so on). Most post offices will hold your mail for up to 1 month, and are open Monday to Friday from 8am to 6pm, and Saturday from 9am to 3pm.

Generally found at intersections, mailboxes are blue with a red-and-white stripe and carry the inscription U.S. MAIL. If your mail is addressed to a U.S. destination, don't forget to add the five-digit postal code (or zip code), after the two-letter abbreviation of the state to which the mail is addressed. This is essential to prompt delivery.

At press time, domestic postage rates were 22¢ for a postcard and 37¢ for a letter. For international mail, a first-class letter of up to ½ ounce costs 60¢ (46¢ to Canada and 40¢ to Mexico); a first-class postcard costs 50¢ (including Canada and Mexico); and a preprinted postal aerogramme costs 50¢.

Newspapers & Magazines In addition to the *New York Times* and other city papers, many newsstands carry a selection of international newspapers and magazines. For major newspapers and magazines from around the world, visit **Universal News & Magazines,** at 234 W. 42nd St. (btwn 7th and 8th aves.; *©* 212/221-1809), and 977 8th Ave. (btwn 57th and 58th sts.; *©* 212/459-0932); or **Hotalings News Agency,** 624 W. 52nd St. (btwn 11th and 12th aves.; *©* 212/974-9419). Other good bets include the **Hudson** newsdealers, located in Grand Central Terminal, at 42nd Street and Lexington Avenue, and Penn Station, at 34th Street and 7th Avenue.

Taxes The United States has no value-added tax (VAT) or other indirect tax at the national level. Every state, county, and city has the right to levy its own local tax on all purchases, including hotel and restaurant checks, airline tickets, and so on. The sales tax in New York City is 8.625%.

Telephone, Telegraph, Telex & Fax The telephone system in the United States is run by private corporations, so rates, especially for long-distance service and operator-assisted calls, can vary widely. Generally, hotel surcharges on long-distance and local calls are astronomical, so you're usually better off using a **public pay telephone,** which you'll find clearly marked in most public buildings and private establishments as well as on the street. Convenience grocery stores and gas stations always have them. Many convenience groceries and packaging services sell **prepaid calling cards** in denominations up to $50; these can be the least expensive way to call home. Many public phones at airports now accept American Express, MasterCard, and Visa credit cards. **Local calls** made from public pay phones in most locales cost either 25¢ or 35¢. Pay phones do not accept pennies, and few will take anything larger than a quarter.

You may want to look into leasing a cellphone for the duration of your trip (see "Using a Cellphone Across the U.S." in chapter 2.)

Most long-distance and international calls can be dialed directly from any phone. **For calls within the United States and to Canada,** dial 1 followed by the area code and the seven-digit number. **For other international calls,** dial 011 followed by the country code, the city code, and the telephone number of the person you are calling.

Calls to area codes **800, 888,** and **877** are toll-free. However, calls to numbers in area codes **700** and **900** (chat lines, bulletin boards, "dating" services, and so on) can be very expensive—usually a charge of 95¢ to $3 or more per minute, and they sometimes have minimum charges that can run as high as $15 or more.

For **reversed-charge or collect calls,** and for person-to-person calls, dial 0 (zero, not the letter O) followed by the area code and number you want; an operator will then come on the line, and you should specify that you are calling collect, or person-to-person, or both. If your operator-assisted call is international, ask for the overseas operator.

For **local directory assistance** ("information"), dial 411; for long-distance information, dial 1, then the appropriate area code and 555-1212.

Telegraph and telex services are provided primarily by Western Union. You can bring your telegram into the nearest Western Union office (there are hundreds across the country) or dictate it over the phone (𝒞 **800/325-6000**). You can also telegraph money, or have it telegraphed to you, very quickly over the Western Union system, but this service can cost as much as 15% to 20% of the amount sent.

Most hotels have **fax machines** available for guest use (be sure to ask about the charge to use it). Many hotel rooms are even wired for guests' fax machines. A less expensive way to send and receive faxes may be at stores such as The UPS Store, a national chain of packing service shops. (Look in the Yellow Pages directory under "Packing Services.")

There are two kinds of telephone directories in the United States. The so-called **White Pages** list private households and business subscribers in alphabetical order. The inside front cover lists emergency numbers for police, fire, ambulance, the Coast Guard, poison-control center, crime-victims hot line, and so on. The first few pages will tell you how to make long-distance and international calls, complete with country codes and area codes. Government numbers are usually printed on blue paper within the White Pages. Printed on yellow paper, the so-called **Yellow Pages** list all local services, businesses, industries, and houses of worship according to activity, with an index at the front or back. (Drugstores/pharmacies and restaurants are also listed by geographic location.) The Yellow Pages also include city plans or detailed area maps, postal zip codes, and public transportation routes.

Time The continental United States is divided into **four time zones:** Eastern Standard Time (EST), Central Standard Time (CST), Mountain Standard Time (MST), and Pacific Standard Time (PST). Alaska and Hawaii have their own zones. For example, noon in New York City (EST) is 11am in Chicago (CST), 10am in Denver (MST), 9am in Los Angeles (PST), 8am in Anchorage (AST), and 7am in Honolulu (HST).

New York City is in the Eastern Time Zone (GMT minus 5 hr.).

Daylight saving time is in effect from 1am on the first Sunday in April through 1am on the last Sunday in October, except in Arizona, Hawaii, part of Indiana, and Puerto Rico. Daylight saving time moves the clock 1 hour ahead of standard time.

For the correct local time in New York, dial ② **212/976-1616.**

Tipping Tipping is so ingrained in the American way of life that the annual income tax of tip-earning service personnel is based on how much they should have received in light of their employers' gross revenues. Accordingly, they may have to pay tax on a tip you didn't actually give them.

Here are some rules of thumb:

In hotels, tip **bellhops** at least $1 per bag ($2–$3 if you have a lot of luggage) and tip the **chamber staff** $1 to $2 per day (more if you've left a disaster area for him or her to clean up, or if you're traveling with kids and/or pets). Tip the **doorman** or **concierge** only if he or she has provided you with some specific service (for example, calling a cab for you or obtaining difficult-to-get theater tickets). Tip the **valet-parking attendant** $1 every time you get your car.

In restaurants, bars, and nightclubs, tip **service staff** 15% to 20% of the check, tip **bartenders** 10% to 15%, tip **checkroom attendants** $1 per garment, and tip **valet-parking attendants** $1 per vehicle. Tip the **doorman** only if he has provided you with some specific service (such as calling a cab for you). Tipping is not expected in cafeterias and fast-food restaurants.

Tip **cab drivers** 15% of the fare.

As for other service personnel, tip **skycaps** at airports at least $1 per bag ($2–$3 if you have a lot of luggage) and tip **hairdressers** and **barbers** 15% to 20%.

Tipping ushers at movies and theaters, and gas-station attendants, is not expected.

Toilets You won't find public toilets or "restrooms" on the streets in most U.S. cities, but they can be found in hotel lobbies, bars, restaurants, museums, department stores, railway and bus stations, and service stations. Large hotels and fast-food restaurants are probably the best bet for good, clean facilities. If possible, avoid the toilets at parks and beaches, which tend to be dirty; some may be unsafe. Restaurants and bars in resorts or heavily visited areas may reserve their restrooms for patrons. Some establishments display a notice indicating this. You can ignore this sign or, better yet, avoid arguments by paying for a cup of coffee or a soft drink, which will qualify you as a patron. See "Restrooms" under "Fast Facts: New York City," in chapter 4.

4

Getting to Know New York City

"The Bronx is up and the Battery's down . . ." These lyrics from the musical *On the Town* are actually a useful hint to the layout of the city (thank you, Comden and Green). This chapter gives you a *little* more detail on the lay of the land; it's an insider's take on Manhattan's most distinctive neighborhoods and streets, tells you how to get around, and serves as a reference to everything from personal safety to libraries and liquor laws. We also recommend (along with *On the Town*), other New York–centric books and films you might use to whet your appetite for your visit.

1 Orientation

VISITOR INFORMATION

INFORMATION OFFICES

- The **Times Square Visitors Center,** 1560 Broadway (btwn 46th and 47th sts., where Broadway meets 7th Ave.), across from the TKTS booth (© **212/ 869-1890;** www.timessquarebid.org), is the city's top info stop. This attractive center features an info desk offering loads of information. There's also a Metropolitan Transportation Authority (MTA) desk that sells MetroCards, offers transit maps, and answers your questions on the transit system; a Broadway Ticket Center providing show information and selling full-price tickets; ATMs and currency-exchange machines; and computers with free Internet access. It's open daily from 8am to 8pm.
- The **New York Convention and Visitors Bureau** runs the **NYCVB Visitor Information Center** at 810 7th Ave. (btwn 52nd and 53rd sts.). In addition to information on attractions and a multilingual counselor, the center has interactive terminals that provide touch-screen access to visitor information via Citysearch and sell advance tickets to major attractions, which can save you from standing in long lines (you can also buy a CityPass using these; p. 190). There's also an ATM, a gift shop, and phones that connect you directly with American Express card member services. The center is open Monday through Friday from 8:30am to 6pm, Saturday and Sunday from 9am to 5pm. For phone assistance, call © **212/484-1222.**

PUBLICATIONS

For comprehensive listings of films, concerts, performances, sports, museum and gallery exhibits, street fairs, and special events, the following are your best bets:

- The *New York Times* (**www.nytimes.com** or **www.nytoday.com**) features great arts and entertainment coverage, particularly in the Friday "Weekend" section and Sunday's "Arts & Leisure" section. Both days have full guides to the latest happenings in theater, music, dance, film, and the art world. Friday is good for cabaret, family fun, and general-interest events.

- *Time Out New York* (**www.timeoutny.com**) is an attractive, well-organized, and easy-to-use magazine. *TONY* features excellent coverage in categories from music, theater, and clubs (gay and straight) to museums, dance, book and poetry readings, and kids' stuff. The regular "Check Out" section, unequaled in any other listings magazine, will fill you in on upcoming sample and closeout sales, crafts and antiques shows, and other shopping scoops. A new issue hits newsstands every Thursday.
- The free weekly *Village Voice* (**www.villagevoice.com**) is available late Tuesday downtown and early Wednesday elsewhere. From classical music to clubs, the arts and entertainment coverage couldn't be more extensive, and just about every music venue advertises its shows. NYPress (www.nypress.com), also offers comprehensive listings and reviews.

Other useful weeklies include the glossy *New York* magazine (**www.nymetro. com**), which offers restaurant reviews and whose "Cue" section is a selective guide to city arts and entertainment; and *The New Yorker* (**www.newyorker.com**), which features "Goings On About Town" at the front of the magazine. Monthly *Paper* (**www.papermag.com**) is a glossy alternamag that serves as good prep for those of you who want to experience the hipper side of the city.

CITY LAYOUT

Open the sheet map that comes with this book and you'll see the city is comprised of five boroughs: **Manhattan,** where most of the visitor action is; the **Bronx,** the only NYC borough on the mainland United States; **Queens,** where Kennedy and LaGuardia airports are located; **Brooklyn,** south of Queens, which is also on Long Island and is famed for its attitude, accent, and Atlantic-front Coney Island; and **Staten Island,** the least populous borough, bordering Upper New York Bay on one side and the Atlantic Ocean on the other.

It is Manhattan, the finger-shaped island pointing southwest off the mainland—surrounded by the Harlem River to the north, the Hudson River to the west, the East River (really an estuary) to the east, and Upper New York Bay to the south—that most visitors think of when they envision New York City. Despite the fact that it's the city's smallest borough (13½ miles long, 2¼ miles wide, 22 sq. miles), Manhattan contains the city's most famous attractions, buildings, and institutions. For that reason, almost all of the accommodations and restaurants in this book are in Manhattan.

In most of Manhattan, finding your way around is a snap because of the grid system by which the streets are numbered. If you can discern uptown and downtown, and East Side and West Side, you can find your way around pretty easily. In real terms, **uptown** means north of where you happen to be and **downtown** means south, although sometimes these labels have deeper meanings (generally speaking, "uptown" chic vs. "downtown" bohemianism).

Avenues run north and south (uptown and downtown). Most are numbered. **Fifth Avenue** divides the East Side from the West Side of town and serves as the eastern border of Central Park north of 59th Street. **First Avenue** is all the way east and **12th Avenue** is all the way west. The three most important unnumbered avenues on the East Side you should know are between 3rd and 5th avenues: **Madison** (east of 5th), **Park** (east of Madison), and **Lexington** (east of Park, just west of 3rd). Important unnumbered avenues on the West Side are **Avenue of the Americas,** which all New Yorkers call 6th Avenue; **Central Park West,** which is what 8th Avenue north of 59th Street is called as it borders Central Park on the west (hence the name); **Columbus Avenue,** 9th Avenue north of 59th Street; and **Amsterdam Avenue,** or 10th Avenue north of 59th.

Broadway is the exception to the rule—it's the only major avenue that doesn't run uptown to downtown. It cuts a diagonal path across the island, from the northwest tip down to the southeast corner. As it crosses most major avenues, it creates **squares** (Times Square, Herald Square, and Union Square, for example).

Streets run east to west (crosstown) and are numbered as they proceed uptown from Houston (*house*-ton) Street. To go uptown, walk north of, or to a higher-numbered street than, where you are. Downtown is south of (or a lower-numbered street than) your current location. If you can see a landmark like the Empire State Building, it's easy to determine uptown and downtown if you know what street you are on; remember that the Empire State Building is on 34th Street.

Fifth Avenue is the dividing line between the **East Side** and **West Side** of town (except below Washington Square, where Broadway serves that function). On the east side of 5th Avenue, streets are numbered with the distinction "East"; on the west side of 5th Avenue, they are numbered "West." East 51st Street, for example, begins at 5th Avenue and runs east to the East River, while West 51st Street begins at 5th Avenue and runs west to the Hudson River.

If you're looking for a particular address, remember that even-numbered street addresses are on the south side of streets and odd-numbered addresses are on the north. Street addresses increase by about 50 per block starting at 5th Avenue. For example, nos. 1 to 50 East are just about between 5th and Madison avenues, while nos. 1 to 50 West are just about between 5th and 6th avenues. Traffic generally runs east on even-numbered streets and west on odd-numbered streets, with a few exceptions, like the major east-west thoroughfares—**14th, 23rd, 34th, 42nd, 57th, 72nd, 79th, 86th**—which have two-way traffic. Therefore, 28 W. 23rd St. is a short walk west of 5th Avenue; 325 E. 35th St. would be a few blocks east of 5th.

Avenue addresses are irregular. For example, 994 2nd Ave. is at East 51st Street, but so is 320 Park Ave. Thus, it's quite important to know a building's cross street to find it. If you don't have the cross street and want to figure out the exact location using just the address, use the **Manhattan Address Locator,** later in this chapter.

Unfortunately, the rules don't apply to neighborhoods in Lower Manhattan, south of 14th Street—like Wall Street, Chinatown, SoHo, TriBeCa, the Village— since they sprang up before engineers devised this brilliant grid scheme. A good map is essential when exploring these areas.

Tips Orientation Tips

I've indicated the cross streets for every destination in this book, but be sure to ask for the cross street (or avenue) if you call for an address.

When you give a taxi driver an address, always specify the cross streets. New Yorkers, even most cab drivers, probably wouldn't know where to find 284 E. 81st St., but they *do* know where to find 81st and 2nd. If you're heading to the Afghan Kebab House, for example, tell them that it's on 9th Avenue between 51st and 52nd.

If you have only the numbered address on an avenue, you can figure out the cross street using the **Manhattan Address Locator** on p. 77.

STREET MAPS You'll find a pullout map of Manhattan at the back of this book. There's also a decent one available for free as part of the **Official NYC Visitor Kit** if you write ahead for information (see "Visitor Information," in chapter 2); you can also pick it up for free at the visitor centers listed above.

Even with all these freebies, I suggest investing in a map with more features if you want to zip around the city like a pro. **Hagstrom** maps are my favorites because they feature block-by-block street numbering—so instead of trying to guess the cross street for 125 Prince St., you can see that it's Greene Street. Hagstrom and other visitor-friendly maps are available at any good bookstore. You might also want to look for *The New York Map Guide: The Essential Guide to Manhattan* (Penguin), by Michael Middleditch, a 64-page book that maps the entire city, including attractions, restaurants, and nightlife spots.

Because there are always disruptions or changes in service, don't rely on any subway map that hasn't been printed by the Metropolitan Transit Authority; more on this in "Getting Around," later in this chapter.

MANHATTAN'S NEIGHBORHOODS IN BRIEF

Since they grew up over the course of hundreds of years, Manhattan's neighborhoods have multiple personalities and fluid boundaries. Still, it's relatively easy to agree upon what they stand for in general—so if you stop a New Yorker and ask him or her to point you to, say, the Upper West Side or the Flatiron District, they'll know where you want to go. From south to north, here is how I've defined Manhattan's neighborhoods throughout this book.

Downtown

Lower Manhattan: South Street Seaport & the Financial District

At one time, this was New York—period. Originally established by the Dutch in 1625 (hence the city's original name, Nieuw Amsterdam), New York's first settlements sprung up here, on the southern tip of Manhattan island; everything uptown was farm country and wilderness. While all that's changed, this is still the best place in the city to search for the past.

Lower Manhattan constitutes everything south of Chambers Street. **Battery Park,** the point of departure for the Statue of Liberty, Ellis Island, and Staten Island, is on the very south tip of the island. The **South Street Seaport,** now touristy but still a reminder of times when shipping was the lifeblood of the city, lies a bit north on the east coast; it's just south of the Brooklyn Bridge, which stands proudly as the ultimate engineering achievement of New York's 19th-century Industrial Age.

The rest of the area is considered the **Financial District,** but may be more famous now as the site of **Ground Zero.** Until September 11, 2001, the Financial District was anchored by the **World Trade Center,** with the World Financial Center complex and residential Battery Park City to the west, and **Wall Street** running crosstown a little south and to the east. Now, a gaping hole sits where the Twin Towers and its five sister buildings stood.

Ground Zero has been cleared and the PATH station has reopened; it's better than ever. The Freedom Tower plans were approved and ground was broken for their construction in the summer of 2004, but it will still be years before the tower is completed.

Wall Street, the South Street Seaport, and Battery Park are all open and ready for business. **City Hall** remains the northern border of the district, abutting Chambers Street (look for City Hall Park on the map). Most of the streets of this neighborhood are narrow concrete

Downtown Revival

After September 11, 2001, the rebuilding process has been long and difficult for downtown New York, the area hardest hit economically by the terrorist attacks. But Lower Manhattan has so much to offer that the local community has united to revitalize and promote the area. Here are two websites you can check for useful information on new developments and exciting events that you'll find downtown. Both www.lowermanhattan.info and www.downtownny.com, the website for the Alliance for Downtown New York, Inc., are updated daily.

canyons, with Broadway serving as the main uptown–downtown artery.

Just about all of the major subway lines congregate here before they either end up in or head to Brooklyn. See "Getting Around," later in this chapter, for information on where to gather the latest subway information.

TriBeCa Bordered by the Hudson River to the west, the area north of Chambers Street, west of Broadway, and south of Canal Street is the *Tri*angle *Be*low *Ca*nal Street, or TriBeCa. Since the 1980s, as SoHo became saturated with chic, the spillover has been quietly transforming TriBeCa into one of the city's hippest residential neighborhoods, where celebrities and families quietly coexist in cast-iron warehouses converted into spacious, expensive loft apartments. Artists' lofts and galleries as well as hip antiques and design shops pepper the area, as do some of the city's best restaurants. Standing in the north shadow of the World Trade Center, TriBeCa suffered in the wake of the disaster; however, it has recovered beautifully.

Robert DeNiro gave the neighborhood a tremendous boost when he established the TriBeCa Film Center, and Miramax headquarters gave the area further capitalist-chic cachet. Still, historic streets like White (especially the Federal-style building at no. 2) and Harrison

(the complete stretch west from Greenwich St.) evoke a bygone, more human-scaled New York, as do a few holdout businesses and old-world pubs.

The main uptown-downtown drag is **West Broadway** (2 blocks to the west of Broadway). Consider the Franklin Street subway station on the 1/9 line to be your gateway to the heart of the action.

Chinatown New York City's most famous ethnic enclave is bursting past its traditional boundaries and has encroached on Little Italy. The former marshlands northeast of City Hall and below Canal Street, from Broadway to the Bowery, are where Chinese immigrants arriving from San Francisco were forced to live in the 1870s. This booming neighborhood is now a conglomeration of Asian populations. It offers tasty, cheap eats in cuisines from Szechuan to Hunan to Cantonese to Vietnamese to Thai. Exotic shops offer strange foods, herbs, and souvenirs; bargains on clothing and leather are plentiful. It's a blast to walk down Canal Street, peering into the myriad electronics and luggage stores and watching crabs wiggle loose from their handlers at the exotic fish markets.

The Canal Street (J, M, Z, N, R, 6, Q, W) station will get you to the heart of the action. The streets are crowded during the day and empty

Manhattan Neighborhoods

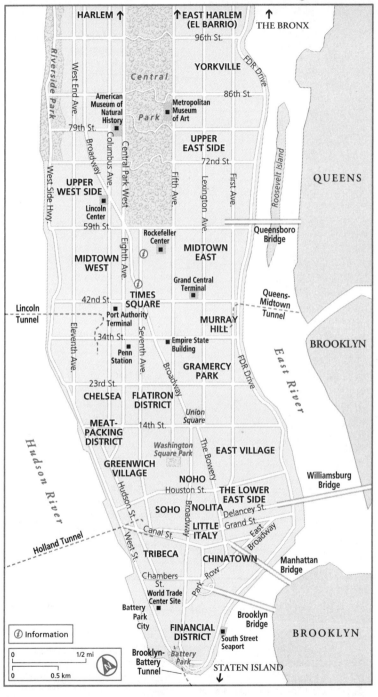

out after around 9pm; they remain quite safe, but the neighborhood is more enjoyable during the bustle.

Little Italy Little Italy, traditionally the area east of Broadway between Houston and north of Canal streets, is a shrinking community today, due to the encroachment of thriving Chinatown. It's now limited mainly to **Mulberry Street,** where you'll find most restaurants, and just a few offshoots. With rents going up in the increasingly trendy Lower East Side, a few chic spots are moving in, further intruding upon the old-world landscape. The best way to reach Little Italy is to walk east from the Spring Street station, on the no. 6 line, to Mulberry Street; turn south for Little Italy (you can't miss the year-round red, green, and white street decorations).

The Lower East Side The Lower East Side boasts the best of both old and new New York: Witness the stretch of Houston between Forsyth and Allen streets, where Yoneh Shimmel's Knish Shop sits shoulder-to-shoulder with the city's newest art house cinema—and both are thriving, thank you very much. Some say that the Lower East Side has come full circle: Hipster 20-somethings with Ivy League educations and well-honed senses of entitlement have been drawn back to the neighborhood their immigrant grandparents worked their fingers to the bone to escape.

Of all the successive waves of immigrants and refugees who passed through this densely populated tenement neighborhood from the mid–19th century to the 1920s, Eastern European Jews left the most lasting impression here. The Jewish communities, which first popped up between Houston and Canal streets, east of the Bowery, have been ultimately supplanted by drugs and crime, dragging the Lower East Side into the gutter—until now, that is. The neighborhood has experienced quite a renaissance over the last few years, and makes a fascinating itinerary stop for both nostalgists and nightlife hounds. Still, the blocks well south of Houston can be grungy in spots, so walk them with confidence and care after dark.

There are some remnants of what was once the largest Jewish population in America along **Orchard Street,** where you'll find great bargain hunting in its many old-world fabric and clothing stores still thriving between the club-clothes boutiques and trendy lounges. Keep in mind that the old-world shops close early on Friday afternoon and all day on Saturday (the Jewish Sabbath). The exponentially expanding trendy set can be found in the blocks between Allen and Clinton streets south of Houston and north of Delancey, with more new shops, bars, and restaurants popping up in the blocks to the east every day.

Visiting the Lower East Side

The **Lower East Side Business Improvement District** operates a neighborhood visitor center at 261 Broome St. (btwn Orchard and Allen sts.; © **866/224-0206** or 212/226-9010), that's open daily from 10am to 4pm (sometimes later). Stop in for an Orchard Street Bargain District shopping guide (which they can also send you in advance), plus other information on this historic yet freshly hip 'hood. You can also find shopping, dining, and nightlife directories online at **www.lowereastsideny.com**.

This area is not well served by the subway system (one cause for its years of decline), so your best bet is to take the F train to 2nd Avenue and walk east on Houston; when you see Katz's Deli, you'll know you've arrived. You can also reach the neighborhood from the Delancey Street station on the F line, and the Essex Street station on the J, M, and Z lines.

SoHo & NoLita No relation to the London neighborhood of the same name, **SoHo** got its moniker as an abbreviation of "*So*uth of *Ho*uston Street." This fashionable neighborhood extends down to Canal Street, between 6th Avenue to the west and Lafayette Street (1 block east of Broadway) to the east. It's easily accessible by subway: Take the N or R to the Prince Street station; the C, E, or 6 to Spring Street; or the F or V train to the Broadway-Lafayette stop (note that the B, D, and Q trains are not currently serving Broadway-Lafayette due to construction on the Manhattan Bridge).

An industrial zone during the 19th century, SoHo retains the impressive cast-iron architecture of the era, and in many places, cobblestone peeks out from beneath the asphalt. In the early 1960s, cutting-edge artists began occupying the drab, deteriorating buildings, soon turning it into the trendiest neighborhood in the city. SoHo is now a prime example of urban gentrification and a major New York attraction thanks to its impeccably restored buildings, fashionable restaurants, and boutiques. On weekends, the cobbled streets and narrow sidewalks are packed with shoppers, with the prime action between Broadway and Sullivan Street north of Grand Street.

Some critics claim that SoHo is a victim of its popularity—witness the departure of several imaginative galleries and independent boutiques for TriBeCa and Chelsea, as well as the influx of suburban chains like J. Crew and Victoria's Secret. However, SoHo is still one of the best shopping neighborhoods in the city, and few are more fun to browse. High-end peddlers set up along the boutique-lined sidewalks, hawking jewelry, coffee-table books, and their own art. At night, the neighborhood is a terrific, albeit pricey, dining and barhopping neighborhood (I recommend some affordable options in chapter 6).

In recent years, SoHo has been crawling east, taking over Mott and Mulberry streets—and Elizabeth Street in particular—north of Kenmare Street, an area now known as **NoLita** for its *No*rth of *Li*ttle *Ita*ly location. NoLita is increasingly well known for its shopping. Some of the city's most promising clothing designers have set up shop, but don't expect bargains. Good, affordable restaurants abound, making the neighborhood well worth a browse. Taking the 6 to Spring Street will get you closest by subway, but it's a short walk east from SoHo proper.

The East Village & NoHo The **East Village,** which extends between 14th Street and Houston Street, from Broadway east to 1st Avenue and beyond to Alphabet City— avenues A, B, C, and D—is where the city's real bohemia has gone. Once, flower children tripped along St. Marks Place and listened to music at the Fillmore East; now the East Village is a fascinating mix of affordable ethnic and trendy restaurants, upstart clothing designers and kitschy boutiques, punk-rock clubs (yep, still), and folk cafes. A half-dozen or so Off- and Off-Off-Broadway theaters also call this place home.

The gentrification that has swept the city has made a huge impact on the East Village, but there's still a seedy element that some of you won't find appealing—and some of you will. Now yuppies and other ladder-climbing types make their homes alongside old-world Russian immigrants who have lived in the neighborhood forever, and the cross-dressers and squatters who settled here in between. The neighborhood still embraces ethnic diversity, with strong elements of its Ukrainian and Irish heritage, while more recent immigrants have taken over 6th Street between 1st and 2nd avenues, turning it into a Little India.

The East Village isn't very accessible by subway; unless you're traveling along 14th Street (the L line will drop you off at 3rd and 1st aves.), your best bet is to take the 4, 5, 6, N, Q, R, or W to 14th Street/Union Square; the N or R to 8th Street; or the 6 to Astor Place and walk east.

Until 1998 or so, **Alphabet City** resisted gentrification and remained a haven of drug dealers and other unsavory types—but no more. Bolstered by a major real estate boom, this way-east area of the East Village has blossomed. French bistros and smart shops have popped up on every corner. Nevertheless, the neighborhood can be deserted late at night, since it's generally the province of locals. It's far off the subway lines, so know where you're going if you venture out here.

The southwestern section of the East Village, around Broadway and Lafayette between Bleecker and 4th streets, is called **NoHo** (for *No*rth of *Ho*uston), and has a completely different character. As you might have guessed from its name, this area has developed much more like its neighbor to the south, SoHo. Here you'll find a crop of trendy lounges, stylish restaurants, cutting-edge designers, and upscale antiques shops. NoHo is fun to browse; the Bleecker Street stop on the 6 line will land you in the heart of it, and the Broadway-Lafayette stop on the F or V line will drop you at its southern edge.

Greenwich Village   Tree-lined streets crisscross and wind, following ancient streams and cow paths. Each block reveals yet another row of Greek Revival town houses, a well-preserved Federal-style house, or a peaceful courtyard or square. This is "the Village," from Broadway west to the Hudson River, bordered by Houston Street to the south and 14th Street to the north. It defies Manhattan's orderly grid system with streets that predate it, virtually every one chockablock with activity, and unless you live here, it may be impossible to master the lay of the land—so be sure to take a map along as you explore.

The 7th Avenue line (1, 2, 3, or 9) is the area's main subway artery, while the West 4th Street stop (where the A, C, B, D, and E lines meet the F and V lines) serves as its central hub.

Nineteenth-century artists such as Mark Twain, Edgar Allan Poe, Henry James, and Winslow Homer first gave the Village its reputation for embracing the unconventional. Groundbreaking artists such as Edward Hopper and Jackson Pollack were drawn in, as were writers such as Eugene O'Neill, e. e. cummings, and Dylan Thomas. Radical thinkers from John Reed to Upton Sinclair basked in the neighborhood's liberal ethos, and beatniks Allen Ginsberg, Jack Kerouac, and William Burroughs dug the free-swinging atmosphere. Now the Village is the roost of choice for the young celebrity set, with the likes of Gwyneth Paltrow, Matthew Broderick, and Sarah Jessica Parker

> ## Tips Touring Tip
>
> If you'd like to tour a particular neighborhood with an expert, call **Big Apple Greeter** (© **212/669-8159**; www.bigapplegreeter.org) at least 1 week ahead of your arrival. This nonprofit organization has specially trained volunteers who take visitors around town for a 2- to 4-hour tour of a specific neighborhood. And they say New York isn't friendly!

drawn by its historic, low-rise, laid-back charms. Gentrification and escalating real-estate values conspire to push out the artistic element, but culture and counterculture still rub shoulders in cafes, internationally renowned jazz clubs, neighborhood bars, Off-Broadway theaters, and an endless variety of tiny shops and restaurants. With a few charming and affordable hotels (see chapter 5), the Village makes a great base for visitors who prefer to avoid more touristy areas in favor of a quirkier, residential view of the city.

The Village is probably the most chameleon-like of Manhattan's neighborhoods. Some of the highest-priced real estate in the city runs along lower 5th Avenue, which dead-ends at **Washington Square Park.** Serpentine **Bleecker Street** stretches through most of the neighborhood and is emblematic of the area's historical bent. The tolerant anything-goes attitude in the Village has fostered a large gay community, which is still largely in evidence around **Christopher Street** and Sheridan Square. The streets west of 7th Avenue, an area known as the **West Village,** boast a more relaxed vibe and some of the city's most charming and historic brownstones. Three colleges—New York University, Parsons School of Design, and the New School for Social Research—keep the area thinking young.

Streets are often crowded with weekend warriors and teenagers, especially on Bleecker, West 4th, 8th, and surrounding streets, and have been known to become increasingly sketchy west of 7th Avenue in the very late hours, especially on weekends. Keep an eye on your wallet when navigating the weekend throngs. Washington Square Park was cleaned up a couple of years back, but it's still best to stay out of the area after dark.

Midtown

Chelsea & the Meat Packing District Chelsea
has come on strong in recent years as a hip address, especially for the gay community. A low-rise composite of town houses, tenements, lofts, and factories, the neighborhood comprises roughly the area west of 6th Avenue from 14th to 30th streets. (Sixth Ave. below 23rd St. is considered part of the Flatiron District; see below.) Chelsea has also evolved into one of the city's best-value accommodations neighborhoods for travelers looking for something special as well as affordable (see chapter 5). Its main arteries are 7th and 8th avenues, and it's primarily served by the C, E, 1, or 9 subway lines.

The **Chelsea Piers** sports complex to the far west and a host of shops (both unique boutiques and big names like Williams-Sonoma), well-priced bistros, and bars along the main drags have contributed to the area's rebirth. Even the Hotel Chelsea—the neighborhood's most famous architectural and literary landmark, where Thomas Wolfe and Arthur Miller wrote, Bob Dylan composed "Sad-Eyed Lady of the Low Land," Viva and Edie Sedgwick of Andy Warhol fame lived, and Sid Vicious killed girlfriend Nancy Spungeon—has undergone a renovation. Prices put it beyond reach of most budget travelers, but pop into the lobby if you're a pop-culture buff. You'll find a number of popular flea markets in parking lots along 6th Avenue, between 24th and 27th streets, on the weekends.

One of the most recent trends in Chelsea has been the establishment of **West Chelsea** (from 9th Ave. west) and the adjacent **Meat Packing District** (south of West Chelsea in the far west Village, roughly from 17th St. to Little West 12th St.) as the style-setting neighborhoods for the 21st century. What SoHo was in the '60s, this industrial west world (dubbed "the Lower West Side" by *New York* magazine, and MePa by others) is today. New restaurants, cutting-edge shopping, and hot nightspots pop up daily in the still-beefy Meat Packing District, while the area from West 22nd to West 29th streets between 10th and 11th avenues is home to the cutting edge of today's art scene, with West 26th the unofficial "gallery row." This area is still quite industrial and in the early stages of transition. With galleries and bars in converted warehouses and meat lockers, browsing can be frustrating, and the sometimes-desolate streets a tad intimidating. Your best bet is to have a destination in mind, be it a restaurant, gallery, or nightclub, before you come.

The Flatiron District, Union Square & Gramercy Park These adjoining, and at some points, overlapping neighborhoods contain some of the city's most appealing streets. They have been rediscovered by New Yorkers and visitors alike, largely thanks to the boom-to-bust dot-com revolution of the last half-dozen or so years; the Flatiron District earned the nickname "Silicon Alley" during those heady times. These neighborhoods boast great shopping and dining, plus a central location that's hard to beat (and a handful of affordable hotels). The commercial spaces are often large expanses with witty designs and graceful columns.

The **Flatiron District** lies south of 23rd Street to 14th Street, between Broadway and 6th Avenue, and centers around the historic Flatiron Building on 23rd (so named for its triangular shape) and Park Avenue South, which has become a sophisticated Restaurant Row. Below 23rd Street along 6th Avenue (once known as the Ladies' Mile shopping district), discounters like Filene's Basement, Bed Bath & Beyond, and others have moved in. The shopping gets classier on 5th Avenue, where you'll find a mix of national names and hip boutiques. Lined with Oriental carpet dealers and high-end fixture stores, Broadway has become the city's home-furnishings alley; its crowning jewel is the justifiably famous ABC Carpet & Home.

Union Square is the hub of the area; the N, R, 4, 5, 6, and L trains stop here, as do Q and W trains, making it easy to reach. Long in the shadows of the more bustling (Times and Herald) and high-toned (Washington) squares, Union Square has experienced a renaissance in the last decade. Local businesses joined forces with the city to rid the park of drug dealers, and now it's a delightful place to spend an afternoon. Union Square is best known as the setting for New York's premier greenmarket every Monday, Wednesday, Friday, and Saturday. In-line skaters take over the space in the after-work hours. During the winter holidays, a series of booths and tents becomes a minimall for clothing, gifts, books, and ornaments. A number of hip and affordable restaurants rim the square, as do stores like Toys "R" Us, the city's best Barnes & Noble, and a Virgin Megastore.

From about 16th to 23rd streets, east from Park Avenue South to about 2nd Avenue, is the leafy, largely residential district known as **Gramercy Park.** The pity of the district is that so few can enjoy the park: Built by Samuel Ruggles in the 1830s to attract buyers to the area, it is the only private park in the city and locked to all but those who live on its perimeter (your windows have to look over the park for you to have a key). At the southern end of Lexington Avenue (at 21st St.), it is one of the most peaceful spots in the city. If you know someone who has a key, go there.

At the northern edge, fronting the Flatiron Building on 23rd Street and 5th Avenue, is lovely little **Madison Square.** Across from its northeast corner stood Stanford White's original Madison Square Garden (in whose roof garden White was murdered in 1906 by jealous millionaire Harry K. Thaw). It's now presided over by the New York Life Insurance Building, the New York State Supreme Court, and the Metropolitan Life Insurance Company, whose tower, at 700 feet, was the tallest in the world when it was built in 1909.

Midtown West & Times Square
Midtown West, the area from 34th to 59th streets west of 5th Avenue to the Hudson River, encompasses several famous names: Madison Square Garden, the Garment District, Rockefeller Center, the Theater District, and Times Square. This is

New York's tourism central, where you'll find the bright lights and bustle that draw people from all over the world. This is the city's biggest hotel neighborhood. While there are a lot of budget and midpriced choices, rates can fluctuate dramatically, since this is where everybody wants to stay; in periods of high demand, even "budget" hotels can price around the $200 mark. You're likely to find your best bargains elsewhere, especially in fall and the holiday season.

The 1, 2, 3, or 9 subway line serves the massive neon station at the heart of Times Square, at 42nd Street between Broadway and 7th Avenue, while the F, V line runs up 6th Avenue to Rockefeller Center (B and D lines also serve Rockefeller Center, but travel only as far south as 34th St. until Manhattan Bridge work is complete in 2005). The N/R line cuts diagonally across the neighborhood, following the path of Broadway before heading up 7th Avenue at 42nd Street (the Q and W trains also use this line until 2004). The A, C, and E line serves the west side, running along 8th Avenue.

If you know New York but haven't been here in a few years, you'll be quite surprised by the "new" **Times Square.** Longtime New Yorkers kvetch about the glory days of the peep-show-and-porn-shop Times Square that this cleaned-up version supplanted, but the truth is that it's a successful gentrification. Old theaters have come back to life as Broadway and children's playhouses, and scores of family-friendly restaurants and shops have opened (including the Virgin Megastore on Broadway). Plenty of businesses have moved in—MTV studios overlook Times Square at 1515 Broadway, and *Good Morning America* has its own studio at Broadway and 44th Street. The lights have never been brighter, and Middle America has never been more welcome. Expect dense crowds; it's often tough just to make your way along the sidewalks.

Most of the Broadway theaters light up the streets just off Times Square, in the West 40s just east and west of Broadway. At the heart of the **Theater District,** where Broadway meets 7th Avenue, is the TKTS booth, where crowds line up to buy discount tickets.

To the west, in the 40s and 50s between 8th and 10th avenues, is **Hell's Kitchen,** an area that is much nicer than its ghoulish name and one of my favorites in the city. The neighborhood resisted gentrification until the mid-1990s, but has grown into a charming, less touristy adjunct to the Theater District. Ninth Avenue has blossomed into one of the city's finest dining avenues; stroll along and you'll have a world of affordable cuisine to choose from, from American diner to hearty German to traditional Thai. Stylish boutiques and bars have also popped up in this area. Realtors tried to rename the area Clinton, but locals hold fast to Hell's Kitchen, clearly delighting in the increasing juxtaposition.

Unlike Times Square, **Rockefeller Center** has needed no renovation. Between 46th and 50th streets from 6th Avenue east to 5th, this Art Deco complex contains some of the city's great architectural gems, which house offices, a number of NBC studios (including *Saturday Night Live, Late Night with Conan O'Brien,* and the glass-walled *Today* show studio at 48th St.), and some boutiques. If you can negotiate the crowds, the winter holidays are a great time to be here, as ice skaters take over the central plaza, the huge Christmas tree twinkles against the night sky, and lines wind past the holiday windows of Saks Fifth Avenue, across the street.

Along 7th Avenue south of 42nd Street is the **Garment District,** of little interest to tourists except for its sample sales, where some great new fashions are sold to serious bargain hunters willing to scour the racks (see chapter 8 for details). Other than that, it's a grim commercial area. Between 7th and 8th avenues and 31st and 33rd streets, **Penn Station** sits beneath ugly **Madison Square Garden,** where the Rangers, Knicks, and Liberty play. Taking up 34th Street between 6th and 7th avenues is **Macy's,** the world's largest department store; exit Macy's at the southeast corner and you'll find more famous-label shopping around **Herald Square.** The blocks around 32nd Street west of 5th Avenue have developed into a Koreatown, with midpriced hotels and Asian restaurants that offer some of the best-value stays and eats in Midtown.

Midtown West is also home to some of the city's most revered museums and institutions, including **Carnegie Hall,** the **Museum of Modern Art, Radio City Music Hall,** and the *Intrepid* **Sea-Air-Space Museum,** to name just a few.

Midtown East & Murray Hill Midtown East, the area including 5th Avenue and everything east from 34th to 59th streets, is the more upscale side of Midtown. This side of town is short of subway trains, served mostly by the Lexington Avenue 4, 5, or 6 lines.

Midtown East is where you'll find many of the city's grand hotels along Lexington Avenue and near the park at the top of 5th. The stretch of **5th Avenue** from Saks at 49th Street extending to the famous Plaza Hotel at 59th is home to the city's most high profile haute shopping, including Tiffany & Co. and Bergdorf Goodman, but midpriced names like

Manhattan Address Locator

To locate avenue addresses, cancel the last figure, divide by 2, and add (or subtract) the key number below. The answer is the nearest numbered cross street, approximately.

Avenue A:	add 3	11th Avenue:	add 15
Avenue B:	add 3	Amsterdam Avenue:	add 59
Avenue C:	add 3	Columbus Avenue:	add 59 or 60
1st Avenue:	add 3	Lexington Avenue:	add 22
2nd Avenue:	add 3	Madison Avenue:	add 27
3rd Avenue:	add 10	Park Avenue:	add 34
6th Avenue:	subtract 12	Park Avenue South:	add 8
8th Avenue:	add 9	West End Avenue:	add 59
9th Avenue:	add 13	York Avenue:	add 4
10th Avenue:	add 14		

Note special instructions for finding address locations on the following:

5th Avenue

63 to 108:	add 11	776 to 1286: cancel last figure of
109 to 200:	add 13	house number and subtract 18 (do
201 to 400:	add 16	not divide house number by 2)
401 to 600:	add 18	For 1310 to 1494: cancel last figure
601 to 775:	add 20	of house number. For 1310, subtract
		20 and for every additional 20 street
		numbers, increase deduction by 1.

7th Avenue

1 to 1800:	add 12	above 1800:	add 20

Broadway

Anything from 1 to 754 is south of 8th Street, and hence a named street.

756 to 846:	subtract 29	Above 953:	subtract 31
847 to 953:	subtract 25		

Central Park West

Cancel last figure and add 60

Riverside Drive

Cancel last figure and

Up to 567:	add 72	568 and up:	add 78

Banana Republic and Liz Claiborne have moved in over the last 5 years. The stretch of 57th Street between 5th and Lexington avenues is also known for high-fashion boutiques (Chanel, Hermès) and galleries, but change is underway since names like Levi's and Niketown have arrived.

You'll find more spillover along **Madison Avenue,** a great strip for shoe shopping in particular.

Architectural highlights include the recently repolished **Chrysler Building,** with its stylized gargoyles glaring down on passersby; the Beaux Arts tour de force that is

Grand Central Terminal; St. Patrick's Cathedral; and the glorious Empire State Building.

Far east, swank Sutton and Beekman places are enclaves of beautiful town houses and tiny pocket parks that look out over the East River. Along the river is the United Nations, which isn't officially in New York City, or even the United States, but on a parcel of land belonging to member nations.

Claiming territory east from Madison Avenue, Murray Hill begins somewhere north of 23rd Street (the line between it and Gramercy Park is fuzzy), and is most clearly recognizable north of 30th Street to 42nd Street. This brownstone-lined quarter is residential, notable for its handful of budget and mid-priced hotels. The stretch of Lexington Avenue in the high 20s is Curry Hill, and is a destination for inexpensive, good Indian and Pakistani food.

Uptown

Upper West Side North of 59th Street and encompassing everything west of Central Park, the Upper West Side contains Lincoln Center, arguably the world's premier performing arts venue; the new (in 2004) Time Warner Center with its upscale shops, such as Hugo Boss, A/X Armani, and Sephora; Jazz at Lincoln Center; the Mandarin Oriental Hotel; and the gargantuan Whole Foods Market. The Upper West Side is also the home of the American Museum of Natural History, whose renovated Dinosaur Halls and magnificent new Rose Center for Earth and Space garner justifiably rave reviews. You'll also find a growing number of midpriced hotels whose larger-than-Midtown rooms and nice residential location make them some of the best values —and some of my favorite places to stay—in the entire city.

Unlike the more stratified Upper East Side, the Upper West Side is home to an egalitarian mix of middle-class yuppiedom, laid-back wealth (lots of celebs and moneyed media types call the grand apartments along Central Park West home), and ethnic families who were here before the gentrification.

The neighborhood runs all the way up to Harlem, around 125th Street, and encompasses Morningside Heights, where you'll find Columbia University and the perennial construction project known as the Cathedral of St. John the Divine. But prime Upper West Side—the part you're most likely to explore—is the area running from Columbus Circle at 59th Street into the 80s, between the park and Broadway. North of 59th Street is where 8th Avenue becomes Central Park West, the eastern border of the neighborhood (and the western border of Central Park); 9th Avenue becomes Columbus Avenue, lined with attractive boutiques and cafes; and 10th Avenue becomes Amsterdam Avenue, less charming than Columbus to the east and less trafficked than bustling Broadway (whose highlights are the gourmet megamarts Zabar's and Fairway) to the west; still, Amsterdam has blossomed into quite a happening restaurant and bar strip over the last couple of years. You'll find Lincoln Center in the mid-60s, where Broadway crosscuts Amsterdam.

Two major subway lines service the area: the 1, 2, 3, or 9 line runs up Broadway, while the B and C trains run up glamorous Central Park West, stopping right at the historic Dakota apartment building (where John Lennon was shot and Yoko Ono still lives) at 72nd Street, and at the Museum of Natural History at 81st Street.

Upper East Side North of 59th Street and east of Central Park is some of the city's most expensive residential real estate. This is New York at its most gentrified: Walk along 5th and Park avenues, especially between 60th and 80th streets, and you're sure to encounter some of the wizened WASPs and Chanel-suited socialites that make up the most rarefied of the city's population. Madison Avenue from 60th Street well into the 80s is the moneyed crowd's main shopping strip, in recent years vaunting ahead of Hong Kong's Causeway Bay to become the most expensive retail real estate *in the world*. The main attraction of this neighborhood is **Museum Mile,** the stretch of 5th Avenue fronting Central Park that's home to no fewer than 10 cultural institutions, including Frank Lloyd Wright's **Guggenheim,** and anchored by the **Metropolitan Museum of Art.** But the elegant rows of town houses are worth a look: East 70th Street, from Madison to Lexington, is one of the world's most charming residential streets. If you want to see where real people live, move east to 3rd Avenue and beyond, called Yorkville, where affordable restaurants and street life start popping up.

A second subway line is in the works, but that's years away. For now, the Upper East Side is served by the crowded Lexington Avenue line (4, 5, or 6 trains) and rather slow buses, so wear your walking shoes (or bring taxi fare) if you head here to explore.

Harlem Now that Bill Clinton has moved his post-presidential office —and more than a few Secret Service agents—into this uptown neighborhood, the world has again heard about Harlem, which has benefited from a dramatic image makeover in the last few years.

Harlem is really two areas: Harlem proper stretches from river to river, beginning at 125th Street on the West Side and 96th Street on the East Side. East of 5th Avenue, **Spanish Harlem** *(El Barrio)* runs between East 100th and East 125th streets. Harlem proper is benefiting from the revitalization that has swept much of the city, with national retailers moving in, restaurants and nightspots opening, and visitors touring historic sites related to the Golden Age of African-American culture, when bands like the Count Basie and Duke Ellington orchestras played the Cotton Club and Sugar Cane Club, and literary giants like Langston Hughes and James Baldwin soaked up the scene. Some houses date back to when the area was a country retreat and represent some of the best brownstone mansions in the city. On **Sugar Hill** (from 143rd to 155th sts., btwn St. Nicholas and Edgecombe aves.) and **Striver's Row** (W. 139th St. btwn Adam Clayton Powell Jr. and Frederick Douglass blvds.) are a significant number of fine town houses. For cultural visits, there's the Morris-Jumel Mansion, the Schomburg Center, the Studio Museum, and the Apollo Theatre.

Do come to Harlem—it's one of the city's most vital, historic neighborhoods, and no other feels quite so energized. Your best bet is to take a guided tour (see "Affordable Sightseeing Tours," in chapter 7); if you come on your own, do it during the day. Don't wander without a plan, especially at night. If you head up after dark to a restaurant or club, be clear about where you're going and stay alert.

Washington Heights & Inwood At the northern tip of Manhattan, Washington Heights (the area from 155th St. to Dyckman St., with adjacent Inwood running to the tip) is home to a large segment of Manhattan's Latino community, plus an increasing number of yuppies who don't mind trading a half-hour subway commute to Midtown for lower rents. **Fort Tryon Park** and **the Cloisters** are the two big reasons visitors come up this way. The Cloisters houses the Metropolitan Museum of Art's medieval collection, with excellent views across the Hudson to the Palisades.

The Boroughs

Manhattan is just one of the five boroughs that make up the very Big Apple. The others are Brooklyn, the Bronx, Queens, and Staten Island.

Brooklyn Brooklynites are quick to tell you that their borough is the fourth-largest city in the United States. That's because this borough is about pride and attitude. And though it has been over 45 years since the team left, don't even talk to them about the Dodgers.

Brooklyn is also about neighborhoods and diversity; the borough is a pleasure to explore. Some of the highlights include New York's first historic district, **Brooklyn Heights,** with its elegant brownstones; the Promenade, with its spectacular view of Manhattan; and the River Cafe. To get to Brooklyn Heights, take the A, C, or F to Jay Street; the 2, 3, 4, or 5 to Clark Street; or the N or R to Court Street.

Brooklyn's newest trendy neighborhood is the creation called **DUMBO** (Down Under the Manhattan Bridge Overpass). What was once a scattering of warehouses was gentrified by artists, with those former warehouses now converted into expensive lofts. The main drag is **Washington Street,** and businesses are beginning to populate the area. It's here where you'll find **Jacques Torres Chocolate,** the **Brooklyn**

Ice Cream Factory, and **Grimaldi's Pizza.** The best way to get to DUMBO is the F train to York Street or the A or C to High Street.

Brooklyn's hippest neighborhood (though once it's *known* as hip, some say it's over), is **Williamsburg.** In the early 1990s, artists began to flee Manhattan's high rents to live here among the Hispanic and Hasidic communities already there. Now, though, the hipsters are seeing their once independent and inexpensive enclave being slowly transformed into SoHo/Brooklyn. There are a number of funky, youth-oriented boutiques along the neighborhood's main drag, **Bedford Avenue,** but Williamsburg is also the home of that venerable red meat institution, **Peter Luger.** The best train to get to Williamsburg from Manhattan is the L to Bedford Avenue.

Other emerging neighborhoods are **Carroll Gardens, Cobble Hill,** and **Boerum Hill** (which are attempting to adopt the acronym CoBoCa, with mixed results). **Smith Street** cuts through all three and has become a booming restaurant destination. To get to Smith Street the best train is the F, with stops at either Carroll Street or Bergen Street.

Downtown Brooklyn off Flatbush Avenue is probably best known for **BAM,** the **Brooklyn Academy of Music.** You'll also find a number of chain department stores and one of the borough's most beloved landmarks, **Junior's,** the diner noted for its famous cheesecakes. Many trains converge in downtown Brooklyn at the Pacific Street/Atlantic Avenue station, including the 2, 3, 4, 5, M, N, Q, R, and W.

Park Slope is probably the heart of Brooklyn; it is here and in nearby Prospect Heights where you find the **Brooklyn Museum,** the **Brooklyn Botanical Gardens,** and **Prospect**

Park. The 2, 3, 4, or 5 trains to Grand Army Plaza will land you close to all of the above.

In its heyday during the early 20th century, **Coney Island** was to New York what South Beach is now to Miami. This was where everyone flocked to escape the heat and grime of a New York summer day. A few remnants of Coney Island's past remain, such as the long-defunct parachute ride. But during the summer you can still ride on one of the best roller coasters anywhere, the famous **Cyclone.** Coney Island is also the home of the **New York Aquarium** and the minor league baseball team the Cyclones. To get to Coney Island, take the D or F to West 8th Street, Brooklyn.

The Bronx Perhaps the most famous destination in the Bronx, and next to Rome's Coliseum maybe one of the most celebrated sports arenas in the world, is **Yankee Stadium.** Even if you are a Yankee hater, you will be awed by the stadium. The 4, D, and B trains all stop there.

The Bronx is also the home of the United States's largest metropolitan animal park, the **Bronx Zoo,** and the national landmark **Bronx Botanical Gardens.** Both are wonders very worthy of an excursion from Manhattan. To get to the Bronx Zoo, you can take the 2 train to Pelham Parkway and walk to the Bronxdale entrance of the zoo. To get to the Botanical Gardens, you can take Metro-North from Grand Central Station to the Botanical Gardens station.

While visiting either the Bronx Zoo or the Botanical Gardens, stop at the Little Italy of the Bronx, **Arthur Avenue,** for a mouthwatering walk past meat markets, delis, vegetable stands, fish markets, cafes, and restaurants. To get to Arthur Avenue, take the 4 or D train to Fordham Road, and transfer to the no. 12 bus east or the 2 or 5 train to Pelham Parkway and the no. 12 bus west.

Queens At 109 square miles, Queens is the largest borough in New York and it's also the city's most ethnically diverse. There are more languages spoken here than anywhere else on the planet. All that ethnicity translates into an adventurous eater's paradise. I've dined on Thai, Peruvian, Indian, Guyanese, Greek, Colombian, and Brazilian here, and I've barely scratched the surface. But there's more to Queens than just food.

Astoria, with its large Greek community, is also the home of the **American Museum of the Moving Image,** dedicated to the movies—film, video, and digital. To get to Astoria, take the N/W to Broadway.

Long Island City, directly across the river from Manhattan's Upper East Side, is where you'll find **Socrates Park,** the **Museum of African Art,** and the **P.S. 1 Contemporary Art Center.** The best train to get to Long Island City is the 7. The 7 train is really the heartbeat of Queens, also known as the International Express, running through one ethnic community after another; get off at just about any spot and you'll see signs in an assortment of languages. The 7 train will also take you to Flushing, where you'll find **Shea Stadium,** home of the Mets; the Louis Armstrong Stadium and the Arthur Ashe Stadium at **Flushing Meadow Park,** where the **U.S. Open** is held each September; and the **Queens Museum of Art** on the grounds of the 1964 World's Fair.

Staten Island Staten Island is the most remote of the boroughs and best reached by ferry. There is a suburban feel to the borough, making it a haven for commuters. The free **Staten Island Ferry** gets you to the borough. If you decide to spend time in Staten Island, take in a **Staten Island Yankees** minor-league baseball game. The stadium is within walking distance from the ferry and has lovely views of downtown Manhattan.

2 Getting Around

Frankly, Manhattan's transportation systems are a marvel. It's miraculous that so many people can gather on this little island and move around on it. For the most part, you can get where you're going pretty easily using some combination of subways, buses, and cabs; this section will tell you how to do just that.

But between traffic gridlock and subway delays, sometimes you just can't get there from here—unless you walk. Walking can be the fastest way to navigate the island. During rush hours, you'll beat car traffic on foot, as taxis and buses stop and groan at gridlocked corners (don't even *try* going crosstown in a cab or bus in Midtown at midday). You'll also see a lot more by walking than by riding beneath the street or flying by in a cab. So pack comfortable shoes and hit the pavement—it's the best, cheapest, and most appealing way to experience the city.

BY SUBWAY

Run by the **Metropolitan Transit Authority (MTA),** the much-maligned subway system is actually the best way to travel around New York, especially during rush hours. Some 3.5 million people a day agree, as it's their primary mode of transportation. The subway is quick, inexpensive, relatively safe, and pretty efficient, as well as being a genuine New York experience.

The subway runs 24 hours a day, 7 days a week. The rush-hour crushes are roughly from 8 to 9:30am and 5 to 6:30pm on weekdays; the rest of the time the trains are relatively uncrowded.

PAYING YOUR WAY

The venerable New York city token is now a thing of the past, having been eliminated in 2003, so now you need a **MetroCard,** a magnetically encoded card that debits the fare when swiped through the turnstile (or the fare box on any city bus). Once you're in the system, you can transfer freely to any subway line that you can reach without exiting your station. MetroCards—not tokens—also allow you **free transfers** between the bus and subway within a 2-hour period.

⌒ *Tips* **On the Sidewalks**

New Yorkers stride across wide, crowded pavements without any regard for the traffic light, weaving through crowds, dodging taxis and buses. **Never take your walking cues from the locals.** Wait for walk signals and always use crosswalks—don't jaywalk. Do otherwise and you could quickly end up as a flattened statistic.

Always pay attention to the traffic flow. Walk as if you're driving, staying to the right. At intersections, keep an eye out for drivers who don't yield, turn without looking, or think a yellow traffic light means "Hurry up!" Unfortunately, most bicyclists seem to think that the traffic laws don't apply to them; they'll often blithely fly through red lights and dash the wrong way on one-way streets, so be on your guard.

For more safety tips, see "Playing It Safe," later in this chapter.

Subway Service Interruption Notes

The subway map featured on the inside back cover of this book was as accurate as possible at press time, but service is always subject to change, especially on weekends, so your best bet is to contact the **Metropolitan Transit Authority (MTA)** for the latest details; call ✆ **718/330-1234** or visit **www.mta.nyc.ny.us**, where you'll find system updates that are thorough, timely, and clear. Once you're in town, you can also stop at the MTA desk at the **Times Square Visitors Center**, 1560 Broadway (btwn 46th and 47th sts., where Broadway meets 7th Ave.) to pick up the latest subway map. (You can also ask for one at any token booth, but they might not always be stocked.)

MetroCards can be purchased primarily from ATM-style vending machines located in all stations or at one of the few remaining staffed station booths, where you can only pay with cash. The ATM-style vending machines accept cash, credit cards, and debit cards. You can also purchase MetroCards from a MetroCard merchant, such as most Rite-Aid drugstores or Hudson News at Penn Station and Grand Central Terminal; or at the MTA information desk at the Times Square Visitors Center, 1560 Broadway, between 46th and 47th streets.

MetroCards come in a few different configurations:

- **Pay-Per-Ride MetroCards,** which can be used for up to four people by swiping up to four times (bring the whole family). You can put any amount from $4 (two rides) to $80 on your card. Every time you put $10 on your Pay-Per-Ride MetroCard, you get an extra ride added to your total. (For example, if you buy a $10 MetroCard, you get six rides.) You can buy Pay-Per-Ride MetroCards in any denomination at any subway station at automated MetroCard vending machines, which allow you to buy MetroCards using your major credit card. MetroCards are also available from shops and newsstands around town in $10 and $20 values. You can refill your card at any time until the expiration date on the card, usually about a year from the date of purchase, at any subway station.

- **Unlimited-Ride MetroCards,** which can't be used for more than one person at a time or more frequently than 18-minute intervals, are available in four values: the **daily Fun Pass,** which allows you a day's worth of unlimited subway and bus rides for $7; the **7-Day MetroCard,** for $21; and the **30-Day MetroCard,** for $70. Seven- and 30-day Unlimited-Ride MetroCards can be purchased at any subway station or from a MetroCard merchant. Fun Passes *cannot* be purchased at booths—you can only buy them at a MetroCard machine, from a MetroCard merchant, or at the MTA information desk at the Times Square Visitors Center. Unlimited-Ride MetroCards go into effect the first time you use them—so if you buy a card on Monday and don't use it until Wednesday, Wednesday is when the clock starts ticking. A Fun Pass is good from the first time you use it until 3am the next day, while 7- and 30-day MetroCards run out at midnight on the last day. These MetroCards cannot be refilled; throw them out once they've expired and buy a new one.

Tips for using your MetroCard: The MetroCard swiping mechanisms at turnstiles are the source of much grousing among subway riders. If you swipe too fast or too slow, the turnstile will ask you to swipe again. If this happens, *do not move to a different turnstile,* or you may end up paying twice. If you've tried repeatedly and really can't make it work, tell the token-booth clerk; chances are good, though, that you'll get the movement down after a couple of uses.

If you're not sure how much money you have left, or when the card expires, use the station's MetroCard reader, usually near the station entrance or the token booth (on buses, the fare box will also provide you with this information).

To locate the nearest MetroCard merchant, or for any other MetroCard questions, call © **800/METRO-CARD** or 212/METRO-CARD (212/638-7622) Monday through Friday from 7am to 11pm, Saturday and Sunday from 9am to 5pm. Or go online to **www.mta.nyc.ny.us/metrocard**, which can give you a full rundown of MetroCard merchants in the tri-state (New York, New Jersey, and Connecticut) area.

Note: At press time, the MTA was considering (yet another) fare increase on the 30-day unlimited-Ride Metro Card from $70 to $76 and the 7-Day Metro Card from $21 to $24. Check online at www.mta.nyc.ny.us/metrocard to see if these changes have been implemented when you visit.

USING THE SYSTEM

As you can see from the full-color subway map on the inside back cover, the subway system basically mimics the lay of the land above ground, with most lines in Manhattan running north and south, and a few running east and west.

To go up and down the east side of Manhattan (and to the Bronx and Brooklyn), take the 4, 5, or 6 train.

To travel up and down the west side (and also to the Bronx and Brooklyn), take the 1, 2, 3, or 9 line; the A, C, E, or F line; or the B or D line.

⌒Tips For More Bus & Subway Information

For transit information, call the Metropolitan Transit Authority's **MTA/New York City Transit Travel Information Center** at © **718/330-1234.** Automated information is available 24 hours a day, and agents are on hand daily from 6am to 9pm. For online information, visit **www.mta.nyc.ny.us**; kudos to the MTA, because the information on the site is always current.

To request maps, call the Customer Assistance Line at © **718/330-3322** (although recent service changes may not be reflected on printed maps). Riders with disabilities should direct inquiries to © **718/596-8585;** hearing-impaired riders can call © **718/596-8273.** For Metro-Card information, call © **212/638-7622** weekdays from 7 to 11am, weekends from 9am to 5pm, or go online to **www.mta.nyc.ny.us/metrocard**.

You can get bus and subway maps and additional information at most information centers (see "Visitor Information," earlier in this chapter). A helpful MTA transit information desk is located at the Times Square Visitors Center, 1560 Broadway (btwn 46th and 47th sts.), where you can also buy MetroCards. Maps are sometimes available in subway stations (ask at the token booth), but rarely on buses.

The N, R, Q, and W lines first cut diagonally across town from east to west and then snake under 7th Avenue before shooting out to Queens or Brooklyn.

The crosstown S line, the Shuttle, runs back and forth between Times Square and Grand Central Terminal (as does the 7 line). Farther downtown, across 14th Street, the L line works its own crosstown magic.

Note: For service changes, see "Subway Service Interruption Notes," above.

Lines have assigned colors on subway maps and trains—red for the 1, 2, 3, 9 line; green for the 4, 5, and 6 trains; and so on—but nobody refers to them by color. Always use the number or letter when asking questions. Within Manhattan, the distinction between numbered trains that share the same line is usually that some are express and others are local. **Express trains** often skip about three stops for each one that they make; express stops are indicated on subway maps with a white (rather than solid) circle. Local stops usually come about 9 blocks apart.

Directions are almost always indicated using "uptown" (northbound) and "downtown" (southbound), so be sure to know what direction you want to head in. The outsides of some subway entrances are marked UPTOWN ONLY or DOWNTOWN ONLY; read carefully, as it's easy to head in the wrong direction. Once you're on the platform, check the signs overhead to make sure that the train you're waiting for will be traveling in the right direction. If you do make a mistake, it's a good idea to wait for an express station, like 14th Street or 42nd Street, so you can get off and change for the other direction without paying again.

The days of graffiti-covered cars are gone, but the stations—and an increasing number of trains—are not nearly as clean as they could be. Trains are air-conditioned (move to the next car if yours isn't), though during the dog days of summer the platforms can be sweltering. In theory, all subway cars have PA systems to allow you to hear the conductor's announcements, but they don't always work well. It's a good idea to move to a car with a working PA system in case sudden service changes are announced that you'll want to know about.

For **subway safety tips,** see "Playing It Safe," later in this chapter.

BY BUS

Less expensive than taxis and more pleasant than subways (they provide a mobile sightseeing window on Manhattan), MTA buses are a good transportation option. Their big drawback: They can get stuck in traffic, sometimes making it quicker to walk. They also stop every couple of blocks, rather than the 8 or 9 blocks that local subways traverse between stops. So for long distances, the subway is your best bet; but for short distances or traveling crosstown, try the bus.

PAYING YOUR WAY

Like the subway fare, **bus fare** is $2, half price for seniors and riders with disabilities, free for children under 44 inches (up to three per adult). The fare is payable with a **MetroCard** or **exact change.** Bus drivers don't make change, and fare boxes don't accept dollar bills or pennies, so bring lots of quarters. You can't purchase MetroCards on the bus, so get them before you board; for details on where to get them, see "Paying Your Way" under "By Subway," above.

USING THE SYSTEM

You can't flag down a city bus—you have to wait at a bus stop. **Bus stops** are located every 2 or 3 blocks on the right-side corner of the street (facing the direction of traffic flow). They're marked by a curb painted yellow and a blue-and-white sign with a bus emblem and the route number or numbers. Guide-A-Ride boxes at most stops show a route map and a somewhat optimistic schedule.

Almost every major avenue has its own **bus route.** They run either north or south: downtown on 5th, uptown on Madison, downtown on Lexington, uptown on 3rd, and so on. There are **crosstown buses** at strategic locations all around town: 8th Street (eastbound); 9th (westbound); 14th, 23rd, 34th, and 42nd (east- and westbound); 49th (eastbound); 50th (westbound); 57th (east- and westbound); 65th (eastbound across the West Side, through the park, and then north on Madison, continuing east on 68th to York Ave.); 67th (west-bound on the East Side to 5th Ave. and then south on 5th, continuing west on 66th St. through the park and across the West Side to West End Ave.); and 79th, 86th, 96th, 116th, and 125th (east- and westbound). Some bus routes, however, are erratic: The M104, for example, starts at the East River, then turns at 8th Avenue and goes up Broadway. The buses of the 5th Avenue line go up Madison or 6th and follow various routes around the city.

Most routes operate 24 hours a day, but service is infrequent at night. Some say that New York buses have a herding instinct: They come only in groups. During rush hour, main routes have "limited-stop" buses, identifiable by the orange card in the front window; they stop only at major cross streets.

To make sure the bus you're boarding goes where you're going, check the maps on the sign that's at every bus stop, get your hands on a route map (see "For More Bus & Subway Information," above), or *just ask.* The drivers are helpful, as long as you don't hold up the line too long.

While traveling, look out the window not only to take in the sights, but also to keep track of cross streets. You can signal for a stop by pressing the tape strip above and beside the windows and along the metal straps, about 1 block before you want to stop. Exit through the back doors (not the front door) by pushing on the yellow tape strip; the doors open automatically (pushing on the handles is useless). Most city buses are equipped with wheelchair lifts, making buses the preferable mode of public transportation for wheelchair-bound travelers (if you're in a seat that converts for wheelchair use, you'll be expected to vacate it if

---

Value Money-Saving Transit Tips: Free Transfers

If you pay your subway or bus fare with a **MetroCard,** you can transfer to another bus or to the subway (or from the subway to a bus) for up to 2 hours. You don't need to do anything special; just swipe your card at the turnstile, and the automated system keeps track.

If you use coins to board a bus and need to transfer to another line, request a free **transfer slip** that allows you to change to an intersecting bus route only (transfer points are listed on the transfer itself) within 1 hour of issue. Transfer slips cannot be used to enter the subway.

When you're waiting on the street for a taxi, look at the **medallion light** on the top of the coming cabs. If the light is out, the taxi is in use. When the center part (the number) is lit, the taxi is available: Raise your hand to flag the cab. If all the lights are on, the driver is off-duty.

Note: A taxi can't take more than four people.

---

the bus stops to pick up a person in a chair); for more on this topic, see "Travelers with Disabilities," under "Specialized Travel Resources," in chapter 2. Buses also "kneel," lowering down to the curb to make boarding easier.

BY TAXI

If you don't want to deal with public transportation, finding an address that might be a few blocks from the subway station, or sharing your ride with 3.5 million other people, take a taxi. The biggest advantages are that cabs can be hailed on any street (provided you find an empty one—often simple, yet at other times nearly impossible) and will take you right to your destination.

Official New York City taxis, licensed by the Taxi and Limousine Commission, are yellow, with the rates printed on the door and a light with a medallion number on the roof. You can hail a taxi on any street. *Never* accept a ride from any other car except an official city yellow cab (private livery cars are not allowed to pick up fares on the street).

Lobbying by taxi drivers led to fare increases in the spring of 2004. The base fare on entering the cab is $2.50. The cost is 40¢ for every ⅕ mile or 40¢ per 2 minutes in stopped or very slow-moving traffic (or for waiting time). There's no extra charge for each passenger or for luggage. However, you must pay bridge or tunnel tolls (sometimes the driver will front the toll and add it to your bill at the end; most times, however, you pay the driver before the toll). You'll also pay a $1 night surcharge after 8pm and before 6am. A 15% to 20% tip is customary.

Because it's going to cost you at least $2.50 just to get in the car, taxis are far more expensive than other forms of transportation. Visitors on a limited budget are generally better off relying on subways and buses, using taxis only late at night (after 11pm or midnight, when buses and subway trains start getting fewer and farther between) or to reach an out-of-the-way destination (maybe a bar or restaurant on the Lower East Side or the far East Village, neighborhoods not well served by the subway). You'll also get your money's worth out of a taxi at night, when there's little traffic to keep them from speeding you to your destination.

Although taxis are generally far more expensive than the subway or a bus, consider taking cabs for short hauls if there are three or four in your group. A taxi might not actually save you money, but you'll get door-to-door service for about the same price: It costs four people $6 to take the subway, which is no less than you'd pay for a short taxi ride from Times Square to the West Village, say, or from Carnegie Hall to your Murray Hill hotel. Skip taxis entirely at rush hour, when it's more convenient and cheaper to take the subway, because you don't want to end up stuck in traffic, delayed, and paying for unnecessary wait time.

Forget about hopping into the back seat and having some double-chinned, cigar-chomping driver slowly turn and ask, "Where to, Mac?" Nowadays most taxi drivers speak only an approximation of English and drive in engagingly exotic ways. Always wear your seat belt—taxis are required to provide them.

The TLC has posted a **Taxi Rider's Bill of Rights** in every cab. Drivers are required to take you anywhere in the five boroughs, to Nassau or Westchester counties, or to Newark Airport. They are supposed to know how to get you to any address in Manhattan and major points in the outer boroughs. They are required to provide air-conditioning and turn off the radio on demand, and they cannot smoke while you're in the cab. They are required to be polite.

You are allowed to dictate the route that is taken. It's a good idea to look at a map before you get in a taxi. Taxi drivers have been known to jack up the fare on visitors who don't know better by taking very circuitous routes. Know enough about where you're going to know that something's wrong if you hop in a cab at 6th Avenue and 57th Street to go to the Empire State Building (5th Ave. and 34th St.), say, and you suddenly find yourself on 9th Avenue.

On the other hand, listen to drivers who propose an alternate route. These guys spend 8 or 10 hours a day on these streets, and they know them well—where the worst traffic is, or where Con Ed has dug up an intersection. A knowledgeable driver will know how to get you to your destination quickly and efficiently.

Another important tip: Always make sure the meter is turned on at the start of the ride. You'll see the red readout register the initial $2.50 and start calculating the fare as you go. I've witnessed unscrupulous drivers hauling unsuspecting visitors around with the meter off, and then overcharging them at drop-off time.

Always ask for the receipt—it comes in handy if you need to make a complaint or if you leave something behind. It's a good idea to make a mental note of the driver's four-digit medallion number (usually posted on the divider between the front and back seats). You probably won't need it, but it's a good idea.

A taxi driver is obligated to take you to your desired destination. If the taxi driver is on duty and after giving your desired destination, the taxi driver refuses to take you there, write down the driver's name and medallion number and file a complaint with the Taxi and Limousine Commission.

For driver complaints and lost property, call the 24-hour Consumer Hot Line at © **212/NYC-TAXI.** For details on getting to and from the local airports by taxi, see "By Plane" under "Getting There," in chapter 2. For further taxi information—including a complete rundown of your rights as a taxi rider—point your Web browser to **www.ci.nyc.ny.us/taxi**.

BY CAR

Forget driving yourself around the city. It's not worth it. Traffic is horrible, the streets have all the civility of the Wild West, street parking is nearly impossible (not to mention the security risks), and garage parking *will* cost you a fortune.

If you arrive in New York City by car, park it in a garage and leave it there. If you drive a rental car in, return it as soon as you arrive and rent another on the day you leave. Just about all of the major car-rental companies, including **National** (© **800/227-7368;** www.nationalcar.com), **Hertz** (© **800/654-3131;** www.hertz.com), and **Avis** (© **800/230-4898;** www.avis.com), have multiple Manhattan locations.

> **Impressions**
> *Traffic signals in New York are just rough guidelines.*
> —David Letterman

TRAVELING FROM THE CITY TO THE SUBURBS

The **PATH** (© **800/234-7284;** www.panynj.gov/path) system connects urban communities in New Jersey, including Hoboken and Newark, to Manhattan by subway-style trains. Stops in Manhattan are at Christopher and 9th streets, and along 6th Avenue at 14th, 23rd, and 33rd streets. A new lower-Manhattan station, to replace the one destroyed underneath the World Trade Center, is not expected to be up and running until sometime in late 2004. The fare is $1.50.

New Jersey Transit (© **973/772-2222;** www.njtransit.com) operates commuter trains from Penn Station, and buses from the Port Authority at 8th Avenue and 42nd Street, to points throughout New Jersey.

The **Long Island Rail Road** (© **718/217-LIRR;** www.mta.nyc.ny.us/lirr) runs from Penn Station, at 7th Avenue between 31st and 33rd streets, to Queens and points beyond on Long Island.

Metro-North (© **800/METRO-INFO** or 212/532-4900; www.mta.nyc.ny. us/mnr) departs from Grand Central Terminal, at 42nd Street and Lexington Avenue, for areas north of the city, including Westchester County, the lovely Hudson Valley, and Connecticut.

If you'd prefer to rely on substantially cheaper buses to reach your suburban destination, visit **www.panynj.gov/tbt/pabframe.HTM**, where you'll find a complete list of bus companies (in addition to NJ Transit, above) that service Manhattan's Port Authority bus terminal at 8th Avenue and 42nd Street.

3 Playing It Safe

Sure, there's crime in New York City, but millions of people spend their lives here without being robbed and assaulted. In fact, New York is safer than any other large American city. The city ranked 210th out of 229 cities across the nation in the FBI's 2003 crime index. While that's quite encouraging, it's still important to take precautions. Criminals are expert at spotting newcomers who appear disoriented or vulnerable.

Men should carry their wallets in their front pockets and women should keep hold of their purse straps. Cross camera and purse straps over one shoulder, across your front, and under the other arm. Never hang a purse on the back of a chair or on a hook in a bathroom stall; keep it in your lap or between your feet with one foot through a strap. Avoid carrying large amounts of cash. You might carry your money in several pockets so that if one is picked, the others might escape. Skip the flashy jewelry and keep valuables out of sight on the street.

Panhandlers are seldom dangerous and can usually be ignored (more aggressive pleas can be answered, "Not today"). If a stranger walks up to you

> **Impressions**
>
> *I like it here in New York. I like the idea of having to keep eyes in the back of your head all the time.*
>
> —John Cale

on the street with a sob story ("I live in the suburbs and was attacked and don't have the money to get home . . ."), it's likely a scam. You have every right to walk away. Be wary of an individual who "accidentally" falls in front of you or causes some other commotion, because he or she may be working with someone else who will take your wallet when you try to help. And remember: You *will* lose if you place a bet on a sidewalk card game or shell game.

Certain areas should be avoided late at night. I don't recommend going to the Lower East Side, Alphabet City in the far East Village, Harlem, or the Meat Packing District unless you know where you're going. Don't be afraid to go, but head straight for your destination and don't wander onto deserted side streets. Times Square has been cleaned up, and there'll be crowds around until midnight, when

---

Tips **Top Safety Tips**

Trust your instincts, because they're usually right. You'll rarely be hassled, but it's always best to walk with a sense of purpose, and don't stop in the middle of the sidewalk to look at your map. If you find yourself on a deserted street that feels unsafe, it probably is; leave as quickly as possible. If you do find yourself accosted by someone with or without a weapon, remember to keep your anger in check and that the most reasonable response (maddening though it may be) is not to resist.

---

theater- and moviegoers leave the area. Still, stick to the main streets, such as Broadway or 9th Avenue, Midtown West's newest restaurant row. The areas south of Times Square are best avoided after dark, as they're largely abandoned once the business day ends. Take a cab or bus when visiting the Jacob Javits Center on 34th Street and the Hudson River. Don't wander the parks after dark, unless you're going to a performance; if that's the case, stick with the crowd.

If you plan on visiting the outer boroughs, go during the daylight hours. If the subway doesn't go directly to your destination, your best bet is to take a taxi. Don't wander the side streets; many areas in the outer boroughs are absolutely safe, but neighborhoods change quickly, and it's easy to get lost.

All this said, don't panic. New York has experienced a dramatic drop in crime and is safer than many other major U.S. cities these days, especially in the neighborhoods that visitors frequent. There's a good police presence on the street, so don't be afraid to stop an officer, or even a friendly-looking New Yorker (trust me—you can tell) if you need help getting your bearings.

SUBWAY SAFETY TIPS   In general, the subways are safe, especially in Manhattan. Still, stay alert and trust your instincts. Always keep a hand on your personal belongings.

When using the subway, *do not wait for trains near the edge of the platform* or on extreme ends of a station. During non-rush hours, wait for the train in view of the token-booth clerk or under the yellow DURING OFF HOURS TRAINS STOP HERE signs, and ride in the train operator's or conductor's car (usually in the center of the train; you'll see his or her head stick out of the window when the doors open). Choose crowded cars over empty ones—there's safety in numbers.

Avoid subways late at night, and take a cab after about 10 or 11pm—it's money well spent to avoid a long wait on a deserted platform. Or take the bus.

FAST FACTS: New York City

American Express Travel service offices are at many Manhattan locations, including 1185 6th Ave., at 47th Street (✆ 212/398-8585); at the New York Marriott Marquis, 1535 Broadway, in the eighth-floor lobby (✆ 212/575-6580); on the mezzanine level at Macy's Herald Square, 34th Street and Broadway (✆ 212/695-8075); and at 374 Park Ave., at 53rd Street (✆ 212/421-8240). Call ✆ 800/AXP-TRIP or go online to **www.americanexpress.com** for other city locations or general information.

Area Codes There are four area codes in the city: two in Manhattan, the original **212** and the new **646**, and two in the outer boroughs, the original

718 and the new **347.** Also common is the **917** area code, which is assigned to cellphones, pagers, and a few land lines. *Note:* All calls between these area codes are local calls, but you'll have to dial 1 + the area code + the seven digits for all calls, even ones in the same area code.

Doctors For emergencies requiring immediate attention, head to the nearest emergency room (see "Hospitals," below). New York also has several walk-in centers, like **DOCS at New York Healthcare,** 55 E. 34th St. (btwn Park and Madison aves.; (✆ **212/252-6001),** for non-emergency illnesses. The clinic, affiliated with Beth Israel Medical Center, is open Monday through Thursday from 8am to 8pm, Friday from 8am to 7pm, Saturday from 9am to 3pm, and Sunday from 9am to 2pm. The **NYU Downtown Hospital** offers referrals at ✆ **888/698-3362.**

Embassies & Consulates See "Fast Facts: For the International Traveler," in chapter 3.

Emergencies Dial ✆ **911** for fire, police, and ambulance. The **Poison Control Center** is at ✆ **800/222-1222,** toll-free from any phone.

Hospitals The following hospitals have 24-hour emergency rooms. Don't forget your insurance card.

Downtown: New York Downtown Hospital, 170 William St. (btwn Beekman and Spruce sts.; ✆ 212/312-5063 or 212/312-5000); **St. Vincents Hospital and Medical Center,** 153 W. 11th St. (at 7th Ave.l ✆ 212/604-7000); and **Beth Israel Medical Center,** 1st Avenue and 16th Street (✆ 212/420-2000).

Midtown: Bellevue Hospital Center, 462 1st Ave., at 27th Street (✆ 212/562-4141); **New York University Medical Center,** 560 1st Ave., at 33rd Street (✆ 212/263-7300); and **Roosevelt Hospital,** 425 W. 59th St. (btwn 9th and 10th aves.; ✆ 212/523-6800).

Upper West Side: St. Luke's Hospital Center, Amsterdam Avenue and 113th Street (✆ 212/523-3335); and **Columbia Presbyterian Medical Center,** 622 W. 168th St. (btwn Broadway and Fort Washington Ave.; ✆ 212/305-2500).

Upper East Side: New York Presbyterian Hospital, 525 E. 68th St. (at York Ave.; ✆ 212/472-5454); **Lenox Hill Hospital,** 100 E. 77th St. (btwn Park and Lexington aves.; ✆ 212/434-2000); and **Mount Sinai Medical Center,** 5th Avenue at 100th Street (✆ 212/241-6500).

Hot Lines The 24-hour **Rape and Sexual Abuse Hot Line** is ✆ 212/267-7273. The **Bias Crimes Hot Line** is ✆ 212/662-2427. The **LIFENET hot line** for suicide prevention, substance abuse, and other crises is ✆ 800/543-3638. For **Mental Health and Alcoholism Services Crisis Intervention,** call ✆ 212/219-5599. You can reach **Alcoholics Anonymous** at ✆ 212/870-3400 (general office) or 212/647-1680 (for alcoholics who need immediate counseling from a sober, recovering alcoholic). The **Domestic Violence Hot Line** is ✆ 800/621-4673. Other useful numbers are the **Crisis Help Line** ✆ 212/532-2400; **Samaritans' Suicide Prevention Line** ✆ 212/673-3000; to locate local **police** precincts ✆ 646/610-5000 or 718/610-5000; **Department of Consumer Affairs** ✆ 212/487-4444; and **taxi complaints** ✆ 212/NYC-TAXI or 212/676-1000. If you suspect your car was towed, call the **Department of Transportation TOWAWAY Help Line** at ✆ 212/869-2929.

Information To receive information and access to city government services, call the city information line at ✆ **311.** Call takers answer questions, take service requests, and refer callers to government agencies. (For example, if your car is towed, staff members can help you track it or direct you to the car pound.)

Libraries The **New York Public Library** is on 5th Avenue at 42nd Street (② **212/930-0830**). This Beaux Arts beauty houses more than 38 million volumes, and the reading rooms have been restored to their former glory. More efficient and modern, if less charming, is the mid-Manhattan annex at 455 5th Ave., at 40th Street, across from the main library (② **212/340-0833**). For other branches, see the list online at **www.nypl.org**.

Liquor Laws The minimum legal age to purchase and consume alcoholic beverages in New York is 21. Liquor and wine are sold only in licensed stores, which are open 6 days a week, with most choosing to close on Sundays. Liquor stores are closed on holidays, and election days while the polls are open. Beer can be purchased in grocery stores and delis 24 hours a day, except Sunday before noon. Last call in bars is at 4am, although many close earlier.

Newspapers & Magazines There are three major daily newspapers: the *New York Times,* the *Daily News,* and the *New York Post.* For details on where to find arts and entertainment listings, see "Publications," under "Visitor Information," earlier in this chapter.

If you want to find your hometown paper, visit **Universal News & Magazines,** at 234 W. 42nd St. (btwn 7th and 8th aves.; ② **212/221-1809**); and 977 8th Ave. (btwn 57th and 58th sts.; ② **212/459-0932**); or **Hotalings News Agency,** 624 W. 52nd St. (btwn 11th and 12th aves.; ② **212/974-9419**).

Pharmacies **Duane Reade (www.duanereade.com)** has 24-hour pharmacies in Midtown at 224 W. 57th St., at Broadway (② **212/541-9708**); on the Upper West Side at 2465 Broadway, at 91st Street (② **212/799-3172**); and on the Upper East Side at 1279 3rd Ave., at 74th Street (② **212/744-2668**).

Police Dial ② **911** in an emergency; otherwise, call ② **311** for non-emergencies or 718/610-5000 (NYPD headquarters) for the number of the nearest precinct.

Restrooms There are public restrooms at the visitor centers in Midtown (1560 Broadway, btwn 46th and 47th sts.; and 810 7th Ave., btwn 52nd and 53rd sts.). Grand Central Terminal, at 42nd Street between Park and Lexington avenues, also has clean restrooms. On the street, try Starbucks or another java chain—there's one on practically every block. The big bookstores are good for restrooms, too. You can also head to hotel lobbies (especially the big Midtown ones) and department stores like Macy's and Bloomingdale's. On the Lower East Side, stop into the Lower East Side BID Visitor Center, 261 Broome St. (btwn Orchard and Allen sts.; Sun–Fri 10am–4pm, sometimes later).

Smoking Smoking is prohibited on public transportation, in the lobbies of hotels and office buildings, in taxis, in restaurants, in bars, and in most shops. In this town, if you want to smoke, take it outside.

Taxes **Sales tax** is 8.25% on meals, most goods, and some services, but is not charged on clothing and footwear under $110. **Hotel tax** is 13.25% plus $2 per room per night (including sales tax). **Parking-garage tax** is 18.25%.

Time For the correct time, dial ⓒ **212/976-1616.**

Transit Information For information on getting to and from the airport, see "Getting There" in chapter 2, or call **Air-Ride** at ⓒ **800/247-7433.** For information on subways and buses, call the **MTA** at ⓒ **718/330-1234,** or see "Getting Around," earlier in this chapter.

Traveler's Assistance **Travelers Aid International (www.travelersaid.org)** helps distressed travelers with all kinds of problems, including accidents, sickness, and lost or stolen luggage. There is an office on the second floor of the International Arrivals Building at John F. Kennedy International Airport (ⓒ **718/656-4870**), and one in Newark International Airport's Terminal B (ⓒ **973/623-5052**).

Weather For the current temperature and next day's forecast, look in the upper-right corner of the front page of the *New York Times* or call ⓒ **212/976-1212.** If you want to know how to pack before you arrive, point your browser to **www.cnn.com/weather** or **www.weather.com**.

5

Accommodations
You Can Afford

New York may be the most expensive place to live in the United States. It only follows that hotel rates here will also be more expensive than almost any other city in the country. So understanding that from the get-go will help you get over any notions that you might find rates comparable to those back home.

While the city does have a handful of good inexpensive hotels, it can be difficult to score a room with a private bathroom, nice furniture, closet space, and elevator for $100 or less. Still, there are bargains if you know where to look.

To stay in New York on a tight budget, you must weigh what you're willing to spend versus what you're willing to put up with. If you only want to spend 100 bucks a night—a very budget rate in this city—you're going to have to live with some inconveniences.

First, be aware that many of New York's budget hotels have **shared bathrooms.** There are a few exceptions—but in general, don't count on a double room with its own bathroom for less than $100.

Even if you're willing to spend a bit more, don't expect much in the way of **space,** New York's most coveted commodity. Don't be surprised if your hotel room isn't much bigger than the bed in it, the closet is a rack screwed to the wall, and the bathroom is the smallest you've ever seen. Pack light.

It's almost always more expensive to stay in the Theater District than in a residential **neighborhood** like Chelsea, Murray Hill, the Upper West Side, or Harlem; in fact, uptown has become a haven for travelers looking for the highest value-for-dollar ratio. Staying in a residential area is almost always quieter, and will give you better access to affordable restaurants where locals eat. Most travelers who choose residential areas end up thrilled with their advantages.

Remember: Hotel rooms are subject to **13.25% tax plus $2 per night,** unless otherwise noted.

22 WAYS TO SAVE ON YOUR HOTEL ROOM

1. **Stay uptown or downtown.** The advantages of a Midtown location are overrated, especially when saving money is your object. You'll get the best value by staying in the neighborhoods where real New Yorkers live, such as Greenwich Village, Chelsea, Murray Hill, or—my favorite neighborhood for space-seekers and bargain hunters—the Upper West Side.

2. **Visit over a weekend.** If your trip includes a weekend, you might save big. Business hotels tend to empty, and rooms that go for $300 or more Monday through Thursday can drop to as low as $150 or less once the execs have gone home. These deals are prevalent in the Financial District, but are often available in Midtown, too.

Tips **No Room Service, but . . .**

Hotels in this price range rarely offer room service, but many will provide you with menus from nearby restaurants, diners, and delis that deliver. If you're just too pooped to set foot outside the room, the amount you'll pay to order in from the nearby Chinese restaurant, sushi joint, or pizzeria won't set you back a fortune (remember to tip your delivery person!).

---

3. **Watch for advertised discounts.** Scan ads in the travel section of your Sunday paper, which can be an excellent source for up-to-the-minute hotel deals. Also check the back of the travel section of the Sunday *New York Times,* where the best weekend deals and other bargains are usually listed.

4. **Don't be afraid to bargain.** Always ask for a lower price than the first one quoted. Most rack rates include commissions for travel agents, which many hotels will cut if you make your own reservations and haggle a bit. Ask whether a less-expensive room is available than the first one mentioned or if any special rates apply: corporate, student, military, seniors. Mention membership in AAA, AARP, frequent-flier programs, corporate or military organizations, or unions, which might entitle you to deals. The chains, such as Best Western and Comfort Inn, tend to be good about trying to save you money, but reservations agents often won't volunteer the information; you have to pull it out of them.

5. **Dial direct.** When booking a room in a chain hotel, call the hotel's local line, as well as the toll-free number, and see where you get the best deal. The clerk who runs the place is more likely to know about booking patterns and will often grant deep discounts in order to fill up.

6. **Rely on a qualified professional.** Certain hotels give travel agents discounts in exchange for steering business their way, so if you're shy about bargaining, an agent may be better equipped to negotiate discounts for you.

7. **Shop online.** New York hotels often offer "Internet-only" deals that can save you 10% to 20% off what you'd pay if you booked by telephone. Also, hotels often advertise all of their available weekend and other package deals on their websites. For more, see "Surfing for Hotels" in chapter 2.

8. **Investigate reservations services.** These work like consolidators, buying up or reserving rooms in bulk, and then dealing them to customers at a profit. You can get 10% to 50% off; but remember, these discounts apply to rack rates, prices that people rarely end up paying. You may get a decent rate, but call the hotel directly to see if you can do better.

   Start with **Quikbook** (© 800/789-9887 or 212/779-7666; www. quikbook.com), the best of the bunch since they book more than 100 hotels, require no prepayment, and allow you to make changes and cancellations (penalties depend on the hotel). Another good bet is **Hotel ConXions** (© 800/522-9991 or 212/840-8686; www.hotelconxions.com). Both Quikbook and Hotel ConXions have guaranteed room blocks in select properties, and can sometimes get you into a hotel that's otherwise sold out. You can also try the **Hotel Reservations Network,** also known as HotelDiscount!com (© 800/715-7666; www.180096HOTEL.com or www.hoteldiscount.com).

   Important tips: Never just rely on a reservations service. Do a little homework; compare the rack rates to the discount rates to see what kind of deal you're getting. Always compare the rate a reservations service offers you with the rate from the hotel. If you're being offered a stay in a hotel I haven't recommended, do more research on it. *It's not a deal if you end up at a dump.*

9. **Take a chance with Priceline.** Tales abound of the jackpots people have hit on the "name your price" site Priceline.com (**www.priceline.com**). I know someone who's scored a room in a suite hotel on the East Side for $50 a night (albeit in Jan). I also put out-of-town relatives into the Sheraton Four Points in Chelsea for $90 a night in July. Priceline can be a great way to win the budget war. You won't know the name of your hotel until it's paid for, but you can choose your neighborhood and the class of hotel (from economy to deluxe), and Priceline guarantees you'll stay in a nationally recognized, name-brand or independent hotel trusted for its quality, service, and amenities.

10. **If you find a rate that seems like a good value, book it early.** If somebody quotes you a good rate, don't assume it'll be waiting for you in a month, a week, or even a day. As hotels fill up and the number of empty rooms goes down, rates go up.

11. **If you find yourself without a room at the last minute, work it to your advantage.** I never recommend coming to town without reservations. But if you find yourself without a room, you might be able to strike a bargain. As the hours progress, the hotel becomes more anxious to fill empty rooms and will lower the rate to get your business. I've seen desk clerks sell $179 rooms for $79. But remember—this is a risky way to go, because if the hotel is full, you're out of luck.

12. **Be willing to share a bathroom.** For the best bargains, do as the Europeans do: Share a hall bathroom with your fellow travelers. Usually there are two or three bathrooms to a floor, often with separate rooms for the toilet and the shower and/or tub so all the facilities aren't tied up at once. If you're on a tight budget, you'll be able to stay at a nicer hotel than if you insist on a private bathroom. Many rooms have private sinks, so you can brush your teeth or wash your face in your room. A couple of very good bargain-rate places, the Chelsea Lodge and the Chelsea Pines Inn, have private in-room showers, so the only thing you have to share is the toilet.

13. **Consider a suite.** It sounds like a splurge, but if you're traveling with another couple or your family, a suite can be a bargain. They're cheaper than two hotel rooms. The living room almost always features a sofa bed, and there's often a kitchenette where you can prepare coffee and light meals. Some places charge for more than two guests; some don't.

14. **If you're traveling with the kids, stay at a hotel that lets them stay for free.** Most hotels add a surcharge—from $10 to $30 per night—for each extra person beyond two sharing a room. So if you're traveling with kids, choose a hotel that lets them stay free. Age limits for free kid stays can range from 10 to 18. Even if the hotel usually charges for kids, it might be willing to drop this charge to draw you in, so do ask.

15. **Save on hotel tax by booking an apartment or home stay.** Booking a hosted or unhosted apartment stay can save you dollars on taxes. These agencies are able to charge just 8¼% sales tax, as opposed to 13¼% plus $2 per night for a regular hotel room. Even better: Tax is often included in the rates quoted by booking agencies; thus, a $130 room is just $130, while a regular hotel will charge you $149 per night for a $130 room. A tax loophole eliminated the tax on many 7-night or longer stays (which are classified as short-term leases rather than hotel stays). Be sure to get the specific rules

at booking to avoid any surprises at bill time. See "Home Stay Sweet Home Stay," later in this chapter, for recommended agencies.

16. **Look into group or long-stay discounts.** If you come as part of a group, you may be able to negotiate a bargain because the hotel can guarantee occupancy in a number of rooms. If you're planning a long stay (5–7 days or more), you might qualify for a discount, so be sure to ask.

17. **If you're on a shoestring budget, book a hostel bed.** You'll have no privacy—you'll share a room with fellow travelers and all facilities are common—but there's no arguing with the rate. The largest hostel in the **Hostelling International–American Youth Hostels** system houses travelers in bunk-bedded rooms for $29 to $35 per person per night. You'll save about $3 a night if you become an AYH member. Also consider the dorms at the **Chelsea Star,** the **Chelsea International Hostel, Chelsea Center Hostel,** the **Big Apple Hostel,** the East Village's **Whitehouse Hotel of New York,** Harlem's **Park View Hostel** and **Sugar Hill International House,** and the **Central Park Hostel & Inn.** For additional hostel possibilities, surf to **The Hostel Handbook** (www.hostelhandbook.com) and **Hostels.com** on the Internet.

18. **Try the Y.** The Y isn't as cheap as hostel living, but the facilities are better. The **YMCA of Greater New York** (✆ 212/630-9600; www.ymcanyc.org) has eight residences throughout the city's five boroughs. You'll have a private room (some have private bathrooms) and access to the on-site fitness center—many feature state-of-the-art equipment, pools, and exercise classes—free. The Y is popular with families, older travelers, and singles. Contact the **West Side YMCA,** adjacent to Central Park at 5 W. 63rd St. (off Central Park W.; ✆ 212/875-4100), and the **Vanderbilt Y,** 224 E. 47th St. (btwn 2nd and 3rd aves.; ✆ 212/756-9600), as far in advance as possible. Manhattan locations are the most expensive, with prices starting around $80; if you can stay in Harlem, Brooklyn, or Queens, nightly rates start as low as $40. For information, visit www.ymcanyc.org and click on "Guest Rooms & Group Rates."

19. **Dorm it.** At Columbia University, **International House,** 500 Riverside Dr. on the Upper West Side (✆ 212/316-8436 or 212/316-8473; www.ihousenyc.org), offers dormitory-style accommodations in July and August, priced at $40 or $45 depending on your length of stay (up to 20 nights); you must be 18 or older to stay. International House has 11 guest rooms with private bathrooms and maid service, ranging from $110 to $150 for up to four people. These are especially reasonable if there are three or four of you, or if you're traveling in the autumn, when everybody else is charging an arm and a leg. Book well ahead.

20. **Make a spiritual connection.** Fully outfitted and maid-serviced guest rooms are offered at Columbia's **Union Theological Seminary** (✆ 212/662-7100; www.uts.columbia.edu), for a pricey $130 to $175 per night.

More affordable accommodations are offered at **The House of the Redeemer,** a former Vanderbilt mansion on the Upper East Side, just steps from Museum Mile, at 7 E. 95th St. (btwn 5th and Madison aves.; ✆ 212/289-0399; www.houseoftheredeemer.org). This Episcopal worship center offers short-term accommodations (2–6 nights) to adult travelers of all faiths when groups are not in residence. Accommodations are $60 single, $75 double with hall bathroom, $100 double with private bathroom. Rooms are not available from late June to early September.

The Community of the Holy Spirit, an Episcopal monastic community of nuns, welcomes guests into their simple but neat private rooms (most with shared bathrooms) at **St. Hilda's House,** 621 W. 113th St. (btwn Broadway and Riverside Dr.; ✆ **212/932-8098;** www.chssisters.org). Rates are $65 single, $110 to $130 double, and $165 triple. Because this is a contemplative environment, it's best suited for visitors looking for the same. You are welcome to share meals with the sisters, but no meals are served and no guests are welcomed on Monday. Reserve well in advance, as these accommodations fill up early.

21. **Do as little business as possible through the hotel.** Any service the hotel offers will cost you dearly. You can find dry cleaners or other services in most areas of Manhattan. Find out before you dial whether your hotel imposes a surcharge on local or long-distance calls.

22. **If you're driving into the city and will need to garage your car, check parking rates with the hotel before you book.** Many hotels offer discounts at nearby garages. Choose a hotel that has a good rate, or you could pay a fortune to park.

The **rates** quoted in the listings are the rack rates (the maximum rates that a hotel charges). But rack rates are only guidelines, and there are ways around them.

The hotels below have provided us with their best rate estimates for 2005, and all quoted rates were correct at press time. Be aware that **rates can change at any time,** subject to availability, seasonal fluctuations, and plain old increases. All bets are off at Christmas; expect everyone to charge over their rack rates.

1 TriBeCa

Cosmopolitan Hotel–Tribeca ✦ (Value) Hiding behind a plain-vanilla TriBeCa awning is one of the best hotel deals in Manhattan for travelers who insist on a private bathroom. Everything is budget but nice: The IKEA-ish furniture includes a work desk and an armoire (a few rooms have a dresser and hanging rack instead); for a few more bucks, you can have a love seat. Beds are comfy, and sheets and towels are of good quality. Rooms are small but make the most of the limited space, and the whole place is pristine. The two-level minilofts have lots of character, but expect to duck on the second level: Downstairs is the bathroom, TV, closet, desk, and club chair, while upstairs is a low-ceilinged bedroom. Management does a great job keeping everything fresh. The TriBeCa location is safe, hip, and subway-convenient. There's no room service, but a range of restaurants will deliver. In fact, all services are kept at a bare minimum to keep costs down, so you must be a low-maintenance guest to be happy here. If you are, this place is a great deal.

95 W. Broadway (at Chambers St.), New York, NY 10007. ✆ **888/895-9400** or 212/566-1900. Fax 212/566-6909. www.cosmohotel.com. 113 units. $119–$159 double. Inquire about discounts. AE, DC, MC, V. Parking $20, 1 block away. Subway: 1, 2, 3, or 9 to Chambers St. *In room:* A/C, TV, dataport, ceiling fan.

2 On the Bowery

Off SoHo Suites Hotel (Value) Clean, welcoming rooms with full kitchen facilities at surprisingly low prices make this hotel a good downtown choice. Just a stone's throw from the city's coolest dining, shopping, and nightlife: NoLita's Elizabeth Street is 2 blocks west, and the Lower East Side's Orchard and Ludlow streets are a half-dozen blocks east, not to mention Chinatown's nearby cheap eats. You'll get a lot for your dough: Each deluxe suite has a living and dining area with a pullout sofa, kitchen, private bathroom with hair dryer, and separate bedroom. In the economy suites, kitchens and bathrooms (with hair dryers) are shared with another room; if four of you are traveling, you can combine two economy suites into a sizable apartment. Everything is basic and the beds are a bit harder than you might like, but the whole place is nicely kept. Telephones have voice mail and dataports.

11 Rivington St. (btwn Chrystie St. and the Bowery), New York, NY 10002. © **800/OFF-SOHO** (633-7646) or 212/979-9808. Fax 212/979-9801. www.offsoho.com. 38 units, 10 with shared bathroom. $89–$99 economy suite (2 people maximum); $179–$209 deluxe suite (4 people maximum). AE, MC, V. Parking $20 nearby. Subway: F to 2nd Ave.; 6 to Spring St. Pets allowed (in deluxe suites only). **Amenities:** Cafe (for breakfast and lunch); exercise room; activities desk; limited room service; laundry service; dry cleaning; coin-op laundry. *In room:* A/C, TV w/free movies, dataport, kitchen w/fridge and coffeemaker, hair dryer, iron.

SoHotel ★ *Finds*   Formerly the Pioneer, this little Euro-style hotel has done something no other Manhattan hotel has managed: It offers clean, quiet, friendly accommodations with private bathrooms for as little as $69 double (tax not included) on a year-round basis.

This older hotel (it claims to be the oldest in the city) has come into its own, and the friendly manager continues to make improvements. The same can be said for the neighborhood: The hotel is in a four-story walkup off a stretch of the Bowery, lined with restaurant suppliers, that was crusty and desolate a few years ago. But these days it's clean, safe, and convenient.

It's one level up to the lobby, which is older but bright and agreeable. Here you'll find a professional staff and morning coffee. Decorative painting adds an attractive flair to rooms, and hanging plants add color in the halls. Rooms have black linoleum floors, lamps and chairs, ceiling fans, and fresh and firm platform beds (which may be a tad too firm for some). Most rooms have a tiny but spotless bathroom with a shower stall (a handful have tubs). Shared-bathroom units (which have small sinks) are petite, but many spacious configurations are available, and the standard doubles are a good size. Room no. 11D is a family-friendly triple with two doubles and a twin and a sizable bathroom with a tub, while a room with three twins is a great configuration for friends. A few rooms have no windows, but they're blissfully silent and will even save you a few dollars. Ask for a renovated room (most are). Service is delightfully old-fashioned; a wake-up call consists of a clerk who'll knock on your door (BYO alarm and hair dryer if you'll want them).

341 Broome St. (btwn Elizabeth St. and the Bowery), New York, NY 10013. © **800/737-0702** or 212/226-1482. Fax 212/226-3525. www.pioneerhotel.com. 125 units, about 35 with shared bathroom. $59–$69 single or double with shared bathroom; $69 $99 double with private bathroom; $109–$129 triple, quad, or family room with private bathroom. Rates include tax. AE, DC, DISC, MC, V. Parking $10–$15 nearby. Subway: F to 2nd Ave.; 6 to Spring St. **Amenities:** Free coffee in lobby. *In room:* A/C, TV, ceiling fan, no phone.

3 The Lower East Side

New York City Howard Johnson Express Inn ★★ *Value*   This hotel is a boon to travelers looking for quality at a great price, a trendy location, or both. It sits on a wide thoroughfare next to a renovated Yiddish vaudeville house that houses a state-of-the-art movie complex. Bars, live-music clubs, restaurants, and offbeat shops abound on the surrounding blocks; East Village action is across Houston Street, and SoHo is to the west. The neighborhood may be on the cutting edge, but this HoJo is wonderfully predictable. In the second-floor lobby, we found a welcome bowl of Tootsie Rolls and a staff that's more attentive than most working in this price range. Rooms are small, but furnishings and textiles are attractive and of good quality: Mattresses are firm, work desks boast desk-level inputs and an ergonomic chair, and the granite bathrooms are nicer than those in some luxury hotels (some even have Jacuzzis).

Most rooms have queen-size beds, while some have two doubles; don't expect much elbowroom in either configuration. Those with room numbers ending in 01, 02, or 03 are the largest. Not much noise comes off of Houston, but request a back-facing or high-floor room for total quiet. Coffee's on all day in the lobby, and a basic continental breakfast (Danishes, doughnuts) is laid out in the morning.

135 E. Houston St. (at Forsyth St.), New York, NY 10002. ② **800/406-1411** or 212/358-8844. Fax 212/473-3500. www.hojo.com. 54 units. $109–$229 double. Rates include continental breakfast. Inquire about AAA, AARP, and corporate discounts. AE, DC, DISC, MC, V. Parking $29, 4 blocks away. Subway: F to 2nd Ave. **Amenities:** Laundry service; dry cleaning. *In room:* A/C, TV, dataport, hair dryer, iron.

4 The East Village

East Village Bed & Coffee *(Finds* *Fair warning:* If you're turned off by the idea of staying behind a graffiti-covered facade in a work-in-progress, in an up-and-coming neighborhood, skip this. But if you're an adventurous traveler and are willing to put up with a few eccentricities for a super deal, read on.

Friendly innkeeper Carlos Delfin has created a series of private guest rooms on two floors. All are small and basic, with little more than a high-quality bed and a work desk. Best is the sunlit French room, with a queen-size bed and a chest of drawers. Also on the second floor are some very petite rooms, including the Mexican room, plus a common kitchen, living room with TV, and bathroom. Downstairs is a loftlike space with Carlos's workroom, office, and the main kitchen; a second bathroom; and two more Japanese-style bedrooms (with low ceilings and low platform beds) built as enclosed lofts over the main space (best for heavy sleepers). Furnishings are hodgepodge; everything is well worn but clean and comfortable—Carlos makes constant improvements—and a wonderful art collection brightens the mix. The back garden is open in warm weather. The Alphabet City neighborhood is gentrifying, but it's still the hinterlands as far as most visitors are concerned. Subways are a significant walk away, so use the money you save on your room to take cabs back late at night.

110 Ave. C (btwn 7th and 8th sts.), New York, NY 10009. ②/fax **212/533-4175.** Fax 212/979-9743. www.eastvillagebed.citysearch.com or www.bedandcoffee.com. 6 units, all with shared bathroom. $60–$90 single; $70–$100 double. Rates include tax. AE, MC, V. Subway: L to 1st Ave.; 6 to Astor Place. **Amenities:** Common kitchen w/coffee and tea; living room w/TV/VCR; Internet connection for guest use; fax; free local calls from common phone. *In room:* A/C, no phone.

St. Mark's Hotel   This four-story walkup is on St. Marks Place, the hot spot for the East Village's youth, lined with used-record stores, restaurants and bars, and a parade of tattooed hipsters. Folks in search of peace and quiet will abhor the location, but anybody interested in being in the heart of the action will love it.

In a city where dingy paint and 20-year-old carpet is the norm in budget hotels, St. Mark's pretty Parisian mural (in the stairwell leading up to the second-floor front desk), lighting, finished oak, and marble floors are a welcome sight. Rooms are basic and furnishings are simple, but even the smallest—one double bed—is a decent size and boasts new carpet, a firm bed, a TV, a phone with voice mail, and a tiled bathroom with a tiny sink, shower, and nice towels; butter-yellow walls and framed prints brighten most rooms. Services are minimal, but the staff is professional. There's no dedicated public space, but a pub sits on the ground level. Some of New York's best affordable restaurants are within shouting distance.

Village and Downtown Accommodations

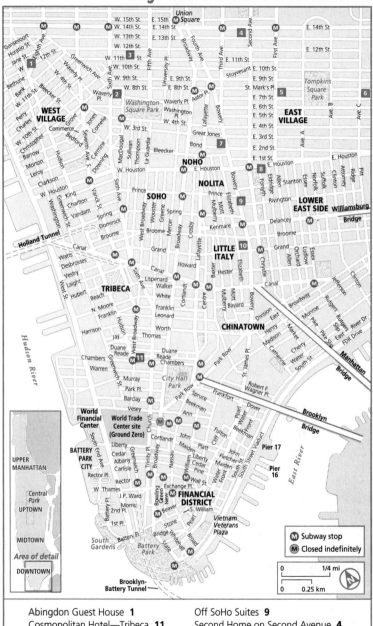

Abingdon Guest House **1**
Cosmopolitan Hotel—Tribeca **11**
East Village Bed & Coffee **6**
Larchmont Hotel **3**
New York City
  Howard Johnson Express Inn **8**
Off SoHo Suites **9**
Second Home on Second Avenue **4**
SoHotel **10**
St. Mark's Hotel **5**
Washington Square Hotel **2**
Whitehouse Hotel of New York **7**

2 St. Marks Place (at 3rd Ave.), New York, NY 10003. (C) 212/674-0100 or 212/674-2192. Fax 212/420-0854. www.stmarkshotel.qpg.com. 67 units. $100–$130 single or double. No credit cards. Subway: 6 to Astor Place. *In room:* A/C, TV.

Second Home on Second Avenue ★ *Finds* Here's another guesthouse run by gregarious innkeeper Carlos Delfin, this one a big step up in quality, location, and price from his East Village Bed & Coffee (see above). It's a guesthouse for young, independent-minded travelers who prefer the restaurant- and club-heavy East Village. The rooms are large and eclectically furnished. Each is outfitted with two full beds, good closet space, a large TV with VCR, a CD player (unheard of in this price category), an alarm, and a phone (free local calls!) with answering machine in every room. If there are more than two of you, the suite, which has a separate living room with a leather sofa that pulls out into a queen-size bed and a big private bathroom, is a good bet. Bathrooms are older but clean. A nice, new common kitchen is fully outfitted and offers free coffee and tea.

A few words of caution: Don't expect lots in the way of service, as Carlos lives off-site. Rooms are on the third and fourth floors of a walk-up. The guesthouse is popular with European travelers, who tend to smoke; you may still want to stay elsewhere if the possibility bothers you.

221 2nd Ave. (btwn E. 13th and 14th sts.), New York, NY 10003. (C)/fax 212/677-3161. www.secondhome. citysearch.com. 6 units, 2 with private bathroom. $85–$175 single; $105–$185 double. Rates include tax. Extra person $20. 2-night minimum stay required. AE, MC, V. Parking about $20 nearby. Subway: L to 3rd Ave.; N, R, 4, 5, or 6 to Union Square. **Amenities:** Common kitchen. *In room:* A/C, TV/VCR, CD player.

Whitehouse Hotel of New York ★ *Value* This newly renovated, youth-oriented hotel is a wonderful addition because it offers private rooms at hostel prices, and the location is smashing. Rooms are tiny and plain, each with either a full bed or twins, so expect no perks; but everything is clean, well maintained, and relatively new. Good-quality linens and towels are provided. All rooms share simple shower-stall bathrooms off the hall. There's a lobby lounge with a TV, tables and chairs for lounging, a cafe area selling continental-style breakfast items, and friendly, grandfatherly service around the clock. A coin-op laundry and an Internet-access machine in the lobby add to the convenience. The city's best budget dining lines the East Village blocks; the heart of Greenwich Village is to the west, and SoHo and the Lower East Side are both just a 5-minute walk away. No smoking allowed, and no travelers under 18.

340 Bowery (btwn 2nd and Great Jones/3rd sts.), New York, NY 10012. (C) 212/477-5623. Fax 212/473-3150. www.whitehousehotelofny.com. 468 beds, all with shared bathroom. $27–$32 single; $50–$63 double; $67–$91 triple. Rates include tax. AE, DC, MC, V. Subway: 6 to Bleecker St. No children under 18 accepted. **Amenities:** Continental breakfast for a charge (daily 6–10am); common kitchen w/microwave; Internet access machine and dataport in lobby; coin-op laundry. *In room:* A/C.

5 Greenwich Village

Abingdon Guest House ★★ *Finds* Steve Austin and his partner, Zachary Stass, run this lovely guesthouse (and its downstairs coffee bar, **Brewbar**) in a retail-and-residential West Village neighborhood. Both men have an eye for style—the Abingdon is beautifully outfitted and professionally run. Accommodations with in-room bathrooms are pricey for most wallet-watching travelers (but worth the price if you feel like a splurge). All of the rooms are done in bold colors and outfitted with well-chosen art and furnishings. No matter which you choose, you'll get a quality mattress and linens, soft bathrobes, an alarm clock, a telephone with free local calls and your own answering machine (a splitter can be provided for your laptop), and maid service.

The neighborhood is terrific, with good restaurants and shops. The Abingdon is best for mature, independent travelers, because there's no regular staff on-site, and the area is geared to locals rather than tourists. The thoughtful style and privacy make it ideal for a romantic escape, but friends traveling won't feel out of place (in fact, two rooms feature two twin beds). It's a nonsmoking property.

13 8th Ave. (btwn W. 12th and Jane sts.), New York, NY 10014. ✆ 212/243-5384. Fax 212/807-7473. www.abingdonguesthouse.com. 9 units. $149–$239 double. 4-night minimum on weekends, 2-night minimum on weekdays. Rates $10 less for single travelers. Extra person $25. AE, DC, DISC, MC, V. Parking $20 nearby. Subway: A, C, E, L, 1, 2, 3, or 9 to 14th St. **Amenities:** Coffee bar. *In room:* A/C, TV, dataport, hair dryer, iron, safe.

Larchmont Hotel ★★ *Value*   On a tree-lined block in a quiet part of the Village, this European-style hotel is a gem. If you're willing to share a bathroom, it's hard to do better for the money. The entire place has an air of warmth and sophistication. Each bright guest room is done in rattan and outfitted with a writing desk, a mini-library, an alarm clock, a washbasin, and a few extras you normally have to pay a lot more for, such as bathrobes, slippers, and ceiling fans. Every floor has two shared bathrooms (with hair dryers) and a small kitchen. The management is constantly renovating, so everything feels clean and fresh. Those looking for a hip downtown base couldn't be better situated, because some of the city's best shopping, dining, and sightseeing—plus your choice of subway lines—is all close. A free continental breakfast that includes fresh-baked goods every morning is the crowning touch that makes the Larchmont a terrific deal. Book *well* in advance (the management suggests 6–7 weeks' lead time).

27 W. 11th St. (btwn 5th and 6th aves.), New York, NY 10011. ✆ 212/989-9333. Fax 212/989-9496. www.larchmonthotel.com. 58 units, all with shared bathroom. $70–$95 single; $90–$125 double. Rates include continental breakfast. Children under 13 stay free in parent's room. AE, MC, V. Parking $18 nearby. Subway: A, C, E, F, or V to W. 4th St. (use 8th St. exit); F to 14th St. **Amenities:** Common kitchenette; tour desk; fax service; room service (10am–6pm). *In room:* A/C, TV, hair dryer, safe, wash basin, ceiling fan.

Washington Square Hotel   Popular with a young international crowd, this affordable hotel sits behind a pretty facade facing Washington Square Park (historically Henry James territory, now the heart of New York University) in the heart of Greenwich Village. The lobby was recently renovated and is now a pleasant place for tea in the afternoon and cocktails in the evening. The rooms are tiny, but pleasant. Each comes with a firm bed, a private bathroom, and a small closet with a pint-size safe. It's worth paying a few extra dollars for a south-facing room on a high floor, since others can be a bit dark. Bathrooms were also renovated, with the addition of granite counters; high-speed Internet access is in all of the rooms. On-site is a very good restaurant and lounge, **North Square Lounge,** which even draws locals with its stylish design, well-priced cocktails and international bistro fare, and Sunday jazz brunch.

103 Waverly Place (btwn 5th and 6th aves.), New York, NY 10011. ✆ 800/222-0418 or 212/777-9515. Fax 212/979-8373. www.wshotel.com. 165 units. $127–$141 single; $150–$179 double; $184–$204 quad. Rates include continental breakfast. Rollaway $20. Inquire about special rates and jazz packages. AE, MC, V. Parking $20 nearby. Subway: A, C, E, F, or V to W. 4th St. (use 3rd St. exit). **Amenities:** Restaurant and lounge; exercise room; laundry service; dry cleaning. *In room:* A/C, TV, dataport, hair dryer, iron, safe.

6 Chelsea

Chelsea Lodge ★★ *Finds*   In a brownstone on a landmarked block, this small hotel is charming and a terrific value—arguably the best in the city for budget-minded travelers. The husband-and-wife owners, Paul and GG Weisenfeld, have put in an incredible effort: Renovations have restored original woodwork and created a country-in-the-city vibe with beautiful wallpapers and wainscoting, vintage furniture, and lovely touches like Hershey's Kisses on the pillows. The beds are the finest and best outfitted I've seen in this price category. Ongoing renovations show how much Paul and GG continue to care.

The only place with a similar grown-up sensibility for the same money is Greenwich Village's Larchmont (p. 103), but there, bathroom facilities are shared; at Chelsea Lodge, each room has its own sink and in-room shower stall, so you only have to share a toilet. The rooms are petite, the closets are small, and beds are full-size (queens wouldn't cut it). But considering the stylishness, the amenities—which include TV, a ceiling fan, a desk, and an alarm clock—and the neighborhood, you'd be hard-pressed to do better. Best for couples rather than shares. *Tip:* Try to book no. 2A, which is bigger than most, or one of the first-floor rooms, whose high ceilings make them feel more spacious.

318 W. 20th St. (btwn 8th and 9th aves.), New York, NY 10011. (C) 800/373-1116 or 212/243-4499. Fax 212/243-7852. www.chelsealodge.com. 24 units, all with semiprivate bathroom. $90 single; $105 double. AE, DC, DISC, MC, V. Parking about $20 nearby. Subway: 1 or 9 to 18th St.; C or E to 23rd St. *In room:* A/C, TV, ceiling fan.

Chelsea Pines Inn ★★ *Value*   This inn caters largely to gay travelers, but all adult travelers are welcome as long as they'll be comfortable in a gay-oriented atmosphere. The inn straddles the border of the West Village, the heart of New York's gay community, and Chelsea, the hip neighborhood for the GLBT scene.

The rooms have comfortable furnishings, floral-print textiles, and a terrific collection of movie posters. Each room is dedicated to a Golden-Age-of-Hollywood star; the Paul Newman room boasts posters from movies such as *Hud* and *The Drowning Pool.* Rooms aren't big, but are well outfitted and arranged. Each has a minifridge, free HBO, a clock radio, and an answering machine; most have queen-size beds and daybeds for extra seating, and a half-dozen have breakfast areas with cafe tables and microwaves. Private bathrooms are bright and new; the cheapest (semiprivate) rooms have showers and sinks, so you just have to share a hall toilet. There's a payoff if you're willing to stay at the top of the five-story walkup: The Rock Hudson room sleeps four and has a terrific green-and-white bathroom with a skylight. The friendly staff mans the front desk around the clock, and continental breakfast is served in a cute breakfast room. There's also a greenhouselike enclosed patio and a backyard garden with blooming flowers.

317 W. 14th St. (btwn 8th and 9th aves.), New York, NY 10014. (C) 888/546-2700 or 212/929-1023. Fax 212/620-5646. www.chelseapinesinn.com. 23 units, 15 with private bathroom. $89–$109 double with semiprivate bathroom, $129–$139 double with private bathroom; $129–$139 deluxe. Rates include expanded continental breakfast. Check website for specials. Extra person $20. 3-night minimum stay on weekends. AE, DC, DISC, MC, V. Parking $25 nearby. Subway: A, C, or E to 14th St. Not appropriate for children. *In room:* A/C, TV, dataport, fridge, hair dryer, iron.

Chelsea Savoy Hotel ★★ *Kids*   The six-story Savoy was built from the ground up in 1995, so it isn't subject to the eccentricities of older hotels. The hallways are attractive and wide, the elevators swift and silent, and the cheery rooms of good size with big closets and roomy, immaculate bathrooms with tons of counter space. The reasonably priced quad rooms are suitable for a family of four (children stay free). Creature comforts abound: The rooms boast mattresses, furniture, and linens of high quality, plus the kinds of amenities you usually have to pay more for, like minifridges, in-room safes, and toiletries. Free continental breakfast makes a good value even better. Most rooms are street-facing and sunny; corner rooms tend to be brightest but noisiest. Ask for a back-facing room if you crave total silence. The staff is young and helpful, and the increasingly hip neighborhood makes a good base for exploring both Midtown and downtown. A plain but pleasant sitting room off the lobby makes an excellent place to enjoy your morning coffee over a selection of newspapers and magazines.

204 W. 23rd St. (at 7th Ave.), New York, NY 10011. ℂ 866/929-9353 or 212/929-9353. Fax 212/741-6309. www.chelseasavoynyc.com. 90 units. $99–$115 single; $135–$175 double; $145–$195 quad. Rates include continental breakfast. Children stay free in parent's room. AE, MC, V. Parking $25 nearby. Subway: 1 or 9 to 23rd St. *In room:* A/C, TV, dataport, fridge, hair dryer, iron, safe.

Chelsea Star Hotel/Chelsea Suites

Industrial-chic hallways lead to private rooms that are minuscule and bare-bones basic at this Generation Y–targeted hotel—more hostel than hotel-like, with nothing more than a firm bed and an open closet. But they're spotless, and the mattresses and linens are of such good quality that they don't feel as dour as most supercheap sleeps. They're individually dressed in cheeky themes ranging from the Disco Room (graced by a *Fever*-era poster of Travolta in all his white-suited glory) to the Asian mod Madame Butterfly Room (tiny but lovely) to the glow-in-the-dark cosmos of the Orbit Room (complete with black light). Try to grab the Madonna Room, a relatively spacious quad where Mrs. Ritchie lived for a year in leaner days. The shared hallway bathrooms have showers only, but they're smart and clean. Shoestring travelers who don't mind snoozing with strangers can opt for a single bunk in one of the serviceable dorms.

For a bit more, you can have your own pad: a stylish, fully loaded apartment with an equipped kitchen, private bathroom, and TV in the furnished living room. These are the best values in the house—and some of the best in Midtown—so book way ahead. *Tip:* The courtyard-facing apartments are quietest.

The Chelsea Star is a great addition to the budget hotel scene, but a word of warning: It is decidedly youth-oriented; mature travelers looking for standard amenities may be disappointed. The location—at the back door of Penn Station, more Midtown than Chelsea—may not be New York's finest, but it's cleaner and safer than ever, and cheap eateries and Irish pubs abound.

300 W. 30th St. (at 8th Ave.), New York, NY 10001. ℂ 877/827-6969 or 212/244-7827. Fax 212/279-9018. www.chelseastar.com or www.chelseasuites.com. 25 rooms, all with shared bathroom; 5 apts; 24 dorm beds. $59–$69 single; $79–$89 double; $89–$99 triple or quad. $30 per person in dorm. $159–$179 apt (sleeps up to 4). AE, DISC, MC, V. Parking about $25 nearby. Subway: A, C, or E to 34th St./Penn Station. No children under 18 accepted. **Amenities:** Pay Internet PC; fax service; laundry service; dry cleaning; shared pay phones. *In room:* A/C, no phone (TV, phone, and dataport in apts).

Colonial House Inn ⭐

This charming 1850 brownstone, on a pretty residential block in the heart of gay-friendly Chelsea, was the first permanent home of the Gay Men's Health Crisis. The four-story walk-up caters to a largely gay and lesbian clientele, but the friendly staff welcomes everyone. The place is beautifully maintained and professionally run. Rooms are small and basic but clean; all have radios, and those that share a hall bathroom (at a ratio of about three rooms per bathroom) have in-room sinks. Deluxe rooms—those with private bathrooms—have minifridges, and a few have working fireplaces. Both private and shared bathrooms are basic but nice. A terrific art collection brightens the public spaces. Book at least a month in advance for weekend stays. At parlor level is a breakfast room where a continental spread is put out from 8am to noon daily; coffee and tea are available all day. Rooms don't have hair dryers and irons, but the front desk will lend them. There's a nice roof deck split by a privacy fence (the area behind the fence is clothing optional). The neighborhood is chock-full of great restaurants and shopping, and offers easy access to the rest of the city.

Tips **Deal-Making with the Chains**

Most hotels—particularly chains like Comfort Inn, Holiday Inn, and Best Western—are market-sensitive. Because they hate to see rooms sit empty, they'll often negotiate good rates at the last minute and in slow seasons.

The chains are also where you can ask for all kinds of discounts, from auto-club membership to senior status. And you might be able to take advantage of corporate or government rates or discounted weekend stays. Most chain hotels let the kids stay with parents for free. Ask for every possible kind of discount; if you find that you get an unhelpful reservation agent, call back and try again. And it's worth calling the hotel direct, where the front-desk staff will deal to keep their occupancy rate high.

Of course, there's no guarantee. Your chances of getting a deal aren't great if you're visiting in a busy season. But if you're willing to make a few extra calls, or spend some time surfing online—which might net you a 10% discount for booking online—you might get a deal at hotels that would otherwise be out of your price range.

Best Western's (℮ **800/826-4667**; www.bestwestern.com) rack rates for its New York hotels are higher than you'd expect. At the **Best Western President Hotel**, in the Theater District at 234 W. 48th St. (℮ **800/ 826-4667** or 212/246-8800), doubles go for $129 to $229 but can drop to $99—a great deal on a centrally located hotel. Ditto for **Hampshire Hotels & Suites (www.bestnyhotels.com)**, the company that manages this and chain hotels such as the **Quality Hotel on Broadway** (p. 126) where rooms can go as low as $72 (with breakfast), as well as two Midtown Best Westerns and Howard Johnsons on Park Avenue; check their website for all the details.

At these and other franchised hotels—such as the ones run by **Apple Core Hotels** (℮ **800/567-7720**; www.applecorehotels.com), a management company that handles the **Comfort Inn Midtown** (p. 113), the

318 W. 22nd St. (btwn 8th and 9th aves.), New York, NY 10011. ℮ **800/689-3779** or 212/243-9669. Fax 212/633-1612. www.colonialhouseinn.com. 20 units, 12 with shared bathroom. $80–$125 single or double with shared bathroom; $125–$140 double with private bathroom. Rates include expanded continental breakfast. 2-night minimum on weekends. Extra person $15. Weekly rates available. MC, V. Parking $20 nearby. Subway: C or E to 23rd St. **Amenities:** Internet-access PC in lounge; fax service. *In room:* A/C, TV, dataport.

SUPERCHEAP SLEEPS

Also consider the dorm beds ($26) at the **Chelsea Star Hotel** (see above).

Chelsea Center Hostel   Going strong since 1981, this small, pleasant hostel is ideal for travelers who prefer a laidback ambience and a good night's sleep over the standard hostel bustle. It's on two floors of a Chelsea brownstone. Rooms are bunk-bedded and hostel-simple, but everything is bright and clean, and rates include decent-quality sheets and blankets; each bed also has its own night light for late-night reading and writing. Plenty of top-flight dining and nightlife is nearby; there's no curfew, and the owners will be happy to point you in the right direction. One of the nicest perks is the light continental breakfast included in the

Ramada Inn Eastside (p. 122), Manhattan's first Red Roof Inn (p. 118), the Super 8 Hotel Times Square (p. 119), and the La Quinta Inn, 17 W. 32nd St. (📞 212/736-1600), doubles can go for as little as $89. Check with the franchiser directly if you're not quoted a good advance-booking rate, or go through the management company's online reservations system; their global 800 and online reservations systems will often garner you a better rate, which might include a promotion—or, at minimum, an "Internet User's Rate" that's 10% lower than the standard.

A good source for deals is Choice Hotels (📞 877/426-6423; www.hotelchoice.com), which oversees Comfort Inn, Quality Hotel, and Clarion Hotel chains, all of which have terrific Manhattan branches.

Also try Holiday Inn (📞 800/HOLIDAY; www.holiday-inn.com), which has a handful of terrific hotels in Manhattan, all of which carry rack rates that are too high for most budget travelers. However, discounted weekend and slow-season rates can drop as low as $109 double at the Holiday Inn Wall Street, 15 Gold St. (📞 212/232-7800; www.holidayinnwsd.com), New York's most high-tech hotel. Shoppers might like the Holiday Inn Downtown/SoHo, 138 Lafayette St. (📞 212/966-8898; www.holidayinn-nyc.com), straddling the border between Chinatown and SoHo.

Another hotel to try is the Days Hotel Midtown, 790 8th Ave., at 48th Street (📞 800/544-8313 or 212/581-7000; www.daysinn.com). The bistro Pigalle (p. 165) gives it a better-than-budget flair, and the motel-like rooms are worth the $95-to-$130 rate you might be able to snare in slower seasons. Be sure to ask about senior, AAA, corporate, and promotional rates at all three (Choice, Holiday Inns, and Days Hotel), and check for online-booking discounts.

rate; guests sit around their morning table to chat. There's also a common room, plus a garden for warm-weather relaxation. You can request a dorm bed at their eastside location, in the East Village (exact location provided upon booking).

313 W. 29th St. (just west of 8th Ave.), New York, NY 10031. 📞 212/643-0214. www.chelseacenterhostel.com. 20 dorm beds in each location, all with shared bathroom. $33 dorm bed. Rate includes continental breakfast and tax. No credit cards. Subway: C or E to 23rd St. **Amenities:** Common kitchen and lounge rooms. *In room:* No phone.

Chelsea International Hostel As hostels go, this is a good one. The only other private hostel in this league, both in terms of cleanliness and location, is the Big Apple Hostel (p. 120). The well-managed, well-maintained Chelsea International consists of a warren of low-rise buildings around a central courtyard, like a cottage complex. It's hugely popular with international travelers.

Accommodations and shared bathrooms are older and plain but fine; the shared rooms come with nice extras such as wall hooks, sinks, and in-room lockers big enough for most backpacks (BYO combination lock and towels). The miniscule private rooms have little more than a double bed and some shelf units, but you can call one your own for just 60 bucks. Some rooms have air-conditioning, so request one if it matters to you.

The two fully equipped common kitchens (with microwaves) are the best I've seen in a hostel, and free coffee, tea, sugar, and cream is on hand. The private courtyard has picnic tables and barbecues. There are also dining and lounge areas with TV, Internet-access machines, self-service laundry, and soda machines; free luggage storage is another plus. The neighborhood is great, the desk is attended 24 hours, and maintenance is on hand around the clock. Free pizza is part of the package for guests on Wednesday nights.

251 W. 20th St. (btwn 7th and 8th aves.), New York, NY 10011. ℂ 212/647-0010. Fax 212/727-7289. www.chelseahostel.com. 288 dorm beds; 57 private units, all with shared bathroom. $28 dorm bed; $70 double. Rates include tax. AE, MC, V. Subway: 1 or 9 to 18th St. **Amenities:** 2 kitchens; dining areas; Internet access; fax; coin-op laundry. *In room:* No phone.

7 Union Square, the Flatiron District & Gramercy Park

Carlton Arms   The motto here is THIS AIN'T NO HOLIDAY INN! The spirit of bohemianism and artistic freedom reigns in this backpacker's delight, where every room is a work of art by an artist given license to go hog wild. Think of this as the legendary Hotel Chelsea as it used to be. Some spaces are sublime, such as Robin Banks's Cartoon Room (no. 5B), Thias Charbonet's Underwater Room (no. 1A), Olivia Hamlin's super-realist room no. 12A, the ocean-blue lobby (complete with fish in the TV), and the first-floor mosaic bathroom; others are simply bizarre. Whether you end up with a mermaid mural or a wall of teddy bears, you'll see why this is one of the most extraordinary hotels in the city.

But if you're looking for creature comforts, this is *not* the place for you. The cramped rooms are *very* basic. The beds are lumpy, and there's no air-conditioning. Each room has a sink, but you'll most likely end up sharing a bathroom with your fellow travelers (mainly students, international travelers, and existentialists). The place is clean, but there's no maid service. Still, the staff is friendly, and they'll be happy to take messages (rooms don't have phones; there's a pay phone in the lobby). The neighborhood isn't glitzy, but it's safe, quiet, residential, and overflowing with affordable restaurants. Reserve 1 to 2 months in advance, because despite the inconveniences, this place is almost always full.

160 E. 25th St. (btwn Lexington and 3rd aves.), New York, NY 10010. ℂ 212/679-0680 or 212/684-8337. www.carltonarms.com. 54 units, 20 with private bathroom. $60–$85 single or double with shared bathroom; $99–$111 triple or quad with shared bathroom; $75–$95 single or double with private bathroom; $111–$140 triple or quad with private bathroom. 10% discount on 7-night stays paid upon arrival. MC, V. Subway: 6 to 23rd St. *In room:* No phone.

Chelsea Inn   The name may say Chelsea, but the east-of-6th-Avenue address is really Flatiron. It's still a great location, what with Union Square just a stone's throw in one direction and Chelsea in the other.

The inn is in two 19th-century brownstones, but don't expect too much. Staying here is like living in your own New York City tenement for a few days: The rooms feature a mix of thrift-store furniture, the beds in the twin rooms are little more than rollaways, and the quality of the mattresses is a crapshoot. Everything's faded, but the place is clean and well kept. More on the upside: Closets are big, bathrooms are fine, and all rooms feature a hot plate, minifridge, coffeemaker, cups and utensils, a safe, voice mail, and free coffee; those without a bathroom have their own sinks. Shared bathrooms are livened with murals, and you'll have to split yours with only one other room. If there's more than two of you, pair up two doubles that share a bathroom, and you can usually negotiate a discount. Groups of three or four will like no. 102, a spacious suite with a private bathroom, a dining table, and a kitchenette. The staff is accommodating, and deals are often available. It's a reasonable, well-priced budget choice.

46 W. 17th St. (btwn 5th and 6th aves.), New York, NY 10011. (© 800/640-6469 or 212/645-8989. Fax 212/645-1903. www.chelseainn.com. 26 units, 18 with private bathroom. $89–$109 double with shared bathroom; $159–$189 double with private bathroom; $179–$219 suite (for up to 4). Check website for available specials (as low as $89 at press time). AE, DISC, MC, V. Parking about $20 nearby. Subway: 4, 5, 6, N, R, Q, or W to 14th St./Union Square. *In room:* A/C, TV, kitchenette, coffeemaker, safe.

Gershwin Hotel ⭐ (Kids)   Nestled between Le Trapeze, an S&M club, and the Museum of Sex, and with its own glowing protruding horns as your landmark, the close proximity to erotica is really just a coincidence. This creative-minded, Warholesque hotel caters to up-and-coming artistic types—and well-established names with an eye for good value—with its bold modern art collection and wild style. The lobby was renovated in 2003, and along with a new bar, **Gallery at the Gershwin,** much of the original art remains. The standard rooms are clean and bright, with Picasso-style wall murals and Philippe Starck–ish takes on motel furnishings. Superior rooms are best, as they're newly renovated, and well worth the extra $10; all have either a queen-size bed, two twins, or two doubles, plus a newish private bathroom with cute, colorful tile. If you're bringing the brood, two-room suites, or Family Rooms, are a good option.

The hotel is more service-oriented than you usually see at this price level, and the staff is very professional.

7 E. 27th St. (btwn 5th and Madison aves.), New York, NY 10016. (© 212/545-8000. Fax 212/684-5546. www.gershwinhotel.com. 150 units. $99–$189 double (usually less than $150); $189–$219 family room. Extra person $10. Check website for discounts, 3rd-night-free specials, or other value-added packages. AE, MC, V. Parking $25 3 blocks away. Subway: N, R, or 6 to 28th St. **Amenities:** Bar; tour desk; babysitting; laundry service; dry cleaning; Internet-access PC. *In room:* A/C, TV, dataport, hair dryer, iron.

Hotel 17   Hotel 17 has managed to garner a hip reputation: Madonna, David Bowie, and Maxwell have all been photographed in the eclectic, eccentric rooms. The neighborhood is great, the block is peaceful, and the individually decorated rooms are attractive and recently refreshed. Look beyond the stylish veneer and you'll find rooms that are cramped, dark, and basic—not for travelers looking for creature comforts. Each has its own sink, hair dryer, and alarm clock, and phones have recently been installed. The shared bathrooms are clean and have recently been renovated. The lobby has a funky, modern feel, but the security glass separating you from the staff detracts from the ambience. It's a decent deal, especially if you're the sort who requires some individuality in your lodgings. Expect lots of younger and international travelers, who don't mind the inconveniences and the lingering smell of smoke.

225 E. 17th St. (btwn 2nd and 3rd aves.), New York, NY 10003. (© 212/475-2845. Fax 212/677-8178. www. hotel17.ny.com. 120 units, all with shared bathroom. $60–$80 single; $60–$100 double; $85–$125 triple. MC, V. Parking about $20 nearby. Subway: 4, 5, or 6 to 14th St.; L to 3rd Ave. No children under 18 accepted. **Amenities:** Coin-op laundry. *In room:* A/C, TV, hair dryer (no A/C or TV in singles).

The Marcel ⭐ (Finds)   Being budget-challenged doesn't mean you have to settle for boring. This Gramercy Park hotel offers high style and a superhip scene at low, low prices. Thanks to the design firm Goodman Charlton, which loves to infuse retro styles with futuristic freshness, the Marcel sits on the cutting edge style-wise. Fab faux *Mod Squad*–era Scandinavian stylings in the lobby lead to

Finds   Home Stay Sweet Home Stay

New York apartment or home stays can be a great way to go. They usually fall on the lower end of the price continuum and can range from spartan to splendid, and from a hosted bedroom in a private home to an unhosted, fully equipped apartment. No matter what, you can pretty much guarantee that you'll get more for your money than with a regular hotel room.

The city's best-kept accommodations secret is **Homestay New York** ★ (*C*/fax **718/434-2071;** www.homestayny.com). Lovely owner Helayne Wagner can book you into a private room with a family (including her own) that welcomes travelers. Homes are in residential neighborhoods in Brooklyn, Queens, or Upper Manhattan, all within a half-hour of Midtown or downtown via subway or bus, and most are beautifully restored 19th- and early-20th-century houses. Not only can this save you money, it can be fun, too: Visitors are matched to hosts by age, interests, and occupation, and the hosts are more than happy to provide advice and assistance. You'll be the only in-house guest, so it's much like staying with a friend who delights in seeing you happy and enjoying the city.

Rates run $100 to $130 single or double, with shared or private bathroom depending on the home. Most rooms have TV, air-conditioning, and a small fridge, and towels are provided. Buffet breakfast is included; the price also often includes a welcome dinner, plus a farewell dinner if your stay lasts 5 or more days. Also included are free MetroCards and phone cards (values depend on the length of your stay), plus Broadway show information and discount coupons for live performances, comedy clubs, and other entertainment. In summer, guests staying 7 nights or more get a 3-hour evening cruise. With these extras, Homestay New York is an excellent value. Tax is included, which saves you an additional 13.25% plus $2 per night over what you'd pay in a hotel. Helayne also has access to theater discounts that you can't get on your own. A 3-night minimum is requested, and no credit cards are accepted. Children 3 and over are welcome.

guest rooms boasting gorgeous blond-wood built-ins that make clever use of limited space, and a bold geometric cushioned headboard adds a downright luxurious flair. The designer furnishings and textiles look and feel expensive, even if the somewhat lumpy beds don't; still, budget travelers will be thrilled. Even if the service isn't fabulous or the little details aren't perfect, you should feel like you're getting a great deal here.

One of the strongest appeals of the Marcel is **Spread** (*C* **212/683-8880;** www.spreadnyc.com), a restaurant/lounge hybrid offering a creative small plates menu, a first-rate sushi bar, terrific cocktails, and a blast of an after-dark scene. The subterranean lounge **Coal** is an even more seductive space.

201 E. 24th St. (at 3rd Ave.), New York, NY 10011. *C* **888/66-HOTEL** or 212/696-3800. Fax 212/696-0077. www.nychotels.com. 97 units. $99–$175 double. AE, DISC, MC, V. Parking $24. Subway: 6 to 28th St. **Amenities:** Restaurant; stylish lounge; all-day coffee and cappuccino bar; limited room service; laundry service; dry cleaning. *In room:* A/C, TV w/pay movies, dataport, hair dryer, iron, CD player.

A number of agencies can book you into a B&B room (hosted or unhosted) or a private apartment. The place to start is **Manhattan Getaways** ✸ (© 212/956-2010; www.manhattangetaways.com). Judith Glynn maintains a beautifully kept and managed network of bed-and-breakfast rooms (from $100 nightly) and unhosted apartments (from $145) around the city. There's a 3-night minimum, and credit cards are accepted. Another decent bet is **A Hospitality Company** (© 800/987-1235 or 212/813-2244; www.hospitalityco.com), with more than 300 apartments they own and manage around Manhattan starting at $125 a night, or $675 weekly for a basic studio. These are rather sparsely furnished apartments and the company offers little in the way of service, but the apartments are clean and do the trick. There's no minimum stay, and credit cards are accepted. Optional cleaning services are available for longer stays. Additional agencies that can book you into a B&B room or a private apartment, with prices starting at $90 nightly, include **As You Like It** (© 800/277-0413 or 212/695-0191; www.furnapts.com), **Abode Apartment Rentals** (© 800/835-8880 or 212/472-2000; www.abodenyc.com), **CitySonnet** (© 212/614-3034; www.citysonnet.com), **Manhattan Lodgings** (© 212/677-7616; www.manhattanlodgings.com), and **New York Habitat** (© 212/255-8018; www.nyhabitat.com).

Another advantage to booking B&B or apartment accommodations is that taxes are lower, usually just 8.25% (as opposed to 13.25% plus $2 per night for a regular hotel room).

A few words of warning: If you go this route, keep in mind that you won't have the amenities that a hotel—even a budget hotel—can offer, such as maid service and tour planning. In fact, many accommodations called "B&Bs" don't even offer breakfast, so be sure to ask. You'll have a host on hand to offer personal assistance if you book through Homestay New York. I've received complaints about agencies that offer one thing and deliver another, so get all promises in writing and an exact total up front. Try to pay by credit card if possible, so you can dispute payment if the agency fails to live up to its promises.

Union Square Inn ✸ *Value*   A stone's throw east of Union Square, on the fringe of the energetic East Village, this unassuming little hotel is a welcome addition to the budget hotel scene. Rooms here aren't quite as cheap as those at its sister hotel, the Murray Hill Inn, but comforts are better quality; every room has a private bathroom, and everything feels fresh and new. Four standard rooms are tiny twins with trundle beds, and a handful in the deluxe category are spacious rooms with two double beds that can accommodate more than two if necessary. Most fall in the moderate category, with one double bed and little room to spare. All rooms boast quality mattresses and bedding, and pretty Italian-tile bathrooms. On the downside, the rooms lack views, open wall racks substitute for closets, most bathrooms have showers only, halls are narrow, and there's no elevator—but those are minimal sacrifices considering the low prices. Services are virtually nonexistent in order to keep costs down, but everything you'll need—from restaurants to dry cleaners to a slate of subway lines—is right at hand in the hip, central-to-everything location.

209 E. 14th St. (btwn 2nd and 3rd aves.), New York, NY 10003. ℂ **212/614-0500.** Fax 212/614-0512. www.unionsquareinn.com or www.nyinns.com. 40 units. $90–$149 double. Extra person $20. Rates include basic continental breakfast. AE, MC, V. Parking $25 nearby. Subway: L to 3rd Ave.; 4, 5, 6, N, or R to 14th St./Union Square. **Amenities:** Coffee bar serving light meals; access to local fitness club. *In room:* A/C, TV, dataport.

8 Times Square & Midtown West

Americana Inn ★ *Value* The cheapest hotel from the Empire Hotel Group— the people behind the Upper West Side's Newton and pricier properties—is a star in the budget category. Linoleum floors give the rooms a somewhat institutional quality, but the hotel is well run and immaculately kept. Rooms are spacious, with good-size closets, private sinks, and an alarm built into the TV; the beds are the most comfortable I've found at this price. Most rooms come with a double bed or two twins; a few can accommodate three guests in two twin beds and a pullout sofa or three twins. One hall bathroom accommodates every three rooms or so; all are spacious and spotless, and the front desk lends hair dryers. Every floor has a kitchenette with microwave, stove, and fridge (BYO cooking utensils, or go plastic). The five-story building has an elevator (uncommon at this price), and four rooms are accessible for travelers with disabilities. Ask for a back-facing room away from the street noise.

69 W. 38th St. (at 6th Ave.), New York, NY 10018. ℂ **888/HOTEL-58** (468-3558) or 212/840-6700. Fax 212/840-1830. www.newyorkhotel.com. 50 units, all with shared bathroom. $65–$75 single; $75–$115 double. Check website for specials (winter rates as low as $60 double). Extra person $10. AE, MC, V. Parking $25–$35 nearby. Subway: B, D, F, or V to 34th St. **Amenities:** Kitchenettes on each floor; safety-deposit boxes. *In room:* A/C, TV.

Broadway Inn ★★ *Finds* More like a San Francisco B&B than a Theater District hotel, this lovely, welcoming inn is a real charmer. The second-floor lobby sets the homey, easygoing tone with stocked bookcases, cushy seating, and cafe tables where breakfast is served. The rooms are basic but comfy, outfitted in an appealing neo-deco style with firm beds, good-quality linens and textiles, and nice bathrooms (about half have showers only). The whole place is impeccably kept. Two rooms have king-size beds and whirlpool tubs, but the standard doubles are just fine for two if you're looking to save some dough. If there are more than two of you, or you're staying a while, the suites—with pullout sofa, microwave, minifridge, and lots of closet space—are a great deal. The location can be noisy, but double-paned windows keep the rooms surprisingly peaceful; still, ask for a back-facing one if you're extra sensitive.

The inn's biggest asset is its terrific staff, who go above and beyond the call to make guests happy; they'll even give you a hot line number so you can call while you're on the town for directions, advice, and other assistance. Service doesn't get any better in this price range. The inn has inspired a loyal following, so reserve early. However, there's no elevator in the four-story building, so overpackers and travelers with limited mobility should book elsewhere.

264 W. 46th St. (at 8th Ave.), New York, NY 10036. ℂ **800/826-6300** or 212/997-9200. Fax 212/768-2807. www.broadwayinn.com. 41 units. $99–$115 single; $135–$225 double; $189–$249 suite. Extra person $10. Children under 12 stay free in parent's room. Rates include continental breakfast. Check website for specials. AE, DC, DISC, MC, V. Parking $20 3 blocks away. Subway: A, C, or E to 42nd St. **Amenities:** 2 neighboring restaurants where inn guests have special discounts; concierge; fax and copy service. *In room:* A/C, TV, dataport, fridge, hair dryer, iron.

Comfort Inn Manhattan   This centrally located hotel is a good choice for those who prefer to go with a national chain. It's on a block near some of Midtown's biggest attractions, including the Empire State Building and Macy's. This is a standard chain hotel, but the rooms are clean, well maintained, and large by Manhattan standards. In fact, Choice Hotels (Comfort Inn's parent company) presented this location its gold award for the quality of its professionalism, housekeeping, and hospitality. Nice extras include big closets, hair dryers, in-room safes, on-command movies, and voice mail on the phones. A number of rooms have microwaves and minifridges, and about 30 king-size-bed rooms come with sleeper sofas. The lobby is attractive enough to invite lounging, and the front-desk staff is friendly and helpful. The expanded continental breakfast that's included in the rates is a big plus.

42 W. 35th St. (btwn 5th and 6th aves.), New York, NY 10001. (*) **800/228-5150** or 212/947-0200. Fax 212/594-3047. www.comfortinnmanhattan.com or www.comfortinn.com. 131 units. $99–$219 double. Rates include continental breakfast. Ask about senior, AAA, corporate, and other discounts. Extra person $15. Children under 19 stay free in parent's room. AE, DC, DISC, MC, V. Parking $18 nearby. Subway: B, D, F, N, Q, R, V, or W to 34th St. **Amenities:** Restaurant; laundry service; dry cleaning. *In room:* A/C, TV, dataport, hair dryer, iron, wireless Internet.

Comfort Inn Midtown *(Value*   Rates can climb in autumn or at Christmas, but low-season rates can make the rooms one of Midtown's best bargains. A mahogany-and-marble lobby leads to the petite but comfortable and nicely outfitted guest rooms, which boast neo-Shaker furnishings, coffeemakers, blackout drapes, and marble-and-tile bathrooms; all rooms have tub/shower combinations. Every room formerly in the "smoking allowed" category has been disinfected. Don't expect much in the way of service, but the location is excellent—steps from Times Square, Rockefeller Center, Broadway theaters, and a wealth of dining options.

129 W. 46th St. (btwn 6th Ave. and Broadway), New York, NY 10036. (*) **800/567-7720** or 212/221-2600. Fax 212/790-2760. www.applecorehotels.com or www.comfortinn.com. 79 units. $89–$329 double. Rates include continental breakfast. Ask about senior, AAA, corporate, and other discounts; check www.comfort inn.com for online discounts. Extra person $10. Children under 14 stay free in parent's room. AE, DC, DISC, MC, V. Parking $20 nearby. Subway: 1, 2, 3, or 9 to 42nd St./Times Square; N or R to 49th St.; B, D, F, or V to 47–50th sts./Rockefeller Center. **Amenities:** Small fitness room; self-serve business center; laundry service; dry cleaning. *In room:* A/C, TV, dataport, coffeemaker, hair dryer, iron, wireless Internet.

Herald Square Hotel   Presiding regally over the entrance, Philip Martiny's gilded sculpture *Winged Life* is emblematic of the new life in this older Manhattan hotel. The owners took the Carrère & Hastings Beaux Arts building that was once home to *Life* magazine and reinvented it as a budget hotel with a sense of history. *Life* covers decorate the lobby and some of the rooms. The rooms are small and basic, with laminated furniture, fluorescent lighting, and good-size but older bathrooms, plus voice mail and in-room safes. Still, if you're looking for a great location, this is a good bet (although I'd try the Portland Square, the Herald Square's sister hotel, first; see below). The hotel is popular with Europeans and other visitors who love the nearby shopping (Macy's, Lord & Taylor, the Manhattan Mall) and sightseeing (the Empire State Building). The friendly staff can arrange bus tours and airport transportation.

19 W. 31st St. (btwn 5th Ave. and Broadway), New York, NY 10001. (*) **800/727-1888** or 212/279-4017. Fax 212/643-9208. www.heraldsquarehotel.com. 120 units, 109 with private bathroom. $69–$99 single; $99–$120 double; $130–$140 triple or quad. Extra person $10. Children under 12 stay free in parent's room. AE, DISC, MC, V. Parking from $21 nearby. Subway: N or R to 28th St.; B, D, F, N, Q, R, V, or W to 34th St. *In room:* A/C, TV, dataport, hair dryer, iron, safe, wireless Internet.

Midtown, Chelsea & Union Square Accommodations

UPPER EAST SIDE

E. 66th St.
E. 65th St.
E. 64th St.
E. 63rd St.
E. 62nd St.
E. 61st St.
E. 60th St.
E. 59th St.
E. 58th St.
E. 57th St.
E. 56th St.
E. 55th St.
E. 54th St.
E. 53rd St.
E. 52nd St.
E. 51st St.
E. 50th St.
E. 49th St.
E. 48th St.
E. 47th St.
E. 46th St.
E. 45th St.
E. 44th St.
E. 43rd St.
E. 42nd St.
E. 41st St.
E. 40th St.
E. 39th St.
E. 38th St.
E 37th St.
E 36th St.
E. 35th St.
E. 34th St.
E. 33rd St.
E. 32nd St.
E. 31st St.
E. 30th St.
E. 29th St.
E. 28th St.
E. 27th St.
E. 26th St.
E. 25th St.
E. 24th St.
E. 23rd St.
E. 22nd St.
E. 21st St.
E. 20th St.
E. 19th St.
E. 18th St.
E. 17th St.
E. 16th St.
E. 15th St.
E. 14th St.
E. 13th St.

From Lower Level
Roosevelt Island Tram
Queensboro Bridge
To Upper Level

Fifth Ave.
Madison Ave.
Park Ave.
Lexington Ave.
First Ave.
York Ave.

MIDTOWN EAST

Sutton Pl.
Sutton Pl. South

Beekman Place

Mitchell Place

Third Ave.
Second Ave.
First Ave.

United Nations

Queensboro Bridge

ROOSEVELT ISLAND

QUEENS

Queens–Midtown Tunnel

East River

FDR Drive

Queens–Midtown Tunnel

Tunnel Exit
Tunnel Entrance

Grand Army Plaza
The Pond
Central Park South

PARK
Transverse
East Drive

Rockefeller Center

Sixth Ave. (Ave. of the Americas)

Fifth Ave.
Madison Ave.
Vanderbilt Ave.
Park Ave.
Lexington Ave.

Grand Central Terminal

Bryant Park
New York Public Library

MURRAY HILL

Empire State Bldg.

Broadway

Fifth Ave.
Madison Ave.
Park Ave. S.
Lexington Ave.

Madison Square Park

Asser Levy Pl.
Ave C

Peter Cooper Village

Stuyvesant Town

FLATIRON DISTRICT

GRAMERCY PARK

Gramercy Park

Sixth Ave. (Ave. of the Americas)

Fifth Ave.
Union Sq. W.
Union Sq. E.
Irving Pl.
N.D. Perlman Pl.

Union Square

2
3
4
5
6
7
16
17
18
19
20
21
22
23
24
25
26
27
28
29
30
31
32

M Subway stop

UPPER MANHATTAN
Central Park
UPTOWN
Area of detail
DOWNTOWN

0   1/4 mi
0   0.25 km

Hotel Edison *(Kids)*   A classic Art Deco lobby and a 1940s feel along with some attractive prices, make the Edison a good Theater District option. Don't expect much more than the basics, but you will find a firm bed, decor that's more attractive than most in this category, and a clean tile bathroom. Most double rooms feature two twins or a full bed, but there are some queens; request one at booking and show up early for your best chance at one. The larger quad rooms, with two doubles, are the best reason to consider the Edison, especially if you're traveling with the kids. Off the lobby is the **Cafe Edison,** an old-style Polish deli that's a favorite among theater types and downmarket ladies who lunch; **Sofia's,** a just-fine Italian restaurant; and the **Rum House Tavern,** which has a Caribbean flair and live entertainment most nights.

228 W. 47th St. (btwn Broadway and 8th Ave.), New York, NY 10036. (¢ **800/637-7070** or 212/840-5000. Fax 212/596-6850. www.edisonhotelnyc.com. 780 units. $140–$160 single; $160–$180 double; $175–$190 triple or quad; $180–$245 suite. Extra person $15. AE, DC, DISC, MC, V. Parking $35. Subway: N or R to 49th St.; 1 or 9 to 50th St. **Amenities:** 2 restaurants; cocktail lounge; exercise room; tour desk; laundry service; dry cleaning. *In room:* A/C, TV, dataport.

Hotel Metro ★★ *(Kids)*   One of my favorites, the Metro is the best choice in Midtown for those who don't want to sacrifice style or comfort for affordability. This Art Deco–style jewel has larger rooms than you'd expect. The rooms and halls are outfitted with retro furnishings, playful fabrics, fluffy pillows, alarm clocks, and small but beautiful marble bathrooms. Only about half the bathrooms have tubs, but the others have huge shower stalls (junior suites have whirlpool tubs). The family room—a two-room suite with a second bedroom in lieu of a sitting area—is an ingenious invention, while families on tighter budgets can opt for a roomy double/double. There's a comfy, fire-lit library/lounge area off the lobby, where complimentary buffet breakfast is laid out and the coffeepot's on all day. The well-furnished rooftop terrace boasts a breathtaking view of the Empire State Building, and makes a great place to order up room service from the stylish and very good **Metro Grill.**

Prices typically rise in fall, but it's relatively easy to score a rate between $150 and $180 through August, as long as you book well ahead; also check with airlines and other package operators for great-value package deals.

45 W. 35th St. (btwn 5th and 6th aves.), New York, NY 10001. (¢ **800/356-3870** or 212/947-2500. Fax 212/279-1310. www.hotelmetronyc.com. 179 units. $145–$250 double; $155–$300 triple or quad; $175–$350 family room; $210–$400 suite. Rates include continental breakfast. Check with airlines and other package operators for great-value package deals. Extra person $25. 1 child under 14 stays free in parent's room. AE, DC, MC, V. Parking $17 nearby. Subway: B, D, F, V, N, or R to 34th St. **Amenities:** Restaurant; rooftop bar in summer; fitness room; salon; limited room service; laundry service; dry cleaning. *In room:* A/C, TV, dataport, fridge, hair dryer, iron.

Hotel Wolcott   Once one of the grande dames of Manhattan hotels, the Wolcott has been reinvented as a good-value option for bargain hunters. Only the lobby hints at its former grandeur; these days, the rooms are motel-standard, but they're rather large, well kept, and quite serviceable. Plusses include spacious bathrooms and phones with voice mail, plus minifridges in most rooms. On the downside, the decor is less than stylish and the closets tend to be small—but these are small sacrifices for prices this low. Some of the triples are poorly configured—but they're big enough for three, and come with two beds (as do the suites). What's more, the services—fitness room, business center, coin-op laundry, Nintendo, a free "express" breakfast (coffee and muffins), and TV Internet access in every room—far exceed most competitors in the budget category. All in all, you get your money's worth here.

4 W. 31st St. (at 5th Ave.), New York, NY 10001. ℂ **212/268-2900**. Fax 212/563-0096. www.wolcott.com. 250 units. $99–$160 single or double; $115–$180 triple; $120–$220 junior suite for 2 or 3. Discounted AAA, AARP, and promo rates may be available. AE, MC, V. Parking $17 next door. Subway: B, D, F, V, N, or R to 34th St. **Amenities:** Exercise room; tour desk; business center; coin-op laundry. *In room:* A/C, TV w/pay movies, dataport, fridge, hair dryer, video games, Internet access.

La Quinta Inn Manhattan ✿ The newest of the Apple Core group's properties and the first and only La Quinta Inn in Manhattan is another excellent midtown budget choice. Housed in a 1904 Beaux Arts structure on the block known as Little Korea, La Quinta Inn offers standard motel amenities along with very motel-like prices. Like the other Apple Core properties, including the Red Roof Inn across the street, service is friendly and a continental breakfast adds to the value. The rooms are basic motel-room decor and size, but there's nothing wrong with that especially at these prices. Bathrooms are comparably small, but clean and well equipped. There's even a cozy rooftop bar that offers indoor and outdoor seating in the shadow of the majestic Empire State Building. And if you like Korean barbecue and dumplings, you won't have to travel far; the block is packed with some very good Korean restaurants.

17 W. 32nd St (btwn 5th and 6th aves.), New York, N.Y. 10001. ℂ **800/567-7720** or 212/790-2710. www.applecorehotels.com. 182 units. $89–$329 double (usually less than $159). Rates include continental breakfast. Children under 14 stay free in parent's room. AE, DC, DISC, MC, V. Parking $22. Subway: B, D, F, V, N, or R to 34th St. **Amenities:** Breakfast room; bar; exercise room; concierge; business center; laundry service; dry cleaning. *In room:* A/C, TV w/pay movies, dataport, coffeemaker, iron, video games, wireless Internet access.

Mayfair Hotel Be prepared—the rooms here are *tiny*. The elevator is, too. That's it for the bad news. Now the good: The Mayfair is one of the Theater District's friendliest and best-kept budget hotels. Each room boasts a smallish but nice black-and-white tile bathroom (all but a few singles have tub/shower combos) and unstylish but perfectly nice decor. The wood-paneled lobby is more elegant than most in this price range; just off it is the cute French bistro Le Garrick, an attraction in its own right. A supernice staff is the icing on the cake. Don't be frightened off by the rack-rate range; while prices can soar in peak seasons, rates generally stay well below $200 (which they should—if you're quoted more, stay elsewhere).

242 W. 49th St. (btwn Broadway and 8th Ave.), New York, NY 10019. ℂ **800/55-MAYFAIR** or 212/586-0300. Fax 212/307-5226. www.mayfairnewyork.com. 78 units. $95–$250 single or double ($100–$150 in most seasons). Check for low-season specials. AE, DC, MC, V. Parking $18 nearby. Subway: 1, 9, C, or E to 50th St. **Amenities:** Restaurant; concierge. *In room:* A/C, TV, dataport, hair dryer, iron, safe.

New York Inn Don't expect much from this dingy little hotel on a still-ratty block of 8th Avenue. But if you're committed to finding a room with private bathroom, TV, and phone in the Theater District for a low rate, this is probably your best choice—especially in the second half of the year, when prices skyrocket at most neighboring budget hotels. A half-staircase leads up to the lobby, where you'll check in and proceed up a narrow staircase to three floors of rooms. Guest rooms are small and dark but have firm beds with relatively new spreads, new desktop TVs with cable, telephones with voice mail, and cramped bathrooms with stall showers that could use some serious retiling. Maintenance is less than perfect, but everything is clean—frankly, as good as can be expected considering the location and rate. I'd choose the St. Mark's Hotel (p. 100) first—but it's not in the heart of the Theater District. While this specific block is less than pretty, this area is gentrifying well, and great, affordable eats abound.

765 8th Ave. (btwn 46th and 47th sts.), New York, NY 10036. ℂ **888/450-5555** or 212/247-5400. Fax 212/541-4674. www.newyorkinn.com. 40 units. $89–$130 single or double. Rates include continental breakfast and tax. AE, DISC, MC, V. Subway: C or E to 50th St. *In room:* A/C, TV, hair dryer.

Park Savoy Hotel   The Park Savoy isn't as nice as its sibling, the Chelsea Savoy (p. 104), but the lower prices reflect the quality difference, making it a good deal. Rooms are basic, and a few were in need of a fresh coat of paint. All have voice mail and alarm clocks, most have walk-in closets, and a few have minifridges. All rooms have tiled private bathrooms that are petite (with showers only, no tubs) but attractive and clean. If your budget is tight, two of you can make do in the smallest rooms; the biggest ones can accommodate three or four in two double beds. Services are kept to a minimum to keep rates low, but there's a decent restaurant next door. Best of all is the convenient location—a block from Central Park and a stone's throw from Carnegie Hall, Lincoln Center, and the Columbus Circle subways, which give easy access to the rest of the city.

158 W. 58th St. (btwn 6th and 7th aves.), New York, NY 10019. ☎ **212/245-5755.** Fax 212/765-0668. www. parksavoyhotel.com. 70 units. $79–$145 single or double. AE, MC, V. Parking $20 next door. Subway: A, B, C, D, 1, or 9 to 59th St./Columbus Circle; N or R to 57th St. **Amenities:** Limited room service. *In room:* A/C, TV.

Portland Square Hotel   Another Puchall family project (see the Herald Square Hotel, above), the Portland Square is a good Theater District bet for budget travelers. Some prefer this hotel to the comparable Herald Square: The public spaces have been renovated, and everything seems to be in good shape. The rooms are small, simple, and cheaply furnished (laminated furniture, fluorescent lighting), but clean. Ask for one with an extralarge bathroom; some are almost as big as the bedroom. Avoid the shared-bathroom singles if you can: The ratio is a high four rooms to a bathroom, some of the hall bathrooms were on the crusty side, and most of the shared bathrooms had a smoky odor. But the private bathrooms are a decent deal if money's tight. The staff is friendly and cooperative, but don't expect much in the way of service (that's one way they keep rates low).

132 W. 47th St. (btwn 6th and 7th aves.), New York, NY 10036. ☎ **800/388-8988** or 212/382-0600. Fax 212/382-0684. www.portlandsquarehotel.com. 145 units, 115 with private bathroom. $65–$75 single or double with shared bathroom; $99–$120 single with private bathroom; $125–$135 double with private bathroom; $135–$170 triple or quad with private bathroom. Extra person $10. AE, MC, V. Parking $24 across the street. Subway: B, D, F, or V to 47th–50th sts./Rockefeller Center. **Amenities:** Luggage lockers. *In room:* A/C, TV, dataport.

Red Roof Inn ☆☆   Manhattan's first, and only Red Roof Inn offers relief from Midtown's high-priced hotel scene. The hotel occupies a former office building that was gutted and laid out fresh, allowing for more spacious rooms and bathrooms than you'll usually find in this price category. The lobby feels smart, and elevators are quiet and efficient. In-room amenities—including coffeemakers and TVs with on-screen Web access—are better than most competitors', and furnishings are new and comfortable. Wi-Fi wireless Internet is available throughout the property. The location—on a bustling block lined with nice hotels and affordable Korean restaurants, just a stone's throw from the Empire State Building and Herald Square—is excellent.

Be sure to compare the rates offered by Apple Core Hotel's reservation line (the management company) and those quoted on Red Roof's national reservation line and website, as they can vary significantly. Complimentary continental breakfast adds to the good value.

6 W. 32nd St. (btwn Broadway and 5th Ave.), New York, NY 10001. ☎ **800/567-7720,** 800/RED-ROOF, or 212/643-7100. Fax 212/643-7101. www.applecorehotels.com or www.redroof.com. 171 units. $89–$329 double (usually less than $159). Rates include continental breakfast. Children under 14 stay free in parent's room. AE, DC, DISC, MC, V. Parking $22. Subway: B, D, F, V, N, or R to 34th St. **Amenities:** Breakfast room; wine-and-beer lounge; exercise room; concierge; business center; laundry service; dry cleaning. *In room:* A/C, TV w/pay movies, dataport, fridge, coffeemaker, hair dryer, iron, video games, wireless Internet.

Skyline Hotel *(Kids)*   This nice, newly renovated motor hotel offers predictable comforts and some uncommon extras—inexpensive storage parking ($8 a day) and a lovely indoor pool—that make it a very good value. A pleasant lobby leads to motel-standard rooms that are a far cry from stylish, but are bigger than most in this price range. There are two room categories: standard, with two twin beds; and deluxe, with either a king-size bed with sofa or a queen-size bed. The deluxe with king-size and sofa is best for families. They boast decent-size closets, small work desks (in most), and double-paned windows that open to let fresh air in, and shut out a surprising amount of street noise when closed. Some rooms have brand-new bathrooms, but the older ones are still fine. Everything is very well kept. Another plus for the family is the pool, which has a nicely tiled deck and plush deck chairs; but it's open limited hours, so call ahead if it matters.

725 10th Ave. (at 49th St.), New York, NY 10019. ℂ **212/586-3400.** Fax 212/582-4604. www.skylinehotel ny.com. 230 units. $109–$179 standard; $139–$229 deluxe. Check website or inquire about special rates (as low as $89 at press time). Extra person $15. Children 14 and under stay free in parent's room. AE, DC, DISC, MC, V. Parking $8 (charge for in/out privileges). Subway: A, C, or E to 50th St. Pets accepted with $200 deposit. **Amenities:** Restaurant (American/Italian); bar, big-screen TV and live entertainment; indoor pool; Gray Line tour desk; Internet-access machine in lobby. *In room:* A/C, TV w/pay movies, dataport, hair dryer, iron, safe, video games, Internet access.

Super 8 Hotel Times Square *★★ (Value)*   The Super 8 folks, in alliance with Apple Core Hotels (the franchisee behind such hotels as the Comfort Inn Midtown and Red Roof Inn), have done a terrific job reinventing the former Hotel Wentworth into a bright, attractive hotel offering better-than-budget accommodations in the heart of Midtown. The Wentworth was built in 1902 as a hotel for women, so it boasts extralarge rooms (by New York standards), outfitted with a king-size bed or two doubles, and all-new bathrooms. Decor isn't what you'd call stylish, but it's attractive, with woods, pastel wallpaper, green carpeting, and floral spreads. All rooms are well outfitted with fridges, coffeemakers, small work desks, hair dryers, irons, and alarm clocks, plus Nintendo and on-screen e-mail access. Mom and Dad will love the family suite, which features a king-size bed in one room and two twin beds (in lieu of a sitting area) in the other; be flexible in your travel and you may be able to snare this suite for as little as $129.

The lobby is bright and elegant, and service is professional. Perks include a state-of-the-art exercise room and a breakfast room serving a continental meal that's included in the rate—for as little as $89 double! Even in high seasons, when Super 8 rates can climb into the mid-$100s, you'll still get your money's worth. In fact, Apple Core always keeps its hotels priced ahead of the curve.

59 W. 46th St. (btwn 5th and 6th aves.), New York, NY 10036. ℂ **800/567-7720** or 212/719-2300. Fax 212/790-2760. www.applecorehotels.com or www.super8.com. 206 units. $89–$329 double (usually less than $179); family suite from $129. Rates include continental breakfast. Check for AAA, AARP, and other discounts. Children under 14 stay free in parent's room. AE, DC, DISC, MC, V. Parking $20 next door. Subway: B, D, F, or V to 42nd St. **Amenities:** Breakfast room; exercise room; business center w/computer, fax, copier; laundry service; dry cleaning. *In room:* A/C, TV w/pay movies, dataport, fridge, coffeemaker, hair dryer, iron, video games, wireless Internet.

Travel Inn *(Kids)*   Extras like a huge outdoor pool and sun deck, a sunny, up-to-date fitness room, and the *only* hotel I've found for this guide that offers free parking (with in-and-out privileges!) make the Travel Inn another terrific deal. Like the Skyline (see above), the Travel Inn may not be loaded with personality, but it offers the clean, bright regularity of a good chain hotel—an attractive trait in a city where "quirky" is the catchword at most affordable hotels. Rooms are oversize and comfortable, furnished with extrafirm beds and desks; even the smallest double is sizable and has a roomy bathroom, and double/doubles make affordable shares for families. A renovation over the last couple of years has made everything feel like new, even the tiled bathrooms. The neighborhood has gentrified and isn't as far off as you might think: Off-Broadway theaters and good restaurants are nearby, and it's a 10-minute walk to the Theater District. It's a good bet even if you don't have a car.

515 W. 42nd St. (just west of 10th Ave.), New York, NY 10036. ℂ 888/HOTEL-58 (468-3558), 800/869-4630, or 212/695-7171. Fax 212/967-5025. www.newyorkhotel.com. 160 units. $125–$250 double. AAA discounts available. Check website for Internet deals (as low as $105 at press time). Extra person $10. Children under 16 stay free in parent's room. AE, DC, DISC, MC, V. Free self-parking. Subway: A, C, or E to 42nd St./Port Authority. **Amenities:** Coffee shop; outdoor pool; fitness center; tour desk; 24-hr. room service. *In room:* A/C, TV, dataport, hair dryer, iron.

The Wyndham 🌟 *Finds* This hotel isn't part of the upscale chain of the same name; rather, it's a family-owned charmer that's one of Midtown's best hotel deals: perfectly located, on a great block steps away from 5th Avenue and Central Park. The Wyndham is stuck in the '70s on all fronts, but its guest rooms are enormous, comfortable, and loaded with character. The hotel features a wild collection of wallpaper, from candy stripes to crushed velvets, so some rooms cross the ticky-tacky line. If you're put in a room that's not to your taste, just ask politely to see another one; the staff is usually willing to accommodate.

Most important, it's a great deal: The rooms are quite large and feature huge walk-in closets (the biggest I've seen). The surprisingly affordable suites also have full living rooms, dressing areas, and cold kitchenettes (fridge only). You'll need a two-bedroom suite if you bring the kids (only two guests are allowed in standard rooms or one-bedroom suites), but the rate is a steal considering the space. Don't expect an alarm clock, hair dryer, luxury toiletries, or other modern amenities. But at these prices, you can afford to invest in travel sizes.

42 W. 58th St. (btwn 5th and 6th aves.), New York, NY 10019. ℂ 800/257-1111 or 212/753-3500. Fax 212/ 754-5638. 212 units. $140–$175 single or double; $190–$250 1-bedroom suite; $335–$390 2-bedroom suite (up to 4 guests included in rate). AE, DC, MC, V. Parking $40 nearby. Subway: N or R to 5th Ave.; B or Q to 57th St. **Amenities:** Restaurant w/excellent cocktail lounge; salon; laundry service; dry cleaning. *In room:* A/C, TV, dataport.

SUPERCHEAP SLEEPS

Big Apple Hostel 🌟 This is the nicest hostel in Midtown, if not in all of Manhattan. It's not fancy, but it's well run, spotlessly clean, and in the heart of the Theater District; many luxury hotels wish they had it so good. All dorm rooms are four-bedded; they're well spaced and well kept, with metal bunks and good mattresses with blankets and linens. Only guests in private rooms get towels, so dormers should bring their own. Private rooms are basic but better than most in hostels; all have phones (free local calls!), TVs, radios, and alarm clocks, and some have a table and chairs. The shared bathrooms are better than average. There's a stocked kitchen with microwave, a backyard patio with barbecue, and a luggage storage room. It's popular with Japanese and other international travelers who like the location. It doesn't get much better at bargain-basement prices—Big Apple Hostel is superior to the better-known Aladdin Hostel farther west on 45th Street.

119 W. 45th St. (btwn 6th and 7th aves.), New York, NY 10036. ℂ 212/302-2603. Fax 212/302-2605. www.bigapplehostel.com. 112 dorm beds; 11 private doubles. $28–$38 dorm bed; $78–$109 double. MC, V. Subway: N, R, S, 1, 2, 3, 7, or 9 to Times Square/42nd St. **Amenities:** Common kitchen. *In room:* Fan, no phone in dorm units.

9 Midtown East & Murray Hill

Habitat Hotel ⚝   Marketed as "upscale budget," this hotel features rooms dressed to appeal to travelers who are short on funds but big on style. They're well designed in a natural palette accented with black-and-white photos. Everything is of better quality and more attractive than in most hotels in this price range, from the firm mattresses to the plush towels to the pedestal sinks in every room. The bathrooms are all new; choose between shared (one for every three to four rooms), private, or a semiprivate "minisuite" (two rooms sharing an adjacent bathroom—great for friends traveling together).

The only downside—and it may be a big one for romance-seeking couples—is the sleeping accommodations. A few queens are available (at the highest end of the price spectrum), but most of the double rooms consist of a twin bed with a pullout trundle, which takes up most of the width of the room when it's open. Despite that drawback, rates are attractive, especially for the rooms with shared bathroom, considering the *Metropolitan Home* mindset and the location. I prefer the private-bathroom rooms at sister hotel **Thirty Thirty** (below), because they don't have the space limitations these have, but this hotel has a more thrilling location and a more exciting vibe thanks to the popular restaurant and bar, **Opia.**

130 E. 57th St. (at Lexington Ave.), New York, NY 10022. © **800/497-6028** or 212/753-8841. Fax 212/838-4767. www.habitatny.com. 330 units, about 40 with private bathroom. $75–$115 single or double with shared bathroom; $125–$185 single or double with private bathroom; $240–$270 minisuite (2 rooms with shared bathroom). Rates include continental breakfast. Call or check website for student rates and promotions (from $79 at press time). AE, DC, DISC, MC, V. Parking $25. Subway: 4, 5, or 6 to 59th St.; E or F to Lexington Ave. **Amenities:** Restaurant/bar; tour desk. *In room:* A/C, TV, dataport.

Helmsley Middletowne ⚝   This value-laden member of the Helmsley chain (yes, as in Leona Helmsley) boasts little in the way of style, but rooms and suites are large, comfortable, and well priced, and the location is fantastic—you usually have to spend more to stay in this 'hood. The hotel started life as an apartment building and as a result, the lobby is virtually nonexistent, but the front-desk staff—most of whom have worked here for *years*—is brisk and friendly. Room decor is generic and furnishings are older, but beds are firm and everything is well kept. Each room has a refrigerator (usually with a wet bar), multiple-line phones, a dated but fine bathroom, and a wealth of closet space. The one- and two-bedroom suites are well priced and big enough to accommodate families. They also boast walk-in kitchenettes (some lack dishware, though, so request it or bring plastic); some have fireplaces and/or balconies as well. Business travelers can request an in-room fax machine. Not sexy but a nice choice in the midprice range.

148 E. 48th St. (btwn 3rd and Lexington aves.), New York, NY 10017. © **800/221-4982** or 212/755-3000. Fax 212/832-0261. www.helmsleyhotels.com. 192 units. $195–$205 double; from $235 1-bedroom suite. Rates include continental breakfast. Ask about packages. Children under 12 stay free in parent's room. AE, DC, MC, V. Parking $30. Subway: 6 to 51st St. **Amenities:** Restaurant; laundry service; dry cleaning. *In room:* A/C, TV, kitchenettes (in suites), fridge, hair dryer, iron.

Hotel Grand Union   This centrally-located hotel is big with budget-minded international travelers. A pleasant white-on-white lobby leads to clean, spacious rooms with nice extras that are uncommon in this price category, like hair dryers and free HBO. Bad fluorescent lighting, unattractive furniture, and a lack of natural light dampen the mood—but considering the roominess, rates, and central-to-everything location, the Grand Union is a deal. A nicely configured quad with two twins and a queen-size bed in a separate alcove, no. 309 is a great bet for families. Most bathrooms have been outfitted in granite or tile; ask for a newly renovated one. The staff is helpful, there's a pleasant sitting room off the lobby, and an adjacent coffee shop is convenient for morning coffee or a quickie burger.

34 E. 32nd St. (btwn Madison and Park aves.), New York, NY 10016. ✆ **212/683-5890.** Fax 212/689-7397. www.hotelgrandunion.com. 95 units. $120 single or double; $140 twin or triple; $165 quad. Call or check website for special rates. AE, DC, DISC, MC, V. Parking $22 nearby. Subway: 6 to 33rd St. **Amenities:** Coffee shop; tour desk; fax service. *In room:* A/C, TV, dataport, fridge, hair dryer.

Pickwick Arms Hotel *(Value)*   For a Midtown hotel on the East Side, this is like entering an economic time warp. The location couldn't be better. The older, sometimes astoundingly small rooms are spare (think monk's cell), but they're well kept, and the place is safe and well run. There are a few doubles and twins with private bathrooms (the larger deluxe twins can accommodate a rollaway), but the majority of rooms are singles with private, semiprivate, or shared hall bathrooms. Two friends traveling together can take advantage of the semiprivate situation: Two singles (each with sink, TV, desk, closet, and telephone) that share a bathroom can be had for the same price as a twin room. All of the bathrooms are worn-looking and have showers only, but they're clean. A renovation has spiffed up the halls and rooms. If you want a great location for a low price, this is the place. On-site is a rooftop patio with skyline views, and an affordable restaurant serving three squares a day.

230 E. 51st St. (btwn 2nd and 3rd aves.), New York, NY 10022. ✆ **800/742-5945** in the U.S., 800/874-0074 in Canada, or 212/355-0300. Fax 212/755-5029. www.pickwickarms.com. 320 units, 200 with private bathroom. $69–$114 single; $125–$150 double or twin; $165–$175 triple. AE, DC, MC, V. Parking $30–$35 nearby. Subway: 6 to 51st St. **Amenities:** Restaurant; roof patio. *In room:* A/C, TV, dataport.

Ramada Inn Eastside   The most affordable of the Apple Core Hotels (which also include the Red Roof Inn, the Comfort Inn Midtown, and the Super 8

Tips **Queens for a Day (and a Night)**

If you come to New York on a whim with no advance planning (not recommended) and find yourself without Manhattan accommodations, look across the river to Queens for a couple of low-priced options. The new in 2004, basic **Comfort Inn Long Island City,** 42-24 Crescent Ave. (✆ **718/303-3700**), features standard Comfort Inn amenities including complimentary continental breakfast. The hotel is just a few blocks from the 7 train and only 10 to 15 minutes to midtown Manhattan.

Also in Long Island City is the **Best Western City View,** 33-17 Greenpoint Ave. (✆ **718/392-8400**). Located in a renovated schoolhouse, the hotel claims to offer free shuttle service to LaGuardia Airport. When I called to inquire about that service, the response was vague, so if that is important to you, double-check before you book. Like the Comfort Inn, the Best Western is also near the 7 train. Rates for both hotels range from $99 to $130.

You might also consider these hotels if you're coming to town for the U.S. Open (held in Flushing, which is at the other end of the 7 line) or to see a game at Shea Stadium. Long Island City is convenient to both the National Tennis Center/Shea and Midtown.

Hotel), this former Quality Hotel is nothing special—small, basic rooms with older bathrooms—but a renovation has given them a fresh look in greens and beige. Its other features are the location, in quiet Murray Hill, which abounds with affordable restaurants; the value-added amenities, which include free continental breakfast, free local phone calls, business center, and fitness room; and the usually low rates. Don't expect anything in the way of service, but considering how expensive an average room has become, this hotel is a value. It's quite easy to score a room for $139 or less most of the year.

161 Lexington Ave. (at 30th St.), New York, NY 10016. ℂ **800/567-7720** or 212/545-1800. Fax 212/790-2760. www.applecorehotels.com. 96 units. $89–$209 double. Rates include continental breakfast. Inquire about seasonal/weekend discounts (as low as $79 at press time). Children under 13 stay free in parent's room. AE, DC, DISC, MC, V. Parking $20 nearby. Subway: 6 to 33rd St. **Amenities:** Coffee shop; exercise room and business center (both under renovation at press time). *In room:* A/C, TV w/pay movies, dataport, coffeemaker, hair dryer, iron, video games, wireless Internet.

Thirty Thirty ★★ *Value*   Thirty Thirty is just right for bargain-hunting travelers looking for a splash of style with an affordable price tag. The building—which formerly housed the well-known Martha Washington women's hotel and the legendary nightclub Danceteria, where Madonna got her start—was gutted, renovated, and redone with brand-new everything.

The design-conscious tone is set in the loftlike industrial-modern lobby. Rooms are mostly on the smallish side, but do the trick for those who intend to spend their days out on the town rather than holed up here. They're done in a natural palette with a creative edge—purplish carpet, khaki bedspread, woven wallpaper—that comes together more attractively than you might expect. Configurations are split among twin/twins (great for friends), queen-size beds, and queen-size/queen-size (great for triples, budget-minded quads, or shares that want more spreading-out room). Nice features include cushioned headboards, firm mattresses, two-line phones, nice built-in wardrobes, and spacious, nicely tiled bathrooms. A few larger units have kitchenettes, great if you're staying in town for a while, as you'll appreciate the extra room and the fridge. No room service, but delivery is available from nearby restaurants.

30 E. 30th St. (btwn Madison and Park aves.), New York, NY 10016. ℂ **800/497-6028** or 212/689-1900. Fax 212/689-0023. www.thirtythirty-nyc.com. 243 units. $115–$145 double; $145–$195 double with kitchenette; $185–$245 quad. Call for last-minute deals, or check website for special promotions (as low as $99 at press time). AE, DC, DISC, MC, V. Parking $35 1 block away. Subway: 6 to 28th St. Pets accepted with advance approval. **Amenities:** Restaurant; concierge; laundry service; dry cleaning. *In room:* A/C, TV, dataport, hair dryer.

10 The Upper West Side

Amsterdam Inn ★ *Value*   This renovated five-story walk-up offers basic accommodations that add up to a great value in a terrific neighborhood. The inn's biggest assets are its Upper West Side location, its newness, its cleanliness, and its professional management.

The rooms are small and narrow, with a bed, a rack to hang your clothes on, a set of drawers with a TV on top, a side table with a lamp and a phone that requires a deposit to activate, and a sink if there's no private bathroom. The Euro-style rooms share the in-hall bathrooms at a ratio of about 2½ to 1. The bathrooms are new but have showers only. If you book a double, make sure it's a *real* double, with a double bed. The singles with trundles can (theoretically) accommodate two, but don't expect to have any space left over. Management seems willing to negotiate, so always ask for a lower rate.

340 Amsterdam Ave. (at 76th St.), New York, NY 10024. ✆ **212/579-7500.** Fax 212/579-6127. www.amsterdam inn.com. 25 units, 18 with private bathroom. $60–$75 single with shared bathroom; $75–$95 bunk-bed twin or double with shared bathroom; $95–$115 double with private bathroom. Extra person $20. Children under 12 stay free in parent's room. AE, MC, V. Parking $20–$25 nearby. Subway: 1 or 9 to 79th St. *In room:* A/C, TV.

Hotel Belleclaire This Beaux Arts hotel that underwent a face-lift in 2004 boasts a great Upper West Side location and renovated, stylish guest rooms that are larger than most. The accommodations, though simple, do the job, and the management seems intent on pleasing. The rooms have small, freshly tiled bathrooms with tub/shower combos (six have roll-in showers to accommodate travelers with disabilities). Cushioned headboards, nice fabric-covered cubes for modular seating, small TVs, minifridges, and alarm clocks are the main amenities. Closets are small. The shared-bathroom units are the same but have in-room sinks and share hall bathrooms at a ratio of 3 to 1. The family suite features two attached, semi-private bedrooms with a bathroom, a minifridge, and a big walk-in closet. This is a decent choice in a first-class residential neighborhood.

250 W. 77th St. (at Broadway), New York, NY 10024. ✆ **877/HOTEL-BC** (468-3522) or 212/362-7700. Fax 212/362-1004. www.hotelbelleclaire.com. 189 units, 39 with shared bathroom. $109 double with shared bathroom; $169–$189 double with private bathroom; $229 family suite. Ask about AAA, corporate, group, and other discounts. AE, DC, DISC, MC, V. Parking $25 nearby. Subway: 1 or 9 to 79th St. **Amenities:** Access to nearby health club; tour desk; fax; laundry service; dry cleaning. *In room:* A/C, TV w/pay movies and games, dataport, fridge, hair dryer, iron.

Hotel Newton ☆ *Value* On the burgeoning northern extreme of the Upper West Side, the Newton, unlike many of its peers, doesn't scream "budget" at every turn. As you enter the pretty lobby, you're greeted by a uniformed staff that's attentive and professional. The rooms are generally large, with good, firm beds, a work desk, and a sizable new bathroom, plus roomy closets in most (a few of the cheapest have wall racks only). Some are big enough to accommodate families, with two doubles or two queen-size beds. The suites feature two queen-size beds in the bedroom, a sofa in the sitting room, plus niceties such as microwave, minifridge, and iron, making them well worth the few extra dollars. The bigger rooms and suites have been upgraded with cherrywood furnishings, but even the older laminated furniture is much nicer than I usually see in this price range. The AAA–approved hotel is impeccably kept. The 96th Street express subway stop is just a block away, providing convenient access to the rest of the city, and the Key West Diner next door is a favorite for huge, cheap breakfasts.

2528 Broadway (btwn 94th and 95th sts.), New York, NY 10025. ✆ **888/HOTEL-58** or 212/678-6500. Fax 212/678-6758. www.newyorkhotel.com. 110 units. $95–$160 double or junior suite. Extra person $10. Children under 15 stay free in parent's room. AAA, corporate, senior, and group rates available; check website for special Internet deals. AE, DC, DISC, MC, V. Parking $20 nearby. Subway: 1, 2, 3, or 9 to 96th St. **Amenities:** 24-hr. room service. *In room:* A/C, TV, hair dryer.

The Milburn *Kids* On a quiet Upper West Side street, The Milburn offers reasonably priced rooms and suites with kitchenettes in the same neighborhood—at about half the price. These suites are an excellent value. Every suite is rife with amenities, including a dining area, a bathroom, a kitchenette (with free coffee), two-line phones, and more. Junior and one-bedroom suites boast a pullout queen-size sofa, an extra TV, a CD player, and a desk. Don't expect much from the decor, but everything is attractive and in good shape. The conscientious management keeps the whole place spotless and in good order. In fact, what makes The Milburn a find is that it's more service-oriented than most hotels in this price range: The friendly staff will do everything from providing free copy, fax, and e-mail services to picking up your laundry at the dry cleaner next door.

Amsterdam Inn **6**
Central Park Hostel & Inn **2**
Hostelling International–
   New York **1**
Hotel Belleclaire **5**
Hotel Newton **3**
The Milburn **7**
Quality Hotel on Broadway **4**

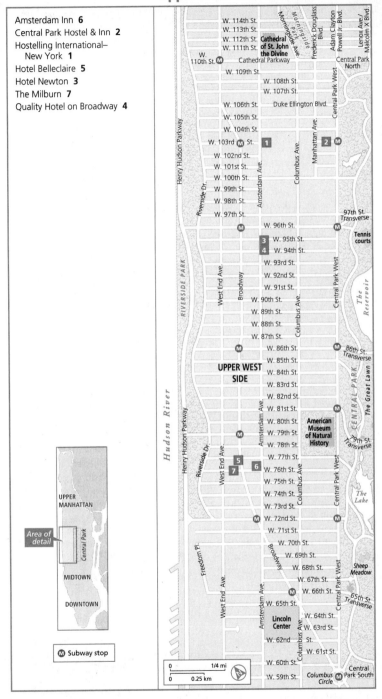

All in all, this is a great choice for bargain hunters—especially families, for whom rollaways and cribs are on hand.

242 W. 76th St. (btwn Broadway and West End Ave.), New York, NY 10023. ☎ **800/833-9622** or 212/362-1006. Fax 212/721-5476. www.milburnhotel.com. 116 units. $129–$169 studio double; $149–$199 junior suite; $169–$239 1-bedroom suite. Check website for seasonal specials (as low as $99 at press time). Extra person $10. Children under 13 stay free in parent's room. AE, DC, MC, V. Parking $20–$29. Subway: 1 or 9 to 79th St. **Amenities:** Fitness room; access to nearby health club; business services; coin-op laundry; free video library. *In room:* A/C, TV/VCR (PlayStation on request), dataport, kitchenette w/fridge and coffeemaker, hair dryer, iron, safe, CD player in suites, wireless Internet.

Quality Hotel on Broadway *(Value* Stay at this reliable, freshly renovated hotel if you like lots of space; some rooms are large enough for two doubles or a king-size bed. Rooms feature dark-wood, hotel-standard furnishings that include a work desk with a good ergonomic chair; an armoire holds the TV and good drawer space. Each room has an alarm clock, two phones with voicemail and free local calls, and a makeup mirror in the bathroom. Some also have a minifridge or a kitchenette; request one when you book. Most bathrooms have spacious granite countertops. A library-style sitting room is off the lobby. The location is terrific—cheaper than staying on the Upper West Side in the 70s and 80s, but just as nice neighborhood-wise, surrounded by affordable restaurants and 2 blocks from an express subway station that will whisk you to Times Square in two stops. Best of all, the online discount deals can be stellar (as low as $70 at press time).

215 W. 94th St. (at Broadway), New York, NY 10025. ☎ **800/228-5151** or 212/866-6400. Fax 212/866-1357. www.bestnyhotels.com. 350 units. $119–$149 single or double; $179–$219 junior suite (sleeps 2 or 3). Ask about senior, AAA, corporate, and promotional discounts; check www.hotelchoice.com for online-booking discounts. Extra person $15. Children under 18 stay free in parent's room. AE, DC, DISC, MC, V. Parking $17. Subway: 1, 2, 3, or 9 to 96th St. **Amenities:** Restaurant; concierge; fax service; laundry service; dry cleaning; coin-op laundry. *In room:* A/C, TV, dataport, coffeemaker, hair dryer, iron.

SUPERCHEAP SLEEPS

Central Park Hostel & Inn There's really no inn here—just a hostel. Run by the folks behind the Amsterdam, Murray Hill, and Union Square inns, this cheap choice offers everything clean, fresh, and of decent quality; mattresses, pillows, and linens are better than in most hostels (BYO towels). The shared bathrooms are brand-new (shared at a ratio of about 10 beds to a bathroom). Each floor has a locker area and the building is generally bright and sunny; the front desk is staffed around the clock, morning coffee and munchies are available at the corner deli, and a basement rec room and TV lounge with Internet access machine was in the works at press time.

Now the downside: Most dorm rooms have one too many bunk beds; there's barely any floor space for luggage. Columbia University is helping by building student housing throughout the area, but the location is still sketchy. It's separated from virtually all commercial activity (along Broadway and Amsterdam Ave.) by a major housing project. Luckily, the B and C trains' stops are at the end of the block. I'd try another city hostel first—the Big Apple (p. 120), Chelsea Center (p. 106), and Chelsea International (p. 107) are as clean and much better located.

19 W. 103rd St. (btwn Central Park W. and Manhattan Ave.), New York, NY 10025. ☎ **877/PARK-BED** (727-5233) or 212/678-0491. Fax 212/678-0453. www.centralparkhostel.com. 150 dorm beds. $26–$36 dorm bed; $75–$85 private twin. Rates include tax. Inquire about discounted rates. No credit cards. Subway: B or C to 103rd St. *In room:* A/C, no phone.

Hostelling International–New York Staying here is like going back to college—a very international college, with clocks set for six different time zones

Kids   Affordable Family-Friendly Hotels

The best way for families on a budget to save is to bunk together in a larger room with two double or queen-size beds. Some hotels have sweet suite deals that allow the kids to sleep on a pullout sofa in the living room, thus giving everybody a little well-deserved privacy.

Chelsea Savoy Hotel (p. 104)   These attractive, affordable rooms are large and comfy enough to accommodate four. Children stay free, and continental breakfast is included.

Gershwin Hotel (p. 109)   Parents in search of a high space-to-dollar ratio will love the family room, a two-room suite that accommodates Mom and Dad in a queen-size bed in one bedroom, two kids in two twin beds in the adjacent one.

Hotel Edison (p. 116)   Quads can accommodate four in two double beds, and value-priced suites with pullout sofas offer even more space.

Hotel Metro (p. 116)   This Art Deco–inspired hotel is an excellent choice for families who want more in the way of room, service, and comforts thanks to the hotel's "family room": a two-room suite with a second bedroom in lieu of a sitting area. This configuration gives Mom and Dad privacy, and kids their own real beds.

The Milburn (p. 124)   This Upper West Sider is a suite deal for any visitor, but their kids-under-12-stay-free policy makes it a stellar choice for families. The neighborhood is kid-friendly, and Central Park is an easy walk away.

Skyline Hotel (p. 119) and **Travel Inn** (p. 119)   If you're driving, take advantage of the low-cost or, at Travel Inn, free parking at these two motor hotels. And you'll like the family-size rooms, and the kids will love the pools (a rarity in affordable hotels). *And* children stay free (under 14 at the Skyline, under 16 at the Travel Inn).

behind the front desk and a backpack-toting clientele from around the globe. Beds are cheap, but expect to bunk it (upper or lower?) with people you don't know in rooms of 4, 6, 8, or 12. Everything is extremely basic, but the mattresses are firm and the shared bathrooms are nicely kept. There are four rooms with one double and two bunk beds that have private bathrooms. The well-managed hostel feels like a student union, with bulletin boards and listings of events posted; a coffee bar with an ample menu and pleasant seating; two TV rooms; a game room; and a library with bill- and credit card–operated Internet access computers. There's also a common kitchen, vending machines, a coin-op laundry, a terrace, and a yard with picnic tables and barbecues in summer. The neighborhood has improved over the years, but it's still a little sketchy; 1 block over is much nicer Broadway, lined with affordable restaurants and shops.

891 Amsterdam Ave. (at 103rd St.), New York, NY 10025. (C) **800/909-4776** or 212/932-2300. Fax 212/932-2574. www.hinewyork.org. 624 beds; 4 units with private bathroom. $29–$38 dorm bed; $120–$135 for family room (sleeps up to 4) or private quad. Travelers must be 18 or older. AE, DC, MC, V. Subway: 1 or 9 to 103rd St. **Amenities:** Coffee bar; access to nearby health club; game room; activities desk; coin-op laundry. *In room:* A/C, locker (BYO lock), no phone.

11 Harlem

If you want the absolute genuine New York brownstone experience, there is only one place to go: Harlem. **The Bed and Breakfast Mont Morris,** 56 W. 120th St., at Lenox Avenue (© **917/617-4354;** www.montmorris.com), is in the middle of one of Harlem's most historic areas and not far from the bustle of 125th

---

Finds   Bed-and-Breakfasting in Brooklyn

Leafy, lovely brownstone Brooklyn is the best-kept secret for B&B-loving budget travelers. The neighborhoods are jewels; these are some of the most desirable areas in the city for folks who don't want to hassle with the bustle of Manhattan. What's more, they're safe and subway-convenient, with Manhattan just 15 to 30 minutes away via subway. Each boasts a good selection of affordable restaurants catering to a local crowd.

The historic neighborhood of Park Slope is the heart of brownstone Brooklyn, and home to **Bed & Breakfast on the Park,** 113 Prospect Park W. (© **718/499-6115;** www.bbnyc.com). Housed in an 1895 Victorian town house across the street from Prospect Park, this inn has two beautifully outfitted shared-bathroom units ($125 or $150 double). A sumptuous breakfast is served in the formal dining room. Six more rooms with private bathrooms are available for guests who are looking to splurge. However, be aware that there is a 10% service charge added to all bills.

Another excellent choice is **Akwaaba Mansion,** 347 MacDonough St. (© **718/455-5958;** www.akwaaba.com), a meticulously restored 1860s Italianate villa in Bedford-Stuyvesant, outfitted with Afrocentric elegance. Four suites are available in the 18-room home, each with private bathroom with either a claw-foot or a Jacuzzi tub, for $120 to $150 double—including a hearty, Southern-style breakfast. The innkeepers are a lovely and helpful couple who love welcoming guests into their home; they also operate an affordably elegant restaurant with live jazz on Friday and Saturday nights, plus an all-you-can-eat Sunday brunch for just $12, just down the street.

In Carroll Gardens is the **Baisley House Bed-and-Breakfast,** 294 Hoyt St. (© **718/935-1959;** www.virtualcities.com/ons/ny/n/nyn1901.htm), a Victorian mansion that offers three guest rooms: one single and two doubles, each with shared bathroom, all including cable TV with VCR and a full breakfast. There's an opulent drawing room for lounging, plus an English-style garden out back. Rates are $95 to $150 double.

Also consider **Garden Green Bed-and-Breakfast,** 641 Carlton Ave. (© **718/783-5717;** www.virtualcities.com/ons/ny/n/nyn7601.htm), in the Prospect Heights section of brownstone Brooklyn, near Park Slope, the Brooklyn Museum of Art, and Prospect Park. Two double rooms (one with a full-size bed, one with two twins) share a hall bathroom, while a full-floor garden apartment—the best value of the three—boasts a queen-size bed, a sleeper sofa, a kitchen, and access to the lovely garden out back. Rates run an affordable $95 to $135 single or double; breakfast is not served.

Be prepared for a 2-night minimum at any bed-and-breakfast.

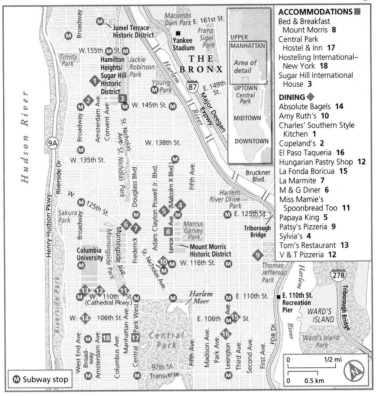

ACCOMMODATIONS ■
Bed & Breakfast
  Mount Morris 8
Central Park
  Hostel & Inn 17
Hostelling International–
  New York 18
Sugar Hill International
  House 3

DINING ◆
Absolute Bagels 14
Amy Ruth's 10
Charles' Southern Style
  Kitchen 1
Copeland's 2
El Paso Taqueria 16
Hungarian Pastry Shop 12
La Fonda Boricua 15
La Marmite 7
M & G Diner 6
Miss Mamie's
  Spoonbread Too 11
Papaya King 5
Patsy's Pizzeria 9
Sylvia's 4
Tom's Restaurant 13
V & T Pizzeria 12

Ⓜ Subway stop

Street. The B&B offers four units, one on each floor, and a continental break-fast from the very good Settepani Bakery just down the block. Rates range from the very friendly $65 to $95.

SUPERCHEAP SLEEPS

Sugar Hill International House   This intimate hostel is a good choice for people looking for a quiet, nonsmoking hostel. It's in two brownstones in the Sugar Hill Historic District, a residential, predominantly African-American sec-tion of Harlem. Owner Jim Williams has been here since 1984, and he and his partners have literally written the book on hostelling—or one of them, anyway: *The Hostel Handbook,* a guide to hostels across North America with an accom-panying website (www.hostelhandbook.com).

Hand-hewn bunk beds fill spacious, high-ceilinged rooms accommodating six to eight; a few highly coveted double rooms are available on a first-come, first-served basis. Accommodations are hostel basic: You'll get a mattress, pillow, and linens (BYO towels), plus plenty of floor space for your stuff; you can store valu-ables in a safe in the main office. Bathrooms are older but well kept, and divided into toilet, shower, and sink sections for easy sharing. The buildings are works in progress, but the place is well kept and well run. The owners are very friendly and helpful, long-term staff lives on-site, and security is tight: A passport ID is required for check-in (required at most private hostels these days), you will be assigned a code for the front door and provided with a key for your specific dorm, and no guests are allowed. One dorm is for women only. There's a common kitchen with a fridge, a cooktop, and basic tools; takeout is available, and St. Nick's Pub is across the street for genuine Harlem jazz.

722 St. Nicholas Ave. (btwn 146th and 147th sts.), New York, NY 10031. ℂ 212/926-7030. www.sugar hillhostel.com. 25 dorm beds. $25 single dorm bed; $30 double $60 bunk-bed twin. No credit cards. Subway: A, B, C, or D to 145th St. **Amenities:** Kitchen; free Internet access. *In room:* No phone.

Great Deals on Dining

Without a doubt, New York is the best restaurant town in the country. Other cities might have particular specialties—Paris has better bistros, Hong Kong better Chinese, Los Angeles better Mexican—but no culinary capital spans the globe as successfully as NYC.

The sheer variety is astounding. That's due in part to New York's vibrant immigrant mix. Let a newcomer arrive and see that his or her native foods aren't being served and *zap!*—there's a restaurant, cafe, or grocery to fill the void. Yet we New Yorkers can be fickle: One moment a restaurant is hot, the next it's passé. Do call ahead to see if it's still there!

But eating in New York ain't cheap. The primary cause? The high rents, which are reflected in your tab. Wherever you're from, New York's restaurants will seem *expensive*. Yet as you peruse this chapter, you'll see that values abound—especially if you eat ethnic and venture beyond tourist zones into the neighborhoods where real New Yorkers eat, such as Chinatown, the Upper West Side, and the East Village. But even if you're not venturing beyond Times Square, I've included inexpensive restaurants in every neighborhood.

RESERVATIONS Reservations are always a good idea, and a virtual necessity if your party consists of more than two people. Do yourself a favor and make them, so you won't be disappointed. If you're booking dinner on a weekend night, call a few days to a week in advance; even further in advance never hurts, especially if you're set on a certain dining hour.

But lots of restaurants, especially at the affordable end of the spectrum, don't take reservations. One of the ways they're able to keep prices down is by packing people in as quickly as possible. This means that the best cheap and mid-priced restaurants often have a wait. Your best bet is to go early or late. Often, you can get in more quickly on a weeknight. Or go knowing that you'll have to wait; there are worse things than sipping a glass of wine or a margarita at the bar.

THE LOWDOWN ON SMOKING With the exception of outdoor dining, New York City law prohibits smoking in any restaurant anywhere in the city.

TIPPING Tipping is easy in New York. Double the 8.625% sales tax and voilà! Happy waitperson. If you check your coat, leave a dollar per item for the checkroom attendant.

1 Restaurants by Cuisine

AFRICAN

La Marmite ✦ (Harlem, p. 180)

AMERICAN

All State Cafe (Upper West Side, p. 170)

Big Nick's Burger and Pizza Joint ✦ (Upper West Side, p. 171)

Bubby's ✦✦ (TriBeCa, Brooklyn, p. 136)

Burger Joint ✦ (Midtown West, p. 167)

Tips Money-Saving Dining Tips

1. **Book a room with a kitchenette.** This allows you to eat some meals in. Even if you only prepare breakfast, you'll save money this way.

2. **Stay at a hotel or bed-and-breakfast that includes breakfast.** And be sure to confirm that it's included before you book, because some city guesthouses keep rates down by not offering breakfast. Ask what's included; the offering will most likely be a limited continental breakfast.

3. **Use any coupons you can get your hands on.** The New York Convention & Visitors Bureau offers a free visitor's guide that includes coupons in the back. Even if you order one in advance, stop in at the local visitor centers, where the wall racks sometimes have coupons and advertisements for freebies, two-for-ones, and dining discounts.

4. **Eat ethnic.** New York probably has the best collection of ethnic restaurants in the country, and the best offer first-class eats for low, low prices. Chinatown is always a good bet for top-quality meals for a pittance, as are the restaurants on East 6th Street east of 2nd Avenue, known as Little India. Jewish delis are first-rate in Manhattan—and the pastrami can keep you fueled for days.

5. **During warm weather, picnic.** New York is full of marvelous delis, greenmarkets, and gourmet groceries where you can assemble a delicious, affordable meal. The city is rich with parks that serve as great picnic spots: Battery Park, Bryant Park, and Union Square—and perhaps best of all, Central Park.

6. **Eat street food.** Although dirty-water hot dogs and rock-hard pretzels still have their appeal, New York's street-food offerings have expanded considerably. You'll find vendors all over the city hawking soups, gyros, falafels, baked potatoes with a variety of toppings, fresh fruit, and more. The best vendors congregate in high-end business districts, such as around Rockefeller Center in Midtown (vendors often line up just off 6th Ave.; 50th St. is a hot corner) and in the Financial District. Sixth Avenue is lined with plazas where you can enjoy your alfresco lunch, and Lower Manhattan offers a wealth of even more pleasant open spaces. (See "Dining Alfresco in NYC [Who's Al Fresco?]" on p. 162.)

7. **Order the prix-fixe special.** Fixed-price specials that include appetizers, side dishes, and dessert (as well as beverages in some cases) will almost always get you more bang for your buck. Just one example: Diners willing to eat between 5 and 7pm can have three courses for just $14 at authentic French wine bar **Le Pere Pinard** ✪ (p. 142).

8. **Bring your own wine or beer.** Some restaurants, even those with their own wine lists, will let you bring your own if you call and ask. At press time, places that are BYOB include **Snack,** the **Zen Palate** in Union Square, **Afghan Kebab House,** and just about any restaurant in Little India; all these places are happy to open your bottle and provide glasses.

Chat 'n' Chew (Union Square,
p. 157)

Clinton St. Baking Co. ✺ (Lower
East Side, p. 142)

Corner Bistro (Greenwich Village,
p. 150)

EJ's Luncheonette (Greenwich
Village, Upper East Side, and
Upper West Side, p. 150)

Empire Diner (Chelsea, p. 154)

Fanelli's Cafe (SoHo, p. 144)

Good Enough to Eat ✺✺ (Upper
West Side, p. 174)

Gray's Papaya (Greenwich Village,
Upper East Side, and Upper
West Side, p. 153)

Joe Allen ✺✺ (Midtown West/
Times Square, p. 164)

Kitchenette (TriBeCa, p. 138)

Lyric Diner (Gramercy Park,
p. 157)

Nathan's Famous (Brooklyn,
p. 181)

Old Town Bar & Restaurant ✺
(Flatiron District, p. 157)

Papaya King (Times Square, Upper
East Side, and Harlem, p. 177)

Popover Cafe (Upper West Side,
p. 175)

Prime Burger (Midtown East,
p. 169)

Serendipity 3 ✺ (Upper East Side,
p. 177)

Tom's Restaurant (Upper West
Side, p. 176)

Vynl ✺ (Midtown West, p. 167)

Walker's ✺ (TriBeCa, p. 138)

ASIAN FUSION/PAN-ASIAN

Republic (Union Square, p. 158)

Rice ✺ (NoLita, p. 145)

Zen Palate ✺ (Union Square,
Midtown West, Upper West
Side, p. 158)

BELGIAN

Le Pain Quotidien ✺✺ (SoHo,
Flatiron District, Midtown East,
Upper East Side, and Upper
West Side, p. 144)

Petite Abeille (Chelsea, TriBeCa,
and Greenwich Village, p. 155)

BRAZILIAN

Rice 'n' Beans (Midtown West,
p. 165)

BRITISH

A Salt & Battery (Greenwich Village and East Village, p. 149)

Christer's (Midtown East, p. 169)

Tea & Sympathy (Greenwich
Village, p. 153)

CHINESE

Big Wong King ✺ (Chinatown,
p. 139)

Flor de Mayo (Upper West Side,
p. 174)

Funky Broome ✺ (Chinatown,
p. 139)

Grand Sichuan International ✺
(Chelsea and Midtown West,
p. 154)

Joe's Shanghai ✺ (Chinatown and
Midtown West, p. 139)

New York Noodletown ✺✺
(Chinatown, p. 139)

Sweet-n-Tart Cafe (Chinatown,
p. 140)

FILIPPINO

Ihawan (Queens, p. 182)

FRENCH

Florent (Meat Packing District,
p. 150)

La Bonne Soupe ✺ (Midtown
West, p. 164)

Le Pain Quotidien ✺✺ (SoHo,
Flatiron District, Midtown
East, Upper East Side, and
Upper West Side, p. 144)

Le Pere Pinard ✺ (Lower East
Side, p. 142)

Le Zinc ✺✺✺ (TriBeCa,
p. 138)

Pigalle ✺ (Midtown West,
p. 165)

Rue des Crepes ✺ (Chelsea,
p. 155)

GERMAN

Hallo! Berlin ✺ (Midtown West,
p. 163)

Knödel (Midtown East, p. 169)

GOURMET SANDWICHES/ CAFE/TAKEOUT

Absolute Bagels (Upper West Side, p. 171)

Amy's Bread (Midtown West, Chelsea, and Upper East Side, p. 168)

Caffé Roma ⚘ (Little Italy, p. 141)

Dean & Deluca (Greenwich Village, SoHo, and Midtown West, p. 168)

Eisenberg's Coffee Shop (Flatiron District, p. 157)

Ess-A-Bagel (Midtown East, p. 171)

F&B ⚘ (Chelsea, p. 154)

Ferrara (Little Italy, p. 141)

H&H Bagels ⚘ (Upper West Side, Midtown West, and Upper East Side, p. 171)

Housing Works Used Books Cafe ⚘ (SoHo, p. 146)

Hungarian Pastry Shop (Upper West Side, p. 176)

Island Burgers & Shakes (Midtown West, p. 163)

Junior's (Midtown East and Brooklyn, p. 169)

Le Pain Quotidien ⚘⚘ (SoHo, Flatiron District, Midtown East, Upper East Side, and Upper West Side, p. 144)

Little Pie Company (Chelsea and Midtown East, p. 155)

Mike's Take-Away (Midtown East, p. 169)

Murray's Bagels (Greenwich Village, p. 171)

P&W's Sandwich & More Shop (Upper West Side, p. 176)

Silver Moon Bakery (Upper West Side, p. 176)

Yura & Company (Upper East Side, p. 177)

GREEK

Snack (SoHo, p. 145)

Uncle Nick's (Midtown West, p. 166)

ICE CREAM

Brooklyn Ice Cream Factory ⚘ (Brooklyn, p. 156)

Chinatown Ice Cream Factory (Chinatown, p. 156)

Cold Stone Creamery (Upper East Side and Midtown West p. 156)

Custard Beach (Midtown East, p. 156)

Il Laboratorio del Gelato (Lower East Side, p. 156)

INDIAN

Bombay Dining (East Village, p. 147)

Cafe Spice Express (Midtown East, p. 169)

Curry in a Hurry ⚘ (Midtown East, p. 168)

Gandhi (East Village, p. 147)

Rose of India (East Village, p. 147)

Sonali (East Village, p. 147)

INTERNATIONAL

F&B ⚘ (Chelsea, p. 154)

ITALIAN

Bar Pitti ⚘ (Greenwich Village, p. 149)

Barocco to Go (Greenwich Village, p. 153)

Becco ⚘ (Midtown West, p. 162)

Bread ⚘ (NoLita, p. 142)

Bread Tribeca ⚘⚘ (TriBeCa, p. 136)

Celeste ⚘⚘ (Upper West Side, p. 174)

Cucina di Pesce (East Village, p. 147)

Dominick's (Bronx, p. 180)

Ferrara (Little Italy, p. 141)

Ferdinando's Focacceria ⚘ (Brooklyn, p. 181)

Frankie and Johnnies's Pine (Bronx, p. 181)

44 Southwest ⚘ (Midtown West, p. 163)

Frutti di Mare (East Village, p. 147)

Mario's Restaurant (Bronx, p. 180)

Nick's Family-Style Restaurant and Pizzeria 🍴 (Upper East Side, p. 176)

Via Emilia 🍴 (Flatiron District, p. 158)

JAPANESE

Go Sushi (Midtown East, Greenwich Village, and Midtown West, p. 168)

Jeollado (East Village, p. 147)

Katsu-Hama (Midtown East, p. 168)

Ony (Greenwich Village, p. 153)

Otafuku (East Village, p. 148)

Sandobe Sushi (East Village, p. 148)

Sapporo 🍴 (Midtown West/Times Square and East Village, p. 166)

JEWISH

Artie's Delicatessen (Upper West Side, p. 170)

Barney Greengrass, the Sturgeon King (Upper West Side, p. 171)

Carnegie Deli (Midtown West, p. 164)

Junior's (Midtown East and Brooklyn, p. 181)

Katz's Delicatessen 🍴🍴 (Lower East Side, p. 142)

Second Avenue Deli (East Village, p. 146)

Stage Deli (Midtown West, p. 164)

KOREAN

Jeollado (East Village, p. 147)

Mandoo Bar (Midtown West, p. 164)

Sandobe Sushi (East Village, p. 148)

LATIN AMERICAN/ CARIBBEAN

Cafe Habana (NoLita, p. 144)

Flor de Mayo 🍴 (Upper West Side, p. 174)

La Fonda Boricua 🍴 (Harlem, p. 179)

La Nacional 🍴 (Chelsea, p. 154)

La Pollada de Laura (Queens, p. 182)

Mojo 🍴🍴 (East Village, p. 148)

Rice 🍴 (NoLita and Brooklyn, p. 145)

MALAYSIAN

Nyonya 🍴 (Chinatown, p. 140)

MEXICAN/TEX-MEX

El Paso Taqueria 🍴 (Harlem, p. 178)

Noche Mexicana 🍴 (Upper West Side, p. 175)

MIDDLE EASTERN

Afghan Kebab House (Midtown West, p. 159)

Bereket 🍴 (Lower East Side, p. 141)

Moustache (Greenwich Village and East Village, p. 150)

PIZZA

Big Nick's Burger and Pizza Joint 🍴 (Upper West Side, p. 171)

Grimaldi's Pizzeria 🍴 (Brooklyn, p. 152)

John's Pizzeria (Times Square, Greenwich Village, and Upper East Side, p. 152)

Lil' Frankie's Pizza (East Village, p. 149)

Lombardi's (SoHo/Little Italy, p. 152)

Nick's Family-Style Restaurant and Pizzeria 🍴 (Upper East Side, p. 176)

Patsy's Pizzeria 🍴🍴 (Harlem, p. 152)

Pintaile's Pizza (Union Square and Upper East Side, p. 159)

Totonno's Pizzeria Napolitano (Upper East Side, p. 152)

Two Boots (East Village, Greenwich Village, and Midtown East, p. 169)

V&T Pizzeria (Upper West Side, p. 176)

SEAFOOD

New York Noodletown 🍴🍴 (Chinatown, p. 139)

SOUTHERN/SOUL FOOD/ BARBECUE

Acme Bar & Grill (NoHo, p. 146)

Amy Ruth's (Harlem, p. 156)

Blue Smoke ⍟ (Flatiron District, p. 178)

Charles' Southern Style Kitchen ⍟ (Harlem, p. 178)

Copeland's (Harlem, p. 178)

M&G Diner (Harlem, p. 178)

Miss Mamie's Spoonbread Too ⍟ (Harlem, p. 178)

Sylvia's (Harlem, p. 178)

Virgil's Real BBQ ⍟⍟ (Times Square, p. 167)

THAI

Arunee Thai (Queens, p. 182)

Siam Inn ⍟ (Midtown West, p. 166)

UKRAINIAN

Veselka ⍟ (East Village, p. 148)

VEGETARIAN/HEALTH-CONSCIOUS

Angelica Kitchen (East Village, p. 146)

The Pump (Murray Hill and Midtown West, p. 169)

Zen Palate ⍟ (Union Square, Midtown West, and Upper West Side, p. 158)

VIETNAMESE

Nha Trang ⍟ (Chinatown, p. 140)

Saigon Grill ⍟ (Upper West Side, p. 175)

2 TriBeCa

Bread Tribeca ⍟⍟ ITALIAN   Bread Tribeca is one of the few restaurants in New York to feature the cuisine of Italy's Liguria region. What is Ligurian cuisine? Seafood is a big part of it and Bread Tribeca does a good job with its *fritto misto,* a mixture of fried fish (such as calamari, cod, and mussels) and vegetables; and its *zuppa de pesce,* assorted seafood in a saffron-tomato sauce. Homemade pastas are another trademark of Ligurian food, and at Bread Tribeca you'll find pansotti, ravioli-like dumplings served with a walnut sauce; and fresh taglierini, a spaghetti-like pasta that was slightly overwhelmed by the dense combination of haricots verts, potatoes, and a surprisingly subtle pesto. A wood-burning oven turns out excellent thin-crust pizzas and roasted meats and, like its sister restaurant, the breads are superb, including a remarkable sardine, tomato, and peperoncini slathered on a baguette. Most of the tables are communal, so if the restaurant is crowded don't expect intimacy; and the 50-inch television above the bar that runs movies (when I was there last, *Chocolat*) is often a distraction, not a complement, to the food. On weekends, a DJ spins calming, low-key music to accompany the rustic food.

301 Church St. (at Walker St.). ⍟ **212/334-8282.** Reservations recommended. Main courses $13–$23 at dinner. AE, DC, DISC, MC, V. Daily 11:30am–7pm. Subway: A, C, or E to Canal St.

Bubby's ⍟⍟ AMERICAN   You might have to wait on line to eat at Bubby's. You might get squeezed into a table perilously close to another couple. And you might have to talk very loudly to carry on a conversation. But your level of discomfort will immediately subside as soon as you begin to consume Bubby's comfort food. Whether it is the slow-cooked pulled barbecue pork, the magnificent, lighter-than-air meatloaf, or the buttermilk-fried half chicken, coupled with sides like collard greens, sautéed spinach, macaroni and cheese, and baked beans, Bubby's dishes define comfort. Take Bubby's advice and save room for the desserts, especially the homemade pies; one taste of the chocolate peanut-butter pie immediately brought on happy childhood flashbacks. Breakfast is big here

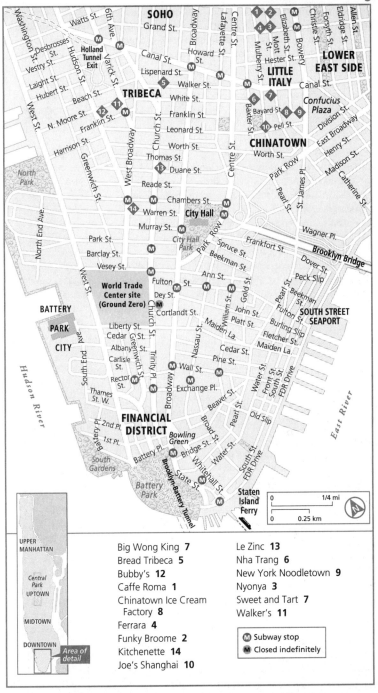

Big Wong King **7**
Bread Tribeca **5**
Bubby's **12**
Caffe Roma **1**
Chinatown Ice Cream
 Factory **8**
Ferrara **4**
Funky Broome **2**
Kitchenette **14**
Joe's Shanghai **10**

Le Zinc **13**
Nha Trang **6**
New York Noodletown **9**
Nyonya **3**
Sweet and Tart **7**
Walker's **11**

Ⓜ Subway stop
Ⓜ Closed indefinitely

and lasts well into the middle of the day. On weekends, though, here in trendy TriBeCa, the wait for brunch can be very lengthy. Celebrities need comfort too and you might spot one or two at Bubby's seeking anonymity and down-home chow. And now Bubby's has opened a branch across the river in the DUMBO neighborhood of Brooklyn.

120 Hudson St. (at N. Moore St.). (C) 212/219-0666. www.bubbys.com. Reservations recommended for dinner (not accepted for brunch). Main courses $2–$7 at breakfast, brunch, and lunch, $9–$19 at dinner. AE, DC, DISC, MC, V. Mon–Thurs 8am–11pm; Fri 8am–midnight; Sat 9am–4:30pm and 6pm–midnight; Sun 9am–10pm. Subway: 1 or 9 to Franklin St. Bubby's Brooklyn: 1 Main St. (at Water St.). (C) 718/222-0666. Subway: A or C to High St.; F to York St.

Kitchenette AMERICAN   This TriBeCa luncheonette has become a prime contender on the comfort-food circuit, thanks to Hungry Man–size breakfasts and just-like-home cooking. The little room has the feel of a New England diner, with folk art on the walls and country-rustic chairs at the tables. Expect high-cholesterol breakfasts and hearty salads and sandwiches. Weekly lunchtime blue-plate specials include shepherd's pie with mashed-potato crust on Tuesday and gooey four-cheese mac and cheese on Friday (specials are subject to change). Everything is well prepared and filling. Service is sit-down at breakfast, but lunch is more cafeteria-style, with orders taken at the counter.

80 W. Broadway (at Warren St.). (C) 212/267-6740. www.kitchenettenyc.com. Main courses $4.50–$7 at breakfast, $5.25–$9.25 at lunch and brunch, $9.50–$17 at dinner. AE ($20 minimum). Mon–Fri 7:30am–4:30pm; Sat–Sun 9am–4:30pm. Subway: 1, 2, 3, or 9 to Chambers St.

Le Zinc ★★★ *Value* FRENCH   The new restaurant from David and Karen Waltuck (the team behind glorious, big-ticket Chanterelle) is this affordable and authentic French bistro. Despite its TriBeCa address, Le Zinc is unfussy and unpretentious, boasting genuine warmth and creative bistro cuisine. The space is open and comfortable, with big, well-spaced tables, banquette seating, unframed art posters glazed into the walls, and soft, sexy lighting.

The menu features bistro favorites with gentle accents, some of which reach beyond France to Eastern Europe, Asia, and even New Orleans. Winning choices include a skate wing browned in butter and capers; Grandma Gaby's Hungarian stuffed cabbage; mussels in snail butter; an excellent duck, foie gras, and pistachio terrine from the charcuterie; rib steak and frites; and a thick, juicy bacon cheeseburger. Reservations aren't taken, but any wait is worth it—put yourself in the competent hands of the bartenders at the mahogany bar. The crowd is grown-up and easygoing. This is a real winner—and reason enough to visit TriBeCa.

139 Duane St. (btwn W. Broadway and Church St.). (C) 212/513-0001. www.lezincnyc.com. Reservations not accepted. Main courses $3–$7 at breakfast, $7–$16 at lunch, $10–$21 at dinner. AE, DISC, MC, V. Sun–Thurs 8am–1am; Fri–Sat 8am–3am. Subway: 1, 2, 3, or 9 to Chambers St.

Walker's ★ AMERICAN   Down-to-earth as ever, Walker's is an old holdout from pre-fabulous TriBeCa. The space is charming, with a tin ceiling, a long wooden bar, oldies on the sound system, friendly bartenders, cozy tables, and low prices. The meat-and-potatoes fare includes an 8-ounce sirloin burger, a delicious grilled rib-eye, and well-roasted organic chicken with mashies among an extensive list of entrees and specials, plus crisp, fresh salads. The fried oysters with Cajun aioli make a great starter. Low lighting sets a nice dinnertime mood, and service is friendly and attentive enough, as long as you're not in a hurry.

16 N. Moore St. (at Varick St.). (C) 212/941-0142. Reservations accepted for dinner. Main courses $8–$15 at dinner. AE, DC, DISC, MC, V. Daily noon–1am (bar usually open to 4am). Subway: 1 or 9 to Franklin St.; 2 or 3 to Chambers St.

3 Chinatown & Little Italy

Big Wong King ⭐ CHINESE   Last year, Big Wong was called New Big Wong; this year they want to be called Big Wong King. No matter. They will always be Big Wong and that's a good thing. Why mess with success? For over 30 years, Big Wong has been an institution for workers from the nearby courthouses and Chinese families who come to feast on *congee* (rice porridge) and fried crullers for breakfast. They come not only for the congee, but the superb roasted meats, the pork and duck seen hanging in the window, the comforting noodle soups, and the terrific barbecued ribs. This is simple, down-home Cantonese food—lo mein, chow fun, bok choy in oyster sauce—cooked lovingly, and so very cheap. If you don't mind sharing a table, Big Wong is a must at any time of day.

67 Mott St. (btwn Canal and Bayard sts.). ℂ 212/964-0540. Appetizers $1.50–$5; congee $1.50–$6; soups $3–$5; Cantonese noodles $5.25–$11. No credit cards. Daily 8:30am–9pm. Subway: N, R, or 6 to Canal St.

Funky Broome ⭐ CHINESE   This neon-bright Chinese joint straddles the NoLita/Chinatown border geographically and in attitude—and the crowd, a mix of hipsters and Chinese nationals, loves the fusion. The mind-set is evident in the playful decor and the mainly Cantonese menu. The kitchen keeps preparations authentic. You'll get traditional favorites like crispy intestines, duck tongues with chives, and smoked meats with jellyfish. Too traditional for ya? Not to worry, there are also the old standbys like sweet and sour chicken, and beef with snow peas. Last time I visited I tried the crispy squab. You'll need your chopsticks to pull off the meat from the tiny bird, especially if you want to pick its brain (yes, it's served with the head on). Now that's funky!

176 Mott St. (at Broome St.). ℂ 212/941-8628. Reservations accepted. Main courses $3.50–$16 (most less than $12). AE, MC, V. Sun–Thurs 11:30am–11pm; Fri–Sat 11:30am–midnight. Subway: 6 to Spring St.

Joe's Shanghai ⭐ CHINESE   Tucked away on a little side street off the Bowery is this Chinatown institution, which serves up authentic cuisine. The stars of the extensive menu are the soup dumplings, quivering steamed pockets filled with broth and your choice of pork or crab, accompanied by a side of seasoned soy. Listed as "steamed buns" (item nos. 1 and 2), these culinary marvels never disappoint. Neither does the rest of the Shanghai-inspired menu, which boasts such main courses as whole yellowfish bathed in spicy sauce; and an excellent "mock duck," a saucy bean-curd dish similar to Japanese *yuba* that's a hit with vegetarians and carnivores alike. The room is set mostly with round tables of 10 or so, and you'll be asked if you're willing to share. It's a great way to watch and learn from your neighbors (many of whom are Chinese), who are usually happy to tell you what they're eating. If you want a private table, expect a wait. ***Note:*** The Midtown location is geared more to Western diners, and is more expensive across the board, but it takes major credit cards.

9 Pell St. (btwn Bowery and Mott sts.). ℂ 212/233-8888. Reservations recommended for 10 or more. Main courses $4.25–$17. No credit cards. Daily 11am–11pm. Subway: N, R, Q, W, or 6 to Canal St.; F to Delancey St. Also at 24 W. 56th St. (btwn 5th and 6th aves.; ℂ 212/333-3868; subway: B or Q to 57th St.).

New York Noodletown ⭐⭐ CHINESE/SEAFOOD   So what if the fluorescent-lit room has all the ambience of a school cafeteria? This is my favorite Chinatown restaurant of the moment. If I'm in the vicinity, I'll always sit down for a bowl of chicken noodle soup, the broth a combination of seafood and chicken stock. Or I'll just settle for a mound of barbecued pork. Anything with shrimp here is a winner, especially the salt and pepper shrimp. The quick-woked Chinese broccoli or the crisp sautéed baby bok choy are great accompaniments.

Other special dishes are various sandy pot casseroles: hearty, flavorful affairs slow-simmered in clay vessels. New York Noodletown keeps very long hours, which makes it the best late-night bet in the neighborhood, too.

28½ Bowery (at Bayard St.). ✆ 212/349-0923. Reservations accepted. Main courses $4–$13. No credit cards. Daily 9am–3:30am. Subway: N, R, or 6 to Canal St.

Nha Trang ⭐ VIETNAMESE   The decor may be standard-issue, Chinatown (glass-topped tables, linoleum floors, mirrored walls), but this friendly, bustling place serves up the best Vietnamese fare in Chinatown. A plate of six crispy, fin-ger-size spring rolls is a nice way to start; the slightly spicy pork-and-shrimp fill-ing is offset by the wrapping of lettuce, cucumber, and mint. The *pho* noodle soup comes in a quart-size bowl brimming with bright vegetables and meats and seafood. But my favorite dish is the simple barbecued pork chops—sliced paper-thin, soaked in a soy/sugar cane marinade, and grilled to utter perfection. Every-thing is well prepared, though, and your waiter will be glad to help you design a meal to suit your tastes.

If there's a line and you don't want to wait, head a couple of blocks over to the nice second location, **Nha Trang Centre,** which accepts credit cards.

87 Baxter St. (btwn Canal and Bayard sts.). ✆ 212/233-5948. Reservations accepted. Main courses $4–$13. No credit cards. Daily 11am–9:30pm. Subway: N, R, or 6 to Canal St. Also at 148 Centre St. (at Walker St.; ✆ 212/941-9292; MC, V; subway: N, R, or 6 to Canal St.).

Nyonya ⭐ *(Finds* MALAYSIAN   You won't find many Malaysian restaurants in New York, but this is one of the best. This spacious, bustling restaurant designed like a South Asian Tiki hut offers efficient, friendly service, but it's the huge por-tions of exotic, spicy food that are the real treat. Coconut milk, curry, and chile-pepper-laden dishes are staples of Malaysian cuisine. The Malaysian national dish, *roti canai,* an Indian pancake with a curry-chicken dipping sauce, is out-standing. The noodle soups are meals in themselves; *prawn mee,* egg noodles, shredded pork, and large shrimp in a spicy shrimp broth was sinus-clearing, while the curry spareribs were spectacular. Even the drinks and desserts are exotic, including *sooi pooi* drink (sour plum) and *pulut hitam,* creamy black glutinous rice with coconut milk. But vegans beware: There's not much on the menu for you here; most dishes are prepared in either a meat or fish broth.

194 Grand St. (btwn Mulberry and Mott sts.). ✆ 212/334-3669. Appetizers $2.25–$8; noodle soups $4.25–$6; main dishes $5.25–$16. No credit cards. Sun–Thurs 11am–11:30pm; Fri–Sat 11am–midnight. Sub-way: 6 to Spring St.

Sweet-n-Tart Cafe *(Value* CHINESE   Supercheap, there's almost nothing over $6—and, considering the prices, the quality is stellar. Rarely is Chinese food described as airy and light, but this is, especially the noodle soups. The scallion pancake is beautifully seasoned, and the Taiwan-style salt-baked chicken, served

---

⟮ **Tips**   **Sweet, Not Sour**

To help cool my palate after a spicy Asian meal, one of my favorite stops in Chinatown is the **Chinatown Ice Cream Factory,** 65 Bayard St. (btwn Mott and Elizabeth sts.; ✆ 212/608-4170). The ice cream is made on the premises and is a contender for best in the city. But what separates the Chinatown Ice Cream Factory from the others are the Asian-inspired flavors such as ginger, mango, almond cookie, litchi, green tea, and the incredible red bean. If you have room after your Chinatown feast, don't miss it.

Espresso, Anyone?

With the encroachment of Chinatown upon what was formerly Little Italy north of Canal Street, the neighborhood made famous in movies like *The Godfather* has lost much of its appeal. More important, the quality restaurants are gone. Though there are still many Italian restaurants, especially along Mulberry Street, there are none I can recommend. Sadly, the street has become a tourist trap with waiters trying to lure customers off the streets by waving menus at them. I do recommend the appetizing combination of a dinner in Chinatown at an Asian restaurant followed by coffee and a pastry at one of Little Italy's *pasticcerias.* My favorite is **Caffé Roma** ☆, 385 Broome St., on the corner of Mulberry (✆ **212/226-8413**). The cannolis (try the chocolate-covered one) and tiramisu are spectacular. Open from 8am to midnight daily. Another you might try is **Ferrara,** 195 Grand St. (btwn Mott and Mulberry sts.; ✆ **212/226-6150**). Founded in 1892, the pasticceria claims to be America's first espresso bar. Cafe seating is available, so you can enjoy instant, sweet gratification. Open daily from 8am to midnight (to 1am on Sat).

---

on broth-soaked rice, is a don't-miss. There are plenty of familiar dishes—fried rice, lo mein, pan-fried dumplings, and the like—but this is also a good bet for adventurous diners who'd like to try something new, be it shredded jellyfish, chicken with sea cucumber, or broiled frog. Consider the quail eggs with lotus seed in a light, peppery broth. Sweet-n-Tart's specialty is *tong shui,* a broth or gelatin made with herbal, nut, or fruit essences. Served cold or hot, they're taken as invigorating medicinal tonics. You can have yours at any time during the meal, but I've found they offer a clean, fresh finish.

There's zero ambience, but it's pleasant enough, and the service is some of the best I've experienced in Chinatown. No alcohol is served, but the servers keep your glass filled with tea, and a juicer blends papaya and other fresh-fruit shakes.

76 Mott St. (just south of Canal St.). ✆ 212/334-8088. www.sweetntart.com. Reservations not accepted. Main courses $4–$10. No credit cards. Sun–Thurs 9am–11pm; Fri–Sat 9am–midnight. Subway: N, R, W, or 6 to Canal St.; F to E. Broadway. Also at 20 Mott St. (✆ 212/964-0380).

4 The Lower East Side

Bereket ☆ *Value* MIDDLE EASTERN This popular kabob house has undergone an expansion that more than doubled the number of tables and upgraded its hole-in-the-wall ambience to shiny diner-style decor—and the quality of their grilled meats is as excellent as ever. Order at the counter, where you'll see the kabobs displayed behind glass, waiting to hit the grill, and then snare a table as your plate is being prepared. The *kofte,* ground lamb with spices, is a favorite, but you won't go wrong with any of the choices. Complete dinners—two skewers of your choice, rice, and salad—are a steal for a 10 spot, especially the mixed grill, which features chicken, *shish* (beef), and *doner* (lamb) kabobs. Vegetarians have a lot to choose from, including excellently herbed hummus, falafel, great *piyaz* (white-bean salad with chopped onions and parsley), and babaganoush. Everything is freshly prepared in-house, and the counter staff is friendly and accommodating. No alcohol is served, but Turkish coffee should provide the necessary jolt.

187 E. Houston St. (at Orchard St.). ✆ 212/475-7700. Reservations not accepted. Main courses $3.50–$14. No credit cards. Daily 24 hr. Subway: F to 2nd Ave.

Clinton St. Baking Company ⭐ *Finds* AMERICAN   Though they are open all day, breakfast and desserts are best here. The blueberry pancakes with maple butter and the buttermilk-biscuit egg sandwich are worth braving the morning lines for, while the desserts, all homemade and topped with a scoop or two of ice cream from the Brooklyn Ice Cream factory, are good any time of day.

4 Clinton St., at Houston St. ℭ 646/602-6263. Main courses $7–$14. No credit cards. Mon–Sat 8am–11pm; Sun 10am–6pm. Subway: F or V to 2nd Ave.

Katz's Delicatessen ⭐⭐ *Value* JEWISH   Arguably the city's best Jewish deli. The motto is, "There's Nothing More New York than Katz's," and it's spot-on. Founded in 1888, this cavernous, brightly lit place is suitably *Noo Yawk,* with dill pickles, Dr. Brown's cream soda, and old-world attitude to spare. You are handed a ticket as you come in, and it's marked by the server for each item you buy; you can choose to sit in the waiter-serviced area, or grab a tray and stand in line to order your meal. (Tip the carver who prepares your sandwich and gives you a slice of whatever you've ordered on a small plate while he's at work.)

All of Katz's traditional eats are first-rate: matzo-ball and chicken-noodle soups, potato knishes, cheese blintzes, egg creams (made with Katz's very own seltzer), and all-beef hot dogs. There's no faulting the pastrami—smoked to perfection and piled high on rye—or the dry-cured roast beef, either. All of the well-stuffed sandwiches are substantially cheaper than you'll find at any other deli in town. What's more, Katz's is one of the only delis cool enough to let you split one with your travel partner without adding a bogus $2 to $3 "sharing" charge.

Note: A great New York souvenir is a Katz's T-shirt, admonishing the wearer to "Send a Salami to Your Boy in the Army!"

205 E. Houston St. (at Ludlow St.). ℭ 212/254-2246. Reservations not accepted. Sandwiches $2.15–$10; other main courses $5–$18. AE, MC, V ($20 minimum). Sun–Tues 8am–10pm; Wed–Thurs 8am–11pm; Fri–Sat 8am–2:30am. Subway: F to 2nd Ave.

Le Pere Pinard ⭐ *Finds* FRENCH   This authentic French wine bar and bistro is a charming slice of Le Marais, with high ceilings, burnished brick walls, well-spaced tables with mix-and-match chairs, and an authentic come-as-you-are air. Everything is well worn in a comfortable way. The kitchen specializes in the Gallic version of comfort food: steak frites, shell steak with Roquefort sauce, shepherd's pie with a delightfully cheesy crust, a terrific *brandade* (a dish of salt fish puréed with olive oil, milk, and garlic), and a charcuterie and cheese plate—the perfect match for the sublime crusty-on-the-outside, soft-in-the-middle bread that accompanies every meal. Greens are fresh and well prepared; even a simple mesclun salad wears a just-right vinaigrette.

There's a wonderful and affordable wine selection by the bottle, carafe, and glass. Service is attentive and easygoing. There's also a pleasant garden in warm weather. Attention diners happy to eat on the early side (before 7pm): The pre-theater meal is a stellar deal.

175 Ludlow St. (south of Houston St.). ℭ 212/777-4917. Reservations recommended. Main courses $12–$20; pre-theater menu daily 5–7pm, $14 for 3 courses. AE. Mon–Thurs 5pm–midnight; Fri 5pm–1am; Sat 11am–1am; Sun 11am–midnight. Subway: F to 2nd Ave.

5 SoHo & NoLita

Also consider **Lombardi's,** 32 Spring St. (btwn Mott and Mulberry sts.; ℭ 212/941-7994; see "Pizza New York Style" on p. 152).

Bread ⭐⭐ ITALIAN   The older, yet smaller sibling of Bread Tribeca (p. 136) does bread like no other sandwich shop. The bread at Bread comes from Balthazar

A Salt & Battery **9**
Acme Bar & Grill **12**
Angelica Kitchen **1**
Bereket **15**
Bombay Dining **7**
Bread **26**
Café Habana **27**
Clinton St. Baking
  Company **17**
Cucina de Pesce **11**
Dean & Deluca **22**

Fanelli's Café **20**
Gandhi **7**
Housing Works
  Used Books Café **19**
Jeollado **10**
Katz's Delicatessen **16**
Le Pain Quotidien **23**
Le Pere Pinard **18**
Lil' Frankie's Pizza **13**
Lombardi's Pizza **24**
Mojo **8**

Moustache **4**
Otafuku **6**
Rice **25**
Rose of India **7**
Sapporo East **3**
Second Avenue Deli **2**
Snack **21**
Sonali **7**
Two Boots **14**
Veselka **5**

Bakery down the street, but it's what they do with the bread that makes Bread so special. They take a rustic ciabatta loaf, slather it with, say, Sicilian sardines, Thai mayonnaise, tomato, and lettuce, and then press it in their very capable panini press. The result is a gooey convergence of flavors that you will attempt to gobble down. And when you do, the whole sandwich will fall apart. That's okay; someone will be along very shortly with more napkins. Besides the spectacular sardine sandwich, the Italian tuna with mesclun greens and tomatoes in a lemon dressing and the fontini with grilled zucchini, eggplant, arugula, and tomato in a balsamic vinaigrette are also standouts. Really there are no losers on the bread side of Bread's menu, which also includes salads, pastas, and "plates." The 32-seat restaurant is located in fashionably chic NoLita and if you are luck you might even be treated by the unusual sight of a breathtakingly thin model doing her best to keep the contents of one of Bread's sandwiches from staining her custom-made designer duds.

20 Spring St (btwn Mott and Elizabeth sts.). © 212/334-1015. Breads $7–$9; plates $6–$16. AE, DC, MC, V. Daily noon–midnight. Subway: 6 to Spring St.

Cafe Habana LATIN AMERICAN   This is a sleek update of a typical Hispanic luncheonette. It's hip without being the least bit pretentious, and what the food may lack in authenticity it more than makes up for in quality and flavor: Shrimps are big and hearty; pork is moist and flavorful; cilantro and other spices are fresh and aromatic. Winning starters include *pozole,* hominy corn stew with shredded chicken or pork in a clear broth that you season to taste with oregano, chile, and lime; and the hugely popular Mexican corn on the cob, which is skewered, coated with lime juice and grated cheese, sprinkled with chile powder, and grilled into a messy but sweet popcorny treat. Main courses include the ultramoist roast pork (perfect with a squeeze of lime) and *camarones al ajillo,* shrimp in spicy garlic sauce. Most everything comes with your choice of red or black beans and rice. Wine and a handful of Mexican beers are served, but I really enjoyed the not-too-sweet red hibiscus tea.

The room is narrow and tables are petite (especially those for two), but a middle aisle keeps the place from feeling too crowded, and service is easygoing and friendly. Don't be surprised if there's a wait for a table.

17 Prince St. (at Elizabeth St.). © 212/625-2001. Reservations not accepted. Main courses $5–$15. AE, MC, V. Daily 9am–midnight. Subway: B, D, F, or Q to Broadway/Lafayette St.; 6 to Spring St.

Fanelli's Cafe AMERICAN   Once upon a time, SoHo consisted of a few galleries, some artists living in loft space no one wanted, a few Italian bakeries, and Fanelli's. It couldn't be more different now: The galleries have given way to Banana Republic, the bakeries have moved over for Balthazar, and people pay millions for the lofts. Thankfully, Fanelli's remains. This is a classic New York pub, with a long bar propped up by regulars, and a corner door and pressed-tin ceiling that have locked in the 1847 atmosphere. The giant burgers are great, the pastas are fresh, and the beer is served in pint glasses. The daring will give the mussels a shot. Wine? House red. The Bloody Marys are a godsend for a hangover (white wine is the secret ingredient). If you're coming for dinner, especially on a weekend, your best bet is to arrive before 7pm, which is when the noise level really starts to escalate.

94 Prince St. (at Mercer St.). © 212/226-9412. Reservations not accepted. Main courses $6–$15 (most less than $12). AE, MC, V. Sun–Thurs 10am–12:30am; Fri–Sat 10am–1am. Subway: N or R to Prince St.

Le Pain Quotidien ★★ BELGIAN/FRENCH   This big, airy neoclassical-goes-farmhouse cafe (a Franco-Belgian transplant) is one of my favorites for a sophisticated casual meal at a bargain-basement price. Take a seat at a table for two or cozy up to one of the generous and comfy common tables (the one in the sunlit front room is best). The light menu is made up mostly of beautifully crafted sandwiches and salads. Excellent choices include the open-faced beef carpaccio sandwich dressed with basil, Parmesan, and virgin olive oil on dark country bread; Paris ham with three mustards on crusty French; and a board of fine French cheeses—brie, chavignol, Gruyère—and your choice of walnut bread, rye, wheat, or a crusty baguette. Salads are a particularly good value, because they come piled high and accompanied by a plate of French bread. Soups are homemade, hearty, and warming. Breads are baked five times daily in small batches to ensure freshness. Save room for the divine desserts—fruit tarts, pies, brownies, cookies, brioches—or stop by just for a sweet and a cappuccino. Tables are waiter-serviced, but an up-front counter serves walk-ins and takeout.

100 Grand St. (btwn Mercer and Greene sts.). ℂ 212/625-9009. www.painquotidien.com. Reservations not accepted. Breakfast $3–$7.50; sandwiches and salads $7.50–$18 (most less than $12). No credit cards. Daily 8am–7pm. Subway: N or R to Canal St. Also at ABC Carpet & Home, 38 E. 19th St. (btwn Broadway and Park Ave. S.; ℂ 212/673-7900; subway: 4, 5, 6, N, R, or L to 14th St./Union Square); 50 W. 72nd St. (btwn Columbus Ave. and Central Park W.; ℂ 212/712-9700; subway: B or C to 72nd St.); 833 Lexington Ave. (btwn 63rd and 64th sts.; ℂ 212/755-5810; subway: 4, 5, or 6 to 59th St., N or R to Lexington Ave.); 1336 1st Ave. (btwn 71st and 72nd sts.; ℂ 212/717-4800; subway: 6 to 68th St); 1131 Madison Ave. (btwn 84th and 85th sts.; ℂ 212/327-4900; subway: 4, 5, or 6 to 86th St.).

Rice 🍴 *Value* PAN-ASIAN/CARIBBEAN This sleek, but tiny restaurant has a cool Japanese vibe and a superaffordable seasonal menu built around—you guessed it—rice. You pick your grain from the seven options, which range from healthy brown to Bhutanese red or Thai black, and pair it with any 1 of 10 toppings. Vietnamese-grilled lemon-grass chicken goes well with either short-grain Japanese or sticky rice, while Jamaican jerk chicken wings is an ideal match for yellow rice and peas. Basmati is a must for the warm lentil salad or Indian curry. If you're just not sure, go with the pairing suggestions on the short but appealing menu. Thick Portuguese soup, flavored with potatoes and distinctive caraway-flavored rice, is a vegan's delight; it pairs up well with grilled eggplant maki or rice balls topped with tomato cumin sauce for a complete vegetarian meal for about $10. Rice bowls come small or large to suit your appetite, but all portions tend to be on the daintier side, so big appetites should order accordingly.

A takeout outlet is in the adjacent storefront and a second location opened in the DUMBO neighborhood of Brooklyn.

227 Mott St. (btwn Prince and Spring sts.). ℂ 212/226-5775. Reservations not accepted. Main courses $6–$13. No credit cards. Daily noon–midnight. Subway: 6 to Spring St. In Brooklyn: 81 Washington St. (btwn Front and York sts.; ℂ 718/222-9880; subway: F to York St.).

Snack GREEK It's hard to find quality Greek food at prices like these, but Snack does just that. Tables are tiny and seating is tight, but a tin ceiling, Art Nouveau light fixtures, and shelves lined with Greek grocery items transform the storefront dining room into a real charmer. Even with paper plates and plastic utensils, this place is atmospheric enough to enjoy a wallet-friendly date (you're welcome to BYO wine or beer). The menu is traditional Greek cooking, and the kitchen usually strikes gold. The *taramosalata* (carp roe dip) is the best I've had, and the *spanikopitakia* (spinach squares) come close. Dressed with fresh tomatoes, roasted red onions, and a roasted tomato aioli and served on fresh, crusty *ciabatta*, the braised lamb sandwich was terrific. If the wait is too long at lunch and the weather's nice, order to go and head down the block to the park, where chess tables and benches come in handy for alfresco dining.

105 Thompson St. (btwn Prince and Spring sts.). ℂ 212/925-1040. Reservations not accepted. Main courses $6–$14. No credit cards. Sun–Mon 11am–8:30pm; Tues–Sat 11am–10:30pm. Subway: C or E to Spring St.

QUICK BITES

If you need a coffee break, head to **Housing Works Used Books Cafe** 🎯, 126 Crosby St. (1 block east of Broadway), south of Houston Street (© **212/334-3324;** www.housingworksubc.com). This attractive and airy used-book shop (whose proceeds support AIDS charities) has a cafe that serves coffee and tea, salads, sandwiches, sweets, and other light bites. There are tables where you can pull up a chair, and you're welcome to read while you nosh. Beer and wine are served, and such events as readings and wine tastings are held in the evenings.

Dean & Deluca also has a walk-up cafe for coffee, sandwiches, and sweets at the front of their store at 560 Broadway, at Prince Street (© **212/431-1691**).

6 The East Village & NoHo

In addition to the choices below, a great choice for wallet-friendly Middle Eastern fare is **Moustache** (p. 150), at 265 E. 10th St. (btwn 1st Ave. and Ave. A; © **212/228-2022**). There's also an East Village branch of **Sapporo** 🎯 (p. 166) called **Sapporo East,** on the corner of 1st Avenue and 10th Street (© **212/ 260-1330**), with a good sushi bar in addition to the cheap-eats Japanese menu offered here and at the sushi-less Theater District location.

Additionally, a second location of British chippery **A Salt & Battery** (p. 149) is at 80 2nd Ave. (btwn 4th and 5th sts.; © **212/254-6610**). Also consider the kosher **Second Avenue Deli,** 156 2nd Ave., at 10th Street (© **212/677-0606**), for Jewish deli fare extraordinaire.

Acme Bar & Grill *Kids* SOUTHERN/BARBECUE   Acme's motto is AN OKAY PLACE TO EAT. This NoHo joint is divey in a pleasing way, with a good-natured staff, a Louisiana roadhouse theme, and the ambience of a well-worn neighborhood favorite. Acme serves up platters of Southern cooking and barbecue, including po' boys, crawfish, jambalaya, seafood gumbo, thick-cut pork chops, chicken-fried steak, baby back ribs—good, cheap, filling eats. Kids are welcome, and there are plenty of choices for them on the menu. The restaurant is a hot-sauce lover's delight, with dozens of bottles lining the walls. Fresh-baked corn bread starts the meal, and a range of beers is available.

9 Great Jones St. (at Lafayette St.). © **212/420-1934.** Reservations accepted for parties of 8 or more. Main courses $6–$14 at lunch, $7–$16 at dinner; fixed-price weekend brunch $10 (includes coffee and tea, plus juice, Bloody Mary, beer, or mimosa). AE, DC, DISC, MC, V. Mon–Thurs 11:30am–midnight; Fri–Sat 11am–1am; Sun 11am–11pm. Subway: 6 to Bleecker St.

Angelica Kitchen VEGETARIAN   This cheerful restaurant is serious about vegan cuisine. The kitchen prepares everything fresh daily; they guarantee at least 95% of all ingredients are organically grown. But good-for-you (and good-for-the-environment) doesn't have to mean boring—this is flavorful, beautifully prepared cuisine served in a country-kitchen-style setting. Salads spill over with sprouts and crisp veggies and are crowned with homemade dressings. The Dragon Bowls, a specialty, are heaping portions of rice, beans, tofu, and steamed vegetables. The daily specials feature the best of what's fresh and in season in such dishes as fiery three-bean chili, slow-simmered with sun-dried tomatoes and a blend of chile peppers; baked tempeh in a sourdough baguette dressed in mushroom gravy; and lemon-herb baked tofu layered with roasted vegetables and fresh pesto on mixed-grain bread. Breads and desserts are fresh-baked and similarly wholesome (and made without eggs, of course).

300 E. 12th St. (just east of 2nd Ave.). © **212/228-2909.** Reservations accepted for parties of 6 or more. Main courses $6–$15. No credit cards. Daily 11:30am–10:30pm. Subway: L, N, R, 4, 5, or 6 to 14th St./Union Square.

Cucina di Pesce *Value* ITALIAN   This crowded East Village stalwart—left over from the neighborhood's pretrendy days—is legendary for its value. It's charming, too, if a little loud. The focus is on old-world basics like lasagna, marinara-topped pasta, shrimp scampi, and veal Marsala. Every once in a while somebody in the kitchen goes too far with a shellfish-and-mollusk combo, but by and large the offerings satisfy. The wide selection of pastas (fettuccine primavera, linguine with clam sauce) is always fresh-made and properly sauced, the veal tender, and the calamari well seasoned and crisp. The great-meal/low-price combo means that the place can be a mob scene (so to speak), but free mussels marinara at the bar makes the wait easier to take. Try to snare a seat in the garden if the weather suits. As for wine, stick with the house red, or opt for beer instead.

Note: If the wait is too long, head across the street to **Frutti di Mare,** 84 E. 4th St., at 2nd Avenue (© 212/979-2034), which offers up basically the same schtick, minus the mussels at the bar.

87 E. 4th St. (btwn 2nd and 3rd aves.). © 212/260-6800. www.cucinadipesce.com. Main courses $8–$13 (specials may be slightly higher); 3-course pre-theater dinner with glass of wine $10 (daily 3–6:30pm). No credit cards. Daily 2:30pm–midnight. Subway: F to 2nd Ave.

Jeollado *Value* JAPANESE/KOREAN   Sushi chef Kirjin Kim expanded to this cavernous space, which he named after his South Korean hometown. Just like its plain-Jane sister, Sandobe Sushi, Jeollado offers one of the best price-to-quality ratios in the city for sushi lovers. Take it from this sushi hound: You'll pay significantly more—and wait just as long—for sushi of this quality anywhere else. The fresh fish is generously and expertly cut. The sushi combos are a good-value starting point; supplement with some sea-salty *edamame* (soybean pods) and one or two of the creative house rolls, such as the Hawaiian (ruby-red tuna and real crabmeat). The Korean side of the menu features Korean pancakes,

Dining Zone: Little India

East 6th Street, between 1st and 2nd avenues in the East Village, is better know as "Little India," thanks to the dozen or more Indian restaurants that line the block (subway: F to 2nd Ave.). Dining here isn't exactly high style, but the restaurants offer decent food at discount prices, sometimes accompanied by live sitar music. It's fun to grab a bottle of wine or a six-pack (many of Little India's restaurants don't serve alcohol, but even those that do will often let you bring in your own) and cruise the strip. In warm weather, each usually stations a hawker out front to convince you that theirs is *so* much better than the competition.

Some people speculate that there's one big kitchen behind East 6th, but a few of Little India's restaurants deserve special attention. **Bombay Dining,** 320 E. 6th St. (© 212/260-8229), is a standout, serving excellent *samosa* (vegetable-and-meat patties), *pakora* (banana fritters), and *papadum* (crispy bean wafers with coarse peppercorns). Also try **Gandhi,** 345 E. 6th St. (© 212/614-9718), for a touch of low-light romance; **Rose of India,** 308 E. 6th St. (© 212/533-5011), most notable for the pure spectacle of its every-day-is-Christmas decor; and my sentimental favorite, **Sonali,** 326 E. 6th St (© 212/505-7515), whose low, low prices kept me well fed during some very lean years.

teriyaki and noodle dishes, and *bibimbop* (spiced vegetables served over rice). Service can be slow, the room can get loud, and it's almost always packed, but the efficient servers turn the tables over quickly, and the payoff is worth it.

Note: If you're in the neighborhood, Kim's original no-decor **Sandobe Sushi,** 330 E. 11th St. (btwn 1st and 2nd aves.; © **212/780-0328**), still offers excellent sushi-meal deals at similarly low prices.

116 E. 4th St. (btwn 1st and 2nd aves.). © 212/260-7696. Reservations not accepted. Sushi rolls $3.40–$12; sushi combos $9.75–$18; nonsushi entrees $8–$15. No credit cards. Daily 5pm–1am. Subway: F to 2nd Ave.

Mojo (★★ (*Finds* LATIN   Austin Powers spent an entire movie searching for his elusive and indefinable "mojo." The Mojo in the East Village, though small, is not too hard to find, but it is indefinable. How do we describe a restaurant that features Latin ingredients and pairs them with Southern specialties, with outcomes like catfish with chipotle mayo, tacos filled with short ribs, hanger steak rubbed with chiles, grilled apple/blue cheese quesadilla with smoked bacon, or macaroni and cheese with oven-dried tomatoes and chorizo? Even the desserts, like the Mexican brownie with pecan graham crust and cinnamon ice cream, and the cocktails, like "Johnny's Mommy," a mix of Jack Daniels with ginger beer, reflect this unusual fusion. So do we call it Southern Latino cuisine? Why bother labeling it at all? The culinary creations at Mojo are not only original, but good enough to enrich your own elusive mojo. But arrive early or, with only 28 tables available, be prepared to dull the wait by experiencing numerous inventive cocktails.

309 E. 5th St. (btwn 1st and 2nd aves.). © 212/539-1515. www.mojony.com. Main courses $11–$19. AE, DC, MC, V. Sun–Wed 6–11pm; Thurs 6pm–midnight; Fri–Sat 6pm–2am; brunch Sat noon–4pm, Sun noon–10pm. Subway: F to 2nd Ave.; 6 to Astor Place.

Veselka (★ UKRAINIAN   Whenever the craving hits for hearty Eastern European fare at old-world prices, Veselka fits the bill with divine *pirogi* (small doughy envelopes filled with potatoes, cheese, or sauerkraut), *kasha varnishkes* (cracked buckwheat and noodles with mushroom sauce), stuffed cabbage, grilled Polish kielbasa, freshly made potato pancakes, and classic soups, like a sublime borscht. Breakfast is special here. The Christmas borscht, which hits the menu in early December and stays through January, is a simple but beautiful rendering of the Eastern European classic. But if all you want is a burger don't worry—it's a classic, too.

Despite the authentic fare, the diner is comfortable, modern, and appealing, with an artsy slant and house-made desserts. Regional beers from Ukraine and Poland and a nice selection of wines from California and South America add a sophisticated touch. No wonder Veselka surpasses its status as a popular after-hours hangout with club kids and other night owls to be a favorite at any hour.

144 2nd Ave. (at 9th St.). © 212/228-9682. Reservations not accepted. Main courses $5–$13. AE, DC, DISC, MC, V. Daily 24 hr. Subway: 6 to Astor Place.

QUICK BITES

Adventuresome diners should seek out **Otafuku,** 236 E. 9th St. btwn 2nd and 3rd aves.; © **212/353-8503**). Run by two Japanese women, this tiny takeout specializes in *okonomiyaki,* a Japanese pancake made with egg and flour, blended with shredded cabbage and either meat or seafood, then grilled on a hot plate and topped with a traditional sauce and curly dried bonito flakes. *Okonomiyaki* means, "cook what you like," and you can choose your ingredients: beef, pork, shrimp, or squid. It's a delicious, filling, and healthy one-dish meal that's also dirt cheap—I defy you to spend $10 here. There are no tables, but you can take your food to the Starbucks across 3rd Avenue, which has plenty of outdoor seating, or head to a bench in Union Square Park a few blocks north.

You'll find better-than-average, thin-crust pizza at **Lil' Frankie's Pizza,** 19 1st Ave. (btwn 1st and 2nd sts.; ℂ **212/420-4900**). Try the Sicilian with the salted anchovies; you'll never scorn an anchovy pizza again. If you like your pizza on the funky side, head to the original **Two Boots** , 37–45 Ave. A (btwn 2nd and 3rd sts.; ℂ **212/505-2276** or 212/254-1919; www.twoboots.com). The East Village location also boasts two entertainment spaces: The **Pioneer Theater** (ℂ **212/254-3300**), hosting indie films, and the **Den of Cin** at Two Boots Video (ℂ **212/254-1441**), a lounge hosting cult films, music, comedy, and other entertainment. Call or check the website for a schedule.

7 Greenwich Village & the Meat Packing District

In addition to the choices below, there's the ultrafresh, cheap **Go Sushi** (p. 168) at 3 Greenwich Ave. (6th Ave. at 8th St.; ℂ **212/366-9272**). There's also a branch of the Belgian **Petite Abeille** (p. 155) in the West Village at 466 Hudson St., at Barrow Street (ℂ **212/741-6479**), and another at 200 W. 14th St. (btwn 9th and 10th aves.; ℂ **212/727-1505**). The original, best **John's Pizzeria** is at 278 Bleecker St. (btwn 6th and 7th aves.; ℂ **212/243-1680**); see "Pizza New York Style" on p. 152. Two spinoffs from the popular Two Boots pizzerias can be found in Greenwich Village at **Two Boots to Go West,** 201 W. 11th St., at 7th Avenue (ℂ **212/633-9096**), or **Two Boots to Go-Go,** 74 Bleecker St., at Broadway (ℂ **212/777-1033**).

Also you'll find **Murray's Bagels** at 500 6th Ave. (btwn 12th and 13th sts.; ℂ **212/466-2830**); see "Bagel Power" on p. 171.

A Salt & Battery BRITISH   Adjacent to tearoom Tea & Sympathy (see below) and a shop selling Cadbury Flake bars, Hob Nob biscuits, and other English groceries and trinkets, this is this newest addition to Nicky Perry's burgeoning Pax Brittania. This shop is so genuine that they serve the goods wrapped in newspaper. Stick with the traditional varieties (halibut, cod) and you'll enjoy the real thing (crisp-battered outside, flaky and greaseless inside). The room is tiny, with no more than six or eight seats, so come at an off hour or be prepared to wait—but it's worth it. English beers are available, of course.

112 Greenwich Ave. (btwn 12th and 13th sts.). ℂ **212/691-2713.** www.asaltandbattery.com. Reservations not accepted. Main courses $5–$13. AE, MC, V. Daily noon–10pm. Subway: A, C, E, 1, 2, 3, or 9 to 14th St. Also at 80 2nd Ave. (btwn 4th and 5th sts.; ℂ **212/254-6610**; subway: F to 2nd Ave.).

Bar Pitti (Value ITALIAN   This indoor/outdoor trattoria is a hip sidewalk scene, and one of downtown's best dining bargains. Waiting for a table can be a chore, but all is forgiven once you take a seat, thanks to authentic, affordably priced cuisine and some of the friendliest waiters in town. Despite the packed seating, Bar Pitti wins you over with Italian charm—it's the kind of place where the waiter brings over the list of daily specials on a blackboard, and if you want more cheese, a block of Parmesan and a grater suddenly appear. Peruse the menu, but don't get your heart set on anything until you see the board, which boasts the best of what the kitchen has to offer; on my last visit, they wowed me with fabulous veal meatballs. Winners off the regular menu, which focuses heavily on pastas and panini, include excellent beef carpaccio; grilled country bread with prosciutto, garlic, and olive oil; and spinach-and-ricotta ravioli in a creamy sage and Parmesan sauce. The all-Italian wine list is high-priced compared to the menu, but you'll find a few good-value choices.

268 6th Ave. (btwn Bleecker and Houston sts.). © 212/982-3300. Reservations accepted for parties of 4 or more. Main courses $7.50–$16 (some specials may be higher). No credit cards. Daily noon–midnight. Subway: A, C, E, F, or V to W. 4th St. (use 3rd St. exit).

Corner Bistro AMERICAN   This old-time neighborhood bar serves up what some people (including *The Daily Show*'s Jon Stewart) consider to be the best burger in the city. Its well-charred, beefy burgers are deservedly famous—and you'd be hard-pressed to dine so well for so little anywhere else. The top of the line is the bistro burger, with bacon, cheese, lettuce, and tomato, for five bucks. The thin, crispy fries, served up on a paper plate, are an appropriate accompaniment. Head elsewhere if you want something besides a burger, because the other offerings are limited and halfhearted, except for the chili. Service can be slow, but why bother being in a rush at an atmospheric neighborhood locale like this?

331 W. 4th St. (at Jane St., near 8th Ave.). © 212/242-9502. Reservations not accepted. Burgers and sandwiches $2.50–$6. No credit cards. Mon–Sat 11am–3:30am; Sun noon–3:30am. Subway: A, C, or E to 14th St.

EJ's Luncheonette *(Kids* AMERICAN   This retro diner is popular with all Village types, including families, who come for hearty American fare in a 1950s setting—turquoise vinyl booths, formica tabletops, a soda fountain, and a lunch counter with stools that spin. Breakfast is king here, but there's also a terrific selection of burgers (including a veggie version), well-stuffed sandwiches, green salads, and main dishes such as meatloaf with mashed potatoes. Everything is better than you'd expect from a joint like this, and service is friendly. Don't miss the sweet-potato fries.

432 6th Ave. (btwn 9th and 10th sts.). © 212/473-5555. Reservations not accepted. Main courses $4–$12. AE. Sun–Thurs 8:30am–10:30pm; Fri–Sat 8:30am–11pm. Subway: A, B, C, D, E, F, or Q to W. 4th St. (use 8th St. exit). Also at 447 Amsterdam Ave. (btwn 81st and 82nd sts.; © 212/873-3444; subway: 1 or 9 to 79th St.); 1271 3rd Ave. (at 73rd St.; © 212/472-0600; subway: 6 to 77th St.).

Florent *(Kids* FRENCH   In the heart of the Meat Packing District, Florent, the nearly 24-hour French bistro dressed up as a '50s-style diner, is a perennial hot spot no matter what the time of day; a children's menu makes this the perfect place to bring the kids for lunch or early dinner. But it's after the clubs close when the joint really jumps. Tables are tightly packed, almost uncomfortably so in some cases, but it's all part of the late-night festivities. This place has a real sense of humor (check out the menu boards above the bar) and a CD catalog full of the latest indie sounds, all adding to the hipster fun. The food's good, too: The grilled chicken with herbs and mustard sauce is a winner, moist and flavorful, as is the French onion soup crowned with melted Gruyère. There are always diner faves like burgers and chili in addition to Gallic standards like *moules frites* (mussels and fries), and the comfort food specialties such as chicken potpie make regular appearances. The fries are light, crispy, and addictive.

69 Gansevoort St. (2 blocks south of 14th St. and 1 block west of 9th Ave., btwn Greenwich and Washington sts.). © 212/989-5779. www.restaurantflorent.com. Reservations recommended for dinner. Main courses $4.50–$15 at brunch and lunch, $8–$21 at dinner (most less than $15); 2-course fixed-price lunches $8.25–$12; 3-course fixed-price dinner $19 before 7:30pm, $21 7:30pm–midnight. No credit cards. Mon–Thurs 9am–5am; Fri–Sun 24 hr. Subway: A, C, E, or L to 14th St.

Moustache *(Value* MIDDLE EASTERN   Moustache (pronounced moo-*stahsh*) is the sort of exotic neighborhood spot that's just right. On a side street in the West Village, this charming hole-in-the-wall boasts a Middle Eastern vibe and fare that's both palate-pleasing and wallet-friendly. Delicately seasoned

Greenwich Village Dining

W. 14th St. — W. 14th St.
W. 13th St. — W. 13th St.
Little W. 12th St. — W. 12th St.
Greenwich Ave. — W. 11th St.

MEAT-PACKING DISTRICT

Gansevoort St.
Horatio St.
Jane St.
W. 12th St.
Bethune St.
Bank St.

Hudson St.
Greenwich St.
Washington St.
West St.

Eighth Ave.
W. 4th St.
Seventh Ave.
Bleecker St.
W. 11th St.
Perry St.
Charles St.
W. 10th St.
Christopher St.

Waverly Pl.
Patchin Pl.

Sixth Ave. (Ave. of the Americas)
Fifth Ave.

W. 13th St.
W. 12th St.
W. 11th St.
W. 10th St.
W. 9th St.
W. 8th St.

Washington Sq. North
Washington Square Park
Washington Sq. South
W. 3rd St.

WEST VILLAGE
Grove St.
Bedford St.
Barrow St.
Jones St.
Cornelia St.
Commerce St.
Leroy St.
Carmine St.
Downing St.
Minetta La.
MacDougal St.
Bleecker St.
LaGuardia Pl.

Waverly Pl.
Washington Pl.
W. 4th St.

Barrow St.
Morton St.
Leroy St.
Clarkson St.
St. Luke's Pl.
W. Houston St.
King St.
Charlton St.
Vandam St.
Spring St.
Dominick St.
Broome St.

Greenwich St.
Washington St.
Hudson St.
Varick St.

Prince St.
Sullivan St.
Thompson St.
West Broadway

SOHO
Spring St.
Broome St.

Hudson River

Holland Tunnel
Holland Tunnel Entrance

Watts St.
Desbrosses St.
Vestry St.
Grand St.
Canal St.
Laight St.
N. Moore St.

TRIBECA

0 — 1/4 mi
0 — 0.25 km

Ⓜ Subway stop

MANHATTAN
Central Park
Area of detail

A Salt & Battery /
  Tea & Sympathy **3**
Barocco to Go **4**
Bar Pitti **13**
Corner Bistro **2**
Dean & Deluca Café **7**
E.J.'s Luncheonette **8**
Florent **1**
Go Sushi **9**

Gray's Papaya **10**
John's Pizza **12**
Moustache **14**
Murray's Bagels **6**
Ony **11**
Petite Abeille **15**
Two Boots to Go **5**

Pizza New York Style

Once the domain of countless first-rate pizzerias, Manhattan's pizza offerings have noticeably dropped in quality. The proliferation of Domino's Pizza, Pizza Hut, and other fast-food chains into the market have lowered pizza standards. Still, there is plenty of good pizza to be found. Don't be tempted by sad imitations; when it comes to pizza, search out the real deal. Here are some of the best.

Grimaldi's Pizzeria, 19 Old Fulton St. (btwn Front and Water sts.; ℂ **718/ 858-4300**). If you need incentive to walk across the Brooklyn Bridge, Grimaldi's, in Brooklyn Heights, easily provides it. In fact, the pizza is so good, made in a coal oven with a rich flavorful sauce and homemade mozzarella, you might run across the bridge to get to it. Be warned: It can get very crowded at dinnertime.

John's Pizzeria 🌟, 278 Bleecker St., near 7th Avenue South (ℂ **212/ 243-1680**). Since it expanded from this original location—there are now three outlets in the city—the once-gleaming luster of John's has faded slightly, but the pizza is still a cut above the rest. Thin-crusted, and out of a coal oven with the proper ratio of tomato sauce to cheese, John's pizza has a loyal following. Though the quality at all of the four locations is good, the original Bleecker Street location is the most romantic and my favorite. Also at 260 W. 44th St. (btwn Broadway and 8th Ave.; ℂ **212/391-1560**); and 408 E. 64th St. (btwn York and 1st aves.; ℂ **212/935-2895**).

Lombardi's, 32 Spring St. (btwn Mulberry and Mott sts.; ℂ **212/941- 7994**). Claiming to be New York's first "licensed" pizzeria, Lombardi's opened in 1905 and still uses a generations-old Neapolitan family pizza recipe. The coal oven kicks out perfectly cooked pies, some topped with pancetta, homemade sausage, and even fresh-shucked clams. It's hard to go wrong here no matter what tops the pizza. A garden in the back makes it even more inviting during warm weather.

Patsy's Pizzeria 🌟🌟, 2287 1st Ave. (btwn 117th and 118th sts.; ℂ **212/ 534-9783**). My favorite, and also the favorite of Frank Sinatra, who liked it so much he had pies flown out to him in Las Vegas. The coal oven has been burning since 1932 and though its neighborhood in East Harlem has had its ups and downs, the quality of pizza at Patsy's has never wavered. Try the marinara pizza, a pie with fresh marinara sauce but no cheese that's so good you won't miss the mozzarella. Unlike the other pizzerias mentioned here, you can order by the slice at Patsy's. Don't be fooled by imitators using Patsy's name; this is the original and the best.

Totonno's, 1524 Neptune Ave. (btwn W. 15th and W. 16th sts., Coney Island, Brooklyn; ℂ **718/372-8606**). This unassuming pizzeria has been at the same spot since 1924 and it makes pizzas almost exactly as it did 80 years ago—thin crust, fresh sauce, and mozzarella, and that's about it. Don't even think about asking for an exotic topping (and why would you?). Enjoy it in all its simple unadorned glory. Totonno's second branch, on the Upper East Side, 1544 2nd Ave. (btwn 80th and 81st sts; ℂ **212/327-2800**), opened about 10 years ago—go ahead and order the exotic toppings there, but for the real deal, go to Coney Island.

dishes bear little resemblance to the food at your average falafel joint. Expect subtly flavored hummus, tabbouleh, and spinach-chickpea-tomato salad (or a large plate of all three); oven-roasted "pitzas," thin, matzolike pita crusts topped with spicy minced lamb and other ingredients; and—best of all—homemade pita bread, which puts any of those store-bought Frisbees to shame. Moustache is hugely popular, so don't be surprised if there's a line—but it's worth the wait.

90 Bedford St. (btwn Barrow and Grove sts.). ✆ **212/229-2220.** Reservations not accepted. Main courses $5–$12. No credit cards. Daily noon–midnight (last order at 11pm). Subway: 1 or 9 to Christopher St. Also at 265 E. 10th St. (btwn 1st Ave. and Ave. A; ✆ **212/228-2022**; subway: L to 1st Ave.).

Ony JAPANESE   The specialty at this smart, stylish noodle shop is *menchanko,* a ramen-noodle soup served in a soy, miso, or tomato broth with your choice of fresh ingredients, from chicken and shrimp to tofu to kimchee and fresh vegetables—or all of the above. Menchanko arrives piping hot at your table in a large metal bowl, with both chopsticks and a ladle for easy sipping and slurping. A handful of other noodle dishes are also on hand, including udon bowls and cold soba (buckwheat) noodle dishes, plus a short sushi-roll menu— but this place is all about the noodles. The room is attractive and service professional. Pony up to the sleek noodle bar if you're in a hurry.

357 6th Ave. (btwn W. 4th St. and Washington Place). ✆ **212/414-8429.** www.ony.usa.com. Reservations not accepted. Noodle bowls $7.75–$9.75; sushi $4.50–$11. AE, MC, V. Daily 11am–1am. Subway: A, C, E, F, or V to W. 4th St. (use 3rd St. exit). Also at 158 W. 72nd St. (btwn Broadway/Columbus Ave.; ✆ **212/ 362-5531**; subway: 1, 2, 3, or 9 to 72nd St.).

Tea & Sympathy BRITISH   When Londoner Nicky Perry moved to New York, she was disappointed to find no proper British tearoom, so she opened her own. Tea & Sympathy seems transplanted wholesale from Greenwich or Highgate, complete with an oddball collection of creamers and teapots, snappy British waitstaff, and plenty of charm. Elbow room is at a minimum and the place is usually packed, but it's worth the squeeze for the full afternoon tea, which comes on a tiered tray with crust-off finger sandwiches like chicken salad and egg and watercress, scones with jam and Devonshire cream, and cakes and cookies for a sugary finish. The menu also features such traditional British comforts as shepherd's pie, bangers and mash, and a chicken-and-leek pie. Anglophiles line up for the Sunday dinner—roast beef and Yorkshire pudding, of course. For dessert, try the treacle pudding, ginger cake, or yummy sherry trifle.

108 Greenwich Ave. (btwn 12th and 13th sts.). ✆ **212/807-8329** or 212/989-9735. www.teaandsympathy newyork.com. Reservations not accepted. Main courses $5.50–$12 at lunch and brunch, $11–$17 at dinner; full afternoon tea $19 ($35 for 2). MC, V. Daily 11:30am–10pm. Subway: 1, 2, 3, 9, A, C, or E to 14th St.

QUICK BITES

There's a downtown location of Upper West Side classic **Gray's Papaya,** 402 6th Ave., at 8th Street (✆ **212/260-3532**). Hot dogs are just as cheap, but beware: Don't eat more than two. They're rather greasy.

Gourmet grocer **Dean & Deluca** has a cafe at 11th Street and University Place (✆ **212/473-1908**), a great stop for a sandwich or cafe au lait and pastry.

For very good Tuscan-style sandwiches and pastas, **Barocco to Go,** 94 Greenwich Avenue (btwn 11th and 12th sts.; ✆ **212/366-6110**), is a treat especially in warm weather when its charming garden is open.

8 Chelsea

Empire Diner *(Overrated)* AMERICAN   This throwback to the all-American diner looks like an Airstream camper plunked down on the corner. This classic joint boasts an Art Deco vibe, honest coffee, and great mashed potatoes. The food is diner fare: eggs, omelets, burgers, sandwiches, and a nice turkey platter. Frankly, I think it's overrated—you'll find better breakfast fare elsewhere—but there's no denying its status as a fixture on the late-night scene. If you want quiet, go early. If you want an eyeful, wait for the after-hours crowd; 1 to 3am offers the best people-watching. There's live music courtesy of a regular pianist. When the weather's warm, a pleasing sidewalk cafe appears, and the limited traffic this far West keeps the soot-and-fumes factor down.

210 10th Ave. (at 22nd St.). ✆ **212/243-2736.** Reservations not accepted. Main courses $9–$18. AE, DC, DISC, MC, V. Daily 24 hr. Subway: C or E to 23rd St.

F&B ✿ *(Finds)* INTERNATIONAL/GOURMET SANDWICHES   Budget-minded New Yorkers have rejoiced at the arrival of F&B, which serves a global menu of European street food (Danish and German hot dogs, Swedish meatballs, Belgian frites, New Orleans beignets) in a stylish powder-blue space. The signature dog comes in a variety of styles, from the Great Dane, a Danish dog dressed with rémoulade, roast onions, marinated cucumber slices, Danish mustard, and ketchup on a toasted bun; to Pups in a Blanket, minidogs in puff pastry served with honey mustard. A veggie dog is also available. The warm beignets come brushed with powdered sugar and your choice of dips, including chocolate, maple syrup, and crème anglaise. The twice-cooked frites come accompanied with your choice of a range of flavored butters, oils, and dips, including a tangy garlic aioli. You can wash it down with Belgian-style beers, ciders, wine, even champagne. Delivery is available if you're staying in the area.

269 W. 23rd St. (btwn 7th and 8th aves.). ✆ **646/486-4441.** Reservations not accepted. Main courses $1.50–$10. AE, MC, V. Daily 11am–11pm. Subway: C or E to 23rd St.

Grand Sichuan International ✿ *(Value)* CHINESE   Finally, a Szechuan restaurant that doesn't alter its standards to appease those with an aversion to the heat of chile peppers. The food here is intensely spiced, the way Szechuan food should be. And the heat does not compromise the flavors that remain complex and strong, especially in such top choices as Szechuan wontons in red oil, Chairman Mao's pork with chestnuts, and my favorite, boneless whole fish with pine nuts in a modified sweet-and-sour sauce. The house bean curd in spicy sauce is another winner and so hot it's best washed down with a cold beer.

229 9th Ave. (at 24th St.). ✆ **212/620-5200.** Reservations accepted for parties of 3 or more. Main courses $3.25–$14. AE, DC, MC, V. Daily 11:30am–11pm. Subway: C or E to 23rd St. Also at 745 9th Ave. (btwn 50th and 51st sts.; ✆ **212/582-2288;** subway: C or E to 50th St.).

La Nacional ✿ *(Finds)* LATIN AMERICAN   It's not easy finding the oldest Spanish restaurant in New York. In fact, the search for this unmarked restaurant on West 14th Street might get you a bit frustrated, but once you find it, your frustration will soon be rewarded. Founded in 1868 as a gathering spot for the Benevolent Spanish Society, La Nacional, a social club is a real hidden treat. At one time food was secondary to the company of Spanish expatriates who congregated here, filling the room with smoke and loud talk of Spanish politics and football. It was here where Gabriel Garcia Lorca spent countless hours documenting his New York City experience. The cigarette smoke is now gone replaced only by the smoke coming from the grill which turns out extremely tasty tapas like sardines, octopus, and shrimp. There is a somewhat formal dining room in the front while in the back, next to the open kitchen there are a few tables and televisions usually tuned to soccer matches. Come and share a bottle of Spanish wine and make a meal out of the tapas; the *albóndigas* (Spanish meatballs), *boquerones* (white anchovy filets) and the aforementioned octopus are my favorites, or order the restaurant's excellent paella. Tapas range from $4 to $9 while no entree is more than $18. In a ballroom on the second level, the club sponsors flamenco performances and dance lessons.

239 W. 14th St (btwn 7th and 8th aves.). © 212/243-9308. Tapas $4–$9; entrees $15–$18. Subway: A, C, or E to 14th St.; 1, 2, 3, or 9 to 14th St.

Petite Abeille BELGIAN   This delightful cafe serves Belgian fare to a loyal local crowd that returns each day for morning pastries, quiches, salads, sandwiches, and sweets. Start with a fresh-from-the-oven *pain au chocolat* or cream-cheese croissant, and return at lunch for a fresh-baked quiche; panini bread dressed with Black Forest ham, Swiss cheese, and pineapple; a beautiful niçoise salad; or a traditional Belgian dish like *les carbonnades à la Flamande,* a classic Belgian stew. In addition to a first-rate espresso bar, a full selection of Samantha and Looza Nectar juices are on hand.

107 W. 18th St. (at 6th Ave.). © 212/604-9350 or 212/367-9062. Main courses $5.25–$11 (most under $8). AE, MC, V. Mon–Fri 7am–7pm; Sat–Sun 9am–5pm. Subway: F to 14th St. Also at 400 W. 14th St. (btwn 9th and 10th aves.; © 212/727-1505; subway: A, C, or E to 14th St.); 466 Hudson St. (at Barrow St.; © 212/741-6479; subway: 1 or 9 to Christopher St.); 134 W. Broadway (btwn Duane and Thomas sts.; © 212/791-1360; subway: 1, 2, 3, or 9 to Chambers St.).

Rue des Crepes ⭐ *Value* FRENCH   Seldom do decor, quality, and service come together so well in such an affordable restaurant. Evoking a Parisian cafe with muraled walls, tiled floors, Art Nouveau lamps, and petite tables, the dining room is comfortable and romantic. The light-as-air buckwheat (and cholesterol-free) crepes are folded around a host of savory fillings, from classics like turkey and Brie to spicy Moroccan *merguez* sausage accompanied by white beans and roasted garlic. Vegetarian options are available, including homemade hummus and roasted veggies. Soups and salads are also served; sandwiches are made on fresh baguettes from Amy's Bread, and premade ones are ready to go in the takeout case. Dessert crepes come with your choice of fillings; my favorite is the "Sidewalk," a classic preparation with butter, sugar, lemon, and chocolate, but fresh-fruit and fat-free vanilla-cream options are on hand for waist-watchers. You'll order at the counter, but a server takes over from there. Beer and wine are available. *Money-saving tip:* Check the website for a 10%-off coupon.

104 8th Ave. (btwn 15th and 16th sts.). © 212/242-9900. www.ruedescrepes.com. Reservations not accepted. Main courses $6–$9. AE, MC, V. Sun–Thurs 11am–11pm; Fri–Sat 11am–1am. Subway: A, C, or E to 14th St.

QUICK BITES

At Chelsea Market, 75 9th Ave. (btwn 15th and 16th sts.), a second branch of **Amy's Bread** (© 212/462-4338; p. 168) has cafe tables where you can enjoy a light bite for breakfast or lunch.

There's also the wonderful **Little Pie Company** at 407 W. 14th St., west of 9th Avenue (© 212/414-2324), where you can sit at a table or pull up a stool at the counter and dig in to one of the classic pies and cakes, which many consider New York's best; the sour-cream apple is divine.

Ice-Cream Fever

It's an addiction. I have cravings almost daily that are satisfied only by a decadently sweet fix. Like so many others, I am an ice-cream junkie. But I am fortunate to live in New York, where I can fulfill this need with some of the finest quality stuff anywhere. If you suffer as I do, here are some of the city's best sources to help get you through the day.

Brooklyn Ice Cream Factory ⭐, Fulton Ferry Landing Pier, Brooklyn (📞 718/246-3963). The best ice cream in New York can be found right over the Brooklyn Bridge. Everything is freshly made, including the hot fudge for your sundae.

Chinatown Ice Cream Factory, 65 Bayard St. (btwn Mott and Elizabeth sts.; 📞 212/608-4170). In Chinatown, this is perfect after a spicy Chinese meal. The ice cream here features exotic Asian flavors like almond cookie, litchi, and an incredible green tea.

Custard Beach, 2 World Financial Center (📞 212/786-4707). This is the best soft ice cream I've had since my summers down the shore.

Il Laboratorio del Gelato, 95 Orchard St. (btwn Broome and Delancey sts.; 📞 212/343-9922; www.laboratoriodelgelato.com). Jon Snyder, the owner of this remarkable little ice-cream/gelato shop on the Lower East Side, creates sweet magic in his laboratory. I, for one, am willing to sacrifice in the name of science by taste-testing any of his new delicious concoctions.

Cold Stone Creamery, 253 W. 42nd St. (btwn 7th and 8th aves.; 📞 212/398-1882; www.coldstonecreamery.com), and 1651 2nd Ave. (at 86th St.; 📞 212/249-7080). This Arizona-based ice-cream franchise broke into the New York market in 2003 and I'm not complaining. No, the more options to satisfy my insatiable need, the better. At Cold Stone, or "Stone Cold" as I refer to them, the rich, "creamy" ice cream is mixed on a frozen granite stone and made into creations like "mud pie mojo," "coconut cream pie," and "our strawberry blonde."

9 The Flatiron District, Union Square & Gramercy Park

For baked goods and sandwiches and salads, try **Le Pain Quotidien** ⭐⭐ (p. 144) at ABC Carpet & Home, 38 E. 19th St. (btwn Broadway and Park Ave. S.; 📞 212/625-9009).

Blue Smoke ⭐ *(Finds* SOUTHERN/BARBECUE   Leave it to Danny Meyer, the impresario behind classic restaurants like the Union Square Café and the Gramercy Tavern, to create a restaurant where you can order a smoked bologna sandwich. For many, that might be a culinary risk; for Meyer, it is another triumph. The big chunk of smoked homemade bologna is nothing like what you used to throw between two slices of bread. Meyer claims that Blue Smoke was his effort to replicate the barbecue he grew up on in St. Louis. He even had a high-tech smoker built to slowly, lovingly cook the meats. The ribs come in three varieties: Memphis baby backs, salt and pepper dry-rubbed, and St. Louis spare ribs, all tender to the bone, with the St. Louis variety, glazed in a mild barbecue sauce, the clear winner. Though the meats are the attraction, the side dishes are as good as I've tasted anywhere, especially the collard greens, speckled with pieces of pork, and the slow-cooked green beans, oozing with flavor. The house Blue Smoke Ale is the perfect hearty complement to the rich food.

116 E. 27th St. (btwn Park and Lexington aves.). © 212/447-7733. www.bluesmoke.com. Reservations suggested. Main courses $10–$22. AE, DC, DISC, MC, V. Daily 11:30am–11pm; late-night menu Wed–Sat 11pm–1am. Subway: 6 to 28th St.

Chat 'n' Chew AMERICAN   Chat 'n' Chew is so down-homey it's on the brink of becoming a theme restaurant, but the chow's the real thing. Look for honey-dipped fried chicken, roast turkey with all the fixins, barbecue pork chops with skin-on mashed potatoes, and mac 'n' cheese as crispy on the outside as it is gooey on the inside. The only real misstep is the meatloaf, which is a disappointment. Weekend brunch sees such standards as oatmeal with brown sugar and omelets with honey-baked ham on the side. Portions are all large, service is snappy, and beer's available. Desserts are of the Duncan Hines layer-cake variety (is there any better?), and the soda fountain serves up everything from egg creams to Häagen-Dazs shakes. The crowd mainly consists of the young and hip (who can afford to throw caution to the wind when it comes to calories), but everyone will feel perfectly welcome.

10 E. 16th St. (btwn 5th Ave. and Union Sq. W.). © 212/243-1616. www.chatnchew.citysearch.com. Reservations not accepted. Sandwiches and salads $6–$11; main courses $7–$14. AE, MC, V. Mon–Fri 11:30am–midnight; Sat 10:30am–midnight; Sun 10:30am–11pm. Subway: L, N, R, Q, W, 4, 5, or 6 to 14th St./Union Square.

Eisenberg's Coffee Shop *(Finds* GOURMET SANDWICHES   Eisenberg's has always been, and remains, the real deal. This old-world luncheonette has been dishing up the same eggs/bacon/burgers/sandwiches since 1929, at pretty much the same prices—adjusted for inflation, of course, but still welcomingly wallet-friendly.

One of the best things about Eisenberg's is the folks who work there, some of whom have seemingly been there since the Eisenhower era. More likely than not, you'll be greeted with a growled "Hiya, sweetheart," or a gravelly "What'll it be, love?" Pony up to the long counter or nab one of the four or five tables and place your order. Is this the best tuna in town as often proclaimed? Decide for yourself. Or try the egg or chicken salad. Either way, you won't go wrong. Morning diners can choose from a number of egg dishes, including a Western omelet or pastrami and eggs. The egg cream—that frothy mix of milk, chocolate syrup, and real from-the-bottle seltzer—is a New York classic.

174 5th Ave. (at 22nd St.). © 212/675-5096. Reservations not accepted. Main courses $2.25–$7.25. No credit cards. Mon–Fri 6am–5pm; Sat 7:30am–4pm. Subway: N or R to 23rd St.

Lyric Diner AMERICAN   Want to know where the good diners are? Follow the cops. On the East Side, you'll find 'em at the Lyric, which dishes out good, straightforward diner fare in a clean, bright, well-lit space. Expect all the diner standards: hot open sandwiches, Monte Cristos and Reubens, burgers, and stuffed baked potatoes. Breakfast is served round the clock, of course.

283 3rd Ave. (at 22nd St.). © 212/213-2222. Reservations not accepted. Breakfast (served all day) $2.75–$11 (most less than $7); sandwiches and salads $2.25–$11; dinner $10–$18 (including soup or salad). AE, MC, V. Daily 24 hr. Subway: 6 to 23rd St.

Old Town Bar & Restaurant ⊛ AMERICAN   If you've watched TV at all over the last couple of decades, this place should look familiar: It was featured in the old *Late Night with David Letterman* intro, starred as Riff's Bar in *Mad About You,* and appeared in such movies as *The Devil's Own, Bullets Over Broadway,* and *The Last Days of Disco.* But this is no stage set—it's a genuine tin-ceilinged 19th-century bar serving up good pub grub, lots of beers on tap, and a sense of history. Sure, there are salads on the menu, but everybody comes for the burgers. Whether you go low-fat turkey or bacon-chili-cheddar, they're perfect every time. You have your choice of sides, but go with the shoestring fries. Other good choices include Buffalo wings, fiery bowls of chili with cheddar cheese and sour cream, and a Herculean Caesar salad slathered with mayo and topped with anchovies. Food comes up from the basement kitchen courtesy of ancient dumbwaiters behind the bar, where equally crusty bartenders would rather *not* make you a Cosmopolitan, thank you very much.

45 E. 18th St. (btwn Broadway and Park Ave. S.). © 212/529-6732. Reservations not accepted. Main courses $6–$12. AE, MC, V. Mon–Fri 11:30am–midnight; Sat–Sun 12:30pm–midnight. Subway: L, N, R, Q, W, 4, 5, or 6 to 14th St./Union Square.

Republic PAN-ASIAN   Proving once and for all that you don't have to sacrifice style for wallet-friendly prices, this chic noodle joint serves up affordable food in a neighborhood where it's getting harder to find an affordable meal. Cushionless, backless benches pulled up to pine-and-steel tables don't encourage lingering, but that's the point: This is the kind of place that knows how to make you feel happy and get you out the door quickly. The Chinese, Vietnamese, and Thai-inspired noodle menu attracts a stream of on-the-go customers. For a one-bowl meal, try the spicy coconut chicken (chicken slices in coconut milk, lime juice, lemon grass, and galangal) or spicy beef (rare beef with wheat noodles spiced with chiles, garlic, and lemon grass). Service is friendly. The long, curving bar is perfect for solitary diners in the daytime and during the early-dinner hour; later, it livens up with a crowd who come to enjoy such libations as the Sake Dragon (sake and Chambord) and Fuji apple Cosmopolitan.

37 Union Sq. W. (btwn 16th and 17th sts.). © 212/627-7172. Reservations accepted for parties of 10 or more. Main courses $7–$9. AE, DISC, MC, V. Sun–Wed 11:30am–11pm; Thurs–Sat 11:30am–11:30pm. Subway: L, N, R, Q, W, 4, 5, or 6 to 14th St./Union Square.

Via Emilia 🕏 *Value* ITALIAN   This candlelit, brick-walled trattoria is a haven for budget diners in the high-priced Park Avenue South area. The menu is simple but satisfying, with an emphasis on house-made pastas—as you might expect from a restaurant that emphasizes the cuisine of Emilia-Romagna. The specialty is tortellini; the *tortellini in brodo,* meat-stuffed tortellini in a chicken broth, is a great way to start your meal. Other starters include fresh-grilled squid or thin-sliced tenderloin carpaccio, served with shaved Parmesan and leafy arugula. There's not a dud among the pastas, all of which are oversize, none exceeding $12. There's also a handful of nonpasta entrees, including veal scaloppine in an aromatic sauce with diced asparagus, and the *cosciotto d'agnello,* a thinly sliced leg of lamb with mushrooms, cannelloni beans, and tomatoes, like a lighter, Italian cassoulet. Wines are well priced, too, and service is better than you'd expect at a restaurant this affordable.

240 Park Ave. S. (btwn 19th and 20th sts.). © 212/505-3072. Reservations not accepted. Main courses $7.50–$15. No credit cards. Mon–Sat 5–11pm. Subway: N, R, or 6 to 23rd St.

Zen Palate 🕏 PAN-ASIAN/VEGETARIAN   Zen Palate has adopted the healthy, less-is-more approach to Asian cuisine. Each location shares the same Japanese-influenced postmodern decor, with teak and patinated copper; the Union Square flagship is a standout, with a counter downstairs for on-the-run eaters and a warren of spare but attractive dining rooms upstairs, including some with Japanese-style seating.

Tofu is king here, but you're not limited to it. Stars on the wide-ranging menu include taro spring rolls and basil moo-shu rolls for something creative, as well as veggie dumplings and buns for a more traditional Asian choice. Despite the good-for-you approach, main courses such as Rose Petals (homemade soy pasta in a sweet rice-ginger sauce with garden vegetables) and Curry Supreme (with tofu, potatoes, and carrots) are very flavorful, and some will particularly appeal to spicy-food lovers. Even more affordable casual grazing dishes are served in the all-day gourmet shop downstairs. All in all, a good bet for health-minded diners.

And as an added attraction, you're welcome to BYOB with no corkage fee in the upstairs dining room at this location.

34 Union Sq. E. (at 16th St.). ℂ 212/614-9345. www.zenpalate.com. Reservations accepted. Main courses $7–$18 ($3–$8 in gourmet shop). AE, MC, V. Mon–Sat 11am–10:45pm; Sun noon–10:45pm. Subway: L, N, R, Q, W, 4, 5, or 6 to 14th St./Union Square. Also at 663 9th Ave. (at 46th St.; ℂ 212/582-1669; subway: A, C, or E to 42nd St.); 2170 Broadway (btwn 76th and 77th sts.; ℂ 212/501-7768; subway: 1 or 9 to 79th St.).

QUICK BITES

Pintaile's Pizza, 124 4th Ave. (btwn 12th and 13th sts.; ℂ **212/475-4977;** www.pintailespizza.com), dresses their crisp organic crusts with layers of plum tomatoes, extra-virgin olive oil, and other fresh ingredients. This new branch of the East Side favorite even has lots of seating for in-house eating.

From May through early November, Danny Meyer, of **Blue Smoke** (p. 156) and Gramercy Tavern, opens his **Shake Shack** in Madison Square Park at 24th Street, an old-fashioned roadside hot dog, hamburger and ice-cream shack. Grab a hot dog and shake and sit and watch the nonstop baby stroller parade.

10 Times Square & Midtown West

Check out the Asian-nouvelle vegetarian cuisine at **Zen Palate** (p. 158), at 663 9th Ave., at 46th Street (ℂ **212/582-1669). Joe's Shanghai** (p. 139) has a Midtown branch at 24 W. 56th St., west of 5th Avenue (ℂ **212/333-3868**), offering soup dumplings and other dishes—but expect to pay a bit more here than in Chinatown. An outpost of **Grand Sichuan International** (p. 154) dishes up killer Szechuan fare at 745 9th Ave. (btwn 50th and 51st sts.; ℂ **212/ 582-2288**). A branch of the ultrafresh, cheap eat-in/takeout sushi joint, **Go Sushi** (p. 168), is at 756 9th Ave., at 51st Street (ℂ **212/459-2288**).

For wraps and smoothies, healthy eaters will enjoy the all-natural eats at **The Pump** (p. 169), 40 W. 55th St. (btwn 5th and 6th aves.; ℂ **212/246-6844**), too. There is a very nice outlet of **John's Pizzeria** in Times Square, 260 W. 44th St. (btwn 7th and 8th aves.; ℂ **212/391-7560**); see "Pizza New York Style" on p. 152.

If you're over by the *Intrepid,* stop into the sister location of **H&H Bagels,** 639 W. 46th St., at 12th Avenue (ℂ **212/595-8000**), to sample incredible fresh-baked bagels; see "Bagel Power" on p. 171.

Afghan Kebab House *Value* MIDDLE EASTERN   You'll find Afghan Kebab Houses all over the city. Are they related? Who knows, but I like this one the best for heaping plates of first-rate Middle Eastern fare. Kabobs are the first order of business: All are pleasing, but my favorite is the *sultani,* chunks of ground lamb marinated in aromatic spices and broiled over wood charcoal with green peppers and tomatoes. The *tikka kebabs*—lamb and beef—are impressive, as is the chicken korma, slow-cooked with fresh onions, tomatoes, peppers, and

Midtown, Chelsea & Union Square Dining

Afghan Kebab House **5**
Amy's Bread **11, 24**
Becco **12**
Blue Smoke **37**
Burger Joint **48**
Carnegie Deli **1**
Chat 'n' Chew **29**
Cold Stone Creamery **20**
Curry in a Hurry **38**
Eisenberg's Coffee Shop **36**
Empire Diner **23**
Ess-A-Bagel **44**
F&B **22**
44 Southwest **16**
Go Sushi **6, 45**
Grand Central Terminal **41**
  Cafe Spice Express
  Christer's
  Junior's
  Knodel
  Little Pie Company
  Mike's Take Away
  Two Boots
Grand Sichuan
  International **8, 21**
H&H Bagels **14**
Hallo! Berlin **7, 15**
Island Burgers & Shakes **5**
Joe Allen **12**
Joe's Shanghai **47**
John's Pizza **17**
Katsu-Hama **42**
La Bonne Soupe **46**
Le Pain Quotidien **33**
La Nacional **27**
Little Pie Company **25**
Lyric Diner **35**
Mandoo Bar **40**
Old Town Bar
  & Restaurant **32**
Papaya King **19**
Petite Abeille **28**
Pigalle **10**
Prime Burger **43**
Republic **30**
Rice 'n' Beans **5**
Rue des Crepes **26**
Sapporo **9**
Siam Inn **4**
Stage Deli **3**
The Pump **39, 46**
Uncle Nick's **8**
Via Emelia **34**
Virgil's Real BBQ **18**
Vynl **2**
Zen Palate **13, 31**

fresh herbs. All plates come with amazingly aromatic brown Indian basmati rice and flat Afghan bread. The room is simple and well worn but evocative, with Oriental carpets serving as table runners, and service is attentive.

764 9th Ave. (btwn 51st and 52nd sts.). ℂ **212/307-1612** or 212/307-1629. Reservations accepted. Main courses $10–$16 (most less than $12). AE, DC, DISC, MC, V. Daily 11:30am–10:30pm. Subway: C or E to 50th St.

Becco ✪ *Finds* ITALIAN   If you're a fan of *Lidia's Italian-American Kitchen* on PBS, you'll be happy to know you can sample Lidia Bastianich's simple, hearty Italian cooking here. Becco, on Restaurant Row, is designed to serve her meals "at a different price point" (read: cheaper) than her East Side restaurant Felidia. The prices are not rock-bottom, but in terms of service, portions and quality, you get tremendous bang for your buck at Becco (which means to "peck, nibble, or savor something in a discriminating way." The main courses can head north of the $20 mark, but take a look at the prix-fixe menu for $17 at lunch, $22 at dinner, which includes either a Caesar salad or antipasto plate, followed

---

> *Tips* **Dining Alfresco in NYC (Who's Al Fresco?)**
>
> It started with a cart filled with hot dogs, sauerkraut, spicy onions, and mustard. Then the cart included warm pretzels and, when the weather turned cool, hot chestnuts. You could find these carts all over the city—providing sustenance for workers on lunch breaks or tourists who did not want to miss a minute of sightseeing. But hot dogs were not enough for New Yorkers who crave variety and enterprising immigrants began to sell foods from their homelands, most typically from the Middle East, Pakistan, India, and Israel. Carts where you could get excellent falafel emerged, or basmati rice and chicken, or grilled lamb shish kebab, or vegetable roti. Now, the fare sold from carts is like an international food festival.
>
> I can't predict or pinpoint where you might locate a particular cart, but the highest concentration of them can be found along 6th Avenue from 43rd to 50th streets. Most have no name—they are known only by the friendly men and women who work them. There are, however, a few that do have names that are quite good including **Kwik Meal,** specializing in halal food, or Muslim-approved food including lamb, chicken, falafel, and vegetables usually served on pita bread.
>
> On 46th Street the Kosher contingent sets up, including **Miriam's** on the west side of the street and **Moishe's** on the east side. Both make excellent falafel.
>
> On 50th Street, the carts line the west side of the street including one for tacos, more falafel, and the newest addition, **Daisy Mae's BBQ.** At Daisy Mae's, you can sample slow-cooked pulled pork, chopped beef, or some of the best Texas chili I've sampled in the city.
>
> Most street-cart food will set you back around $5 and you'll be hard pressed to spend more than $10. If the weather's good, find a seat around the fountains or promenades of the office buildings that surround the area and take in some sun like the people around you on their breaks.

by a "Symphony of Pasta," unlimited servings of the three fresh-made daily pastas. There's also an excellent selection of Italian wines at $20 a bottle. If you can't make up your mind about dessert, have them all: a tasting plate includes gelato, cheesecake, and whatever else the dessert chef has whipped up that day. Lidia herself does turn up at Becco and Felidia regularly; you can even "Dine with Lidia" (see website for details).

345 W. 46th St. (btwn 8th and 9th aves.). © 212/387-7597. www.becconyc.com. Reservations recommended. Main courses lunch $13–$25, dinner $19–$28. AE, DC, DISC, MC, V. Mon–Tues and Thurs–Fri noon–3pm; Wed 11:30am–3pm; Sat 11:30am–2:30pm; Mon 5–10pm; Tues–Wed 4:30pm–midnight; Thurs–Fri 5pm–midnight; Sat 4pm–midnight; Sun noon–10pm.

44 Southwest 🌟 *Finds* ITALIAN   This mom-and-pop restaurant serves up the best Italian food in Midtown for the money. It's simple but charming, with an original tin ceiling, red-checkered tablecloths, and soft lighting; the result is a romantic first-date ambience (very *Lady and the Tramp* sharing spaghetti). The dishes are generously portioned and very satisfying. Pastas are perfectly al dente; I especially love the thick and hearty meat sauce on the linguine Bolognese. The chicken Parmesan is classically yummy, and personal pizzas arrive with wonderfully chewy crusts. The wine list is affordable and the service attentive, making 44 Southwest a winner on all fronts for wallet-watching visitors.

621 9th Ave. (at 44th St.). © 212/315-4582 or 212/315-4681. Reservations accepted (recommended for pre-theater dining). Main courses $8–$14. AE, MC, V. Sun–Thurs noon–11pm; Fri–Sat noon–midnight. Subway: A, C, or E to 42nd St.

Hallo! Berlin 🌟 GERMAN   Hallo! Berlin bills itself as "New York's Wurst Restaurant"—and indeed it is. If wurst is best in your book, don't miss it. Hallo! Berlin is straight outta Deutschland, serving up eight varieties of sausage, from boiled beef-and-pork knockwurst to pan-fried veal Bavarian wurst and beef currywurst. Sandwiches come with all the fixings, including red cabbage, sauerkraut, onions, and mustard, but I prefer the combo, which lets me choose two kinds of sausage (substitute spaetzle for German fries for maximum satisfaction). There's also a terrific Wiener schnitzel. The potato pancakes make a great starter; one generous order is enough for a few friends to share. A big bowl of lentil, split pea, or potato soup with cut-up wurst and bread and butter makes a satisfying lunch for just $5. The main location is petite and pleasant, with efficient table service and a couple of taps pouring German brews, while the 10th Avenue location is a full-scale beer hall well equipped for larger parties (and a back patio which you can enjoy in the warm weather).

402 W. 51st St. (just west of 9th Ave.). © 212/541-6248. Reservations not accepted. Sandwiches $3–$3.75; main courses (with soup) $6.50–$15; lunch specials (until 5pm) $5.25–$6.50. MC, V. Mon–Sat 11am–11pm; Sun 4–11pm. Subway: C or E to 50th St. Also at 626 10th Ave. (at 44th St.; © 212/977-1944; subway: A, C, or E to 42nd St./Port Authority).

Island Burgers & Shakes GOURMET SANDWICHES   This aisle-size diner glows with the wild colors of a California surf shop. Service is minimal and tables are tiny, but the food is top-notch. A small selection of sandwiches and salads are on hand, but as the name implies, folks come here for the Goliath-size burgers—either beef hamburgers or, the specialty of the house, *churrascos* (flattened grilled chicken breasts). Innovation strikes with the more than 40 topping combinations. Though Island Burgers doesn't serve fries, they do have very tasty "dirty" potato chips.

766 9th Ave. (btwn 51st and 52nd sts.). © 212/307-7934. www.island.citysearch.com. Reservations not accepted. Sandwiches and salads $6.50–$9. No credit cards. Sun–Thurs noon–10:30pm; Fri–Sat noon–11:30pm. Subway: C or E to 50th St.

Tips **The Midtown Deli News**

If you're in Midtown and looking for one of the Big Apple's quintessential delis, head to the **Stage Deli**, 834 7th Ave. (btwn 53rd and 54th sts.; © **212/ 245-7850**; www.stagedeli.com), known for its celebrity sandwiches, from the Joe DiMaggio (corned beef, pastrami, chopped liver, and Bermuda onion) to the Julia Roberts (chicken salad, hard-boiled egg, lettuce, and tomato); or the **Carnegie Deli**, 854 7th Ave., at 55th Street (© **212/757- 2245**; www.carnegiedeli.com), for pastrami, corned beef, and cheesecake. *Note:* These landmarks specialize in tourist-target pricing, with sandwiches coming in between $12 and $20. You get your money's worth—they're more than most mortals can consume in one sitting—but you'll be charged $2 to $3 to split one with your travel partner. Head down to **Katz's** ✰✰ (p. 142) or up to **Barney Greengrass** (p. 171) for less touristy, less expensive deli experiences.

Joe Allen ✰✰ AMERICAN   This Restaurant Row pub is a glorious throwback to yesteryear, when theater types went to places like Sardi's and Lüchow's— and yep, Joe Allen. Joe Allen is still going strong; don't be surprised if you spot a stage star or two. The straightforward pub food is reliable and well priced, and served at big, comfortable tables (the kind that restaurant managers don't order anymore because they take up too much room) covered with red-checked cloths. The meatloaf is terrific, but you can't go wrong with the chili, the Greek salad, the burgers, or anything that comes with mashed potatoes. More than 30 beers are available, and some good wines by the glass. The staff is a congenial and neighborhood-appropriate mix of career waiters and aspiring thespians. You'll enjoy perusing the walls covered with posters and other memorabilia from legendary Broadway flops.

326 W. 46th St. (btwn 8th and 9th aves.). © **212/581-6464**. Reservations recommended (a must for pre-theater dining). Main courses $9–$22 (most less than $17). MC, V. Mon–Tues and Thurs–Fri noon–11:45pm; Wed and Sat–Sun 11:30am–11:45pm. Subway: A, C, or E to 42nd St./Port Authority.

La Bonne Soupe ✰ *Kids* FRENCH   This slice of Paris has been around forever, and for gourmet at good prices, it's still hard to beat it. You'll even see French natives elbow-to-elbow in the newly renovated dining room. "Les bonnes soupes" are satisfying noontime meals of salad, bread, a big bowl of soup (mushroom and barley with lamb is a favorite), dessert (chocolate mousse, crème caramel, or ice cream), and wine or coffee—a great bargain at just $14. The menu also features entree-size salads (including a good niçoise), burgers, and bistro fare like omelets, quiche Lorraine, croque monsieur, and fancier fare like steak frites and filet mignon *au poivre*. Rounding out the menu are French fondues: Emmethal cheese, beef, and creamy chocolate to finish off the meal; the silky-smooth chocolate mousse is yummy. A kids' menu is available, offering a burger or chicken and fries, plus dessert, for $10. Bon appétit!

48 W. 55th St. (btwn 5th and 6th aves.). © **212/586-7650**. www.labonnesoupe.com. Reservations recommended for parties of 3 or more. Main courses $9–$19 (most less than $15); "les bonnes soupes" fixed price $14; 3-course fixed price $20 at lunch and dinner. AE, DC, MC, V. Mon–Sat 11:30am–midnight; Sun 11:30am–11pm. Subway: E or F to 5th Ave.; B or Q to 57th St.

Mandoo Bar *Finds* KOREAN   The heart of Manhattan's Koreatown is 32nd Street between 5th and 6th avenues—and the number of Korean restaurants on that 1 block is dizzying. You'll know you've found Mandoo Bar when you see the two women in the window lovingly rolling and stuffing fresh *mandoo* (Korean for dumpling). Because of the constant preparation, the dumplings, stuffed with a variety of ingredients, are incredibly fresh. There's the Mool Mandoo (basic white dumplings filled with pork and vegetables), the Kimchee Mandoo (steamed dumplings stuffed with potent kimchi [Korean spiced cabbage], tofu, pork, and vegetables), the green Vegetable Mool Mandoo (boiled dumplings filled with mixed vegetables), and the Goon Mandoo (pan-fried dumplings filled with pork and vegetables). You really can't go wrong with any of these dumplings, so sample them all with a Combo Mandoo. Soups are also special here; try the beef noodle in a spicy, sinus-clearing broth. With seating that is nothing more than wooden benches, Mandoo Bar is better suited for quick eats rather than a lingering meal—a perfect lunch break from shopping in Herald Square or visiting the nearby Empire State Building.

2 W. 32nd St. (just west of 5th Ave.). ℂ 212/279-3075. Reservations not accepted. Main courses $6–$14. AE, DC, MC, V. Daily 11:30am–11pm. Subway: B, D, F, N, Q, R, V, or W to 34th St./Herald Square. Also at 71 University Place (btwn 10th and 11th sts.; ℂ **212/358-0400**; subway: N, R, W, Q, 4, 5, 6, or L to 14th St./Union Square).

Pigalle ⭐ FRENCH   This brasserie is a wonderful Theater District choice, thanks to its winning combination of high-quality fare, low prices, and location—not to mention 24-hour service that makes it the best place to satisfy post-anything munchies. The beautifully designed room by Nancy Mah boasts all the trimmings of a traditional brasserie—zinc-topped bar, colorful rattan, soft ocher lighting—with a designer edge. The room is big, airy, and comfortable, great for couples and larger parties alike. The menu offers true-to-form versions of brasserie fare, including onion soup gratinée, *classique* cassoulet, duck confit, and steak au poivre. Stick to the classics and you'll enjoy yourself. Also check out the inspired cocktail menu, reason enough to come in. The Violet Martini is perfectly shaken with Grey Goose and a hint of violet essence, then dressed with a single purple petal. ***Note:*** If you're going before the theater, make it clear from the moment you sit.

790 8th Ave. (at 48th St.), adjacent to the Days Hotel. ℂ 212/489-2233. Reservations recommended. Main courses $6.50–$14 at breakfast and lunch, $8–$18 at dinner. AE, DC, DISC, MC, V. Daily 24 hr. Subway: C or E to 50th St.

Rice 'n' Beans BRAZILIAN   This cool, dark, hallway-size restaurant dishes up bold-flavored, stick-to-your-ribs fare that'll make you want to stand up and samba. Among the highlights are *feijoada,* the national dish of Brazil, a hearty stew of black beans, pork ribs, and linguica (Portuguese sausage); and a roasted chicken seasoned with tomato and cilantro. Prices have climbed a bit in recent years, but big eaters will still get a bang for their buck. The best bargain is the restaurant's namesake: For less than $10 you get a large plate mounded with rice, beans, mixed vegetables, collard greens, and plantains—a vegetarian's delight. Portions are monstrous. The weekday lunch specials—full meals with rice, beans, plantains, and your choice of roasted or sautéed chicken, beef stew, thin-cut sautéed pork chops, or the day's fried fish—are a steal. ***Be forewarned:*** Service can be slow at times and ambience is almost nonexistent.

744 9th Ave. (btwn 50th and 51st sts.). ℂ 212/265-4444. Reservations not accepted. Full plates $5–$8.25 at lunch, $6–$17 at dinner. AE, DISC, MC, V. Sun–Thurs 11am–10pm; Fri–Sat 11am–10:30pm. Subway: C or E to 50th St.

Sapporo ⭐ *Value* JAPANESE   Peruse the community bulletin board as you enter Sapporo and you might find yourself a deal on an apartment—that is, if you can read Japanese characters. Thankfully, the menu is in English in this longtime Theater District Japanese noodle shop. If the mostly Japanese clientele doesn't convince you of Sapporo's authenticity, the din of satisfied diners slurping at huge bowls of steaming ramen (noodle soup with meat and vegetables) surely will. And though the ramen is Sapporo's well-deserved specialty, the *gyoza* (Japanese dumplings) and the *donburi* (pork or chicken over rice with soy-flavored sauce) are also terrific. Best of all, nothing on the menu is over $10 and that's not easy to accomplish in the oft-overpriced Theater District.

152 W. 49th St. (btwn 6th and 7th aves.). ℭ 212/869-8972. Reservations not accepted. Main courses $6–$9. No credit cards. Mon–Sat 11am–11pm; Sun 11am–10pm. Subway: N or R to 49th St.

Siam Inn ⭐ THAI   Situated on an unremarkable stretch of 8th Avenue, Siam Inn is an attractive outpost of very good Thai food. All of your Thai favorites are here, well prepared and served by a brightly attired and courteous waitstaff. *Tom kah gai soup* (with chicken, mushrooms, and coconut milk), chicken satay with peanut sauce, and light, flaky curry puffs all make good starters. Among noteworthy entrees are the masaman and red curries (the former rich and peanutty, the latter quite spicy), spicy sautéed squid with fresh basil and chiles, and perfect pad Thai. The decor is pretty and pleasing—black deco tables and chairs, cushy rugs underfoot, and soft lighting.

854 8th Ave. (btwn 51st and 52nd sts.). ℭ 212/757-4006. www.siaminn.com. Reservations suggested. Main courses $8–$12 at lunch, $8–$16 at dinner. AE, DC, MC, V. Mon–Fri noon–11:30pm; Sat–Sun 4–11:30pm. Subway: C or E to 50th St.

Uncle Nick's GREEK   For stupendous portions of surprisingly good traditional Greek food at ridiculous prices, come to Uncle Nick's. Turn off your cellphone

---

Kids Family-Friendly Restaurants

While it's always smart to call ahead to make sure a restaurant has kids' menus and high chairs, you can count on the following to be especially accommodating. Additionally, you and the kids might also consider **Acme Bar & Grill** (p. 146), **Florent** (p. 150), and **Artie's Delicatessen** (p. 170). And don't forget the pizzerias, **John's** (p. 152) and **Lombardi's** (p. 152).

Here are some other choices for the whole family:

EJ's Luncheonette (p. 150). There's a kids' menu featuring peanut-butter-and-jelly sandwiches along with downsized versions of the classics. Order up a milkshake on the side, and your kid will be in hog heaven.

Good Enough to Eat (p. 174). Comfort food for kids like macaroni and cheese, pizza, and great desserts.

Serendipity 3 (p. 177). Kids of all ages will love this whimsical restaurant and ice-cream shop, which serves up a huge menu of American favorites, followed up by colossal ice-cream treats.

Virgil's Real BBQ (p. 167). This pleasing Times Square barbecue joint welcomes kids with open arms—and Junior will be more than happy, I'm sure, to be *allowed* to eat with his hands.

upon entering, not because you might disturb your neighbors, but because there is no way you will be able to have a phone conversation in this very loud restaurant. But how can you talk anyway if your mouth is filled with one or more of Nick's Greek dips like taramosalata or tzatziki, or his perfectly tender, grilled baby octopus. If you haven't filled up on his appetizers, order one of Nick's grilled specialties; the grilled lamb kabob is an absolute winner and guaranteed for leftovers while the gyro plate is a challenge for those with even the heartiest appetites. Seafood is also very good, especially the swordfish kabobs. Desserts are standard; you won't have room for them anyway. Service is friendly to match the rollicking atmosphere here. Next door is the slightly more intimate, Uncle Nick's Ouzeria specializing in mezedes, Greek small dishes like tapas.

747 9th Ave. (btwn 50th and 51st sts.). (C) 212/245-7992. Appetizers $5–$10; main courses $10–$17. Sun–Thurs 11:30am–11pm; Fri–Sat noon–11:30pm. Subway: C or E to 50th St. Also at 749 9th Ave. ((C) 212/397-2892).

Virgil's Real BBQ 🍴🍴 _Kids_ SOUTHERN/BARBECUE   In the heart of the theme restaurant wasteland known as Times Square is a theme restaurant that actually has good food. The "theme" is Southern barbecue and the restaurant, sprawling with dining on two levels, is made to look and feel like a Southern roadhouse with good ol' boy decorations on the walls and blues on the soundtrack. Virgil's does an admirable job recreating that authentic flavor so hard to find north of the Mason-Dixon line. The spice-rubbed ribs are slow-cooked and meaty, but it's the Owensboro Lamb (smoked slices of lamb) and the Texas beef brisket that are the standouts. Both are melt-in-your-mouth tender; the lamb is sprinkled with a flavorful mustard sauce, while the brisket is perfect with a few dabs of Virgil's homemade spicy barbecue sauce. For starters, the corn dogs with poblano mustard is something New Yorkers rarely have the pleasure of experiencing, while the BBQ nachos—tortilla chips slathered with melted cheese and barbecued pulled pork—is a meal in itself. Desserts are what you would expect from a restaurant emulating a Southern theme: big and sweet. Try the ice-cream sandwich made with the cookie of the day. Virgil's is a great place to bring the kids; they can make as much noise as they want and no one will notice.

152 W. 44th St. (btwn 6th and 7th aves.). (C) 212/921-9494. www.virgilsbbq.com. Reservations recommended. Sandwiches $6–$11; main courses and barbecue platters $13–$26 (most less than $19). AE, DC, DISC, MC, V. Sun–Mon 11:30am–11pm; Tues–Sat 11:30am–midnight. Subway: 1, 2, 3, 7, 9, N, or R to 42nd St./Times Square.

Vynl 🍴 AMERICAN   Vynl adds a hip quotient to the traditional diner formula with Lucite and Bakelite decor, a collection of action figures through the ages (from Captain and Tennille to Tyson Beckford), a 1970s-to-now soundtrack, and an affordable menu in a gatefold album cover (ours were from Lionel Richie and Three Dog Night). But Vynl isn't all veneer—the food is terrific. The brioche French toast with sautéed apples and caramel sauce is a great way to launch a weekend. For daytime and evening, the fare runs the gamut from diner fare to Asian-accented dishes including Thai curries, a veggie stir-fry, and Chinese chicken salad. Service is friendly and attentive. Pay with a credit card so you can sign the bill with the coolest pen in town (yours to purchase, if you wish).

824 9th Ave. (at 54th St.). (C) 212/974-2003. Reservations not accepted. Main courses $4.50–$11. AE, MC, V. Mon–Tues 11:30am–11pm; Wed–Fri 11:30am–midnight; Sat 9:30am–midnight; Sun 9:30am–11pm. Subway: C or E to 50th St.

QUICK BITES

Burger Joint 🍴, at Le Parker Meridien hotel, 118 W. 57th St. (btw 6th and 7th aves.; (C) 212/708-7460). Who woulda thunk that a fancy hotel like **Le Parker**

Meridien would be the home to a place called Burger Joint that serves great burgers at great prices ($5.95 for a cheeseburger). Will wonders never cease?

Amy's Bread, 672 9th Ave. (btwn 46th and 47th sts.; ✆ **212/977-2670;** www.amysbread.com), makes a great daytime stop. The brick-walled bakery/cafe serves up fresh-baked pastries, quiches, sandwiches made on some of the city's best bread, homemade soups, and excellent sweets (including divine old-fashioned layer cake), as well as cappuccino. Pastries are $1 to $4, sandwiches $3 to $6. A few tables are on hand in addition to the takeout counter.

Papaya King (p. 177) is at 255 W. 43rd St., just off 8th Avenue (✆ **212/944-4590**). The two-all-beef-franks-and-an-all-natural-fruit-drink combo is a bargain at $4.30.

Gourmet grocer **Dean & Deluca** runs a bustling, airy cafe at 9 Rockefeller Center, at 49th Street, across from the *Today* show studio (✆ **212/664-1363**).

11 Midtown East & Murray Hill

In addition to the listings below consider **Le Pain Quotidien,** at 833 Lexington Ave. (btwn 63rd and 64th sts.; ✆ **212/755-5810**), and the scrumptious **Ess-A-Bagel** at 831 3rd Ave. (at 51st St.; ✆ **212/980-1010**); see "Bagel Power" on p. 171.

Curry In A Hurry ⚝ *Value* INDIAN   The Murray Hill area of Lexington Avenue in the upper 20s is so rife with East Asian (Pakistani and Indian) restaurants it has been labeled Curry Hill and Curry in a Hurry, one of the best dining bargains in the city, has long been my favorite. Select what you want downstairs, including fresh Indian breads and dosas and bring it upstairs to the dining area where there is a salad bar featuring enough condiments to make a meal. Prices are ridiculously low and because the place is always busy, the food stays fresh. With a name like Curry in a Hurry, the curries better be good, and they are; my favorite is the fish curry in a thick, mild green curry sauce. For spicy, try the lamb vindaloo, while vegetarians can opt for the masala dosa, a vegetarian pancake stuffed with potatoes and peas. You can mix and match by making your own combo platters, a good way to sample different items.

119 Lexington Ave (at 28th St). ✆ **212/683-0900.** Main courses $5.50–$12, most around $9 including all-you-can-eat Indian salad bar. Daily 11am–midnight. AE, MC, V. Subway: 6 to 28th St.

Go Sushi *Value* JAPANESE   This bright, attractive chain of eat-in/takeout joints serves up excellent sushi for wallet-watching fans. It's boxed in bento-style containers, but everything is prepared fresh by a bevy of chefs behind the counter, so you never have to worry about quality; you can also place orders if what you want is not ready-made. In addition to sashimi, nigiri, and cut-roll choices, you can choose from a selection of fresh-made noodle bowls as well as bentos with teriyaki or tempura. I know locals who eat at Go Sushi three times a week. It's a wallet-friendly choice for a quick, healthy meal. No alcohol is served.

982 2nd Ave. (at 52nd St.). ✆ **212/593-3883.** Reservations not accepted. A la carte sushi $1.50–$2; rolls $3.80–$9 (most less than $6); sushi combos and bentos $5–$17 (most less than $10); noodle soups $5.50–$6.50. AE, MC, V. Daily 11:30am–11:10pm. Subway: 6 to 51st St. Also at 511 3rd Ave. (btwn 34th and 35th sts.; ✆ **212/679-1999;** subway: 6 to 33rd St.); 756 9th Ave. (at 51st St.; ✆ **212/459-2288;** subway: C or E to 50th St.); 3 Greenwich Ave. (6th Ave. at 8th St.; ✆ **212/366-9272;** subway: A, C, E, F, V, or S to W. 4th St.).

Katsu-Hama *Finds* JAPANESE   Even if you've never dined on Japanese cuisine, give this restaurant a try. It specializes in *katsu,* breaded and cleanly fried cutlets, usually pork, friendly to American palates. Katsu-Hama also katsus

Moments Grand Dining at Grand Central

The lower concourse of **Grand Central Terminal** ⭐⭐, 42nd Street at Park Avenue, is a haven of cheap eats—and the setting is an architecture-lover's delight. Head downstairs and you'll find everything from bratwurst to sushi. Standouts include **Junior's,** a branch of the Brooklyn stalwart, serving deli sandwiches, burgers, and their world-famous cheesecake in a waiter-serviced dining area. (With a few exceptions, most of the outlets are takeout counters; there's abundant seating at the center of the concourse.) **Mike's Take-Away** serves up soups, salads, and sandwiches, including a mushroom stew in winter. **Little Pie Company** serves up the Big Apple's best pies, plus fresh-baked muffins and the concourse's best coffee. **Cafe Spice Express** serves Indian fare, while **Christer's** and **Knödel** specialize, respectively, in fish and chips and German-style brats, wieners, and sausages. There's also an outpost of pizzeria **Two Boots.** If you want beer or wine, visit one of the two **bar cars,** which sit near tracks 105 and 112. For a complete list of vendors, check out www.grandcentralterminal.com.

chicken, prawns, and potatoes ("cream croquettes") in addition to moist pork tenderloin. Dinners start at $8.95 and come with as much rice, miso, and cabbage salad as you can eat. Japanese curries and skewers (yakitori) are also on hand, and there's a kids' menu. The butter-yellow room features modern art and comfy seating. Service is welcoming, knowledgeable, and generous with seconds. Beer and a short but good sake selection are on hand. It's an excellent value offering a more pleasing all-around dining experience than most in this price range.

11 E. 47th St. (btwn 5th and Madison aves.). ✆ 212/758-5909. www.katsuhama.com. Reservations accepted. Main courses and complete meals $7–$16. AE, DC, DISC, MC, V. Mon–Thurs 11:30am–3pm and 5–10:30pm; Fri 11:30am–10:30pm; Sat–Sun 11:30am–9:30pm. Subway: B, D, F, or V to 47th–50th sts./Rockefeller Center.

Prime Burger AMERICAN   In 2004 this no-frills coffee shop, located across the street from St. Patrick's Cathedral, was honored as an "American Classic" by the James Beard Foundation. For serving reasonably priced juicy burgers and well-stuffed sandwiches in such a high-priced neighborhood, Prime Burger is more than worthy of its many accolades. The front seats, which might remind you of old wooden grammar-school desks, are great fun—especially when business-suited New Yorkers take their places at these oddities. A great stop during a day of 5th Avenue shopping.

5 E. 51st St. (btwn 5th and Madison aves.). ✆ 212/759-4729. Reservations not accepted. Main courses $3.25–$9. No credit cards. Mon–Fri 6am–6:30pm; Sat 6am–5pm. Subway: 6 to 51st St.

The Pump HEALTH-CONSCIOUS   Here's a terrific stop for diners watching their figures as well as their wallets. An appealing mix of retro-cute and future-chic, with a counter in back and a few tables, The Pump espouses a philosophy that eating right doesn't have to mean boring. Everything is low fat and high in protein but doesn't sacrifice flavor for healthfulness. This is casual food with natural ingredients: salads, sandwiches, "supercharged" combo platters, fresh juices, and high-protein and health shakes. Although they serve up a great nature burger (a blend of brown rice, sunflower seeds, herbs, and veggies), The

Pump isn't a vegetarian restaurant; lean beef, turkey, and chicken are served. Because they cater to a workout crowd that needs energy, portions are substantial. Salad dressings are fat-free, using tahini and honey mustard, and pizzas are prepared with nonfat mozzarella, low-sodium tomato sauce, and whole-wheat crust. At breakfast, eggs, pancakes, and potatoes are baked, never fried—so you can indulge in a steak-and-egg sandwich (served on a whole-wheat pita).

113 E. 31st St. (btwn Park and Lexington aves.). ℂ 212/213-5733. www.thepumpenergyfood.com. Reservations not accepted. Breakfast $3.75–$8.50; sandwiches and salads $4.75–$7; full plates $8–$14. AE, MC, V. Mon–Thurs 9:30am–9:30pm; Fri 9:30am–8pm; Sat 11am–6:30pm. Subway: 6 to 33rd St. Also at 40 W. 55th St. (btwn 5th and 6th aves.; ℂ 212/246-6844; subway: F to 57th St.).

12 The Upper West Side

For good burgers and diner fare, visit **EJ's Luncheonette** (p. 150), 447 Amsterdam Ave. (btwn 81st and 82nd sts.; ℂ 212/873-3444). Vegetarians and health-minded diners might also consider **Zen Palate** ☆ (p. 158), 2170 Broadway (btwn 76th and 77th sts.; ℂ 212/501-7768).

For French baked goods, sandwiches, and salads of a divine order, also consider **Le Pain Quotidien** ☆☆ (p. 144), at 50 W. 72nd St. (btwn Columbus Ave. and Central Park W.; ℂ 212/712-9700).

You'll find some of the best bagels in New York on the Upper West Side, including **H&H Bagels,** 2239 Broadway, at 80th Street (ℂ 212/595-8003), and **Absolute Bagels,** 2788 Broadway (btwn 106th and 107th sts.; ℂ 212/932-2105); for more information, see "Bagel Power" on p. 171.

For one of the most satisfying meal deals in the city, head for the original **Gray's Papaya** (p. 153), 2090 Broadway, at 72nd Street (ℂ 212/799-0243). Try the "recession special": $2.45 for two beef dogs and a fruit drink. The good thing is that at Gray's, there is always a recession.

All State Cafe *(Finds* AMERICAN   This subterranean pub is one of Manhattan's undiscovered treasures—a classic neighborhood "snugger." It's easy to miss, and the regulars like it that way. The All State attracts a crowd drawn in by the casual ambience, the outstanding jukebox, and the superior burgers. If you're not in the burger mood, dig in to a variety of fresh salads and sandwiches, plus main courses like homemade fusilli with sautéed shrimp and scallops in a shiitake-mushroom sauce. The dining room behind the bar has casual, rough-hewn tables and chairs and an easygoing ambience; a fireplace makes it inviting in cold weather. Draft beers, a wine list featuring affordable labels from the United States and Australia, and a full bar round out the comfortable picture.

250 W. 72nd St. (btwn Broadway and West End Ave.). ℂ 212/874-1883. Reservations not accepted. Main courses $10–$14. No credit cards. Daily 11:30am–4am (sometimes earlier; food nightly until 12:45am). Subway: 1, 2, 3, or 9 to 72nd St.

Artie's Delicatessen *(Kids* JEWISH   Artie's opened in 1999 but already has the vibe of an institution. What's more, it's as good as many of the best delis in Manhattan (I prefer it over tourist traps like the Carnegie and the Stage), and far more cheery. In other words, Artie's is tourist-friendly, but in a good way; even New Yorkers appreciate it. All of your favorites are here—from corned beef to chopped liver to tongue on rye—and arrive at your table in top form. The pastrami is everything it should be, and the chicken soup with kreplach is a sore throat's worst nightmare. Artie's chili dogs deserve special note—they may be the best in town. Burgers, omelets, and salads are also on hand. Nostalgia-inducing desserts include Jell-O, baked apple, New York black-and-white cookies, very good homemade ruggelach, and sliced birthday cake every day ("No birthday necessary—song not included").

2290 Broadway (btwn 82nd and 83rd sts.). ⓒ 212/579-5959. www.arties.com. Reservations not accepted. Main courses $6–$12 at breakfast, $6–$17 at lunch and dinner. AE, DISC, MC, V. Sun–Thurs 9am–11pm; Fri–Sat 9am–11:30pm. Subway: 1 or 9 to 86th St.

Barney Greengrass, the Sturgeon King JEWISH   This daytime-only deli, going strong since 1908, is different from other delis; it's small and quiet, with an emphasis on smoked fish and service that's friendly rather than attitude-laden. It's a legend for its high-quality salmon (sable, gravlax, Nova Scotia, kippered, lox, pastrami—you choose), whitefish, and sturgeon (of course). But meat-lovers won't be disappointed: The triple-deckers are terrific (and much cheaper than at Midtown's delis), and the chicken liver inspired a raging, months-long debate among restaurant critics a few years back.

541 Amsterdam Ave. (btwn 86th and 87th sts.). ⓒ 212/724-4707. Reservations not accepted. Breakfast $3.50–$14; sandwiches $2.50–$16 (most less than $10); smoked fish platters $16–$36 (most less than $22). No credit cards. Tues–Fri 8:30am–4pm (takeout 8am–6pm); Sat–Sun 8:30am–5pm (takeout 8am–6pm). Subway: 1 or 9 to 86th St.

Big Nick's Burger and Pizza Joint ⋆ *Kids* AMERICAN/PIZZA   A neighborhood landmark since 1962, Big Nick's has a menu that seems to have grown each year of its existence. Trying to decide if you want the Madrid burger, with olives, feta, and pimentos, with or without buffalo meat; a slice of Hawaiian

---

Tips **Bagel Power**

Bagels are a quintessential New York food. People here are very loyal to their favorite bagels, and discussions about who makes the best bagel in New York often can lead to heated arguments. I have my favorite (see "Best Low-Cost Dining Bets" in chapter 1), but you won't go wrong with a bagel from any of the places I've listed below.

Absolute Bagels, 2708 Broadway (btwn 107th and 108th sts.; ⓒ 212/ 932-2105). A new player on the bagel scene. Their egg bagels, hot out of the oven, melt in your mouth, and their whitefish salad is perfectly smoky though not overpowering.

Ess-A-Bagel, 359 1st Ave., at 21st Street (ⓒ 212/260-2252; www.ess-a-bagel.com). When it comes to size, Ess-a-Bagel's are the best of the biggest; plump, chewy, and oh so satisfying. Also at 831 3rd Ave. (btwn 50th and 51st sts.; ⓒ 212/980-1010).

H&H Bagels, 2239 Broadway, at 80th Street (ⓒ 212/595-8003; www.handhbagel.com). Long reputed as the best bagel in New York—which may have resulted in the arrogant price hike to $1 a bagel. Some complain they are a bit too sweet, but I disagree. The bagels here are always fresh and warm, the bagel aficionado's prerequisite. Also at 639 W. 46th St., at 12th Avenue (ⓒ 212/595-8000). Takeout only.

Murray's Bagels, 500 6th Ave. (btwn 12th and 13th sts.; ⓒ 212/462-2830); and 242 8th Ave., at 23rd St. (ⓒ 646/638-1334). There's nothing like a soft, warm bagel to begin your day with, and Murray's does them beautifully. Their smoked fish goes perfectly on their bagels.

Uptown Dining

Absolute Bagels **2**
All State Cafe **15**
Amy's Bread **22**
Artie's Delicatessen **10**
Barney Greengrass,
  the Sturgeon King **7**
Big Nick's Burger Joint/
  Pizza Joint **13**
Celeste **8**
Cold Stone Creamery **28**
E.J.'s Luncheonette **11, 24**
El Paso Taqueria **32, 33**
Flor de Mayo **4, 9**
Good Enough to Eat **9**
Gray's Papaya **16**
H&H Bagels **12**
Hungarian Pastry Shop **1**
John's Pizzeria **21**
Le Pain Quotidien **17, 19, 23, 26**
Nick's Family-Style Restaurant
  and Pizzeria **31**
Noche Mexicana **5**
P&W Sandwich & More Shop **1**
Papaya King **27**
Pintaile's Pizza **20, 30**
Popover Cafe **7**
Saigon Grill **6**
Serendipity 3 **18**
Silver Moon Bakery **3**
Tom's Restaurant **2**
Totonno's Pizzeria
  Napolitano **25**
V&T Pizzeria **1**
Yura & Company **29**
Zen Palate **14**

Ⓜ Subway stop

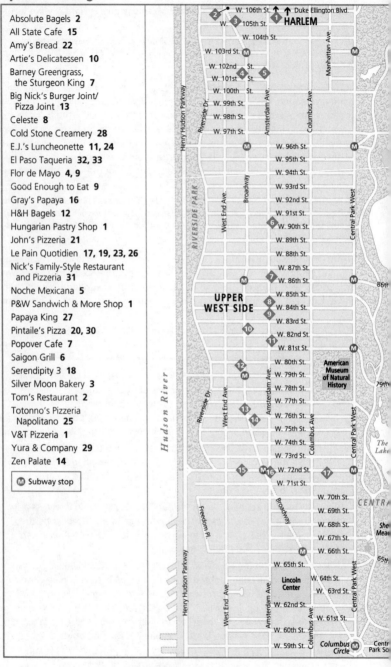

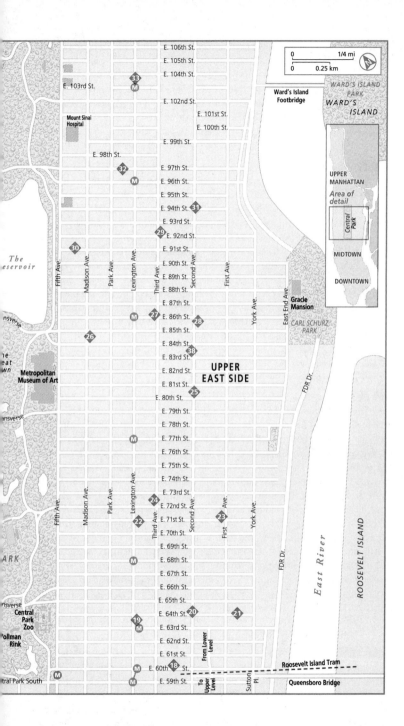

E. 106th St.
E. 105th St.
E. 104th St.
E. 103rd St.
E. 102nd St.
E. 101st St.
E. 100th St.
E. 99th St.
E. 98th St.
E. 97th St.
E. 96th St.
E. 95th St.
E. 94th St.
E. 93rd St.
E. 92nd St.
E. 91st St.
E. 90th St.
E. 89th St.
E. 88th St.
E. 87th St.
E. 86th St.
E. 85th St.
E. 84th St.
E. 83rd St.
E. 82nd St.
E. 81st St.
E. 80th St.
E. 79th St.
E. 78th St.
E. 77th St.
E. 76th St.
E. 75th St.
E. 74th St.
E. 73rd St.
E. 72nd St.
E. 71st St.
E. 70th St.
E. 69th St.
E. 68th St.
E. 67th St.
E. 66th St.
E. 65th St.
E. 64th St.
E. 63rd St.
E. 62nd St.
E. 61st St.
E. 60th St.
E. 59th St.

Mount Sinai
Hospital

Ward's Island
Footbridge

WARD'S ISLAND
PARK

WARD'S
ISLAND

UPPER
MANHATTAN

*Area of
detail*

Central
Park

MIDTOWN

DOWNTOWN

*The
Reservoir*

Fifth Ave.
Madison Ave.
Park Ave.
Lexington Ave.
Third Ave.
Second Ave.
First Ave.
York Ave.
East End Ave.

Gracie
Mansion

CARL SCHURZ
PARK

Metropolitan
Museum of Art

UPPER
EAST SIDE

FDR Dr.

East River

ROOSEVELT ISLAND

FDR Dr.

Central
Park
Zoo

Wollman
Rink

Central Park South

From Lower Level
To Upper Level

Sutton Pl.

Roosevelt Island Tram

Queensboro Bridge

0   1/4 mi
0   0.25 km

PARK

0   1/4 mi
0   0.25 km

pizza; or just an order of the spinach pie can be exhausting. If reading the menu is too much for you, peruse the numerous photos of celebrities who have supposedly chowed at Big Nick's over the years, or just keep your eyes on the nonstop "Three Stooges" marathon playing on the restaurant's televisions. Whatever you do, you'll never forget your Big Nick's experience. With all those diversions, it's a great place to take the kids; they'll never be bored.

2175 Broadway (at 77th St.). ℂ 212/362-9238. www.bignicksnyc.com. Reservations not accepted. Main courses $3.50–$19 (most less than $10). MC, V. Daily 24 hr. Subway: 1 or 9 to 79th St.

Celeste ★★ *Finds* ITALIAN   In the land of smoked fish and Chinese restaurants, this fabulous Italian restaurant is a godsend to the Upper West Side dining scene. Tiny but charming, Celeste features its own wood-burning pizza oven, which churns out thin-crust, simple but delicious pizzas. But pizza is not the only attraction; the "fritti" (fried) course is unique; the *fritto misto de pesce* (fried mixed seafood) is delectable, but really special are the fried zucchini blossoms, usually available in the summer and fall. The fresh pastas are better than the dried pasta; I never thought the fresh egg noodles with cabbage, shrimp, and sheep's cheese would work, but it was delicious. Not on the menu, but usually available, are artisanal plates of rare Italian cheeses served with homemade jams. Though the main courses are also good, stick with the pizzas, antipasto, frittis, and pastas. For dessert, try the gelato; the pistachio was the best I've had in New York. The restaurant has been "discovered," so go early or go late—or expect a wait.

502 Amsterdam Ave. (btwn 84th and 85th sts). ℂ 212/874-4559. Reservations not accepted. Pizzas $10–$12; antipasto $7–$10; pastas $10; main courses $14–$16. No credit cards. Mon–Sat 5–11pm; Sun noon–3:30pm. Subway: 1 or 9 to 86th St.

Flor de Mayo ★ *Finds* CHINESE/CARIBBEAN   Cuban-Chinese cuisine is a New York phenomenon that started in the late 1950s when Cubans of Chinese heritage immigrated to New York after the revolution. Most of the immigrants took up residence on the Upper West Side, and Cuban-Chinese restaurants flourished. Many have disappeared, but the best one, Flor de Mayo, still remains and is so popular that a new branch opened farther south on Amsterdam Avenue. The kitchen excels at both sides of the massive menu, but the best dish is the *la brasa* half-chicken lunch special—beautifully spiced and slow-roasted until it's fork tender and falling off the bone, served with a giant pile of fried rice, bounteous with roast pork, shrimp, and veggies. Offered Monday through Saturday until 4:30pm, the whole meal is just $6.95, and it's enough to fortify you for the day. Service and atmosphere are reminiscent of Chinatown: efficient and lightning-quick. My favorite combo: the hearty, noodles-, greens-, shrimp-, and pork-laden Chinese soup with an order of yellow rice and black beans.

2651 Broadway (btwn 100th and 101st sts.). ℂ 212/663-5520 or 212/595-2525. Reservations not accepted. Main courses $4.50–$19 (most under $10); lunch specials $5–$7 (Mon–Sat to 4:30pm). AE, MC, V ($15 minimum). Daily noon–midnight. Subway: 1 or 9 to 103rd St. Also at 484 Amsterdam Ave. (btwn 83rd and 84th sts.; ℂ 212/787-3388; subway: 1 or 9 to 86th St.).

Good Enough to Eat ★★ *Kids* AMERICAN   For 23 years, the crowds have been lining up on weekends outside Good Enough to Eat to experience chef/owner Carrie Levin's incredible breakfasts; as a result, lunch and dinner at the restaurant have been somewhat overlooked, which is too bad, because those meals can be as good as the breakfasts. The restaurant's cow motif, the cozy throw pillows, and farmhouse knickknacks imply hearty, home-cooked food; and that is what is done best here. Don't waver from ordering the mainstays: meatloaf with gravy and mashed potatoes; traditional turkey dinner with cranberry relish, gravy, and corn-bread stuffing; macaroni and cheese; griddled corn bread; Vermont spinach salad; and the barbecue sandwich, roasted chicken with barbecue sauce and home-made potato chips. And save room for the homemade desserts; though the selection is often overwhelming, I can never resist the coconut cake. This is food you loved as a kid, one reason why the kids will love it as well. There are only 20 tables here, so expect a wait on weekends during the day or for dinner after 6pm.

483 Amsterdam Ave. (btwn 83rd and 84th sts). ℭ 212/496-0163. www.citysearch.com/nyc/goodenough. Breakfast $4.50–$9; lunch $8.50–$15; dinner $8.50–$23 (most under $18). AE, MC, V. Breakfast Mon–Fri 8am–4pm, Sat–Sun 9am–4pm; lunch Mon–Fri 11:30am–4pm; dinner Mon–Thurs 5:30–10:30pm, Fri–Sat 5:30–11pm, Sun 5:30–10pm. Subway: 1 or 9 to 86th St.

Noche Mexicana ℛ *Finds* MEXICAN   This tiny, new Mexican restaurant serves some of the best tamales in New York. Wrapped in cornhusks, as good tamales should be, they come in two varieties: in a red mole sauce with shredded chicken or in a green tomatillo sauce with shredded pork. There are three tamales in each order, which costs only $5, making it a cheap and almost perfect lunch. The burritos are authentic and meals unto themselves. The *tinga* burrito, shredded chicken in a tomato-and-onion chipotle sauce, is my favorite. Each is stuffed with rice, beans, and guacamole. Don't get fancy here; stick with the tamales, burritos, and soft tacos, the best being the taco *al pastor,* a taco stuffed with pork marinated with pineapple and onions.

852 Amsterdam Ave. (btwn 101st and 102nd sts.). ℭ 212/662-6900 or 212/662-7400. Burritos $6–$7.50; tacos $2; tamales $5; Mexican dishes $8.50–$9.50. AE, DISC, MC, V. Sun–Thurs 10am–11pm; Fri–Sat 10am–midnight. Subway: 1 or 9 to 103rd St.

Popover Cafe *Kids* AMERICAN   The first thing people usually call Popover's is kid-friendly, a nod to its child-size burger, PBJ sandwiches, and decor that's chockablock with teddy bears. But grownups will like it just as much. Everybody gets addicted to the fluffy popovers with strawberry butter or preserves. The full dinner entrees are a bit pricey, but Popover's forte is comfort food that makes hearty and affordable breakfasts and lunches: omelets and scrambles, chili and soups, and salads and sandwiches. A bowl of one of the day's homemade soups (vegetarian three-bean and split-pea are two of my favorites) accompanied by a popover makes a more-than-satisfying lunch for a few dollars. Service is warm and welcoming; in fact, eating here feels like stepping into somebody's big, old, hospitable New England home. Well worth a stop. Beware the crowds at brunch, however, which can ruin the mood.

551 Amsterdam Ave. (btwn 86th and 87th sts.). ℭ 212/595-8555. Reservations not accepted. Main courses $6–$11 at breakfast and brunch, $9–$15 at lunch, $8.50–$21 at dinner (most less than $15). AE, MC, V. Mon–Fri 8am–10pm; Sat–Sun 9am–10pm. Subway: 1 or 9 to 86th St.

Saigon Grill ℛ *Value* VIETNAMESE   This cafeteria-like restaurant isn't very fancy, but the artistry in the food preparation, along with whopping portions at bargain-basement prices, more than makes up for the too-bright lighting and uncomfortable seating. I always judge Vietnamese restaurants by their salads, and Saigon Grill's are outstanding. The *goi du du,* shredded green papaya salad with grilled beef and crushed peanuts, is a Vietnamese specialty and is done perfectly here. But my favorite salad is the bean curd and baby-green salad, fresh mesclun greens with slivers of fried bean curd topped by crushed peanuts in a spicy *nuac cham* sauce. The soups can be meals here; *pho bo* is comforting, with oxtail stock and thin slices of rare beef, while the *canh chua* (hot-and-sour soups) will help clear your sinuses. The curries are popular here, but I prefer the basil dishes, in particular the basil prawns: jumbo shrimp with vegetables and Thai basil in a spicy fish sauce. If you crave noodles, try the *bun xao,* stir-fried rice noodles with shredded vegetables, egg, and crushed peanuts with your choice of chicken, shrimp, beef, or vegetarian. Come with a group and be prepared to share; there will be more than enough for everyone.

620 Amsterdam Ave. (at 90th St.) Ⓒ 212/875-9072. Lunch special $4.95–$7.50; soups $2.95–$6.50; main courses $8–$14 (most under $10). AE, DISC, DC, MC, V. Daily 11am–midnight. Subway: 1 or 9 to 86th St.

Tom's Restaurant AMERICAN   Tom's would be just any other diner if it weren't for its famous connections: This is the restaurant that served as the exterior for Monk's on *Seinfeld* and inspired Suzanne Vega to write *Tom's Diner.* It's worth a pilgrimage if you're a Jerry fan or if you're in the neighborhood. It's popular with Columbia University students, thanks to its long hours and cheap coffee-shop fare. Expect the standards, from three-egg omelets to tuna salad. The '70s-era waitstaff emits the requisite attitude and won't think twice of rushing you when it's crowded.

2880 Broadway (at 112th St.). Ⓒ 212/864-6137. Reservations not accepted. Main courses $3–$10. No credit cards. Sun–Wed 6am–1:30am; Thurs–Sat 24 hr. Subway: 1 or 9 to 110th St.

QUICK BITES

Farther uptown, the place to go is **V&T Pizzeria** 𝔊, 1024 Amsterdam Ave. (btwn 110th and 111th sts.; Ⓒ **212/666-8051** or 212/663-1708). This is a sit-down (or carryout) restaurant with red-checked tablecloths and traditional pies with red sauce and a chewy crust. V&T caters to a Columbia University crowd, so prices stay low—how can you *not* splurge on one of the mascarpone-filled cannolis for dessert, right?

After pizza at the V&T, head next door to the lovely, worn **Hungarian Pastry Shop,** 1030 Amsterdam Ave. (btwn 110th and 111th sts.; Ⓒ **212/866-4230**)—a landmark for 40 years. It's an ideal stop for coffee and pastry or a plateful of crumbly, buttery cookies. For something more substantial, head next door to **P&W's Sandwich & More Shop** (Ⓒ **212/222-2245**), specializing in homemade soups, bagels, made-to-order sandwiches, by-the-pound salads, and the like. There are no tables, but you're welcome to pick up your food and take it over to the pastry shop to enjoy. If you're staying in the area and your room has kitchen facilities, P&W's also makes a good spot at which to stock up on supplies like milk, cereal, peanut butter, coffee, paper plates, plastic utensils, and the like.

Silver Moon Bakery, 2740 Broadway, at 105th Street (Ⓒ **212/866-4717**), is bright, airy, and alive with fresh-baked pastry smells. Come by for a first-rate java fix and a fresh-from-the-oven brioche, a muffin, or other baked goods.

13 The Upper East Side

There's also a branch of **EJ's Luncheonette** (p. 150), the retro all-American diner, at 1271 3rd Ave., at 73rd Street (Ⓒ **212/472-0600**).

John's Pizzeria (p. 152) has a location at 408 E. 64th St. (btwn 1st and York aves.; Ⓒ **212/935-2895**); see "Pizza New York Style" on p. 152.

For baked goods and sandwiches and salads, consider **Le Pain Quotidien** 𝔊𝔊 (p. 144), which has three Upper East Side locations: 833 Lexington Ave. (btwn 63rd and 64th sts.; Ⓒ **212/755-5810**); 1336 1st Ave. (btwn 71st and 72nd sts.; Ⓒ **212/717-4800**); and an easy walk from Museum Mile at 1131 Madison Ave. (btwn 84th and 85th sts.; Ⓒ **212/327-4900**).

Nick's Family-Style Restaurant and Pizzeria 𝔊 *Kids*   ITALIAN/PIZZA Since 1994, Nick Angelis has wowed them in Forest Hills, Queens, with his pizzas.

In 2003, he took his act to Manhattan, where the pizza is garnering equally high praise. The pizza is thin-crust, with the proper proportions of creamy, homemade mozzarella and fresh tomato sauce. But this is much more than a pizzeria; try the light, lemony baked clams or "Josephine's" perfectly breaded eggplant parmigiana. If you dare combine pizza with a calzone, this is the place; Nick's calzone, stuffed with ricotta and mozzarella cheese, is spectacular. The *orecchiette* with broccoli rabe and sausage is the pasta winner, while the filet of sole oreganato Livornese with mussels is the standout main course. Save room for an extra-large cannoli for dessert; the shell is perfectly flaky and the filling ultra-creamy. Full orders are enough to feed two or three and are a great bargain for a group, but half-orders are also available. The room is comfortable and far from fancy. Go early or be prepared to wait.

1814 2nd Ave. (at 94th St.). (C) 212/987-5700. Pizzas $11–$13; macaroni half-orders $5–$11, full orders $11–$22; main courses half-orders $7.50–$11, full orders $15–$22. AE, DC, DISC, MC, V. Sun–Thurs 11:30am–11pm; Sat–Sun 11:30am–midnight. Subway: 6 to 96th St.

Serendipity 3 (☆) (Kids) AMERICAN   You'd never guess that this whimsical place was once a top stop on Andy Warhol's agenda. Wonders never cease—and neither does the confection at this delightful restaurant and sweet shop. Tucked into a brownstone a few steps from Bloomingdale's, Serendipity's small front-room curiosity shop overflows with odd objects, from jigsaw puzzles to silly jewelry. But the real action is behind the shop, where the quintessential American soda fountain still reigns supreme. Happy people gather at marble-topped ice-cream parlor tables for burgers and foot-long hot dogs, meat loaf with mashed potatoes and gravy, and salads and sandwiches with cute names like "The Catcher in the Rye" (their own twist on the BLT, with chicken and Russian dressing—on rye, of course). The food isn't great, but the main courses aren't the point—they're just an excuse to get to the desserts. The restaurant's signature is Frozen Hot Chocolate, a slushie version of everybody's cold-weather favorite, but other crowd pleasers include dark double devil mousse, celestial carrot cake, lemon icebox pie, and anything with hot fudge. So cast that willpower aside and come on in—Serendipity is an irony-free charmer to be appreciated by adults and kids alike.

225 E. 60th St. (btwn 2nd and 3rd aves.). (C) 212/838-3531. www.serendipity3.com. Reservations accepted for lunch and dinner (not dessert only). Main courses $7–$18; sweets and sundaes $5–$17 (most under $10). AE, DC, DISC, MC, V. Sun–Thurs 11:30am–midnight; Fri 11:30am–1am; Sat 11:30am–2am. Subway: N or R to Lexington Ave.; 4, 5, or 6 to 59th St.

QUICK BITES

The original **Papaya King,** 179 E. 86th St., at 3rd Avenue ((C) 212/369-0648), is Gray's Papaya's (p. 153) chief rival. It's not as good and a bit more expensive, but they still cook a pretty fair hot dog here.

For more refined tastes, there's **Yura & Company,** 6045 3rd Ave., at 92nd Street ((C) 212/860-8060), one of the Upper East Side's best-kept secrets. This gourmet bakery/cafe serves good coffee, scones, and muffins, and a selection of foods that are perfect for a Central Park picnic (the 90th St. entrance is a few blocks away). Or you can opt for table service in the country-style dining room, a cute spot for breakfast or a well-made sandwich. Good angel-food cake, too.

Pintaile's Pizza, at 26 E. 91st St. (btwn 5th and Madison aves.; (C) 212/722-1967; daily 11am–9:30pm), dresses its organic crusts with tomatoes, extra-virgin olive oil, and fresh ingredients. Pintaile's is also at 1237 2nd Ave. (btwn 64th and 65th sts.; (C) 212/752-6222; daily 11am–10:30pm).

The Soul of Harlem

There is much soul to go around in Manhattan, but Harlem seems to possess the mother lode—at least when it comes to food. Here is one man's primer to Harlem's soul food:

Amy Ruth's, 112 W. 116th St. (btwn Lenox and 7th aves.; ✆ **212/280-8779**). Claiming to be authentic soul, Amy Ruth's has become a mecca for Harlem celebs, with the gimmick of naming platters after some of them, such as the Rev. Al Sharpton (chicken and waffles) and the Rev. Calvin O. Butts III (chicken wings and waffles). Most of the celebrities are probably only household names in Harlem, but the food is famous all over: those chicken and waffles, or fried whiting and waffles, or steak and waffles are *stars*. You can't go wrong with anything here as long as waffles are included.

Charles' Southern Style Kitchen ✿, 2841 8th Ave. (btwn 151st and 152nd sts.; ✆ **877/813-2920** or 212/926-4313). Nothing fancy about this place, just a brightly lit, 25-seater on a not very attractive block in upper Harlem. But you don't come here for fancy; you come for soul food at its simplest and freshest. And you better come hungry. The $11 all-you-can-eat buffet features crunchy, incredibly moist, pan-fried chicken; ribs in a tangy sauce, with meat falling off the bone; smoky stewed oxtails in a thick brown onion gravy; macaroni and cheese; collard greens with bits of smoked turkey; black-eyed peas; and corn bread, warm and not overly sweet. Hours can be erratic, so call ahead before you make the trek.

Copeland's, 547 W. 145th St. (btwn Broadway and Amsterdam Ave.; ✆ **212/234-2357**; www.copelands-ny.com). With food almost as good as Charles', but in a much more elegant setting (you'll find tables adorned with china and white tablecloths), Copeland's has been dishing out excellent soul food for 40 years. Fried chicken is their trademark, but I favor the braised short ribs. The jazz buffet on Tuesday, Wednesday, and Thursday nights is a double treat.

For a more traditional pie, head to **Totonno's Pizzeria Napolitano,** 1544 2nd Ave. (btwn 80th and 81st sts.; ✆ **212/327-2800**). Recently opened on the Upper East Side scene for coffee and pastry is **Amy's Bread** (p. 168), 972 Lexington Ave. (btwn 70th and 71st sts.; ✆ **212/537-0270**).

14 Harlem

El Paso Taqueria ✿ MEXICAN   In the past decade, Spanish Harlem, predominately an enclave for Puerto Ricans, has become more a Mexican community and as a result some very authentic Mexican restaurants and groceries have emerged. El Paso Taqueria is the best of the new Mexican restaurants in the neighborhood. The menu here is extensive with tamales, *flautas*, enchiladas, *chalupas*, and tacos on the menu in many varieties including some not so familiar to the gringo palate like tripe, tongue, and salted beef. The mole poblano, the "famous Puebla stew" was chocolaty rich while the *sopes*, a thick tortilla covered with salted beef and soft cheese, ranked high on my personal spice meter. You'll

M&G Diner, 383 W. 125th St., at St. Nicholas Avenue (© **212/864-7325**). All the soul food joints I've listed here serve top-notch fried chicken, but the best I've had is the perfectly pan-fried, super moist bird at the M&G. This small, no-frills diner, open 24 hours, is a treat any time of day. Start your day here with a soul breakfast of eggs with salmon croquettes or eggs with grits or finish it with the celebrated chicken, chitterlings, or meatloaf. All the sides are freshly made and the desserts, especially the sweet-potato pie, are phenomenal. There's also a great jukebox loaded with soul to complement the food.

Miss Mamie's Spoonbread Too ⭐, 366 W. 110th St. (btwn Columbus and Manhattan aves.; © **212/865-6744**). Entering this bright, strawberry-curtained charmer is like stepping straight into South Carolina. But you are in Harlem, or at least the southern fringe of Harlem, and you won't be paying South Carolina soul prices, or Harlem soul prices, either. Still, despite the somewhat inflated prices, Miss Mamie's is the real deal, especially their barbecued ribs, falling off the bone and smothered in a sweet peppery sauce, and the smothered chicken, fried and then covered with thick pan gravy.

Sylvia's, 328 Lenox Ave. (btwn 126th and 127th sts.; © **212/996-0660**; www.sylviassoulfood.com). Sylvia is the self-proclaimed queen of not only Harlem soul food, but all soul food. Sylvia's now has become a franchise, with canned food products, beauty and hair products, and fragrances and colognes. With all that attention to merchandising, the food at her original Harlem restaurant has suffered and now has regressed into a tourist trap. If you plan to go, however, make it on Sunday for the gospel brunch, which is an absolute joy.

Also consider **Patsy's Pizzeria** (p. 152).

eat hearty here for few pesos. If you are an early riser, come for breakfast where you can sample eggs with chorizo or eggs with cactus.

1642 Lexington Ave. (btwn 103rd and 104th sts.). © 212/831-9831. Tacos $2; poblanos $8–$11. Subway: 6 to 103rd St. Also at 64 E. 97th St. (btwn Park and Madison aves.; © 212/996-1739; subway: 6 to 96th St.).

La Fonda Boricua ⭐ *Value* *Finds* CARIBBEAN   The food of Puerto Rico is vastly underrated, and the best of that cuisine can be found in the heart of El Barrio at La Fonda Boricua. Was that Marc Anthony sitting across from New York Yankee Bernie Williams? This stylish, 75-seat former diner is a hangout for leaders of the local Latino community and beyond; politicians, artists, writers, musicians, and ballplayers convene for delicious Puerto Rican staples. Excellent choices include tender, succulent octopus salad; crispy *chicharrones* of pork; slightly smoky *arroz con pollo;* garlic-laden *lechón asado* (roasted pork shoulder); thinly pounded citrus-marinated steak smothered with onions; rice and beans in many varieties; and that artery-clogging favorite, *mofongo* (fried mashed plantains with garlic and crispy pieces of pork rind). The diverse crowd also comes for the creative vibes encouraged by the engaging owners, brothers Jorge and Roberto Ayala, who have adorned the restaurant with paintings from local artists, promote impromptu jams from visiting musicians, and foster an atmosphere of Latino sophistication. The portions are more than generous and the prices easily affordable. The only disappointment is the lack of variety for dessert; flan, though excellent, is the only option.

169 E. 106th St. (btwn 3rd and Lexington aves.). ℂ 212/410-7292. Lunch $5–$8; dinner $7–$10. No credit cards. Daily 10am–10pm. Subway: 6 to 103rd St.

La Marmite ☆ *(Finds* AFRICAN   The concentration of African restaurants in the area around 116th and Frederick Douglass Boulevard in Harlem is probably denser than anywhere outside of Dakar, with most being from West Africa—Senegal in particular. Of the ones I have sampled, La Marmite is my favorite. Though it's tiny, you'll rarely have a problem finding a table since most of the business is takeout. The wobbly television will be tuned to news from France or West African music videos will be playing—hope for the latter. The traditional West African dish, *thiebou djoun,* a combination of rice and fish in a piquant tomato-based sauce is usually available. Give it a try if it is. The *poulet braise,* baked half-chicken in a sweet brown onion sauce and the *mafe,* lamb chunks in a peanut butter sauce, are also winners. You really won't go wrong with anything here. Portions are sizable; you definitely won't leave hungry. Just don't expect typically rushed New York service; this is an authentic African experience in every way including the slow pace. No alcohol is served, but if you want a beer to accompany the spicy food, there's a bodega (Hispanic deli) next door.

2264 Frederick Douglass Blvd. (at 120th St.). ℂ 212/666-0653. Main courses $8–$11. No credit cards. Open 24 hr. (but call ahead to make sure). Subway: C or B to 116th St.

QUICK BITES
Papaya King (p. 177) has another location at 121 W. 125th St. (btwn Lenox Ave. and Adam Clayton Powell Blvd.; ℂ 212/665-5732). The two-all-beef-franks-and-an-all-natural-fruit-drink combo is a bargain at $4.30.

15 The Outer Boroughs
THE BRONX
MODERATE
If you are looking for old-fashioned, Italian-American food—the kind you used to get before waiters began asking if you want your water tap or sparkling—look no further than the Bronx. The best concentration of Italian-American "red sauce" restaurants can be found in the Little Italy of the Bronx, on and around **Arthur Avenue.** One of my favorites is **Mario's Restaurant,** 2342 Arthur Ave. (btwn Crescent Ave. and E. 187th St.; ℂ 718/584-1188), where the Neapolitan pizza is magnificent and the ziti with broccoli unforgettable. Reservations are accepted, as are American Express, Discover, Diners Club, MasterCard, and Visa. Wonderful **Dominick's,** on the same block at 2335 Arthur Ave. (ℂ 718/733-2807), is the inspiration behind family-style creations like Carmine's. There's no menu here, but trust your waiter to ramble off what is on the day's menu, which almost always includes tender calamari marinara and luscious veal francese. There's always a crowd so go early or expect to wait for a communal table. Reservations are not accepted and please, cash only.

To get to Arthur Avenue, take the 4 or D train to Fordham Road and then the no. 12 bus east; the 2 or 5 train to Pelham Parkway, and the no. 12 bus west;

or the Metro-North Harlem line to Fordham Road, and the shuttle bus to Belmont and Bronx Zoo.

A few miles east of Arthur Avenue you'll find another classic Italian "red sauce" restaurant. This one, **Frankie and Johnnie's Pine,** 1913 Bronxdale Ave. (btwn Matthews and Muliner aves.; © **718/792-5956**), has been around so long, I remember watching the Times Square ball drop on a black-and-white television in the dining room while devouring a big bowl of *zuppa di pesce* one lonely New Year's Eve many years ago. I remember that New Year's, though lonely, very fondly mainly because of that *zuppa di pesce.* Now The Pine, as it's known, has become very popular as a hangout for New York Yankees who crave pasta after their games at Yankee Stadium. As a result, you'll find plenty of baseball memorabilia on the walls. No reservations accepted, cash only. To get there, take the 2 or 5 train to Bronx Park East.

BROOKLYN

In addition to **Ferdinando's Focacceria** ✸ (below), consider the DUMBO outposts of the comforting, comfort-food legend **Bubby's** ✸✸ (p. 136), **Bubby's Brooklyn,** 1 Main St., at Water Street (© **718/222-0666**), and **Rice** ✸ (p. 145), 81 Washington St. (btwn Front and York sts.; © **718/222-9880**), where you can load up on carbs for a walk back into Manhattan across the Brooklyn Bridge.

The fabulous **Grimaldi's Pizzeria** is located at 19 Old Fulton St. (btwn Front and Water sts.; © **718/858-4300**); and out in Coney Island, the 1924-established and little-changed **Totonno's** is at 1524 Neptune Ave. (btwn W. 15th and W. 16th sts.; © **718/372-8606**). See "Pizza New York Style," on p. 152, for more information.

Also in Coney Island is the famous **Nathan's Famous,** 1310 Surf Ave., at Stillwell Avenue (© **718/946-2202**), for hot dogs by the beach. See how many you can eat.

If you are traveling to BAM to see a show, you'll be tempted to have your pre- or post-theater meal at **Junior's,** 386 Flatbush Ave., at DeKalb Avenue (© **718/852-5257**). Everyone knows about Junior's world-famous cheesecake, the epitome of New York cheesecake; but don't miss the opportunity to experience the authentic Brooklyn atmosphere here, complete with old-school waiters you'll not soon forget. Don't expect anything fancy, but do expect great cheesecake.

Ferdinando's Focacceria ✸ ITALIAN   You might think that focaccia, that wonderful Italian bread coated with olive oil, herbs, and tomato sauce is a recent culinary innovation. Think again. They've been making focaccia at Ferdinando's since 1904. But the focaccia they make at this Sicilian restaurant, in the increasingly trendy neighborhood of Cobble Hill, is nothing like the focaccia you've tasted. Here the specialty focaccia is panelle, a deep-fried pancake made of chickpea flour. You can have your panelle plain, or you can have it topped with ricotta and grated cheese. Trust me, any way you have it is good. The restaurant also features Sicilian specials like marinated octopus, stuffed calamari, tripe in tomato sauce, and a magnificent *caponatina,* or eggplant salad.

151 Union St. (btwn Columbia and Hicks sts.), Cobble Hill. © 718/855-1545. Panelle $3; main courses $10–$13. No credit cards. Mon–Thurs 10:30am–6pm; Fri–Sat 10:30am–9pm. Subway: F or G to Carroll St.

QUEENS

The 7 train is sometimes known as the International Express. Take it out of Manhattan and through the borough of Queens and you will pass one ethnic neighborhood after another. You could write a book on all the different restaurants located around the 7 train in Queens. Here are a few of my favorites:

Get off at the 69th Street stop in Woodside, walk 1 block north, and you might begin to detect the aroma of barbecued meats. That smell is coming from **Ihawan,** 40-06 70th St. (© 718/205-1480), which claims to be home of the best barbecue in town. But unless you've been to the Philippines, Ihawan's country of origin, this is barbecue unlike any you've tasted before. Here you can sample barbecue pork on bamboo skewers, grilled marinated pork chops, and the local favorite, grilled marinated pork belly. The menu here also includes other Filipino specialties such as *dinuguan,* pork stewed in pork-blood gravy, and *lapu-lapu,* a whitefish, served in tamarind soup.

If you get off the train at the 82nd St./Jackson Heights stop, just a few steps from the elevated tracks, you'll find **Arunee Thai,** 37-68 79th St., off Roosevelt Avenue (© 718/205-5559). Here, the Thai food is so authentic (and the clientele mostly Thai) that the menus are written in both Thai and English. Everything is delicious, and thankfully the spice level is not toned down to appease those with delicate palates. The fish, served whole on the bone, with chile, garlic, and hot-and-sour sauce, will either take the chill off a cold winter's day or, if it's summer, the chiles will cool down your overheated body and soul.

Farther down the 7 line, get off at 103rd Street and Corona Plaza and take the no. Q23 bus to Northern Boulevard. You are in Corona now where you will find the marvelous Peruvian restaurant **La Pollada de Laura,** 102–03 Northern Blvd. (© 718/426-7818). If you like ceviche, you've come to the right place. The restaurant makes over 15 varieties, including the mythical *leche de tigre,* also known as Peruvian Viagra, a few pieces of raw shrimp and crab smothered in coconut milk, lime juice, and hot chiles and served in a wine glass. If you prefer your fish cooked, the *jalea,* a gigantic platter of fried fish, squid, and shrimp served with salsa criolla, is unforgettable. *Note:* La Pollada de Laura is within walking distance of the **Louis Armstrong House Museum** (see chapter 7), and combining the two will make a memorable excursion to Queens.

7

Exploring New York City

If this is your first trip to New York, you'll soon realize that it's impossible to take in the entire city. Because New York is almost unfathomably big and constantly changing, you could live your whole life here and still make fascinating daily discoveries (I certainly do!). This chapter is designed to give you an overview so you can narrow your choices to the itinerary that best captures your needs, interests, and time available.

Decide on a few things you absolutely must see and do, and then let the city take you on its own ride. Inevitably, you'll be blown off course by unplanned diversions that are as much fun as what you meant to see.

1 Sights & Attractions by Neighborhood

Downtown Attractions

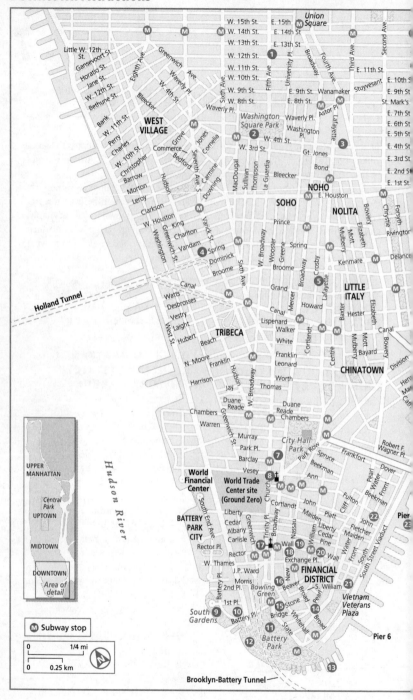

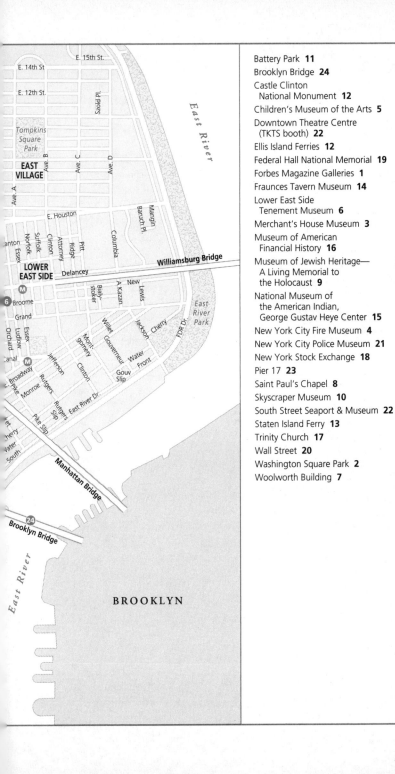

Map labels:

E. 15th St.
E. 14th St
E. 12th St.
Szold Pl.
East River
Tompkins Square Park
EAST VILLAGE
Ave. B
Ave. C
Ave. D
Ave. A
E. Houston
Mangin
Baruch Pl.
Columbia
anton
Norfolk
Essex
Suffolk
Clinton
Attorney
Pitt
Ridge
LOWER EAST SIDE
Delancey
Williamsburg Bridge
Broome
Bialy-stoker
A Kazan
New
Lewis
East River Park
Grand
Willet
Jackson
Cherry
FDR Dr.
Essex
Ludlow
Orchard
Mont-gomery
Gouverneur
Water Front
Broadway
Jefferson
Clinton
Gouv Slip
anal
Pike
Monroe
Rutgers
Rutgers Slip
East River Dr.
East River Dr.
herry
Pike Slip
Water
South
Manhattan Bridge
Brooklyn Bridge
East River
BROOKLYN

Midtown Attractions

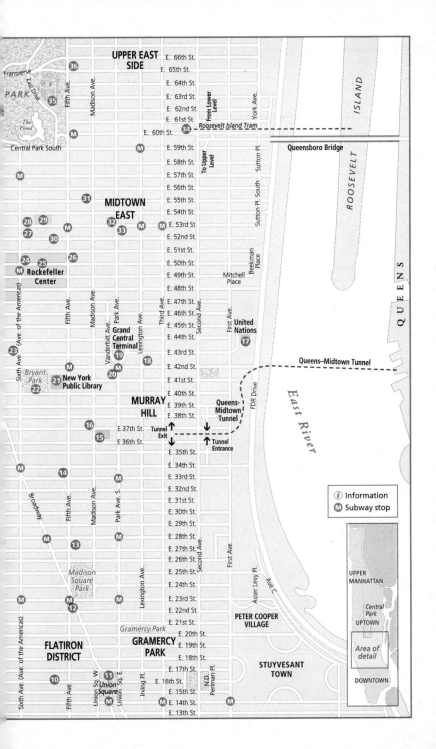

Uptown Attractions

Ⓜ Subway stop

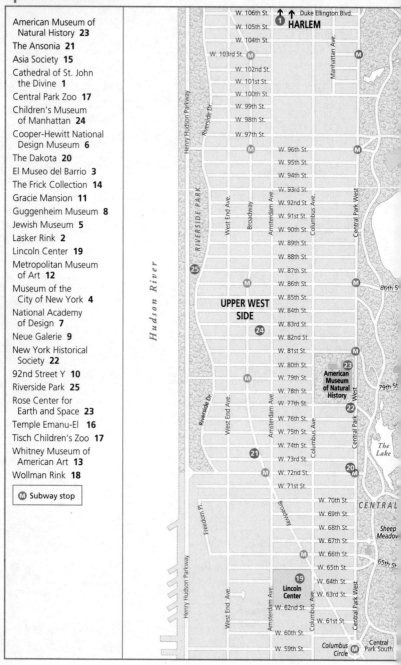

Scale	
0	1/4 mi
0	0.25 km

E. 106th St.
E. 105th St.
E. 104th St.
E. 103rd St.
E. 102nd St.
E. 101st St.
E. 100th St.
E. 99th St.
E. 98th St.
E. 97th St.
E. 96th St.
E. 95th St.
E. 94th St.
E. 93rd St.
E. 92nd St.
E. 91st St.
E. 90th St.
E. 89th St.
E. 88th St.
E. 87th St.
E. 86th St.
E. 85th St.
E. 84th St.
E. 83rd St.
E. 82nd St.
E. 81st St.
E. 80th St.
E. 79th St.
E. 78th St.
E. 77th St.
E. 76th St.
E. 75th St.
E. 74th St.
E. 73rd St.
E. 72nd St.
E. 71st St.
E. 70th St.
E. 69th St.
E. 68th St.
E. 67th St.
E. 66th St.
E. 65th St.
E. 64th St.
E. 63rd St.
E. 62nd St.
E. 61st St.
E. 60th St.
E. 59th St.

Ward's Island Footbridge

WARD'S ISLAND PARK
WARD'S ISLAND

UPPER MANHATTAN
Area of detail
Central Park
MIDTOWN
DOWNTOWN

Mount Sinai Hospital

MUSEUM MILE

The Reservoir

Transverse

The Great Lawn

Metropolitan Museum of Art

Transverse

Fifth Ave.
Madison Ave.
Park Ave.
Lexington Ave.
Third Ave.
Second Ave.
First Ave.
York Ave.
East End Ave.

CARL SCHURZ PARK

UPPER EAST SIDE

FDR Dr.

East River

ROOSEVELT ISLAND

PARK

Transverse

Central Park Zoo

Wollman Rink

Central Park South

From Lower Level
To Upper Level
Sutton Pl.

Roosevelt Island Tram
Queensboro Bridge

Upper Manhattan Attractions

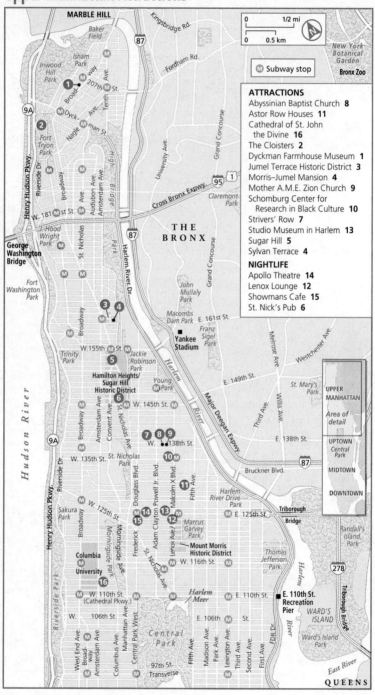

MARBLE HILL

Kingsbridge Rd.

Baker Field

87

Fordham Rd.

New York Botanical Garden

Bronx Zoo

| 0 | 1/2 mi |
| 0 | 0.5 km |

Ⓜ Subway stop

Inwood Hill Park

Isham Park

Broadway

207th St.

Ⓜ Dyck-

Ⓜ man St.

Tenth Ave.

Nagle Ave.

1

2

Fort Tryon Park

Riverside Dr.

Broadway

Audubon Ave.

Amsterdam Ave.

9A

Henry Hudson Pkwy.

W. 181st St. Ⓜ

J. Hood Wright Park

George Washington Bridge

Fort Washington Park

St. Nicholas

University Ave.

Grand Concourse

95   1

Cross Bronx Expwy.

Claremont Park

THE BRONX

Harlem River Dr.

Harlem River Park Bridge

87

John Mullaly Park

Grand Concourse

Macombs Dam Park

E. 161st St.

3 **4**

Franz Sigel Park

■ Yankee Stadium

W.155th St. Ⓜ

Trinity Park

Broadway

5

Jackie Robinson Park

Melrose Ave.

Westchester Ave.

Hamilton Heights/ Sugar Hill Historic District

Amsterdam Ave.

Convent Ave.

St. Nicholas Ave.

6

Young Park

W. 145th St. Ⓜ

Major Deegan Expwy.

Harlem River

E. 149th St.

St. Mary's Park

Third Ave.

Willis Ave.

7 **8** **9**

W. 138th St.

10

Ⓜ W. 135th St.

St. Nicholas Park

Douglass Blvd.

Adam Clayton Powell Jr. Blvd.

Malcolm X Blvd.

Fifth Ave.

E. 138th St.

Bruckner Blvd.

87

9A

11

Harlem River Drive Park

ATTRACTIONS
Abyssinian Baptist Church **8**
Astor Row Houses **11**
Cathedral of St. John
  the Divine **16**
The Cloisters **2**
Dyckman Farmhouse Museum **1**
Jumel Terrace Historic District **3**
Morris–Jumel Mansion **4**
Mother A.M.E. Zion Church **9**
Schomburg Center for
  Research in Black Culture **10**
Strivers' Row **7**
Studio Museum in Harlem **13**
Sugar Hill **5**
Sylvan Terrace **4**

NIGHTLIFE
Apollo Theatre **14**
Lenox Lounge **12**
Showmans Cafe **15**
St. Nick's Pub **6**

W. 125th St.

Morningside Ave.

Broadway

14 **13**

15 **12**

Frederick

St. Nicholas Ave.

Lenox Ave.

Marcus Garvey Park

■ Mount Morris Historic District

W. 116th St.

Triborough Bridge

E. 125th St.

278

Columbia University

16

Morningside Park

W. 110th St. (Cathedral Pkwy.)

W. 106th St.

Harlem Meer

Thomas Jefferson Park

Harlem River

E. 110th St.

E. 106th   St.

■ E. 110th St. Recreation Pier

WARD'S ISLAND

Ward's Island Park

Triborough Bridge

Randall's Island Park

Riverside Park

Sakura Park

Hudson River

Riverside Dr.

Henry Hudson Pkwy.

Central Park

West End Ave.

Broadway

Amsterdam Ave.

Manhattan Ave.

Columbus Ave.

Central Park West

Fifth Ave.

Madison Ave.

Park Ave.

Lexington Ave.

Third Ave.

Second Ave.

First Ave.

FDR Dr.

97th St. Transverse

East River

QUEENS

UPPER MANHATTAN

Area of detail

UPTOWN
Central Park

MIDTOWN

DOWNTOWN

> ## *Tips* Money-Saving Sightseeing Tips
>
> 1. **Buy a CityPass.** CityPass may be New York's best sightseeing deal. Pay one price ($45, or $39 for kids 12–17) for admission to seven major attractions: The American Museum of Natural History (does not include Space Show), the Solomon R. Guggenheim Museum, the Empire State Building, the *Intrepid* Sea-Air-Space Museum, Museum of Modern Art (MoMa), and a 2-hour Circle Line cruise. If you purchased separate admission to each of these, you'd spend more than twice as much.
>
>   CityPass is not a coupon book. It contains actual tickets, so you can bypass ticket lines. This can save you hours, since sights like the Empire State Building often have waits of an hour or more.
>
>   CityPass is good for 9 days from the first time you use it. It's sold at all participating attractions and online at **www.city-pass.net**. Your best bet is to buy it at the first attraction you visit because online orders rack up service and shipping fees. Start sightseeing at an attraction that's likely to have the shortest admission line, like the Guggenheim or the Whitney, or arrive before opening to avoid a wait. A preorder may be the way to go, however, if that's not convenient for you or you're starting your sightseeing on a weekend or during holiday time, when even those museums can have ugly ticket lines.
>
>   Get more info by calling CityPass at ✆ **208/787-4300** (CityPass is not sold over the phone).
>
> 2. **Take advantage of freebies.** Many of the best things to do and see in Manhattan are free, from walking the Brooklyn Bridge to riding the Staten Island Ferry to exploring Central Park to attending TV show tapings. Additionally, some organizations offer free walking tours. Many museums and attractions that charge admission have free or pay-as-you-wish programs 1 day or evening a week. See "Where to Find Free Culture" (p. 208) and "Absolutely Free Walking Tours" (p. 238).
>
> 3. Pick up a copy of *Frommer's NYC Free & Dirt Cheap,* by Ethan Wolff (Wiley Publishing, Inc.) for even more detailed information about free and reduced-admission attractions in the city, from theater to museums to TV show tapings.

Staten Island Ferry ★★ (p. 202)

Statue of Liberty ★★★ (p. 202)

Trinity Church (p. 226)

U.S. Customs House ★ (p. 207)

Wall Street ★★ (p. 203)

Woolworth Building ★ (p. 223)

World Trade Center site (Ground Zero) (p. 204)

MIDTOWN EAST

Chrysler Building ★★ (p. 221)

Empire State Building ★★★ (p. 197)

Grand Central Terminal ★★ (p. 198)

Lever House (p. 220)

New York Public Library ★★ (p. 222)

Tips **Advance-Planning Tip**

If you're planning your itinerary around specific attractions, make sure they'll be open while you're in town. This is also a good way to check current programming, such as museum schedules, and prioritize your time—there will always be more to see and do than you'll have time for.

OUTER BOROUGHS
THE BRONX

Bronx Zoo Wildlife Conservation
   Park ✸✸✸ (p. 247)
Edgar Allan Poe Cottage (p. 223)
New York Botanical Garden ✸
   (p. 247)
Wave Hill ✸ (p. 248)
Yankee Stadium (p. 256)

BROOKLYN

Brooklyn Botanic Garden ✸
   (p. 249)
Brooklyn Bridge ✸✸ (p. 196)
Brooklyn Heights Historic
   District ✸ (p. 252)
Brooklyn Museum of Art ✸✸
   (p. 249)
Brooklyn Tabernacle ✸ (p. 249)
Coney Island ✸✸ (p. 250)
Grand Army Plaza (p. 249)

New York Aquarium (p. 250)
New York Transit Museum (p. 251)
Prospect Park ✸✸ (p. 252)

QUEENS

American Museum of the Moving
   Image ✸ (p. 253)
Flushing Meadows–Corona Park
   (p. 245)
Isamu Noguchi Garden
   Museum ✸ (p. 254)
Louis Armstrong House
   Museum ✸ (p. 254)
Museum for African Art (p. 254)
New York Hall of Science ✸
   (p. 245)
P.S. 1 Contemporary Art Center ✸
   (p. 254)
Queens Museum of Art (p. 255)
Shea Stadium (p. 255)
Socrates Sculpture Park (p. 255)

2 Suggested Itineraries

If you're a first-time visitor and you'd like a blueprint with which to begin planning your time, consider the following 5-day game plan. Mix and match as you will!

Day 1   Start your day off just like the city itself did: at Manhattan's southern tip, New York's oldest precinct. Leave early to catch the first ferry to the **Statue of Liberty** ✸✸✸ and **Ellis Island** ✸✸. This will occupy your morning.

Once back on the mainland, pop over to the downtown **TKTS booth** at South Street Seaport (the line is usually shorter than at Times Square) to pick up some half-price tickets for a **Broadway** or **Off-Broadway show** (something's always available for the evening, or tomorrow afternoon if you prefer a matinee).

Then hop the subway to Brooklyn (the A/C line will whisk you from Manhattan to High St. in minutes), have lunch at **Grimaldi's Pizzeria** (p. 152), and then stroll back to the 212 area code over the **Brooklyn Bridge** ✸✸, which offers one of my favorite views of the Manhattan skyline.

Or use the time to enjoy one of Lower Manhattan's many historic or cultural attractions, such as the moving **Museum of Jewish Heritage—a Living Memorial to the Holocaust** ✸; surprisingly diminutive **Wall Street** ✸✸; or the **National Museum of the American Indian,** housed in the stunning 1907 Beaux Arts **U.S. Customs House,** worth a visit for the architecture alone.

Head back to your hotel to freshen up so you can enjoy a leisurely dinner at one of the city's many fantastic and inexpensive restaurants.

Day 2   Spend most of the day at one of the big museums like the **Metropolitan Museum of Art** ✸✸✸ or the **American Museum of Natural History** ✸✸✸. You could spend a week at either, so you might want to take a Highlights Tour. Don't miss the new Harrison Ford–narrated Space Show at the Natural History Museum's **Rose Center for Earth and Space** ✸.

After you've had enough museum going (you'll give out before you exhaust these collections), head into **Central Park** ✿✿✿; both museums sit right on its fringe. If you still have some energy left, you might stroll out of the south end to do a bit of window-shopping on **5th Avenue.** Plan on dinner at one of the city's ethnic enclaves (see chapter 6 for recommendations).

Day 3   Start your morning with a 3-hour cruise with either **Circle Line** or **New York Waterway,** which circumnavigates Manhattan and offers a fascinating perspective on the island. If you're strapped for time, opt for the 1-hour cruise that ferries you around New York Harbor and halfway up the East River. In the afternoon, explore one or two of the downtown neighborhoods—perhaps the cast-iron canyons of **SoHo,** the 19th-century streets of **Greenwich Village,** or exotic **Chinatown.** Walk the thoroughfares, poke your head into shops, or sit at a cafe and watch the world go by. If you prefer to have a guide, schedule a **guided walking tour** (see "Affordable Sightseeing Tours," later in this chapter).

Stay downtown for the evening, catching dinner in a stylish (or authentically old-world) restaurant and following up with some out-on-the-town time, perhaps in a live-music or comedy venue, a dance club, a hipper-than-thou cocktail lounge, or a neighborhood tavern (see chapter 9 for recommendations). Or, if you've had enough of downtown, head uptown for some down-home cooking in Harlem, and then some jazz at **St. Nick's Pub.**

Day 4   Head to **Rockefeller Center** ✿✿ to start your day with Matt and Katie outside the *Today* show studio, or to score standby tickets for Conan O'Brien. Make your way to the **Empire State Building** ✿✿✿ to see the view from the 86th floor of New York's ultimate landmark skyscraper.

Once you're done, head to **Grand Central Terminal** ✿ (a pleasant walk on a nice day) to admire the marvelous Beaux Arts monument to modern transportation, and to have lunch. Head for the **food concourse,** which boasts a wealth of full-service and casual options (see chapter 6).

Spend the afternoon browsing one or two of the smaller museums—maybe the *Intrepid* **Sea-Air-Space Museum,** the **Frick Collection** ✿✿, or the **Whitney.** Afterward, enjoy another evening at the theater; or, if it's summer, catch one of the city's free alfresco entertainment events (see chapter 9). Or catch a **baseball game;** the Yankees or the Mets are likely to be in residence (sometimes both); you might get lucky and get some bleacher seats.

Day 5   Use the morning to explore one of the major attractions you've missed thus far. If you spent day 2 at the Met, spend today at the **American Museum of Natural History.** Or go see Frank Lloyd Wright's iconic **Guggenheim Museum.** Tour the nerve center of international relations, the **United Nations.** Or, if you haven't seen **Central Park** yet, go now; you cannot leave New York without visiting it.

After lunch, take stock: What haven't you done yet that you don't want to miss? What did you do that you want to do more of? Perhaps do a bit more shopping or take a trip to one of the outer boroughs. Explore **Brooklyn Heights, Park Slope, Williamsburg,** or some of the other neighborhoods of Brooklyn; take the 7 train, the "International Express," to the **Louis Armstrong House Museum** in Queens, passing one ethnic enclave after another; or venture up to the Bronx to the **Bronx Zoo,** the **Bronx Botanical Gardens,** or **Arthur Avenue,** the Little Italy of the Bronx.

After lunch, take stock: What haven't you done yet that you don't want to miss? What do you want to do more of? Perhaps a bit of shopping (see chapter 8), or a visit to a museum that focuses on your interests, such as the **International Center of Photography** ✵, the **Museum of Arts and Design** ✵, or the **Museum of Television & Radio.** You're becoming a pro at exploring the city by now, so take the bull by the horns and make the most of your afternoon.

In the evening, celebrate the end of a great vacation with some live music. Splurge on a night of jazz at one of the Big Apple's legendary clubs, or take in a night of laughs at one of the city's comedy clubs, such as the **Comedy Cellar.** If you're the party type, don your glad rags and dance the night away at one of the city's outrageous clubs. No matter what you choose, make it a night to remember!

3 The Top Attractions

In addition to the choices below, don't forget **Central Park** ✵✵✵, the great green swath that is, by virtue of its existence, New York City's greatest marvel. Central Park is so big and multifaceted that it earns its own section (p. 227).

American Museum of Natural History ✵✵✵   This is one of the hottest museum tickets in town, thanks to the $210-million **Rose Center for Earth and Space** ✵, whose four-story-tall planetarium sphere hosts the excellent Harrison Ford–narrated Space Show *Are We Alone?,* the most technologically advanced sky show on the planet. Prepare to be blown away. The show is short—less than a half-hour from start to finish—but phenomenal. (*New York* magazine has called it "the world's largest, most powerful virtual-reality simulator.")

Buy your tickets in advance for the Space Show in order to guarantee admission (they're available online); I also recommend buying tickets in advance for a specific IMAX film or special exhibition, such as the Butterfly Conservatory (see below), especially during peak seasons (summer, autumn, holiday time) and for weekend visits; otherwise, you might miss out.

Other must-sees include the Big Bang Theater, which re-creates the theoretical birth of the universe; the main Hall of the Universe, with its very own 16-ton meteorite; and the terrific Hall of Planet Earth, which focuses on the geologic processes of our home planet (great volcano display!). All in all, you'll need a minimum of 2 hours to fully explore the Rose Center. *Tip:* Friday night is a great time to plan your visit, as the center isn't overcrowded, live jazz and food fill the Hall of the Universe, and, bathed in blue light, the sphere looks magical.

The rest of the 4-square-block museum is nothing to sneeze at, either. Founded in 1869, it houses the world's greatest natural science collection in a square-block group of buildings made of towers and turrets, pink granite and red brick. The diversity of the holdings is astounding: some 36 million specimens, ranging from microscopic organisms to the world's largest cut gem, the Brazilian Princess Topaz (21,005 carats). Rose Center aside, it would take you all day to see the entire museum, and then you *still* wouldn't get to everything. If you don't have a lot of time, you can see the best of the best on free **highlights tours** offered daily every hour at 15 minutes after the hour from 10:15am to 3:15pm. Free daily **spotlight tours,** thematic tours that change monthly, are also offered; stop by an information desk for the day's schedule. **Audio Expeditions,** high-tech audio tours that allow you to access narration in the order you choose, are also available to help you make sense of it all.

If you only see one exhibit, see the **dinosaurs** ✵, which take up the entire fourth floor.

The **Hall of Biodiversity** is an impressive multimedia exhibit, but its doom-and-gloom story about the future of rainforests and other natural habitats might be too much for the little ones. Kids 5 and up should head to the **Discovery Room,** with lots of hands-on exhibits and experiments. (*Parents, be prepared:* There seems to be a gift shop overflowing with fuzzy stuffed animals at every turn.) After a renovation, the **Arthur Ross Hall of Meteorites** opened in late 2003, transformed into a hands-on exhibit.

The museum excels at **special exhibitions,** so check to see what will be on while you're in town in case any advance planning is required. The magical **Butterfly Conservatory** ⊛, a walk-in enclosure housing nearly 500 free-flying tropical butterflies, has developed into a can't-miss fixture from October through May; check to see if it's in the house while you're in town.

Central Park West (btwn 77th and 81st sts.). ⓒ **212/769-5100** for information, or 212/769-5200 for tickets (tickets can also be ordered online). www.amnh.org. Suggested admission $12 adults, $9 seniors and students, $7 children 2–12; Space Show and museum admission $19 adults, $14 seniors and students, $12 children under 12. Additional charges for IMAX movies and some special exhibitions. Daily 10am–5:45pm; Rose Center Fri to 8:45pm. Subway: B or C to 81st St.; 1 or 9 to 79th St.

Brooklyn Bridge ⊛⊛ *(Moments)*   Its Gothic-inspired stone pylons and intricate steel-cable webs have moved poets like Walt Whitman and Hart Crane to sing the praises of this great span, the first to cross the East River and connect Manhattan to Brooklyn. Begun in 1867 and ultimately completed in 1883, the beautiful Brooklyn Bridge is now the city's best-known symbol of the age of growth that seized the city during the late 19th century. Walk across the bridge and imagine the awe that New Yorkers of that age felt at seeing two boroughs joined by this monumental span. It's still astounding.

Walking the Bridge: Walking the Brooklyn Bridge is one of my all-time favorite New York activities, although there's no doubt that the Lower Manhattan views from the bridge now have a painful resonance as well as a joyous spirit. A wide wood-plank pedestrian walkway is elevated above the traffic, making it a relatively peaceful, and popular, walk. It's a great vantage point from which to contemplate the New York skyline and the East River.

There's a sidewalk entrance on Park Row, just across from City Hall Park (take the 4, 5, or 6 train to Brooklyn Bridge/City Hall). But why do this walk *away* from Manhattan, toward the far less impressive Brooklyn skyline? Instead, for Manhattan skyline views, take an A or C train to High Street, one stop into Brooklyn. From there, you'll be on the bridge in no time: Come above ground, then walk through the little park to Cadman Plaza East and head downslope (left) to the stairwell that will take you up to the footpath. (Following Prospect Place under the bridge, turning right onto Cadman Plaza E., will also take you directly to the stairwell.) It's a 20- to 40-minute stroll over the bridge to Manhattan, depending on your pace, the amount of foot traffic, and the number of stops you make to behold the spectacular views (there are benches along the way). The footpath will deposit you right at City Hall Park.

Tasty tips: The perfect complement to your stroll over the Brooklyn Bridge is a stop for pizza at **Grimaldi's** (see "Pizza New York Style" on p. 152), followed by delicious homemade ice cream at the **Brooklyn Ice Cream Factory** (ⓒ **718/ 246-3963**), located at the Fulton Ferry Fire Boat House on the river and in the shadow of the bridge. The pizza and ice cream will fortify you for your return stroll into Manhattan.

Subway: A or C to High St.; 4, 5, or 6 to Brooklyn Bridge/City Hall.

Ellis Island ⊛⊛ *(Moments)*   Roughly 40% of Americans can trace their heritage back to an ancestor who came through here. For the 62 years when it was America's main entry point for immigrants (1892–1954), Ellis Island processed some

12 million people. The greeting was often brusque—especially in the early years when as many as 12,000 came through in a single day. The **Immigration Museum** skillfully relates the story of Ellis Island and immigration in America by placing the emphasis on personal experience.

It's difficult to leave the museum unmoved. Today you enter the Main Building's baggage room, just as the immigrants did, and then climb the stairs to the **Registry Room,** with its vaulted tiled ceiling, where millions waited anxiously for medical and legal processing. A step-by-step account of the immigrants' voyage is detailed in the exhibit, with haunting photos and oral histories. What might be the most poignant exhibit is *Treasures from Home,* 1,000 objects and photos donated by descendants of immigrants, including family heirlooms, religious articles, and clothing and jewelry. Outside, the **American Immigrant Wall of Honor** commemorates the names of more than 500,000 immigrants and their families, from Myles Standish to Jay Leno. You can research your own family's history at the **American Family Immigration History Center;** start your research at home at www.ellisislandrecords.org. You might also make time to see the award-winning short film *Island of Hope, Island of Tears,* which plays on a continuous loop in two theaters. Short live performances are also often part of the day's events.

Touring tips: Ferries run daily to Ellis Island and Liberty Island from Battery Park and Liberty State Park (in New Jersey) at frequent intervals; see the Statue of Liberty listing (p. 202) for details.

In New York Harbor. ℰ **212/363-3200** (general info), or 212/269-5755 (ticket/ferry info). www.nps.gov/elis or www.ellisisland.org. Free admission (ferry ticket charge). Daily 9:30am–5:50pm (last ferry departs around 3:30pm). For subway and ferry details, see the Statue of Liberty listing on p. 202 (ferry trip includes stops at both sights).

Empire State Building ★★★   It took 60,000 tons of steel, 10 million bricks, 2.5 million feet of electrical wire, 120 miles of pipe, and 7 million man-hours to build. King Kong climbed it in 1933. A plane slammed into it in 1945. The World Trade Center superseded it in 1970 as the island's tallest building. On September 11, 2001, it regained its status as New York City's tallest building after 31 years of taking second place. Through it all, the Empire State Building has remained one of the city's favorite landmarks, and its signature high-rise. Completed in 1931, the limestone-and-stainless-steel streamline deco dazzler climbs 102 stories (1,454 ft.) and now harbors the offices of fashion firms, and, in its upper reaches, a jumble of broadcast equipment.

Always a conversation piece, the Empire State Building glows every night, bathed in colored floodlights to commemorate events of significance—red, white, and blue for all U.S. holidays; green for St. Patrick's Day; red, black, and green for Martin Luther King Day; blue and white for the first night of Hanukkah; even lavender and white for Gay Pride Day (you can find a lighting schedule online). The silver spire can be seen from all over the city. On a lovely day, stand at the base of the Flatiron Building (p. 221) and gaze up 5th; the crisp, gleaming deco tower jumps out, soaring above the sooty office buildings that surround it.

But the views that keep nearly 3.5 million visitors a year coming are the ones from the 86th-story **observatory,** where you can walk out on a windy deck and look through coin-operated viewers (bring quarters!) over what, on a clear day, can be as much as an 80-mile radius. The panorama is magnificent. The higher observation deck is glass-enclosed and cramped.

Light fog can create an admirably moody effect, but it goes without saying that a clear day is best. Dusk brings the most remarkable views and the biggest crowds. Consider going in the morning, when the light is still low on the horizon, keeping glare to a minimum. Starry nights are pure magic.

In your haste to go up, don't rush through the beautiful marble **lobby** without pausing to admire its features, which include a wonderful streamline mural as well as the 5th Avenue gallery which features New York City–themed artists.

Time-saving tip: If you don't mind spending about $1 more per ticket, you can avoid ticket lines by buying advance tickets online. It's money well spent in the busy seasons. Place your order well before you leave home.

350 5th Ave. (at 34th St.). ℭ **877/NYC-VIEW** or 212/736-3100. www.esbnyc.com. Observatory admission $12 adults, $11 seniors and children 12–17, $6 children 5–11, free for children under 5. Mon–Fri 10am–midnight; Sat–Sun 9:30am–midnight; tickets sold until 11pm. Subway: B, D, F, N, R, V, Q, or W to 34th St.; 6 to 33rd St.

Grand Central Terminal ⚑⚑   Even if you're not catching one of the subway lines or Metro-North commuter trains that rumble through Grand Central Terminal, come for a visit; it's one of the most magnificent public places in the country. And even if you arrive and leave by subway, be sure to exit the station, walking a couple of blocks south, to about 40th Street, before you turn around to admire Jules-Alexis Coutan's neoclassical sculpture *Transportation* hovering over the south entrance, with a majestically buff Mercury, the Roman god of commerce and travel, as its central figure.

The greatest visual impact comes when you enter the vast majestic **main concourse.** The high windows allow sunlight to penetrate the space, glinting off the half-acre Tennessee marble floor. The brass clock over the central kiosk gleams, as do the gold- and nickel-plated chandeliers piercing the side archways. The masterful **sky ceiling,** a brilliant greenish blue, depicts the constellations of the winter sky above New York. They're lit with 59 stars, surrounded by dazzling 24-carat gold and emitting light fed through fiber-optic cables, their intensities roughly replicating the magnitude of the actual stars as seen from Earth. Look carefully and you'll see a patch near one corner left unrestored as a reminder of the neglect once visited on this splendid overhead masterpiece. On the east end of the main concourse is a grand **marble staircase.**

This dramatic Beaux Arts splendor serves as a hub of social activity as well. Excellent-quality retail shops and restaurants have taken over the mezzanine and lower levels. Off the main concourse at street level, there's a nice mix of specialty shops and national retailers, as well as the truly grand **Grand Central Market** for gourmet foods. The **New York Transit Museum Store** (p. 282), in the shuttle passage, houses city transit-related exhibitions and a terrific gift shop that's worth a look for transit buffs. The **lower dining concourse** ⚑ houses a stellar food court and the famous **Oyster Bar & Restaurant.**

The **Municipal Art Society** (ℭ **212/935-3960;** www.mas.org) offers a free walking tour of Grand Central Terminal on Wednesday at 12:30pm, which meets at the information booth on the Grand Concourse. The **Grand Central Partnership** (ℭ **212/697-1245**) runs its own free tour every Friday at 12:30pm, which meets outside the station in front of the Whitney Museum at the Altria gallery, at 42nd Street and Park Avenue. Call to confirm before you set out to meet either tour.

42nd St. at Park Ave. ℭ **212/340-2210** (events hot line). www.grandcentralterminal.com. Subway: S, 4, 5, 6, or 7 to 42nd St./Grand Central.

Metropolitan Museum of Art ★★★ Home of blockbuster after blockbuster exhibition, the Metropolitan Museum of Art attracts some five million people a year, more than any other spot in New York City. And it's no wonder—this place is magnificent. At 1.6 million square feet, this is the largest museum in the western hemisphere. Nearly all the world's cultures are on display through the ages—from Egyptian mummies to ancient Greek statuary to Islamic carvings to Renaissance paintings to Native American masks to 20th-century decorative arts—and masterpieces are the rule. You could go once a week for a lifetime and still find something new on each visit.

So unless you plan on spending your entire vacation in the museum (some people do), you cannot see the entire collection. My recommendation is to give it a good day—or better yet, 2 half-days so you don't burn out. One good way to get an overview is to take advantage of the little-known **Museum Highlights Tour,** offered every day at various times throughout the day (usually 10:15am–3:15pm; tours also offered in Spanish, Italian, German, and Korean). Even some New Yorkers who've spent many hours in the museum could profit from this once-over. Visit the museum's website for a schedule of this and subject-specific walking tours (Old Master Paintings, American Period Rooms, Arts of China, Islamic Art, and so on); you can also get a schedule of the day's tours at the Visitor Services desk when you arrive. A daily schedule of **Gallery Talks** is available as well.

The least overwhelming way to see the Met on your own is to pick up a map at the round desk in the entry hall and choose to concentrate on what you like, whether it's 17th-century paintings, American furniture, or the art of the South Pacific. Highlights include the American Wing's **Garden Court,** with its 19th-century sculpture; the terrific ground-level **Costume Hall;** and the **Frank Lloyd Wright room.** The beautifully renovated **Roman and Greek galleries** are overwhelming, but in a marvelous way, as are the collections of **Byzantine Art** and later **Chinese art.** The highlight of the astounding **Egyptian collection** is the **Temple of Dendur,** in a dramatic, purpose-built glass-walled gallery with Central Park views. The **Greek Galleries,** which at last fully realize McKim, Mead & White's grand neoclassical plans of 1917, and the **Ancient Near East Galleries,** are particularly of note. But it all depends on what your interests are. **Special exhibitions** can range from *Orazio and Artemisia Gentileschi: Father and Daughter Painters in Baroque Italy* to *Earthly Bodies: Irving Penn's Nudes, 1949–50.*

In a response to the huge crowds, in 2003 the Met began opening "Holiday Mondays." On those Mondays, such as Memorial Day or Labor Day, the museum is open from 9:30am to 5:30pm.

To purchase tickets for concerts and lectures, call ☎ **212/570-3949** (Mon–Sat 9:30am–5pm). The museum contains several dining facilities, including a **full-service restaurant** serving Continental cuisine (☎ **212/570-3964** for reservations). The roof garden is worth visiting if you're here from spring to autumn, offering peaceful views over Central Park and the city.

Money-saving tip: The Met's medieval collections are housed in Upper Manhattan at the **Cloisters** ★ (p. 206); admission is included with your Met ticket purchase, but seeing both satisfactorily in a single day is more than only the most die-hard budget travelers should try to accomplish. If you're committed to seeing both on one ticket, start at the Cloisters at opening time on a Friday or Saturday (the Met's extended-hour days, so you can maximize your time), then move downtown to the main museum in the afternoon.

5th Ave. at 82nd St. ☎ 212/535-7710. www.metmuseum.org. Admission (includes same-day entrance to the Cloisters) $12 adults, $7 seniors and students, free for children under 12 when accompanied by an adult.

Moments **Evening Events at the Met**

On **Friday and Saturday evenings,** the Met remains open for art viewing and cocktails in the Great Hall Balcony Bar (5–8pm) and live classical music. A slate of after-hours programs (gallery talks, tours) changes by the week; call for schedule. The restaurant stays open until 10pm (last reservation at 8:30pm); dinner is usually accompanied by piano music.

Sun, holiday Mon (Labor Day, Memorial Day, and so forth), and Tues–Thurs 9:30am–5:30pm; Fri–Sat 9:30am–9pm. No strollers allowed Sun (back carriers available at 81st St. entrance coat-check area). Subway: 4, 5, or 6 to 86th St.

Museum of Modern Art *✫*   The Museum of Modern Art (or MoMa, as it's usually called) boasts the world's greatest collection of painting and sculpture from the late 19th century to the present, including everything from Monet's *Water Lilies* and Klimt's *The Kiss* to later masterworks by Frida Kahlo, Edward Hopper, Andy Warhol, Robert Rauschenberg, and many others. Top that off with an extensive collection of modern drawings, photography, architectural models and furniture, iconic design objects ranging from tableware to sports cars, and film and video (including the world's largest collection of D. W. Griffith films), and you have quite a museum. If you're into modernism, this is the place to be.

The good news is that after a $650-million renovation of its West 53rd Street building under the guidance of Japanese architect Yoshio Taniguchi, MoMa returned to Manhattan from its temporary home in Queens in November 2004 with more than double the previous exhibit space. The bad news is that the admission charge has gone up to a whopping $20! (This, however, covers all exhibits and galleries.) However, like most other Manhattan museums, there are designated free entry times, in MoMa's case, 4 to 8pm on Friday.

11 W. 53rd St. (btwn 5th and 6th aves.). ✆ 212/708-9480. www.moma.org. Admission $12 adults, $8.50 seniors and students, free for children under 16 when accompanied by an adult, pay what you wish Fri 4:30–8:15pm. You can purchase tickets on the website. Sat–Tues and Thurs 10:30am–5:45pm; Fri 10:30am–8:15pm; closed Wed. Subway: E or F to 5th Ave.

Rockefeller Center *✫✫ Moments*   A streamline masterpiece, Rockefeller Center is one of New York's central gathering spots. A prime example of the city's skyscraper spirit, it was erected in the 1930s, when the city was deep in the Depression as well as its most passionate Art Deco phase. Designated a National Historic Landmark in 1988, it's the world's largest privately owned business-and-entertainment center, with 18 buildings on 21 acres.

For a dramatic approach to the entire complex, start at 5th Avenue between 49th and 50th streets. The builders purposely created the gentle slope of the Promenade, known here as the **Channel Gardens** because it's flanked to the south by La Maison Française and to the north by the British Building. You'll also find a number of shops along here, including a branch of the **Metropolitan Museum of Art Store,** a good stop for elegant gifts (some quite affordable). The Promenade leads to the **Lower Plaza,** home to the famous ice-skating rink and alfresco dining in summer in the shadow of Paul Manship's gilded bronze statue *Prometheus.* All around the flags of the United Nations' member countries flap in the breeze. Just behind *Prometheus,* in December and early January, towers the city's majestic official Christmas tree.

The **Rink at Rockefeller Plaza** (© 212/332-7654; www.rockefellercenter. com) is tiny but romantic, especially during the holidays, when the Christmas tree's lights twinkle. It's open from mid-October to mid-March, and you'll skate under the tree from early December through the holiday season.

The focal point of this "city within a city" is the **GE Building**, at 30 Rockefeller Plaza, a 70-story showpiece. It's still one of the city's most impressive buildings; walk through for a look at the granite-and-marble lobby, lined with sepia-toned murals by José Maria Sert. You can pick up a walking-tour brochure highlighting the center's art and architecture at the main information desk. **NBC** maintains studios throughout the complex. Shows like *Saturday Night Live, Dateline NBC,* and *Late Night with Conan O'Brien* originate in the GE Building (see "Talk of the Town: Free TV Tapings" on p. 240 for tips on getting tickets). NBC's *Today* show is broadcast live on weekdays from 7 to 10am from the glass-enclosed studio on the corner of 49th Street and Rockefeller Plaza; come early if you want a visible spot, and bring your HI MOM! sign.

The 70-minute **NBC Studio Tour** (© 212/664-3700; www.shopnbc.com/ nbcstore/default.aspx) will take you behind the scenes, but it's not worth the expenditure for wallet-watching budget travelers ($18 adults, $15 seniors and kids 6–16). If you're committed to the notion, you can reserve your tickets for either tour in advance or buy them right up to tour time at the **NBC Experience** store, on Rockefeller Plaza at 49th Street.

Other notable buildings include the **International Building,** on 5th Avenue between 50th and 51st streets, worth a look for its Atlas statue; and the **McGraw-Hill Building,** on 6th Avenue between 48th and 49th streets, with its 50-foot sun triangle on the plaza. Designed by Donald Deskey, the restored **Radio City Music Hall**, 1260 6th Ave., at 50th Street (© 212/247-4777; www.radiocity.com), is one of the city's largest indoor theaters, with 6,200 seats, but its true grandeur derives from its Art Deco appointments. From the distant seats, the stage's proscenium arch evokes a faraway sun setting on the horizon. The men's and women's lounges are also splendid. The theater hosts the annual **Christmas Spectacular,** starring the Rockettes. The 1-hour **Stage Door Tour,** offered Monday through Saturday, is $16 for adults, $10 for children under 12.

Btwn 48th and 50th sts., from 5th to 6th aves. © 212/332-6868. www.rockefellercenter.com. Subway: B, D, F, or V to 47th–50th sts./Rockefeller Center.

Solomon R. Guggenheim Museum   It's been called a bun, a snail, a concrete tornado, and even a giant wedding cake; bring your kids, and they'll probably see it as New York's coolest opportunity for skateboarding. Whatever description you choose to apply, Frank Lloyd Wright's only New York building, completed in 1959, is best summed up as a brilliant work of architecture—so consistently brilliant that it competes with the art for your attention. If you're

---

Tips **Avoiding the Crowds at Big Apple Museums**

Many of the city's top museums—including the Natural History Museum, the Met, the Guggenheim, and the Whitney—have late hours on Friday and/or Saturday nights. Take advantage of them. You'll largely have the place to yourself by 5 or 6pm—which, in most cases, leaves you hours left to explore, unfettered by crowds or screaming kids. The other option, as I've stressed through the book, is to avoid weekends and come early on weekdays, preferably when the doors open.

looking for the city's best modern art, head to MoMa or the Whitney first; come to the Guggenheim to see the house.

It's easy to see the bulk of what's on display in 2 to 4 hours. Inside, a spiraling rotunda circles over a slowly inclined ramp that leads you past changing exhibits that, in the past, have ranged from *Matthew Barney: The Cremaster Cycle* to *Norman Rockwell: Pictures for the American People,* said to be the most comprehensive exhibit ever of the beloved painter's works. Usually the progression is counterintuitive: from the first floor up, rather than from the sixth floor down. If you're not sure, ask a guard before you begin. Permanent exhibits of 19th- and 20th-century art, including strong holdings of Kandinsky, Klee, Picasso, and French Impressionists, occupy a stark annex called the **Tower Galleries,** an addition (accessible at every level) that some critics claimed made the entire structure look like a toilet bowl backed by a water tank (judge for yourself—I think there may be something to that view).

The Guggenheim runs some interesting special programs, including free docent tours daily, a limited schedule of lectures, free family films, avant-garde screenings for grown-ups, curator-led guided gallery tours on select Friday afternoons, and the **World Beat Jazz Series,** which resounds through the rotunda on Friday and Saturday from 5 to 8pm.

1071 5th Ave. (at 89th St.). ✆ **212/423-3500.** www.guggenheim.org. Admission $15 adults, $10 seniors and students, free for children under 12, pay what you wish Fri 6–8pm. Sat–Wed 10am–5:45pm; Fri 10am–8pm. Subway: 4, 5, or 6 to 86th St.

Staten Island Ferry ★★ *Value*   Here's New York's best freebie—especially if you just want to glimpse the Statue of Liberty and not climb its steps. You get an hour-long excursion (round-trip) into the world's biggest harbor. This is not strictly a sightseeing ride, but commuter transportation to and from Staten Island. During business hours you'll share the boat with working stiffs reading papers and drinking coffee, blissfully unaware of the sights outside.

You, however, should go on deck and enjoy the busy harbor traffic. The old orange-and-green boats usually have open decks along the sides or at the bow and stern; try to catch one of these boats if you can, because the newer white boats don't have decks. Grab a seat on the right side of the boat for the best view. On the way out of Manhattan, you'll pass the Statue of Liberty, Ellis Island, and from the left side of the boat, Governor's Island; you'll see the Verrazano Narrows Bridge spanning the distance from Brooklyn to Staten Island in the distance.

When the boat arrives at St. George, Staten Island, everyone must disembark. Follow the boat-loading sign on your right as you get off; you'll circle around to the next loading dock. It's all well worth the time spent.

Departs from the Whitehall Ferry Terminal at the southern tip of Manhattan. ✆ **718/815-BOAT.** www. ci.nyc.ny.us/html/dot. Free admission ($3 for car transport on select ferries). 24 hrs.; every 20–30 min. weekdays, less frequently off-peak and weekend hours. Subway: N or R to Whitehall St.; 4 or 5 to Bowling Green; 1 or 9 to South Ferry (ride in one of the 1st 5 cars).

Statue of Liberty ★★★ *Kids*   For the millions who first came by ship to America in the last 2 centuries—either as privileged tourists or needy, hopeful immigrants—Lady Liberty, standing in the Upper Bay, was their first glimpse of America. No monument so embodies the nation's, and the world's, notion of political freedom and economic potential. Even if you don't make it out to Liberty Island, you can get a spine-tingling glimpse from Battery Park, from the New Jersey side of the bay, or during a free ride on the Staten Island Ferry (see above). It's always reassuring to see her torch lighting the way.

Proposed by French statesman Edouard de Laboulaye as a gift from France to the United States, commemorating the two nations' friendship and joint notions of liberty, the statue was designed by sculptor Frédéric-Auguste Bartholdi with the engineering help of Alexandre-Gustave Eiffel (who was responsible for the famed Paris tower) and unveiled on October 28, 1886. *Touring tips:* Ferries leave daily every half-hour to 45 minutes from 9am to about 3:30pm, with more frequent ferries in the morning and extended hours in summer. Try to go as early as you can on a weekday to avoid the crowds in the afternoon, on weekends, and on holidays.

A stop at **Ellis Island** (p. 196) is included in the fare, but if you catch the last ferry, you can only visit the statue or Ellis Island, not both.

Note that you can **buy ferry tickets in advance** via **www.statueoflibertyferry. com**, which will allow you to board the boat without standing in the sometimes-long ticket line; however, there is an additional service charge attached. Even if you've already purchased tickets, arrive as much as 30 minutes before your desired ferry time to allow for increased security procedures prior to boarding the ferry. The ferry ride takes about 20 minutes.

Once on Liberty Island, you'll start to get an idea of the statue's immensity: She weighs 225 tons and measures 152 feet from foot to flame. Her nose alone is 4½ feet long, and her index finger is 8 feet long.

After September 11, 2001, access to the base of the statue was prohibited, but in the summer of 2004, access, albeit still somewhat limited (you can't climb to the Statue's crown), was once again allowed. Now you can explore the Statue of Liberty Museum, peer into the inner structure through a glass ceiling near the base of the Statue, and enjoy views from the observation deck on top a 16-story pedestal.

On Liberty Island in New York Harbor. © 212/363-3200 (general info), or 212/269-5755 (ticket/ferry info). www.nps.gov/stli or www.statueoflibertyferry.com. Free admission; ferry ticket to Statue of Liberty and Ellis Island $10 adults, $8 seniors, $4 children 3–17. Daily 9am–5pm (last ferry departs around 4pm); extended hours in summer. Subway: 4 or 5 to Bowling Green; 1 or 9 to South Ferry. Walk south through Battery Park to Castle Clinton, the fort housing the ferry ticket booth.

Times Square *Overrated*   There's no doubting that Times Square has evolved into something much different than it was over a decade ago when it had a deservedly sleazy reputation. Yet there is much debate among New Yorkers about which incarnation was better. For New Yorkers, Times Square is a place we go out of our way to avoid. The crowds, even by New York standards, are stifling; the restaurants, mostly national chains, aren't very good; the shopping, also mostly national chains, are unimaginative; and the attractions, like **Madame Tussaud's New York** wax museum, are kitschy. I suppose it's a little too Vegas for us. Still, you've come all this way; you've got to at least take a peek, if only for the amazing neon spectacle of it.

Most of the Broadway shows are centered around Times Square, so plan your visit around your show tickets. For your predinner meal, walk 2 blocks west to 9th Avenue where you'll find a number of relatively inexpensive, good restaurants. If you are with the kids, the Ferris wheel in the **Toys "R" Us** store makes a visit to Times Square worthwhile.

Subway: 1, 2, 3, 7, S, A, C, E, N, R, or W to Times Square.

Wall Street & the New York Stock Exchange ★★ *Value*   Wall Street—it's an iconic name, and the world's prime hub for bulls and bears everywhere. This 18th-century lane (you'll be surprised at how little it is) is appropriately monumental,

World Trade Center Site (Ground Zero)

Do you call a place where over 3,000 people lost their lives an "attraction"? Or do you now call it a shrine? This is the quandary of the World Trade Center site. And as you read this book it is still just a site, but ground was broken in the summer of 2004 and in a few years it will no longer be a site but a gleaming complex and at its center a Freedom Tower. There will also be a memorial to the innocent victims lost in the attack of September 11, 2001, consisting of two large voids with pools cascading 30 feet into the footprints of the Twin Towers.

While construction is going on, you can see the site through a viewing wall on the Church Street side of the site; on that "Wall of Heroes" are the names of those who lost their lives that day along with the history of the site, including photos of the construction of the World Trade Center in the late 1960s and how, after it opened in 1972, it changed the New York skyline and downtown. A walk along the Wall of Heroes remains a painfully moving experience.

The site is bounded by Church, Barclay, Liberty, and West streets. Call ℭ 212/484-1222, or go to www.nycvisit.com or www.southstseaport. org for viewing information; go to www.downtownny.com for Lower Manhattan area information and rebuilding updates.

lined with neoclassical towers that reach as far skyward as the dreams of investors who built it into the world's most famous financial market.

At the heart of the action is the **New York Stock Exchange (NYSE),** the world's largest securities trader, where you can watch the billions change hands and get an idea of how the money merchants work. NYSE came into being in 1792, when merchants met daily under a buttonwood tree to pass off to each other the U.S. bonds that had been sold to fund the Revolutionary War. By 1903, they were trading stocks of publicly held companies in this Corinthian-columned Beaux Arts "temple" designed by George Post. About 3,000 companies are listed on the exchange, trading nearly 314 billion shares valued at about $16 trillion. Until September 11, 2001, visitors could acquire free tickets to tour a small interactive museum and watch the action on the trading floor from the glass-lined, mezzanine-level observation gallery. However, the facility has been closed to the public since the terrorist attack. The website says it is closed "indefinitely."

20 Broad St. (btwn Wall St. and Exchange Place). ℭ 212/656-5165. www.nyse.com. Subway: J, M, or Z to Broad St.; 2, 3, 4, or 5 to Wall St.

Whitney Museum of American Art 🎭🎭   What is arguably the finest collection of 20th-century American art in the world belongs to the Whitney thanks to the efforts of Gertrude Vanderbilt Whitney. A sculptor herself, Whitney organized exhibitions by American artists shunned by traditional academies, assembled a sizable personal collection, and founded the museum in 1930 in Greenwich Village.

Today's museum is an imposing presence on Madison Avenue—an inverted three-tiered pyramid of concrete and gray granite with seven seemingly random windows designed by Marcel Breuer, a leader of the Bauhaus movement. The rotating permanent collection consists of an intelligent selection of major works by Edward Hopper, George Bellows, Georgia O'Keeffe, Roy Lichtenstein, Jasper

Johns, and other significant artists. A pleasing second-floor exhibit space is devoted exclusively to works from its permanent collection from 1900 to 1950, while the rest of the space is dedicated to rotating exhibits.

Shows are usually all well curated and more edgy than what you'd see at the MoMa or the Guggenheim (though not as left-of-mainstream as what you'll find at the New Museum). Topics range from topical surveys, such as *American Art in the Age of Technology* and *The Warhol Look: Glamour Style Fashion* to in-depth retrospectives of famous or lesser-known movements (such as Fluxus, the movement that spawned Yoko Ono, among others) and artists (Mark Rothko, Keith Haring, Duane Hanson, Bob Thompson). Free **gallery tours** are offered daily, and music, screenings, and lectures fill the calendar. For details on the exhibits at the Whitney's small satellite branch, the **Whitney Museum of American Art at Altria,** which is located in the lobby of the Altria building across the Grand Central Station; see the website.

945 Madison Ave. (at 75th St.). (© 877/WHITNEY or 212/570-3676. www.whitney.org. Admission $12 adults, $9.50 seniors and students, free for children under 12, pay what you wish Fri 6–9pm. Mon–Tues, Thurs, and Sat–Sun 11am–6pm; Fri 1–9pm. Subway: 6 to 77th St.

4 More Manhattan Museums

In 1978, New York's finest cultural institutions on 5th Avenue from 82nd to 104th streets formed a consortium called **Museum Mile,** the name New York City gave to the stretch several years later. The "mile" begins at the **Metropolitan Museum of Art** 𝍩𝍩𝍩 (see "The Top Attractions," above) and moves north to **El Museo del Barrio.** However, even the smallest museums require some time; so don't plan on just popping into a few as you stroll along. Your best bet is to head directly to the museum that's tops on your list, then proceed to your second choice if you have time. If you're heading to the Metropolitan, you'll only see a portion of the collection there in a full day.

For the **Brooklyn Museum of Art** 𝍩𝍩, the **New York Transit Museum,** the **American Museum of the Moving Image** 𝍩, the **Queens Museum of Art,** the **Isamu Noguchi Garden Museum** 𝍩, and the **P.S. 1 Contemporary Art Center** 𝍩, see "Highlights of the Outer Boroughs" (p. 247).

If you're traveling with the kids, consider the museums in "Especially for Kids" (p. 244), which include the **Children's Museum of Manhattan** 𝍩, the **Sony Wonder Technology Lab,** and the **New York Hall of Science** 𝍩.

If you're interested in historic-house museums, see "In Search of Historic Homes" (p. 223).

Also, don't forget to see what's on at the **New York Public Library** 𝍩𝍩, which regularly holds excellent free exhibitions; see p. 222.

American Folk Art Museum 𝍩𝍩 This gorgeous, ultramodern boutique museum has been called by *House & Garden* no less than the city's greatest new (when it opened in 2001) museum and best work of architecture since Frank Lloyd Wright built the Guggenheim in 1959, while *New York* magazine called it "brilliant" and "a tour de force." Not only is it a stunning structure, but it also heralds American folk art's entry into the top echelon of museum-worthy art.

The modified open-plan interior features an extraordinary collection of traditional works from the 18th century to the self-taught artists and craftspeople of the present, reflecting the breadth and vitality of the American folk-art tradition. A splendid variety of quilts, in particular, makes the textiles collection the museum's most popular. The book- and gift shop is outstanding, filled with one-of-a-kind objects.

45 W. 53rd St. (btwn 5th and 6th aves.). ☎ 212/265-1040. www.folkartmuseum.org. Admission $9 adults, $7 seniors and students, free for children under 12, free to all Fri 6–8pm. Tues–Thurs and Sat–Sun 10:30am–5:30pm; Fri 10:30am–7:30pm. Subway: E or V to 5th Ave.

Asia Society   The Asia Society was founded in 1956 by John D. Rockefeller III with the goal of increasing understanding between Americans and Asians through art exhibits, lectures, films, performances, and conferences. The society is a leader in presenting contemporary Asian and Asian-American art. Now, after a $30-million renovation that doubled the exhibition space, the society's headquarters is bigger, smarter, and better than ever. Never has so much of the core collection, comprised of Rockefeller's Pan-Asian acquisitions dating from 2000 B.C. to the 19th century, been on display before. Well-curated temporary exhibits run the gamut from *The New Way of Tea,* exploring Japan's elaborate tea ceremony, to *Through Afghan Eyes: A Culture in Conflict, 1987–1995,* a study in photographs and video. The mammoth calendar of events ranges from films to lectures to discussions featuring experts in Pan-Asian and global politics, business, and more.

725 Park Ave. (at 70th St.). ☎ 212/288-6400. www.asiasociety.org. Gallery admission $7 adults, $5 seniors and students, free for children under 16, free to all Fri 6–9pm. Tues–Thurs and Sat–Sun 11am–6pm; Fri 11am–9pm. Subway: 6 to 68th St./Hunter College.

Center for Jewish History *(Finds)*   This 125,000-square-foot complex is the largest repository of Jewish history, art, and literature in the Diaspora. It unites five of America's leading institutions of Jewish scholarship: the **American Jewish Historical Society** (www.ajhs.org), the national archives of the Jewish people in the Americas; the **Leo Baeck Institute** (www.lbi.org), documenting the history of German-speaking Jewry from the 17th century until the Nazis; the **Yeshiva University Museum** (www.yu.edu/museum), which includes general-interest exhibits, plus a collection of Judaica objects confiscated by the Nazis; the **YIVO Institute for Jewish Research** (www.yivoinstitute.org), focusing on exhibits exploring the diversity of the Jewish experience; and the **American Sephardi Federation** (www.asfonline.org), representing the spiritual, cultural, and social traditions of the American Sephardic communities (Jews from southern Europe, North Africa, and the Middle East). This union represents about 100 million archival documents, 500,000 books, and thousands of objects of art and ephemera, ranging from Thomas Jefferson's letter denouncing anti-Semitism to memorabilia of famous Jewish athletes.

The main gallery space is the Yeshiva Museum, which comprises four galleries, an outdoor sculpture garden, and a children's workshop; a range of exhibits also showcase holdings belonging to the other institutions. A central feature is the **Reading Room,** home to stacks accessible by serious researchers and lay historians alike, as well as the **Center Genealogy Institute,** which offers assistance in family-history research. Another huge component of the center is its 250-seat auditorium, home to a packed schedule of events. There's also a kosher cafe.

15 W. 16th St. (btwn 5th and 6th aves.). ☎ 212/294-8301. www.cjh.org. Admission to Yeshiva University Museum $6 adults, $4 seniors and students, free to all other facilities. Yeshiva University Museum Sun and Tues–Wed 11am–5pm; Thurs 11am–8pm. Reading Room and Genealogy Institute Mon–Thurs 9:30am–4:30pm; Fri by appt. All other galleries Mon–Thurs 9am–5pm; Fri 9am–4pm. Subway: 4, 5, 6, N, R, L, Q, or W to 14th St./Union Square; F or V to 14th St.

The Cloisters *(★) (Moments)*   If it weren't for this branch of the Metropolitan Museum of Art, many New Yorkers would never get to the northernmost point in Manhattan. This remote yet lovely spot is devoted to the art and architecture of medieval Europe. Atop a cliff overlooking the Hudson River, you'll find a

12th-century chapter house, parts of five cloisters from medieval monasteries, a Romanesque chapel, and a 12th-century Spanish apse brought intact from Europe. Surrounded by peaceful gardens, this is the one place on the island that can even approximate the kind of solitude suitable to such a collection. Inside

Downtown Relics

New York is neither Rome nor Athens, yet the city can boast a few old structures, at least New World "old." To find a good sampling of "ancient" New York, head downtown, where it all began.

You might want to first stop at the southern tip of the island at Battery Park where an old fort called **Castle Clinton National Monument** (© 212/344-7220; www.nps.gov/cacl) still stands. The fort, or what remains of it, was built between 1808 and 1811 to defend New York Harbor against the British. In the mid–19th century the fort was the city's first immigration center. A small museum was added to the monument in 1986, with exhibits that follow the evolution of the fort.

Not far from Castle Clinton at 1 Bowling Green is the relatively modern 1907-built **U.S. Customs House** 🍴, which houses the National Museum of the American Indian, George Gustav Heye Center (p. 207). Designed by Cass Gilbert and now a National Historic Landmark, the granite structure features giant statues carved by Daniel Chester French (of Lincoln Memorial fame) lining the front that personify Asia (pondering philosophically), America (bright-eyed and bushy-tailed), Europe (decadent, whose time has passed), and Africa (sleeping). Inside, the airy oval rotunda designed by Spanish engineer Raphael Guastavino was frescoed by Reginald Marsh to glorify the shipping industry (and, by extension, the Customs office once housed here).

One of Wall Street's most recognizable sights is the imposing, majestic **Federal Hall National Memorial,** 26 Wall St. (© 212/825-6888; www.nps.gov/feha). Built in 1842, the memorial, with the 1883-built statue of George Washington on the steps, and directly across from the New York Stock Exchange, was erected on the site of New York's first City Hall. Inside it's now a museum, with exhibits that elucidate the events surrounding the memorial and other aspects of American history. The infrastructure of the memorial suffered from the massive shock of the nearby attack on the World Trade Center; as a result, it is undergoing a $16-million rehabilitation to repair cracks.

George Washington was a visible presence in 18th-century New York and he worshipped at the still-standing **St. Paul's Chapel,** built in 1766 and part of the Trinity Church (p. 226) at 74 Trinity Place (© 212/602-0800). The chapel now serves as a memorial to the victims of 9/11.

So now we know where Washington worshipped, but where did he eat? The answer is at **Fraunces Tavern,** the same place where Washington bade farewell to his officers at the end of the American Revolution. This 1907-built tavern is an exact replica of the original 1717 tavern. It's now a museum, 54 Pearl St., near Broad Street (© 212/425-1778; www.frauncestavernmuseum.org), and an actual restaurant.

⌒Value Where to Find Free Culture

New York's gargantuan stash of museums, galleries, and attractions makes this city one of the cultural capitals of the world. But the cost of this culture can be high, especially because many museums now charge $10 or more. But don't get discouraged; there are ways around these steep fees.

Some city attractions are free all the time. Some set aside an afternoon, an evening, or a day during the week when you can explore at no charge. Others offer "pay what you wish" times, be it $1 or the full admission price.

Most museums keep pretty solid schedules, but it's always a good idea to call ahead and confirm free and "pay what you wish" times—because these, like everything else, are always subject to change.

ALWAYS FREE
- **Abyssinian Baptist Church** (p. 204)
- **American Folk Art Museum's Eva and Morris Feld Gallery** (p. 205)
- **Brooklyn Tabernacle** (p. 249)
- **Center for Jewish History** (all galleries except Yeshiva University Museum; p. 206)
- **Federal Hall National Memorial** (p. 207)
- **Forbes Magazine Galleries** (p. 210)
- **Mother A.M.E. Zion Church** (p. 225)
- **National Museum of the American Indian** (p. 216)
- **New York City Police Museum** (p. 217)
- **New York Public Library** (p. 222)
- **New York Stock Exchange** (p. 203)
- **New York Transit Museum's Gallery Annex** (p. 251)
- **St. Patrick's Cathedral** (p. 225)
- **Schomburg Center for Research in Black Culture** (p. 218)
- **Socrates Sculpture Park** (p. 255)
- **Sony Wonder Technology Lab** (p. 246)
- **South Street Seaport** (charge for museum admission; p. 219)
- **Staten Island Ferry** (p. 202)
- **Temple Emanu-El** (p. 226)
- **Trinity Church** ($2 donation requested for noonday concerts; p. 226)
- **Whitney Museum of American Art at Philip Morris** (p. 204)
- **Zenith Media Lounge** at the New Museum of Contemporary Art (p. 217)

SOMETIMES FREE (OR PAY WHAT YOU WISH)
- **Museum of Arts and Design:** Thursday from 6 to 8pm; regular admission $9 (p. 213)

you'll find extraordinary works that include the famed Unicorn tapestries, sculpture, illuminated manuscripts, stained glass, ivory, and precious metal work.

Despite its remoteness, the Cloisters are extremely popular, especially in fine weather, so try to schedule your visit on a weekday. A free guided **Highlights Tour** is offered Tuesday through Friday at 3pm and Sunday at noon; gallery talks

- **American Folk Art Museum:** Friday 6 to 8pm; regular admission $9 (p. 205)
- **Asia Society:** Friday 6 to 9pm; regular admission $10 (p. 206)
- **Bronx Zoo Wildlife Conservation Park:** All day Wednesday; regular admission $11 (p. 247)
- **Brooklyn Botanic Garden:** All day Tuesday and Saturday from 10am to noon year-round, plus all day Wednesday, Thursday, and Friday from mid-November to mid-March; regular admission $5 (p. 249)
- **Brooklyn Museum of Art:** First Saturday of the month from 5 to 11pm; regular admission $8 donation (p. 249)
- **Children's Museum of the Arts:** Thursday from 4 to 6pm; regular admission $6 (p. 209)
- **Cooper-Hewitt National Design Museum:** Tuesday from 5 to 9pm; regular admission $10 (p. 209)
- **The Jewish Museum:** Tuesday from 5 to 8pm; regular admission $10 (p. 211)
- **Museum of Modern Art:** Friday from 4:30 to 8:15pm; regular admission $20 (p. 200)
- **New York Hall of Science:** Friday from 2 to 5pm; regular admission $9 (p. 245)
- **New York Transit Museum:** Seniors enter free Tuesday from noon to 4pm; regular senior admission $3, regular admission $5 (p. 251)
- **Solomon R. Guggenheim Museum:** Friday from 6 to 8pm; regular admission $15 (p. 201)
- **Studio Museum in Harlem:** First Saturday of the month; regular admission $7 (p. 220)
- **Wave Hill:** All day Tuesday and Saturday mornings in summer, every day in winter; regular admission $4 (p. 248)
- **Whitney Museum of American Art:** Friday from 6 to 9pm; regular admission $12 (p. 204)

ALMOST FREE (ADMISSION OF $3 OR LESS)
- **Cathedral of St. John the Divine:** $2 ($3 for guided tour; p. 225)
- **Edgar Allan Poe Cottage:** $2 (p. 223)
- **Fraunces Tavern Museum:** $3 (p. 207)
- **Morris-Jumel Mansion:** $3 (p. 223)
- **Museum of American Financial History:** $2 (p. 213)
- **New Museum of Contemporary Art:** Thursday from 6 to 8pm, $3; regular admission $6 (p. 217)
- **New York Botanical Garden:** $3 (p. 247)
- **Scandinavia House:** $3 (p. 218)

are also a regular feature. **Garden Tours** are offered Tuesday through Sunday at 1pm in May, June, September, and October; lectures and other programming are on Sunday from noon to 2pm; medieval-music concerts are held in the 12th-century Spanish chapel.

At the north end of Fort Tryon Park. ℂ **212/923-3700.** www.metmuseum.org. Suggested admission (includes same-day entrance to the Metropolitan Museum of Art) $12 adults, $7 seniors and students, free for children under 12. Nov–Feb Tues–Sun 9:30am–4:45pm; Mar–Oct Tues–Sun 9:30am–5:15pm. Subway: A to 190th St., then a 10-min. walk north along Margaret Corbin Dr., or pick up the M4 bus at the station (1 stop to Cloisters). Bus: M4 Madison Ave. (Fort Tryon Park/The Cloisters).

Cooper-Hewitt National Design Museum 🔎   Part of the Smithsonian Institution, the Cooper-Hewitt is in the Carnegie Mansion, built by Andrew Carnegie in 1901 and renovated in 1996. Some 11,000 square feet of space is devoted to changing exhibits that are well conceived, engaging, and educational. Shows are both historic and contemporary in nature, and topics range from *The Work of Charles and Ray Eames: A Legacy of Invention* to *The Architecture of Reassurance: Designing the Disney Theme Parks.*

Note the Art Nouveau–style copper-and-glass canopy above the entrance. And visit the garden, ringed with Central Park benches from various eras.

2 E. 91st St. (at 5th Ave.). ℂ **212/849-8400.** www.si.edu/ndm. Admission $10 adults, $7 seniors and students, free for children under 12, free to all Tues 5–9pm. Tues 10am–9pm; Wed–Sat 10am–5pm; Sun noon–5pm. Subway: 4, 5, or 6 to 86th St.

El Museo del Barrio   What started in 1969 with a display in a school classroom is today the only museum in America dedicated to Puerto Rican, Caribbean, and Latin American art. The northernmost Museum Mile institution has a permanent exhibit ranging from pre-Columbian artifacts to photographic art and video. The display of *santos de palo,* woodcarved religious figurines, is worth noting, as is *Taíno, Ancient Voyagers of the Caribbean,* dedicated to the cultures that Columbus encountered when he landed in the "New World." The changing exhibitions focus on 20th-century artists and contemporary subjects.

1230 5th Ave. (at 104th St.). ℂ **212/831-7272.** www.elmuseo.org. Suggested admission $6 adults, $4 seniors and students, free for children under 12. Wed–Sun 11am–5pm. Subway: 6 to 103rd St.

Forbes Magazine Galleries *Kids*   The late publishing magnate Malcolm Forbes may have been a self-described "capitalist tool," but he had esoteric, almost childish, tastes. With its model boats, toy soldiers, old Monopoly games, trophies, miniature rooms, presidential memorabilia, and Fabergé eggs, this is a great little museum for you and the kids. Personal anecdotes explain why certain objects attracted Forbes's attention and turn the collection into an interesting biographical portrait. The Picture and Autograph Galleries, where you can find Abraham Lincoln's Emancipation Proclamation, are also intriguing.

62 5th Ave. (at 12th St.). ℂ **212/206-5548.** www.forbes.com/forbescollection. Free admission. Tues–Wed and Fri–Sat 10am–4pm (hours vary, call ahead). Subway: L, N, R, 4, 5, or 6 to 14th St./Union Square.

The Frick Collection 🔎🔎   Henry Clay Frick could afford to be an avid collector of European art after amassing a fortune as a pioneer in the coke and steel industries at the turn of the 20th century. To house his treasures and himself, he hired architects Carrère & Hastings to build this 18th-century French-style mansion (1914), one of the most beautiful remaining on 5th Avenue.

Most appealing about the Frick is its intimate size and setting. This is a living testament to New York's Gilded Age—the interior still feels like a private home (albeit a really, really rich guy's home) graced with beautiful paintings, rather than a museum. Come here to see the classics by some of the world's most famous painters: Titian, Bellini, Rembrandt, Turner, Vermeer, El Greco, and Goya, to name only a few. A highlight of the collection is the **Fragonard Room,** graced with the sensual rococo series *The Progress of Love.* The portrait of Montesquieu by Whistler is also stunning. Included in the price of admission, the AcousticGuide audio tour is particularly useful because it allows you to follow your own path rather than a set route. A free 22-minute video presentation is screened in the Music Room every half-hour from 10am to 4:30pm (from 1:30pm on Sun); starting with this helps to set the tone for what you'll see.

In addition, free **chamber music concerts** are held twice a month, generally every other Sunday at 5pm in fall and winter and select Thursdays at 5:45pm in warm weather, and once-a-month **lectures** are offered select Wednesdays at 5:30pm; call or visit the website for the current schedule and ticket information.

1 E. 70th St. (at 5th Ave.). © 212/288-0700. www.frick.org. Admission $12 adults, $8 seniors, $5 students. Children under 10 not admitted; children under 16 must be accompanied by an adult. Tues and Thurs–Sat 10am–6pm; Fri 10am–9pm; Sun 1–6pm. Closed Wed and all major holidays. Subway: 6 to 68th St./Hunter College.

International Center of Photography *Finds* The state-of-the-art gallery space is ideal for viewing exhibitions of the museum's 50,000-plus prints, as well as visiting shows. The emphasis is on contemporary photographic works, but historically important photographers aren't ignored.

1133 6th Ave. (at 43rd St.). © 212/857-0000. www.icp.org. Admission $10 adults, $7 seniors and students. Tues–Thurs 10am–5pm; Fri 10am–8pm; Sat–Sun 10am–6pm. Subway: B, D, F, or V to 42nd St.

Intrepid Sea-Air-Space Museum *Kids* The most astonishing thing about the aircraft carrier USS *Intrepid* is how it can be simultaneously so big and so small. It's a few football fields long, weighs 40,000 tons, holds 40 aircraft, and sometimes doubles as a ballroom for society functions. But stand there and think about landing an A-12 jet on the deck and suddenly it's minuscule. Furthermore, in the narrow passageways below, you'll find it isn't quite the roomiest of vessels. Now a National Historic Landmark, the exhibit also includes the naval destroyer USS *Edson,* and the submarine USS *Growler,* the only intact strategic missile submarine open to the public anywhere in the world, as well as a collection of vintage and modern aircraft, including the A-12 Blackbird, the world's fastest spy plane, and the newest addition to the museum, a retired British Airways Concorde jet.

Kids just love this place. They, and you, can climb inside a replica Revolutionary War submarine, sit in an A-6 Intruder cockpit, and follow the progress of America's astronauts as they work in space. There are even navy flight simulators—including a "Fly with the Blue Angels" program—for educational thrill rides in the Technologies Hall. Look for family-oriented activities and events at least one Saturday a month.

The program "All Hands on Deck" teaches both children and adults how things work on ships, plus there's a new AH-1 Cobra attack helicopter. The action-packed *Intrepid Wings* shows aircraft carrier take-offs and recoveries in the new Allison and Howard Lutnick Theater; the film runs continuously throughout the day. The exhibit *Remembering 9-11* recalls those lost, both civilians and rescuers. The grand visitor center makes for an impressive entrance, and the massive museum store is well stocked; goods include NYPD and FDNY logo gear. Dress warmly for a winter visit—it's almost impossible to heat an aircraft carrier.

Pier 86 (W. 46th St. at 12th Ave.). © 212/245-0072. www.intrepidmuseum.org. Admission $15 adults, $11 veterans, seniors, and students, $7.50 children 6–11, $2 children 2–5. $5 extra for flight simulator rides. Apr–Sept Mon–Fri 10am–5pm, Sat–Sun 10am–7pm; Oct–Mar Tues–Sun 10am–5pm. Last admission 1 hr. before closing. Subway: A, C, or E to 42nd St./Port Authority. Bus: M42 crosstown.

The Jewish Museum Housed in a Gothic-style mansion renovated in 1993 by AIA Gold Medal winner Kevin Roche, this museum now has the world-class

space it deserves to showcase its collections, which chronicle 4,000 years of Jewish history. The permanent exhibit, *Culture and Continuity: The Jewish Journey,* tells the story of the Jewish experience from ancient times through today. Artifacts include daily objects that might have served the authors of the books of Genesis, Psalms, and Job, and an assemblage of Torahs. A collection of classic TV and radio programs is available for viewing through the Goodkind Resource Center (as any fan of television's golden age knows, its finest comic moments were Jewish comedy). The scope of the exhibit is phenomenal, and its story an enlightening—and intense—one. A random-access audio guide is geared to families (free with admission). In addition to the in-house shop, don't miss the Jewish Museum Design Shop in the adjacent brownstone. *Money-saving tip:* Check the website for online admission discounts (50% off at press time).

1109 5th Ave. (at 92nd St.). ✆ 212/423-3200. www.thejewishmuseum.org. Admission $10 adults, $7.50 seniors and students, free for children under 12, pay what you wish Thurs 5–8pm. Sun 10am–5:45pm; Mon–Wed 11am–5:45pm; Thurs 11am–8pm; Fri 11am–3pm. Subway: 4 or 5 to 86th St.; 6 to 96th St.

Lower East Side Tenement Museum ⊛ This museum is the first-ever National Trust for Historic Preservation site that was not the home of someone rich or famous. It's a five-story tenement that 10,000 people from 25 countries called home between 1863 and 1935—people who had come to the United States looking for the American dream. The museum tells the story of the immigration boom of the late 19th and early 20th centuries, when the Lower East Side was considered the "Gateway to America." A visit here is a good follow-up to an Ellis Island trip—what happened to the people who passed through that way station?

The only way to see the museum is by guided tour. Two tenement tours, held on all open days and lasting an hour, offer an exploration of the museum: **Piecing It Together: Immigrants in the Garment Industry,** which focuses on the apartment and the lives of its turn-of-the-20th-century tenants, an immigrant Jewish family named Levine from Poland; and **Getting By: Weathering the Great Depressions of 1873 and 1929,** featuring the homes of the German-Jewish Gumpertz family and the Sicilian-Catholic Baldizzi family, respectively. A guide leads you into each dingy urban time capsule, where several apartments have been restored to their lived-in condition, and recounts the stories of the families who occupied them. You can pair them for an in-depth look at the museum.

These tours are not really for kids, who won't enjoy the serious tone and "don't touch" policy. Much better for them is the 45-minute, weekends-only **Confino Family Apartment** tour, a living-history program geared to families, which allows kids to converse with an interpreter playing teenage immigrant Victoria Confino (ca. 1916); kids can handle whatever they like and try on period clothes.

The hour-long **Streets Where We Lived** neighborhood-heritage walking tour is offered on weekends from April to December. Small permanent and rotating exhibits, including photos, videos, and a model tenement, are housed in the Visitor Center and exhibition space in the tenement building at 97 Orchard St. Special tours and programs are sometimes on the schedule.

Tours are limited in number and sell out quickly, so it pays to buy tickets in advance, which you can do online, or over the phone by calling **Ticketweb** at ✆ **800/965-4827.** Note that the potential acquisition of a neighboring tenement at 99 Orchard St. may change programming, so confirm schedules.

Visitor Center at 90 Orchard St. (at Broome St.). ✆ 212/431-0233. www.tenement.org. Tenement and walking tours $9 adults, $7 seniors and students; Confino Apartment $8 adults, $6 seniors and students. Tenement tours depart every 40 min. Tues–Fri 1–4pm; Sat–Sun every half-hour 11am–4:45pm. Confino Apartment tour Sat–Sun hourly noon–3pm. Walking tour Apr–Dec Sat–Sun 1 and 2:30pm. Subway: F to Delancey St.; J, M, or Z to Essex St.

Museum of American Financial History   Real money buffs (and who among us isn't?) may want to make a stop here. The exhibits housed in this Smithsonian-affiliate museum include numismatic and vintage ticker-tape displays; murals and photos depicting historic Wall Street scenes; and interactive financial news terminals, so little bulls and bears can learn how to keep up with the market. Temporary installations have run the gamut from *Morgan,* a chronicle of the lasting influence of J. Pierpont Morgan, to *High Notes,* an oddly compelling exhibit of high-denomination currency.

28 Broadway (just north of Bowling Green Park). (*C*) **212/908-4110.** www.financialhistory.org. Admission $2. Tues–Sat 10am–4pm. Subway: 4 or 5 to Bowling Green; J or M to Broad St.; 2 or 3 to Wall St.

Museum of Arts and Design 𝒜 *Finds*   Formerly called the American Craft Museum, this small but aesthetically pleasing museum is the nation's top showcase for contemporary crafts. The collection focuses on objects that are prime examples of form and function, ranging from jewelry to baskets to vessels to furniture. You'll see a strong emphasis on material as well as craft, whether it be fiber, ceramics, or metal. Special exhibitions can range from expressionist clay sculpture to fine bookbinding, and can celebrate movements or single artisans. Or just take your chances and stop in—you're unlikely to be disappointed. Stop into the gorgeous shop even if you don't make it into the museum (p. 282).

40 W. 53rd St. (btwn 5th and 6th aves.). (*C*) **212/956-3535.** www.americancraftmuseum.org. Admission $9 adults, $6 students and seniors, free for children under 12, pay as you wish Thurs 6–8pm. Tues–Wed and Fri–Sun 10am–6pm; Thurs 10am–8pm. Subway: E or V to 5th Ave.

Museum of Jewish Heritage—A Living Memorial to the Holocaust 𝒜   Located in the south end of Battery Park City, the Museum of Jewish Heritage occupies a strikingly spare six-sided building designed by award-winning architect Kevin Roche, with a six-tier roof alluding to the Star of David and the six million Jews murdered in the Holocaust. The permanent exhibits—*Jewish Life a Century Ago, The War Against the Jews,* and *Jewish Renewal*—recount the daily prewar lives, the unforgettable horror that destroyed them, and the tenacious renewal experienced by European and immigrant Jews in the years from the late 19th century to the present. The museum's power derives from the way it tells that story: through the objects, photographs, documents, and, most poignantly, through the videotaped testimonies of Holocaust victims, survivors, and their families, all chronicled by Steven Spielberg's Survivors of the Shoah Visual History Foundation. Thursday evenings are dedicated to panel discussions, performances, and music, while Sundays are dedicated to family programs and workshops; a film series is also a regular part of the calendar. In the fall of 2003, the East Wing opened and includes a kosher cafe, Abigael's, run by celebrity chef Jeff Nathan.

While advance tickets are not usually necessary, you may want to purchase them to guarantee admission; call (*C*) **212/945-0039.** Audio tours narrated by Meryl Streep and Itzhak Perlman are available at the museum for an additional $5. ***Money-saving tip:*** Check the website for a $2-off admission coupon (available at press time), which you'll need to print out and bring with you.

36 Battery Place (at 1st Place), Battery Park City. (*C*) **212/968-1800.** www.mjhnyc.org. Admission $10 adults, $7 seniors, $5 students, free for children under 5. Sun–Wed 10am–5:45pm; Thurs 10am–8pm; Fri and eves of Jewish holidays 10am–3pm. Subway: 4 or 5 to Bowling Green.

Art for Art's Sake: The Gallery Scene

Manhattan has more than 500 private art galleries, selling everything from old masters to tomorrow's news. Galleries are free to the public, generally Tuesday through Saturday from 10am to 6pm. Nobody will expect you to buy—it's all about looking.

The best way to choose where to browse is by perusing the "Art Guide" in the Friday "Weekend" section of the *New York Times,* or the Sunday "Arts & Leisure" section; the "Cue" section of *New York* magazine; the Art section in *Time Out New York;* or the *New Yorker's* "Goings on About Town." You can find the latest listings at **www.nymetro.com**, whose Arts page gives you access to *New York* magazine's listings; **www. newyork.citysearch.com** (click on "Arts"); **www.artnet.com**; and **www. galleryguide.org**. An excellent source—more for practicals on the galleries and the artists and genres—is **www.artincontext.org**. The *Gallery Guide* is available at most galleries.

I suggest picking a gallery or a show in a neighborhood that seems to suit your taste, and just start browsing from there. Be aware that my list below doesn't even begin to scratch the surface. There are many, many more galleries in each neighborhood, as well as smaller concentrations of galleries in areas like the East Village, TriBeCa, and Brooklyn (check the Art in Context site).

Keep in mind that uptown galleries tend to be more traditional and exclusive-feeling, downtown galleries more high-ticket contemporary, and far west Chelsea galleries the most cutting edge. Museum-quality works dominate uptown, while raw talent and emerging artists are most common in west Chelsea. But there are constant surprises in all neighborhoods.

UPTOWN   Uptown galleries are clustered in and around the glamorous crossroads of 5th Avenue and 57th Street as well as on and off stylish Madison Avenue in the 60s, 70s, and 80s. Unlike their upstart Chelsea and SoHo counterparts, these blue-chip galleries maintain a quiet white-glove demeanor. They include art-world powerhouses **Gagosian Gallery,** 980 Madison Ave. (*©* 212/744-2313; www.gagosian.com), and **PaceWildenstein,** 32 E. 57th St. (*©* 212/421-3292), whose focus is on classic modernism, representing such artists as Jim Dine, Barbara Hepworth, and Claes Oldenburg; **Richard Gray Gallery,** 1018 Madison Ave., fourth floor (*©* 212/472-8787; www.richardgraygallery.com), featuring American and European contemporary works, with artists ranging from Joan Miró to David Hockney; the **Margo Feiden Galleries,** 699 Madison Ave. (*©* 212/ 677-5330; www.alhirschfeld.com), the sole authorized representative of the works of the late master ink caricaturist Al Hirschfeld; the **Mary Boone Gallery,** 745 5th Ave. (*©* 212/752-2929), known for success with such artists as Ross Bleckner and Nancy Ellison; and **Wildenstein & Co.,**

Museum of Sex *(Finds* How many cities can claim their own Museum of Sex? Not too many in the U.S., for sure. This one debuted in 2002 and despite its provocative title, offers a studied, historical look at the history of sex in our

Inc., the classical big brother of **PaceWildenstein,** 19 E. 64th St. (© 212/
879-0500; www.wildenstein.com), both specializing in big-ticket works:
old masters, Impressionism, and Renaissance paintings and drawings.

CHELSEA   The area in the West 20s between 10th and 11th avenues is
home to the avant-garde of today's New York art scene, with West 26th
serving as the unofficial "gallery row." Most galleries are not in storefronts but in the large spaces of multistory former garages and warehouses. Galleries worth seeking out include **Paula Cooper,** 534 W. 21st St.
(© 212/255-1105), a heavyweight in the modern art world, specializing in
conceptual and minimal art; **George Billis Gallery,** 511 W. 25th St., 9F
(© 212/645-2621; www.georgebillis.com), who shows works by talented
emerging artists; **Barbara Gladstone Gallery,** 515 W. 24th St. (© 212/
206-9300; www.gladstonegallery.com); uptown powerhouse **Gagosian
Gallery,** 555 W. 24th St. (© 212/741-1111; www.gagosian.com), which
shows such major modern artists as Richard Serra and Julian Schnabel;
Feigen Contemporary, 535 W. 20th St. (© 212/929-0500), the modern
counterpart to the uptown Old Masters gallery; **Cheim & Read,** 547 W.
25th St. (© 212/242-7727), which often shows works by such high-profile
pop artists as Diane Arbus and Robert Mapplethorpe Goldin; **DCA Gallery,**
525 W. 22nd St. (© 212/255-5511; www.dcagallery.com), specializing in
contemporary Danish artists; **Alexander and Bonin,** 132 10th Ave. (© 212/
367-7474; www.alexanderandbonin.com), which mounts excellent solo
exhibitions; **James Cohan Gallery,** 533 W. 26th St. (© 212/714-9500; www.
jamescohan.com), particularly strong in modern photography; and
Lehmann Maupin, 540 W. 26th St. (© 212/255-2923; www.lehmann
maupin.com), whose roster runs the gamut from young unknowns to
contemporary masters like Ross Bleckner.

DOWNTOWN   SoHo remains colorful, if less edgy than it used to be,
with the action centered around West Broadway and encroaching onto
the edge of Chinatown of late. Start with **Bronwyn Keenan,** 3 Crosby St.
(© 212/431-5083), who's known for a keen eye for spotting emerging
talent; **Peter Blum Gallery,** 99 Wooster St. (© 212/343-0441), who show-
cased the divine Kim Sooja, a Korean artist who uses traditional Korean
bedcovers to comment on the promise of wedded bliss; **O. K. Harris,** 383
W. Broadway (© 212/431-3600; www.okharris.com), which shows a
wide and fascinating variety of contemporary painting, sculpture, and
photography; and **Louis K. Meisel,** 141 Prince St. (© 212/677-1340;
www.meiselgallery.com), specializing in photo-realism and American
pinup art (yep, Petty and Vargas girls). In TriBeCa, try **Cheryl Hazan Arts
Gallery,** 35 N. Moore St. (© 212/343-8964; www.cherylhazanarts.com),
or **DFN Gallery,** 176 Franklin St. (© 212/334-3400; www.dfngallery.com),
both of which focus on fresh and distinctive contemporary art.

culture. The museum's first exhibit, *NYC Sex: How New York City Transformed
Sex in America,* featured displays about S&M and 19th-century brothels and
videos of Times Square in its sleazy heyday of the 1970s. In 2004, *Sex Among*

the Lotus: 2,500 Years of Chinese Erotic Obsession opened, displaying explicit imagery dating from the 2nd century B.C. Don't miss a trip through the gift shop—definitely not your typical museum shop. How about a $1,375 snakeskin souvenir to show your friends back home? The price of admission is high (though MoMa's is now higher—where do you get more bang for your buck?). Check the website for discount specials. *Note:* Many of the displays are graphic, so the museum may not be for everyone.

233 5th Ave. (at 27th St.). (✆ 866/MOSEX-NYC. www.museumofsex.com. Admission $15 adults, $14 students and seniors. No one under 18 admitted. Mon–Tues and Thurs–Fri 11am–6:30pm; Sat 10am–9pm; Sun 10am–6pm. Subway: N or R to 28th St.

Museum of Television & Radio

If you can resist the allure of this museum, I'd wager you've spent the last 70 years in a bubble. You can watch and hear the great personalities of TV and radio—from Uncle Miltie to Johnny Carson to Jerry Seinfeld—at a private console. You can conduct computer searches to pick out the great moments of history, viewing almost anything that made its way onto the airwaves, from the Beatles' appearance on *The Ed Sullivan Show* to the crumbling of the Berlin Wall. The collection consists of 75,000 programs and commercials, only a fraction of which are available for instant viewing (call at least a week in advance to arrange for a specific reel); you're allowed to watch up to four shows in one sitting. Selected programs are also presented in two theaters and two screening rooms.

25 W. 52nd St. (btwn 5th and 6th aves.). (✆ 212/621-6800 or 212/621-6600. www.mtr.org. Admission $10 adults, $8 seniors and students, $5 children under 13. Tues–Sun noon–6pm (Thurs until 8pm, Fri theater programs until 9pm). Subway: B, D, F, or V to 47th–50th sts./Rockefeller Center; E or V to 53rd St.

Museum of the City of New York

A wide variety of objects—costumes, photographs, prints, maps, dioramas, and memorabilia—trace the history of New York City from its beginnings as a humble Dutch colony in the 16th century to its present-day prominence. Two outstanding permanent exhibits are the re-creation of John D. Rockefeller's master bedroom and dressing room, and the space devoted to *Broadway!*, a history of New York theater. Kids will love *New York Toy Stories*, a permanent exhibit showcasing toys and dolls owned and adored by centuries of New York children. The permanent *Painting the Town: Cityscapes of New York* explores the changing cityscape from 1809 to 1997, and carries new profundity in the wake of the September 11, 2001, terrorist attacks.

1220 5th Ave. (at 103rd St.). (✆ 212/534-1672. www.mcny.org. Suggested admission $7 adults; $4 seniors, students, and children; $12 families. Wed–Sun 10am–5pm. Subway: 6 to 103rd St.

National Museum of the American Indian, George Gustav Heye Center

This impressive collection, a branch that predates the fabulous new museum that opened in Washington, D.C., in the fall of 2004, is part of the Smithsonian Institution. The collection spans more than 10,000 years of native heritage, gathered a century ago mainly by New York banking millionaire George Gustav Heye. About 70% of the collection is dedicated to the natives of North America and Hawaii; the rest represents the cultures of Mexico and Central and South America. There's a wealth of material here, but it's not as well organized as it could be. The museum also hosts temporary themed exhibitions and interpretive programs, plus free storytelling, music, and dance presentations.

The museum is housed in the beautiful 1907 Beaux Arts **U.S. Customs House** (✮, designed by Cass Gilbert and a National Historic Landmark that's worth a look in its own right (see "Downtown Relics" on p. 207).

1 Bowling Green (btwn State and Whitehall sts.). (✆ 212/514-3700. www.nmai.si.edu. Free admission. Daily 10am–5pm (Thurs until 8pm). Subway: 4 or 5 to Bowling Green; N or R to Whitehall.

Neue Galerie New York *(Finds)*   This museum is dedicated to German and Austrian art and design, with a focus on the early 20th century. The collection features painting, works on paper, decorative arts, and other media from such artists as Klimt, Kokoschka, Kandinsky, Klee, and leaders of the Wiener Werkstätte decorative arts and Bauhaus movements such as Adolf Loos and Mies van der Rohe. Once occupied by Mrs. Cornelius Vanderbilt III, the landmark-designated 1914 Carrère & Hastings building (they built the New York Public Library as well) is worth a look. Cafe Sabarsky is modeled on a Viennese cafe, so museumgoers in need of a snack break can expect a fine Linzer torte.

1048 5th Ave. (at 86th St.). (*) 212/628-6200. www.neuegalerie.org. Admission $10 adults, $7 seniors. Fri–Mon 11am–7pm. Subway: 4, 5, or 6 to 86th St.

New Museum of Contemporary Art ★   This contemporary arts museum has moved closer to the mainstream in recent years, but it's only a safety margin in from the edge as far as most of us are concerned. Expect adventurous and well-curated exhibitions. The 2005 exhibition calendar had not been announced at press time, but previous schedules have included *Portrait of the Lost Boys,* New Zealander Jacqueline Fraser's moving narrative made of sumptuous fabric and fragile wire sculptures that examines the high incidence of suicide among teenage boys in New Zealand, and *John Waters: Change of Life,* photographs by the filmmaker who brought us *Pink Flamingos* and *Hairspray.* The **Zenith Media Lounge,** a digital- and media-arts technology space housing rotating installations, is free to the public. In 2006, the museum will move to a new 60,000-square-foot, $35-million home on the Bowery at Prince Street. In the meantime, exhibitions will be displayed at the Chelsea address below.

556 W. 22nd St. (at 11th Ave.). (*) 212/219-1222. www.newmuseum.org. Admission $6 adults, $3 seniors and students, free to visitors 18 and under Thurs 6–8pm. Tues–Sun noon–6pm; Thurs noon–8pm (Zenith Media Lounge to 6:30pm). Subway: C or E to 23rd St.

New York City Fire Museum ★ *(Kids)*   Housed in a 1904 firehouse, the former quarters of FDNY Engine Co. 30, this museum houses one of the country's most extensive collections of fire-service memorabilia from the 18th century to the present. It's also the best place to pay tribute to the 343 heroic firefighters who lost their lives in the World Trade Center disaster. Expect changing exhibits relating to the September 11, 2001, terrorist attacks. Other displays range from vintage fire marks to fire trucks to the gear and tools of modern firefighters. Also look for leather hoses, fireboats, and Currier & Ives prints, plus a new exhibit on fire safety and burn prevention geared to families. Real firefighters are almost always on hand to share stories and fire-safety information. The retail store sells FDNY logo wear and souvenirs. Call ahead for details on scheduling a guided tour.

278 Spring St. (btwn Varick and Hudson sts.). (*) 212/691-1303. www.nycfiremuseum.org. Admission $4 adults, $2 seniors and students, $1 children under 12. Tues–Sat 10am–5pm; Sun 10am–4pm. Subway: C or E to Spring St.

New York City Police Museum *(Kids)*   Newly opened in this Lower Manhattan location in early 2002, this small museum tells the story of the NYPD and offers a look at the present-day world of law enforcement through the eyes of NYPD officers. Exhibits include arrest records of famous criminals, fingerprinting and forensic art stations, and crime-fighting weapons galore.

100 Old Slip (at South St., 2 blocks south of Wall St.). (*) 212/480-3100. www.nycpolicemuseum.org. Free admission (donation suggested). Tues–Sat 10am–5pm. Subway: N or R to Whitehall St.; 2 or 3 to Wall St.

New-York Historical Society ⚑ Launched in 1804, the New-York Historical Society is a major repository of American history, culture, and art, with a focus on New York. The neoclassical edifice near the Museum of Natural History has emerged from the renovation tent. Now open on the fourth floor is the Henry Luce III Center for the Study of American Culture, a state-of-the-art facility and gallery of fine and decorative arts, which displays more than 40,000 objects amassed over 200 years—including paintings, sculpture, Tiffany lamps, textiles, furniture, even carriages—that had been in storage for decades. Also look for paintings from Hudson River School artists Thomas Cole, Asher Durand, and Frederic Church, including Cole's five-part masterpiece, *The Course of Empire*. Of particular interest to scholars and ephemera buffs are the extensive Library Collections, which include books, manuscripts, maps, newspapers, photographs, and more documents chronicling the American experience. (An appointment may be necessary to view some or all of the Library Collections, so call ahead.)

Also of note are the society's temporary exhibits; a series called *History Responds* was one of the best in the city dealing with the September 11, 2001, terrorist attacks and the aftermath. World Trade Center–related exhibits are likely to continue, so interested visitors should be sure to check the exhibition schedule.

An extensive calendar of public programs runs the gamut from family story hours to Irving Berlin music nights to lectures by such luminaries as Ric Burns and Susan Sontag to expert-led walks through Manhattan neighborhoods.

2 W. 77th St. (at Central Park W.). © 212/873-3400. www.nyhistory.org. Admission $8 adults, $6 seniors and students, free for children 12 and under. Tues–Sun 11am–6pm. Subway: B or C to 81st St.; 1 or 9 to 79th St.

Scandinavia House: The Nordic Center in America *Finds* Dedicated to both the shared and unique cultures of Denmark, Finland, Iceland, Norway, and Sweden, Scandinavia House features two floors of galleries and an outdoor sculpture terrace display rotating art and design exhibits that can range from *Scandia: Important Early Maps of the Northern Regions* to *Strictly Swedish: An Exhibition of Contemporary Design*. The rest of the space, including the 168-seat Victor Borge Hall, is dedicated to a calendar full of lectures, film screenings, music and drama performances, and scholarly presentations, all of a Nordic ilk. The exquisite modern building—designed to showcase Scandinavian materials and aesthetics—is worth a look in itself, especially if you're a modern-architecture buff. Guided tours are offered Tuesdays and Thursdays at 2pm and last a half-hour; they're free, but reservations are recommended.

The shop is a riot of fine Scandinavian design, and the excellent **AQ Café** serves up Swedish meatballs and other Scandinavian delicacies.

58 Park Ave. (btwn 37th and 38th sts.). © 212/879-9779. www.scandinaviahouse.org. Suggested admission to 3rd- and 4th-floor galleries $3, $2 seniors and students; free admission to other spaces. Exhibitions Tues–Sun noon–6pm; cafe Mon–Sat 10am–5pm; store Mon–Sat 10am–6pm. Subway: 6 to 33rd St.; 4, 5, 6, 7, or S to 42nd St./Grand Central.

Schomburg Center for Research in Black Culture *Value* Arturo Alfonso Schomburg, a black Puerto Rican, set himself to accumulating materials about blacks in America, and his massive collection is now housed and preserved at this research branch of the New York Public Library. The Exhibition Hall, the Latimer/Edison Gallery, and the Reading Room host exhibits related to black culture, such as *Lest We Forget: The Triumph over Slavery* and *Masterpieces of African Motherhood*. A rich calendar of talks and performing arts events is part of the continuing program. Make an appointment for a guided tour so you can see the 1930s murals by Harlem Renaissance artist Aaron Douglas; it'll be worth your while. Academics and others interested in a more complete look at the center's holdings can preview what's available online. Call to inquire about current exhibitions and information on tours and public programs.

515 Malcolm X Blvd. (Lenox Ave., btwn 135th and 136th sts.). ⌀ **212/491-2200.** www.nypl.org. Free admission. Gallery Mon–Sat 10am–6pm; Sun 1–5pm. Subway: 2 or 3 to 135th St.

Skyscraper Museum   Here's a museum about those structures that you've craned your neck to get a look at, the first of its kind about skyscrapers. After years of seeking a permanent home, finally, in 2004, the museum opened in the 38-story Skidmore, Owings & Merrill tower that also houses the Ritz-Carlton New York, Battery Park. The new space comprises two galleries, one housing a permanent exhibition dedication to the evolution of Manhattan's commercial skyline, the other for changing shows.

2 West St., Battery Park City. ⌀ **212/968-1961.** www.skyscraper.org. $5 adults, $2.50 students and seniors. Wed–Sun noon–6pm. Check website for updates. Subway: 4 or 5 to Bowling Green.

South Street Seaport & Museum (*Kids*)   This landmark district encompasses 11 blocks of historic buildings, a museum, several piers, shops, and restaurants.

You can explore most of the Seaport on your own. It's an odd place. The 18th- and 19th-century buildings lining the cobbled streets and alleyways are beautifully restored but have a theme-park air about them, no doubt due to the mall-familiar shops housed within. The height of the Seaport's cheesiness is Pier 17, a barge converted into a mall, complete with food court and jewelry kiosks.

Despite its rampant commercialism, the Seaport is worth a look. There's a good amount of history to be discovered here, most of it around the **South Street Seaport Museum,** a fitting tribute to the sea commerce that once thrived here.

In addition to the galleries—which house paintings and prints, ship models, scrimshaw, and nautical designs, as well as exhibitions—there are a number of historic ships berthed at the pier, including the 1911 *Peking* and the 1893 Gloucester fishing schooner *Lettie G. Howard.* The museum also offers a number of guided **walking tours;** call or check **www.southstseaport.org** for details.

Even **Pier 17** has its merits. Head up to the third-level deck overlooking the East River, where the wooden chairs will have you thinking about what it was like to cross the Atlantic on the *Normandie.* From here, you can see south to the Statue of Liberty, north to the Brooklyn Bridge, and across to Brooklyn Heights.

At the gateway to the Seaport, at Fulton and Water streets, is the ***Titanic Memorial Lighthouse,*** a monument to those who lost their lives when the ocean liner sank on April 15, 1912. It was erected overlooking the East River in 1913 and moved to this spot in 1968, just after the historic district was so designated.

A variety of events take place year-round, ranging from street performers to concerts to fireworks; check the website or dial ⌀ **212/SEA-PORT.**

(*Tips*) **Alert: Subway Access Update**

Changes in normal subway service happen almost every weekend. Stops are skipped, routes changed . . . it's enough to frustrate a veteran New York subway rider. I *strongly* recommend you check with the **Metropolitan Transit Authority** (⌀ **718/330-1234;** www.mta.nyc.ny.us) before you plan your travel routes; your hotel concierge or any token booth clerk should also be able to assist you.

At Water and South sts.; museum Visitor Center is at 12 Fulton St. ℂ 212/748-8600 or 212/SEA-PORT. www. southstseaport.org or www.southstreetseaport.com. Museum admission $5. Museum Apr–Sept Fri–Wed 10am–6pm, Thurs 10am–8pm; Oct–Mar Wed–Mon 10am–5pm. Subway: 2, 3, 4, or 5 to Fulton St. (walk east, or downslope, on Fulton St. to Water St.).

Studio Museum in Harlem   The small but lovely museum is devoted to 19th- and 20th-century African-American art as well as 20th-century African and Caribbean art and traditional African art and artifacts. Rotating exhibitions are a big part of the museum's focus, such as *Smithsonian African-American Photography: The First 100 Years, 1842–1942;* the silk-screens and lithographs of Jacob Lawrence; and an annual exhibition of works by emerging artists as part of its Artists-in-Residence program. There's also a small sculpture garden, a good gift shop, and a full calendar of special events.

144 W. 125th St. (btwn Lenox Ave. and Adam Clayton Powell Blvd.). ℂ 212/864-4500. www.studiomuseumin harlem.org. Admission $7 adults, $3 seniors, $1 children under 12, free for all on lst Sat of the month. Sun and Wed–Fri noon–6pm; Sat 10am–6pm. Subway: 2 or 3 to 125th St.

Whitney Museum of American Art at Philip Morris *(Value)*   This Midtown branch of the Whitney Museum of American Art (p. 204) features an airy sculpture court and a petite gallery that hosts changing exhibits, usually the works of living contemporary artists. Well worth peeking into if you happen to be in the neighborhood; I popped in recently and found a wonderful exhibition that juxtaposed the organic-inspired sculptures and drawings of Isamu Noguchi and Ellsworth Kelly. Free gallery talks are offered Wednesday and Friday at 1pm.

120 Park Ave. (at 42nd St., opposite Grand Central Terminal). ℂ **917/663-2453.** www.whitney.org. Free admission. Gallery Mon–Wed and Fri 11am–6pm; Thurs 11am–7:30pm. Sculpture Court Mon–Sat 7:30am–9:30pm; Sun 11am–7pm. Subway: S, 4, 5, 6, or 7 to 42nd St./Grand Central.

5 Skyscrapers & Other Architectural Highlights

For details on the **Empire State Building** 𝕽𝕽𝕽, see p. 197; **Grand Central Terminal** 𝕽𝕽, see p. 198; **Rockefeller Center** 𝕽𝕽, see p. 200; the **U.S. Customs House,** p. 207; and the **Brooklyn Bridge** 𝕽𝕽, p. 196. "Places of Worship," below, covers **St. Patrick's Cathedral, Temple Emanu-El,** and the **Cathedral of St. John the Divine** 𝕽.

In addition to the landmarks below, architecture buffs may want to seek out the **Lever House,** at 390 Park Ave. (btwn 53rd and 54th sts.), and the **Seagram Building** (1958), at 375 Park Ave., which are the city's best examples of the glass-and-steel International style, with the latter designed by master architect Mies van der Rohe himself. Also in Midtown East is the **Sony Building,** at 550 Madison Ave., designed in 1984 by Philip Johnson with a rose-granite facade and a playful Chippendale-style top that puts it a cut above the rest on the block.

The Upper West Side is home to two of the city's prime examples of residential architecture. On Broadway, between 73rd and 74th streets, is **The Ansonia,** looking like a flamboyant architectural wedding cake. This splendid Beaux Arts building has been home to the likes of Stravinsky, Toscanini, and Caruso, thanks to its virtually soundproof apartments. (It was also the spot where members of the Chicago White Sox plotted to throw the 1919 World Series.) Even more notable is **The Dakota,** at 72nd Street and Central Park West. Legend has it that the angular 1884 apartment house—accented with gables, dormers, and oriel windows that give it a brooding appeal—earned its name when its developer, Edward S. Clark, was teased by friends that he was building so far north of the city that he might as well be building in the Dakotas. One of the building's most

> ## *Fun Fact* Harlem's Architectural Treasures
>
> Originally conceived as a suburb for 19th-century Manhattan's moneyed set, Harlem has always had more than its share of historic treasures. Pay a call on the **Astor Row Houses,** 130th Street between 5th and Lenox avenues, a series of 28 town houses built in the early 1880s by the Astors, graced with wooden porches, yards, and ornamental ironwork.
>
> Equally impressive is **Strivers' Row,** West 139th Street between Adam Clayton Powell Jr. and Frederick Douglass boulevards, where hardly a brick has changed among the McKim, Mead & White neo-Italian Renaissance town houses since 1890. Once the original white owners had moved out, these houses attracted the cream of Harlem, "strivers" like Eubie Blake and W. C. Handy.
>
> Handsome brownstones, town houses, and row houses are atop **Sugar Hill,** 145th to 155th streets, between St. Nicholas and Edgecombe avenues, named for the "sweet life" enjoyed by its residents. In the early 20th century, such prominent blacks as W. E. B. DuBois, Thurgood Marshall, and Roy Wilkins lived in the building at 409 Edgecombe Ave.
>
> While you're uptown, don't miss the **Jumel Terrace Historic District,** west of St. Nicholas Avenue between 160th and 162nd streets. Of particular note is **Sylvan Terrace,** which feels more like a Hudson River town than a part of Harlem. A walk along it will lead you to the **Morris-Jumel Mansion** ⍟ (see "In Search of Historic Homes," below).

famous residents, John Lennon, was gunned down outside the 72nd Street entrance on December 8, 1980; Yoko Ono still lives there.

Chrysler Building ⍟⍟   Built as Chrysler Corporation headquarters in 1930, this is perhaps the 20th century's most romantic architectural achievement, especially at night, when the lights in its triangular openings play off its steely crown. As you admire its facade, be sure to note the gargoyles reaching out from the upper floors, looking for all the world like streamline-Gothic hood ornaments.

There's a fascinating tale behind this building. While it was under construction, architect William Van Alen hid his final plans for the spire that now tops it. Working at a furious pace in the last days of construction, the workers assembled the elegant pointy top in secrecy—and then they raised it right through what people had assumed was going to be the roof, and for a brief moment it was the world's tallest building (a distinction taken by the Empire State Building a few months later). The observation deck closed long ago, but you can visit its lavish ground-floor interior, which is Art Deco to the max. The ceiling mural depicting airplanes and other marvels of the first decades of the 20th century evince the bright promise of technology. The elevators are works of art, covered in exotic woods (especially note the lotus-shaped marquetry on the doors).

405 Lexington Ave. (at 42nd St.). Subway: S, 4, 5, 6, or 7 to 42nd St./Grand Central.

Flatiron Building   This triangular masterpiece was one of the first skyscrapers. Its knife-blade wedge shape is the only way the building could fill the triangular property at the intersection of 5th Avenue and Broadway, and that coincidence created one of the city's most distinctive buildings. Built in 1902 and fronted with limestone and terra cotta, the Flatiron measures only 6 feet across at its narrow end. It was originally named the Fuller Building, then later

"Burnham's Folly," because folks were certain that architect Daniel Burnham's 21-story structure would fall down. It didn't. There's no observation deck, and the building mainly houses publishing offices, but there are a few shops on the ground floor. The building's existence has served to name the neighborhood around it—the Flatiron District, home to a bevy of smart restaurants and shops.
175 5th Ave. (at 23rd St.). Subway: N or R to 23rd St.

New York Public Library *★★* *(Value)* The New York Public Library, adjacent to Bryant Park (p. 234) and designed by Carrère & Hastings (1911), is one of the country's finest examples of Beaux Arts architecture, a majestic structure of white Vermont marble with Corinthian columns and allegorical statues. Before climbing the broad flight of steps to the 5th Avenue entrance, take note of the famous lion sculptures—*Fortitude* on the right and *Patience* on the left. At Christmastime they don natty wreaths to keep warm.

This library is actually the **Humanities and Social Sciences Library,** only one of the research libraries in the New York Public Library system. The interior is one of the finest in the city and features **Astor Hall,** with arched marble ceilings and grand staircases. The **Main Reading Rooms** have now reopened after a massive restoration and modernization that brought them back to their stately glory and moved them into the computer age (goodbye, card catalogs!).

Even if you don't stop in to peruse the periodicals, you may want to check out one of the excellent rotating **exhibitions.** Call or check the website to see what's on while you're in town. There's also a full calendar of **lecture programs,** with past speakers ranging from Tom Stoppard to Cokie Roberts; popular speakers often sell out, so it's a good idea to purchase tickets in advance.

5th Ave. and 42nd St. *(C)* **212/869-8089** (exhibits and events), or 212/661-7220 (library hours). www.nypl.org. Free admission to exhibitions. Mon and Thurs–Sat 10am–6pm; Tues–Wed 11am–7:30pm. Subway: B, D, F, or V to 42nd St.; S, 4, 5, 6, or 7 to Grand Central/42nd St.

United Nations The U.N. headquarters occupies 18 acres of international territory—neither New York City nor the United States has jurisdiction here—along the East River from 42nd to 48th streets. Designed by an international team of architects (led by American Wallace K. Harrison and including Le Corbusier), the complex along the East River weds the 39-story glass slab Secretariat with the free-form General Assembly on grounds donated by John D. Rockefeller Jr. One hundred eighty nations use the facilities to arbitrate worldwide disputes.

Guided tours last 45 minutes to an hour and take you to the General Assembly Hall and the Security Council Chamber, and introduce the history and activities of the United Nations and its related organizations. Along the tour you'll see donated objects and artwork, including charred artifacts that survived the atomic bombs at Hiroshima and Nagasaki, stained-glass windows by Chagall, a replica of the first *Sputnik,* and a colorful mosaic called *The Golden Rule,* based on a Norman Rockwell drawing, which was a gift from the United States in 1985.

If you take the time to wander the landscaped **grounds,** you'll be rewarded with lovely views and some surprises. The monument *Good Defeats Evil,* donated by the Soviet Union in 1990, fashioned a contemporary St. George slaying a dragon from parts of Russian and American missiles. At press time, the **Delegates' Dining Room** was closed to the public for lunch; feel free to call *(C)* **212/963-7625** to see if it has reopened to visitors.

At 1st Ave. and 46th St. *(C)* **212/963-8687.** www.un.org/tours. Guided tours $11 adults, $8 seniors, $7 high school and college students, $6 children 5–14. Children under 5 not admitted. Daily tours every half-hour 9:30am–4:45pm; closed weekends Jan–Feb; limited schedule may be in effect during the general debate (late Sept to mid-Oct). Subway: S, 4, 5, 6, or 7 to 42nd St./Grand Central.

Finds In Search of Historic Homes

New York's appetite for change often means that older architecture is torn down so that money-earning high-rises can go up. Surprisingly, the city maintains a fine collection of often-overlooked historic houses that are more than a tale of architecture—they're the stories of the people who passed their lives in buildings that range from humble to magnificent.

The **Historic House Trust of New York City** preserves 19 houses in all five boroughs. Those worth seeking out include the **Morris-Jumel Mansion** ✦, in Harlem at 65 Jumel Terrace (at 160th St. east of St. Nicholas Ave.; ✆ **212/923-8008;** Wed–Sun 10am–4pm; admission $3, $2 seniors and students), a grand colonial mansion built in the Palladian style around 1765 and now Manhattan's oldest surviving house.

The **Edgar Allan Poe Cottage,** 2460 Grand Concourse, at East Kingsbridge Road, the Bronx (✆ **718/881-8900;** www.bronxhistoricalsociety. org; Sat 10am–4pm, Sun 1–5pm; admission $2), was the final home of the poet and author, who moved his wife here because he thought the "country air" would be good for her tuberculosis. Among the works he penned in residence (1846–49) are "The Bells" and "Annabel Lee." The house is outfitted with period furnishings and exhibits on Poe's life and times.

The **Merchant's House Museum** ✦, 29 E. 4th St. between Lafayette Street and Bowery in NoHo (✆ **212/777-1089;** www.merchantshouse. com; Thurs–Mon 1–5pm; admission $6, $4 for seniors and students), is a rare jewel: a perfectly preserved 19th-century home, complete with intact interiors, whose last resident is said to have been the inspiration for Catherine Sloper in Henry James's *Washington Square*. The house is a prime example of Greek Revival architecture. Seven rooms are outfitted with the belongings of the original inhabitants, offering a prime look at domesticity in the 19th century.

Each of the others has its own fascinating story, and admission is generally around $2 or $3. A brochure listing the locations and touring details of all 19 of the historic homes is available by calling ✆ **212/360-8282;** recorded information is available at ✆ **212/360-3448.** You'll find information online at **www.preserve.org/hht** (click on "Things to Do," then "Attractions").

Woolworth Building ✦   This soaring "Cathedral of Commerce" cost Frank W. Woolworth $13.5 million worth of nickels and dimes in 1913. Designed by Cass Gilbert, it was the world's tallest edifice until 1930, when the Chrysler Building surpassed it. At its opening, President Woodrow Wilson pressed a button from the White House that illuminated the building's 80,000 electric light bulbs. The neo-Gothic architecture is rife with spires, gargoyles, flying buttresses, vaulted ceilings, 16th-century-style stone-as-lace traceries, turrets, and a churchlike interior.

Step into the marble entrance arcade to view the mosaic Byzantine-style ceiling and gold-leafed neo-Gothic cornices. The corbels (carved figures under the crossbeams) in the lobby include portraits of the building's engineer Gunwald

---

Moments A View from (next to) the Bridge

Want to impress your family and friends with a little known, but spectacular view of the New York skyline? Take them for a ride on the Roosevelt Island Tram (𝄪 **212/832-4543**, ext. 1). This is the same tram that King Kong "attacks" in the Universal Studio Theme Park in Florida. The same tram you have probably seen in countless movies, most recently *Spider-Man*. The tram originates at 59th Street and 2nd Avenue, costs $2 each way ($2 round-trip for seniors), and takes 4 minutes to traverse the East River to Roosevelt Island, where there are a series of apartment complexes and parks. During those 4 minutes you will be treated to a gorgeous view down the East River and the East Side skyline, with views of the United Nations and four bridges: the Queensboro, Williamsburg, Manhattan, and Brooklyn Bridge. On a clear day you might even spot Lady Liberty. And don't worry, despite what you've seen in the movies, the tram is safe, the Green Goblin is dead, and your friendly neighborhood Spiderman has everything under control. The tram operates daily from 6am until 2:30am and until 3:30am on weekends.

Aus measuring a girder (above the staircase to the left of the main door), Gilbert holding a model of the building, and Woolworth counting coins (both above the left-hand corridor of elevators). Stand near the security guard's podium and crane your neck for a glimpse of Paul Jennewein's murals of *Commerce* and *Labor*, half hidden on the mezzanine. Cross Broadway for the best view of the exterior.

233 Broadway (at Park Place, near City Hall Park). Subway: 2 or 3 to Park Place; N or R to City Hall.

6 Places of Worship

New York has an incredible range of religious institutions, notable for their history, architecture, and/or inspirational music. I've listed two of Harlem's premier gospel institutions below; if you would rather go to one of these gospel services in the company of a guide, see "Affordable Sightseeing Tours," on p. 236. Those who would like to hear the rousing gospel of the multiple Grammy Award–winning **Brooklyn Tabernacle Choir** should see p. 250.

If you do plan to attend a gospel service, be prepared to stay for the entire 1½- to 2-hour service. It is impolite to exit early. (Services are extremely popular, so you'll find it just plain difficult to leave before the end, anyway.)

Abyssinian Baptist Church 𝄪 The most famous of Harlem's more than 400 houses of worship is this Baptist church, founded downtown in 1808 by African-American and Ethiopian merchants. It was moved uptown to Harlem back in the 1920s by Adam Clayton Powell, Sr., who built it into the largest Protestant congregation in America. His son, Adam Clayton Powell, Jr. (for whom the adjoining boulevard was named), carried on his tradition, and also became a U.S. congressman. Abyssinian is now the domain of the activist-minded Rev. Calvin O. Butts, whom the chamber of commerce has declared a "Living Treasure." The Sunday-morning services—at 9 and 11am—offer a wonderful opportunity to experience the Harlem gospel tradition.

132 Odell Clark Place (W. 138th St., btwn Adam Clayton Powell Blvd. and Lenox Ave.). 𝄪 **212/862-7474.** www.abyssinian.org. Subway: 2, 3, B, or C to 135th St.

Cathedral of St. John the Divine ⚶   The world's largest Gothic cathedral has been a work in progress since 1892. Its sheer size is amazing enough—a nave that stretches two football fields and a seating capacity of 5,000—but keep in mind that there is no steel structural support. The church is being built using Gothic engineering; blocks of granite and limestone are carved by master masons and their apprentices—which may explain why construction is still ongoing, more than 100 years after it began, with no end in sight. That's precisely what makes this place so wonderful: Finishing isn't necessarily the point. A December 2001 fire destroyed the north transept, which housed the gift shop. But this phoenix rose from the ashes; the cathedral was reopened to visitors within a month, even though the scent of charred wood was still in the air.

Though the seat of the Episcopal Diocese of New York, St. John's embraces an interfaith tradition. Each chapel is dedicated to a different national, ethnic, or social group. The genocide memorial in the Missionary chapel—dedicated to the victims of the Ottoman Empire in Armenia (1915–23), of the Holocaust (1939–45), and in Bosnia-Herzegovina since 1992—moved me to tears, as did the FDNY memorial in the Labor chapel. Although it was originally conceived to honor 12 firefighters killed in 1966, hundreds of personal note cards and trinkets of remembrance have evolved it into a moving tribute to the 343 firefighting heroes murdered in the September 11, 2001, terrorist attacks.

You can explore the cathedral on your own, or on the **Public Tour,** offered 6 days a week; also inquire about periodic (usually twice-monthly) **Vertical Tours,** which take you on a hike up the 11-flight circular staircase to the top, for spectacular views. St. John the Divine is also known for presenting outstanding workshops, musical events, and important speakers. The free **New Year's Eve concert** draws thousands of New Yorkers; so, too, does its annual **Blessing of the Animals,** held in early October (see "New York City Calendar of Events" in chapter 2). To hear the pipe organ in action, attend the weekly **Choral Evensong and Organ Meditation** service Sunday at 6pm.

1047 Amsterdam Ave. (at 112th St.). ✆ 212/316-7540, 212/932-7347 (tour information and reservations), or 212/662-2133 (event information and tickets). www.stjohndivine.org. Suggested admission $2, tour $3, vertical tour $10. Mon–Sat 7am–6pm; Sun 7am–8pm. Tours offered Tues–Sat 11am, Sun 1pm. Worship services Mon–Sat 8 and 8:30am (morning prayer and holy Eucharist), 12:15pm, and 5:30pm (1st Thurs service 7:15am); Sun 8, 9, and 11am and 6pm; AIDS memorial service 4th Sat of the month at 1pm. Subway: B, C, 1, or 9 to Cathedral Pkwy.

Mother A.M.E. Zion Church   Another of Harlem's great gospel churches is this African Methodist Episcopal house of worship, the first black church to be founded in New York State. Established on John Street in Lower Manhattan in 1796, Mother A.M.E. was known as the "Freedom Church" for the central role it played in the Underground Railroad. Among the escaped slaves the church hid was Frederick Douglass; other famous congregants have included Sojourner Truth and Paul Robeson. Rousing Sunday services are at 11am.

140 W. 137th St. (btwn Adam Clayton Powell Blvd. and Lenox Ave.). ✆ 212/234-1544. www.motherafrican methodistezchurch.com. Subway: 2, 3, B, or C to 135th St.

St. Patrick's Cathedral   This Gothic white-marble and stone structure is the largest Catholic cathedral in the United States, as well as the seat of the Archdiocese of New York. Designed by James Renwick, begun in 1859, and consecrated in 1879, St. Patrick's wasn't completed until 1906. Irish Catholics picked one of the city's WASPiest neighborhoods for St. Patrick's. If you don't wish to attend Mass, you can pop in between services to get a look at the impressive interior. The St. Michael and St. Louis altar came from Tiffany and Co. (also on

5th Ave.), while the St. Elizabeth altar—honoring Mother Elizabeth Seton, the first American-born saint—was designed by Paolo Medici of Rome.

5th Ave. (btwn 50th and 51st sts.). © 212/753-2261. www.ny-archdiocese.org/pastoral/cathedral_about.html. Free admission. Sun–Fri 7am–8:30pm; Sat 8am–8:30pm. Mass Mon–Fri 7, 7:30, 8, and 8:30am, noon, and 12:30, 1, and 5:30pm; Sat 8 and 8:30am, noon, and 12:30 and 5:30pm; Sun 7, 8, 9, and 10:15am (Cardinal's Mass), noon, and 1, 4, and 5:30pm; holy days 7, 7:30, 8, 8:30, 9, 11, and 11:30am, noon, and 12:30, 1, 5:30, and 6:30pm. Subway: B, D, F, or V to 47th–50th sts./Rockefeller Center.

Temple Emanu-El Many of New York's most prominent families are members of this Reform congregation—the first established in New York City. The largest house of Jewish worship in the world is a blend of Moorish and Romanesque styles, symbolizing the mingling of Eastern and Western cultures. The temple houses a remarkable collection of Judaica in the Herbert & Eileen Bernard Museum, including a collection of Hanukkah lamps ranging from the 14th to the 20th centuries. Three galleries also tell the story of the congregation from 1845 to the present. Free **tours** are given after services Saturday at noon. Inquire for a schedule of lectures, films, music, and symposiums.

1 E. 65th St. (at 5th Ave.). © 212/744-1400. www.emanuelnyc.org. Free admission. Daily 10am–5pm. Services Sun–Thurs 5:30pm; Fri 5:15pm; Sat 10:30am. Subway: N or R to 5th Ave.; 6 to 68th St.

Trinity Church Serving God and Mammon, this Wall Street house of worship—with neo-Gothic flying buttresses, stained-glass windows, and vaulted ceilings—was designed by Richard Upjohn and consecrated in 1846. At that time, its 280-foot spire dominated the skyline. Its main doors, embellished with biblical scenes, were inspired in part by Ghiberti's famed doors on Florence's Baptistery. The historic church stood strong while office towers crumbled around it on September 11, 2001. The gates to the historic church serve as an impromptu memorial to the victims of the September 11, 2001, terrorist attacks, with countless tokens of remembrance left by both locals and visitors alike.

The church runs a brief free **tour** daily at 2pm (a second Sun tour follows the 11:15am Eucharist); groups of five or more should call © **212/602-0872** to reserve. There's a small museum at the end of the left aisle displaying documents (including the 1697 church charter from William III), photographs, replicas of the Hamilton-Burr duel pistols, and other items. Surrounding the church is a churchyard whose monuments read like a history book: a tribute to martyrs of the American Revolution, Alexander Hamilton, Robert Fulton, and many more. Lined with benches, this makes a wonderful picnic spot on warm days.

Also part of Trinity Church is **St. Paul's Chapel,** at Broadway and Fulton Street, New York's only surviving pre-Revolutionary church, and a transition shelter for homeless men until it was transformed into a relief center after the September 11, 2001, terrorist attacks; it returned to its former duties in mid-2002. Built by Thomas McBean, with a templelike portico and Ionic columns supporting a massive pediment, the chapel resembles London's St. Martin-in-the-Fields. In the small graveyard, 18th- and early-19th-century notables rest in peace and modern businesspeople sit for lunch.

Trinity holds its **Noonday Concert series** of chamber music and orchestral concerts Monday and Thursday at 1pm; call © **212/602-0747** or visit the website for a schedule, and to see if programming has resumed at St. Paul's.

At Broadway and Wall St. © 212/602-0800, 212/602-0872, or 212/602-0747 (concert information). www. trinitywallstreet.org. Free admission and tours; $2 suggested donation for noonday concerts. Museum Mon–Fri 9–11:45am and 1–3:45pm; Sat 10am–3:45pm; Sun 1–3:45pm. Services Mon–Fri 8:15am, 12:05, and 5:15pm (additional healing service Thurs at 12:30pm); Sat 8:45am; Sun 9 and 11:15am (also 8am Eucharist service at St. Paul's Chapel, btwn Vesey and Fulton sts.). Subway: 4 or 5 to Wall St.

7 Central Park ✶✶✶ & Other Places to Play

CENTRAL PARK

Without the miracle of civic planning that is Central Park, Manhattan would be an unbroken block of buildings. Instead, in the middle of Gotham, an 843-acre retreat provides an escape valve and tranquilizer for millions of New Yorkers.

While you're here, take advantage of the park's many charms—not the least of which is its layout. Frederick Law Olmsted and Calvert Vaux won a competition with a plan that marries flowing paths with sinewy bridges, integrating them into the natural landscape with its rocky outcroppings, man-made lakes, and wooded pockets. The park's construction, between 1859 and 1870, provided employment during a depression and drew the city's population into the upper reaches of the island, which at that time were still quite rural. Nevertheless, designers predicted the hustle and bustle to come, and hid traffic from the eyes and ears of park-goers by building roads that are largely hidden from the bucolic view.

On just about any day, Central Park is crowded with New Yorkers and visitors alike. On nice days, especially weekend days, it's the city's party central. Families come to play in the snow or the sun, depending on the season; in-line skaters come to fly through the crisp air and twirl in front of the band shell; couples come to stroll or paddle the lake; dog owners come to hike and throw Frisbees to Bowser; and just about everybody comes to sunbathe at the first sign of summer. On beautiful days, the crowds are part of the appeal—folks come here to peel off their urban armor and relax, and the common goal puts a general feeling of camaraderie in the air. On these days, the people-watching is more compelling than anywhere else in the city. But even on the most crowded days, there's always somewhere to get away from it all, if you just want a little peace and quiet, and a moment to commune with nature.

ORIENTATION & GETTING THERE   Look at your map—that great green swath in the center of Manhattan is Central Park. It runs from 59th Street (also known as Central Park S.) at the south end to 110th Street at the north end, and from 5th Avenue on the east side to Central Park West (the equivalent of 8th Ave.) on the west side. A 6-mile rolling road, **Central Park Drive,** circles the park, and has a lane set aside for bikers, joggers, and in-line skaters. A number of **transverse (crosstown) roads** cross the park at major points—at 65th, 79th, 86th, and 97th streets—but they're built down a level, largely out of view, to minimize intrusion on the bucolic nature of the park.

A number of subway stops and lines serve the park. To reach the southernmost entrance on the west side, take an A, B, C, D, 1, or 9 to 59th Street/Columbus Circle. To reach the southeast corner, take the N or R to 5th Avenue; from this stop, it's an easy walk to the Information Center in the **Dairy** (🕾 212/794-6564; daily 11am–5pm, to 4pm in winter), midpark at about 65th Street. Here you can ask questions, pick up information, and purchase a good park map.

If your time for exploring is limited, I suggest entering the park at 72nd or 79th streets (subway: B or C to 72nd St. or 81st St./Museum of Natural History). From here, you can pick up information at the visitor center at **Belvedere Castle** (🕾 212/772-0210; Tues–Sun 10am–5pm, to 4pm in winter), midpark at 79th Street. There's also a visitor center at the **Charles A. Dana Discovery Center** (🕾 212/860-1370; daily 11am–5pm, to 4pm in winter), at the northeast corner of the park at Harlem Meer, at 110th Street between 5th and Lenox avenues (subway: 2 or 3 to 110th St.). The Dana Center is an environmental center hosting workshops, exhibits, music programs, and park tours, and lends fishing poles for fishing in Harlem Meer (park policy is catch-and-release).

Food carts and vendors are at all of the park's main gathering points, so finding a bite is never a problem. You'll also find food counters at the **Conservatory,** on the east side of the park, north of the 72nd Street entrance; and at **The Boat House,** on the lake near 72nd Street and Park Drive North, which also offers a full-service menu (© **212/517-2233**).

GUIDED WALKS The **Central Park Conservancy** offers a slate of free walking tours; call © **212/360-2726** or check **www.centralparknyc.org** for the current schedule (click on the "Walking Tours" button on the left). The Dana Center hosts ranger-guided tours on occasion (call © **800/201-PARK** or 212/860-1370 for the schedule).

FOR FURTHER INFORMATION Call the main number at © **212/360-3444** for recorded information, or 212/310-6600 or 212/628-1036 to speak to a live person. Call © **888/NY-PARKS** for events information. The park also has two websites: The city parks department's site at **www.centralpark.org**, and the Central Park Conservancy's site at **www.centralparknyc.org**, each of which features maps and a rundown of attractions and activities. For a park **emergency,** dial © **800/201-PARK,** which will link you to the park rangers.

SAFETY TIP Even though the park has the lowest crime rate of any of the city's precincts, keep your wits about you, especially in the more remote northern end. It's a good idea to avoid the park entirely after dark, unless you're heading to one of the restaurants for dinner or to a SummerStage or Shakespeare in the Park event (see chapter 9), when you should stick with the crowds.

EXPLORING THE PARK

The best way to see Central Park is to wander along the park's 58 miles of winding pedestrian paths, keeping in mind the following highlights.

Before starting your stroll, stop by the **Information Center** in the Dairy (© **212/794-6464;** daily 11am–5pm, to 4pm in winter), midpark in a 19th-century-style building overlooking Wollman Rink at about 65th Street, to get a good park map and other information on sights and events.

The southern part of Central Park is more formally designed and heavily visited than the relatively rugged and remote northern end. Not far from the Dairy is the **carousel,** with 58 hand-carved horses (© **212/879-0244;** daily 10:30am–6pm, to 5pm in winter; rides 90¢); the zoo (see "Central Park Zoo," below); and the Wollman Rink for roller- or ice-skating (see "Activities," below).

Tips **Softball for the Stars**

Every spring and summer, Central Park is home to many softball leagues. One of the oldest and most celebrated is the Broadway Show League, which plays at Hecksher Fields, around 63rd Street on the west side of the park. The league features representatives from all the major Broadway productions. The coed games, which are open for all to watch, can get pretty intense, and you might be surprised who you see out there shagging flies; Al Pacino, Matthew Broderick, and Robert Redford have all played in the league. I once witnessed Edie Falco slide headfirst into second base. And yes, she was safe.

Central Park

i Information

Ⓜ Subway stop

0   1/5 mi

0   0.2 km

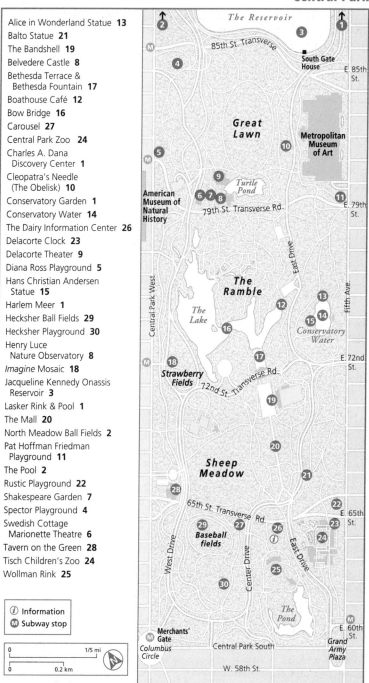

The **Mall,** a long, formal walkway lined with elms shading benches and sculptures of sometimes-forgotten writers, leads to the focal point of Central Park, **Bethesda Fountain** ✿ (along the 72nd St. transverse road). **Bethesda Terrace** and its sculpted entryway border a large **lake** where dogs fetch sticks, boaters glide by, and anglers try their luck at catching carp, perch, catfish, and bass. You can rent a rowboat at or take a gondola ride from **Loeb Boathouse,** on the eastern end of the lake (see "Activities," below). Boats of another kind are at **Conservatory Water** (on the east side at 73rd St.), a stone-walled pond flanked by statues of both **Hans Christian Andersen** and **Alice in Wonderland.** On Saturday at 10am, die-hard yachtsmen race remote-controlled sailboats in fierce competitions following Olympic regulations. (Sorry, model boats aren't for rent.)

Sheep Meadow on the southwestern side of the park is a designated quiet zone, where Frisbee throwing and kite flying are as energetic as things get. Another respite is **Strawberry Fields** ✿, at 72nd Street on the west side. This memorial to John Lennon, who was murdered across the street at The Dakota apartment building, is a gorgeous garden centered around an Italian mosaic bearing the title of this Beatle's most famous solo song, and his lifelong message: IMAGINE. In keeping with its goal of promoting world peace, the garden has 161 varieties of plants, donated by each of the 161 nations in existence when it was designed in 1985. This is a wonderful place for peaceful contemplation.

Bow Bridge, a graceful lacework of cast iron designed by Calvert Vaux, crosses over the lake and leads to the most bucolic area of Central Park, the **Ramble.** This dense 38-acre woodland with spiraling paths, rocky outcroppings, and a stream is the best spot for bird-watching and feeling as if you've discovered an unimaginably leafy forest right in the middle of the city.

North of the Ramble, **Belvedere Castle** ✿ is home to the **Henry Luce Nature Observatory** (✆ 212/772-0210), worth a visit if you're with children. From the castle, set on Vista Rock (the park's highest point at 135 ft.), you can look down on the **Great Lawn,** where softball players and sun worshipers compete for coveted greenery, and the **Delacorte Theater,** home to Shakespeare in the Park (p. 304). The small **Shakespeare Garden** south of the theater is scruffy, but it does have plants, herbs, and trees mentioned by the playwright. Behind Belvedere Castle is the **Swedish Cottage Marionette Theatre** ✿ (✆ 212/988-9093), hosting marionette plays for children.

Continue north along the east side of the Great Lawn, parallel to East Drive. Near the glass-enclosed back of the **Metropolitan Museum of Art** ✿✿✿ (p. 199) is **Cleopatra's Needle,** a 69-foot obelisk originally erected in Heliopolis around 1475 B.C. It was given to the city by the khedive of Egypt in 1880. (The khedive bestowed on London a similar obelisk, which now sits on the Embankment of the Thames.)

North of the 86th Street Transverse Road is the **Jacqueline Kennedy Onassis Reservoir,** so named after the death of the First Lady, who lived nearby and often enjoyed a run along the 1.5-mile jogging track around the reservoir.

North of the reservoir is my favorite part of the park. It's much less traversed, and in some areas, absolutely tranquil. The **North Meadow** (at 96th St.) features 12 baseball and softball fields. Sadly, the North Meadow is circled by a not very attractive fence, and 6 months of the year that fence is locked and the Meadow closed. An unfortunate recent trend in Central Park has been the proliferation of fences. They have become so prevalent that at times you get the feeling you are not really in a park, but a museum.

North of the North Meadow, at the northeast end of the park, is the **Conservatory Garden** ✦ (at 105th St. and 5th Ave.), Central Park's only formal garden, with a magnificent display of flowers and trees reflected in calm pools of water. (The gates to the garden once fronted the 5th Ave. mansion of Cornelius Vanderbilt II.) **The Lasker Rink and Pool** (© **212/534-7639**) is the only swimming pool in Central Park; and in the winter it converts to a skating rink, offering a less hectic alternative to Wollman Rink (see "Activities," below). **Harlem Meer** and its boathouse were recently renovated and look beautiful. The boathouse now berths the **Charles A. Dana Discovery Center,** near 110th Street between 5th and Lenox avenues (© **212/860-1370**), where children learn about the environment and borrow fishing poles for catch-and-release at no charge. **The Pool** (at W. 100th St.), possibly the most idyllic spot in all of Central Park, was recently renovated and features willows, grassy banks, and a small pond populated by some very well-fed ducks. You might even spot an egret and a hawk or two lurking around here.

GOING TO THE ZOO

Central Park Zoo ✦ *Kids*   It has been a decade since the zoo in Central Park was renovated, making it both more human and more humane. Sea lions frolic in the central pool area. The gigantic, graceful polar bears (one of whom, by the way, made himself a true New Yorker when he began regular visits to a shrink) glide back and forth across a watery pool that has glass walls, through which you can observe very large paws doing very smooth strokes. The monkeys seem to regard those on the other side of the fence with knowing disdain. In the hot and humid Tropic Zone, large, colorful birds swoop around in freedom, sometimes landing next to nonplused visitors.

The indoor Tropic Zone is a real highlight; its steamy rainforest is home to everything from black-and-white Colobus monkeys to emerald tree boa constrictors to a leaf-cutter ant farm; look for the dart poison frog exhibit, which is very cool. So is the large penguin enclosure in the Polar Circle, which is better than the one at San Diego's Sea World. In the Temperate Territory, look for the Asian red pandas (cousins to the black-and-white ones), which look like beautiful raccoons. Despite their pool and piles of ice, the polar bears still look sad.

The entire zoo is good for short attention spans; you can cover the whole thing in 1½ to 3 hours, depending on the size of the crowds and how long you like to linger. It's also very kid-friendly, with lots of well-written and -illustrated placards that older kids can understand. For the littlest ones, there's the $6-million **Tisch Children's Zoo.** With sheep, llamas, potbellied pigs, and more, this petting zoo and playground is a real blast for the 5-and-under set.

830 5th Ave. (at 64th St., just inside Central Park). © 212/861-6030. www.wcs.org/zoos. Admission $6 adults, $1.25 seniors, $1.50 children 3–12, free for children under 3. Apr–Oct Mon–Fri 10am–5pm, Sat–Sun 10am–5:30pm; Nov–Mar daily 10am–4:30pm. Subway: N or R to 5th Ave.

ACTIVITIES

The 6-mile rolling road circling the park, **Central Park Drive,** has a lane for bikers, joggers, and in-line skaters. The best time to use it is when the park is closed to traffic: Monday through Friday from 10am to 3pm (except Thanksgiving to New Year's) and 7 to 10pm. It's also closed from 7pm Friday to 6am Monday, but when the weather is nice, the crowds can be hellish.

BIKING   Off-road mountain biking isn't permitted; stay on Central Park Drive or your bike may be confiscated by park police.

You can rent 3- and 10-speed bikes as well as tandems in Central Park at the **Loeb Boathouse,** midpark near 72nd Street and Park Drive North, just in from 5th Avenue (© **212/517-2233** or 212/517-3623), for $9 to $20 an hour, with a complete selection of kids' bikes, cruisers, tandems, and the like ($200 deposit required); at **Metro Bicycles,** 1311 Lexington Ave., at 88th Street (© **212/427-4450**), for about $7 an hour, or $35 a day; and at **Toga Bike Shop,** 110 West End Ave., at 64th Street (© **212/799-9625;** www.togabikes.com), for $30 a day. No matter where you rent, be prepared to leave a credit card deposit.

BOATING   March through November, gondola rides and rowboat rentals are available at the **Loeb Boathouse,** midpark near 74th Street and Park Drive North, just in from 5th Avenue (© **212/517-2233** or 212/517-3623). Rowboats are $10 for the first hour, $2.50 every 15 minutes thereafter, and a $30 deposit is required; reservations are accepted.

HORSE-DRAWN CARRIAGE RIDES   At the entrance to the park at 59th Street and Central Park South, you'll see a line of **horse-drawn carriages** waiting to take passengers through the park or along certain of the city's streets. Horses belong on city streets as much as chamber pots belong in our homes. You won't need me to tell you how forlorn most of these horses look—skip it.

ICE-SKATING   **Wollman Rink** ⚘, on the east side of the park between 62nd and 63rd streets (© **212/439-6900;** www.wollmanskatingrink.com), is the city's best outdoor skating spot, more spacious than the rink at Rockefeller Center. It's open for skating from mid-October to mid-April, depending on the weather. Rates are $8.50 for adults, $4.25 for seniors and kids under 12, and skate rental is $4.75; lockers are available (locks are $6.75). **Lasker Rink** (© **212/534-7639**) on the east side around 106th Street, is a less-expensive alternative to the much more crowded Wollman Rink. It's open November through March. Rates are $4.50 for adults, $2.25 for kids under 12; skate rental is $4.75.

IN-LINE SKATING   Central Park is the city's most popular place for blading. See the beginning of this section for details on Central Park Drive, the main drag for skaters. On weekends, head to West Drive at 67th Street, behind Tavern on the Green, where you'll find trick skaters weaving through an NYRSA slalom course at full speed, or the Mall in front of the band shell (above Bethesda Fountain) for twirling to tunes. In summer, **Wollman Rink** converts to a hotshot roller rink, with half-pipes and lessons available (see "Ice-Skating," above).
     You can rent skates for $20 a day from **Blades Board and Skate,** 120 W. 72nd St. (btwn Broadway and Columbus Ave.; © **212/787-3911;** www.blades.com). Wollman Rink (see above) also rents in-line skates for park use at similar rates.

PLAYGROUNDS   Nineteen Adventure Playgrounds are scattered throughout the park, perfect for jumping, sliding, swinging, and digging. At Central Park West and 81st Street is the **Diana Ross Playground** ⚘, voted the city's best by *New York* magazine. Also on the west side is the **Spector Playground,** at 85th Street and Central Park West, and, farther north, the **Wild West Playground** at 93rd Street. On the east side is the **Rustic Playground,** at 67th Street and 5th Avenue, a delightfully landscaped space rife with islands, bridges, and slides; and the **Pat Hoffman Friedman Playground,** behind the Metropolitan Museum of Art at East 79th Street, is geared toward older toddlers.

RUNNING   Marathoners and wannabes run in Central Park along the 6-mile **Central Park Drive,** which circles the park (run toward traffic to avoid being mowed down by wayward cyclists and in-line skaters). For a shorter loop, try the midpark 1.5-mile track around the **Jacqueline Kennedy Onassis Reservoir**

Tips **Running the City**

Here, as suggested by the **New York Road Runner's Club,** are the five best running routes in Manhattan.

Central Park Reservoir: Possibly the most famous running route in the world; presidential candidates have run this route as well as the famous former first lady for whom it is now named.

The **Loop** in Central Park: I used to run past Madonna and her male bodyguards when she was a frequenter of the 6-mile loop. Now I see Howard Stern jogging, no bodyguards in sight, but usually with a female companion or two.

East River: Entering on 63rd Street and York Avenue and running up to 125th Street and back is a 6-mile jog where you will pass Gracie Mansion, high-rises overlooking the river, and fishermen testing the river waters.

Hudson River South: Entering at Chelsea Piers at West 23rd Street and continuing down to Battery Park City is approximately a 5-mile run. In the warm months it's a carnival downtown, with in-line skaters, kayakers, musicians, and cyclists crowding the slim downtown park.

Hudson River North: Entering at Riverbank State Park at 145th Street on the Hudson River and running down lovely Riverside Park, passing the 79th Street Boat Basin, and ending at the Intrepid Sea-Air-Space Museum is approximately a 6-mile run.

(keep your eyes ready for spotting Madonna and other famous bodies). It's safest to jog only during daylight hours and where everybody else does. Avoid the small walks in the Ramble and at the north end of the park.

SWIMMING   Lasker Pool, around 106th Street on the east side (✆ **212/534-7639**), is the only pool in Central Park. It is open from July 1 to Labor Day weekend. Rates are $4 for adults, $2 for kids under 12. Bring a towel.

OTHER PARKS

For parks in Brooklyn and Queens, see "Highlights of the Outer Boroughs" (p. 247). For more information on these and other city parks, go online to **nyc-parks.completeinet.net.**

Battery Park ⭐⭐   As you traverse Manhattan's concrete canyons, it's easy to forget you're on an island. But at Manhattan's southernmost tip, you get the real sense that just past Liberty, Ellis, and Staten islands is the Atlantic Ocean.

The 21-acre park is named for the cannons built to defend residents after the American Revolution. **Castle Clinton National Monument** (the place to purchase tickets for the Statue of Liberty and Ellis Island ferry) was built as a fort before the War of 1812, though it was never used as such. The 22-ton **bronze sphere** by Fritz Koenig that was recovered from the rubble of the World Trade Center, where it stood between the Twin Towers as a symbol of global peace, now stands—damaged but still whole—in the park as a temporary memorial to the victims of the World Trade Center terrorist attack. This may be the finest place in the city to pay tribute to those who were lost.

Finds   A Park with a View

I acknowledge that Central Park is the king of New York parks, but if I can't have Central Park, I'll take **Riverside Park** 🎯🎯—any day. I spent many of my early years in New York in Riverside Park (© **212/408-0264**; www.nycgov parks.org) staring at the New Jersey skyline, jogging along the Hudson river, playing hoops at the courts on 77th Street (when I still could jump), taking strolls along the promenade on hot summer nights, and watching the comings or goings of the unusual community that lives in the boats at the 79th Street Boat Basin. This underrated beauty designed by Frederick Law Olmstead, the same man who designed Central Park, stretches 4 miles from 72nd Street to 158th Street. The serpentine route along the Hudson River offers a variety of lovely river vistas, 14 playgrounds, two tennis courts, softball and soccer fields, a skate park, beach volleyball, the aforementioned Boat Basin, two cafes—the **Boat Basin Café** at 79th Street (© **212/496-5542**) and **Hurley's Hudson Beach Café** at 105th Street (© **917/370-3448**), open April through September only—and monuments such as the Eleanor Roosevelt statue at 72nd Street, the Soldiers and Sailors Monument at 90th Street, and Grant's Tomb at 122nd Street (© **212/666-1640**).

But here's the best part: On a hot summer day, when Central Park is teeming with joggers, sunbathers, and in-line skaters, Riverside Park, just a few blocks from Central Park's western fringe, is comparatively serene.

You'll likely recognize Battery Park for the role it played in *Desperately Seeking Susan*. Besides the T-shirt vendors and hot-dog carts, you'll find several statues and memorials throughout the park. This is quite the civilized park, with lots of STAY OFF THE GRASS! signs and Wall Streeters eating sandwiches on the park benches. Pull up your own bench for a good view across the harbor.

From State St. to New York Harbor. Subway: N or R to Whitehall St.; 1 or 9 to South Ferry; 4 or 5 to Bowling Green.

Bryant Park 🎯   Another success story in urban redevelopment, Bryant Park is the latest incarnation of a 4-acre site that was, at various times, a graveyard and a reservoir. Named for poet and *New York Evening Post* editor William Cullen Bryant (look for his statue on the east end), the park rests atop the New York Public Library's underground stacks. Another notable statue is a squat and evocative stone portrait of Gertrude Stein.

This simple green swath is welcome relief from Midtown's concrete, taxi-choked jungle, and good weather attracts brown-baggers from neighboring office buildings. Just behind the library is **Bryant Park Grill** (© **212/840-6500**; www. bryantpark.org/amenities/dining.php), a gorgeous, airy bistro with spectacular views but merely decent food. The grill's two summer alfresco restaurants—**The Terrace,** on the Grill's roof, and the **Cafe** are extremely pleasant on a nice day.

Adding to the charm of Bryant Park is **Le Carrousel**; a working merry-go-round created to complement the park's French classical style. It's not as big as the Central Park Carrousel, but truly romantic, with 14 different animals that revolve to the sounds of French cabaret music. Le Carrousel is open year-round, weather permitting, from 11am to 7pm, and costs $1.50 to ride.

Additionally, the park plays host to New York's **Seventh on Sixth** fashion shows, set up in billowy white tents (open to the trade only) in the spring and fall.

In the summer, you can head for the **Bryant Park Summer Film Festival,** in which a classic film—*Dr. Zhivago, Viva Las Vegas,* and the like—is shown on a 20-by-50-foot screen under the stars every Monday evening at sunset. Admission is free; just bring a blanket and a picnic. Rain dates are Tuesdays. For the current schedule, call ✆ **212/512-5700** or visit www.hbobryantparkfilm.com.

Behind the New York Public Library, at 6th Ave. btwn 40th and 42nd sts. www.bryantpark.org. Subway: B, D, F, or V to 42nd St.; 7 to 5th Ave.

Union Square Park   Reclaimed from drug dealers and abject ruin in the late '80s, Union Square Park is now one of the city's best assets. This patch of green is the focal point of the fashionable Flatiron and Gramercy Park neighborhoods. Don't miss the grand equestrian statue of George Washington at the south end, or the bronze statue (by Bartholdi, the sculptor of the Statue of Liberty) of the marquis de Lafayette at the eastern end, gracefully glancing toward France.

This charming square is the site of New York's premier **Greenmarket.** Every Monday, Wednesday, Friday, and Saturday, vendors hawk fresh veggies and fruits, organic baked goods, cider, wine, and even fresh fish and lobsters in booths that flank the north and west sides of the square. Fresh-cut flowers and plants are also for sale, as are books and postcards. During summer and fall, you can graze the bazaar and assemble a cheap and healthy lunch to munch under the trees or at the picnic tables at the park's north end. Musical acts play the small pavilion at the north end of the park, and in-line skaters take over the market space in the after-work hours. A **cafe** is open at the north end of the park in warm weather.

From 14th to 17th sts., btwn Park Ave. S. and Broadway. Subway: 4, 5, 6, L, N, R, Q, or W to 14th St./Union Square.

Washington Square Park   You'll be hard-pressed to find much "park" in this mostly concrete square—a burial ground in the late 18th century—but it's undeniably the focal point of Greenwich Village. Chess players, skateboarders,

---

⌐Tips The Greening of New York

Whenever I travel to a city anywhere around the world, I make it a priority to visit that city's greenmarket, or farmer's market. I've been to some great ones, and I might be a tad bit prejudiced, but I haven't been to many better than the **Union Square Greenmarket** ⍟⍟ here in New York City. New York has greenmarkets throughout the city on different days of the week, but the biggest and the best is at Union Square every Monday, Wednesday, Friday, and Saturday. You'll find pickings from upstate and New Jersey farms, fresh fish from Long Island, homemade cheese and other dairy products, baked goods, plants, and organic herbs and spices. It's a true New York scene with everyone from models to celebrated chefs poring through the bounty. The Union Square Greenmarket is open year-round, but is at its peak August through October when the local harvest—tomatoes, corn, greens, grapes, peppers, and apples—flourishes. If you are lucky enough to be in the city during this period, don't miss the bonanza and do pick up some apples or grapes for your travels around the city—but even if you're not, check it out no matter what the season. If you find the right ingredients (say, a crusty loaf of bread, cheese, cider), you can sit down and have an impromptu picnic! For more information and locations and schedules, refer to the Council on the Environment of New York City website at www.cenyc.org or call ✆ **212/477-3220.**

street musicians, New York University students, couples, the occasional film crew, and not a few homeless people compete for attention throughout the day and most of the night. (If anyone issues a challenge to play you in the ancient and complex Chinese game of Go, don't take him up on it—you'll lose money.)

The lively scene belies a macabre past. Once marshland traversed by Minetta Brook, it became in 1797 a potter's field, and the remains of some 10,000 bodies are buried here. In the early 1800s, the square, or the infamous Hanging Elm in the northwest corner where MacDougal Street meets the park, was used for public executions. It wasn't until the 1830s that the Greek Revival town houses on **Washington Square North** known as "The Row" (note especially nos. 21–26) attracted the elite. Stanford White designed Washington Arch (1891–92) to commemorate the centenary of George Washington's inauguration as president. While in the neighborhood, peek down MacDougal Alley and Washington Mews, both lined with delightful old carriage houses. The arch was refurbished in 2004 and now features exterior lighting.

At the southern end of 5th Ave. (where it intersects Waverly Place btwn MacDougal and Wooster sts.). Subway: A, C, E, F, or V to W. 4th St./Washington Square.

8 Affordable Sightseeing Tours

Reservations are required on some of the tours listed below, but even if they're not, it's always best to call ahead to confirm prices, times, and meeting places.

HARBOR CRUISES

Circle Line Sightseeing Cruises ☆☆   A New York institution, the Circle Line is famous for its 3-hour tour around the entire 35 miles of Manhattan. This **Full Island** cruise passes by the Statue of Liberty, Ellis Island, the Brooklyn Bridge, the United Nations, Yankee Stadium, the George Washington Bridge, and more, including Manhattan's wild northern tip. The panorama is riveting, and the commentary isn't bad. The big boats are basic but fine, with lots of deck room for everybody to enjoy the view. Snacks, soft drinks, coffee, and beer are available onboard for purchase.

If 3 hours is more than you or the kids can handle, go for either the 2-hour **Semi-Circle** or the **Sunset/Harbor Lights** cruise, both of which show you the highlights of the skyline. There's also a 1-hour **Seaport Liberty** version that sticks close to the south end of the island. But of all the tours, the kids might like **The Beast** best, a thrill-a-minute speedboat ride offered in summer only.

In addition, a number of adults-only **Live Music and DJ Cruises** sail regularly from the seaport from May through September ($20–$40 per person). Depending on the night of the week, you can groove to the sounds of jazz, Latin, gospel, dance tunes, or blues as you sail along the skyline.

Departing from Pier 83, at W. 42nd St. and 12th Ave. Also departing from Pier 16 at South St. Seaport, 207 Front St. ⓒ **212/563-3200.** www.circleline42.com, www.ridethebeast.com, or www.seaportmusiccruises.com. Sightseeing cruises $16–$25 adults, $17–$20 seniors, $10–$13 children 12 and under. Subway to Pier 83: A, C, or E to 42nd St. Subway to Pier 16: J, M, Z, 2, 3, 4, or 5 to Fulton St.

New York Waterway ☆☆   New York Waterway, the nation's largest privately held ferry service and cruise operator, like Circle Line, also does the 35-mile trip around Manhattan, but does it in 2 hours, taking in all the same sights. They also offer a staggering number of different sightseeing options, including a very good 90-minute New York Harbor Cruise, a Romantic Twilight Cruise, a Friday Dance Party Cruise, and Baseball Cruises to Mets and Yankee games.

Departing from 38th St. Ferry Terminal, at W. 38th St and 12th Ave. ✆ **800/533-3779**. www.nywaterway. com. Sightseeing cruises $14–$25 adults, $13–$20 seniors, $7–$12 children. Free bus transportation from 57th, 49th, 42nd, and 34th sts. to 38th St. Terminal; you can flag down any of the big red buses labeled NYWATERWAY or wait at any of the bus stops along those streets.

SPECIALTY TOURS
MUSEUMS & CULTURAL ORGANIZATIONS

In addition to the choices below, those interested in touring the Financial District with a guide should also consider the **World of Finance Walking Tour** offered Fridays at 10am by the Museum of American Financial History; see p. 238.

The **Municipal Art Society** ✪ (✆ **212/439-1049** or 212/935-3960; www. mas.org) offers excellent historical and architectural walking tours aimed at intelligent, individualistic travelers. A highly qualified guide who gives insights into the significance of buildings, neighborhoods, and history leads each tour. Topics range from the urban history of Greenwich Village to *Mies and the Moderns,* examining the architectural legacy of Mies van der Rohe, to an examination of the "new" Times Square. Weekday walking tours cost $12; weekend tours cost $15. Reservations may be required depending on the tour, so call ahead. A full schedule is available online or by calling ✆ **212/439-1049.**

The Alliance for Downtown New York, the Business Improvement District in charge of Lower Manhattan, offers a free, 90-minute **Wall Street Walking Tour** ✪ every Thursday and Saturday at noon, rain or shine. (See "Absolutely Free Walking Tours," below). Reservations are not required (unless you're a group), but you can call ✆ **212/606-4064** or visit **www.downtownny.com** to confirm the schedule.

The **92nd Street Y** ✪ (✆ **212/415-5500** or 212/415-5628; www.92ndsty.org) offers a variety of walking and bus tours, many featuring funky themes or behind-the-scenes visits. Subjects can range from "Diplomat for a Day at the U.N." to "Secrets of the Chelsea Hotel," from "Artists of the Meat Packing District" to "Jewish Harlem." Prices range from $20 to $60 (sometimes more for bus tours), but many include ferry rides, afternoon tea, dinner, or whatever suits the program. Guides are experts on their subjects, ranging from historians to an East Village poet, mystic, and art critic (for "Allen Ginsberg's New York" and "East Village Night Spots"), and many routes travel into the outer boroughs; some day trips even reach beyond the city. Advance registration is required for all walking and bus tours. Schedules are planned a few months in advance, so check the website for tours that might interest you.

INDEPENDENT OPERATORS

One of the most highly praised sightseeing organizations in New York is **Big Onion Walking Tours** ✪ (✆ **212/439-1090;** www.bigonion.com). Enthusiastic Big Onion guides (all hold degrees in American history) peel back the layers of history to reveal the city's secrets. The 2-hour tours are offered mostly on weekends, and subjects include the "The Bowery," "Presidential New York," "Irish New York," "Central Park," "Greenwich Village in Twilight," "Historic Harlem," "Jewish Ellis Island," "Brooklyn Bridge & Brooklyn Heights at Twilight," and historic takes on Lower Manhattan. One of the most popular is the "Multiethnic Eating Tour" of the Lower East Side, where you munch on everything from dim sum and dill pickles to fresh mozzarella. Tour prices range from $12 to $18 for adults, $10 to $16 for students and seniors. No reservations are necessary, but Big Onion *recommends that you call to verify schedules.*

Value Absolutely Free Walking Tours

A number of neighborhood organizations and Business Improvement Districts (BIDs) offer free guided walks of their neighborhoods. For travelers on a budget, these introductory freebies are well worth taking advantage of:

The **Municipal Art Society** (© 212/935-3960; www.mas.org) offers a free walking tour of Grand Central Terminal on Wednesday at 12:30pm, which meets at the information booth on the Grand Concourse. The **Grand Central Partnership** (© 212/697-1245) runs its own free tour every Friday at 12:30pm, meeting outside the station in front of the Whitney Museum at Philip Morris gallery, at 42nd Street and Park Avenue. It's a real joy now that Grand Central has been restored. Call to confirm the schedule and meeting spot before you set out to meet either tour.

The Alliance for Downtown New York, the Business Improvement District in charge of Lower Manhattan, offers a free 90-minute **Wall Street Walking Tour** ⚡ every Thursday and Saturday at noon, rain or shine. This guided tour explores the history and architecture of the nation's first capital and the world center of finance. Stops include the New York Stock Exchange, Trinity Church, Federal Hall National Monument, and other sites of historic and cultural importance. Tours meet on the steps of the U.S. Customs House (p. 207), at 1 Bowling Green (subway: 4 or 5 to Bowling Green). Reservations are not required (unless you're a group), but you can call © 212/606-4064 or visit **www.downtownny.com** to confirm the schedule.

The **Orchard Street Bargain District Tour** (© 866/224-0206 or 212/226-9010; www.lowereastsideny.com) explores the history and retail culture of this neighborhood. This is a good bet for bargain-hunters, who will learn about the old-world shops and newer outlet stores in this discount-shopping destination. The free tours are given Sunday at 11am from April to December, rain or shine, and no reservation is required. Meet up with the guide in front of Katz's Delicatessen, 205 E. Houston St., at Ludlow Street.

If you're looking to tour a specific neighborhood with an expert guide, call **Big Apple Greeter** (© 212/669-8159; www.bigapplegreeter. org). This nonprofit organization consists of specially trained New Yorkers who volunteer to take visitors around town for a free 2- to 4-hour tour of a particular neighborhood. Reservations must be made in advance, preferably at least 1 week ahead of your arrival. Big Apple Greeter is also well suited to accommodate travelers with disabilities; see "Specialized Travel Resources" in chapter 2 for details.

All tours from **Joyce Gold History Tours of New York** ⚡ (© 212/242-5762; www.nyctours.com) are offered by Joyce Gold herself, an instructor of Manhattan history at New York University and the New School, who has been conducting walks around New York since 1975. Her tours can cut to the core of this town; Joyce is full of fascinating stories about Manhattan and its people.

Tours are arranged around themes like "The Colonial Settlers of Wall Street," "The Genius and Elegance of Gramercy Park," "Downtown Graveyards," "The Old Jewish Lower East Side," "Historic Harlem," and "TriBeCa: The Creative Explosion." Tours are offered most weekends March through December and last from 2 to 4 hours, and the price is $12 per person; no reservations are required. Private tours can be arranged year-round, either for individuals or groups.

Myra Alperson, founder and lead tour guide for **NoshWalks** (② 212/222-2243; www.noshwalks.com), knows food in New York City and knows where to find it. For the past 5 years, Alperson has been leading adventurous, hungry walkers to some of the city's most delicious neighborhoods. From the Uzbek, Tadjik, and Russian markets of Rego Park, Queens, to the Dominican coffee shops of Washington Heights in upper Manhattan, Alperson has left no ethnic neighborhood unexplored. Tours are conducted on Saturday and Sunday, leaving around 11am. The preferred means of transportation is subway and the tours generally last around 3 hours and cost $15, not including the food you will undoubtedly buy on the tour. Space is limited, so book well in advance.

Alfred Pommer has conducted **New York City Cultural Walking Tours** (② 212/979-2388; www.nycwalk.com) in nearly every Manhattan neighborhood for over 15 years. He focuses on history and architecture, making the past come alive via photographs and stories. A number of his tours focus on specific subjects, such as "Gargoyles in Manhattan." His 2½-hour tours take place most Sundays at 2pm. The charge is $10 per person, and no reservation is needed; just show up at the assigned spot. Mr. Pommer also offers weekday walking tours that cost $20 per person and require reservations; call ② **212/334-2211,** ext. 101, or go to www.imar.com/nycwalk. Private tours are available at $35 per hour for individuals or groups.

Would you like to cruise by Monica and Chandler's apartment building? How about the courthouse where the prosecutors of *Law & Order* fight the good fight? **On Location Tours** (② 212/209-3370 or 212/935-0168; www.sceneontv.com) offers narrated minibus tours on their **Manhattan TV Tour;** tickets are $20 for adults, $10 for kids 6 to 9, free for 5 and under. Or, if you want to see Carrie Bradshaw's Big Apple, take the 2½-hour *Sex and the City* **Tour;** tickets cost $33. Most tours take place on Saturdays and depart from the Times Square Visitors Center, at noon and 2:30pm. There's a 3-hour *Sopranos* **Tour** that will take you to New Jersey for $35. Reservations are a must.

Harlem Spirituals (② 800/660-2166 or 212/391-0900; www.harlemspirituals. com) specializes in gospel and jazz tours of Harlem that can be combined with a traditional soul-food meal. A variety of options are available, including a tour of Harlem sights with gospel service, and a soul-food lunch or brunch as an optional add-on. The Harlem jazz tour includes a neighborhood tour, dinner at a family-style soul-food restaurant, and a visit to a local jazz club; there's also an Apollo Theater variation on this tour. Bronx and Brooklyn tours are also an option for those who want a taste of the outer boroughs. Prices start at $30, $23 for children, for a Harlem Heritage tour, and go up from there based on length and inclusions (tours that include food and entertainment are pay-one-price). All tours leave from Harlem Spirituals' Midtown office (690 8th Ave., btwn 43rd and 44th sts.), and transportation is included.

New York Like a Native ⚑ (② **718/393-7537;** www.nylikeanative.com) offers the city's best introduction to Brooklyn. The tours focus mainly on the best of brownstone Brooklyn, and you can choose from a 2½-hour version ($13), or an extended 4½-hour version ($35); the longer tour includes lunch, but you

Finds **Offbeat New York Tours**

So maybe you've taken a harbor cruise or the double-decker bus tour, but you just don't feel you got a taste of the gritty, quirky, neurotic elements that make New York so unique. You want to see those sights that even many native New Yorkers have never seen. Here are a few alternatives to the conventional tours that might satisfy that need.

Soundwalk (www.soundwalk.com): This innovative company behind the audio self-guided tour CDs debuted in 2003, with audio tours offering insider's peeks at Chinatown, the Lower East Side, Times Square, DUMBO, and the Meat Packing District. All of these are great fun and will take you places no double-decker bus ever will, but my favorite is the three-CD set **"Bronx Soundwalk."** The CD set includes *Baseball*, a tour of Yankee Stadium and environs, narrated by longtime employee Tony Morante; *Graffiti*, a tour of Hunts Point and the trail of some of the legendary graffiti artists, narrated by BG183 (aka Sotero Ortiz), founding member of the TATS Cru and Mural Kings of the Bronx; and *Hip Hop*, a Bronx River tour narrated by hip-hop DJ, the Original Jazzy Jay, which takes you to the birthplace of hip-hop and the haunts of rap pioneers like Afrika Bambaataa and Cool Herc. These tours are so authentic you'll even visit the G&R Pastry Shop where Mr. Steinbrenner, we learn, is a big fan of the shop's cheese Danish. CDs range from $13 to $19; all you need is a portable CD player, map, MetroCard, walking shoes, and an adventurous spirit. You can purchase CDs on the website, or at specific retailers listed on the site.

Wildman Steve Brill (www.wildmanstevebrill.com): If you ever get stranded in Central Park, a tour with Wildman Steve Brill might help you survive. I've seen him in the park, raggedy beard, shorts, hiking boots, and pith helmet, leading groups of eager-eyed followers while instructing them on what flora and fauna they can forage—breaking

must cover your own bus and subway fares. Tours are generally offered on Saturdays April through December, and meet at the Brooklyn Library on Grand Army Plaza (subway: 2 or 3 to Grand Army Plaza). *Prepaid reservations are required;* visit the website or call © **212/239-1124** to order.

9 Talk of the Town: Free TV Tapings

The trick to getting tickets for TV tapings in this city is to be from out of town. Visitors have a much better chance than we New Yorkers; producers are gun-shy about filling their audiences with obnoxious locals and see everybody who's not from New York as being from the heartland—their target TV audience.

If your heart's set on getting tickets to a show, request them as early as possible—6 months ahead isn't too early. You're usually asked to send a postcard. Always include the number of tickets you want, your preferred dates of attendance (be as flexible as you can), and your address *and* phone number. Tickets are always free. The shows tend to be pretty good about trying to meet your specific date requests, but don't be surprised if Ricki or Montel are far more responsive

off a stick of some edible tree and gnawing on it as an example. Brill's Central Park tours occur twice monthly and are not only hilarious, they are truly educational. If you're lucky, maybe he'll regale you with his tale of his arrest by a park ranger for eating a dandelion. Reservations must be made in advance; call © **914/835-2153**. Suggested donation is $10.

Radical Walking Tours: Led by self-proclaimed "radical historian" Bruce Kayton, these are unconventional tours of conventional tourist sights. A tour to Harlem covers the Black Panthers, Malcolm X, and the Communist party in addition to the Apollo Theater and the Schomburg Center. My favorite is the Non-Jerry Seinfeld Upper West Side Tour, which stops at the home of Fidel Castro when he lived in the neighborhood in the late 1940s, the site of the shootout with Black Panther H. Rap Brown and police, and Lincoln Center and how it destroyed what once was a thriving Puerto Rican community. Call © **718/492-0069** or visit www.he. net/~radtours for more information. Tours are $10 and no reservations are necessary.

Adventures on a Shoestring: One of the earliest entrants into the now booming walking tour market, host Howard Goldberg has provided unique views of New York since 1963, exploring New York with a breezy, man-of-the-people style. Tours, which go behind the scenes of neighborhoods, range from a variety of Greenwich Village tours—haunted, picturesque, historic—to Historic Roosevelt Island, which includes taking the Roosevelt Island Tram. He even does theme walks such as "Marilyn Monroe's Manhattan" and a "Salute to Katherine Hepburn." Tours are a bargain at $5 for 90 minutes and are conducted year-round, rain or shine. Call © **212/265-2663** for more info.

than, say, Dave Letterman. And even if you send in your request early, don't be surprised if tickets arrive as late as 1 or 2 weeks before tape date.

If you come to town without any tickets, all hope is not lost. Because they know that not every ticket holder will make it, many studios give out standby tickets on the day of taping. If you can get up early and don't mind standing in line for a couple (or a few) hours, you may get one. Now, the bad news: Only one standby ticket per person is allowed, so everybody who wants to get in has to get up at the crack of dawn and stand in line. And even if you get your hands on a standby ticket, it doesn't guarantee admission; they usually start seating standbys only after the regular ticket holders are in. Still, chances are good.

For additional information on getting tickets, call the NYCVB at © **212/484-1222.** And remember—you don't need a ticket to be on the *Today* show.

If you attend a taping, bring a sweater! As anybody who watches Letterman knows, it's *cold* in those studios. And bring ID, as proof of age may be required.

The Daily Show with Jon Stewart   Comedy Central's irreverent, often hilarious mock newscast tapes every Monday through Thursday at 5:45pm, at 513 W.

54th St. (btwn 10th and West End aves.). Make your advance ticket requests by phone at ☏ **212/586-2477,** or check with them for any cancellation tickets for the upcoming week; the line is open Monday through Thursday from 10:30am to 4pm for tickets.

The Tony Danza Show   The Brooklyn native and star of *Who's the Boss?* comes home to host his own talk show. For tickets to attend the live show, send a request in a SASE to The Tony Danza Show, Ansonia Station, P.O. Box 234095, New York, NY 10023-9426 or call ☏ **212/479-8422.** The show is taped Monday through Thursday at 10 am at ABC Studios at 30 W. 67th St. (btwn Central Park W. and Amsterdam Ave.).

Good Morning America   Fans of ABC's weekday-morning show can join Diane Sawyer and Charlie Gibson in their street-facing studio at Broadway and 44th Street as part of the live audience. To witness the 7-to-9am broadcast, fill out the online request at www.abcnews.go.com/sections/GMA (click on "GMA Tickets"), or call ☏ **212/580-5176** during business hours.

The Jane Pauley Show   What goes around comes around . . . and around . . . and around. The former *Today* and *Dateline* host is back with her own morning gabfest. If you are interested in attending one of the shows, call ☏ **212/664-3056.** For standby tickets, arrive at the NBC Studios marquee (on the 50th St. side of 30 Rockefeller Plaza) no later than 9am on the morning of the taping. You may choose standby tickets for either the 11:30am or 3:30pm show. The show tapes twice a day Tuesday to Friday. Only one ticket will be issued per person. Audience members must bring photo ID and a reservation confirmation, and are advised not to bring any unnecessary electronic devices.

Last Call with Carson Daly   Tapings of the MTV heartthrob's NBC late-night gabfest are much like a grown-up TRL, without the countdown or screaming sweet 16s. Tapings are on select weeknights at 7 and/or 9pm. You can reserve up to four tickets by calling ☏ **212/664-3056.** Standby tickets are distributed on the day of taping at 9am outside 30 Rockefeller Plaza, on the 49th Street side of the building, on a first-come, first-served basis (read: Come early if you actually want to get one). Note that a standby ticket does not guarantee admission.

Late Night with Conan O'Brien   Conan tix might not have quite the cachet of a Dave ticket, but they're a very hot commodity—so start planning now. Tapings are Tuesday through Friday at 5:30pm (arrive by 4:45pm), and you must be 16 or older to attend. You can reserve up to four tickets by calling ☏ **212/664-3056.** Standby tickets are distributed on the day of taping at 9am outside 30 Rockefeller Plaza, on the 49th Street side of the building (under the NBC Studios awning), on a first-come, first-served basis.

The Late Show with David Letterman   Here's the most in-demand TV ticket in town. Tapings are Monday through Thursday at 5:30pm (arrive by 4:15pm), with a second taping Thursday at 8pm (arrive by 6:45pm). You must be 18 or older to attend. You can try for tickets in three ways: (1) Fill out a form at **www.cbs.com/latenight/lateshow** to submit an online request. (2) Submit a request in person Monday to Friday from 9:30am to 12:30pm, Saturday and Sunday from 10am to 6pm. Requests are awarded monthly and you will be notified by phone. You can submit requests up to 1 month in advance. The more dates you select, the better chance you have, but you can only apply once within a 6-month period. (3) Call the standby phone line at 11am of the day you wish to attend. Good luck!

Live! with Regis and Kelly   Tapings with Regis Philbin and Kelly Ripa are Monday through Friday at 9am at the ABC Studios at 7 Lincoln Sq. (Columbus Ave. and W. 67th St.) on the Upper West Side. You must be 10 or older to attend (under 18s must be accompanied by a parent). Send your postcard (four tickets max) at least a *full year* in advance to *Live!* Tickets, Ansonia Station, P.O. Box 230777, New York, NY 10023-0777 (**℃** **212/456-3054**). Standby tickets are sometimes available. Arrive at the studio no later than 7am and request a standby number; standby tickets are handed out on a first-come, first-served basis.

Saturday Night Live   SNL tapings are Saturday at 11:30pm (arrival time 10pm); there's also a full dress rehearsal at 8pm (arrival time 7pm). You must be 16 or older to attend. Here's the catch: Written requests are taken only in August and the odds are always long. However, you can try for standby tickets on the day of the taping, which are distributed at 7am outside 30 Rockefeller Plaza, on the 49th Street side of the building (under the NBC Studios awning), on a first-come, first-served basis; only one ticket per person will be issued. If you want to try your luck with advance tickets, call **℃** **212/664-3056** *as far in advance of your arrival in New York as possible* to determine the current ticket-request procedure.

The *Today* Show   Anybody can be on TV with Katie, Matt, and weatherman Al Roker. All you have to do is show up outside *Today*'s glass-walled studio at Rockefeller Center, on the southwest corner of 49th Street and Rockefeller Plaza, with your very own HI, MOM! sign. Tapings are Monday through Friday from 7 to 10am, but come at the crack of dawn if your heart's set on being in front. Who knows? If it's a nice day, you may even get to chat with Katie, Matt, or Al in a segment. Come extra early to attend a Friday Summer Concert Series show.

Total Request Live   The countdown show that made Carson Daly a household name is broadcast live from MTV's second-floor glass-walled studio at 1515 Broadway, at 44th Street in Times Square, weekdays at 3:30pm. Crowds start gathering below at all hours, depending on the drawing power of the day's guest.

(Tips **Who Wants to Be on a Game Show?**

The syndicated daily version of *Who Wants to Be a Millionaire*, hosted by Meredith Viera, goes through a lot of contestants, and is always on the lookout for smart cookies to sit in the Hot Seat. Check the website (www.millionaretv.com/audience.html) to see if auditions are being held while you're in town (auditions are usually held Aug–Dec). You can sign up over the Net to attend a taping or take the test on a specific date, and will receive an e-mail confirmation. When the show is taping, you'll be expected to attend the taping of a couple of episodes in addition to taking the test (all the better to practice your skills as part of "Ask the Audience.") On your audition date, report to the ABC studios at 30 W. 67th St. (off of Central Park West). Expect the whole process (including attending a taping) to take about half a day. If you're testing before the season starts, it will take about 90 minutes. You'll take a multiple-choice test and if you score in the top 10% or so, you'll have a brief interview with show staff. If you're chosen for the contestant pool, you'll receive a postcard in the mail. If you're selected from the pool to go into the Hot Seat, you'll have to plan another trip to New York City, so remember where you put this book!

Audience tickets can sometimes be reserved by calling the **TRL Ticket Reservation Hot Line** at ✆ **212/398-8549;** you must be between the ages of 16 and 24 to attend. If you're not able to score reservations, arrive by 2pm (preferably earlier) if you want a prayer of making it into the in-studio audience; a producer usually roams the crowd asking music-trivia questions and giving away standby tickets for correct answers. And don't forget to make your WE LOVE YOU, CARSON! signs large enough to be captured on camera. You may also be able to watch or participate in other tapings; stop into the MTV Store on the corner of 44th and Broadway, where flyers for tapings and events are sometimes stacked next to the register.

The View   ABC's popular girl-power gabfest tapes live Monday through Friday at 11am (ticket holders must arrive by 9:30am). Requests, which should be made 12 to 16 weeks in advance, can be submitted online (www.abc.go.com/theview) or via postcard to Tickets, *The View,* 320 W. 66th St., New York, NY 10023. Because exact date requests are not usually accommodated, try standby: Arrive at the studio before 10am and put your name on the standby list; earlier is better, because tickets are handed out on a first-come, first-served basis. You must be 18 or older to attend.

Who Wants to Be a Millionaire   The syndicated version and the evening version of the popular trivia show are filmed at ABC's Upper West Side studios. To request tickets to be an audience member (or sign up to take the contestant test), send a postcard to *Who Wants to Be a Millionaire,* Columbia University Station, P.O. Box 250225, New York, NY 10025. Ticket requests are limited to four, and you must be 18 or older to attend. You can also request tickets online at www.millionairetv.com or call ✆ **212/479-7755.**

10 Especially for Kids

Some of New York's sights and attractions are designed specifically with kids in mind. But many of those I've discussed in the rest of this chapter are terrific for kids as well as adults; I've also included cross-references to the best of them.

Probably the best place to entertain the kids is in **Central Park** 🟀🟀🟀, which has kid-friendly diversions galore (p. 227). For general tips and additional resources, see "Family Travel" under "Specialized Travel Resources," in chapter 2.

MUSEUMS

In addition to the museums specifically for kids, also consider the following: The **American Museum of Natural History** 🟀🟀🟀 (p. 195), whose dinosaur displays are guaranteed to wow both you and the kids; the *Intrepid* **Sea-Air-Space Museum** 🟀🟀 (p. 211), on a battleship with an amazing collection of vintage and high-tech airplanes; the **Forbes Magazine Galleries** (p. 210), whose collection includes a number of vintage toys and games; the **New York City Police Museum** (p. 217); the **New York City Fire Museum** 🟀 (p. 217), housed in a real firehouse; the **American Museum of the Moving Image** 🟀 (p. 253), where you and the kids can learn how movies are made; the **Lower East Side Tenement Museum** 🟀 (p. 212), whose weekend living-history program really intrigues school-age kids; the **New York Transit Museum** (p. 251), where kids can explore vintage subway cars and other hands-on exhibits; and the **South Street Seaport & Museum** (p. 219), which little ones will love for its theme park–like atmosphere and old boats bobbing in the harbor.

Children's Museum of Manhattan 🟀   Designed for ages 2 to 12, this museum is strictly hands-on. Interactive exhibits and activity centers encourage

Value Museum & Entertainment Deals for Teens

High 5 Tickets to the Arts (℡ 212/HI5-TKTS; www.high5tix.org) makes theater and culture more accessible for kids between the ages of 13 and 18. Teens can buy tickets for select theatrical performances and events for $5 each for weekend performances, or $5 for two (for the teen and a guest of any age) for Monday-through-Thursday performances. High 5 also offers discounted museum passes at the wallet-friendly price of two for $5 (for the teen and a guest of any age). Check the website for details on obtaining theater or museum tickets, which can usually be purchased with proof of age at any New York City Ticketmaster outlet or online. Also check the High 5 website for listings of free and nearly free events going on while you and your teen are in town.

self-discovery—and a recent expansion means there's now even more to keep the kids learning. The Time Warner Media Center takes children through the world of animation and helps them produce their own videos. The Body Odyssey is a zany, scientific journey through the body. This isn't just a museum for the 5-and-up set—there are exhibits designed for babies and toddlers, too. The busy schedule also includes daily art classes and storytellers, and a full slate of entertainment on weekends. Look for *Art Inside Out,* an interactive exhibit dedicated to introducing families to art and museums and featuring a video-making installation from photographer William Wegman, among others, and the exhibit *Oh, Seuss! Off to Great Places* (based on the themes of *Oh, the Places You'll Go!* and other Dr. Seuss classics), running through September 2005.

212 W. 83rd St. (btwn Broadway and Amsterdam Ave.). ℡ 212/721-1234. www.cmom.org. Admission $7 adults and children, $4 seniors. Wed–Sun and school holidays 10am–5pm. Subway: 1 or 9 to 86th St.

Children's Museum of the Arts Interactive workshop programs for children ages 1 to 12 and their families are the attraction here. Kids dabble in puppet making and computer drawing or join in singalongs and live performances. Also look for rotating exhibitions of the museum's permanent collection, featuring WPA work.

182 Lafayette St. (btwn Broome and Grand sts.). ℡ 212/941-9198 or 212/274-0986. www.cmany.org. Admission $6 for visitors 1–65; pay what you wish Thurs 4–6pm. Wed and Fri–Sun noon–5pm; Thurs noon–6pm. Subway: 6 to Spring St.

New York Hall of Science ⭐ Children will love this huge, hands-on museum, which bills itself as "New York's Only Science Playground." This place is amazing for school-age kids. Exhibits let them be engulfed by a giant soap bubble, float on air in an antigravity mirror, compose music by dancing in front of light beams, and explore the world of microbes. There are even video machines that kids can use to retrieve astronomical images, including pictures taken by the *Galileo* in orbit around Jupiter. There's a Preschool Discovery Place for the really little ones. But best of all is the summertime **Outdoor Science Playground** ⭐ for kids 6 and older—ostensibly lessons in physics, but really just a great excuse to laugh, jump, and play on jungle gyms, slides, seesaws, spinners, and more.

The museum is located in **Flushing Meadows–Corona Park,** where kids can enjoy even more fun beyond the Hall of Science. Not only are there more than

1,200 acres of park and playgrounds, there's a zoo, a carousel, an indoor ice-skating rink, an outdoor pool, and bike and boat rentals. Kids and grown-ups will love getting an up-close look at the Unisphere steel globe, which was not really destroyed in *Men in Black*. The park is also home to the **Queens Museum of Art** (p. 255) as well as Shea Stadium and the U.S. Open Tennis Center.

4701 111th St., in Flushing Meadows–Corona Park, Queens. ⓒ 718/699-0005. www.nyhallsci.org. Admission $9 adults, $6 seniors and children 4–17; $2.50 preschoolers. Additional $3 for Science Playground. Mon–Wed 9:30am–2pm (Tues–Wed to 5pm in summer); Thurs–Sun 9:30am–5pm. Subway: 7 to 111th St.

Sony Wonder Technology Lab Kids and adults love this four-level high-tech science-and-technology center, which explores communications and technology. You can experiment with robotics, explore the body through medical imaging, edit a video, mix a song, design a video game, and save the day at an environmental command center. The lab also features the first high-definition interactive theater in the United States. Admission is free; this place is popular, however, so make reservations in advance. Reservations can be made up to 2 weeks in advance by calling ⓒ **212/833-5414** on Monday, Wednesday, or Friday between 11am and 4pm. Otherwise, you may not get in, or you may get tickets that require you to return at a different time.

Sony Plaza, 550 Madison Ave. (at 56th St.). ⓒ **212/833-8100**, or 212/833-5414 for reservations. www.sony wondertechlab.com. Free admission. Tues–Wed and Fri–Sun 10am–6pm; Thurs 10am–8pm; last entrance 30 min. before closing. Subway: E, V, N, or R to 5th Ave.; 4, 5, or 6 to 59th St.

OTHER KID-FRIENDLY DIVERSIONS

In addition to the choices below, don't forget New York's theme restaurants, which are playgrounds unto themselves for kids; see "Family-Friendly Restaurants" in chapter 6. For kid-friendly theater, see "Kids Take the Stage: Family-Friendly Theater " in chapter 9.

ZOOS & AQUARIUMS Bigger kids will love the **Bronx Zoo** ✿✿✿ (see below), while the **Central Park Zoo** ✿ with its Tisch Children's Zoo (p. 231) is suitable for younger kids. At the **New York Aquarium** ✿✿ at Coney Island (p. 250), kids can touch starfish and sea urchins and watch bottlenose dolphins and California sea lions stunt-swim in the outdoor aqua theater. Brooklyn's **Prospect Park** ✿✿ (p. 252) also boasts a wonderful little zoo.

SKY-HIGH VIEW Kids of all ages can't help but turn dizzy with delight at incredible views from atop the **Empire State Building** ✿✿✿ (p. 197).

ARCADES **Lazer Park,** in Times Square at 1560 Broadway (entrance at 163 W. 46th St.; ⓒ **212/398-3060;** www.lazerpark.com), has amusements ranging from old-fashioned pinball to virtual-reality games and a laser-tag arena. Even better is the brand-new **Broadway City** ✿, 241 W. 42nd St. (btwn 7th and 8th aves.; ⓒ **212/997-9797;** www.broadwaycity.com), a neon-bright, multilevel interactive game center designed on a Big Apple theme where you could lose your kids (and a year's supply of quarters) for an entire day.

SPECIAL EVENTS Children's eyes grow wide at the march of **parades** (especially Macy's Thanksgiving Day Parade), **circuses** (both the Big Apple Circus and Ringling Bros. and Barnum & Bailey), and **holiday shows** (the Rockettes' Christmas and Easter performances). See "New York City Calendar of Events," in chapter 2, for details.

11 Highlights of the Outer Boroughs
THE BRONX

In addition to the choices below, literary buffs might also want to visit the **Edgar Allan Poe Cottage,** the final home for the author of *The Raven, The Tell-Tale Heart,* and other masterworks. See "In Search of Historic Homes" (p. 223).

Bronx Zoo Wildlife Conservation Park ★★★ *Kids*   Founded in 1899, the Bronx Zoo is the largest metropolitan animal park in the United States, with more than 4,000 animals on 265 acres. This is an extremely progressive zoo as zoos go—most of the cages have been replaced by more natural settings, ongoing improvements keep it feeling fresh and up-to-date, and it's far more bucolic than you might expect. I think it's one of the city's best attractions.

One of the most impressive exhibits is the **Wild Asia Complex.** This zoo-within-a-zoo comprises the **Wild Asia Plaza** education center; **Jungle World,** an indoor re-creation of Asian forests with birds, lizards, gibbons, and leopards; and the **Bengali Express Monorail** (May–Oct), which takes you on a narrated ride high above free-roaming Siberian tigers, Asian elephants, Indian rhinoceroses, and other nonnative New Yorkers (keep your eyes peeled—the animals aren't as interested in seeing you). The **Himalayan Highlands** is home to some 17 extremely rare snow leopards, as well as red pandas and white-naped cranes. The 6½-acre **Congo Gorilla Forest** is home to Western lowland gorillas, okapi, red river hogs, and other African rainforest animals.

The **Children's Zoo** (Apr–Oct) allows young humans to learn about their wildlife counterparts. Kids can compare their leaps to those of a bullfrog, slide into a turtle shell, climb into a heron's nest, see with the eyes of an owl, and hear with the acute ears of a fox. There's also a petting zoo. Camel rides are another part of the summertime picture, as is the **Butterfly Zone** and the **Skyfari** aerial tram (each an extra $2 charge). *Money-saving tip:* Rather than pay extra for each of the premium attractions, consider purchasing a "P.O.P." pass, which includes one general admission, plus up to six exhibit and/or ride entries good for Bengali Express, Skyfari, Children's Zoo, Zoo Shuttle, Butterfly Zone, and Congo Gorilla Forest. The passes are $20 for adults, $16 for children and seniors.

If the natural settings and breeding programs aren't enough to keep zoo residents entertained, they can choose to ogle the two million annual visitors. But there are ways to beat the crowds. Try to visit on a weekday or on a nice winter's day. In summer, come early, before the heat of the day sends the animals back into their enclosures. Expect to spend an entire day here—you'll need it.

Getting There: Liberty Lines' no. BxM11 express bus, which makes stops on Madison Avenue, will take you to the zoo; call ✆ **718/652-8400.** By subway, take the 2 train to Pelham Parkway and walk west to the Bronxdale entrance.

Fordham Rd. and Bronx River Pkwy., the Bronx. ✆ 718/367-1010. www.wcs.org/zoos. Admission $11 adults, $8 seniors, $8 children 2–12; discounted admission Nov–Mar; free Wed year-round. There may be nominal additional charges for some exhibits. Nov–Mar daily 10am–4:30pm (extended hours for Holiday Lights late Nov to early Jan); Apr–Oct Mon–Fri 10am–5pm, Sat–Sun 10am–5:30pm. Transportation: See "Getting There," above.

New York Botanical Garden ★   A National Historic Landmark, the 250-acre New York Botanical Garden was founded in 1891 and today is one of America's foremost public gardens. The setting is spectacular—a natural terrain of rock outcroppings, a river with waterfalls, hills, ponds, and wetlands.

Highlights of the Botanical Garden include the 27 **specialty gardens,** an exceptional **orchid collection,** and 40 acres of **uncut forest,** as close as New York gets to its virgin state before the arrival of Europeans. The **Enid A. Haupt Conservatory,** a stunning series of Victorian glass pavilions that recall London's former Crystal Palace, shelters a rich collection of tropical, subtropical, and desert plants as well as seasonal flower shows. There's also a **Children's Adventure Garden.** Natural exhibits are augmented by year-round educational programs, musical events, bird-watching excursions, lectures, special family programs, and many more activities. Best of all is the annual **Holiday Train Show** (mid-Nov to early Jan), where railway trains and trolleys wind their way through more than 100 replicas of historic New York buildings and attractions—such as the Statue of Liberty, the Metropolitan Museum of Art, and the Garden's own Enid A. Haupt Conservatory—all made from plant parts and other natural materials. There are so many ways to see the garden—tram, golf cart, walking tours—that it's best to call or check the website for more information.

Getting There: Take Metro-North (© **800/METRO-INFO** or 212/532-4900; www.mta.nyc.ny.us/mnr) from Grand Central Terminal to the New York Botanical Garden station; the easy ride takes about 20 minutes. By subway, take the D or 4 train to Bedford Park, then take bus no. Bx26 or walk southeast on Bedford Park Boulevard for 8 long blocks. The garden operates a shuttle to and from Manhattan April through October on Fridays and weekends, Saturdays only in November and December. Round-trip shuttle and garden tickets are $15 for adults, $12 for seniors and students, $9 for children 2 to 12; call © **718/817-8779** for reservations.

200th St. and Southern Blvd., the Bronx. © **718/817-8700.** www.nybg.org. Admission $3 adults, $2 seniors and students, $1 children 2–12. Extra charges for Everett Children's Adventure Garden, Enid A. Haupt Conservatory, T. H. Everett Rock Garden, Native Plant Garden, and narrated tram tour; entire Garden Passport package $10 adults, $7.50 seniors and students, $4 children 2–12. Apr–Oct Tues–Sun and Mon holidays 10am–6pm; Nov–Mar Tues–Sun and Mon holidays 10am–5pm. Transportation: See "Getting There," above.

Wave Hill ★ *Finds*   Formerly a private estate with panoramic views of the Hudson River and the Palisades, Wave Hill has, at various times, been home to a British U.N. ambassador as well as Mark Twain and Theodore Roosevelt. Set in a bucolic neighborhood that doesn't look anything like you'd expect from the Bronx, its 28 gorgeous acres were bequeathed to the city of New York for use as a public garden that is now one of the most beautiful spots in the city. It's a wonderful place to commune with nature along wooded paths and in herb and flower gardens, where horticulturists have labeled all of the plants. Benches are positioned for quiet contemplation and spectacular views. It's a great spot for taking in the Hudson River vibe without having to travel to Westchester to visit the Rockefeller estate. Programs range from horticulture and environmental education to landscape history and forestry to dance performances and concerts. A new Visitor and Horticultural Center designed by Robert A. M. Stern is currently under construction, and should make this hidden jewel shine even brighter.

Getting There: Take the 1 or 9 subway to 231st Street, then take the no. Bx7 or Bx10 bus to the 252nd Street stop; or take the A subway to 207th Street and pick up the no. Bx7 to 252nd Street. From the 252nd Street stop, walk west across the parkway bridge and turn left; at 249th Street, turn right. Metro North trains (© **212/532-4900**) travel from Grand Central to the Riverdale station; from there, it's a pleasant 5-block uphill walk to Wave Hill.

675 W. 252nd St. (at Independence Ave.), the Bronx. © **718/549-3200.** www.wavehill.org. Admission $4 adults, $2 seniors and students; free in winter and Sat mornings and Tues in summer. Tues–Sun 9am–4:30pm; extended hours in summer (call ahead). Transportation: See "Getting There," above.

BROOKLYN

For details on walking the **Brooklyn Bridge** ★★, see p. 196.

It's easy to link visits to the Brooklyn Botanic Garden, the Brooklyn Museum of Art, and Prospect Park, because they're an easy walk from one another, just off **Grand Army Plaza.** Designed by Frederick Law Olmsted and Calvert Vaux as a suitably grand entrance to their Prospect Park, it boasts a grand Civil War memorial arch designed by John H. Duncan (1892–1901) and the main **Brooklyn Public Library,** an Art Deco masterpiece completed in 1941 (the garden and museum are just on the other side of the library, down Eastern Pkwy.). The entire area is a half-hour subway ride from midtown Manhattan.

Brooklyn Botanic Garden ★ Down the street from the Brooklyn Museum of Art (see below) is the most popular botanic garden in the city. This 52-acre sanctuary is at its most spectacular in May, when the deep-pink blossoms of cherry trees are abloom. Well worth seeing is the **Cranford Rose Garden,** one of the largest and finest in the country; the **Shakespeare Garden,** an English garden featuring plants mentioned in his writings; a **Children's Garden;** the **Osborne Garden,** a 3-acre formal garden; the **Fragrance Garden,** designed for the blind but appreciated by all noses; and the extraordinary **Japanese Hill-and-Pond Garden.** The renowned **C. V. Starr Bonsai Museum** is home to the world's oldest and largest collection of bonsai, while the impressive $2.5-million Steinhardt Conservatory holds the garden's extensive indoor-plant collection.

1000 Washington Ave. (at Eastern Pkwy.), Brooklyn. © 718/623-7200. www.bbg.org. Admission $5 adults, $3 seniors and students, free for children under 16, free to all Tues and Sat 10am–noon year-round, plus Wed–Fri from mid-Nov to mid-Mar. Apr–Sept Tues–Fri 8am–6pm, Sat–Sun 10am–6pm; Oct–Mar Tues–Fri 8am–4:30pm, Sat–Sun 10am–4:30pm. Subway: Q to Prospect Park; 2 or 3 to Eastern Pkwy./Brooklyn Museum.

Brooklyn Museum of Art ★★ One of the nation's premier art institutions, the Brooklyn Museum of Art rocketed back into the public consciousness in 1999 with the controversial *Sensation: Young British Artists from the Saatchi Collection,* which drew international media attention and record crowds who came to see just what an artist—and a few conservative politicians—could make out of a little elephant dung.

Indeed, the museum is best known for its remarkable exhibitions—which ranged from *The Last Expression: Art and Auschwitz* to *Pulp Art: From the Collection of Robert Lesser* in mid-2003 alone—as well as its excellent permanent collection. The museum's grand Beaux Arts building, designed by McKim, Mead & White (1897), befits its outstanding holdings, most notably the Egyptian, Classical, and Ancient Middle Eastern collection of sculpture, wall reliefs, and mummies. The decorative-arts collection includes 28 American period rooms from 1675 to 1928 (the Moorish-style smoking room from John D. Rockefeller's 54th St. mansion is my favorite). Other highlights are the African and Asian arts galleries, dozens of works by Rodin, a good costumes and textiles collection, and a collection of both American and European painting and sculpture that includes works by Homer, O'Keeffe, Monet, Cézanne, and Degas.

200 Eastern Pkwy. (at Washington Ave.), Brooklyn. © 718/638-5000. www.brooklynmuseum.org. Suggested admission $6 adults, $3 seniors and students, free for children under 12; free 1st Sat of the month 11am–11pm. Wed–Fri 10am–5pm; 1st Sat of the month 11am–11pm, each Sat thereafter 11am–6pm; Sun 11am–6pm. Subway: 2 or 3 to Eastern Pkwy./Brooklyn Museum.

Brooklyn Tabernacle ★ Under the direction of passionate orator Pastor Jim Cymbala and his choral-director wife, Carol, this nondenominational Christian revival church has grown into one of the largest—a congregation of nearly 10,000—and most renowned churches in the nation. Folks come from all over the world to see the 275-voice, four-time Grammy Award–winning **Brooklyn Tabernacle Choir,** one of the nation's most celebrated gospel choirs.

Brooklyn Tabernacle relocated to Smith Street, in the heart of downtown Brooklyn, in mid-2002. The gloriously renovated house of worship seats nearly 4,000 for each service. Still, come early for a prime seat, especially when the choir sings (at the noon and 4pm Sun services).

17 Smith St. (btwn Fulton and Livingston sts.), Brooklyn. ⓒ 718/290-2000. www.brooklyntabernacle.org. Services Sun 9am, noon, and 4pm; Tues 7pm. Subway: 1 or 2 to Hoyt St.; 4 or 5 to Borough Hall; A, C, or F to Jay St./Borough Hall; M, N, or R to Lawrence St./Metro Tech.

Coney Island ★★   Sure, Coney Island is just a shell of what it once was in its heyday in the early 20th century. But it's that shell and what remains that make it such an intriguing attraction. The almost mythical Parachute Jump, recently refurbished though long inoperable, stands as a monument to Coney Island. But this is not a dead amusement park; **Astroland,** home of the famed **Cyclone** roller coaster, has some great rides for children and adults. The best amusement of all, however, is the people-watching. Maybe because it is at the extreme edge of New York City, but Coney Island attracts more than its share of the odd, freaky, and funky. It's here where **Nathan's Famous Hot Dogs** holds its annual hot dog eating contest on July 4 at noon; where the wholly entertaining **Mermaid Parade** spoofs the old bathing beauty parades (late June); and where members of the **Polar Bear Swim Club** show their masochistic gusto by taking a plunge into the icy ocean on January 1. There is also the small **Coney Island Museum,** 1208 Surf Ave., near West 12th Street (ⓒ **718/372-5158**), where fun exhibits detail the history of Coney Island. The best time to visit is from Memorial Day until mid-September, when the rides and amusement park are open. Bring your bathing suit and test the waters.

Subway: D, F, Q, or B to Coney Island–Stillwell Ave., Brooklyn.

New York Aquarium *Kids*   Because of the long subway ride (about 1 hr. from Midtown Manhattan) and its proximity to Coney Island, it's best to combine the two attractions, preferably in the summer. This surprisingly good aquarium is home to hundreds of sea creatures. Taking center stage are Atlantic bottle-nosed dolphins and California sea lions that perform daily during summer at the **Aquatheater.** Also basking in the spotlight are gangly Pacific octopuses, sharks, and a brand-new sea horse exhibit. Black-footed penguins, California sea otters, and a variety of seals live at the **Sea Cliffs exhibit,** a re-creation of a Pacific

---

(*Value* **An Arts Party Grows in Brooklyn**

First Saturday is the Brooklyn Museum of Art's popular program that takes place (you guessed it) the first Saturday of each month. It runs from 5 to 11pm and includes free admission and a slate of live music, films, dancing, talks, and other entertainment that can get esoteric—think karaoke, poetry, silent film, experimental jazz, and disco. On a recent Saturday, events included an Irish dance performance, a panel discussion on black photographers, a screening of *Hair,* and a dance party featuring a funk-and-soul DJ. As only-in-New-York events go, First Saturday is a good one—you can always count on a full slate of cool.

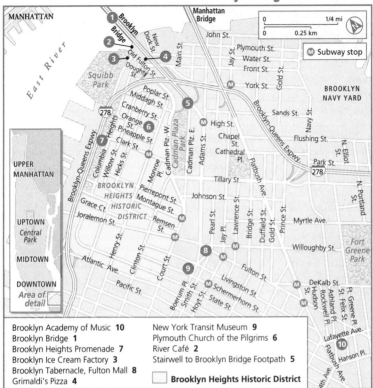

Brooklyn Academy of Music **10**
Brooklyn Bridge **1**
Brooklyn Heights Promenade **7**
Brooklyn Ice Cream Factory **3**
Brooklyn Tabernacle, Fulton Mall **8**
Grimaldi's Pizza **4**

New York Transit Museum **9**
Plymouth Church of the Pilgrims **6**
River Café **2**
Stairwell to Brooklyn Bridge Footpath **5**

☐ **Brooklyn Heights Historic District**

coastal habitat. But my absolute favorites are the beautiful white Beluga whales, which exude buckets of aquatic charm. Children love the hands-on exhibits at **Discovery Cove.** There's an indoor oceanview cafeteria and an outdoor snack bar, plus picnic tables.

502 Surf Ave. (at W. 8th St.), Coney Island, Brooklyn. ⓒ **718/265-3400.** www.nyaquarium.com. Admission $11 adults, $7 seniors and children 2–12. Daily 10am–4:30pm. Subway: D to Coney Island–Stillwell Ave., Brooklyn.

New York Transit Museum _Kids_   Housed in a real (decommissioned) subway station, this recently renovated underground museum is a wonderful place to spend an hour or so. The museum is small but very well done, with good multimedia exhibits exploring the history of the subway from the first shovelful of dirt scooped up at groundbreaking (Mar 24, 1900) to the present. Kids and parents alike will enjoy the interactive elements and the vintage subway cars, old wooden turnstiles, and beautiful station mosaics of yesteryear. A new exhibit dedicated to surface transportation is _On the Streets: New York's Trolleys and Buses._ All in all, a minor but remarkable tribute to an important development in the city's history.

The even smaller **Gallery Annex & Store at Grand Central Station** (aka The New York Transit Museum store) also houses rotating exhibitions and a terrific transit-themed gift shop (see "Museum Stores," in chapter 8). A second museum store, along with a travel information kiosk, is at the **Times Square Visitors Center;** see chapter 4.

Boerum Place and Schermerhorn St., Brooklyn. ✆ 718/694-5100. http://mta.info/mta/museum/index.html. Admission $3 adults, $1.50 seniors and children 3–17, free for seniors Tues noon–4pm. Mon–Fri 10am–4pm; Sat–Sun noon–5pm. Subway: A or C to Hoyt St.; F to Jay St.; M or R to Court St.; 2, 3, 4, or 5 to Borough Hall. Gallery Annex: In Grand Central Terminal (on the main level, in the shuttle passage next to the Station Masters' office), 42nd St. and Lexington Ave. ✆ 212/878-0106. Subway: 4, 5, 6, 7, or S to 42nd St./Grand Central.

Prospect Park 🐾🐾★   Designed by Frederick Law Olmsted and Calvert Vaux after their great success with Central Park, this 562 acres of woodland, meadows, bluffs, and ponds is considered by many to be their masterpiece and the pièce de résistance of Brooklyn.

The best approach is from Grand Army Plaza, presided over by the monumental **Soldiers' and Sailors' Memorial Arch** (1892) honoring Union veterans. For the best view of the lush landscape, follow the path to Meadowport Arch, and proceed through to the Long Meadow, following the path that loops around it (it's about a 1-hr. walk). Other park highlights include the 1857 Italianate mansion **Litchfield Villa** on Prospect Park West; the **Friends' Cemetery** Quaker burial ground (where Montgomery Clift is eternally prone—sorry, it's fenced off to browsers); the wonderful 1906 Beaux Arts **boathouse;** the 1912 **carousel,** with white wooden horses salvaged from a famous Coney Island merry-go-round (Apr–Oct; rides 50¢); and **Lefferts Homestead Children's Historic House Museum** (✆ 718/789-2822), a 1783 Dutch farmhouse with a museum of period furniture and exhibits geared to kids (Apr–Nov Fri–Sun 1–4pm). There's a map at the park entrance that you can use to get your bearings.

On the east side of the park is the **Prospect Park Zoo** (✆ 718/399-7339). This is a thoroughly modern children's zoo where kids can walk among wallabies, explore a prairie-dog town, and much more. Admission is $5 for adults, $1.25 for seniors, $1 for children 3 to 12. April through October, open Monday through Friday 10am to 5pm, to 5:30pm weekends and holidays; November through March, open daily from 10am to 4:30pm.

At Grand Army Plaza, bounded by Prospect Park W., Parkside Ave., and Flatbush Ave., Brooklyn. ✆ 718/965-8951, or 718/965-8999 for events information. www.prospectpark.org. Subway: 2 or 3 to Grand Army Plaza (walk down Plaza St. W. 3 blocks to Prospect Park W. and the entrance) or Eastern Pkwy./Brooklyn Museum.

BROOKLYN HEIGHTS HISTORIC DISTRICT

Just across the Brooklyn Bridge is **Brooklyn Heights** 🐾, a peaceful neighborhood of tree-lined streets, more than 600 historic houses built before 1860, landmark churches, and restaurants. Even with its magnificent promenade providing sweeping views of Lower Manhattan's ragged skyline, it feels more like its own village than part of the larger urban expanse.

This is where Walt Whitman wrote *Leaves of Grass.* In the 19th century, abolitionist Henry Ward Beecher railed against slavery at **Plymouth Church of the Pilgrims** on Orange Street between Henry and Hicks streets. If you walk down **Willow Street** between Clark and Pierrepont, you'll see three houses (nos. 108–112) in the Queen Anne style that was fashionable in the late 19th century, as well as a trio of Federal-style houses (nos. 155–159) built before 1829. Also visit **Montague Street,** the main drag of Brooklyn Heights, full of cafes and shops. On Water Street, under the Brooklyn Bridge, is the **River Café** (✆ 718/522-5200;** www.rivercafe.com), where a drink or dinner at twilight as the lights of Manhattan begin to flicker on will offer an unforgettable view. And don't forget about **Grimaldi's Pizzeria** (p. 152), near the water on historic Old Fulton Street, and the **Brooklyn Ice Cream Factory** (p. 156), on Front Street.

GETTING THERE   Bounded by the East River, Fulton Street, Court Street, and Atlantic Avenue, the Brooklyn Heights Historic District is one of the most easily accessible sights beyond Manhattan. The neighborhood is reachable via several subway trains: the A, C, or F to Jay Street; the 2, 3, 4, or 5 to Clark Street or Borough Hall; and the N or R to Court Street. *Note:* Status of the N, R, and C lines was affected by construction at press time, but all other service should be normal.

It's easy to link a walk around Brooklyn Heights and along its promenade with a walk over the **Brooklyn Bridge** 🌟🌟 (p. 196), a tour that makes for a lovely afternoon. Take a 2 or 3 train to **Clark Street** (the first stop in Brooklyn). Turn right out of the station and walk toward the water, where you'll see the start of the **Brooklyn Promenade.** Stroll along the promenade for the now-heart-breaking views of Lower Manhattan and the multimillion-dollar brownstones, or park yourself on a bench to contemplate.

The promenade ends at Columbia Heights and Orange Street. To head to the bridge from here, turn left and walk toward the Watchtower Building. Before heading downslope, turn right immediately after the playground onto Middagh Street. After 4 or 5 blocks, you'll reach a busy thoroughfare, Cadman Plaza West. Cross the street and follow the walkway through **Cadman Plaza Park;** veer left at the fork. At Cadman Plaza East, turn left (downslope) toward the underpass, where you'll find the stairwell up to the Brooklyn Bridge footpath on your left.

QUEENS

While the Long Island City Art Loop has ceased to run since MoMa returned to Manhattan, you can still catch a lift to the Noguchi Museum and Socrates Sculpture Park on the weekends. The Noguchi Weekend Shuttle Bus Service picks up in front of the Asia Society at Park Avenue and 70th Street in Manhattan and takes you to the Noguchi. Fare is $5 one-way, $10 round-trip. Museum admission is not included. For a schedule, check the Noguchi Museum website.

For details on the **New York Hall of Science** 🌟 and **Flushing Meadows–Corona Park** (home to the Queens Museum of Art), see p. 245.

American Museum of the Moving Image 🌟 *(Kids)* Head here if you truly love movies. Unlike Manhattan's Museum of Television & Radio (p. 216), which is more of a library, this is a thought-provoking museum examining how moving images—film, video, and digital—are made, marketed, and shown. It's housed in part of the Kaufman Astoria Studios, which once were host to W. C. Fields and the Marx Brothers, and more recently have been used by Martin Scorsese *(The Age of Innocence),* Bill Cosby (his *Cosby* TV series), and *Sesame Street.*

The museum's core exhibit, ***Behind the Screen,*** is an engaging two-floor installation that takes you step-by-step through the process of making, marketing, and exhibiting moving images. There are more than 1,000 artifacts, from technological gadgetry to costumes, and interactive exhibits where you can try your hand at sound-effects editing or create animated shorts, among other simulations. Special-effects benchmarks, from the mechanical mouth of *Jaws* to the blending of past and present in *Forrest Gump,* are explored and explained. And in a nod to nostalgia, memorabilia that wasn't swept up by the Planet Hollywood chain is displayed, including a Hopalong Cassidy lunchbox, an E.T. doll, celebrity coloring books, and Dean Martin and Jerry Lewis puppets. Also on display are sets from *Seinfeld.* Even better are the daily hands-on demonstrations, where you can watch film editors, animators, and the like at work.

"Insiders' Hour" tours are offered every day at 2pm. The museum also hosts **free film and video screenings,** often accompanied by artist appearances, lectures, or discussions. Seminars often feature-film and TV pros discussing their craft; past guests have included Spike Lee, Terry Gilliam, Chuck Jones, and Atom Egoyan, so it's worth seeing if someone's on while you're in town. There's a terrific gift shop chock-full of affordable movie- and TV-themed gifts, too.

35th Ave. at 36th St., Astoria, Queens. (C) 718/784-0077. www.ammi.org. Admission $10 adults, $7.50 seniors and college students, $5 children 5–18. Tues–Fri noon–5pm; Sat–Sun 11am–6pm (evening screenings Sat–Sun 6:30pm). Subway: R to Steinway St.; N to Broadway.

Isamu Noguchi Garden Museum ⭐ *Finds* No place in the city is more Zen than this marvelous indoor/outdoor garden museum showcasing the work of Japanese-American sculptor Isamu Noguchi (1904–88). In 2004, after a 2½-year renovation, the museum returned to its original site and once again showcases the beautifully curated collection of the artist's masterworks in stone, metal, wood, and clay; you'll even see theater sets, furniture, and models for public gardens and playgrounds that Noguchi designed. A new gallery highlights the artist's work in interior design.

9-01 33rd Rd. (at Vernon Blvd.), Long Island City, Queens. (C) 718/545-8842. www.noguchi.org. Suggested admission $4 adults, $2 seniors and students. Wed–Fri 10am–5pm; Sat–Sun 11am–6pm. Subway: N to Broadway. Walk west on Broadway toward Manhattan until Broadway ends at Vernon Blvd.; turn left on Vernon and go 2 blocks.

Louis Armstrong House Museum ⭐ *Finds* What is it about celebrities' homes that we find so fascinating? Is it that we get to see how they lived away from the glare of the cameras; how they functioned on a daily basis just like the rest of us? Armstrong was an international celebrity and could have lived anywhere, yet this unassuming, bi-level house in the working-class neighborhood of Corona, Queens, was the great Satchmo's home from 1943 until his death in 1971. It was bought and designed by his fourth wife, Lucille, who lived in it until her death in 1983. No one has lived in the house since and in 2003, the house, a National Historic Landmark and a New York City landmark, opened its doors to the public as a museum. The 40-minute tour takes you through the small, impeccably preserved home and explains the significance of each room to both Louis and Lucille. My favorite is Armstrong's den, where he kept his reel-to-reel tape recordings, cataloging everything he taped—music, conversations, and compositions, some of which are displayed on his desk. The house also includes a small exhibit with some of his memorabilia, including two of his trumpets, and a guest shop, where many of his CDs are for sale along with other Satchmo-centric items. If you have any interest in jazz and in Armstrong, this is a must see.

34–56 107th St., Corona, Queens. (C) 718/478-8274. www.satchmo.net. $8 adults, $6 children and seniors. Tues–Fri 10am–5pm; Sat–Sun noon–5pm. Subway: 7 to 103rd St.–Corona Plaza. Walk north on 103rd St., turn right on 37th Ave., turn left onto 107th St., and the house is ½ block north of 37th Ave.

Museum for African Art *Finds* This captivating museum is a leading organizer of temporary—and usually excellent—exhibits dedicated to historic and contemporary African art and culture. In September 2002, the museum moved out of SoHo into a long-term temporary home in Long Island City, which it will occupy until its Museum Mile home is ready on 5th Avenue between 109th and 110th streets. Weekend and evening programs include music and dance performances, art-making workshops, family events, and more.

36–01 43rd Ave. (at 36th St.), Long Island City, Queens. (C) 212/784-7700. www.africanart.org. Admission $6 adults, $3 seniors, students, and children. Mon and Thurs–Fri 10am–5pm; Sat–Sun 11am–5pm. Subway: 7 to 33rd St. Walk north to 36th St., turn left and go 1 block to 43rd Ave.

P.S. 1 Contemporary Art Center ⭐ If you're interested in contemporary art that's too cutting-edge for most museums, don't miss this MoMa affiliate museum.

The Renaissance Revival building that houses the center was originally a public school (hence the name). This is the world's largest institution exhibiting contemporary art from America and abroad. You can expect to see a kaleidoscopic array of works from artists ranging from Jack Smith to Julian Schnabel; the museum is particularly well known for large-scale exhibitions by artists such as James Turrell.

22–25 Jackson Ave. (at 46th Ave.), Long Island City, Queens. (C) 718/784-2084. www.ps1.org. Suggested admission $5 adults, $2 seniors and students. Wed–Sun noon–6pm. Subway: E or V to 23rd St./Ely Ave. (walk 2 blocks south on Jackson Ave. to 46th Ave.); 7 to 45th Rd./Court House Square (walk 1 block south on Jackson Ave.).

Queens Museum of Art   One way to see New York in the shortest time (albeit without the street life) is to visit the Panorama, created for the 1939 World's Fair and regularly updated, which is a building-for-building architectural model of New York City complete with an airplane that takes off from LaGuardia Airport. The 9,335-square-foot Gotham City is the largest model of its kind, with 895,000 structures built on a scale of 1 inch = 100 feet. A red-white-and-blue ribbon is draped over the Twin Towers, which still stand in this Big Apple.

Also on display is a collection of Tiffany glass made at Tiffany Studios in Queens between 1893 and 1938. The Contemporary Currents series features exhibits focusing on the works of a single artist, often with an international theme (suitable to New York's most diverse borough). History buffs should take note of the museum's NYC Building, which housed the United Nations' General Assembly from 1946 to 1952. Art exhibitions, tours, lectures, films, and performances are part of the program, making this a strong museum on all fronts.

Next to the Unisphere in Flushing Meadows–Corona Park, Queens. (C) **718/592-9700.** www.queensmuse. org. Suggested admission $5 adults, $2.50 seniors and students, free for children under 5. Tues–Fri 10am–5pm; Sat–Sun noon–5pm. Subway: 7 to Willets Point/Shea Stadium (follow the yellow signs for the 10-min. walk through the park to the museum, which sits next to the Unisphere).

Socrates Sculpture Park *Kids*   This former riverside landfill is now the best exhibition space for large-scale outdoor sculpture in the city. No velvet ropes and motion sensors here—interaction with the artwork is encouraged. It's well worth a look, especially on a lovely day. Check the website for the current exhibition schedule—or just let yourself be happily surprised. It's also an excellent spot to bring a picnic and enjoy the great view of Roosevelt Island and the Upper East Side from this riverbank park. Pick up sandwiches, drinks, and fixings from any of the many delis, food carts, and ethnic takeout restaurants along Broadway when you get off the subway.

Broadway at Vernon Blvd., Long Island City, Queens. (C) **718/956-1819.** www.socratessculpturepark.org. Free admission. Daily 10am–sunset. Subway: N or W to Broadway; walk 8 blocks along Broadway toward the East River.

12 Spectator Sports

For details on the **New York City Marathon** and the **U.S. Open Tennis Championships,** see the "New York City Calendar of Events" in chapter 2.

BASEBALL   With two baseball teams in town, you can catch a game almost any day from opening day in April to the beginning of the playoffs in October. (Don't bother trying to get subway series tix, though—they're the hottest seats in town. Ditto for Opening Day or any playoff game.)

Star catcher Mike Piazza and the Amazin' **Mets** play at **Shea Stadium** in Queens (subway: 7 to Willets Point/Shea Stadium). For tickets (which ran $12–$43 for regular-season games in the 2004 season) and information, call the

Mets Ticket Office at ✆ **718/507-TIXX,** or visit **www.mets.com**. Also keep in mind that you can buy game tickets (as well as logo wear and souvenirs, if you want to dress appropriately for the big game) at the **Mets Clubhouse Shop,** which has two Midtown Manhattan locations; see p. 281.

So the **Yankees** haven't won a World Series in 4 years—and were stunned by the Boston Red Sox in 2004. That just means that the team will be raring to go in 2005 (and probably have a few more high-priced stars!). The Yanks play at the House That Ruth Built, otherwise known as Yankee Stadium (subway: C, D, or 4 to 161st St./Yankee Stadium). For tickets ($10–$80 in 2004), contact **Ticketmaster** (✆ **212/307-1212** or 212/307-7171; www.ticketmaster.com) or **Yankee Stadium** (✆ **718/293-6000;** www.yankees.com). Serious baseball fans might check the schedule well in advance and try to catch **Old Timers' Day,** usually held in July, when pinstriped stars of years past return to take a bow.

At Yankee Stadium, upper-tier box seats (which run about $35), especially those behind home plate, give you a great view of all the action. Upper-tier reserve seats are directly behind the box seats and are significantly cheaper ($20). Bleacher seats are even cheaper ($10), and the rowdy commentary from that section's roughneck bleacher creatures is absolutely free. There are always some bleacher seats held back to be sold on game days. Most of the expensive seats (field boxes) are sold out in advance to season ticket holders. You can often purchase these very same seats from scalpers, but you'll pay a premium for them. Tickets can be purchased at the team's **clubhouse shop** in Manhattan; see p. 281.

Minor-league baseball ⚾ made a Big Apple splash when the **Brooklyn Cyclones,** the New York Mets' A-level farm team, and the **Staten Island Yankees,** the Yanks' junior leaguers, came to town. Boasting their very own waterfront stadium, the Brooklyn Cyclones have been a major factor in the revitalization of Coney Island; spanking-new Keyspan Park sits right off the legendary boardwalk (subway: F, N, Q, or W to Stillwell Ave./Coney Island). The SI Yanks also have their own shiny new playing field, the Richmond County Bank Ballpark, just a 5-minute walk from the Staten Island Ferry terminal (subway: N or R to Whitehall St.; 4 or 5 to Bowling Green; 1 or 9 to S. Ferry). What's more, with bargain-basement ticket prices (which topped out at $8 for the Cyclones, $10 for the Yanks in the 2004 season), this is a great way to experience baseball in the city for a fraction of the major-league hassle and cost. Both teams have already developed a rabidly loyal fan base, so it's a good idea to buy your tickets for 2005—which will run from June through September—in advance. For the Cyclones, call ✆ **718/449-8497** or visit **www.brooklyncyclones.com**; to reach the SI Yanks, call ✆ **718/720-9200** or go online to **www.siyanks.com**.

BASKETBALL   Though the New Jersey Nets are rumored to be moving to Brooklyn, there are two pro teams that play in New York at **Madison Square Garden,** 7th Avenue between 31st and 33rd streets (✆ **212/465-6741** or www.thegarden.com; **212/307-7171** or www.ticketmaster.com for tickets; subway: A, C, E, 1, 2, 3, or 9 to 34th St.). Stephon Marbury, Allen Houston, and the rest of the **New York Knicks** (✆ **877/NYK-DUNK** or 212/465-JUMP; www.nyknicks.com)—whose ticket prices range from $10 a pop at the tippy-top of MSG to (gulp) nearly $2,000 for courtside seats—are in residence from late fall through early spring (depending on whether they make the playoffs). The **New York Liberty** (✆ **212/465-6080;** www.wnba.com/liberty), who electrify fans with their tough defense and WNBA All-Stars like Becky Hammon and Elena Baranova, occupy MSG from late May through the fall. Tickets start at $8, and go up to about $65 for courtside, with plenty of good seats available ranging from $14 to $24.

ICE HOCKEY   The **New York Rangers** play at Madison Square Garden, 7th Avenue between 31st and 33rd streets (© **212/465-6741;** www.newyorkrangers. com or www.thegarden.com; subway: A, C, E, 1, 2, 3, or 9 to 34th St.). The Rangers have been going through tough times the last several seasons, but are still a hot ticket in NYC ($27–$139 each), so plan well ahead; call © **212/307-7171,** or visit www.ticketmaster.com for online orders.

8

Shopping for Big Apple Bargains

For many, shopping is their raison d'être—an uncontrollable urge, almost an addiction. What a perfect place New York, to satisfy that urge. No city in the world has the breadth and variety of stores as New York; it's a shopper's paradise.

And included in that paradise is a wealth of values, range, and unparalleled sales. As with anything, you just have to know where to look.

City **sales tax** is 8.625%, so if you're visiting from out of state, consider having your purchases shipped directly home to avoid paying sales tax.

A couple times a year, the state declares "tax free" week in which clothing and footwear under $110 is (you guessed it) sold without sales tax. You'll know if it's a tax-free week because all the clothing and shoe merchants post signs in their windows!

1 The Top Shopping Streets & Neighborhoods

Here's a rundown of New York's most interesting shopping areas, with some highlights of each to give you a feel for the neighborhood. **If addresses and phone numbers are *not* given here,** refer to the store's expanded listing by category in "Shopping A to Z," later in this chapter.

DOWNTOWN
LOWER MANHATTAN & THE FINANCIAL DISTRICT
The Financial District's shopping scene was devastated by the demise of the World Trade Center, whose underground shopping mall had evolved into the city's best by 2001. **South Street Seaport** (© 212/732-8257; subway: 2, 3, 4, or 5 to Fulton St.) carries the neighborhood's torch. Familiar names like Bath & Body Works and the Sunglass Hut line Fulton Street, the Seaport's main cobbled drag, and fill the levels at Pier 17, a barge-turned-shopping-mall. There's nothing here you can't get anywhere else; come for the historic ambience, the harbor views, and to spend a few dollars in Lower Manhattan, which needs all the support it can get. For a complete store list, visit **www.southstreetseaport.com**.

Lower Manhattan continues to shine in the discount department; it's the home of the king of discount department stores, **Century 21.** Electronics megamart **J&R** occupies a full city block with its great prices on everything that you can turn on, plug in, or use to tune out, from cameras and computers to CDs and software.

CHINATOWN
Don't expect to find the purchase of a lifetime, but there's some quality browsing. The fish markets along Canal, Mott, Mulberry, and Elizabeth streets are fun for their bustle and exotica. Dispersed among them (especially along **Canal St.**), you'll find a mind-boggling collection of knockoff sunglasses and watches, backpacks, leather goods, and souvenirs. It's a fun browse, but don't expect quality. Try not to be tempted by the bootleg first-run DVDs you'll see being sold along

> ## (Tips) Money-Saving Shopping Tips
>
> 1. **Ship major purchases home.** If you're buying high-ticket items, you can often save on the 8.65% New York sales tax by having items shipped home. Depending on the laws of your state, you can pay a lesser tax or skip the duty completely.
> 2. **Seek out sample sales.** Garment designers and manufacturers often sell off their newest items (sometimes not even available in stores) for a song to raise quick cash; see "Scouring the Sample Sales" on p. 272.
> 3. **Do your homework and bargain on electronic equipment.** You'll notice a wealth of electronics stores throughout the Theater District, many trumpeting GOING OUT OF BUSINESS sales. These guys have been going out of business since the Stone Age. Trust me: The only way you'll do well is if you know your stuff. And play hard to get; I've seen prices tumble the closer I got to the door.
> 4. **Always ask for a better price on anything used or vintage.** It won't always work, but a lot of vintage, antiques, and collectibles dealers—even those with shops in high-rent districts such as SoHo and the Village—will drop their price if you're just savvy enough to ask. Always be polite, however, and don't push if you're told "no."

Canal Street; the quality will be what you expect from a video taped inside a movie theater—expect to hear the munching of popcorn along with the soundtrack. You'll do a bit better with the bootleg CDs, though still don't expect topnotch sound. **Mott Street,** between Pell Street and Chatham Square, boasts the most interesting off-Canal shopping, with an antiques shop or two among the storefronts selling blue-and-white Chinese dinnerware. The highlight is the **Pearl River** Chinese emporium (see "Gifts & Paper Goods" in "Shopping A to Z," later in this chapter).

THE LOWER EAST SIDE
The bargains aren't what they used to be in the **Historic Orchard Street Shopping District**—which runs from Houston to Canal along Allen, Orchard, and Ludlow streets, spreading outward along both sides of Delancey Street—but prices on leather bags, shoes, luggage, and fabrics are still good. Be aware, though, that the hard sell on Orchard Street can be hard to take. Still, the district is a nice place to discover a part of New York that's disappearing. Come during the week, because most stores are Jewish-owned and therefore close Friday afternoon and all day Saturday. Sunday tends to be a madhouse.

The artists and other trendsetters who have been turning this neighborhood into a bastion of hip have added a cutting edge to its shopping scene. You'll find a growing crop of alterna-shops south of Houston and north of Grand Street, between Allen and Clinton streets to the east and west, specializing in up-to-theminute fashions and club clothes for cutting-edge 20-somethings, plus funky retro furnishings, Japanese toys, and offbeat items. Before you browse, stop into the **Lower East Side Visitor Center,** 261 Broome St. (btwn Orchard and Allen sts.; ✆ **866/224-0206** or 212/226-9010; subway: F to Delancey St.), for a guide that includes vendors both Old World and new. Or you can see the list at www.lowereastsideny.com. *Money-saving tip:* Check the website or call the center for details about the **Go East card,** which will score cardholders discounts at neighborhood merchants.

SOHO

People love to complain about superfashionable SoHo—it's become too trendy, too tony, too Mall of America. True, **J. Crew,** 99 Prince St. (btwn Mercer and Greene; © **212/966-2739**), is one of big names to have supplanted the artists and galleries that used to inhabit the cast-iron buildings. But SoHo is still one of the best shopping neighborhoods in the city, and fun to browse. You'll find few bargains, as merchants have to cover those high rents. This is the epicenter of cutting-edge couture, with designers like Anna Sui and British legend Vivienne Westwood in residence. Most of these designer shops are probably *way* out of your price range, but the streets are full of boutiques, some hawking more affordable wares, and the eye candy is tops. End-of-season sales, when racks are cleared for incoming merchandise, are the best bet if you want to buy.

SoHo's prime shopping grid is from Broadway east to Sullivan Street and from Houston down to Grand Street.

NOLITA

Just a few years ago, **Elizabeth Street** was a nondescript adjunct to Little Italy. Today it's the grooviest shopping strip in town, star of the neighborhood known as NoLita. Elizabeth and **Mott and Mulberry streets** are dotted with an increasing number of shops between Houston and Spring streets, with a few pushing south to Kenmare. But don't expect cheap; NoLita is the stepchild of SoHo. Its boutiques are the province of shopkeepers specializing in high-quality, fashion-forward products and design, but a few yield quirkier, more affordable gifts—and the browsing is excellent. It's an easy walk from the Broadway/Lafayette stop on the F or V line here, since it starts just east of Lafayette Street; you can also take the 6 to Spring Street, or the N or R to Prince Street and walk east. **Prince Street** is probably the best stretch for affordable treasures.

THE EAST VILLAGE

The East Village remains the standard of bohemian hip, and is one of the city's best neighborhoods for wallet-friendly shopping. The easiest subway access is the 6 train to Astor Place, which lets you out by **Kmart** and **Astor Wines & Spirits;** from here, it's just a couple blocks east to the prime hunting grounds.

East 9th Street ⌖ between 2nd Avenue and Avenue A is one of the most fun shopping strips in the city. Lined with an increasingly smart collection of boutiques, it proves that the East Village isn't just for kids anymore. So far, prices have stayed within reach. Up-and-coming designers sell excellent, affordably priced fashions for women here, including **Jill Anderson, a. cheng,** and others, and a small branch of **Eileen Fisher** caters to bargain hunters by serving as the chain's outlet store. This is also an excellent stretch for gifts and little luxuries; see "Gifts & Paper Goods" in "Shopping A to Z," later in this chapter. Most of these shops don't open until around 1pm, and most are closed Mondays. If you're enjoying this 'hood, check out the offerings on surrounding blocks; they aren't as mature, but it won't take long.

If it's strange, illegal, or funky, it's probably available on **St. Marks Place,** 8th Street, running east from 3rd Avenue to Avenue A. It's like a permanent street market, with countless T-shirt and jewelry stands.

LAFAYETTE STREET FROM SOHO TO NOHO

Lafayette Street has a retail character of its own, distinct from the rest of SoHo. It has grown into a full-fledged Antiques Row, strong in mid-20th-century furniture. The quality is high, but prices are higher. Lafayette is great to browse if you have an interest in design trends—stroll between Astor Place and Spring Street—but bargain hunters are better off elsewhere. Browsers should take the 6 train to Astor Place and work their way south, or get off at Spring Street and walk north. Dispersed among the stores are a number of cutting-edge clothiers; this is where skateboard fashion moved from the street to the catwalks.

GREENWICH VILLAGE

The West Village is great for browsing and gift shopping. Specialty book- and record stores, antiques and crafts shops, and gourmet food markets dominate. Except for NYU territory—**8th Street** between Broadway and 6th Avenue for trendy footwear and affordable fashions and Broadway from 8th Street south to Houston, anchored by **Urban Outfitters** and dotted with skate and sneaker shops—the Village isn't much of a destination for fashion hunters.

The prime drag for strolling is **Bleecker Street,** where you'll find lots of leather shops and record stores interspersed with interesting, artsy boutiques. **Christopher Street,** just east of 7th Avenue, is fun and loaded with Village character. Serious browsers should also wander west of **7th Avenue,** where boutiques are tucked among the brownstones, and along **Hudson Street.**

MIDTOWN

THE FLATIRON DISTRICT & UNION SQUARE

The epitome of uptown fashion a hundred years ago, **6th Avenue** from 14th to 23rd streets has grown into the city's discount shopping center. Superstores and off-pricers fill the cast-iron buildings: **Filene's Basement, TJ Maxx,** and **Bed Bath & Beyond** are all at 620 6th Ave., and **Old Navy** is next door; **Barnes & Noble** is at 6th Avenue near 22nd Street.

HERALD SQUARE & THE GARMENT DISTRICT

Herald Square—where 34th Street, 6th Avenue, and Broadway converge—is dominated by **Macy's,** the self-proclaimed world's biggest department store, and other famous-name shopping. At 6th Avenue and 33rd Street is the **Manhattan Mall** (© 212/465-0500; www.manhattanmallny.com), home to mall standards both national and local.

A long block over on 7th Avenue, not much goes on in the Garment District. This is, however, where you'll find that quintessential New York experience, the sample sale; see "Scouring the Sample Sales" on p. 272.

TIMES SQUARE & THE THEATER DISTRICT

This neighborhood has become increasingly family-oriented: with the rollicking **Virgin Megastore; Gap** at 42nd and Broadway; the **Toys "R" Us** flagship on Broadway and 44th Street, with its own Ferris wheel; and the **E-Walk** retail and entertainment complex on 42nd Street between 7th and 8th avenues, overflowing with mall-familiar shops.

West 47th Street between 5th and 6th avenues is the city's **Diamond District.** More than 90% of the diamonds sold the United States come through this neighborhood first, so there are some great deals if you're in the market for a nice rock or a piece of fine jewelry. The street is lined with showrooms; be ready to wheel and deal with the largely Hasidic dealers, who offer quite a juxtaposition to the crowds. For an introduction to the district, visit **www.47th-street.com**. If you're in the market for wedding rings, there's only one place to go: Herman Rotenberg's **1,873 Unusual Wedding Rings,** 4 W. 47th St., booth 86 (© **800/ 877-3874** or 212/944-1713; www.unusualweddingrings.com). For semiprecious stones, head to the **New York Jewelry Mart,** 26 W. 46th St. (© **212/575-9701**). Virtually all dealers are open Monday through Friday only.

Shopper's alert: You'll notice a wealth of electronics stores throughout the neighborhood, many trumpeting GOING OUT OF BUSINESS sales. These guys have been going out of business since the Stone Age. That's the bait and switch; pretty soon you've spent too much money for not enough MP3 player. If you want to check out what they have to offer, go in knowing what the going price is on what you want. You can make a good deal if you know exactly what the market is, but these guys will be happy to suck you dry given half a chance.

5TH AVENUE & 57TH STREET
The heart of Manhattan retail is the corner of 5th and 57th. Home to high-ticket names like Gucci, Chanel, Cartier, and Van Cleef & Arpels, this neighborhood has long been the province of the über-rich. In recent years, however, both 5th Avenue and 57th Street have become more accessible as wallet-friendlier retailers such as the **Niketown** and the **NBA Store** have joined the fold.

High traffic flow and real estate costs keep prices up, and the flagships tend to send their sale merchandise to lower-profile shops. Still, the window-shopping is classic. And if you, like Holly Golightly, always dreamed of shopping at **Tiffany & Co.,** 727 5th Ave., at 57th Street (© **212/755-8000;** www.tiffany.com), the world's most famous jewelry store is worth a stop. The multilevel showroom is so full of tourists that it's easy to browse. If you want to indulge, head upstairs to the gift level, where you'll find a number of items to suit a $75 budget. Everything comes packaged in the classic little blue box with an impeccable white ribbon.

UPTOWN
MADISON AVENUE
Welcome to Rich Man's Land. Madison Avenue from 57th to 79th streets has usurped 5th Avenue as the toniest shopping stretch in the city. It's home to the most luxurious designer boutiques: Calvin, Prada, Versace, Valentino . . . the list goes on. Even the sales are ridiculous. ("This $1,200 sweater is on sale for $575? I'll take it!" Yeah, right!) Still, the window-shopping is unparalleled—even if you're not into fashion, the displays are entertainment in their own right. What's more, a stroll along the superchic avenue on a nice day often results in a star sighting. By all means, make a point of browsing even if you don't intend to buy.

For those of us with limited budgets, stores such as **Crate & Barrel** and the **Ann Taylor** flagship, 645 Madison Ave., at 60th Street (© **212/832-2010;** www.anntaylor.com), make Madison Avenue a little more approachable.

THE UPPER WEST SIDE
The new in 2004 **Shops at Columbus Circle** in the Time Warner Center offers some of the big, and expensive, names in retail; *very* high-end stuff, but fun to window-shop (and maybe pick up something in the massive Whole Foods Market), while the Upper West Side's best shopping street is **Columbus Avenue.** Small shops catering to the neighborhood's mix of young hipsters and families line both sides of the pleasant avenue from 66th Street to about 86th Street. For comfort over style (these city streets can be murder on the feet!), try **Aerosoles,** 310 Columbus Ave. (© **212/579-8659**), or **Sacco** for women's shoes that offer

a bit of both, and **Harry's** and **Tip Top Shoes** for men, women, and children. **Maxilla & Mandible** offers groovy natural science–based gifts (see "Museum Stores" in "Shopping A to Z," later in this chapter).

Boutiques dot Amsterdam Avenue, but main drag Broadway is more notable for its terrific gourmet edibles at **Zabar's** and **Fairway** markets, both legends in their own right (see "Edibles" in "Shopping A to Z," later in this chapter).

2 The Best Department Stores for Bargain Hunters

Bloomingdale's Bloomie's is more accessible than Barneys or Bergdorf's and more affordable than Saks, but still has the pizzazz Macy's and Lord & Taylor now largely lack. Taking up a city block, it has just about anything you could want, from clothing (both designer and everyday basics) and fragrances to a full range of housewares. The frequent sales can yield unbeatable bargains; look for full-page advertisements in the *New York Times*. The main entrance is on 3rd Avenue, but pop up to street level from the 59th Street station and you'll be right at the Lexington Avenue entrance. There's a new, smaller branch of Bloomingdale's in SoHo, but most of the offerings there are decidedly very upscale. 1000 3rd Ave. (Lexington Ave. at 59th St.). ✆ 212/705-2000. www.bloomingdales.com. Subway: 4, 5, 6, N, or R to 59th St. Also at 504 Broadway (btwn Canal and Broome sts.; ✆ 212/729-5900; subway: R or W to Prince, 6 to Spring St.).

Century 21 *Value* Despite suffering severe damage in the terrorist attacks on the World Trade Center, Century 21 reopened its doors on March 1, 2002. The designer discount store is back, and it's better than ever. Prices on designer goods are 40% to 70% off what you would pay at a department store or designer boutique. Don't think that $250 Armani blazer is a bargain? Look again at the tag— the retail price is upward of $800. This is the place to find those $5 Liz Claiborne tees, $20 Todd Oldham pants, or $50 Bally loafers—not to mention underwear, hosiery, and ties that are a bargain-hunter's dream. Kids' clothes, linens, and housewares are also part of the stock. Avoid the weekday lunch hour and Saturdays, if you can. 22 Cortlandt St. (btwn Broadway and Church St.). ✆ 212/227-9092. www.c21stores.com. Subway: 1, 2, 3, 4, 5, or M to Fulton St.; A or C to Broadway/Nassau St.; E to Chambers St.

Kmart Kmart is so out of place in the East Village that it has turned the mundane into camp: Japanese kids stare at gargantuan boxes of detergent as if they were Warhol designed; pierced and tattooed locals navigate the name-brand maze alongside stroller-pushing housewives. Kitsch value aside, this multilevel store is a great bet for discount prices on practical items, from socks to shampoo. You'll also find a pharmacy, a food department (sale prices on snack foods are rock-bottom), and even a photo studio. 770 Broadway (btwn 8th and 9th sts.). ✆ 212/673-1540. Subway: 6 to Astor Place. Also at 250 W. 34th St. (btwn 6th and 7th aves.).

Lord & Taylor Okay, so maybe Lord & Taylor isn't the first place you'd go for a vinyl miniskirt, but you can't deny its elegant mien. Long known as an excellent source of women's dresses and coats, L&T stocks all the major labels for men and women, with a special emphasis on American designers. Their house-brand clothes (khakis, blazers, turtlenecks, and summer sportswear) are well made and a great bargain. Sales, especially around holidays, can be stellar. The store is big enough to have a good selection but doesn't overwhelm. The Christmas window displays are an annual delight. 424 5th Ave. (at 39th St.). ✆ 212/391-3344. www.lordand taylor.com. Subway: F, V, B, or D to 42nd St.

Macy's A four-story sign on the side of the building trumpets MACY'S, THE WORLD'S LARGEST STORE—hard to dispute, since the 10-story behemoth covers an entire block. Macy's is a hard place to shop: The size is unmanageable, the service is dreadful, and the din from the crowds on the ground floor will kick your migraine into action. The store's one-of-a-kind flair that made it legendary is just a memory. But they do sell *everything*. What's more, sales run constantly, so bargains are guaranteed. And the store provides personal guides/shoppers at no charge. At Christmastime, come as late as you can manage (the store is usually open until midnight in the final shopping days).

Tips for sale seekers: One-day sales usually occur on Wednesdays and sometimes on Saturdays. Call the store when you arrive to find out whether your visit overlaps with one. Or check the *New York Times* any day of the week for full-page advertisements, which sometimes include clip-out coupons for additional 10% to 15% discounts. At Herald Square, W. 34th St. and Broadway. ℂ 212/695-4400. www.macys.com. Subway: B, D, F, N, Q, R, 1, 2, 3, or 9 to 34th St.

3 Shopping A to Z
ANTIQUES & COLLECTIBLES

Antiques hounds will dazzle at the bounty that New York has to offer, from Louis XIV settees to vintage DeFranco Family lunchboxes. Be prepared, however—you will pay top dollar for everything.

Traditionalists will love the blocks off **Broadway near 10th and 11th streets,** where the bounty includes Kentshire Galleries (see below); and **East 59th, 60th, and 61st streets** around 2nd Avenue, not far from the Manhattan Art & Antiques Center, where about two dozen high-end dealers line the street and spill over onto surrounding blocks. Fans of midcentury furniture and Americana with a twist should browse **Lafayette Street** in SoHo/NoHo. Just about any dealer you visit will have the current issue of the free *Greyrock Antiques Guide* and/or *Antiques New York,* which will lead you to specialty dealers around the city.

Most call it the 26th Street flea market: The famous **Annex Antiques Fair and Flea Market** (ℂ 212/243-5343; www.annexantiques.citysearch.com) is an outdoor emporium of nostalgia, filling a few parking lots along 6th Avenue between 24th and 27th streets on weekends year-round. The assemblage is hit or miss—some days you'll find treasures galore, and others it seems like there's nothing but junk. A few quality vendors are almost always on hand, though, making it well worth the $1 admission fee. The truly dedicated arrive at 6:30am, but the browsing is still plenty good as late as 4pm. Sunday is always best, since there's double the booty on hand. The website will also link you to other flea markets around the city.

Alphaville This gallery specializes in '40s, '50s, and '60s toys and movie posters, all in mint condition and beautifully displayed. Space toys are an emphasis. Well worth a look for nostalgic baby boomers, even if you have no intention of buying. 226 W. Houston St. (btwn 6th Ave. and Varick St.). ℂ 212/675-6850. www.alphaville.com. Subway: 1 or 9 to Houston St.

Chelsea Antiques Building Right around the corner from New York's best flea market (see the listing for Annex Antiques Fair and Flea Market, above), this 12-floor building houses more than 100 dealers and is open daily. The permanent stalls run the gamut from 18th-century antiques to rare books to early-20th-century radios, jewelry, and toys. Prices are so good that it's known as a dealer's source, and shoppers are the type who love to prowl, touch everything, and sniff out a bargain. 110 W. 25th St. (btwn 6th and 7th aves.). (C) **212/929-0909.** Subway: F to 23rd St.

Kentshire Galleries   Still going strong after a half-century, this large and lovely gallery is the city's prime stop for 18th- and 19th-century English antiques, ranging from jewelry and tabletop items to formal furnishings. Furniture is displayed in richly appointed rooms that make for great browsing. 37 E. 12th St. (btwn University Place and Broadway). (C) **212/673-6644.** www.kentshire.com. Subway: N, R, L, 4, 5, or 6 to 14th St./Union Square.

Lost City Arts   Lost City features vintage modern furnishings and a quirky selection of accessories (station signs, 3-D photos, and the like), plus their own new midcentury-inspired furniture and accessories, including one inspired by the otherwise forbiddingly expensive custom designs of Machine Age genius Warren MacArthur. A real treat. 18 Cooper Sq. (4th Ave. at 5th St.). (C) **212/375-0500.** www.lostcityarts.com. Subway: N or R to 8th St.

Mood Indigo   This dandy of a shop is the city's top dealer in glassware, dishware, and kitchen accessories from the 1930s through the 1950s. The charming shopkeepers also specialize in Bakelite jewelry and 1939 World's Fair memorabilia and boast a whopping collection of '50s novelty salt-and-pepper shakers. Everything is pristine, so expect to pay accordingly. 181 Prince St. (btwn Sullivan and Thompson sts.). (C) **212/254-1176.** Subway: C or E to Spring St.; N or R to Prince St.

BEAUTY

Kiehl's   Kiehl's is more than a store: It's a virtual cult. Models, stockbrokers, foreign visitors, and just about everyone else stops by this always packed, old-time apothecary for its simply packaged, wonderfully formulated products for women and men. Lip Balm no. 1 is the perfect antidote for the biting winds of city or slope. Kiehl's now has a counter at Saks, too (evidence of how they've really moved up in the world), but stop into the original if you can. 109 3rd Ave. (btwn 13th and 14th sts.). (C) **212/677-3171.** Subway: L, N, R, 4, 5, or 6 to 14th St./Union Square.

Ricky's 🅐   This chain of funky drugstores also features a wide range of beauty products. It's a haven for makeup mavens, with multicolored wigs, rainbow-colored lipstick, glitter galore, green nail polish, over 80 kinds of hairbrushes, and even edible undies. Try going into Ricky's and coming out with just a pack of gum. 44 E. 8th St. (at Greene St.). (C) **212/254-5247.** Subway: N or R to 8th St. Also at 466 6th Ave. (at 11th St.; (C) **212/924-3401;** subway: A,C, E, B, D, or F to W. 4th St.), 112 W. 72nd St. (btwn Columbus–and Broadway; (C) **212/769-3670;** subway: 1, 2, 3, or 9 to 72nd St.), and 988 8th Ave. (at 58th St.; (C) **212/957-8343;** subway: A, B, C, D, 1, or 9 to Columbus Circle).

Sephora   The Rock Center branch of the French beauty superstore is a three-floor bonanza of beauty. You'll find everything you could want, from scents to nail color to skin cleansers to bath salts to makeup brushes to hair accessories—in a phenomenal number of lines that run the gamut from upscale lines Babor, Philip Thomas Roth, and Murad to funky bunches like Philosophy, Urban Decay, and Hard Candy. It's an incredible store, with an encyclopedic staff and testers galore. At Rockefeller Center, 636 5th Ave. (at 51st St.). (C) **212/245-1633.** www.sephora.com. Subway: E or F to 51st St. Also at 1500 Broadway (btwn 43rd and 44th sts.; (C) **212/944-6789;** subway: N, R, S, 1, 2, 3, 7, 9 to 42nd St./Times Square), 130 W. 34th St. (btwn Broadway and 7th Ave.; (C) **212/629-9315;** subway: B, D, F, or Q to 34th St./Herald Square), 119 5th Ave. (at 17th St.; (C) **212/674-3570;** subway: N or R to 23rd St.), 555 Broadway (btwn Prince and Spring sts.; (C) **212/625-1309;** subway: N or R to Prince St.), 1129 3rd Ave. (at 67th St.; (C) **212/452-3336;**

subway: 6 to 68th St.), and 2103 Broadway (btwn 73rd and 74th sts.; ℭ **212/362-1500;** subway: 1, 2, 3, or 9 to 72nd St.).

Zitomer's ⭐⭐   This three-story drugstore is more a mini-department store than a pharmacy. You'll find everything from electronics to pet supplies here. But the first floor is where you'll spend most of your time if you are looking for beauty products. They have their own very good line of cosmetics called Z New York. Big Apple lip gloss will make a wonderful souvenir; something you won't find in your local Walgreens. Also, you can say you actually shopped on pricey Madison Avenue. 969 Madison Ave. (at 76th St.). ℭ 212/737-2016. www.zitomer.com. Subway: 6 to 77th St.

BOOKS

In addition to the choices below, there are the big chains: **Barnes & Noble,** with my favorite outlet opposite Union Square, 33 E. 17th St. (ℭ **212/253-0810;** www.bn.com); and **Borders,** which has four stores in Manhattan, including one in the Time Warner Center, 10 Columbus Circle (ℭ **212/823-9775;** www. bordersstores.com).

Argosy Books   Antiquarian book hounds should check out this stately 77-year-old store, with high ceilings, packed shelves, a quietly intellectual air, and an outstanding collection of rarities, including 18th- and 19th-century prints, maps, and autographs. 116 E. 59th St. (btwn Park and Lexington aves.). ℭ 212/753-4455. www.argosybooks.com. Subway: 4, 5, or 6 to 59th St.

Bluestockings   After this community bookstore announced it would close in early 2003, new owners stepped in at the last minute to keep it open. They've changed the focus from a women's bookstore to "radical bookstore, fair-trade cafe, and activist resource center." The small storefront is packed with books to answer literary needs and wants of an eclectic audience, straight and gay, with fiction, nonfiction, memoirs, poetry, self-help, and missives on racism, classism, sexism, empowerment, and more. There's a pleasant cafe, as well as a small but well-chosen section of children's books. A full calendar of readings, meetings, and workshops is always on. 172 Allen St. (south of Houston St.). ℭ 212/777-6028. www. bluestockings.com. Subway: F to 2nd Ave. (use 1st Ave. exit).

Books of Wonder *(Kids)*   You don't have to be a kid to fall in love with this charming bookstore, which served as the model for Meg Ryan's shop in *You've Got Mail.* (Meg even worked here for a spell to train for the role.) Kids will love BOW's story readings; call or check the website for the latest schedule. 16 W. 18th St. (btwn 5th and 6th aves.). ℭ 212/989-3270. www.booksofwonder.net. Subway: L, N, R, 4, 5, or 6 to 14th St./Union Square.

Coliseum Books ⭐⭐ *(Finds)*   Before there were book-selling superstores, there was Coliseum Books. This independent bookstore was my favorite haunt for years when it was located on 57th Street. It closed due to intense competition from the big hitters, but happily, after a 2-year absence, they have found a new home on 42nd Street just opposite Bryant Park. Though not quite as big as the original, the store still has that same independent spirit and many of the original, very helpful, knowledgeable staff have returned. 11 W. 42nd St (btwn 5th and 6th aves.). ℭ 212/803-5890. www.coliseumbooks.com. Subway: B, D, F, or V to 42nd St.

Complete Traveller   Whether your destination is Texas or Tibet, you'll find what you need in this, possibly the world's best, travel bookstore. There are maps and travel accessories as well, plus a rare collection of antiquarian travel books whose facts may be outdated but whose writers' perceptions continue to shine. The staff is attentive. 199 Madison Ave. (at 35th St.). ℭ 212/685-9007. Subway: 6 to 33rd St.

Drama Book Shop   This store has a resident theater company and in-house performance space. It also hosts discussions and book signings with members of the theater community, ranging from playwright Tina Howe to critic Mel Gussow. Offering thousands of plays, from translations of Greek classics to this season's biggest hits, the shop also offers books, magazines, and newspapers on the craft and business of the performing arts. 250 W. 40th St. (btwn 8th and 9th aves.). *©* **212/944-0595.** www.dramabookshop.com. Subway: A, C, or E to 42nd St.

Eichler's   *The* Jewish bookstore of New York City, covering everything from cookbooks to Kaballah. The Brooklyn outlet is even bigger, and features all manner of Judaica, including silver items, garments, music, gifts, and more. 62 W. 45th St. (btwn 5th and 6th aves.). *©* **877/EICHLERS** or 212/719-1918. www.eichlers.com. Subway: B, D, F, or V to 42nd St. Also at 1401 Coney Island Ave. (btwn aves. J and K; *©* **888/EICHLERS** or 718/258-7643; subway: Q or D to Ave. J).

Forbidden Planet   Here's the city's largest collection of sci-fi, comics, and graphic-illustration books. The proudly geeky staff really knows what's what. Great sci-fi-themed toys, too. 840 Broadway (at 13th St.). *©* **212/473-1576.** www.forbiddenplanet nyc.com. Subway: L, N, R, 4, 5, or 6 to 14th St./Union Square.

Gotham Book Mart   Paris may have had its Sylvia Beach, but New York was lucky enough to have Frances Steloff. She opened Gotham Book Mart in 1920, and quickly became a defender of the First Amendment rights of authors. She championed such once-banned works as Henry Miller's *Tropic of Cancer,* and numbered among her admirers Ezra Pound, Saul Bellow, and Jackie Kennedy Onassis. Frances has since passed on, but her aura lives. Although the store has recently relocated, the emphasis, as always, is on poetry, literature, and the arts. 16 E. 46th St. (btwn 5th and Madison aves.). *©* **212/719-4448.** Subway: B, D, F, or V to 47th–50th sts./Rockefeller Center.

Gryphon Bookshop *(value*   Here's the Upper West Side's best used-book store. It's a browser's delight, stacked with used and rare fiction, nonfiction, and art books, plus the occasional reviewer's copy at discounted prices. 2246 Broadway (btwn 80th and 81st sts.). *©* **212/362-0706.** Subway: 1 or 9 to 79th St.

Housing Works Used Books Cafe *(finds*   Here's a way to do something good for yourself and others at the same time: Buy your reading material at this spacious yet quietly cozy used bookshop, sporting 45,000 books and records to browse. It's part of Housing Works, a not-for-profit organization that provides housing, services, and advocacy for homeless people living with HIV and AIDS. The collection is terrific and well organized, with lots of well-priced paperbacks, hardbacks, advance copies, and coffee-table books. There's a comfortable cafe in back that serves coffee and tea as well as freshly prepared sandwiches, sweets, and other light bites, plus beer and wine. The bookstore often hosts readings by well-known writers as well as occasional music performances on Wednesday and Thursday evenings; call or check the website for the current calendar. 126 Crosby St. (south of Houston St.). *©* **212/334-3324.** www.housingworksubc.com. Subway: F or V to Broadway/Lafayette St.; 6 to Spring St.

Hue-Man Bookstore   One of the nation's largest black-owned bookstores, providing the area's largest selection of African-American literature and books. 2319 Frederick Douglass Blvd. (at 8th Ave.). *©* **212/665-7400.** www.huemanbookstore.com. Subway: A, B, C, or D to 125th St.

Kitchen Arts & Letters   Foodies, take note: Here's the ultimate cook's and food-lover's bookstore. You'll be wowed by the depth of the selection, which includes rare, out-of-print, and foreign-language titles focusing on food and wine. The staff will conduct free searches for hard-to-find titles. The shop is an overstuffed jumble, but if this is your bag, you'll be browsing for hours. 1435 Lexington Ave. (btwn 93rd and 94th sts.). © 212/876-5550. Subway: 6 to 96th St.

Oscar Wilde Bookshop   The world's oldest gay and lesbian bookstore was on the brink of extinction until it was thankfully saved by the Lambda Rising chain. The nice staff makes browsing in this landmark a pleasure. 15 Christopher St. (btwn 6th and 7th aves.). © 212/255-8097. www.oscarwildebooks.com. Subway: 1 or 9 to Christopher St.

Rizzoli   This clubby Italian bookstore is the classiest—and most relaxing—spot in town to browse for visual art and design books, plus quality fiction, gourmet cookbooks, and other upscale reading. There's a decent selection of foreign-language, music, and dance titles as well. 31 W. 57th St. (btwn 5th and 6th aves.). © 212/759-2424. Subway: N or R to 5th Ave.

Finds   **Murder, They Wrote**

New York–based mystery writer Lawrence Block once wrote a book titled *Eight Million Ways to Die*, starring his famed detective creation, Matthew Scudder. The title was a spin on the famous line "there are eight million stories in the naked city," culled from the old film *Naked City*. The naked city of the movie was New York, and many of those eight million stories were about crime. That's one reason why New York was and still is fertile fodder for crime writers.

A number of New York's bookstores celebrate the city's reputation as the crime writer's capital. Though you can find many of the same books at chains like Barnes & Noble, these small, independent stores live and breathe mysteries. My favorite of the lot, and one of the oldest in the country, is **The Mysterious Bookshop** ⋆, 129 W. 56th St. (btwn 6th and 7th aves.; © 212/765-0900; www.mysteriousbookshop. com). This two-level shop, where the second floor is reached via a spiral staircase, is owned by mystery publisher Otto Penzler, and is a great source for rare and collectable titles, along with signed first editions. Who knows, that might be Ed McBain next to you perusing the paperbacks . . . or is it Evan Hunter?

Another great mystery bookstore is **Murder Ink,** 2486 Broadway (btwn 92nd and 93rd sts.; © 212/362-8905; www.murderink.com), which claims to be one of the oldest crime bookstores in the *world*. The store, a gathering ground for crime-writing aficionados, also hosts numerous author readings.

As fun as a good thriller is the West Village shop **Partners & Crime,** 44 Greenwich Ave., at Christopher Street (© 212/243-0440; www. crimepays.com). Like the other stores, this one also features a good selection of new and used collections and signed first editions, but the real thrill is the in-store live performance of a 1940s mystery radio show, complete with an organist and sound effects, performed on the first Saturday of the month.

Representing literary murder on the Upper East Side is **Black Orchid Books,** 303 E. 81st St. (btwn 1st and 2nd aves.; © 212/734-5980), where in-store readings and signings are a regular feature.

St. Mark's Bookshop   Established in 1977, this left-of-center East Village bookshop is a great place to browse. You'll find lots of terrific alternative and small-press fiction and poetry, plus cultural criticism, Eastern philosophy, and mainstream literature with an edge. You'll also find art, photography, and design books as well as an alternative 'zine rack. Lots of spoken-word CDs and cassettes, too. 31 3rd Ave. (at 9th St.). © **212/260-7853**. www.stmarksbookshop.com. Subway: 6 to Astor Place.

The Scholastic Store *Kids*   This mammoth store is located at the ground level of the headquarters for children's book publisher Scholastic (which also introduced a boy named Harry Potter to America). The 6,200-foot retail space is a veritable interactive playground for kids. Books, toys, and software products feature Scholastic's top-selling brands, from Clifford the Big Red Dog to Captain Underpants. Needless to say, Hogwarts is well represented. A full slate of in-store events, from author signings to crafts workshops, also keeps kids busy; check the website or call for the current schedule. 557 Broadway (btwn Prince and Spring sts.). © **212/343-6166**. www.scholastic.com/sohostore. Subway: N or R to Prince St.

The Strand *Value*   Something of a New York legend, The Strand is worth a visit for its staggering "eight miles of books" as well as its extensive inventory of review copies and bargain titles at up to 85% off list price. It's unquestionably the city's best book deal—there's almost nothing marked at list price—and the selection is phenomenal in all categories (there's even a rare book department on the third floor). Still, you'll work for it: The narrow aisles mean you're always getting bumped; the books are only roughly alphabetized; and there's no air-conditioning in summer. Nevertheless, it's a used-book-lover's paradise. Note that the Lower Manhattan location is significantly smaller. 828 Broadway (at 12th St.). © **212/473-1452**. www.strandbooks.com. Subway: L, N, R, 4, 5, or 6 to 14th St./Union Square. Strand Annex: 95 Fulton St. (btwn William and Gold sts.). © **212/732-6070**. Subway: 4, 5, or 6 to Fulton St.

Urban Center Books   Housed in an architectural landmark, McKim, Mead & White's 1882 Villard Houses, the Municipal Art Society's bookstore boasts a terrific selection of new books on architecture, urban planning, and landscape design. In the Villard Houses, 457 Madison Ave. (at 51st St.). © **800/352-1880** or 212/935-3592. www.urbancenterbooks.com. Subway: 6 to 51st St.

CLOTHING
RETAIL FASHIONS
Fashion hounds should check out "The Top Shopping Streets & Neighborhoods," earlier in this chapter, for advice on prime hunting grounds for original designs. Also check out the listing for **Century 21** (p. 263), the biggest and best discount department store.

Fashion Flagships
Some New York flagship stores are an experience you won't find in your local mall. These stores are display cases for the complete line of fashions, so you'll often find much more to choose from than in your at-home branch.

Check out **Ann Taylor,** 645 Madison Ave., at 60th Street (© 212/832-2010; www.anntaylor.com); the **Banana Republic** flagship at Rockefeller Center, 626 5th Ave., at 50th Street (© 212/974-2350; www.bananarepublic.com); **Eddie Bauer,** 1960 Broadway, at 67th Street (© 212/877-7629; www.eddiebauer.com), which also carries the AKA Eddie Bauer line and sports and mountaineering line;

Liz Claiborne, 650 5th Ave., at 52nd Street (ℂ 212/338-3888; www.lizclaiborne. com), carrying all of Liz's lines; and the **Original Levi's Store** at 3 E. 57th St. (btwn 5th and Madison; ℂ 212/826-5957). **Old Navy** has a flagship featuring its basics and signature sense of humor at 610 6th Ave., at 18th Street (ℂ 212/ 645-0663; www.oldnavy.com).

For Men & Women

Afterlife   This shop sells cutting-edge sportswear and club-wear accessories to downtowners who aspire to Patricia Field's couture club wear but can't afford it. Expect lots of tiny tees, clingy fabrics, and hip-hugging pants, plus accessories to heighten the hipper-than-thou look. 450 Broadway (btwn Grand and Canal sts.). ℂ **212/ 625-3167** or 212/625-0787. Subway: N, R, Q, W, or 6 to Canal St.

Burlington Coat Factory (Value)   Burlington has a stash of off-price and slightly irregular designer togs for men, women, and kids, but come for the coats. You'll find an exhaustive selection at excellent prices, as well as a fine selection of discounted leather bags and shoes. 707 6th Ave. (btwn 22nd and 23rd sts.). ℂ **212/229-1300.** www.coat.com. Subway: F to 23rd St.

Daffy's (Value)   Long before any of these Johnny-come-lately discounters arrived, Daffy's offered rock-bottom prices. They don't get the big brand names of Century 21, but you'll come across classic European sportswear (cashmere sweaters and the like) and staples, especially for men. The kids' collection— much of it trendy designer—is a well-kept secret among city moms. 111 5th Ave. (at 18th St.). ℂ **212/529-4477.** www.daffys.com. Subway: 4, 5, 6, L, N, R, Q, or W to 14th St./Union Square. Also at 462 Broadway (at Grand St.; ℂ **212/334-7444;** subway: N or R to Canal St.), 335 Madison Ave. (at 44th St.; ℂ **212/557-4422;** subway: 4, 5, 6, 7, or S to 42nd St./Grand Central), 1311 Broadway (at 34th St.; ℂ **212/736-4477;** subway: 1, 2, 3, or 9 to 34th St.), and 125 E. 57th St. (btwn Park and Lexington aves.; ℂ **212/376-4477;** subway: 4, 5, or 6 to 59th St.).

Filene's Basement (Value)   This Boston-based institution's Manhattan satellites pale when compared to the mother store. The stock can be hit-or-miss, but you will find discounts on men's and women's clothing, handbags, accessories, shoes, and a few brands of perfume. Every now and then a big-time European label pops up, but don't count on finding the current season's goods, especially in the downstairs men's store. Inventory turns over lightning-quick here, though, so you never know what a trip through can yield. 620 6th Ave. (btwn 18th and 19th sts.). ℂ **212/620-3100.** www.filenesbasement.com. Subway: F to 14th St. Also at 2222 Broadway (at 79th St.; ℂ **212/873-8000;** subway: 1 or 9 to 79th St.).

H&M (Value)   The Swedish discounter Hennes & Mauritz took New York by storm in 2000 with its high-style fashions at budget-minded prices. The colorful, loud, bustling stores are mammoth, the departments better organized than most full-retail department stores, the men's and women's wearables ultrachic, and the prices low, low, low. It's a fave with teens, in particular. The main Herald Square store carries all lines, including babies, children's, and maternity wear. 1328 Broadway (at 34th St.). ℂ **646/564-9922.** www.hm.com. Subway: B, D, F, N, R, or V to 34th St./Herald Square. Also at 640 5th Ave. (at 51st St.; ℂ **212/489-0390;** subway: E or V to 5th Ave.). Smaller location at 558 Broadway (btwn Prince and Spring sts.; ℂ **212/343-0220;** subway: N or R to Prince St.).

Loehmann's (Value)   This enormous discount outlet occupies a chunk of the original Barneys, and it has latched on to the stylish vibe. But not the prices, though; here, you'll pay 30% to 65% off department-store prices. Two floors of casual wear by makers such as Liz Claiborne and Laundry lead to one of the city's best finds: The "Back Room," where styles by big names—Versace, D&G, Donna Karan, Max Mara—are offered at a fraction of retail. There's also a floor of men's fashions, the best you'll find in the discount realm. Excellent shoes, too, with great prices on top-quality styles. 101 7th Ave. (btwn 16th and 17th sts.). ✆ 212/ 352-0856. www.loehmanns.com. Subway: 1 or 9 to 18th St.

Syms *Value* Syms is the discount store for men and women who need career wear. Designer and brand-name clothes are slashed 40% to 60% off their original retail value. Good buys on kids' clothes, too. *Money-saving tip:* Register at the website for an additional 10% savings. 42 Trinity Place (btwn Rector St. and Battery Park). ✆ 212/797-1199. www.syms.com. Subway: 1, 9, N, or R to Rector St. Also at 400 Park Ave. (at 54th St.; ✆ 212/317-8200; subway: 6 to 51st St.).

Tristan & America This Canadian retailer sells affordable, nicely tailored clothing in muted palettes to men and women who love Banana Republic's clothes but need a break from the high prices there. Look for great men's sweaters, affordable women's suits, and nicely cut trousers and A-line skirts. Excellent sales. 1230 6th Ave. (at 49th St.). ✆ 212/246-2354. www.tristan-america.com. Subway: B, D, F, or V to 47th–50th sts./Rockefeller Center.

Urban Outfitters The store for basics is sort of a Gap for alternative guys and gals: Jeans, oversize and tiny T-shirts, and bright velours and stretchy polyesters. There's a good selection of funky jewelry, as well as a wonderfully offbeat, affordable housewares section with batik bedspreads, candles, glassware, and mod bathroom accessories. You'll also find lots of silly gifts, from *Mad Libs* books to boxes of genuine *South Park* Cheesy Poofs. 628 Broadway (at Bleecker St.). ✆ 212/475-0009. www.urbn.com. Subway: 6 to Bleecker St. Also at 374 6th Ave. (at Waverly Place; ✆ 212/ 677-9350; subway: A, C, E, F, or V to W. 4th St.), 162 2nd Ave. (at 11th St.; ✆ 212/375-1277; subway: L to 3rd Ave.), 526 6th Ave. (at 14th St.; ✆ 646/638-1646; subway: F to 14th St.), and 2081 Broadway (at 72nd St.; ✆ 212/579-3912; subway: 1, 2, 3, or 9 to 72nd St.).

X-Large Your teen will love you for taking him or her to this hot spot (co-owned by Beastie Boy Mike D) for skate and urban street wear. The emphasis is on supercasual, with cutting-edge takes on staples like tees and sweatshirts; it's also big with 20-somethings and hip Japanese. 267 Lafayette St. (btwn Prince and Spring sts.). ✆ 212/334-4480. www.xlarge.com. Subway: 6 to Spring St.

Just Women

a. cheng Alice Cheng's retro-modern styles for women are fresh, pretty, and, best of all, affordable. The petite shop is a breezy delight. 443 E. 9th St. (btwn 1st Ave. and Ave. A). ✆ 212/979-7324. Subway: 6 to Astor Place.

Anthropologie Funky-chic and affordable wearables and accessories mix with gifts and furniture. Geared to young women who've outgrown Urban Outfitters. 375 W. Broadway (btwn Spring and Broome sts.). ✆ 212/343-7070. www.anthropologie.com. Subway: C or E to Spring St. Also at 85 5th Ave. (at 15th St.; ✆ 212/627-5885; subway: L, N, R, 4, 5, or 6 to Union Square).

Eileen Fisher ✮✮ Making their way around the nation in her own shops and through outlets like Saks and the Garnet Hill catalog, Eileen Fisher's separates are a dream come true for stylish women looking for easy-to-wear classic pieces that transcend the latest fads. She designs fluid clothes in a pleasing neutral palette and uses natural fibers that don't sacrifice comfort for chic. The A-line styles look a bit droopy on shorter women, but otherwise suit all figure types well; petites and plus sizes are carried as well. The superior quality, fabrics, and style make

Value   Scouring the Sample Sales

Welcome to the ultimate New York bargain: the sample sale, where top fashion designers recoup some losses by selling off the sample outfits they make for store buyers. Often, they throw in canceled orders, overstock, and discontinued styles. Prices are rock bottom. What's the drawback? Such sales aren't advertised because designers don't want to alienate the big retailers by stealing their customers.

So how do you get the scoop? The **weekly columns** "Sales & Bargains" in *New York* magazine and "Check Out" in *Time Out New York* list current and future sales; you can find *New York* magazine's sale picks online at **www.nymetro.com**. The free site **NYSale (www.nysale.com)** is probably your best source; it'll let you in on otherwise-unadvertised sales. If you're in the Garment District (especially along Broadway and 7th Ave.) in the morning, you'll probably be handed **flyers** advertising sales that day. On the Web, check **www.dailycandy.com**, a daily online newsletter highlighting store openings and where to find the day's sales.

A few tips as you venture into bargain land:

• Don't go at lunch; you'll be elbow-to-elbow with rushed office workers.

• Bring cash. Some designers do accept credit cards, but don't chance it.

• Few, if any, of these spaces have dressing rooms, so be prepared to try things on over your clothes (or hope it fits). Furthermore, because these garments are samples, they don't always come in a wide array of sizes.

• All items are sold "as is," and every sale is final, so inspect merchandise carefully before you buy.

these clothes worth every penny. This beautifully austere SoHo location is Fisher's prime showcase. The semiannual consolidation sales, in March and August, are a bargain hunter's delight. Note that only the SoHo flagship sells the complete line, including both the petite and women's collections. The closet-size East 9th Street location basically functions as an outlet store, with lots of sale merchandise and seconds on hand. 395 W. Broadway (btwn Spring and Broome sts.). © 212/431-4567. www.eileenfisher.com. Subway: C or E to Spring St. Also at 521 Madison Ave. (at 53rd St.; © 212/759-9888; subway: 6 to 51st St.), 341 Columbus Ave. (near 76th St.; © 212/362-3000; subway: B or C to 81st St.), 1039 Madison Ave. (btwn 79th and 80th sts.; © 212/879-7799; subway: 6 to 77th St.), 314 E. 9th St. (btwn 1st and 2nd aves.; © 212/529-5715; subway: 6 to Astor Place), and 166 5th Ave. (at 22nd St.; © 212/924-4777; subway: N or R to 23rd St.).

Foley & Corinna *(Finds)*   The Lower East Side's best boutique specializes in affordable original designs with a '70s flair that's retro in a nonkitschy way. You'll find a few reconstructed vintage pieces mixed in (such as vintage tees with added lace for a sexier look), plus an excellent handbag collection. 108 Stanton St. (btwn Essex and Ludlow sts.). © 212/529-2338. Subway: F to Delancey St.

Intermix   The place to dress and accessorize like your favorite *Sex and the City* gals, at not-too-expensive prices. The Flatiron location is the original, and remains the best. 125 5th Ave. (btwn 19th and 20th sts.). © 212/533-9720. Subway: N or R to 23rd St. Also at 210 Columbus Ave. (btwn 69th and 70th sts.; ⓒ 212/769 9116; subway: B or C to 72nd St.).

Jill Anderson *Finds*   Finally, a New York designer who creates affordable clothes for real women for real life—not just for 22-year-old size-2s. This narrow, peaceful shop and studio is lined with Jill's simple, clean designs, which drape beautifully and accentuate a woman's form without clinging. They're wearable for all ages and many figure types (her small sizes are small enough to fit petites, and her larges generally fit a full-figured size 14). Her clothes are feminine without being frilly, retro-reminiscent but modern, understated but stylish. If this sounds appealing, don't miss her shop. 331 E. 9th St. (btwn 1st and 2nd aves.). ⓒ 212/253-1747. www.jillanderson.com. Subway: 6 to Astor Place.

Liberty House   This Columbia University–area boutique is a find. It specializes in women's wear in easygoing styles that transcend age lines and figure types. Great casual sweaters, tees, cotton pants and skirts, linen separates, and more, all at affordable prices. You'll also find ethnic gifts at the front of the store, jewelry and accessories under the glass-topped counter, and a kids' shop specializing in unique styles that don't cost a fortune. 2878A Broadway (at 112th St.). ⓒ 212/932-1950. Subway: 1 or 9 to Cathedral Pkwy./110th St. Also at 2389 Broadway (btwn 87th and 88th sts.; ⓒ 212/799-7640; subway: 1 or 9 to 86th St.).

Nicolina   This charming and sophisticated shop is a Theater District anomaly. Come for fashionable basics in high-quality materials: wide-legged linen pants, flowing A-line and princess-cut dresses in silk and cotton, sweaters from labels like Beyond Threads and Sarah Arizona in fine wools, cotton, and silk. Great accessories, too, plus a small selection of contemporary and vintage gifts. 247 W. 46th St. (btwn Broadway and 8th Ave.). ⓒ 212/302-NICO. Subway: N, R, S, 1, 2, 3, or 9 to 42nd St./Times Square.

VINTAGE & CONSIGNMENT CLOTHING

Alice Underground   This lovely SoHo shop specializes in cheap-chic vintage wear, from Victoriana to *Mod Squad* era. The goods are displayed in an orderly fashion, and there's a good selection of vintage linens. 481 Broadway (btwn Broome and Grand sts.). ⓒ 212/431-9067. Subway: N, Q, R, W, or 6 to Canal St.

Allan & Suzi *Finds*   Make it past the freaky windows and you'll find one of the best consignment shops in the city. Allan and Suzi have specialized in 20th-century designer wear for over a decade, and the selection is marvelous. Their vintage and contemporary couture collection—which ranges from Chanel to Halston and Versace—is so well priced that it's within reach of the average shopper. The wild one-of-a-kind pieces are worth a look unto themselves. 416 Amsterdam Ave. (at 80th St.). ⓒ 212/724-7445. Subway: 1 or 9 to 79th St.

Andy's Chee-Pees   This vintage-clothing store sports two jam-packed levels of retro-chic wearables, including leather, denim, '50s Hawaiian prints, blazers, and much more. Prices aren't exactly "cheap," but the quality is high. 691 Broadway (btwn 3rd and 4th sts.). ⓒ 212/420-5980. Subway: 6 to Bleecker St.

Argosy   This narrow shop offers a small but pristine collection of '60s and '70s fashions, including an excellent collection of stylish leather jackets. Prices are reasonable considering the quality. 428 E. 9th St. (btwn 1st Ave. and Ave. A). ⓒ 212/982-7918. Subway: 6 to Astor Place.

Encore *Value*   This is one of the city's best resale shops, with two floors of quality women's wear, plus a small men's department and accessories, all sold at a fraction of the original cost. Periodic sales sweeten the deal: The Chanel suit I saw for $650 was the buy of the century, but you don't have to bring that much cash to go home with a bargain. 1132 Madison Ave. (btwn 84th and 85th sts.), 2nd floor. *℗* 212/879-2850. www.encoreresale.com. Subway: 6 to 86th St.

Housing Works Thrift Shop *(Finds* With consistently low prices (most pieces $25 or less), lots of designer names (Todd Oldham, Calvin Klein, Donna Karan), and clothes in excellent condition, why go anywhere else? Styles range from classic to funky. There's also a good used-jeans area and a miniboutique selling couture-ish items at slightly higher prices. There's furniture, too, but good pieces go very fast. A great place to shop—not only will you get a bargain, but sales benefit homeless people living with HIV and AIDS. 143 W. 17th St. (btwn 6th and 7th aves.). *℗* 212/366-0820. www.housingworks.org/thrift. Subway: 1 or 9 to 18th St. Also 202 E. 77th St. (btwn 2nd and 3rd aves.; *℗* 212/772-8461; subway: 6 to 77th St.), 306 Columbus Ave. (btwn 74th and 75th sts.); *℗* 212/579-7566; subway: B or C to 72nd St.), and 157 E. 23rd St. (btwn 3rd and Lexington aves.; *℗* 212/529-5955; subway: 6 to 23rd St.).

Ina *(Finds* This designer consignment boutique specializes in used wearables, vintage and current, for men and women from the world's top couture houses. Labels run the gamut from Halston to Calvin to Prada to Daryl K. A beautiful selection of shoes and accessories is on hand. The locations are so close that you can scour both in one trip. 21 Prince St. (btwn Mott and Elizabeth sts.). *℗* 212/334-9048. Subway: N or R to Prince St.; 6 to Spring St. Also at 101 Thompson St. (btwn Prince and Spring sts.; *℗* 212/941-4757; subway: N or R to Prince St.).

Kimono House This SoHo shop is an excellent stop for low prices on vintage kimono and *yukata* (cotton kimono, which make great bathrobes). The fabrics alone are worth the price for folks looking to dress up their wardrobes and homes with brilliant jewel tones and Asian patterns. 131 Thompson St. (btwn Houston and Prince sts.). *℗* 212/505-0232. Subway: C or E to Spring St.

Metropolis Some of the biggest names in fashion scout this clean, orderly vintage shop for fashion ideas. With good reason: Some of the coolest old clothes in the world turn up here, from skater pants and micro-cords to gingham-checked Western shirts—perfect for your very own hoedown or hullabaloo. 43 3rd Ave. (btwn 9th and 10th sts.). *℗* 212/358-0795. Subway: 6 to Astor Place.

Michael's *(Value* This consignment boutique boasts designer wear for women—including such names as Chanel, YSL, Prada, Gucci, and Escada—at a fraction of the original cost. The bridal salon is an unbeatable find for a top-quality dress at an off-the-rack price. 1041 Madison Ave. (btwn 79th and 80th sts.), 2nd floor. *℗* 212/737-7273. www.michaelsconsignment.com. Subway: 6 to 77th St.

New & Almost New *(Finds* This closet brims with well-chosen contemporary and retro designer wear, all like new and at great prices. 65 Mercer St. (just north of Broome St.). *℗* 212/226-6677. Subway: J, M, N, R, Q, or W to Canal St.

Screaming Mimi's *(Value* Screaming Mimi's is as neat and well organized as any high-priced boutique—yet prices are reasonable, especially given the pricey vintage shops that have popped up in recent years. The clothes and accessories are well chosen, and the display is top-notch. The housewares department is a cornucopia of kitsch, and includes a selection of New York memorabilia; prices start under $10, so this is a great place to find a special souvenir. 382 Lafayette St. (btwn 4th and Great Jones sts.). *℗* 212/677-6464. Subway: 6 to Astor Place.

Tokio 7 *(Value* This designer consignment shop features gently used couture from labels like Helmut Lang, Yohji Yamamoto, Vivienne Westwood, and others, at way-below-retail prices. 64 E. 7th St. (btwn 1st and 2nd aves.). © **212/353-8443.** Subway: 6 to Astor Place; L to 1st Ave.

Tokyo Joe *Value*   This cramped boutique is the designer consignment shop for left-of-mainstream hipsters. Browsing can be hellish, but prices are great. The shoe collection is stellar, often boasting barely (or never) worn Manolos and Jimmy Choos, priced at a fraction of what the *Sex and the City* gals pay at the uptown boutiques. 334 E. 11th St. (btwn 1st and 2nd aves.). © **212/473-0724.** Subway: L to 1st Ave. Also at 240 E. 28th St. (btwn 2nd and 3rd aves.; © **212/532-3605;** subway: 6 to 28th St.).

EDIBLES

Arthur Avenue Retail Market ★★ *Finds*   This colorful, enclosed market opened in the heart of Bronx's Little Italy in 1940 and is my absolute favorite. The market, like the Bronx, has had its ups and downs, but now is thriving. You'll find fresh produce purveyors like the **Biano** fruits and vegetables and **Joe Libertore's Garden of Plenty** where I buy the best tomato plants for my terrace. There is Peter's Market for homemade sausages and braciole, **Mike's Deli** for freshly made mozzarella and sandwiches, and the **Arthur Avenue Baking Company** for loaves of *pane di casa* and Parmesan breadsticks, and even **La Casa Grande Tobacco Company** where they roll their own cigars. 2344 Arthur Ave., the Bronx. © **718/364-4657.** www.arthuravenuebronx.com. Subway: B or D to Fordham Rd.

Chelsea Market   Located in an old Nabisco factory, this big, dazzling food mall is the city's largest. Come for both raw and ready-to-eat foods, including divinely inspired baked goods and cappuccino from **Amy's Bread;** yummy soups from **Hale and Hearty;** Manhattan's best brownie at **Fat Witch Bakery;** and much more, including the wonderful **Chelsea Wine Vault. Chelsea Market Baskets** is a great place to pick up gifts for home. 75 9th Ave. (btwn 15th and 16th sts.). © **212/242-7360.** www.chelseamarket.com. Subway: A, C, E, or L to 14th St.

Dean & Deluca   This bright, clean-lined store offers premier quality across the board: In addition to the excellent butcher, fish, cheese, and dessert counters (check out the stunning cakes and the great character cookies) and beautiful fruits and veggies, you'll find a dried fruit and nut bar, a huge coffee bean selection, a gorgeous cut-flower selection, lots of imported waters and beers in the refrigerator case, and a limited but quality selection of kitchenware in back. A small cafe up front makes a great stop for a cappuccino break from SoHo shopping. 560 Broadway (at Prince St.). © **212/226-6800.** www.dean-deluca.com. Subway: N or R to Prince St.

Dylan's Candy Bar *Finds*   Dylan (daughter of Ralph) Lauren is one of the co-owners of this bazaar for sugar addicts. Located across the street from Bloomingdale's, you'll find candy classics like Necco wafers, Charleston Chews, and both of my favorite childhood chewing gums, Black Jack and Gold Mine. Dylan's also makes signature chocolates, candy creations, candy spa products like hot chocolate bath beads, and custom-made ice cream flavors. 1011 3rd Ave. (at 60th St.) © **646/735-0078.** www.dylanscandybar.com. Subway: 4, 5, 6, N, or R to 59th St.

Fairway ★★ *Value*   There is no better all-in-one market in Manhattan than Fairway. Here you will find the best and most modestly priced vegetables in the city. Cheeses are top of the line and well organized. The fish counter is excellent and again, very modestly priced. The second floor of the Broadway store features hard to find health foods and a wide array of organic fruits and vegetables. Fairway also carries gourmet items you might find at Dean & Deluca but at a fraction of the cost. The Harlem store is huge and features a walk-in freezer complete with down jackets provided for customers. 2127 Broadway (btwn 74th and 75th sts.). © **212/595-1888.** www.fairwaymarket.com. Subway: 1, 2, 3, or 9 to 72nd St. Also at 2328 12th Ave. (at 132nd St.; © **212/234-3883**; subway: 1 or 9 to 125th St.).

Zabar's ⊛   More than any other of New York's gourmet food stores, Zabar's is an institution. This giant deli sells prepared foods, packaged goods from around

Chocolate City

No, I'm not referring to the 1975 Parliament funk album, I'm talking about the Big Apple becoming a city consumed by an almost feverish craving for chocolate. Many sweet shops around the city now are turning out homemade chocolates in every variety that are so good, the stores, like four-star restaurants, are destinations in their own right. The best of these can be found just over the Brooklyn Bridge in DUMBO at **Jacques Torres Chocolate** ⊛⊛, 60 Water St., Brooklyn (© **718/875-9772**; www.mrchocolate.com). Torres, the former celebrated pastry chef at Le Cirque, ventured out on his own a few years ago and opened this mecca to chocolate where your mouth will water as you watch chocolate being made. The variations are staggering here including chocolate peanut brittle, chocolate-covered corn flakes, champagne truffles, and some of the best hot chocolate you've ever tasted. Take home a tin of the "wicked" hot chocolate which features allspice, cinnamon, sweet ancho chile peppers and hot chipotle peppers. In 2004, another outlet of **Jacques Torres Chocolate** opened at 350 Hudson St. (at King St.) in TriBeCa. The new store is the first chocolate manufacturing facility open to the public.

Back in Manhattan in the middle of one of the toniest stretches of Madison Avenue is the import from Paris, **La Maison du Chocolat,** 1018 Madison Ave. (at 78th St.) (© **212/744-7117**; www.lamaisonduchocalt. com). This boutique takes its chocolate very seriously. You won't find any of the foolishness here like adding chile peppers or coating corn flakes with chocolate. What you will find is possibly the best pure chocolate you've ever tasted. They abhor any bitterness in their chocolate and make it a point to claim that they use nothing stronger than 65% cocoa. Now that's taking your chocolate seriously.

One of the oldest chocolate shops in the city is the 1923-established, **Li-Lac Chocolates,** 120 Christopher St. (btwn Bleecker and Hudson sts.; © **800/624-4784** or 212/242-7374). This West Village shop makes their sweets by hand and whips up batches of chocolate fudge daily. In fact, they do chocolate fudge like no one else in the city.

Also in the village is a newcomer to the chocolate scene, **The Chocolate Bar,** 48 8th Ave. (btwn Jane and Horatio sts.; © **212/366-1541;** www. chocolatebarnyc.com). At the Chocolate Bar they make—surprise!— their own chocolate bars that are worthy of their name. I love the mocha, which has flakes of coffee. For those who worship the cocoa gods, go for the super-dark 72%, so dark and rich you might speak in tongues after a few bites.

the world, coffee beans, excellent fresh breads, and much more (no fresh veggies, though). This is the place for lox, and the rice pudding is the best I've ever tasted. You'll also find an excellent—and well-priced—collection of housewares and restaurant-quality cookware on the second floor. Prepare yourself for serious crowds. The attached cafe serves terrific sandwiches and takeout—ideal for a Central Park picnic. 2245 Broadway (at 80th St.). © 212/787-2000. Subway: 1 or 9 to 79th St.

ELECTRONICS

B&H Photo & Video ⭐ *Value*   Looking for a digital camera at a good price? You really won't do any better than B&H, the largest camera store in the country. This camera superstore has everything from lenses to darkroom equipment. If you are a B&H virgin, the store can be somewhat intimidating, but service is helpful. Just follow the signs and they will direct you to whatever you are seeking. *Note:* The store is closed Saturday and all major Jewish holidays. 420 9th Ave. (at 34th St.) © 800/606-6969. www.bhphotovideo.com. Subway: A, C, or E to 34th St.

J&R Music & Computer World ⭐   This block-long Financial District emporium is the city's top discount computer, electronics, small appliance, and office equipment retailer. The sales staff is knowledgeable but can get pushy if you don't buy at once or know exactly what you want. Don't succumb—take your time and find exactly what you need. Or better yet, peruse the store's copious catalog or extensive website, both of which make advance research, mail order, and comparison shopping easy. Park Row (at Ann St., opposite City Hall Park). © 800/426-6027 or 212/238-9000. www.jandr.com. Subway: 2 or 3 to Park Place; 4, 5, or 6 to Brooklyn Bridge/City Hall.

GIFTS & PAPER GOODS

To find a gift for a creative spirit, check out **East 9th Street** in the East Village; the side streets of **SoHo,** where a number of unusual boutiques survive; **NoLita;** and Greenwich Village, especially the one-of-a-kind shops in the **West Village.** See "The Top Shopping Streets & Neighborhoods," earlier.

Alphabets   This playful shop has two halves: one for cards, toys, and tees, the other for creative housewares, from dishware to freeform vases. It's all fun and affordable. 2284 Broadway (btwn 82nd and 83rd sts.). © 212/579-5702. www.alphabets nyc.com. Subway: 1 or 9 to 86th St. Also at 115 Ave. A (at St. Marks Place; © 212/475-7250; subway: 6 to Astor Place; L to 1st Ave.) and 47 Greenwich Ave. (btwn Perry and Charles sts.; © 212/229-2966; subway: 1 or 9 to Christopher St.).

Daily 235   This quirky card and candy store for artsy grown-ups is a great place to pick up creative under-$10 gifts, from small-print books to Buddha-shaped candles. 235 Elizabeth St. (btwn Prince and Houston sts.). © 212/334-9728. Subway: N or R to Prince St.; 6 to Spring St.

Extraordinary* *Finds*   This warm, friendly gallery–cum–gift shop is worth going out of your way to discover. Owner J. R. Sanders, an interior designer who has created exhibits at many museums, has assembled a collection of gifts from around the world. Lacquered crackle-eggshell trays from Vietnam, carved mango bowls from the Philippines, rosewood utensils camouflaged as tree branches from Africa, and much more—all eye candy for those who thrive on whimsy and good design. Best of all, prices are reasonable—you'd pay twice as much at any other gallery or boutique—and late hours (usually daily to 10:30pm) make it easy to visit. Truly extraordinary! 251 E. 57th St. (just west of 2nd Ave.). © 212/223-9151. Subway: 4, 5, or 6 to 59th St.

H   This tranquil shop is a favorite for unusual housewares and gifts. The wonderful collection runs the gamut from Slinky vases to Japanese rice-paper coasters to old French electronics illustrations, suitable for framing. 335 E. 9th St. (btwn 1st and 2nd aves.). ℂ 212/477-2631. Subway: 6 to Spring St.

House of Cards and Curiosities *Finds* This jam-packed shop, the West Village's own funky take on an old-fashioned nickel-and-dime, is a joy to browse for kooky trinkets and cards. 23 8th Ave. (btwn 12th and Jane sts.). ℂ 212/675-6178. Subway: A, C, E, or L to 14th St.

JAM Paper *Value* For stylish stationery at low prices, JAM is the place to go. Most papers are color-block solids, but the spectrum covers the rainbow. You'll also find a large, creative selection of well-priced supplies for your home and office. 111 3rd Ave. (btwn 13th and 14th sts.). ℂ 212/473-6666. www.jampaper.com. Subway: L to 3rd Ave. Also at 611 6th Ave. (btwn 17th and 18th sts.; ℂ 212/255-4593; subway: F to 14th St.).

Kate's Paperie I could browse for hours in this delightful shop's handmade stationery and wrap, innovative invitations and thank-yous, notebooks, writing tools, and other paper products, including lampshades. Lovely art cards, too—perfect for writing the folks back home. A joy! The SoHo location is best. 561 Broadway (btwn Prince and Spring sts.). ℂ 888/941-9169 or 212/941-9816. www.katespaperie.com. Subway: N or R to Prince St. Also at 8 W. 13th St. (btwn 5th and 6th aves.; ℂ 212/633-0570; subway: F to 14th St.), 1282 3rd Ave. (btwn 73rd and 74th sts.; ℂ 212/396-3670; subway: 6 to 77th St.), and 140 W. 57th St. (btwn 6th and 7th aves.; ℂ 212/459-0700; subway: N, R, or W to 57th St.).

Leekan Designs This high-ceilinged shop is packed with Asian, Oceanic, and Moroccan exotica, from beaded jewelry to folk art to tableware to textiles to floor mats. The collection is eye-popping, and prices are quite affordable. 93 Mercer St. (near Spring St.). ℂ 212/226-7226. Subway: N or R to Prince St.

Mascot Studio *Finds* Stop into this rough-hewn custom frame shop for one-of-a-kind picture frames, most extremely affordably priced. The small shop also curates art and photography shows, so you might even find a worthwhile exhibit when you arrive. 328 E. 9th St. (btwn 1st and 2nd aves.). ℂ 212/228-9090. Subway: 6 to Astor Place.

Mxyplyzyk *Value* Come to this unpronounceable Village shop for one of the city's most fun and creative collections of one-of-a-kind housewares, office ware, and gifts. Most everything is reasonably priced. 125 Greenwich Ave. (at 13th St., near 8th Ave.). ℂ 212/989-4300. Subway: A, C, or E to 14th St.

New York Firefighter's Friend *Finds* Purchase FDNY logo wear, including T-shirts, sweatshirts, hats, and more. The goods are all top-quality, and a portion of profits go in support of the widows and children of the 343 firefighters lost in the September 11, 2001, terrorist attacks. 263 Lafayette St. (btwn Prince and Spring sts.). ℂ 212/226-3142. www.nyfirestore.com. Subway: 6 to Spring St.

New York 911 *Finds* Next to Firefighter's Friend (see above), you can shop for NYPD logo wear, and EMT, FBI, and NYC coroner gear. The goods include shirts, caps, patches, logo toys, and more. (Not all of the products are licensed by the city; I suggest trying to stick with those that are.) A portion of the proceeds goes to NYPD-related charities. 263 Lafayette St. (btwn Prince and Spring sts.). ℂ 888/723-3907 or 212/219-3907. www.ny911.com. Subway: 6 to Spring St.

Old Japan Come to this small Village shop for vintage silk kimonos, Japanese dolls, Noguchi lamps, Mingei folk items, and other gifts from the Land of the Rising Sun, including scarves and handbags fashioned out of kimonos and buckwheat pillows covered in kimono cotton. Vintage kimonos run $300 to $1,500, but there's always a year-round sale rack with prices under $100, and small pieces are always affordable. 382 Bleecker St. (btwn Perry and Charles sts.). © 212/ 633-0922. www.oldjapaninc.com. Subway: 1 or 9 to Christopher St.

Pearl River *Value*   Even after moving from tight quarters on Canal Street to a more spacious location, this Chinese mall still overflows with affordable Asian exotica, from paper lanterns to Chinese snack foods to Mandarin-collared silk pajamas to mah-jongg sets to Hong Kong action videos. The new location features a waterfall and a cafe serving 40 different types of tea. This fascinating place can keep you occupied for hours. 477 Broadway (at Grand St.). © 212/431-4770. www.pearlriver.com. Subway: N or R to Canal St. Also at 200 Grand St. (btwn Mott and Mulberry sts.; © 212/966-1010; subway: B, D, or Q to Grand St.).

HOME FASHIONS & HOUSEWARES

ABC Carpet & Home   This 10-floor emporium is the ultimate home-fashions and -furnishings store. The goods run the gamut from Moroccan mosaic-tile end tables to Tuscan pottery to Tiffanyish lamps to distressed bed frames made up with Frette linens to much more, all carefully chosen and exquisitely displayed. Prices aren't bad, but these are high-end goods. Some of the smaller items are affordable, and the sales yield substantial discounts. Whether you buy or browse, you can sit down to a nice snack or lunch at the in-house branch of **Le Pain Quotidien** (p. 144). Across the street is the multifloor carpet store, which boasts a remarkable collection of area rugs. 881 and 888 Broadway (at 19th St.). © 212/473-3000. www.abccarpet.com. Subway: 4, 5, 6, L, N, R, Q, or W to 14th St./Union Square.

Amalgamated Home   Looking for brushed-metal switch plates for your groovy new stainless-steel kitchen? How about a purple velvet love seat straight out of a Looney Tunes cartoon? Or the hippest rice bowls in town? You'll find it all and more at this pair of home shops, which stocks eye-catching household goods you won't see anywhere else. 19 Christopher St. (btwn 6th and 7th aves.). © 212/ 255-4160 (furniture and lighting), or 212/691-8695 (hardware and household sundries). Subway: 1 or 9 to Christopher St.

Broadway Panhandler   If you're looking for restaurant-quality cookware and kitchen tools, this is the place. It has the best combination of selection, prices, and service in town. Don't just take it from me—*New York* magazine gave Broadway Panhandler the "Best Pots and Pans" nod in 2000. 477 Broome St. (btwn Greene and Wooster sts.). © 212/966-3434. www.broadwaypanhandler.com. Subway: C or E to Spring St.

Details   These fun-and-funky home stores are the place to outfit the coolest pad in town with Day-Glo bath accessories, cool-print shower curtains, glassware, and the like. Everything's cute and affordable! 347 Bleecker St. (at W. 10th St.). © 212/414-0039. Subway: 1 or 9 to Christopher St./Sheridan Square. Also at 142 8th Ave. (at 17th St.; © 212/366-9498; subway: A, C, or E to 14th St.) and 188 Columbus Ave. (at 68th St.; © 212/362-7344; subway: 1 or 9 to 66th St.).

Fishs Eddy *Value*   What a great idea—selling remainders of kitschy, custom-designed china. Ever wanted a dish that *really* says "Blue Plate Special"? How about a coffee mug with the terse logo "Cup o' Joe to Go"? The store is Browse Heaven, and prices are low enough. Other items include vintage and retro-inspired flatware, bowls, and restaurant-supply glassware that can be hard to find, like soda fountain and pint glasses. 889 Broadway (at 19th St.). © 212/420-9020. www.fishseddy.com. Subway: 4, 5, 6, L, N, R, Q, or W to 14th St./Union Square. Also at 2176 Broadway (at 77th St.; © 212/873-8819; subway: 1 or 9 to 79th St.).

kar'ikter *(Finds* New York's biggest collection of sleek and playful Alessi house-wares from Italy (including Michael Graves's iconic teakettle with bird whistle), as well as European animation cells and toys starring Tintin, Babar, and Asterix. 19 Prince St. (btwn Elizabeth and Mott sts.). ℂ **212/274-1966.** www.karikter.com. Subway: 6 to Spring St.

Leader Restaurant Equipment & Supplies *(Value* The Bowery is the place to find restaurant-supply-quality kitchenware, and Leader is the best dealer on the block. This big, bustling shop is a good source for Chinese and Japanese wares—chopsticks, rice and noodle bowls, sushi plates, sake cups, and the like. You'll see a lot of the same styles you'd find at the high-end stores in SoHo or the Village, but at a fraction of the prices. 191 Bowery (btwn Spring and Delancey sts.). ℂ **800/666-6888** or 212/677-1982. Subway: 6 to Spring St.

Lighting by Gregory *(Value* The stretch of the Bowery (3rd Ave.) from Hous-ton to Canal streets is considered the "light-fixture district" for its huge selec-tions and great bargains on light fixtures, lamps, and ceiling fans. Gregory's multishowroom shop is by far the best of the bunch, with a first-rate selection of all the name brands (including ultraquiet Casablanca ceiling fans) and terrific prices. 158 Bowery (btwn Delancey and Broome sts.). ℂ **888/811-FANS** or 212/226-1276. www.lightingbygregory.com. Subway: J or M to Bowery.

LEATHER, HANDBAGS & LUGGAGE

Grace Bags *(Value* So you've always wanted a Prada, Gucci, kate spade, or Tod's bag, but your budget's just not up to shelling out the big bucks? Then come to this bargain hunter's delight of a discount shop, where good-quality faux versions of the designer styles sell for just $10 to $45. 190 Orchard St. (btwn Houston and Stanton sts.). ℂ **212/228-6118.** Subway: F to 2nd Ave.

Greenwood This Village shop sells top-quality leather handbags, backpacks, luggage, and wallets from names like Frye and Latico at reasonable prices. The selection is excellent, and service is professional. 263 Bleecker St. (btwn 6th and 7th aves.). ℂ **212/366-0825.** Subway: 1 or 9 to Houston St.

Jobson's *(Value* In business since 1949, Jobson's is a great discount source for name-brand luggage and leather goods. Rather than simply offer a cut off the retail price, management marks most items at 10% above cost, which usually amounts to a whopping 40% to 60% break for the buyer. The shop also does a huge airline and professional flyers business, and they'll be happy to tell you what the pros buy. Negotiators sometimes prevail. 666 Lexington Ave. (btwn 55th and 56th sts.). ℂ **212/355-6846.** Subway: 6 to 51st St.

Jutta Neumann *(Finds* If you stop into this shop, you're likely to find the artist herself behind the counter, cutting and stitching her bold-hued leather goods—bags, wallets, boots, and more. Her mules and strappy sandals have made a big splash. 158 Allen St. (btwn Stanton and Rivington sts.). ℂ **212/982-7048.** www.juttaneumann-newyork.com. Subway: F to Delancey/Essex sts.

Manhattan Portage Ltd. Store Come here for the hippest nylon and can-vas carryalls in town. Manhattan Portage manufactures its bags in the city, and they're made from hard-wearing materials that can stand up to an urban lifestyle. Popular styles include messenger bags, DJ bags, and backpacks (in standard and one-shoulder styles) in a range of colors from bright yellow to camouflage. Man-hattan Portage bags are also sold through other outlets, but you'll find the most complete selection here. 333 E. 9th St. (btwn 1st and 2nd aves.). ℂ **212/995-5490.** www.manhattanportageltd.com. Subway: 6 to Astor Place.

Original Leather   If you're in the market for a leather jacket, pants, or skirt, this is the best of the Village's discount leather shops in terms of quality and price. You'll get good value for your dollar here, and the salespeople aren't *too* hard-sell (comparatively speaking, that is). 171 W. 4th St. (btwn 6th and 7th aves.). © 212/675-2303. www.originalleatherstore.com. Subway: A, C, E, F, V, or S to W. 4th St. Also at 176 Spring St. (btwn Thompson and W. Broadway; © 212/219-8210; subway: C or E to Spring St.), 552 LaGuardia Place (btwn Bleecker and 3rd sts.; © 212/777-4362; subway: A, C, E, F, V, or S to W. 4th St.), 256 Columbus Ave. (at 72nd St.; © 212/595-7051; subway: B or C to 72nd St.), and 1100 Madison Ave. (btwn 82nd and 83rd sts.; © 212/585-4200; subway: 4, 5, or 6 to 86th St.).

Tip: Compare prices and styles to **Janet Woo,** down the block from the West Village location at 189 W. 4th St. (btwn 6th Ave. and 7th Ave. S.; © **646/ 638-3035**), another reasonable outlet.

Village Tannery   The cream of the Greenwich Village leather crop, with gorgeous and well-priced handbags, backpacks, wallets, and organizers. 173 Bleecker St. (btwn MacDougal and Sullivan sts.). © 212/673-5444. Subway: 1 or 9 to Houston St. Also at 742 Broadway (btwn Astor Place and Waverly St.; © 212/979-0013; subway: 6 to Astor Place).

LOGO STORES

Mets Clubhouse Shop   New York's other favorite baseball team has its own logo store in Midtown. Stop in for goods galore—baseball caps, T-shirts, posters, Piazza jerseys, '69 Miracle Mets memorabilia, and much more. You can buy regular-season game tix here, too. 143 E. 54th St. (btwn Lexington and 3rd aves.). © 212/888-7508. www.mets.com. Subway: E or V to Lexington Ave.

The MTV Store   This petite boutique sits street-side, just below the MTV studio. There's not much here—but your kids will surely find something they want, whether it's a *Jackass* bumper sticker, an *Osbournes* T-shirt, or one of any number of *TRL* souvenirs. Flyers are sometimes on hand at the register, advertising for audience members for MTV shows. 1515 Broadway (at 44th St.). © 212/846-5655. Subway: 1, 2, 3, 7, 9, N, R, S, Q, or W to 42nd St./Times Square.

NBA Store   For all things NBA and WNBA, go to this three-level store, a multimedia celebration of pro hoops, complete with bleachers for player appearances and signings. 666 5th Ave. (at 52nd St.). © 212/515-NBA1. www.nbastore.com. Subway: B, D, F, or V to 47th–50th sts./Rockefeller Center.

NBC Experience   This mammoth, neon-lit store sits across from the *Today* show studio and sells all manner of NBC-themed merchandise. Your kids will enjoy the interactive features, like the virtual reality "Conan O'Brien's Wild Desk Ride" or "Al Roker's Weather Challenge," which lets you do the forecast alongside the meteorologist, as well as the candy shop. 30 Rockefeller Plaza (at 49th St.). © 212/ 664-3700. www.nbcsuperstore.com. Subway: B, D, F, or V to 47th–50th sts./Rockefeller Center.

The Pop Shop *(Finds*   For affordable and wearable art that makes supercool souvenirs, come here. This groovy store is full of items based on designs by artist Keith Haring, who died in 1990. T-shirts, posters, calendars, stationery, toys, notebooks, and transparent backpacks—all sport the vivid colors and loopy stick-figure drawings Haring made famous. Best of all, the Pop Shop is a nonprofit, offering continued support to the AIDS-related and children's charities that the young artist championed in life. 292 Lafayette St. (btwn Houston and Prince sts.). © 212/219-2784. www.haring.com. Subway: F or V to Broadway/Lafayette St.

Yankees Clubhouse Shop   For all your Bronx Bombers needs—hats, jerseys, jackets, and so on. Tickets for regular-season home games are also for sale, and there's a limited selection of other New York team jerseys. 245 W. 42nd St. (btwn 7th and 8th aves.). ⓒ **212/768-9555**. www.yankees.com. Subway: A, C, or E to 42nd St. Also at 393 5th Ave. (btwn 36th and 37th sts.; ⓒ **212/685-4693**; subway: 6 to 33rd St.), 110 E. 59th St. (btwn Park and Lexington aves.; ⓒ **212/758-7844**; subway: 4, 5, or 6 to 59th St.), and 8 Fulton St. (in the South St. Seaport; ⓒ **212/514-7182**; subway: 2, 3, 4, or 5 to Fulton St.).

MUSEUM STORES

In addition to these, check out the excellent shops at the New York Public Library, the Museum for African Art, the Jewish Museum, the American Folk Art Museum, the American Museum of the Moving Image, and the Isamu Noguchi Garden Museum; see chapter 7.

Maxilla & Mandible *(Finds* This shop is not affiliated with the Museum of Natural History, but a visit here makes a good adjunct to a trip there (it's right around the corner). It's a fascinating natural-history emporium. Inside, you'll find rocks and shells from around the world, luminescent butterflies in display boxes, even real fossils containing prehistoric fish and insects that come with details on their history. There's also a variety of natural history–themed toys for kids. 451 Columbus Ave. (btwn 81st and 82nd sts.). ⓒ **212/724-6173**. www.maxillaandmandible.com. Subway: B or C to 81st St.

Metropolitan Museum of Art Store Given the scope of the museum, it's no wonder the gift shop is outstanding. Many treasures from the museum's collection have been reproduced as jewelry, china, and other objets d'art. The range of books is dizzying, and there's a comprehensive selection of posters and children's toys. 1000 5th Ave. (at 82nd St.). ⓒ **212/570-3894**. www.metmuseum.org. Subway: 4, 5, or 6 to 86th St. Also at Rockefeller Center, 15 W. 49th St. (ⓒ **212/332-1360**; subway: B, D, F, or Q to 47th–50th sts./Rockefeller Center), 113 Prince St. (at Greene St.; ⓒ **212/614-3000**; subway: N or R to Prince St.), and on the mezzanine level at Macy's (34th St. and 6th Ave.; ⓒ **212/268-7266**; subway: B, D, F, N, R, Q, V, or W to 34th St./Herald Square).

MoMa Design Store Across the street from the Museum of Modern Art in Midtown is this shop, whose stock ranges from posters and clever toys to reproductions of many of the classics of modern design, including free-form Alvar Aalto vases and Frank Lloyd Wright chairs. If these high-design items are out of your reach, don't worry: There are plenty of affordable outré home accessories from which to choose. The new SoHo store is equally fabulous. 44 W. 53rd St. (btwn 5th and 6th aves.). ⓒ **212/767-1050**. www.moma.org. Subway: E or F to 5th Ave.; B, D, F, or V to 47th–50th sts./Rockefeller Center. Also at 81 Spring St. (at Crosby St.; ⓒ **646/613-1367**; subway: 6 to Spring St.).

Museum of Arts and Design The nation's top showcase for contemporary crafts boasts an impressive collection of crafts in its museum store, too. Come for exquisite handblown glassware, one-of-a-kind jewelry, original pottery, and other artistic treasures, all beautifully displayed. 40 W. 53rd St. (btwn 5th and 6th aves.). ⓒ **212/956-3535**. www.americancraftmuseum.org. Subway: E or F to 5th Ave.

New York Transit Museum Store Lots of transportation-themed gifts; the cufflinks made out of subway tokens are great! Grand Central Terminal (on the main level, in the passage next to Station Masters' office), 42nd St. and Lexington Ave. ⓒ **212/878-0106**. Subway: 4, 5, 6, 7, or S to 42nd St./Grand Central.

MUSIC & VIDEO

Academy Records & CDs This Flatiron District shop has a cool intellectual air that's more reminiscent of a good used-book store than your average used-record store. Academy is always filled with classical, opera, and jazz junkies perusing the extensive and well-priced collection of used CDs and vinyl. In addition to the extensive classical and jazz collection is a variety of other audiophile favorites, from rare '60s pop songsters to spoken word. 12 W. 18th St. (btwn 5th and 6th aves.). © 212/242-3000. www.academy-records.com. Subway: L, N, R, 4, 5, or 6 to 14th St./Union Square.

Bleecker St. Records   This sizable, well-lit space is great for one-stop shopping. The clean, well-organized CD and LP collections run the gamut from rock, oldies, jazz, folk, and blues to (oi!) punk. You'll find lots of imports, collectibles, and out-of-print records (including singles), a terrific collection of used CDs, and a mix of casual listeners and serious collectors cruising the bins. 239 Bleecker St. (near Carmine St., just west of 6th Ave.). © 212/255-7899. Subway: A, C, E, F, or V to W. 4th St.

Colony Music Center ⚡   This long-lived Theater District shop ("since 1948") is housed in the legendary Brill Building, the Tin Pan Alley of '50s and '60s pop, where legendary songwriters like Leiber and Stoller and producers like Don Kirschner and Phil Spector crafted the soundtrack for a generation. It's the perfect home for Colony, a nostalgia emporium filled with a pricey but excellent collection of vintage vinyl and new CDs. You'll find a great collection of Broadway scores and cast recordings; decades worth of recordings by pop song stylists both legendary and obscure; the city's best collection of sheet music (including some hard-to-find international stuff); and a great selection of original theater and movie posters. 1619 Broadway (at 49th St.). © 212/265-2050. www.colonymusic.com. Subway: N or R to 49th St.; 1 or 9 to 50th St.

Footlight ⚡ *Finds*   If you like Colony (see above), also check out this dreamy collection of vintage vinyl, strong in jazz and pop vocalists, soundtracks, and show tunes. 113 E. 12th St. (btwn 3rd and 4th aves.). © 212/533-1572. www.footlight.com. Subway: L, N, R, 4, 5, or 6 to 14th St./Union Square.

Generation Records *Value*   This tidy little store sells mostly CDs and is an excellent source for "import" live recordings. Originally specializing in hardcore, punk, and heavy metal, the new collection upstairs still has a heavy edge but has since diversified appreciably. Downstairs is a well-organized and well-priced used CD selection that's not as picked over as most and runs the genre gamut; there's also a good selection of used LPs. Despite the help's tough look, they're actually quite friendly and helpful. 210 Thompson St. (btwn Bleecker and 3rd sts.). © 212/254-1100. Subway: A, C, E, F, or V to W. 4th St.

House of Oldies ⚡   I skipped many a high school class to spend time in this musty old store searching for doo wops. I think it was here that I bought a mint "Woo Woo Train," by the Valentines on Rama Records for less than $5. That same record now probably costs over $60 and you can probably still find it at the House of Oldies. The store has over a million vinyl records in stock in everything from R&B to surf music. So if vinyl oldies are your thing, there's no better place to go. 35 Carmine St. (at Bleecker). © 212/243-0500. www.houseofoldies.com. Subway: A, C, B, D, F, or V to W. 4th.

Jazz Record Center   I have a friend from Paris who lives jazz and this is the first place he hits whenever he visits New York. It's *the* place to find rare and out-of-print jazz records. In addition to the extensive selection of CDs and vinyl (including 78s), videos, books, posters, magazines, photos, and other memorabilia are available. Prices start at $5 for vinyl, $10 for CDs, and soar from there, befitting the rarity of the stock. Owner Frederick Cohen is extremely knowledgeable, so come here if you're trying to track down something obscure.

(Cohen does mail-order business as well). 236 W. 26th St. (btwn 7th and 8th aves.), 8th floor. 🕐 212/675-4480. www.jazzrecordcenter.com. Subway: 1 or 9 to 28th St.

Kim's Video & Audio   This funky minichain is New York's underground alternative to Blockbuster Video, but they also stock a decent selection of indie vinyl and CDs as well as books and 'zines at Mondo Kim's, Kim's West, and Kim's Mediapolis. Kim's Video at 144 Bleecker St. (btwn Thompson St. and LaGuardia Place). 🕐 212/260-1010. Subway: A, C, E, F, V, or S to W. 4th St. Mondo Kim's at 6 St. Marks Place (btwn 2nd and 3rd aves.; 🕐 212/598-9985; subway: 6 to Astor Place); Kim's Mediapolis at 2906 Broadway (at 113th St.; 🕐 212/864-5321; subway: 1 or 9 to 110th St.).

Other Music *Finds*   Head to Other Music for the wildest sounds in town. You won't find a major label here (that's what Tower, across the street, is for). This shop focuses exclusively on small international labels, especially those on the cutting edge. The bizarro runs the gamut from underground Japanese spin doctors to obscure Irish folk; needless to say, the world music selection is terrific—fascinating and bound to be filled with music you've never heard of. The sales staff really knows their stuff, so ask away. 15 E. 4th St. (btwn Broadway and Lafayette St.). 🕐 212/477-8150. www.othermusic.com. Subway: F or V to Broadway/Lafayette St.; 6 to Astor Place.

Tower Records   At press time, this once mighty chain had filed for bankruptcy protection. It's long been my favorite music superstore, so I'm pulling for its survival. Both main locations are huge multimedia superstores brimming with an encyclopedic collection of music—classical, jazz, rock, world, you name it. The Village location also stocks a very good selection of indie and alternative labels. Just behind it at West 4th and Lafayette is **Tower Books and Video** (🕐 212/228-5100), where you'll find videos, books, and magazines (although the video selection isn't as good as you might expect). Look for in-stores by big names in music, usually advertised in the *Time Out New York* and *Village Voice.* 692 Broadway (at W. 4th St.). 🕐 212/505-1500. www.towerrecords.com. Subway: N or R to 8th St.; 6 to Astor Place. Also at 1961 Broadway (at 66th St.; 🕐 212/799-2500; subway: 1 or 9 to 66th St.).

Virgin Megastore   Right in the heart of Times Square, this superstore bustles day and night. For the size of it, the selection isn't as wide as you'd think; still, you're likely to find what you're looking for among the two levels of domestic and imported CDs and cassettes. Other plusses are an extensive singles department, a phenomenal number of listening posts, plus a huge video department. There's also a bookstore, a cafe, and a multiplex movie theater, and you can even arrange airfare on Virgin Atlantic with the on-site travel agent. As at Tower, look for a busy schedule of in-store appearances at both locations. 1540 Broadway (at 45th St.). 🕐 212/921-1020. www.virginmega.com. Subway: N, R, 1, 2, 3, 7, or 9 to Times Square/42nd St. Also at 52 E. 14th St. (at Broadway; 🕐 212/598-4666; subway: 4, 5, 6, N, R, or L to 14th St./Union Square).

SHOES

Designer shoe shops are on **East 57th Street** and up **Madison Avenue,** becoming pricier as you move uptown. **SoHo** is an excellent place to search; the streets are overrun with shoe stores, with **Broadway** below Houston between Spring and Canal streets the place to look for discount prices. Cheaper copies of the trendiest styles are sold in the shops along **8th Street** between Broadway and 6th Avenue in the Village, which some people call Shoe Row. Most department stores have two sizable shoe departments—one for designer stuff and one for daily wearables—and sales can be terrific. The women's shoe department at **Loehmann's** (p. 270) is well stocked and unbelievably priced.

Harry's Shoes ⭐ This shoe store was an Upper West Side institution even before gentrification hit the neighborhood over 20 years ago. They were one of the first shoe stores to carry New Balance in the city and now their selection of brands range from Bruno Magli to retro-Keds. With a huge selection of children's brands, Harry's is the place for kids' shoes which is why you should try to stay away, unless you don't mind parental hysteria, during the back-to-school frenzy of late August as well the pre-summer camp throngs that descend in late June. 2299 Broadway (at 83rd St.) ℂ **212/874-2035.** www.harrys-shoes.com. Subway: 1 or 9 to 86th St.

Sacco Mostly Italian-made women's shoes that cross style with supreme comfort. I especially love the fall and winter boots, which are comfortable enough to carry me around the city on even the most arduous of research days. Lots of terrific basic blacks and browns. Good prices and sales, too. 94 7th Ave. (btwn 15th and 16th sts.). ℂ **212/675-5180.** www.saccoshoes.com. Subway: 1 or 9 to 18th St. Also at 14 E. 17th St. (btwn 5th Ave. and Broadway; ℂ **212/243-2070;** subway: 4, 5, 6, N, R, L, S, Q, or W to 14th St./Union Square), 111 Thompson St. (btwn Prince and Spring sts.; ℂ **212/925-8010;** subway: C or E to Spring St.), 324 Columbus Ave. (btwn 75th and 76th sts.; ℂ **212/799-5229;** subway: B or C to 81st St.), and 2355 Broadway (at 86th St.; ℂ **212/874-8362;** subway: 1 or 9 to 86th St.).

Shoe Mania ⓥₐₗᵤₑ Another terrific discount shoe store for men and women; here, the emphasis is on style and comfort, with brands like Kenneth Cole, Dr. Martens, and Steve Madden dispersed among the Birkenstocks, Mephistos, and Joseph Siebels (great European comfort shoes). 853 Broadway (at 14th St.). ℂ **212/245-5260.** Subway: 4, 5, 6, N, R, L, S, Q, or W to 14th St./Union Square. Also at 331 Madison Ave. (btwn 42nd and 43rd sts.; ℂ **212/557-6627;** subway: 4, 5, 6, 7, or S to 42nd St./Grand Central).

Stapleton Shoe Company ⓥₐₗᵤₑ If Imelda Marcos had been a man, her first stop would have been this shoe store, next to the American Stock Exchange. Stapleton sells men's brands like Bally, Timberland, and Johnston & Murphy, all at discounts so deep it'll feel like insider trading. 68 Trinity Place (at Rector St.). ℂ **212/964-6329.** Subway: N or R to Rector St.

Tip Top Shoes If you find yourself discovering that the shoes you thought were so comfortable just aren't cutting it—trust me, it happens a lot—head over to Tip Top, New York's premier walking-shoe shop (since 1940). You'll find all of the top brands here for men and women, including Rockport, Mephisto, Dansko, Ecco, and hip Campers, plus tennies from New Balance and Puma. 155 W. 72nd St. (btwn Broadway and Columbus Ave.). ℂ **800/WALKING** or 212/787-4960. www.tiptopshoes.com. Subway: 1, 2, 3, or 9 to 72nd St.

SPORTING GOODS

Modell's ⭐ I confess, I, like the annoying ad says, "gotta go to Mo's." But there are good reasons for going to Mo's. The best is the very reasonable prices especially for sneakers and other footwear. Another is the excellent selection of team apparel; I can get my retro New York Giant football cap at half the price they sell it at Giants' Stadium. And there are stores in practically every neighborhood making it very convenient to go to Mo's. 1293 Broadway (at 33rd St.). ℂ **212/244-4544.** www.modells.com. Subway: B, D, F, V, N, or R to 34th St.). Also at 300 W. 125th St. (at Frederick Douglass Blvd.; ℂ **212/280-9100;** subway: A, C, B, or D to 125th St.), 51 E. 42nd St. (at Vanderbilt Ave.; ℂ **212/661-4242;** subway: 4, 5, 6, 7, or S to Grand Central), and 55 Chambers St. (at Broadway; ℂ **212/732-8484;** subway: E to Chambers St.).

Paragon Sporting Goods The emphasis at this excellent all-purpose sporting goods store—New York's best—is on equipment and athletic wear for virtually every sport, from tennis to biking to mountain climbing. End-of-the-season sales, especially on sneakers and outdoor clothing, bring serious discounts. 867 Broadway (at 18th St.). (℃ 800/961-3030 or 212/255-8036. www.paragonsports.com. Subway: L, N, R, 4, 5, or 6 to 14th St./Union Square.

Patagonia Expensive though it may be, Patagonia deserves kudos for its commitment to producing efficient and ecofriendly sports and adventure wear—fleece pullovers made from recycled plastic soda bottles, shell jackets in ultralight weatherproof materials, and organic cotton T-shirts. 101 Wooster St. (btwn Prince and Spring sts.). (℃ 212/343-1776. www.patagonia.com. Subway: N or R to Prince St.; C or E to Spring St. Also at 426 Columbus Ave. (btwn 80th and 81st sts.; (℃ 917/441-0011; subway: B or C to 81st St.).

TOYS

Enchanted Forest *Finds* Here's a shop for kids and grown-ups alike. This joyful shop overflows with stuffed animals and puppets, plus the kinds of simple but absorbing games that parents remember well from the days before PlayStation, like PickUp Sticks and Chinese Checkers. There's also a terrific book nook specializing in reissued classics like *The Phantom Toll Booth* and small-print children's and adult gift books—truly a special place. 85 Mercer St. (btwn Spring and Broome sts.). (℃ 212/925-6677. www.sohotoys.com. Subway: N or R to Prince St.

Kidding Around This boutique stocks pricey high-quality toys, many imported from Europe. The emphasis is on the old-fashioned—low-tech goodies like puzzles, rocking horses, and tops. One wall is devoted exclusively to tub toys, windups, and other stocking stuffers. 60 W. 15th St. (btwn 5th and 6th aves.). (℃ 212/645-6337. Subway: F to 14th St. Also at 68 Bleecker St. (btwn Broadway and Lafayette St.); (℃ 212/598-0228; subway: 6 to Bleecker St.).

Toys "R" Us 🟊 Occupying almost an entire city block in the heart of Times Square, this mammoth "Toys" even boasts its own full-scale Ferris wheel kids can ride for free. The huge collection is very well organized, and the store's "ambassadors" are abundant and very helpful; they'll even point you to restaurants and kid-friendly attractions in the neighborhood. Don't miss it if you're traveling with kids. 1514 Broadway (at 44th St.). (℃ 800/869-7787. Subway: 1, 2, 3, 7, or 9 to 42nd St. Also at 24–30 Union Sq. ((℃ 212/674-8697; subway: 4, 5, 6, N, R, L, or S to 14th St./Union Square).

WINE & SPIRITS

Astor Wines & Spirits *Value* This large store is the source for excellent values on liquor and wine; their stock is deep and diverse. The staff is always willing to recommend a vintage. Astor hosts excellent wine tastings two to three afternoons a week, often paired with edibles from local restaurants and gourmet shops; call or check the website for the schedule. 12 Astor Place (at Lafayette St.). (℃ 212/674-7500. www.astoruncorked.com. Subway: 6 to Astor Place.

Sherry-Lehmann Zagat's has called Sherry-Lehmann "the Rolls Royce" of wine shops, and if you are reading this book, you are asking yourself why is he recommending a wine shop that is the equivalent of a Rolls Royce? Well, we can all dream, and a visit to this store, which the readers of *Decanter* magazine have named as the best wine merchant in the United States is a treat unto itself. Their vast inventory is mind-boggling, service is excellent and there are often free wine tastings. 679 Madison Ave. (btwn 61st and 62nd sts.). (℃ 212/838-7500. www.sherry-lehmann. com. Subway: N or R to Lexington Ave.; 4, 5, or 6 to 59th St.

Union Square Wines and Spirits 🟊 *Finds* This small, cozy wine store squeezes in over 4,000 varieties of wines. There are numerous wine tastings throughout the week and recommendations by sommeliers from local restaurants. The store is ideally located across from the Union Square Greenmarket. If you have loaded up with fresh produce for a picnic, have the very personable clerks pair a wine with your food. 33 Union Sq. W. (btwn 15th and 16th sts.). © **212/675-8100.** www.unionsquarewines.com. Subway: L, N, R, 4, 5, or 6 to Union Square.

9

New York City After Dark

There's so much to see and do in New York at night that your biggest problem is going to be choosing among the many temptations.

There's no way that I can tell you what's going to be on while you're in town. For the latest, most comprehensive listings, from theater and performing arts to live rock, jazz, and dance-club coverage, *Time Out New York* (www.timeoutny.com) is my favorite source; a new issue hits newsstands every Thursday. The free weekly *Village Voice* (www.villagevoice.com) is available late Tuesday downtown and early Wednesday in the rest of the city. The arts and entertainment coverage is extensive. The *New York Times* (www.nytimes.com) features terrific entertainment coverage, particularly in the Friday "Weekend" section; the cabaret, classical-music, and theater guides are particularly useful. Other weekly sources are "Goings on About Town" in

the *New Yorker* (www.newyorker.com); and *New York* magazine, whose "Cue" features the latest happenings. *New York's* www.nymetro.com site is an excellent Web source.

Bar-hoppers shouldn't pass up the comprehensive annual *Shecky's New York Bar, Club & Lounge Guide.* Its website (http://newyork.sheckys.com) is even more current, and all the information is free. **Shecky's Bar Phone** at ✆ 212/777-BARS offers up-to-the minute nightlife news for the cost of a phone call.

NYC/Onstage (✆ 212/768-1818; www.tdf.org) is a recorded service providing schedules, descriptions, and details on theater and the performing arts. The bias is toward plays, but NYC/Onstage is a good source for music (including performances at Lincoln Center), dance, opera, cabaret, and family entertainment.

1 The Theater Scene

Nobody does theater better than New York. No other city—not even London—has a scene with so much breadth and depth, with so many alternatives. Broadway gets the most ink and airplay: This is where you'll find the big stage productions, from crowd-pleasers like *Phantom of the Opera* and *42nd Street* to newer phenomena like *Hairspray* and *Mamma Mia!* But today's scene thrives beyond the bounds of Broadway. With bankable stars on stage, crowds lining up for tickets, and hits popular enough to generate major-label cast albums, Off-Broadway isn't just for culture vultures anymore.

Despite this vitality, plays and musicals close all the time, often with little warning. Before you arrive, or even once you get here, check the **publications** and **websites** at the beginning of this chapter to get an idea of what you might like to see. One useful source is the **Broadway Line** (✆ 888/BROADWAY or 212/302-4111; www.broadway.org), where you can obtain details and descriptions on current Broadway shows, hear about special offers and discounts, and ultimately be transferred to TeleCharge or Ticketmaster to buy tickets. There's

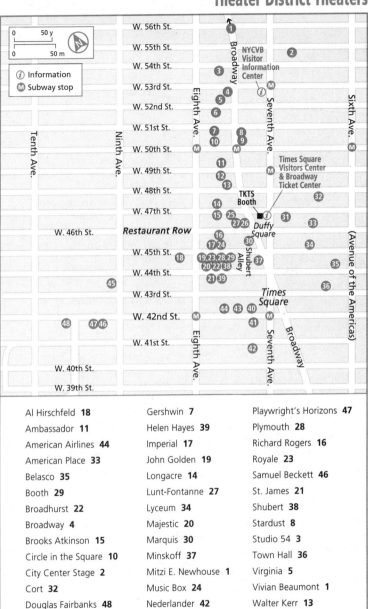

W. 56th St.
W. 55th St.
W. 54th St.
W. 53rd St.
W. 52nd St.
W. 51st St.
W. 50th St.
W. 49th St.
W. 48th St.
W. 47th St.
W. 46th St.
Restaurant Row
W. 45th St.
W. 44th St.
W. 43rd St.
W. 42nd St.
W. 41st St.
W. 40th St.
W. 39th St.

Broadway
Eighth Ave.
Seventh Ave.
Sixth Ave.
Tenth Ave.
Ninth Ave.
(Avenue of the Americas)
Broadway

NYCVB Visitor Information Center
Times Square Visitors Center & Broadway Ticket Center
TKTS Booth
Duffy Square
Shubert Alley
Times Square

0   50 y
0   50 m

ⓘ Information
Ⓜ Subway stop

Al Hirschfeld **18**
Ambassador **11**
American Airlines **44**
American Place **33**
Belasco **35**
Booth **29**
Broadhurst **22**
Broadway **4**
Brooks Atkinson **15**
Circle in the Square **10**
City Center Stage **2**
Cort **32**
Douglas Fairbanks **48**
Duffy **26**
Ethel Barrymore **25**
Eugene O'Neill **12**
Ford Center for the Performing Arts **43**

Gershwin **7**
Helen Hayes **39**
Imperial **17**
John Golden **19**
Longacre **14**
Lunt-Fontanne **27**
Lyceum **34**
Majestic **20**
Marquis **30**
Minskoff **37**
Mitzi E. Newhouse **1**
Music Box **24**
Nederlander **42**
Neil Simon **6**
New Amsterdam **41**
New Victory **40**
Palace **31**

Playwright's Horizons **47**
Plymouth **28**
Richard Rogers **16**
Royale **23**
Samuel Beckett **46**
St. James **21**
Shubert **38**
Stardust **8**
Studio 54 **3**
Town Hall **36**
Virginia **5**
Vivian Beaumont **1**
Walter Kerr **13**
WestSide **45**
Winter Garden **9**

Kids   Kids Take the Stage: Family-Friendly Theater

The family-friendly theater scene is flourishing. There's so much going on that it's best to check *New York* magazine, *Time Out New York,* or the Friday *New York Times* for current listings. Besides Broadway shows, the following are some dependable—and cheaper—entertainment options.

The **New Victory Theater,** 209 W. 42nd St. (btwn 7th and 8th aves.; ℭ 646/252-1619; www.newvictory.org), is the city's first full-time family-oriented performing-arts center and has hosted companies ranging from the Trinity Irish Dance Company to the Flaming Idiots, who juggle everything from fire and swords to bean-bag chairs.

The **Paper Bag Players** (ℭ 212/663-0390; www.paperbagplayers.org), called "the best children's theater in the country" by *Newsweek,* perform funny tales for children 4 to 9 in a set made from bags and boxes, in winter only, at Hunter College's Sylvia and Danny Kaye Playhouse, 68th Street between Park and Lexington avenues (ℭ 212/772-4448). You can also call to inquire whether they'll be staging other performances about town.

TADA! Youth Theater, 120 W. 28th St. (btwn 6th and 7th aves; ℭ 212/627-1732; www.tadatheater.com), is a youth ensemble that performs musicals and plays for kids, teens, and their families.

The **Swedish Cottage Marionette Theatre** (ℭ 212/988-9093; www.centralpark.org) puts on marionette shows for kids at its 19th-century Central Park theater throughout the year. Reservations are a must.

The World Voices Club at the **New Perspectives Theatre,** 750 8th Ave. (btwn 46th and 47th sts.; ℭ 212/730-2030; www.newperspectives theatre.org), presents a new puppet show each month based on fables from various world cultures.

While David Mamet hardly seems like a playwright for the kiddies, the "Atlantic for Kids" series is at the **Atlantic Theater Company,** 453 16th St. (btwn 9th and 10th aves.; ℭ 212/645-8015; www.atlantictheater.org),

also **NYC/Onstage** (ℭ 212/768-1818; www.tdf.org), providing the same kind of service for Broadway and Off-Broadway productions. (Don't buy tickets, though, until you read "Top Ticket-Buying Tips," below.)

Many top stars are heading for the New York stage these days: In recent seasons you could have seen stars like Hugh Jackman, Sean "Puffy" Combs, Antonio Banderas, Kathleen Turner, Patrick Stewart, and Kevin Bacon onstage. But keep in mind that stars' runs are often short, and tickets go fast. If you hear there's an actor you like on the New York stage, check with the box office to find out how long they'll be in the part, or if there are certain performances they don't do (like matinees), before you nail down your travel plans.

THE BASICS

LOCATIONS   Broadway, Off-Broadway, and Off-Off-Broadway refer to theater size, pay, and other arcane details, not location—or, these days, even star wattage. Most of the Broadway theaters are in Times Square, around the thoroughfare for which the scene is named, but not on it: You'll find them on the

which Mamet founded with actor William H. Macy. Another excellent troupe that excels at children's theater is the **Vital Theatre Company,** 432 W. 42nd St. (btwn 9th and 10th aves.; (C) **212/268-2040;** www.vital theatre.org); it's well worth seeing what's on.

If you want to introduce your kids to live opera, check out the "Opera in Brief" program, which runs most Saturdays at 11:30am, at **Amato Opera** (p. 297). For kid-friendly classical music, see what's on at **Bargemusic** (p. 298), which presents chamber-music concerts for kids throughout their season. Look for Young People's Concerts and Kid-zone Live!, in which kids get to interact with orchestra members prior to curtain time, at the **New York Philharmonic** (p. 299). Also check to see what's on at **Carnegie Hall** (p. 302), which offers family concerts for a bargain-basement ticket price of just $5, plus the CarnegieKids program, which introduces kids ages 3 to 6 to basic musical concepts through a 45-minute music-and-storytelling performance. Finally, don't forget "Jazz for Young People," Wynton Marsalis's stellar family concert series at **Jazz at Lincoln Center** (p. 303).

Money-saving tip: High 5 Tickets to the Arts ((C) **212/HI-5-TKTS;** www.high5tix.org) makes theater more accessible for kids 13 to 18. Teens can buy donated tickets for select theatrical performances for $5 each at weekend performances, or $5 for two (for the teen and a guest of any age) for Monday-through-Thursday shows. High 5 also offers discount museum passes at the wallet-friendly price of two for $5 (for the teen and a guest of any age). Check out the website for details on theater or museum tickets, which can usually be purchased with proof of age at any New York City Ticketmaster outlet or online. Also check the High 5 website for listings of free and nearly free events going on while you and your teen are in town.

side streets mostly in the mid-40s between 6th and 8th avenues, running north as far as 53rd Street. There's even a Broadway theater outside Times Square: the Vivian Beaumont in Lincoln Center, at Broadway and 65th Street.

The location of "Off-Broadway," on the other hand, is not that exacting. With the popularization of off-the-beaten-track productions, the distinction between Off- and Off-Off-Broadway has become fuzzier (with the major differences ticket prices, the size of the theater, and the days/number of performances per week). Off-Off-Broadway shows can be more avant-garde and experimental; they're often in intimate spaces with fewer than 100 seats.

TIMETABLES   Broadway shows tend to keep regular schedules. There are usually eight performances a week: evening shows Tuesday through Saturday, plus matinees on Wednesday, Saturday, and Sunday. Evening shows are usually at 8pm, while matinees are usually at 2pm Wednesday and Saturday, and 3pm Sunday. But schedules can vary. Shows usually start on the dot; if you arrive late, you may have to wait until intermission to take your seat.

Value How to Save on Theater Tickets

If you employ a little patience, flexibility, and know-how, there are ways to pay less than full price for your theater tickets—sometimes a lot less.

For Advance Planners Your best bet is to try before you go. You might be able to purchase **reduced-price theater tickets** over the phone (or in person at the box office) by joining one or more of the online theater clubs. Membership is free and can garner you discounts of up to 50% on select Broadway and Off-Broadway shows. The deals are available to registered club members at **Broadway.com (www.broadway.com)**, **Playbill Online (www.playbill.com** or www.playbillclub.com), and **TheaterMania (www.theatermania.com)**. You can sign up to be notified by e-mail as offers change. I like the **Playbill Club** ⚡ best; its discounts tend to be the most wide-ranging, often including the best Broadway and Off-Broadway shows. TheaterMania's **TM Insider** is the runner-up, and offers the most varied range of Off- and Off-Off-Broadway. Nothing prevents you from signing up with all of them and taking advantage of the best deals.

You can sign up with the **Hit Show Club** (℗ **212/581-4211;** www.hit showclub.com), a free subscription club that offers its members discounts to Broadway and Off-Broadway shows. Once you sign up, you can find offers online or stop by their offices at 630 9th Ave. (btwn 44th and 45th sts.), eighth floor (Mon–Fri 9am–4pm), and pick up discount coupons for theater, dining, and attractions. I recommend calling the info line or checking the website before you leave. One advantage of the website is that it will let you "bid" on tickets for the Broadway and Off-Broadway shows in which you're interested. Maybe you can tell the folks back home how you scored *Phantom* tickets for just 20 bucks!

The Theatre Development Fund, which operates the TKTS same-day discount-ticket booth (see below), also runs the **TDF Voucher** program, which gives participants dirt-cheap access to a world of cutting-edge theater and performing arts that even most New Yorkers don't know about. Sign up for $28, and you'll get four vouchers that you can use at any number of events that will be on while you're in town: theater, ballet, light opera, dance, and more. That's $7 a ticket—cheaper than a movie! You can order your vouchers online at the TDF website (**www.tdf. org;** click on "TDF Programs," then "TDF Vouchers"), where you'll be able to review a list of current ongoing events that accept vouchers before you buy.

If You're Already Here The best deal on same-day tickets for Broadway and Off-Broadway shows is the **Times Square Theatre Centre,** better known as the **TKTS** booth run by the nonprofit Theatre Development Fund at Duffy Square, 47th Street and Broadway (3–8pm for evening performances, 10am–2pm for Wed and Sat matinees, from 11am on Sun for all performances). Tickets for that day's performances are usually offered at half-price, with a few reduced 25%, plus a $2.50 per ticket service charge. Boards outside the ticket windows list available shows; you're unlikely to find the biggest hits, but most other shows turn up. Only cash and traveler's checks are accepted (no credit cards). There's often a line, so show up early for the best availability and be prepared to wait—but the crowd is part of the fun. If you don't have a specific show in mind, you can walk up to the window later in the day and something is always available. Sometimes representatives from Off- and Off-Off-Broadway shows that aren't listed offer discount flyers to the people waiting in line.

Run by the same group and offering the same discounts is the **TKTS Downtown Theatre Centre,** at South Street Seaport (Mon–Fri 11am–5:30pm, Sat 11am–3:30pm; subway: 2, 3, 4, 5, E, J, Z, or M to Fulton St.; A or C to Broadway-Nassau). All the same policies apply. The advantages to coming down here are that the lines are generally shorter, and matinee tickets are available the day before, so you can plan ahead.

Visit **www.tdf.org** or call **NYC/Onstage** at © **212/768-1818** and press "8" for the latest TKTS information.

Many shows, particularly long-running ones such as *Cabaret* and *Phantom of the Opera,* offer **twofers,** which allow you to purchase two tickets for the price of one for certain performances. You can find these coupons at many places in the city: hotel lobbies, in banks, in shops, even at restaurant cash registers. They'll definitely be found at the **Times Square Visitors Center,** 1560 Broadway (btwn 46th and 47th sts.; © **212/768-1560**). They're also available at the **NYCVB Visitor Information Center** at 810 7th Ave. (btwn 52nd and 53rd sts.; © **212/484-1222**); and at the information window on the main concourse of **Grand Central Terminal,** East 42nd Street at Vanderbilt Avenue, near the ticket-purchase windows directly across from the information kiosk.

For Theater Fans Willing to Go the Extra Mile   Broadway shows—even blockbusters—sometimes have a limited number of tickets set aside for **students and seniors,** and they might be available at the last minute. Make sure you have ID. Also, some Off-Broadway houses make "rush" seats available to students 30 minutes to an hour before curtain. On Broadway, *Rent* has offered all kinds of bargains to keep younger theatergoers coming. Call the box office of the show in which you're interested to inquire about their discount policies.

If you don't mind staying on your feet, you can save big bucks—and often gain access to sold-out shows—with **standing-room** tickets, offered by many (but not all) Broadway shows. A limited number are usually sold on the day of show, and cost between $10 and $20. Call the box office in advance and they can fill you in on their standing-room policy.

Some Off- and Off-Off Broadway shows, including such fetching performances as the Blue Man Group, will let you see the show for free if you're willing to be an **usher.** This requires some advance legwork and willingness to put in extra hours, but it can pay off for theater fans on shoestring budgets. Again, inquire with the theater directly.

There are so many options for getting cut-rate tickets that any visitor can fill up a week with cheap shows. But there's never any guarantee that last-minute tickets or discounts will be available to a specific show. If there's one you absolutely *must* see, splurge on full-price advance-purchase tickets.

Tips **Where to Find the Drama: Resident Theaters**

When you want a spectacle, there's no place like Broadway: For heli-
copters, dozens of tap dancing chorines, and collapsing chandeliers,
Broadway is your ticket (and a very high-priced one it is, too!).

You can see some amazing work at prices ranging from just-below-
Broadway to less than $20 if you know where to look. For Off-Broad-
way, expect to pay $20 to $60 or so for tickets; Off-Off-Broadway rarely
charges more than $20, and you can sometimes get in for $12 or less
(so you don't feel quite as bad leaving at intermission if the show's a
stinker!).

The theaters mentioned here are just the tip of the iceberg; new
companies pop up all the time, while other companies don't have a
regular production schedule but put on a play when they have the
funding or space.

Where do you find the hidden gems? *The Village Voice* (which sponsors the annual Obie Awards) is a good source. *Timeout New York* has
excellent listings and capsule descriptions for major Off-Broadway
productions. For Off-Off-Broadway, check the reviews on **Theaterma-
nia.com** (which also lets you purchase tickets and offers regular discounts) and **The Off-Off Broadway Review** (www.oobr.com), which
also gives awards to the best productions each season.

Three resident theaters in New York—**Lincoln Center Theater** (p. 303),
the **Roundabout Theatre** (www.roundabouttheatre.org), and **Manhattan Theatre Club** (www.mtc-nyc.org)—present work in Broadway houses,
as well as in smaller venues Off-Broadway. You'll pay Broadway prices
(or whatever discount you can get on TKTS) for the best seats in the big
houses, but you can also usually find special, lower prices for students or
seniors; or last-minute rush tickets.

In their smaller spaces (MTC's Stage II; the Roundabout's Laura Pels
Theatre; Lincoln Center's Mitzi Newhouse) you can find good seats for
less than $50 to see new plays and revivals by the likes of Terence
McNally and John Patrick Shanley, and actors like Laura Linney, Cherry
Jones, Adam Arkin, and Mary Louise Parker.

These theaters and some of the others listed below also offer extra
events like play readings, "talkbacks" with the cast and production
team, and so on—sometimes free, sometimes for a small charge.

TICKET PRICES Ticket prices for Broadway shows vary dramatically. The
high end for any given show is likely to be between $60 and $100, or higher.
The cheapest end of the price range can be as low as $20 or as high as $50,
depending on the theater. If you're buying tickets at the low end of a wide range,
be aware that you may be buying obstructed-view seats. If all tickets are the same
price or the range is small, you can pretty much count on all of the seats being
pretty good. Otherwise, price is your barometer. Legroom can be tight in these
old theaters, and you'll usually get more in the orchestra seats.

Off-Broadway and Off-Off-Broadway shows tend to be cheaper, with tickets
often as low as $10 or $15. In fact, experimental theaters like the award-winning
downtown multi-arts venue **HERE,** 145 6th Ave. (just below Spring St.;

A few of the other Off-Broadway theaters that tend to send their hits to Broadway and garner lots of accolades include:

- The **Joseph Papp Public Theater** ✿, 425 Lafayette St. ((℗ **212/539-8900;** www.publictheater.org; subway: 6 to Astor Place), offers free Shakespeare in the Park (p. 304) and has several performance spaces, including one of the best small music venues in town (Joe's Pub), in the former Astor library. The Public has collected Tonys and Pulitzers, as well as Obies (the Off-Broadway awards) for decades, dating from *A Chorus Line.* Discounted rush tickets are available a half-hour before curtain time to any non-sold-out show, and there are also many free and low-priced events scheduled throughout the season.

- The **Atlantic Theater Company,** 336 W. 20th St. (btwn 8th and 9th aves.; (℗ **212/645-8015;** www.atlantictheater.com; subway: A, C, or E to 23rd St.), "produces great plays simply and truthfully, utilizing an artistic ensemble," according to its mission statement. It's recently presented new work by Woody Allen, Keith Reddin, and Tina Howe's Ionesco translations. It also accepts volunteer ushers.

- **Signature Theatre Company,** 555 W. 42nd St. (btwn 10th and 11th aves.; ((℗ **212/244-PLAY;** www.signaturetheatre.org; subway: A, C, or E to 42nd St.), presents season-long explorations of a living playwright's body of work. In 2004–05, it's Paula Vogel *(How I Learned to Drive).* You can also volunteer usher here.

- **New York Theater Workshop (NYTW),** 79 E. 4th St. (btwn 2nd Ave. and The Bowery; (℗ **212/460-5475;** www.nytw.org; subway: 6 to Astor Place, F or V to Broadway-Lafayette), has been around since 1979, but it was *Rent* (and later, *Dirty Blonde*) that put it on the map. NYTW specializes in new work, rethought revivals (I've never seen Hedda Gabler done *that* way before . . .), and collaborations. All Sunday evening performances are $20; there are discounts for students and opportunities to usher.

- The **Keen Company** ((℗ **212/216-0963;** www.keencompany.org) has a mandate to produce "sincere plays" under the direction of Artistic Director Carl Forsman, who has an eye for old pieces that gleam anew with a heartfelt production.

(℗ **212/647-0202;** www.here.org), offer performances at prices that range from free to $17. However, seats for the most established shows and those with star power can command prices as high as $50 or $60.

Don't let price be a deterrent to enjoying the theater. There are ways to pay less if you're willing to make the effort and be flexible, with a few choices at hand as to what you'd like to see. Read on.

TOP TICKET-BUYING TIPS

BEFORE YOU LEAVE HOME   If you want to guarantee yourself a seat at a particular show by buying tickets in advance, it's almost impossible to get around paying full price. (The only exception is to register for one or more of the online theater clubs, which may offer advance-purchase discounts to members; see "How to Save on Theater Tickets," above.) Phone ahead or go online for tickets to the most successful or popular shows as far in advance as you can—in the case of shows like *The Lion King,* it's never too early.

Buying tickets can be simple, if the show you want to see isn't sold out. You need only call such general numbers as **TeleCharge** (© 212/239-6200; www.telecharge.com), which handles most Broadway and Off-Broadway shows and some concerts; or **Ticketmaster** (© 212/307-4100; www.ticketmaster.com), which also handles Broadway and Off-Broadway shows and most concerts.

Theatre Direct International (TDI) is a ticket broker that sells tickets to select Broadway and Off-Broadway shows—including some of the most popular crowd-pleasers, like *Avenue Q!* and *Wicked*—directly to individuals and travel agents. Check to see if they have seats to the shows you're interested in by calling © 800/BROADWAY or 212/541-8457; you can also order tickets through TDI via its commercial website, **www.broadway.com**. (Disregard the discounted prices, unless you're buying for a group of 20 or more.) Because there's a minimum service charge of $15 per ticket, you'll definitely do better by trying Ticketmaster or TeleCharge first; but because they act as a consolidator, TDI may have tickets left for a specific show even if the major outlets don't.

Other reputable ticket brokers include **Keith Prowse & Co.** (© 800/669-8687; www.keithprowse.com) and **Global Tickets Edwards & Edwards** (© 800/223-6108). For a list of other licensed ticket brokers recommended by the New York Convention & Visitors Bureau, get a copy of the Official NYC Visitor Kit (see "Visitor Information" in chapter 2 for details). All kinds of ticket brokers list ads in the Sunday *New York Times* and other publications, but don't take the risk. Stick with a licensed broker recommended by the NYCVB.

You may have heard about a new development on the Broadway ticket scene: **Broadway Inner Circle** (© 866/847-8587; www.broadwayinnercircle.com), the ticket agency that, in a supposed effort to circumvent scalpers, has arranged with select in-demand shows to sell select premium seats for prices close to $500 a ticket. If price is no object, you might want to try this service.

If you don't want to pay even a service charge, try calling the **box office** directly. Broadway theaters don't sell tickets over the telephone—the one major exception, the **Roundabout Theatre Company** (© 212/719-1300; www.roundabout theatre.org), charges a $5-per-ticket "convenience" fee—but a good number of Off-Broadway theaters do.

WHEN YOU ARRIVE Once you arrive, getting your hands on good tickets can take some smarts—and failing those, cash. Even if it seems unlikely that seats are available, always **call the box office** first. Single seats are often easiest to obtain, so people willing to sit apart may find themselves in luck.

You should also try the **Broadway Ticket Center,** run by the League of American Theaters and Producers at the Times Square Visitors Center, 1560 Broadway (btwn 46th and 47th sts.; Mon–Sat 9am–7pm, Sun 10am–6pm). They often have tickets available for otherwise sold-out shows, both for advance and same-day purchase, and charge about $5 extra per ticket.

If you buy from one of the **scalpers** selling tickets in front of the theater, you're taking a risk. They may be legit—a couple from the burbs whose companions couldn't make it for the evening, say—but they could be swindlers passing off fakes for big money. It's a risk that's not worth taking.

One preferred **insiders' trick** is to make the rounds of Broadway theaters at about 5 or 6pm, when unclaimed house seats are made available to the public.

These tickets—reserved for VIPs, friends of the cast, the press, and so on—offer great seats and are sold at face value without service charge.

Also, note that **Monday** is often a good day to cop big-name tickets. Though most theaters are dark that day, some of the most sought-after choices aren't. Locals are at home the first night of the workweek, so all the odds are in your favor. Your chances will always be better on weeknights, or for Wednesday matinees.

2 Opera, Classical Music & Dance

In addition to the listings below, see what's on at **Carnegie Hall** and the **Brooklyn Academy of Music,** two of the most respected—and enjoyable—performing-arts venues in the city. The **92nd Street Y** also hosts lots of arts events, usually at low prices. I've listed the operatic and symphonic companies at **Lincoln Center;** also check the center's calendar for all offerings. See "Major Concert Halls & Landmark Venues," later in this chapter.

OPERA

In addition to the choices below, you might want to see what's on from the **New York Grand Opera** (© 212/245-8837; www.newyorkgrandopera.org), which puts on free Verdi productions at Central Park's SummerStage (p. 304) as well as workshop programs throughout the year.

Fans with an ear for experimentalism might check out **American Opera Projects** (© 718/398-4024; www.aopinc.org), which develops new American operas and other projects and showcases them at venues around town. Tickets generally run $25 to $30, and discounts may be available for students and seniors.

Amato Opera Theatre _(Value_   This cozy, off-the-beaten-track venue functions as a showcase for talented young American singers. The intimate 100-plus-seat house celebrated its 57th season in 2004 amid a rising reputation and increasing ticket sales. The staple is full productions of Italian classics—Verdi's _La Traviata,_ Puccini's _Madame Butterfly,_ Bizet's _Carmen,_ with an occasional Mozart tossed in—at great prices. Performances, usually held on Saturday and Sunday, now regularly sell out, so it's a good idea to reserve 3 weeks in advance.

**Attention moms and dads:** On one Saturday a month, "Opera in Brief" offers fully costumed, kid-length versions of the classics with narration so Mom and Dad have a forum in which to introduce the little ones to opera. At $15 or so per ticket, these matinees are wallet-friendly, too. 319 Bowery (at 2nd St.). © 212/228-8200. www. amato.org. Tickets $30 adults, $25 seniors and kids. Subway: F to 2nd Ave.; 6 to Bleecker St.

Metropolitan Opera   Tickets can cost a fortune—but for its full productions of the classic repertory and schedule packed with world-class singers, the Met ranks first in the world. Millions are spent on fabulous stagings of new works and repertory favorites, and the venue itself is a wonder of acoustics. To guarantee that its audience understands the words, the Met has outfitted the back of each row of seats with screens for subtitles—translation help for those who want it, minimum intrusion for those who don't. James Levine is the brilliant and popular conductor of the orchestra.

The Met has a number of programs that allow access to cut-rate tickets; for details, see "Lincoln Center Alert: Last-Minute & Discount Ticket-Buying Tips" (p. 300). At the Metropolitan Opera House, Lincoln Center, Broadway and 64th St. © 212/362-6000. www.metopera.org. Tickets $25–$295. Subway: 1 or 9 to 66th St.

New York City Opera   The New York City Opera is a superb company, with a delightful duality to its approach: It not only attempts to reach a wider audience than the Met with its more "human" scale and significantly lower prices, but it's also committed to adventurous premieres, newly composed operas, the occasional avant-garde work, American musicals *(Porgy and Bess)* and novels *(Of Mice and Men)* presented as fresh, innovative operettas, and even obscure works by mainstream or lesser-known composers. Its mix stretches from the "easy" works of Puccini, Verdi, and Gilbert and Sullivan to the more challenging oeuvres of the likes of Arnold Schönberg and Philip Glass. At the New York State Theater, Lincoln Center, Broadway and 64th St. ✆ 212/870-5570 (information or box office), or 212/307-4100 for Ticketmaster. www.nycopera.com or www.ticketmaster.com. Tickets $25–$100. Subway: 1 or 9 to 66th St.

New York Gilbert and Sullivan Players If you're in the mood for light-hearted operetta, try this lively company, which specializes in Gilbert and Sullivan's 19th-century English comic works. The annual calendar generally runs from October through April and includes four shows a year, with some performances held at **City Center** (p. 299). Tickets are affordable. At Symphony Space, Broadway and 95th St. ✆ 212/864-5400 or 212/769-1000. www.nygasp.org. Tickets $40–$85. Subway: 1, 2, 3, or 9 to 96th St.

CLASSICAL MUSIC

Bargemusic *Moments* Many thought Olga Bloom peculiar when she transformed a 40-year-old barge into a chamber-music concert hall. More than 20 years later, Bargemusic is an internationally renowned recital room boasting more than 100 chamber-music performances a year. The musicians perform on a small stage in a cherry-paneled, fireplace-lit room accommodating 130. The barge may creak a bit and an occasional boat may speed by, but the music rivals

---

Value **Bargain Alert: The Classical Learning Curve**

The **Juilliard School,** 60 Lincoln Center Plaza, Broadway at 65th Street (✆ 212/799-5000 or 212/721-0965; www.juilliard.edu), the nation's premier music-education institution, sponsors about 550 performances of high quality—at low prices—throughout the school year. With most concerts free and $20 as a maximum, Juilliard is one of New York's great cultural bargains. Though most would assume that the school presents only classical music, Juilliard offers other music as well as drama, dance, opera, and interdisciplinary works. The best way to find out about the wide array of productions is to call, visit the website (click on "Calendar of Events"), or consult the bulletin board in the building's lobby. Watch for master classes and discussions open to the public featuring celebrity guest teachers.

The **Manhattan School of Music,** at Broadway and 122nd Street (✆ 212/749-2802, ext. 4428; www.msmnyc.edu), hosts student concerts as well as daily recitals during the academic year. Most performances are free, and the top ticket price is usually $15. In addition to orchestral and chamber music, the school is highly regarded for its contemporary music and jazz as well as musical theater programs, so performances run the gamut. Look for free master classes, too. Call the box office weekdays between 9am and 5pm for the latest schedule, or check the website (click on "Concert Calendar"); tickets are usually required even for free events, so plan ahead.

what you'll find in almost any other New York venue—and the panoramic view through the glass wall behind the stage can't be beat. There are three shows per week, on Thursday and Friday evenings at 7:30pm and Sunday afternoon at 4pm. Reserve well in advance. At Fulton Ferry Landing (just south of the Brooklyn Bridge), Brooklyn. 𝄐 **718/624-2083** or 718/624-4061. www.bargemusic.org. Tickets $35 ($25 students), $40 for performances by larger ensembles. Subway: 2 or 3 to Clark St.; A or C to High St.

New York Philharmonic   Symphony-wise, you'd be hard-pressed to do better than the New York Philharmonic. The country's oldest orchestra is now under the guidance of distinguished conductor Lorin Maazel, formerly of the Bavarian Radio Symphony Orchestra. Don't expect quality to falter one bit. There's a summer season in July, when themed classics brighten the hall, as well as free summer concerts in Central Park that are worth checking into.

Opt for a rush-hour concert or a matinee for the lowest across-the-board prices. If you can afford it—and if the tickets are available—it's well worth it to pay for prime seats. The acoustics of the hall are such that, at the midrange price points, I prefer the second tier (especially the boxes) over the more expensive rear orchestra seats. Go cheap if you have to; you're sure to enjoy the program from any vantage. At Avery Fisher Hall, Lincoln Center, Broadway at 65th St. 𝄐 **212/875-5656** for audience services, 212/875-5030 for box office information, or Center Charge at 212/721-6500 for tickets. www.newyorkphilharmonic.org. Tickets $36–$68. Subway: 1 or 9 to 66th St.

DANCE

In addition to the troupes below, some other venues to keep in mind are the **Brooklyn Academy of Music,** the **92nd Street Y, Radio City Music Hall,** and **Town Hall** (see "Major Concert Halls & Landmark Venues," below).

For innovative works, see what's on at the **Dance Theater Workshop,** in the Bessie Schönberg Theater, 219 W. 19th St. (btwn 7th and 8th aves.; 𝄐 **212/691-6500** or 212/924-0077; www.dtw.org), a first-rate launching pad for nearly a quarter-century; and **Danspace Project,** at St. Mark's Church, 131 E. 10th St. (btwn 2nd and 3rd aves.; 𝄐 **212/674-8112** or 212/674-8194; www.danspaceproject.org), whose performances lean toward the avant-garde, with ticket prices usually falling between free and $15, depending on the performance.

In addition to regular appearances at City Center (see below), the **American Ballet Theatre** (www.abt.org) is in residence at Lincoln Center's Metropolitan Opera House (𝄐 **212/477-3030**) for 8 weeks each spring. The same venue also hosts such visiting companies as the Kirov, Royal, and Paris Opéra ballets.

The weekly *Time Out New York,* available on newsstands, maintains a section dedicated to dance events around town that's an invaluable resource to fans.

City Center   Modern dance usually takes center stage in this Moorish dome-topped performing-arts palace. The companies of Merce Cunningham, Martha Graham, Paul Taylor, Alvin Ailey, Twyla Tharp, the Dance Theatre of Harlem (in residence in Sept, and celebrating its 30th year this season), and the American Ballet Theatre are often on the calendar. Don't expect cutting edge—but do expect excellence. Sightlines are terrific from all corners, and a new acoustical shell means the sound is pitch-perfect, so you won't lose out with cheaper tickets. City Center also presents a limited program schedule at the Cathedral of St. John the Divine (p. 225) at lower-than-average ticket prices ($15–$50). 131 W. 55th St. (btwn 6th and 7th aves.). 𝄐 **877/581-1212** or 212/581-1212. www.citycenter.org. Tickets $25–$80, depending on the performance. Subway: F, N, R, Q, or W to 57th St.; B, D, or E to 7th Ave.

Joyce Theater   Housed in an old Art Deco movie house, the Joyce has grown into a modern dance institution. You can see everything from Native American

(Value) Lincoln Center Alert: Last-Minute & Discount Ticket-Buying Tips

Most seats at **New York Philharmonic** performances are sold to subscribers, but there are ways to get tickets.

When subscribers can't attend, they may return their tickets to the theaters, which resell them at the last moment. These can be in the most coveted rows of the orchestra. Ticket holders can return tickets until curtain time, so tickets that are not available in the morning may be available (at full price) later in the day. The hopefuls form "cancellation lines" 2 hours or more before curtain time for a crack at returned tickets.

Periodically, some **same-day orchestra tickets** are set aside at the philharmonic, and sold in the morning for $25 (maximum two). They usually go on sale at 10am weekdays, 1pm Saturday (noon if there's a matinee).

Senior/student/disabled rush tickets may be available for $10 (maximum two) on concert day, but never at Friday matinees or Saturday-evening performances. To check availability for any of these programs at all performances, call **Audience Services** at ✆ **212/875-5656.**

You're also invited to watch the Philharmonic at work by attending an **Open Rehearsal** for just $14. Not only is this a bargain-basement way to see a great orchestra, it's fascinating to watch how the conductor and musicians shape a piece. If you're the sort of person who loves glimpses behind the scenes, this is a real treat. There are usually 30 or so of these each season; call Audience Services or check the website for the schedule.

Families with teenagers can participate in **Phil Teens,** which allows you and your teen between the ages of 12 and 17 to attend a New York Philharmonic Rush Hour Concert for just $10 each. Rush Hour concerts start at 6:45pm and last an hour. Your Phil Teen ticket also allows you to arrive as early at 5:30pm to meet guest artists, soloists, and special guests.

Lincoln Center's **Alice Tully Hall** (where the Chamber Music Society performs and other concerts are held), **Jazz at Lincoln Center,** the

dance to the works of Pilobolus to the Martha Graham Dance Company. In residence annually is Eliot Feld's company, Ballet Tech, which WQXR radio's Francis Mason called "better than a whole month of namby-pamby classical ballets." The Joyce has a second space, the **Joyce SoHo,** where you can see rising young dancers and experimental works in a 70-seat performance space. 175 8th Ave. (at 19th St.). ✆ **212/242-0800.** www.joyce.org. Tickets usually $38 at the main theater, $15 at SoHo location. Subway: C or E to 23rd St.; 1 or 9 to 18th St. Joyce SoHo at 155 Mercer St. (btwn Houston and Prince sts.; ✆ **212/431-9233;** subway: N or R to Prince St.).

New York City Ballet Highly regarded for its unsurpassed technique, the New York City Ballet is the world's best. The company renders with happy regularity the works of two of America's most important choreographers: George Balanchine, its founder, and Jerome Robbins. Under the direction of Ballet Master in Chief Peter Martins, the troupe continues to expand its repertoire and performs to a wide variety of classical and modern music. The cornerstone of the annual season is the

Metropolitan Opera, and the New York City Opera offer last-minute-purchase and discount programs, as do Carnegie Hall and the Brooklyn Academy of Music. Policies differ; for instance, the New York City Ballet offers Student Rush tickets only, at $10 a pop, while the New York City Opera allows students to buy tickets a week in advance at half-price ($13–$53), as well as offering same-day rush tickets (Rush Hot Line: ℂ 212/870-5630). In addition to senior and student rush tickets, Carnegie Hall offers some limited-view tickets for $10 (on sale Sat at 11am for the week's upcoming performances), and presents some totally free events through its neighborhood concert series. Check with the venue directly for details on their specific programs. And call the box office first to check on same-day availability before heading to the theater—or, if you're willing to risk coming away empty-handed, be there at opening time (or before) for first crack.

The Met Opera offers standing-room tickets for $12 to $16, which can be a bargain for budget-minded fans. It's not a bad situation, because you get to lean against plush red bars. (Don't tell the ushers I told you, but if subscribers fail to show, I've seen standees with eagle eyes fill the empty seats at intermission.) Wheelchair-access standing-room places are also available. Tickets go on sale Saturday at 10am for the following week's performances (Sat–Fri). The line sometimes forms much earlier, so plan ahead. Keep in mind that special performances may not be available to potential standees. Call ℂ 212/362-6000 for details. It never hurts to inquire about standing-room availability at other venues as well.

Summer visitors should also keep in mind that both the Philharmonic and the Met Opera offer free concerts in the parks throughout the five boroughs, including Central Park, in July and August. For the current schedule, call ℂ 212/875-5656 or 212/362-6000. The Philharmonic maintains a list of their upcoming park gigs throughout the five boroughs at www.newyorkphilharmonic.org; look under "Events and Performances."

Christmastime production of *The Nutcracker*, for which tickets usually become available in early October. At the New York State Theater at Lincoln Center, Broadway and 64th St. ℂ 212/870-5570. www.nycballet.com. Tickets $28–$66. Subway: 1 or 9 to 66th St.

3 Major Concert Halls & Landmark Venues

Apollo Theatre   Built in 1914, this legendary Harlem theater launched or nurtured the careers of countless musical icons—including Bessie Smith, Billie Holiday, Dinah Washington, Duke Ellington, Ella Fitzgerald, Sarah Vaughan, Count Basie, Aretha Franklin, and James Brown—and is in large part responsible for the development and popularization of black music in America. By the 1970s, it had fallen on hard times, but a 1986 restoration breathed new life into the landmark. Today the Apollo is renowned for its African-American acts of all musical genres, from hip-hop to Wynton Marsalis's "Jazz for Young People" events. Wednesday's "Amateur Night at the Apollo" is a fun-filled night that draws in young talents with high hopes of making it big (a young Lauryn Hill started here—and didn't win!). *Money-saving tip:* For free tickets to *It's Showtime at the Apollo* (www.apollo showtime.com), call ℂ **212/889-3532** or send a self-addressed, stamped envelope and the dates you'll be in the Big Apple to It's Showtime at the Apollo, 3 Park Ave., 40th Floor, New York, NY 10016. 253 W. 125th St. (btwn Adam Clayton Powell and Frederick Douglass blvds.). ℂ **212/531-5300** or 212/531-5301. Tickets usually $16–$24, slightly higher for finalist shows. Subway: 1 or 9 to 125th St.

Brooklyn Academy of Music (BAM) *(Finds)*   BAM is the city's most renowned contemporary-arts institution, presenting cutting-edge theater, opera, dance, and music. Offerings have included presentations of baroque opera by William Christie and Les Arts Florissants; pop opera from Lou Reed; Marianne Faithfull singing Kurt Weill; dance by Mark Morris and Mikhail Baryshnikov; the Philip Glass ensemble accompanying screenings of *Koyannisqatsi* and Lugosi's original *Dracula;* the Royal Dramatic Theater of Sweden directed by Ingmar Bergman; and much more, including visiting companies from all over the world.

Of particular note is the **Next Wave Festival,** from September to December, this country's foremost showcase for new, experimental works. The **BAM Rose Cinemas** show first-run independent films, and there's free live music every Thursday, Friday, and Saturday night at **BAMcafé,** which can range from atmospheric electronica from coronetist Graham Haynes to radical jazz from the Harold Rubin Trio to tango band Tanguardia! ($10 food minimum). 30 Lafayette Ave. (off Flatbush Ave.), Brooklyn. ℂ **718/636-4100.** www.bam.org. Tickets $5–$95, depending on the performance and the seats you choose; most performances offer a $25–$75 range. Subway: 2, 3, 4, 5, M, N, Q, R, or W to Pacific St./Atlantic Ave.

Carnegie Hall *(★★)*   Perhaps the world's most famous performance space, Carnegie Hall offers everything from grand classics to the music of Ravi Shankar. The **Isaac Stern Auditorium,** the 2,804-seat main hall, welcomes visiting orchestras from across the country and the world. Many of the world's premier soloists and ensembles give recitals. The legendary hall is both visually and acoustically brilliant; don't miss an opportunity to experience it if there's something on that interests you.

There's also the intimate 268-seat **Weill Recital Hall,** usually used to showcase chamber music and vocal and instrumental recitals. Carnegie Hall has also, after being occupied by a movie theater for 38 years, reclaimed the ornate underground 650-seat **Zankel Concert Hall.** For last-minute ticket-buying tips, see p. 292. 881 7th Ave. (at 57th St.). ℂ **212/247-7800.** www.carnegiehall.org. Subway: N, Q, R, or W to 57th St.

Lincoln Center for the Performing Arts   New York is the world's premier performing arts city, and Lincoln Center is its premier institution. Whenever you're planning an evening's entertainment, check the offerings here—which can include opera, dance, symphonies, jazz, theater, film, and more, from the classics to the contemporary. Lincoln Center's many buildings serve as permanent homes to their own companies as well as major stops for world-class performance troupes from around the globe.

Resident companies include the following: The **Chamber Music Society of Lincoln Center** (ℂ **212/875-5788;** www.chambermusicsociety.org) performs at Alice Tully Hall or the Daniel and Joanna S. Rose Rehearsal Studio, often in the company of such high-caliber guests as Anne Sofie von Otter and Midori. The **Film Society of Lincoln Center** (ℂ **212/875-5600;** www.filmlinc.com) screens a daily schedule of movies at the Walter Reade Theater, and hosts a number of

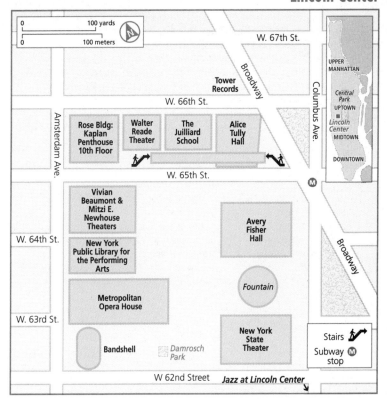

important annual film and video festivals as well as the Reel to Real program for kids, pairing silent-screen classics with live performance. **Jazz at Lincoln Center** (℃ 212/258-9800; www.jazzatlincolncenter.org) is led by the incomparable Wynton Marsalis, with the orchestra now performing at the brand-new $128-million, 100,000-square-foot Frederick P. Rose Hall in the Time Warner Center on Columbus Circle.

Lincoln Center Theater (℃ 212/362-7600; www.lct.org) consists of the Vivian Beaumont Theater, a modern, comfortable venue with great sightlines that has housed many Broadway shows, and the Mitzi E. Newhouse Theater, a well-respected Off-Broadway house that has also boasted numerous theatrical triumphs. Past seasons have included excellent productions of Tom Stoppard's *Arcadia*, Arthur Miller's *After the Fall* in revival, and David Hare's one-man show, *Via Dolorosa*.

For details on the **Metropolitan Opera,** the **New York City Opera,** the **New York City Ballet,** the **Juilliard School,** the phenomenal **New York Philhar-monic,** and the **American Ballet Theatre,** which takes up residence here every spring, see "Opera, Classical Music & Dance," earlier in this chapter.

Most of the companies' **major seasons** run from about September or Octo-ber to April, May, or June. **Special series** like Great Performers and the new American Songbook, showcasing classic American show tunes, help round out the calendar. Indoor and outdoor events are held in warmer months: Summer kicks off with the **JVC Jazz Festival** in June; July sees **Midsummer Night's Swing,** with partner dancing, lessons, and music on the plaza; August's **Mostly**

Value Park It! Shakespeare, Music & Other Free Fun

As the weather warms, New York culture comes outdoors to play.

Shakespeare in the Park, a New York institution since 1957, is as much a part of a New York summer as fireworks on the Fourth of July. The outdoor event was the brainchild of the late Joseph Papp, former director of the Public Theater, who had the bright idea of staging Shakespeare plays each summer at the open-air Delacorte Theater in Central Park. Best of all, and the reason Shakespeare in the Park has become an institution is that the performances are free.

Budget cuts in the last few years have reduced the number of shows offered to one, usually a revival of a Shakespeare play featuring a large company, including at least one or more "names" from film or television. The production runs from the end of June to early August. Depending on the star power of the cast, tickets can be quite scarce. The production of *Much Ado About Nothing* in 2004 featured Jimmy Smits, Sam Waterston, and Kristen Johnson. In years past, Morgan Freeman and Tracey Ullman have starred in *Taming of the Shrew,* and Patrick Stewart in *The Tempest,* which later graduated to a successful Broadway run.

Summer 2004 brought a new program to the Delacorte, with 2 weeks of musical performances, called "Joe's Pub in the Park," an outdoor version of the artists featured at Joe's Pub, the intimate musical venue at the Public Theater. The theater itself, next to Belvedere Castle near 79th Street and West Drive, is a dream—on a starry night, there's no better stage in town. Tickets are given out free on a first-come, first-served basis (two per person), at 1pm on the day of the performance at the theater. The Delacorte might have 1,881 seats, but each is a hot commodity, so people line up next to the theater 2 to 3 hours in advance (even earlier if a big name is involved). You can also pick up same-day tickets between 1 and 3pm at the Public Theater, at 425 Lafayette St., where the Shakespeare Festival continues throughout the year. For more information, call the Public Theater at © **212/ 539-8750** or the Delacorte at © **212/861-7277,** or go online at www. publictheater.org.

With summer also comes the sound of music. The **New York Philharmonic** and the **Metropolitan Opera** hold free concerts beneath the stars in Central Park, and in parks throughout the five boroughs. For the schedule, call © **212/875-5656** or 212/362-6000. The Philharmonic

---

Mozart attracts talents like Alicia de Larrocha and André Watts; **Lincoln Center Festival** celebrates the best of the performing arts; **Lincoln Center Out-of-Doors** is a series of free alfresco music and dance performances; there's also the **New York Film Festival,** and more. Check the "New York City Calendar of Events" in chapter 2, or Lincoln Center's website to see what special events will be on while you're in town.

Tickets for all performances at Avery Fisher and Alice Tully halls can be purchased through **CenterCharge** (© **212/721-6500**) or online at www.lincoln center.org (click on "Event Calendar"). Tickets for all Lincoln Center Theater

maintains a list of their upcoming gigs at www.newyorkphilharmonic.org; look under "Events and Performances."

The most active music stage in Central Park is **SummerStage,** at Rumsey Playfield, midpark around 72nd Street, which has featured everyone from James Brown to Patti Smith. Recent offerings have included concerts by Hugh Masekela, the Jon Spencer Blues Explosion, and Marianne Faithfull; "Viva, Verdi!" festival performances by the New York Grand Opera; cabaret nights; and more. The season usually lasts from mid-June to August. While some big-name shows charge admission, tickets aren't usually required; donations are accepted, however. Call the hot line at © **212/360-2777** or visit www.summerstage.org.

The calendar of free events heats up throughout the city's parks in summertime. You can find out what's happening by calling the **Parks and Recreation Special Events Hot Line** at © **888/NY-PARKS** or 212/360-3456, or pointing your browser to **www.nycgovparks.org/sub_things_to_do/upcoming_events.**

Also each summer is the **Bryant Park Summer Film Festival,** in which a classic film—think *Dr. Zhivago* or *Viva Las Vegas*—is shown on a large screen under the stars every Monday evening at sunset. Admission is free; just bring a blanket and a picnic. Rain dates are Tuesdays. For the schedule and more information, call © **212/512-5700.**

In Lower Manhattan, Trinity Church, at Broadway and Wall Street, hosts a chamber-music and orchestral **Noonday Concert** series year-round each Monday and Thursday at 1pm. This program isn't quite free, but almost: A $2 contribution is requested. Call the concert hot line at © **212/602-0800** or visit www.trinitywallstreet.org; see chapter 7 for further details.

Most of the city's museums offer free music and other programs on select nights. The **Metropolitan Museum of Art** has an extensive slate of offerings, including live classical music and cocktails on Friday and Saturday evenings. There's lots of fun to be had at others as well, including the **Guggenheim,** whose weekend World Beat Jazz series is a big hit; the **American Museum of Natural History,** which features live jazz in the Hall of the Universe in the Rose Center for Earth and Space; and the **Brooklyn Museum of Art,** which hosts the remarkably eclectic **First Saturday** program monthly. For details, see the museum listings in chapter 7.

performances can be purchased thorough **TeleCharge** (© **212/239-6200;** www.telecharge.com). Tickets for New York State Theater productions (New York City Opera and Ballet companies) are available through **Ticketmaster** (© **212/307-4100;** www.ticketmaster.com), while tickets for films showing at the Walter Reade Theater can be bought up to 7 days in advance by calling © **212/496-3809.** For last-minute full-price and discount ticket-buying tips, see p. 292. 70 Lincoln Center Plaza (at Broadway and 64th St.). © **212/546-2656** or 212/875-5456. www.lincoln center.org. Subway: 1 or 9 to 66th St.

Madison Square Garden Monsters of rock and pop fill this 20,000-seat arena, which is also home to the Knicks, the Rangers, and the WNBA's Liberty. The cavernous hulk is better suited to sports than to concerts, or in-the-round events such as Ringling Bros. Barnum & Bailey Circus. End up in the back for U2, and you'd better bring binoculars. You'll find better sightlines at the **Theater at Madison Square Garden,** an amphitheater-style auditorium with 5,600 seats that has played host to some major stars, from Barbra Streisand to Roxy Music. Watch for annual stagings of *The Wizard of Oz, A Christmas Carol,* and such family shows as *Sesame Street Live.* Newest at MSG is the **Comedy Garden** (www.comedygarden.com), the Garden's comedy club at the Theater, where talent runs the gamut from well-known local comics to Robin Williams.

The box office is located at 7th Avenue and 32nd Street. Or you can purchase tickets through **Ticketmaster** (© 212/307-7171; www.ticketmaster.com). On 7th Ave. from 31st to 33rd sts. © 212/465-MSG1. www.thegarden.com. Subway: A, C, E, 1, 2, 3, or 9 to 34th St.

92nd Street Y Tisch Center for the Arts *Value* This generously endowed community center offers a phenomenal slate of cultural happenings, from classical to folk to jazz to world music to cabaret to lyric theater and literary readings. Great classical performers—Janos Starker, Nadja Salerno-Sonnenberg—give recitals here. The concert calendar often includes luminaries such as Max Roach, John Williams, and Judy Collins; Jazz at the Y from Dick Hyman and guests; the longstanding Chamber Music at the Y series; the classical Music from the Jewish Spirit series; and regular cabaret programs. The lectures and literary-readings calendar is unparalleled, with featured speakers ranging from Lorne Michaels to David Halberstam to Jeff Bezos (CEO of Amazon) to Katie Couric to Elie Wiesel. There's a regular schedule of modern dance, too, through the Harkness Dance

---

Moments **Free Music Above & Below the Ground**

The noises of car horns, alarms, and sirens are not the only sounds you will hear in your travels around Manhattan. Music is everywhere. In the warm weather, a bagpiper or violinist will set up at a busy corner and play for hours. In the winter, the musicians head into subway stations, where they are legally not allowed to play, but I've rarely seen the law enforced. Many are very good, while others—well, they are just trying to make a few bucks. Some of the very good ones, who actually audition for the opportunity, perform as part of a program sponsored by the New York Metropolitan Transit Authority (MTA) called **Music Under New York.** If they are chosen, they are allowed to perform at designated subway stations including Times Square/42nd Street, 34th Street/6th Avenue, 14th Street/Union Square, and 59th Street/Columbus Circle. In the summer, there is a Music Under New York festival at Grand Central Station and Bowling Green Park. The variety of music is amazing and the quality as good as you might see at some of New York's clubs. In subway stations I've heard gospel, blues, Cajun, Dixieland jazz, Andean, Brazilian drumming, rumba, and my favorite, doo wop, the original sound of the New York subways. So take a few moments before boarding your train and listen to the music. If you're so moved, toss some change or a dollar into the hat, guitar case, or donation can. For more information, visit the MTA website (www.mta.nyc.ny.us/mta/aft/muny.htm).

Project. Best of all, admission is half or a third of what you'd pay at comparable venues. Additionally, a full calendar of entertainment targeted to the culturally aware in their 20s and 30s—from poetry readings to film screenings to live music including the debut of a very young, talented pianist and singer, Norah Jones—is offered at the Upper West Side community center **Makor,** 35 W. 67th St. (just off Central Park W.; © **212/601-1000;** www.makor.org; subway: 1 or 9 to 66th St.). 1395 Lexington Ave. (at 92nd St.). © **212/415-5500.** www.92ndsty.org. Readings and lectures $20–$30 for nonmembers; dance tickets $20; concert tickets $15–$50. Subway: 4, 5, or 6 to 86th St.; 6 to 96th St.

Radio City Music Hall   This stunning 6,200-seat Art Deco theater, with interior design by Donald Deskey, opened in 1932, and legendary Radio City continues to be a choice venue, where the theater alone adds a dash of panache to any performance. Star of the Christmas season is the **Radio City Music Hall Christmas Spectacular,** starring the legendary Rockettes. Visiting pop chart–toppers, from Neil Young to the Gipsy Kings, also perform here. Thanks to perfect acoustics and uninterrupted sightlines, there's hardly a bad seat in the house. The theater also hosts dance performances; family entertainment; a number of awards shows, such as the Essence Awards, the Grammies, the GQ Man of the Year Awards, and MTV Video Music Awards. 1260 6th Ave. (at 50th St.). © **212/247-4777,** or 212/307-7171 for Ticketmaster. www.radiocity.com or www.ticketmaster.com. Rockettes tickets $36–$119. Subway: B, D, F, or V to 49th–50th sts./Rockefeller Center.

Symphony Space ⚡ *(Finds*   An eclectic mix of culture can be found at this Upper West Side institution that was renovated in 2002. The variety of shows at the **Peter Jay Sharp Theater** include music, with series by the World Music Institute as well as classical, rock, and blues; dance, with marathon tributes to choreographers like George Balanchine; original creations of Israeli Zvi Gotheiner; literature, such as the selected shorts series introduced by writers such as Susan Orleans, Edwidge Danticant, and Walter Mosely; and family, with performances by folk singer Tom Chapin, and the Putayamo Kids. Adjacent to the Sharp Theater is the **Leonard Nimoy Thalia Theater;** the film revival house that was known for its quirky sightlines was rescued by none other than Mr. Spock and has now been totally renovated. Though I'm sure it is much more comfortable now, I'll miss having to peer around a pole to watch a movie like *Plan Nine from Outer Space.* 2537 Broadway (at 95th St.). © **212/864-1414.** www.symphonyspace.org. Subway: 1, 2, 3, or 9 to 96th St.

Town Hall   This intimate landmark theater—a National Historic Site designed by McKim, Mead & White—is blessed with outstanding acoustics, making it an ideal place to enjoy many kinds of performances, including theater, dance, lectures, drama, comedy, film, and pop and world music. The calendar regularly includes such offerings as American tap and Brazilian tango exhibitions; Native American music and global rhythms; comedy from the *Kids in the Hall* Reunion Tour or Eddie Izzard; live tapings of *A Prairie Home Companion* with Garrison Keillor or spoken word from Al Franken; lectures by luminaries such as Marianne Williamson and Frank Gehry; concerts by the likes of David Sanborn or the reunited Blondie; symphony, opera, and ballet companies from around the world; and much more. The grade is extremely steep, so unless Yao Ming sits in front of you, fellow audience members shouldn't block your view. 123 W. 43rd St. (btwn 6th and 7th aves.). © **212/840-2824,** or 212/307-4100 for Ticketmaster. www.the-townhall-nyc.org or www.ticketmaster.com. Ticket prices vary depending on the show but are usually less than $40. Subway: N, Q, R, S, W, 1, 2, 3, 7, or 9 to 42nd St./Times Square; B, D, F, or V to 42nd St.

4 Live Rock, Jazz, Blues & More

I'll give you a thumbnail sketch of the top venues, both large and small, below. But there are many more, and new ones pop up all the time. For the latest, check the publications discussed earlier in this chapter.

LARGER VENUES

For coverage of **Madison Square Garden,** the **Theater at MSG,** and **Town Hall,** see "Major Concert Halls & Landmark Venues," earlier in this chapter.

Beacon Theatre   This pleasing venue—a 1928 Art Deco movie palace with an impressive lobby, stairway, and auditorium seating about 2,700—hosts mainly pop music, usually for the over-30 crowd. Featured acts have ranged from Bryan Ferry to perennial faves the Allman Brothers. You'll also find such events as the bodybuilding "Night of Champions" on the calendar. 2124 Broadway (at 74th St.). ✆ 212/496-7070. www.livetonight.com. Subway: 1, 2, 3, or 9 to 72nd St.

Roseland   This old warhorse, a 1919 ballroom, has been under threat of the wrecking ball for years. Everybody has played at this too-huge-for-its-own-good 2,500-capacity general-admission hall, from Marc Anthony to Hole to Busta Rhymes. Bands who inspire mosh pits like to book here (Nine Inch Nails, No Doubt), because there's plenty of space for slamming and surfing. Thankfully, there's also room to steer clear and enjoy the show. *Money-saving tip:* Purchase advance tickets at Irving Plaza (p. 309) sans the Ticketmaster service fee. 239 W. 52nd St. (btwn Broadway and 8th Ave.). ✆ 212/777-6800, 212/247-0200, or 212/307-7171 for Ticketmaster. www.roselandballroom.com or www.livetonight.com. Subway: C, E, 1, or 9 to 50th St.

MIDSIZE & MULTIGENRE VENUES

For the most part, expect to pay a little more for shows at these venues than you would at smaller clubs—anywhere from $10 to $25, depending on the act.

B.B. King Blues Club & Grill   This 550-seat venue is one of the prime anchors of Times Square's "new" 42nd Street. Despite its name, B.B. King's seldom sticks to the blues; instead, you're likely to find pop, funk, and rock names, mainly from the past. The big-ticket talent runs the gamut from Nile Rodgers and Chic (cool!) to Big Bad Voodoo Daddy to the Turtles (yes, with Flo and Eddie) to the Afro-Cuban All Stars. A few more (relatively) esoteric acts take the stage on occasion, such as Luther "Guitar Junior" Johnson and Shemikia Copeland. Tourist-targeted pricing makes for an expensive night, but there's no arguing with the quality of the talent. The Sunday gospel lunch is a genuine slice of joy. 42nd St. (btwn 7th and 8th aves.). ✆ 212/997-4144, or 212/307-7171 for Ticketmaster. www.bbkingblues.com. Tickets $25–$35, plus minimums. Subway: A, C, E, Q, W, 1, 2, 3, 7, or 9 to 42nd St.

Bowery Ballroom   This marvelous space is run by the same people behind the Mercury Lounge (see below). The Bowery space is bigger, accommodating a crowd of 500 or so. The stage is big and raised to allow good sightlines from every corner. The sound couldn't be better, and Art Deco details give the place a sophistication that doesn't come easy to general-admission halls. My favorite spot is the balcony, which has its own bar and seating alcoves. This place is a favorite with indie-type rockers like the Mooney Suzuki, and singer-songwriters like Dan Bern and Melissa Ferrick, as well as long-time faves like Nick Lowe and Patti Smith, who thrive in an intimate setting. *Money-saving tip:* Buy advance tickets at Mercury's box office; you'll save the service charge and up to $2 to $5 on the day-of-show price. 6 Delancey St. (at Bowery). ✆ 212/533-2111. www.boweryballroom.com. Tickets $13–$30, with most under $20. Subway: F, J, M, or Z to Delancey St.

Tips Ticket-Buying Tips

Tickets for events at all larger theaters and Roseland, Irving Plaza, and B.B. King's can be purchased through **Ticketmaster** (© 212/307-7171; www. ticketmaster.com).

Advance tickets for an increasing number of shows at smaller venues—including CBGB, Bowery Ballroom, Mercury Lounge, Village Underground, Tribeca Blues, and Fez Under Time Cafe, plus Brooklyn's Warsaw and Northsix—can be purchased through **Ticketweb** (© 866/418-7619; www. ticketweb.com). Do note that Ticketweb can sell out its allotted number of tickets without the show being completely sold out. If Ticketweb is sold out, check with the venue directly.

Even if a show is sold out, that doesn't mean you're out of luck. There are usually people hanging around at showtime trying to get rid of extra tickets for friends who didn't show, and they're usually happy to pass them off for face value. You'll also see scalpers, who often peddle forgeries and are best avoided—it doesn't take a rocket scientist to tell the difference. Be aware, of course, that in New York City, it's illegal to sell a ticket for more than $5 above its face value.

Irving Plaza This high-profile, midsize music hall is the prime stop for national-name rock bands that aren't quite big enough yet (or anymore) to sell out Hammerstein, Roseland, or the Beacon. Think Guided by Voices, They Might Be Giants, the Reverend Horton Heat, and Cheap Trick. From time to time, big-name artists also perform—Prince, Bob Dylan, Tom Jones, and Sinead O'Connor have all played intimate shows here. This is a nice place to see a show, with a well-elevated stage and lots of open space, even on sold-out nights. There's an upstairs balcony that offers unparalleled views, but come early for a spot. *Money-saving tip:* Buy tickets prior to the day of show to save $2 to $5. 17 Irving Place (1 block west of 3rd Ave. at 15th St.). © 212/777-1224 or 212/777-6800. www. irvingplaza.com. Tickets $14–$30, with most $25–$30. Subway: 4, 5, 6, L, N, R, Q, or W to 14th St./Union Square.

The Knitting Factory New York's premier avant-garde music venue has four spaces, each showcasing performances ranging from experimental jazz and folk to spoken-word and poetry to multimedia. Regulars who use the Knitting Factory as their lab of choice include former Lounge Lizard John Lurie; around-the-bend experimentalist John Zorn; guitar gods Vernon Reid, Eliot Sharp, and David Torn; and Television's Richard Lloyd. (If these names mean nothing to you, chances are good that the Knitting Factory is not for you.) The schedule is peppered with edgy star turns from the likes of Cibo Matto, Gil Scott Heron, Taj Mahal, Faith No More's Mike Patton, and Lou Reed. There are often two shows a night in the pleasing main performance space, so it's easy to work a show around other activities. The Old Office Lounge offers an extensive list of microbrews and free live entertainment. 74 Leonard St. (btwn Broadway and Church St.). © 212/219-3006. www.knitting factory.com. Tickets $7–$20, with most $10–$15. Subway: 1 or 9 to Franklin St.

ROCK & MIXED-MUSIC CLUBS

Arlene Grocery This casual Lower East Side club boasts a friendly bar and a good sound system; the quality of the acts is usually pretty high. Arlene Grocery serves as a showcase for hot bands looking for a deal or promoting their self-pressed record. The crowd is a mix of club-hoppers, rock fans looking for a new fix, and industry scouts looking for new blood. 95 Stanton St. (btwn Ludlow and Orchard sts.). © 212/358-1633. www.arlene-grocery.com. Cover $7. Subway: F to 2nd Ave.

The Baggot Inn *(value* This easygoing pub has become one of the best showcases in the city for unknown acts, especially if you like quality acoustic and folk-rock music. Blues, Irish music, poetry, acoustic jams, and open-mike nights also regularly pop up on the calendar. The cover is always bargain-priced; happy hour until 7pm and nightly drink specials round out the entertainment value. 82 W. 3rd St. (btwn Thompson and Sullivan sts., below the Boston Comedy Club). © 212/477-0622. www.thebaggotinn.com. Cover free to $5. Subway: A, C, E, F, or V to W. 4th St.

Bitter End Folk rock's legendary Bitter End has been going strong in the heart of the Village since 1960, and it's still a relevant showcase for acoustic and electric rock and experimental sounds. 147 Bleecker St. (btwn Thompson and LaGuardia sts.). © 212/673-7030. www.bitterend.com. Cover $5 (some shows up to $7). Subway: A, C, E, F, or V to W. 4th St.

CBGB The original downtown club has seen better days, but no other spot is so rich with rock history. (The corner of 2nd St. and the Bowery was officially named Joey Ramone Place in 2003.) This was the launching pad for New York punk and New Wave: the Ramones, Blondie, the Talking Heads, Television, Patti Smith, Stiv Bators and the Dead Boys—everybody got started here. These days, you've probably never heard of most acts here. Never mind—CB's still rocks. Come early if you have hopes of actually seeing the stage.

More today than yesterday is **CB's 313 Gallery,** a welcome spinoff that showcases alternative art on the walls and mostly acoustic singer/songwriters on stage; cover is usually $5, never higher than $8. Same goes for CB's **lounge,** which has a more cerebral alt edge to its sounds, including a very popular Sunday night freeform avant jazz series (cover free to $8). Within striking distance of the history, but more pleasant all the way around. 315 Bowery (at Bleecker St.). © 212/982-4052, or 212/677-0455 for CB's 313 Gallery. www.cbgb.com. Cover $6–$10. Subway: F to 2nd Ave.; 6 to Bleecker St.

The C-Note This Alphabet City boîte used to focus on contemporary jazz performers but has branched out to embrace singer-songwriter pop, rock, blues, country, and roots, Latin music, and other genres. The quality tunes are almost always worth the price of admission. 157 Ave. C (at 10th St.). © 212/677-8142. www.the cnote.com. Cover free to $8. Subway: L to 1st Ave.

Continental Artists such as Spacehog occasionally surface among the unknowns at this proudly raunchy joint. It's punk central in the East Village, even more so than CBGB. It was Joey Ramone's headquarters after the Ramones broke up (commemorated by a plaque on the wall by the stage). 25 3rd Ave., at St. Marks Place. © 212/529-6924. www.nytrash.com/continental. Cover free to $10. Subway: 6 to Astor Place.

The Cutting Room This Flatiron District music club and restaurant is co-owned by actor Chris Noth *(Sex and the City, Law & Order),* so don't be surprised if you spot a famous face or two. That said, the environment is usually easygoing, and the mix of entertainment runs the gamut from experimental synth ensemble Mother Mallard's Portable Masterpiece Co. to the terrific Oingo Boingo-ish Niagras. A huge draw is Saturday night's Le Scandal, sort of a feminist take on burlesque, with a dash of Jim Rose Circus Side Show thrown in. 19 W. 24th St. (btwn Broadway and 6th Ave.). © 212/691-1900. www.thecuttingroomnyc.com. Le Scandal tickets $20; $10 food and drink minimum per show. Subway: N, R, or W to 23rd St.

Value Free Music in the Clubs

Rodeo Bar (p. 312) is the city's top no-cover club, but it's not the only free show in town.

Others worth checking out include the **Living Room,** 84 Stanton St., at Allen Street (© **212/533-7235;** www.livingroomny.com), an unpretentious bar/restaurant that's good for acoustic acts (the sound system isn't great for electric). The pass-the-bucket policy allows you to contribute to the performers' earnings (the venue suggests a $5 tip); there is a one-drink minimum. Also on the Lower East Side is **Luna Lounge** ⭐, 171 Ludlow St. (btwn Houston and Stanton sts.; © **212/260-2323;** www.luna lounge.com), which usually hosts two bands a night. Monday's comedy night, Eating It, has become so popular that there's a $7 cover (one drink included).

East Village stalwart **Lakeside Lounge,** 162 Ave. B (btwn 10th and 11th sts.; © **212/529-8463;** www.lakesidelounge.com), regularly hosts excellent-quality live music with no cover charge.

Jazz fans can try **Arthur's Tavern,** in the Village at 57 Grove St., at 7th Avenue South (© **212/675-6879;** www.arthurstavernny.com), a comfortable club and piano bar attracting a mixed gay-and-straight crowd. Beware of the drinks, which can be pricey. In the East Village, "Live Jazz or Die" is the mantra at **Detour** ⭐, 349 E. 13th St., at 1st Avenue (© **212/533-6212;** www.jazzatdetour.com), a high-quality club offering no-cover music nightly (two-drink minimum); $3 happy hour from 4 to 7pm maximizes the fun.

Harlem's **Showmans Cafe,** 375 W. 125th St. (btwn St. Nicholas and Morningside aves.; © **212/864-8941**), hosts free music Monday through Saturday ranging from jazz to funky bebop that attracts music lovers and players from all walks of life. Not far from Duke Ellington's first residence in Manhattan is the **Sugar Hill Bistro,** 485 W. 145th St. (btwn Amsterdam and Convent aves.; © **212/491-5505;** www. sugarhillbistro.com), where on Friday nights you can hear the incomparable Bill Paxton blow sax for free. But when he comes around with his hat, you better drop a few bills in it to keep the man happy.

Also keep in mind that a number of clubs listed in these pages offer free music 1 or more nights a week, such as **Cafe Wha?,** the **Continental,** the **Baggot Inn, Arlene Grocery, Smoke,** the **The C-Note,** the lounge at **CBGB, 55 Bar,** and **Tonic;** and **The Knitting Factory** offers free music in its Old Office Lounge. **Jazz at the Cajun** lets you listen to the finest old-school jazz in town for the price of a meal—and you have to eat anyway, don't you? The easiest way to check for free events while you're in town is to peruse the weekly *Time Out New York,* which announces no-cover shows with an easy-to-spot FREE! Sunday and Monday are big nights for freebies.

Remember that schedules and no-cover policies can change at any time, so always confirm in advance.

Fez Under Time Cafe   You have to reserve a seat a few days ahead for the popular Thursday night Mingus Big Band ($18), when the low-ceilinged basement performance space is filled with the cool sounds of jazz. The rest of the week brings an eclectic live-music-and-performance-art mix, which can range from Patti Rothberg to drag grande-dame Hedda Lettuce to tributes to acts like Queen and ABBA from Loser's Lounge. 380 Lafayette St. (at Great Jones St.). ✆ 212/533-2680. www.feznyc.com. Mingus Big Band tickets $18. Cover $10–$20 (2-drink minimum may be required). Subway: 6 to Bleecker St.

Mercury Lounge   The Merc is everything a top-notch live-music venue should be: unpretentious, civilized, and with a killer sound system. The rooms are nothing special: a front bar and an intimate back-room performance space with a low stage and a few tables lining the brick walls. The calendar is filled with a mix of accomplished local rockers and national acts like Frank Black, Art Alexakis, and the Mekons. The crowd is grown-up and easygoing. The only downside is that it's consistently packed thanks to the high quality of the entertainment and all-around pleasing nature of the experience. 217 E. Houston St. (at Essex St./Ave. A). ✆ 212/260-4700. www.mercuryloungenyc.com. Cover $8–$15 (maybe more for national acts). Subway: F to 2nd Ave.

Rodeo Bar *Value*   Here's New York's oldest—and finest—honky-tonk. Hike up your Wranglers and head inside, where you'll find longhorns on the walls, peanut shells underfoot, and Tex-Mex on the menu. But this place is really about the music: urban-tinged country, bluegrass, swinging rockabilly, and Southern-flavored rock. Bigger names like Brian Setzer and up-and-comers on the tour circuit like Hank Williams III occasionally grace the stage, but regular acts like Dixieland swingers the Flying Neutrinos, cowpunk goddess Rosie Flores, and BBQ Bob and the Spareribs usually supply free music, keeping the urban cowboys plenty happy. A 10-gallon hat full o' fun. It's happy hour until 7pm; the music starts around 9:30pm nightly, and goes until at least 3am. 375 3rd Ave. (at 27th St.). ✆ 212/683-6500. www.rodeobar.com. Subway: 6 to 28th St.

Tonic *Finds*   This intimate, Lower East Side, loftlike space attracts seekers of the alternative in both jazz and rock. It's not for everyone, but if you like your music challenging, to say the least, this is the Tonic for you. Most of the performers are far from household names, but avant-garde artists such as John Zorn, Marc Ribot, Sonic Youth, and Ravi Coltrane occasionally appear on the calendar. 107 Norfolk St. (btwn Rivington and Delancey sts.). ✆ 212/358-7501. www.tonicnyc.com. Cover $8–$10 (when charged). Subway: F or J to Delancey St.

JAZZ, BLUES & MORE

A night at a top-flight jazz club can be expensive. Cover charges can vary dramatically—from as little as $10 to as high as $65, depending on who's taking the stage—and there's likely to be an additional two-drink minimum (or a dinner requirement, if you choose an early show). Call ahead so you know what you're getting into; reservations are also an excellent idea at top spots.

For those of you who like your jazz with an edge, see what's on at **The Knitting Factory** (p. 309), **Tonic** (see above), and **The C-Note** (p. 310), as well as Sunday's freeform avant jazz at **CB's Lounge** (see CBGB on p. ###). Trad fans should also consider the Thursday Mingus Big Band Workshop at **Fez Under Time Cafe** (see above), while swingsters should consider **Swing 46** (p. 329). **Smoke** (p. 314) is probably your best bet for quality jazz without a cover. Lovers of Latin and world music can't do better than terrific **Satalla** (p. 314).

There's also world-beat jazz every Friday and Saturday from 5 to 8pm in the rotunda at the **Guggenheim Museum;** see chapter 7. And don't forget **Jazz at Lincoln Center** (p. 303), the nation's premier forum for the traditional and developing jazz canon.

Birdland   While the legends of Parker, Monk, Gillespie, and other bebop pioneers still hold sway, Birdland isn't a crowded, smoky joint of yesteryear. The big room is spacious, comfy, and classy, with excellent sound and top-notch talent. Expect lots of accomplished big bands and jazz trios, plus occasional appearances by stars like Dave Brubeck. You can't go wrong with the Sunday night show, starring Chico O'Farrell's smokin' Afro-Cuban Jazz Big Band. The Southern-style food is pretty good. At press time, Tuesdays were the domain of the Duke Ellington Orchestra, led by Duke's grandson Paul Ellington every other week. *Money-saving tip:* You can avoid the minimum by sitting at the bar rather than a table, and you'll also score a complimentary beverage (at press time, anyway; check current policy). 315 W. 44th St. (btwn 8th and 9th aves.). ✆ **212/581-3080.** www.birdlandjazz.com. Cover $20–$35; $10 food and drink minimum. Subway: A, C, or E to 42nd St.

Blue Note   The Blue Note has attracted some of the biggest names in jazz to its intimate setting. Those who've played here include just about everyone of note: Dave Brubeck, B.B. King, Manhattan Transfer, Dr. John, George Duke, Chick Corea, David Sanborn, Arturo Sandoval, Gato Barbieri, and the superb Oscar Peterson. The sound system is excellent, and every seat in the house has a sightline to the stage; however, in recent years, the hard edge that once was the Blue Note has faded. Softer, smoother jazz is the domain now, so if that's your thing, enjoy. Prices are high here; there are two shows per night, and dinner is served. 131 W. 3rd St. (at 6th Ave.). ✆ **212/475-8592.** www.bluenote.net. Tickets $20–$30. Subway: A, C, E, F, or V to W. 4th St.

55 Bar *(Value*   This Prohibition-era Village dive hosts high-quality jazz and blues nightly, with guitarists a specialty (think Wayne Krantz, Hiram Bullock). The house guitar trio is definitely worth a listen, and if saxist Ed Palermo is on the bill, go. 55 Christopher St. (just east of 7th Ave.). ✆ **212/929-9883.** www.55bar.com. Cover free to $15, but usually $3–$5 (2-drink minimum). Subway: 1 or 9 to Christopher St.

Iridium   This snazzy jazz club has relocated from its longtime perch across from Lincoln Center to a heart-of-the-Theater-District location. Everything else remains the same, including the talent and big-name acts. Like the Energizer bunny, Les Paul keeps on going, playing every Monday night (tickets $33, plus $15 minimum). Other top-notch performers include Nicholas Payton, Mose Allison, McCoy Tyner and Bobby Hutcherson, and the Jazz Messengers. A full, rather sophisticated dinner menu is served. 1650 Broadway (at 51st St.). ✆ **212/582-2121.** www.iridiumjazzclub.com. Les Paul tickets $33 plus $15 minimum. Subway: 1 or 9 to 50th St.

Jazz at the Cajun *(Finds*   This cozy, casual New Orleans–themed supper club is the best venue in town for prewar big-band and Dixieland jazz—think Jelly Roll Morton, Scott Joplin, early Duke. The crowd comes from all walks of life, united in their love of the old school. Cajun is home base for Vince Giordano's Nighthawks, who are masters of yesteryear—a joy to watch!—but the place jumps no matter what crew takes the stage. Food is affordable and just fine, with entrees in the low and midteens; reserve in advance. 129 8th Ave. (btwn 16th and 17th sts.). ✆ **212/691-6174.** www.jazzatthecajun.com. Subway: A, C, or E to 14th St.; L to 8th Ave.

Jazz Standard 🎯🎯   Kudos to the Jazz Standard, where both the food and music meet all expectations. Boasting a sophisticated retro-speakeasy vibe, the

Jazz Standard is one of the city's largest jazz clubs, with well-spaced tables seating 150. The rule is straightforward, mainstream jazz by new and established musicians, including such stars as Branford Marsalis. On Sunday afternoons, the club features a Jazz for Kids program, A limited menu from Danny's Meyer's barbecue joint, **Blue Smoke** (p. 156), located upstairs, is available. Jazz, blues, and barbecue—hard to go wrong with that. 116 E. 27th St. (btwn Park Ave. S. and Lexington Ave.). ℂ 212/576-2232. Cover $15–$25. www.jazzstandard.net. Subway: 6 to 28th St.

Lenox Lounge *(Finds)* One of Harlem's best jazz clubs, the intimate, Art Deco–cool back room—complete with zebra stripes on the walls and banquettes—hosts top-flight jazz vocalists, trios, and quartets for a crowd that comes to listen and be wowed. Every Monday Patience Higgens and the Sugar Hill Quartet are on tap. Well worth the trip uptown for those who want a genuine Harlem jazz experience. 288 Malcolm X Blvd. (Lenox Ave.; btwn 124th and 125th sts.). ℂ 212/427-0253. Monday cover $5 (2-drink minimum); weekend cover up to $15 (1-drink minimum). Subway: 2 or 3 to 125th St.

St. Nick's Pub ⊹ *(Finds)* As unpretentious a club as you'll find, St. Nick's in Harlem's Sugar Hill district is the real deal, with live entertainment every night. On Tuesday, it's Oldies but Goodies provided by Sexy Charles and Poetry on the Hill, hosted by Chance & Lilah; all the other nights are devoted to jazz, straight up and rarely with a chaser. 773 St. Nicholas Ave. (at 149th St.). ℂ 212/283-9728. Subway: A, C, D, or B to 145th St.

Satalla ⊹ *(Finds)* Satalla was a hit the moment it opened in late 2003. Intimate and innovative, Satalla does a great job of finding hidden (at least hidden from most U.S. audiences) talent from across the globe. The diversity of music that can be heard on any given night is staggering. Flamenco, klezmer, Celtic, Middle-Eastern jazz, Afro-Cuban, and Quebecois are examples of just some of the music you might hear at the club. The room is cozy and sometimes the performers can get cheerily up close and personal with the crowd—and vice versa. 37 W. 26th St. (btwn 6th Ave. and Broadway). ℂ 212/576-1155. www.satalla.com. $10 food and drink minimum (no cover most nights). Subway: F to 23rd St.

Smoke ⊹ *(Value)* A rising star in the New York jazz scene and the best place to hear it on the Upper West Side, Smoke is a welcome throwback to the informal, intimate clubs of the past—the kind of place that on most nights you can just walk in and experience some solid jazz. And though it seats only 65, Smoke still manages to attract big names like the Steve Turre Quartet, Ron Carter, Eddie Henderson, and vocalist Vanessa Rubin. On Sunday through Thursday there is no cover and each night has a theme, including funk on Wednesdays with the rocking Hot Pants Funk Sextet, Latin jazz on Sundays, and my favorite, Hammond organ grooves on Tuesday with Mike LeDonne on the organ and the incomparable Eric Alexander on sax. There are three sets nightly and a very popular happy hour. 2751 Broadway (btwn 105th and 106th sts.). ℂ 212/864-6662. www.smokejazz.com. Cover up to $25. Subway: 1 to 103rd St.

Terra Blues This artsy blues club hosts an active calendar of local and national acts. 149 Bleecker St. (btwn Thompson St. and LaGuardia Place). ℂ 212/777-7776. www.terrablues.com. Cover $5–$10 (2-drink minimum). Subway: A, C, E, F, or V to W. 4th St.

The Village Vanguard ⊹⊹ What CBGB is to rock, the Village Vanguard is to jazz. One look at the photos on the walls will show you who's been through since 1935, from Coltrane, Miles, and Monk to recent appearances by Bill Charlap and Roy Hargrove. Expect a mix of established names and high-quality local talent, including the Vanguard's own jazz orchestra Monday nights. The sound is great, but sightlines aren't, so come early for a front table. If you are looking for serious jazz, this is the place. Sunday through Thursday nights are cheapest. 178 7th Ave. S. (just below 11th St.). ✆ **212/255-4037.** www.villagevanguard.net. Cover $15–$30. Subway: 1, 2, 3, or 9 to 14th St.

5 Stand-Up & Sketch Comedy

Comedy Cellar *(Finds* This intimate subterranean spot is the club of choice for stand-up fans in the know, thanks to the most consistently impressive lineups in the business. He might be the highest-paid sitcom star now, but once an unknown Ray Romano honed his material here. *Money-saving tip:* Check the website to order free tickets and free drinks for select nights. 117 MacDougal St. (btwn Bleecker and W. 3rd sts.). ✆ **212/254-3480.** www.comedycellar.com. Cover $10 weekdays, $15 weekends (2-drink minimum). Subway: A, C, E, F, or V to W. 4th St. (use 3rd St. exit).

New York Comedy Club *(Value* This small club offers the best value for your money. Despite what the owners call their "Wal-Mart approach" to comedy, the club has presented Damon Wayans, Chris Rock, and Brett Butler, among others, in its two showrooms. Monday's Open Mike Night (5pm) is $3 with unlimited soft drinks, and you're welcome to get on stage for your 5 minutes of fame. Weekends set aside time for African-American and Latino comics. Come early for a good seat. *Money-saving tip:* Check the website for half-price specials. 241 E. 24th St. (btwn 2nd and 3rd aves.). ✆ **212/696-5233.** Cover $7 weekdays, $10 weekends (2-drink minimum). www.newyorkcomedyclub.com. Subway: 6 to 23rd St.

Stand-Up New York The Upper West Side's premier stand-up comedy club hosts some of the brightest comics in the business, plus drop-ins like Dennis Leary, Caroline Rhea, Robin Williams, and Mr. Upper West Side himself, Jerry Seinfeld. *Money-saving tip:* Order your tickets for PrimeTime shows (Thurs–Sat) online at the website and you'll save $5 per ticket. 236 W. 78th St. (at Broadway). ✆ **212/595-0850.** www.standupny.com. Cover $10–$15 (2-item food or drink minimum). Subway: 1 or 9 to 79th St.

Upright Citizens Brigade Theater *(Value* You've seen their twisted, highly original sketch comedy on Comedy Central—now you can see the Upright Citizens Brigade, New York's premier alternative comedy troupe, live. The best of the nonstop hilarity is *A.S.S.S.C.A.T.,* the troupe's extremely popular long-form improv show, which often sells out in advance. The company has supplied a few members of the Not-Ready-For-Prime-Time Players in recent years, including Amy Poehler. Reservations are a must. 307 W. 26th St. (btwn 8th and 9th aves.). ✆ **212/366-9176.** www.ucbtheater.com. Tickets $8 or less. Subway: 1 or 9 to 23rd St.

6 Cabaret Rooms & Piano Bars

The city's top supper clubs and cabarets are not for the budget-minded. At places like **CaféCarlyle,** in the Carlyle Hotel, 781 Madison Ave. (✆ **212/744-1600**), home to the legendary Bobby Short (and Woody Allen in the Eddy Davis New Orleans Jazz Band most Mon), and the Algonquin's **Oak Room,** 59 W. 44th St. (✆ **212/840-6800**), covers usually run in the neighborhood of $75, plus two-drink or dinner-check minimums; count on a $300 night on the town.

But never fear: One of these more casual, less-expensive options will result in a wallet-friendly night. Reservations are suggested for cabaret shows, and are not usually necessary for piano bars (although it never hurts to check).

Value   Money-Saving Tip for Cabaret Fans

At **CaféCarlyle,** value-minded cabaret fans can save by reserving standing room (which usually results in a spot at the bar) for just $35.

Brandy's Piano Bar   A mixed crowd—Upper East Side locals, waiters off work, gays, straights, all ages—comes to this intimate, old-school piano bar for the atmosphere and nightly entertainment. The talented waitstaff does most of the singing while waiting for their big breaks, but enthusiastic patrons regularly join in. The sounds tend to familiar adult-contemporary radio hits and cabaret tunes. This place is so unhip that it's downright cool; it makes for a fun and affordable night on the town. 235 E. 84th St. (btwn 2nd and 3rd aves.). © 212/744-4949. 2-drink minimum. Subway: 4, 5, or 6 to 86th St.

Danny's Skylight Room   You'll find this Theater District showroom tucked away in, of all places, the rear of a Thai restaurant. It offers surprisingly strong line-ups, including the fabulous Blossom Dearie and her world-class trio; ask about dinner/show packages. There's no cover in the piano bar, where you'll hear first-class tunes from the American songbook. Happy hour (weekdays 4:30–7pm) means two-for-one beer and wine. At Danny's Grand Sea Palace, 346–348 W. 46th St. (btwn 8th and 9th aves.). © 212/265-8133 or 212/265-8130. www.dannysgrandseapalace.com. Cover $10–$25 (usually under $20) plus $10 minimum. Subway: A, C, or E to 42nd St.

Don't Tell Mama   You'll find an evening of torch songs, comedy, and more in a friendly, and affordable, atmosphere at this wonderful two-room Theater District cabaret. Drinks only, no dinner. The piano bar is particularly lively, and always free (two-drink minimum). 343 W. 46th St. (btwn 8th and 9th aves.). © 212/757-0788. Cover free to $20, depending on show (2-drink minimum). Subway: A, C, or E to 42nd St.

Duplex Cabaret   Expect a high camp factor and lots of good-natured fun in this multilevel space, New York's oldest cabaret. A mixed gay/straight crowd of locals and out-of-towners sit at outdoor tables, gather around the downstairs piano (singalongs from around 9pm), or head upstairs to the cabaret for shows that run from mini-musicals to drag revues to stand-up comedy. No cover at the piano bar (two-drink minimum). 61 Christopher St. (at 7th Ave.). © 212/255-5438. www.theduplex.com. Cover $5–$15. Subway: 1 or 9 to Christopher St.

7 Bars & Cocktail Lounges

TRIBECA

In addition to the choices below, consider **Walker's,** 16 N. Moore St., at Varick Street (© 212/941-0142), a holdout from pre-fabulous TriBeCa; see chapter 6.

Liquor Store Bar   Housed in, yes, a former liquor store, this wonderful little oak-and-brass tavern is the best place for an affordable drink with a dash of style in TriBeCa. Come midweek to beat the Friday and Saturday crowds. 235 W. Broadway (at White St.). © 212/226-7121. Subway: A, C, or E to Canal St.

Puffy's Tavern   Before Nobu—even before Chanterelle and Odeon—Puffy's Tavern was a TriBeCa institution. This was, and still is the place in TriBeCa for no-nonsense drinking. Maybe a beer and a shot while taking in a ball game, or maybe just for marveling at the bar memorabilia to help recall TriBeCa before there was a film festival named after the neighborhood. 81 Hudson St. (btwn Harrison and Jay Sts). © 212/766-9159. www.puffystavern.com. Subway: 1 or 9 to Franklin St.

CHINATOWN & LITTLE ITALY

Double Happiness *(Finds)* The only indicator to the subterranean entrance is a WATCH YOUR STEP sign. Once through the door, you'll find a beautifully designed speakeasy-ish lounge with artistic nods to the neighborhood, plus a low-key vibe. The space is large, but a low ceiling and intimate nooks add a hint of romance (although the loud music mix may deter true wooing). Don't miss the green-tea martini, an inspired house creation. 173 Mott St. (btwn Grand and Broome sts.). *(C)* 212/941-1282. Subway: 6 to Spring St.

Jeremy's Ale House If you want an alternative to the South Street Seaport's chain restaurants and bars, saunter over to Jeremy's. The bar has one of the best views of the Brooklyn Bridge, but maybe that's because the bar is practically under the Bridge. Jeremy's is so close to the river you may think you smell the sea, but what you are really smelling is an endless supply of calamari and clams sizzling in the deep fryers and gallons of Coors beer, served in 32-ounce Styrofoam cups. There's also a space to mingle outside for those who yearn for a smoke or a breath of "fresh" air. 228 Front St. (btwn Peck Slip and Dover St.). *(C)* 212/964-3537. www.jeremysalehouse.com. Subway: 2, 3, 4, or 5 to Fulton St.

Winnie's I usually abhor karaoke bars, but I make an exception for Winnie's. Maybe it's the Asian pop tunes that I'm a sucker for or maybe it's the "Hawaiian Punch," the sickly sweet drink that, after a couple, will have you crooning in Cantonese. Even if you don't partake in the Chinatown version of American Idol, you will enjoy others as they drunkenly embarrass themselves in front of the mike and under the spotlight. 104 Bayard St (btwn Baxter and Mulberry sts.). *(C)* 212/732-2384. Subway: N, R, W, Q, or 6 to Canal St.

THE LOWER EAST SIDE

Also consider **Le Pere Pinard** (p. 142), 175 Ludlow St., south of Houston (*(C)* 212/777-4917), an affordable, terrific, and *très français* wine bar. There's also **Mercury Lounge,** 217 E. Houston St. (*(C)* 212/260-4700), which has a casual, comfortable bar up front; see p. 312.

Barramundi This lounge is notable for its fairy-tale outdoor garden, friendly staff, and settled-in feel in a neighborhood overrun by hipster copycats. Come on a weeknight to snare a table in the little corner of heaven out back. A fireplace makes Barramundi almost as appealing on cool nights. 147 Ludlow St. (btwn Stanton and Rivington sts.). *(C)* 212/569-6900. Subway: F to 2nd Ave.

Good World Bar & Grill *(Finds)* Don't worry about running into your fellow tourists here; this former Chinese barbershop is completely off the beaten track. Despite the location and utter lack of decor, it draws a young alterna-hip crowd with its refreshing lack of pretensions, low prices on good on-tap beers, and surprisingly good—and affordable—Scandinavian eats. 3 Orchard St. (btwn Division and Canal sts.). *(C)* 212/925-9975. Subway: F to E. Broadway.

Rivertown Lounge *(Value)* This spacious, low-key neighborhood boîte is an excellent place to hang with the locals and nurse a beer. Happy hour lasts all day: Enjoy $3 wine and drafts Monday through Friday from 1 to 8pm. There's a dartboard and a pool table. DJs speed up the vibe most nights. 187 Orchard St. (south of Houston St.). *(C)* 212/388-1288. Subway: F to 2nd Ave.

Whiskey Ward *(Finds)* Here's the second-best bar in town for serious whiskey fans (only behind the East Village's dba): first-class single malts and bourbons from which to choose, and no pretensions. Decor is kept to a minimum in traditional saloon style, but the jukebox rocks and a pool table provides additional entertainment. Nice on-tap and bottled beer selection, too. 121 Essex St. (btwn Rivington and Delancey sts.). ✆ **212/477-2998.** Subway: F to Delancey St.

SOHO

Ear Inn   There are many debates about which is the oldest bar in New York, and with its 1870s origins, Ear Inn is a serious contender for that crown. In superchic SoHo, this pub is a welcome cranky relief. They pull an excellent draft of Guinness and make a surprisingly good margarita as well. On Saturday afternoon, the poetry readings just might make you cry into your beer. In warm weather, tables are set up outside within exhaust distance of the nearby UPS depot. *Note:* Respect the no-cellphone policy or suffer the consequences. 326 Spring St. (btwn Greenwich and Washington sts.). ✆ **212/226-9060.** Subway: C or E to Spring St.

Merc Bar   Notable for its long tenure in the fickle world of beautiful-people bars, upscale Merc Bar has mellowed nicely. You'll still find a good-looking crowd in the superbly appointed lounge, but now it's a confident rather than trend-happy one. The decor bespeaks civilized rusticity with warm woods, a canoe over the bar, copper-top tables, and butter-leather banquettes. A great place to nestle into a comfortable couch with your honey, splurge on a classy cocktail, and enjoy the scene. The European martini (Stoli raspberry and Chambord) is divine. Look carefully, because there's no sign. 151 Mercer St. (btwn Prince and Houston sts.). ✆ **212/966-2727.** Subway: N or R to Prince St.

THE EAST VILLAGE & NOHO

In addition to the choices below, also consider **Fez,** 380 Lafayette St., at Great Jones Street (✆ **212/533-2680;** www.feznyc.com), a dimly lit Moroccan-themed bar and lounge that I prefer to the downstairs performance space; see p. 312.

dba *(Finds*   dba has completely bucked the loungey trend that has taken over the city, instead remaining firmly and resolutely an unpretentious neighborhood bar. Everyone is welcome in this beer- and Scotch-lover's paradise, which posts a massive drink menu on chalkboards. Owner Ray Deter specializes in British-style cask-conditioned ales (the kind that you pump by hand) and stocks a phenomenal collection of single-malt scotches. The crowd is a pleasing mix of connoisseurs and casual drinkers who like the choices and egalitarian vibe. Ray has enclosed the back garden, transforming it into an East Village beer garden. Excellent jukebox, too. 41 1st Ave. (btwn 2nd and 3rd sts.). ✆ **212/475-5097.** www.drinkgoodstuff.com. Subway: F to 2nd Ave.

Tips Get Happy at Happy Hour

Many of the city's best bars suddenly become more affordable from 4 to 8pm or thereabouts, when it's definitely a Happy Hour if you snag one of those signature cocktails ($10 martinis anyone?) at half-price, or two-for-one, or free bar food, or some other value-saving offer that might make you very happy. (Hipster Happy Hour trend of fall 2004: PBR cans for $3 or less.) It is during these few hours where you might get to experience some of those pricey places you've heard so much about, the places where a drink normally costs more than dinner. For information on happy hour at many of the city's watering holes, check online at www.sheckys.com or **Murph's NYC Bar Guide** at www.murphguide.com, which is updated daily.

KGB Bar   This former Ukrainian social club still boasts its Soviet-themed decor, but it now draws creative types who like the low-key boho vibe. There's also free entertainment almost every night of the week, thanks to KGB's excellent reading series, where a talented pack of up-and-coming and established writers read their prose in various genres (fiction, science fiction, poetry, and so on) to a receptive crowd starting at 7pm. Past readers have included playwright Tina Howe *(Painting Churches)*, Rick Moody *(The Ice Storm)*, and Kathryn Harrison *(The Kiss)*. 85 E. 4th St. (btwn 2nd and 3rd aves.). ✆ **212/505-3360**. www.kgbbar.com. Subway: 6 to Astor Place.

McSorley's Old Ale House   In business for more than 140 years, McSorley's window proudly claims WE WERE HERE BEFORE YOU WERE BORN. Only McSorley's Ale is served, light or dark, and two at a time. This is an ale-sodden frat-boy madhouse most nights and an Irish Armageddon on St. Patrick's Day, but everybody seems to love it. Although it's also a McSorley's tradition to urinate on the wall outside, they prefer you honor that one in the breach, not in the commission. Weekday afternoons are the best time to go to avoid the crowds. 15 E. 7th St. (btwn 2nd and 3rd aves.). ✆ **212/473-9148**. Subway: 6 to Astor Place.

Tom & Jerry's (288 Bar) *Finds*   Here's a pleasing neighborhood bar minus the grunge factor that usually plagues such joints. The place has an authentic local vibe, and the youngish, artsy crowd is unpretentious and chatty. The beer selection is very good and the mixed drinks are better than average. Flea-market hounds will enjoy the vintage collection of "Tom & Jerry" punchbowl sets behind the bar, and creative types will enjoy the rotating collection of works from local artists, which changes monthly. There's no sign, but you'll spy the action through the plate-glass window on the east side of Elizabeth Street just north of Houston. 288 Elizabeth St. ✆ **212/260-5045**. Subway: 6 to Bleecker St.

Zum Schneider *Finds*   You know New York has just about everything when you can find an authentic indoor German beer garden in the heart of Alphabet City. With long tables and bench seating, this is a fun place for a group. There are more than a dozen varieties of German beer on tap here, and all are served in sturdy steins. To complement those hearty beers you can sample equally hearty German fare such as Bavarian blood sausage and rolled beef filled with pickle, bacon, and mustard. If that seems a bit much, you can just munch on the homemade pretzels. 107 Ave. C (at 7th St.). ✆ **212/598-1098**. www.zumschneider.com. Subway: F to 2nd Ave.; L to 1st Ave.

GREENWICH VILLAGE & THE MEAT PACKING DISTRICT

Bowlmor/Pressure *Finds*   Supercool Bowlmor isn't your daddy's bowling alley: DJs spin, martinis flow, candy-colored balls knock down Day-Glo pins, and strikes and spares are automatically tallied into the wee hours. Frankly, Bowlmor is a blast. Once you're finished with your 10-pin—or while you're waiting for your lane—head upstairs to the rooftop lounge Pressure, housed in a 16,000-square-foot inflated bubble and boasting designer-mod furnishings, a sexy cocktail menu that includes a luscious chocolate martini (infused with Godiva chocolate liqueur), a fleet of pool tables, and always-on movie screens adding an arty-party flair. 110 University Place (btwn 12th and 13th sts.). ✆ **212/255-8188** (Bowlmor), or 212/352-1161 (Pressure). www.bowlmor.com or www.pressurenyc.com. Subway: 4, 5, 6, L, N, or R to 14th St./Union Square.

Chumley's   Many bars in New York date from Prohibition, but Chumley's still has the vibe. The college-age crowd doesn't date back as far, however. Come

Moments The Dive-Bar Experience

Watering holes in New York are many and diverse: There are bars and clubs with cover charges, outrageously expensive cocktails, elegant finger food, beautiful people, and velvet ropes to keep you waiting in the cold until someone determines you are worthy to enter. And then there are places in this city where you should be rewarded for braving, old, dark places where the drinks are cheap and the characters colorful. These are the dive bars, and they are just as much New York as the hottest, trendiest club you've read about back in your hometown. Here are some of my favorite dive bars; stop in one for a real New York experience.

Jimmy's Corner, 140 W. 44th St. (btwn Broadway and 6th Ave.; ℂ 212/ 221-9510). Owned by a former boxing trainer, Jimmy's is a tough-guy's joint that has been around for more than 30 years and survived the Disneyfication of Times Square. Pictures of boxers adorn the walls and the jukebox plays lots of R&B and '70s disco. In the pre-smoking-ban days, the smoke would get so thick in Jimmy's you needed night-vision goggles to see through the haze. Beer is cheap and drinks aren't fancy. Skip the theme bars and restaurants and go for an after-theater pop at Jimmy's.

Rudy's Bar & Grill, 627 9th Ave. (btwn 44th and 45th sts.; ℂ 212/ 974-9169). This Hell's Kitchen establishment is no secret; its happy hour is legendary, and the small place is usually packed with slackers sucking up cheap beer including the house brand, Rudy's Red, a weak, watery brew served in a huge plastic cup for $3. My advice is to get there before Happy Hour, grab a seat on one of the few broken banquettes, and keep your eyes open for the hot-dog guy, who gives out

to warm yourself by the fire and indulge in a once-forbidden pleasure: beer. The door is unmarked, with a metal grille on the small window; another entrance is at 58 Barrow St., which takes you in through a back courtyard. 86 Bedford St. (at Barrow St.). ℂ 212/675-4449. Subway: 1 or 9 to Christopher St.

White Horse Tavern   Poets and literary buffs pop into this 1880 pub to pay their respects to Dylan Thomas, who tipped his last jar here. Best enjoyed in the warm weather when there's outdoor drinking, or at happy hour for the cheap drafts that draw in a big frat-boy and post-frat yuppie crowd. 567 Hudson St. (at 11th St.). ℂ 212/243-9260. Subway: 1 or 9 to Christopher St.

CHELSEA
Chelsea Commons ⟡   The trendy bars come and go in this fashion-conscious neighborhood, but time stands still at Chelsea Commons. This old pub hosts an assortment of locals; artists trying to avoid the pretentiously hip, and workers from the nearby warehouses and depots. A fireplace gives it a homey feel in the winter and an outdoor patio, an urban escape in the summer. The jukebox has a mix of R&B, rock, country, and jazz. A great place for conversation and a pint of beer. Food is available, but don't get fancy; stick with the basic pub fare. 242 10th Ave. (at 24th St.). ℂ 212/929-9424. Subway: C or E to 23rd St.

free hot dogs. You'll need one to balance out a bucket of Rudy's Red. In the summer, Rudy's opens its cement garden for drinks "alfresco."

Subway Inn, 143 E. 60th St. (at Lexington Ave.; © 212/223-9829). My all-time favorite dive, the Subway has been around for over 60 years, and I believe some of the regulars have been on their stools that whole time. The red neon sign beckons from outside, while inside, no matter what time of day, it's midnight dark. The bartender is ancient, and until recently, served Schaeffer on tap. The demise of Schaeffer was troubling, but thankfully not much else has changed. The booths are still wobbly and the models of Godzilla and E.T. along with assorted other dusty junk continue to decorate the shelves behind the bar. If you order a gin and tonic, don't ask for a lime. The last time I visited, I was kept from going into the men's room by police who were rousting one of the regulars during a drug bust. You might find workers from the upscale stores in the neighborhood and writers searching for "material" slumming at the Subway, and occasionally a celebrity "discovers" it, but this joint remains the epitome of a dive.

Tap a Keg, 2731 Broadway (btwn 103rd and 104th sts; © 212/749-1734). The Tap a Keg calls itself a "Hell of a Joint." And hell can mean two things here: very good fun or a nightmare. That's the happy contradiction. There are a few wooden tables and televisions; a great jukebox with jazz, reggae, and R&B; and a popular pool table. But it's the 7-hour happy hour with pints of beer around $3 and the regular gathering of wizened, disheveled characters that give the Tap a Keg its well-deserved dive status.

Gaslight   The ideal cross between a cozy English pub and an elegant Victorian lounge. No taps, though—but a dependably good hangout nonetheless. 400 W. 14th St. (at 9th Ave.). © 212/807-8444. Subway: A, C, or E to 14th St.

Serena   Done in deep, sexy reds, Serena is as hip as can be—I've even spotted mix-master Moby here. It's relatively unpretentious considering its hot-spot status; still, dress the part if you want to make it past the doorman, especially on weekends. The crowd is young and pretty, and the schizophrenic music mix is a blast— think Fatboy Slim meets ABBA meets Foghat, and you'll get the picture. In the basement level of the Hotel Chelsea, 222 W. 23rd St. (btwn 7th and 8th aves.). © 212/255-4646. Subway: C, E, 1, or 9 to 23rd St.

THE FLATIRON DISTRICT, UNION SQUARE & GRAMERCY PARK
Also consider the **Old Town Bar & Restaurant** (p. 157), 45 E. 18th St., (btwn Broadway and Park Ave. S.; © 212/529-6732), a genuine tin-ceilinged 19th-century bar that's a terrific place to soak up some Old New York atmosphere. Sleek noodle house **Republic** (p. 158), 37 Union Square W. (© 212/627-7172), boasts an up-front bar that's popular with a wallet-watching cocktail crowd who come to enjoy such creative libations as the Sake Dragon martini (sake and Chambord) and a Fuji apple Cosmopolitan.

The Bar on Gramercy Park   Who says a hotel bar can't be a dive? But this one is a dive in the best definition of that term. It has a loungey feel to it, with its quasi-antique furnishings and lush red drapes. But it's distinctive, even comforting, in its gauche retro-80s look. The bar was used in the movie *Almost Famous,* about a young journalist covering a rock band for *Rolling Stone,* maybe because rock-'n'-rollers like Sting, Deborah Harry, and The Clash have frequented the place, as have actors Matt Dillon, Ethan Hawke, and Peter O'Toole. And if Peter O'Toole gave it the thumbs up, who are we to argue? 2 Lexington Ave. (at 21st St.). ✆ 212/475-4320. Subway: 6 to 23rd St.

Dusk *Finds*   This casual, artsy lounge is a great choice for a cocktail. There's a fab mirrored mosaic wall, banquettes opposite, a friendly bar serving affordable drinks, a pool table, and mostly U.K. tunes—from drum-and-bass to Super Furry Animals to Blur to Enya—on the sound system. Expect an easygoing, youngish crowd that stays relaxed and unpretentious into the evening. No sign, but look for the three blue lights attached to a dark storefront. 147 W. 24th St. (btwn 6th and 7th aves.). ✆ 212/924-4490. Subway: F to 23rd St.

Pete's Tavern   The oldest continually operating establishment in the city, Pete's opened while Lincoln was president. It reeks of history—and more importantly, there's Guinness on tap and a terrific happy hour. The crowd is a mix of locals from Gramercy Park and more down-to-earth types. 129 E. 18th St. (at Irving Place). ✆ 212/473-7676. www.petestavern.com. Subway: 4, 5, 6, L, N, R, Q, or W to 14th St./Union Square.

TIMES SQUARE & MIDTOWN WEST

Joe Allen (p. 164), the legendary Broadway pub on Restaurant Row, 326 W. 46th St. (btwn 8th and 9th aves.; ✆ 212/581-6464), is great for an after-theater cocktail. A branch of **Heartland Brewery** is across from Radio City at 1285 6th Ave., at 51st Street (✆ 212/582-8244).

Algonquin Bar   The oak-paneled lobby of this venerable literati-favored Arts and Crafts hotel is the comfiest and most welcoming in the city, made to linger over pre- or post-theater cocktails. You'll feel the spirit of Dorothy Parker and the Algonquin Round Table that pervades the room. Try the Matilda, a light blend of orange juice, Absolut Mandarin, triple sec, and champagne, named after the Algonquin's feline in residence. Adjacent is the clubby **Blue Bar,** home to a rotating collection of Hirschfeld drawings. Well worth a few spare bucks if you want to soak in Old New York atmosphere at its finest. 59 W. 44th St. (btwn 5th and 6th aves.). ✆ 212/840-6800. Subway: B, D, F, or V to 42nd St.

M Bar *Finds*   This library-style lounge transcends its hotel-bar status with a circular bar, a first-rate cocktail menu, comfortable seating, a dark and romantic Art Deco mood, and a warmth that will make pretension-phobes feel right at home. Prices are reasonable, too, considering the neighborhood. The weekly Wednesday jazz night has turned into a big hit with locals—so much so that the calendar has expanded to include cabaret nights and wine tastings. A real gem! Adjacent to the Mansfield hotel, 12 W. 44th St. (btwn 5th and 6th aves.). ✆ 212/944-6050. Subway: B, D, F, or V to 42nd St.

Mickey Mantle's   Before Mickey Mantle's officially opened several years ago, I was walking past the restaurant, peered into the window, and there was my boyhood idol, the Mick, sitting at the bar by himself. Through the window I waved—and he waved back. It made my day. And though the food's not very good and the drinks are overpriced, I still have a soft spot for Mickey Mantle's and always will. With plenty of Yankee memorabilia on the walls and sports on all the televisions, it's an ideal place to watch a game, but stick with the basics: beer and burgers. 42 Central Park S. (btwn 5th and 6th aves.). © **212/688-7777**. www.mickey mantles.com. Subway: F to 57th St.

Russian Vodka Room *Finds*   This old-school lounge is a Theater District find. It's not going to win any style awards, but it's comfortable and knows what's what when it comes to vodkas. More than 50 are on hand, plus the RVR's own infusions; you can order an iced rack of six if you can't decide between such yummy flavors as cranberry, apple-cinnamon, ginger, horseradish, and more (the raspberry makes a perfect Cosmo). The 30-something-and-up crowd is peopled with post-Soviet imports as well as New Yorkers in the know. A martini or Cosmo is about $10, but you could do the backstroke in it. Come early if you want to snag a bar table. 265 W. 52nd St. (btwn Broadway and 8th Ave.). © **212/307-5835**. Subway: C, E, 1, or 9 to 50th St.

Tír Na Nóg   This festive place is a standout among the Irish pubs that line 8th Avenue near Penn Station. The decor lends the place a genuine Celtic vibe, as does the Murphy's on tap and the lilt of the bartender. The bar has established itself among both locals and bridge-and-tunnel types for its unpretentious, lively air. There's good, upscale pub grub; a dance floor; and live, foot-stompin' Irish music Friday and Saturday nights. The ideal place to celebrate St. Patrick's Day. 5 Penn Plaza (8th Ave. btwn 33rd and 34th sts.). © **212/630-0249**. www.tirnanognyc.com. Subway: A, C, or E to 34th St./Penn Station.

MIDTOWN EAST & MURRAY HILL

Bull & Bear   The name speaks to its business-minded clientele; there's even a stock ticker in constant service for those three-martini lunches. The Bull & Bear is like a gentlemen's pub, with leather chairs, a waistcoated staff, and a troika-shaped mahogany bar polished to a high sheen at the center of the room. Still, it's plenty comfy for casual drinkers. Ask Oscar, who's been here for more than 30 years, or one of the other accomplished bartenders to blend you a classic cocktail. Or just order a beer—either way, you'll be right at home here. An ideal place to kick back after a hard day of sightseeing. At the Waldorf-Astoria. 301 Park Ave. (btwn 49th and 50th sts.). © **212/872-4900**. Subway: 6 to 51st St.

The Ginger Man   The bait at this appealing upscale bar is the 66 gleaming tap handles lining the wood-and-brass bar, dispensing everything from Sierra Nevada and Hoegaarden to cask-conditioned ales. The cavernous space has a clubby feel, as Wall Streeters and the young men and women they flirt with lounge on sofas and chairs. The limited menu is well prepared, and prices are better than you'd expect from a place like this. 11 E. 36th St. (btwn 5th and Madison aves.). © **212/532-3740**. Subway: 6 to 33rd St.

King Cole Room   The birthplace of the Bloody Mary, this spot may just be New York's best classic hotel bar. The Maxfield Parrish mural is worth the price of a classic cocktail (ask the bartender to tell you about the "hidden" meaning of the painting). The sophisticated setting demands proper attire, so dress for the occasion. The *New York Times* calls the bar nuts "the best in town," but there's an elegant bar-food menu if you'd like something more substantial. Avoid the after-work hours at holiday time, when the crowd can ruin the mood. At the St. Regis hotel, 2 E. 55th St. (at 5th Ave.). © **212/339-6721**. Subway: E or F to 53rd St.

P.J. Clarke's   After being closed for a year, this 120-year-old saloon/restaurant was renovated, preserving most of all the original detail, and reopened in 2003 under new ownership (one of the owners is actor Timothy Hutton). P.J. Clarke's is a New York institution, a late-night hangout for politicians, actors, and athletes. This is where Ray Milland went on a bender in the classic 1948 movie *The Lost Weekend.* Maybe if Milland stopped drinking and had one of P.J. Clarke's legendary hamburgers, he wouldn't have ended up in Bellevue. 915 3rd Ave. (at 55th St.). © **212/317-1616.** www.pjclarkes.com. Subway: E or V to Lexington Ave.

Cocktails Alfresco

One of my favorite moments in the movie *The Producers* is when Max Bialystock (played by Zero Mostel) tries to woo Leo Bloom (Gene Wilder) into helping him carry out his theater scam. Bialystock tells Bloom that he will treat him to dinner and they will dine "alfresco." The next shot is Bialystock buying a hot dog for Bloom from a vendor near Central Park.

But food and drink always *do* taste better alfresco. And for those who crave nicotine, most outdoor spaces allow smoking. Here are some of my favorite places for cocktails out of doors.

On the rooftop of the legendary Gramercy Park Hotel, just opposite pristine and exclusive Gramercy Park, is the very popular **High Bar,** 2 Lexington Ave., at 21st Street (© **212/475-4320**). The scene here, where the views of the Met Life Building, Gramercy Park, and the Empire State Building are gorgeous, has gotten so hot that they actually installed outdoor heaters to extend drinking alfresco into the cooler months.

The view on the roof garden of the Lower East Side, trilevel club, **The Delancey,** 168 Delancey St. (at Clinton St.; © **212/254-9920**), is nothing special, but the fountain, fish pool, and creeping trellises of vines make it a funky, original spot for a drink.

One of my favorite parks is Riverside Park (see chapter 7), and two of the reasons why I love this park are the **79th Street Boat Basin Café,** 79th Street, at the Hudson River (© **212/496-5542**; www.boatbasincafe. com), where you can sip a drink and watch the boats bob on the river as the sun sets, and **Hurley's Hudson Beach Café,** Riverside Park and 103rd Street (© **917/370-3448**), where beach volleyball games and stunning sunsets are the entertainment, marred only by the constant automobile buzz of nearby West Side Highway.

Another park where you can, if you listen closely, hear the birds chirping is Union Square Park, and at **Luna Park,** at the north end of the park at 17th Street (© **212/475-8464**), you can sip a cool glass of sangria under the stars well into a summer evening.

The Lower East Side's **Barramundi** (p. 317) has one of the nicest outdoor spaces for drinking and dining in the city while **Zum Schneider** (p. 319) and **Jeremy's Ale House** (p. 317) both feature beer gardens. And don't forget the outdoor space also referred to as a "garden" at the great dive, **Rudy's Bar & Grill** (see "The Dive-Bar Experience," above).

Under the Volcano *Finds* If you've been shopping crowded Macy's or braving the lines at the Empire State Building and want (need?) a drink, one of the few choices in the area, but a good one, is this Mexican-themed tequila bar. The decor is Mexican folk with Frida Kahlo undertones throughout, but the main attractions are the 16 varieties of tequila and the very smooth, subtly potent margaritas. The bar also features an excellent selection of aged rums. 12 E. 36th St. (btwn 5th and Madison aves.). ℂ 212/213-0093. Subway: B, D, F, N, or R to 34th St.

THE UPPER WEST SIDE

The subterranean **All State Cafe** (p. 170), 250 W. 72nd St. (btwn Broadway and West End Ave.; ℂ 212/874-1883), is one of the best workaday pubs in town, with a loyal and easygoing grown-up crowd, great burgers, a terrific jukebox, and a cozy fireplace.

Also consider the dive **Tap a Keg,** 2731 Broadway (btwn 103rd and 104th sts.; ℂ 212/749-1734). Closer to Columbia, there's also a terrific bar that rollicks well into the wee hours at **Nacho Mama's,** 2893 Broadway (btwn 112th and 113th sts.; ℂ 212/665-2800).

Café del Bar *Finds* This casual reggae lounge in the northern hinterlands of Columbus Avenue is so small, everyone will surely know your name. African and Jamaican roots music adds to the exotic vibe here while the $4 Red Stripes and the special of the house, Mango Mimosas will have you fantasizing about beautiful sandy beaches. 945 Columbus Ave. (at 106th St.). ℂ 212/531-1643. Subway: C or B to 103rd St.

Dublin House For years, like a welcoming beacon, the Dublin House's neon harp has blinked invitingly. This very old pub is a no-frills Irish saloon and the perfect spot for a drink after visiting the Museum of Natural History or Central Park. There's a long, narrow barroom up front and a bigger room in the back that's good for groups. Original wood-veneer detail remains, adding to the pub's charm. The Guinness is cheap and drawn perfectly by the able and sometimes crusty bartenders. It's best enjoyed in the late afternoon or early evening when the regulars populate the bar. Stay away on weekend nights and St. Patrick's Day when the place is overrun with amateurs: frat boys and sorority girls on pub crawls. 225 W. 79th St. (btwn Broadway and Amsterdam Ave.). ℂ 212/874-9528. Subway: 1 or 9 to 79th St.

Eden *Finds* A sleek downtown cocktail lounge has finally found its way uptown. This French-owned lounge features a sleek granite-topped bar, a dark comfy back room with couches, and plush chairs. Happy hour here is happily an extended 4 hours, 5 to 9pm 7 days a week. The DJ comes on after happy hour, and spontaneous dancing has been known to occasionally take place. There is live blues on Wednesday and reggae on Thursday. A belly dancer entertains late on weekends. Bites are available like quesadillas and croque-monsieur. A fashionable refuge in an unfashionable neighborhood. 2728 Broadway (btwn 104th and 105th sts.). ℂ 212/865-5565. Subway: 1 or 9 to 103rd St.

Shark Bar This popular, upscale spot is well known for its good soul food and even better singles' scene. It's also a favorite hangout for sports celebs, so don't be surprised if you spot a New York Knick or Ranger. 307 Amsterdam Ave. (btwn 74th and 75th sts.). ℂ 212/874-8500. Subway: 1, 2, 3, or 9 to 72nd St.

THE UPPER EAST SIDE

You may wish to consider New York's number-one dive: **Subway Inn,** 143 E. 60th St., just east of Lexington Avenue (ℂ 212/223-8929). See "The Dive-Bar Experience," earlier in this chapter.

Author! Author! Where to Hear Spoken Word

Readings can be some of the most inexpensive and entertaining events in New York City. There are several venues dedicated to presenting spoken word, and (like hip clubs) popular series presented in venues ranging from bars to bookstores. Many readings are free; others charge a small cover; and except for the top names, you'll rarely see a charge over $10.

The best sources for finding out who's reading where include the "Books" section of *Timeout New York,* which spotlights top readings in its "Don't Miss" section; and *The Village Voice,* which does the same with its "Voice Choices."

To find out which author (or celebrity who's had a book ghost-written) is reading at a NYC Barnes & Noble (there's *always* a major author in town) go to www.barnesandnoble.com and use the "Event Locator." October 2004, for example, featured free readings by Carson Kressley, Joyce Carol Oates, John Irving, and Dave Navarro.

Who are you likely to see at these venues? Everyone from bestselling authors (Candace Bushell, Tom Wolfe, Norman Mailer), to spoken word artists (Reg E. Gaines and Alix Olson) to whoever's just scribbled a poem on the back of an envelope at an Open Mike event.

Below are some of the top venues/series in town:

- **The Unterberg Poetry Center** at the 92nd Street YMHA (92nd St. at Lexington Ave.; ⓒ **212/415-5740;** www.92y.org; subway: 4, 5, or 6 to 96th St.). The 92nd Street Y has had all the heavy hitters in its lineup since 1939. In addition to talks and readings by the world's top poets, novelists, playwrights, and critics, the Y also offers "Biographers & Brunch," and "Critics & Brunch." Tickets are $16 in the 2004–05 season, which runs from September to June, and features evenings with poet Adrienne Rich, a "Poets Theater" presentation of "Rage of Achilles"; and tributes/commemorations of Richard Wilbur, Truman Capote, and Issac Bashevis Singer. The readings are in a 917-seat auditorium, which does on occasion sell out.

- **Nuyorican Poets Café** (236 E. 3rd St. btwn aves. B and C; ⓒ **212 05-8183;** www.nuyorican.org; subway: F or V to 2nd Ave.). Celebrating 30 years in its East Village location in 2005, the Nuyorican, brainchild of Miguel Algarin, who still runs it, presents poetry, drama, music and film. The raucous, popular **Poetry Slams** (the cafe fields a championship Slam Team) present poetry as a sport: aspiring stars show up and throw down their work in front of an audience and panel of judges, who score them on the quality of the work and presentation. The Friday slams begin around 10pm (cover charge $7) and feature an invited slam poet. Slam Opens are held most Wednesdays (also a $7 cover). The storefront bar gets crowded quickly, so get there early on Slam nights.

- **Bowery Poetry Club,** 308 Bowery (ⓒ **212/614-0505;** www.bowery poetry.com; subway: F or V to 2nd Ave.). "Poetry Czar" (as anointed by the *Village Voice*) Bob Holman opened his "Home for Poetry" in an 1850 building on (you guessed it) the Bowery, across the street from CBGB, in 2002. It's open all day for snacks, coffee and that writer essential, hanging out; a two-for-one happy hour at the bar precedes each evening's festivities. Poetry and fiction readings, open mikes, monologues, words-with-music, and all manner of other spoken word is presented from about 5:30pm each night, with covers ranging from free to $6. National and rising stars on the poetry/spoken word scene show up here. The space can hold up to 200 people.

- **KGB,** 85 E. 4th St. (btwn 2nd Ave. and the Bowery; ⓒ **212/505-3360;** www.kgbbar.com; subway: F or V to 2nd Ave.; 6 to Astor Place). This second-floor bar (it's not handicapped-accessible) in an old East Village brownstone was once a Ukrainian social club and decorated with vintage Communist memorabilia. There's never a cover (but you are urged to refresh your drink between each reader) for the readings held almost every night of the week (check the website) starting at around 7pm. It's a tiny bar, holding perhaps 40 to 50 comfortably, and double that or more for a "hot" reader (think Kathryn Harrison, Rick Moody, A. M. Homes), with "nights" curated by individual writers for poetry, science fiction, and other genres.

FESTIVALS & EVENTS

- *The New Yorker* magazine (**http://festival.newyorker.com**) has gone into the readings business with its high-end "New Yorker Festival" held in early October. You'll pay dearly (up to $30) for the privilege of seeing, say Sherman Alexie or R. Crumb read from or talk about their work at one of several venues, but the events almost always sell out. (Just *try* getting in to see Jumpa Lahiri! *Forget* about Conan O'Brien . . .) There are also free events and book signings scheduled.

- Every New Year's Day, the **Poetry Project at St. Mark's Church,** 131 E. 10th St. (btwn 2nd and 3rd aves.; ⓒ **212/674-0910;** www.poetryproject. com; subway: N, R, or W to Union Square; 6 to Astor Place), presents a marathon poetry reading starting around 2pm, and running till . . . whenever. Poets and performers ranging from Patti Smith to Eric Bogosian, Maggie Estep, Tuli Kupferberg, and many (many) more read to welcome in the New Year and raise money for the Poetry Projects readings, workshops, and other programs. Tickets run about $20.

- **Symphony Space,** 2537 Broadway at 95th St. (ⓒ **212/864-5400;** www. symphonyspace.org; subway: 1, 2, 3, or 9 to 96th St.; B or C to 96th St.) is the home of both **Selected Shorts** (Oct–Dec) and **Bloomsday on Broadway.** In Selected Shorts, modern and classic short stories are read by professional actors, ranging from the likes of Blair Brown, Cynthia Nixon, Eli Wallach, and John Shea in the Peter Jay Sharpe Theater (which seats 760). Authors whose work you might hear include John Cheever, Truman Capote, and Woody Allen. Tickets range from $21 to $25, with discounts for students and seniors. And each June 16 (the day Leopold Bloom took his stroll around Dublin in 1904 in James Joyce's *Ulysses*) an ensemble cast of actors and avid Joyceans do a marathon reading from the masterwork. Its tickets ($20 adults, $17 students and seniors) are usually sold out well in advance.

Great Hall Balcony Bar *(Moments* One of Manhattan's best cocktail bars is only open on Friday and Saturday—and only from 4 to 8:30pm, to boot. The Metropolitan Museum of Art transforms the lobby's mezzanine level into a cocktail-and-classical-music lounge twice weekly, offering an only-in-New-York experience. The music is usually provided by a grand piano and string quartet. The setting couldn't be grander, especially when the hall is transformed into a Christmas paradise at holiday season. You'll have to pay the $10 admission, but the galleries are open until 9pm. At the Metropolitan Museum of Art, 5th Ave. at 82nd St. ✆ 212/535-7710. www.metmuseum.org. Subway: 4, 5, or 6 to 86th St.

Mo's Caribbean Bar & Mexican Grill The poor man's Cancún Spring Break can be found at Mo's, where "Beach Party" nights are common along with live reggae on Tuesdays, sweet and strong rum drinks, a half-price happy hour every day, and disgusting but satisfying munchies such as jalapeño poppers, nachos, and jerk chicken wings to keep you fortified while you drink. 1454 2nd Ave. at 77th St. ✆ 212/650-0561. Subway: 6 to 77th St.

HARLEM

Lenox Lounge More famous for its status as Harlem's best jazz club (p. 314), Lenox Lounge also boasts Harlem's best bar scene. This old-world throwback (Scotch comes Johnnie Walker, not single-malt) is warm, cozy, and popular with grown-ups from all walks of life. 288 Malcolm X Blvd. (Lenox Ave., btwn 124th and 125th sts.). ✆ 212/427-0253. Subway: 2 or 3 to 125th St.

8 Dance Clubs & Party Scenes

No slice of New York nightlife is as mutable as the club scene. In this world, hot spots don't even get 15 minutes of fame—their time in the limelight is usually more like a commercial break.

First things first: Finding and going to the latest hot spot is not worth agonizing over. Clubbers spend their lives obsessing over the scene. My rule of thumb is that if I know about a place, it must be over. Just find someplace that suits you, and enjoy the crowd.

"Clubs" as actual, physical spaces don't mean much anymore. The hungry-for-nightlife crowd follows events of certain party "producers" who switch venues and times each week.

I've concentrated on a wide variety of scenes below, from performance-artsy to perennially popular discos, most of which are generally easy to make your way into. You can find listings for the most current hot spots and movable parties in the **sources** listed in the introduction to this chapter.

New York nightlife starts late. With the exception of places that have scheduled live performances, it's almost useless to show up anywhere before 11pm. Don't depend on plastic; bring cash, and plan on dropping a wad. Cover charges start out anywhere from $5 to $30 and often get more expensive as the night wears on. *Time Out New York* is a great source to check, as it lists cover charges for the week's big events and clearly indicates which are free.

Money-saving tips: Additional online sources that might score you discount admissions to select clubs include **www.promony.com**. No matter what, **always call ahead,** because schedules change and do so at the last minute. Even better: You also may be able to put your name on a guest list that will save you a few bucks at the door. You can also check **http://newyork.sheckys.com** for VIP guest-list access. And always check the clubs' websites directly for special deals.

Avalon   In the old (deconsecrated) church where dance club legend Limelight once reigned supreme, Avalon opened with a big splash in late 2003. The interior has been updated with VIP balconies that overlook the dance floor. Off the dance floor are many small rooms for commingling, if you are tired of dancing. 660 6th Ave. (at 20th St.). (C) 212/807-7780. Subway: F to 23rd St.

Baktun   This club has been hot since the word *go*. Sleek Baktun was conceived in 2000 as a multimedia lounge, and incorporates video projections (shown on a clever double-sided video screen) into its dance parties as well as live cybercasts. The music tends toward electronica, with some live acts. At press time, Saturday's Direct Drive was still the key drum 'n' bass party in town. 418 W. 14th St. (btwn 9th Ave. and Washington St.). (C) 212/206-1590. www.baktun.com. Cover $3–$10. Subway: A, C, E, or L to 14th St.

Cafe Wha?   You'll find a carefree crowd dancing in this casual basement club any night of the week. From Wednesday through Sunday, the stage features the house's own Wha Band, which does an excellent job of cranking out crowd-pleasing covers of familiar rock-'n'-roll hits from the '70s, '80s, and '90s. Monday night is the hugely popular Brazilian Dance Party, while Tuesday night is Classic Funk Night. Expect to be surrounded by lots of Jersey kids and out-of-towners on the weekends, but so what? You'll be having as much fun as they are. Reservations are a good idea. 115 MacDougal St. (btwn Bleecker and 3rd sts.). (C) 212/254-3706. www.cafewha.com. Cover free to $10. Subway: A, B, C, D, E, F, or V to W. 4th St.

Club Shelter   House heads flock to this old-school disco. The big draw is the "Saturday Night Shelter Party," when late-'80s House music takes over. The crowd is racially and sexually diverse and dress is not fancy; wear whatever is comfortable for doing some heavy sweating on the dance floor. At press time, live acts such as Patti LaBelle were set to be added. 20 W. 39th St. (btwn 5th and 6th aves.). (C) 212/719-9867. Subway: B, D, F, Q, V, or 7 to 42nd St.

crobar   With over 25,000 square feet—room enough for 3,000—this is one place where your odds of getting in are very good. The excellent sound system and DJs from around the world—like Paul Van Dyk and Tiesto of Holland—will have you sweating in no time. If you lose your friends or lovers in the crowd, don't worry, you'll find new ones. 530 W. 28th St. (btwn 10th and 11th aves.). (C) 212/629-9000. www.crobar.com. Subway: C or E to 23rd St.

Don Hill's   This long-lived, eccentric, divey club draws a heavily integrated gay-lesbian/straight crowd that comes for rock, glam, and punk some nights, campy parties on others. Röck Cändy is a fun neo-glam resurrection on Wednesday nights, featuring live hair-metal bands (for whom there is still a scene in New York). Drinks are affordable. 511 Greenwich St. (at Spring St.). (C) 212/334-1390. www.donhills.com. Cover $5–$10. Subway: 1 or 9 to Canal St.

Spirit   Mind, Body, and Soul is the theme here. Start with the Body, the 10,000-square-foot dance floor where you'll try to compete with acrobats, aerialists, and professional dancers. The effort will wear you out and you'll need to retreat to the Mind, the club's holistic healing center where you can get a massage or have your palm read, among other New-Agey amenities. Finally, you don't want to leave hungry, so sample Soul, the club's organic vegetarian restaurant. 530 W. 27th St. (btwn 10th and 11th aves.). (C) 212/268-9477. Subway: C or E to 23rd St.

Swing 46   Swing is still a nightly affair at this jazz and supper club (supper not required). Music is live nightly, and runs the gamut from big band to boogie-woogie to jump blues. Don't miss Vince Giordano and His Nighthawks if they're on the bill, especially if sharp-dressed Casey McGill is singing and strumming his ukulele, too. The Harlem Renaissance Orchestra is another great choice. Even first-timers can join in the fun, as free swing lessons are offered nightly at 9:15pm. No jeans or sneakers. 349 W. 46th St. (btwn 8th and 9th aves.). © 212/262-9554. www.swing46.com. Mon–Wed cover $5, Thurs–Sat $15. Subway: C or E to 50th St.

13 *Value*   This little lounge is a great place to dance the night away. It's stylish but unpretentious, with a steady roster of fun weekly parties. Sunday night's no-cover Britpop fest Shout! lives on, as popular as ever—and with no cover, to boot. The rest of the week runs the gamut from '70s and '80s New Wave and glam night to progressive house and trance to poetry slams and performance art. If there's a cover, it's usually $5, occasionally $7 or $10. Happy hour offers two-for-one drinks (and no cover) from 4 to 8pm. 35 E. 13th St. (btwn Broadway and University Place), 2nd floor. © 212/979-6677. www.bar13.com or www.bar13.com. Cover free to $5 (occasionally $7–$10). Subway: 4, 5, 6, N, R, L, Q, or W to 14th St./Union Square.

9 The Gay & Lesbian Scene

To get a thorough, up-to-date take on what's happening in gay and lesbian nightlife, pick up copies of *GONYC* (www.gonycmagazine.com), *HX* (www.hx.com), the *New York Blade* (www.nyblade.com), *Next* (www.nextnyc.com), and *Gay City News* (www.gaycitynews.com), available for free in bars and clubs all around town, at news boxes throughout the city, or at the **Lesbian, Gay, Bisexual & Transgender Community Center,** at 208 W. 13th St. (btwn 7th and 8th aves.; © 212/620-7310; www.gaycenter.org). *Time Out New York* boasts a terrific gay and lesbian section; another great source is the free weekly *Village Voice.* Always remember that asking people in one bar can lead you to discover another that fits your tastes.

In addition to the choices below, be sure to see what's happening at such clubs as **Don Hill's,** which cater to gay and/or gay/straight mixed crowds; see "Dance Clubs & Party Scenes," above. You might also wish to consider **Duplex** and **Don't Tell Mama** if cabaret's more your style (p. 316). Women might wish to see what's on at **Bluestockings** bookstore and cafe (p. 266).

Barracuda   Chelsea is central to gay life—and gay bars. This trendy, loungey place is a continuing favorite, voted "Best Bar" by *HX* and *New York Press* for 2 years running, while *Paper* singles out the hunky bartenders. There's a sexy bar for cruising out front and a comfy lounge in back. Look for the regular drag shows. 275 W. 22nd St. (btwn 7th and 8th aves.). © 212/645-8613. Subway: C, E, 1, or 9 to 23rd St.

Big Cup   Big Cup isn't a bar, but a coffeehouse. Still, you'd be hard-pressed to find a cooler, comfier pickup joint, or a more preening crowd. This is where all the Chelsea boys hang; just think of it as a living room–style lounge without the alcohol. By the way, it also happens to be a fab coffeehouse. 228 8th Ave. (btwn 21st and 22nd sts.). © 212/206-0059. Subway: C or E to 23rd St.

Boiler Room   This East Village bar is everybody's favorite gay dive. Despite the mixed guy-girl crowd, it's a cruising scene for well-sculpted beautiful boys who love to pose, and a fine hangout for those who'd rather play pool. 86 E. 4th St. (btwn 1st and 2nd aves.). © 212/254-7536. Subway: F to 2nd Ave.

The Cock *Finds*   This gleefully seedy East Village joint is the most envelope-pushing gay club in town. A self-proclaimed "rock and sleaze fag bar" is dedicated to good-natured depravity. Head elsewhere if you're the retiring type. 188 Ave. A (at 12th St.). © 212/777-6254. Subway: L to 1st Ave.

The Eagle　Everybody's favorite leather bar has been beautifully re-created in this far west Chelsea bi-level space. 554 W. 28th St. (btwn 10th and 11th aves.). © **646/ 473-1866.** Subway: C or E to 23rd St.

Hell　This glamorous lounge is a sexy haven for a predominantly gay weekend crowd in the hipper-than-hell Meat Packing District. The cocktails are well mixed, and plenty of comfy sofas are on hand for getting cozy. Ahead of its time in the 'hood, Hell is not quite as ultrahot as it used to be, but that just means there's more room for you. 59 Gansevoort St. (btwn Washington and Greenwich sts.). © **212/ 727-1666.** Subway: A, C, or E to 14th St.

Henrietta Hudson *Finds*　This friendly, popular, and sometimes raucous women's bar/lounge is known for drawing in an attractive, upmarket lipstick lesbian crowd that comes for the jukebox and videos as well as the pleasingly low-key atmosphere. On weekends DJs spin tunes (Fri–Sat) and live bands are in the house (Sun). 438 Hudson St. (at Morton St.). © **212/924-3347.** Weekends cover $5–$7. Subway: 1 or 9 to Houston St.

Rubyfruit Bar & Grill　This cozy bar and restaurant is a popular hangout, and less raucous than most of the other all-girl party scenes listed here. Choose a romantic dinner downstairs, or head upstairs for the playful, friendly pickup or hangout scene—whichever you prefer. 531 Hudson St. (btwn Charles and W. 10th sts.). © **212/929-3343.** Subway: 1 or 9 to Christopher St.

Splash/SBNY　Beautiful bartenders, video screens playing campy scenes, New York's best drag queens—Splash has it all. Theme nights are a big deal. The best of the bunch is Musical Mondays, dedicated to Broadway video clips and music. Musical Mondays' now-famous singalongs are such a blast that they regularly draw a crossover gay/straight mixed crowd as well as celebs like Nathan Lane and the cast of the ABBA musical, *Mamma Mia!* 50 W. 17th St. (btwn 5th and 6th aves.). © **212/691-0073.** www.splashbar.com. Subway: F or V to 14th St.; 4, 5, 6, N, R, L, Q, or W to 14th St./Union Square.

Stonewall Bar　Where it all started. A mixed gay and lesbian crowd—old and young—makes this an easy place to begin. At least pop in to relive a defining moment in queer history. 53 Christopher St. (east of 7th Ave.). © **212/463-0950.** Subway: 1 or 9 to Christopher St.

Townhouse Bar　Here's a first-class watering hole for men who want to relax rather than cruise. Friendly and open to all. 236 E. 58th St. (btwn 2nd and 3rd aves.). © **212/754-4649.** Subway: 4, 5, or 6 to 59th St.

Ty's Bar　This friendly, unassuming gay bar has been a part of the Village men's scene for about a million years. The second Tuesday of each month is Firemen's Night, if you want to chat up some of New York's bravest. 114 Christopher St. (btwn Bleecker and Bedford sts.). © **212/741-9641.** www.tys.citysearch.com. Subway: 1 or 9 to Christopher St.

View Bar *Finds*　Up front is a very attractive and comfortable lounge; in back is a pool room with the name-worthy view; throughout you'll find friendly bartenders, affordable drinks, and Kenneth Cole–dressed boys who could pass on either side of bi. A welcome addition to the scene. 232 8th Ave. (btwn 21st and 22nd sts.). © **212/929-2243.** Subway: C or E to 23rd St.

Index

Travel Tip: He who finds the best hotel deal has more to spend on facials involving knobbly vegetables.

Hello, the Roaming Gnome here. I've been nabbed from the garden and taken round the world. The people who took me are so terribly clever. They find the best offerings on Travelocity. For very little cha-ching. And that means I get to be pampered and exfoliated till I'm pink as a bunny's doodah.

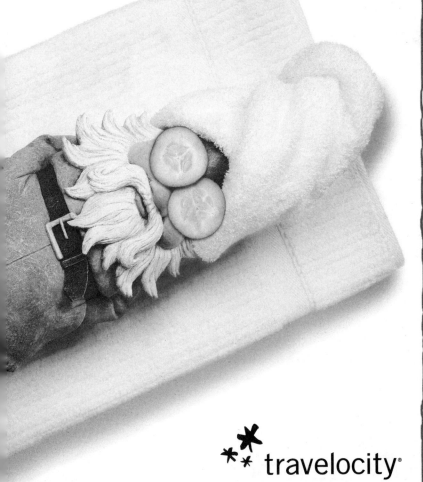

travelocity®

-888-TRAVELOCITY / travelocity.com / America Online Keyword: Travel

Travel Tip: Make sure there's customer service for any change of plans — involving friendly natives, for example.

One can plan and plan, but if you don't book with the right people you can't seize le moment and canoodle with the poodle named Pansy. I, for one, am all for fraternizing with the locals. Better yet, if I need to extend my stay and my gnome nappers are willing, it can all be arranged through the 800 number at, oh look, how convenient, the lovely company coat of arms.

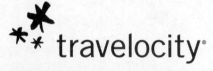